시험에 나오는 것만 **공**부한다!

시나공 토익

7

파트 **7**
실전문제집 시즌2

강진오, 강원기 지음

문제집

길벗
이지:톡

시나공 토익

파트 7 실전문제집 시즌2

초판 1쇄 발행 · 2019년 3월 20일
초판 3쇄 발행 · 2021년 12월 10일

지은이 · 강진오, 강원기
발행인 · 김경숙
발행처 · 길벗이지톡
출판사 등록일 · 2000년 4월 14일
주소 · 서울시 마포구 월드컵로 10길 56 (서교동)
대표전화 · 02) 332-0931 | **팩스** · 02) 322-0586
홈페이지 · www.gilbut.co.kr | **이메일** · eztok@ gilbut.co.kr

책임편집 · 유현우(yhw5719@gilbut.co.kr) | **디자인** · 황애라 | **제작** · 이준호, 손일순, 이진혁
마케팅 · 이수미, 장봉석, 최소영 | **영업관리** · 김명자, 심선숙 | **독자지원** · 윤정아, 홍혜진
편집진행 및 전산편집 · 기본기획 | **CTP 출력 및 인쇄** · 예림인쇄 | **제본** · 예림바인딩

ISBN 979-11-5924-222-9 03740
(이지톡 도서번호 300987)

정가 16,000원

· ·

독자의 1초까지 아껴주는 정성 길벗출판사

(주)도서출판 길벗 | IT실용, IT/일반 수험서, 경제경영, 취미실용, 인문교양(더퀘스트) www.gilbut.co.kr
길벗이지톡 | 어학단행본, 어학수험서 www.eztok.co.kr
길벗스쿨 | 국어학습, 수학학습, 어린이교양, 주니어 어학학습, 교과서 www.gilbutschool.co.kr

12회로 달성하는 파트 7 만점 프로젝트!

신토익이 시행된 지도 어언 3년차에 접어들고 있습니다. 이제 모든 토익 수험생들이 어느 정도 신토익의 유형에 빠르게 적응하고 있는 듯합니다. 하지만 신토익 이전이든, 이후든 변하지 않는 사실 한 가지가 있습니다. 그것은 여전히 파트 7은 수험생들에게 가장 까다롭고 어려운 파트라는 점입니다. 특히 구토익에 비해 문제 수가 6문제나 늘어났고, 삼중지문까지 나오면서 여전히 우리 수험생들을 괴롭히고 있는 대표적인 파트가 되고 있습니다. 이러한 상황 속에서 필자는 파트 7에 대한 수험생들의 고충을 조금이라도 덜어주고자 근 2년 만에 다시 〈시나공 토익 파트 7 실전문제집 시즌 2〉를 출간하게 되었습니다. 새롭게 선보이는 〈시나공 토익 파트 7 실전문제집 시즌 2〉는 다음과 같은 특징을 담고 있습니다.

1. 신토익을 완벽히 반영한 파트 7 12회 문제집!

〈시나공 토익 파트 7 실전문제집 시즌 2〉는 시즌 1에 비해 분량이 2회가 늘어났지만 가격은 오히려 2천 원이나 낮아져 파트별 문제집 중 압도적인 가성비를 지니게 되었습니다. 따라서 주머니 사정이 넉넉하지 못한 수험생들이 파트 7 문제에 부담 없이 접근할 수 있도록 구성하였습니다.

2. YBM 어학원 최다 수강생 보유자인 저자들의 고품질 문제와 해설 수록!

필자는 120회 이상 토익 시험을 본 경험이 있으며, 현재에도 매달 강의 현장에서 1,000명 이상의 수험생을 가르치고 있습니다. 수강생 중에는 필자가 제공하는 노하우와 자료를 바탕으로 950점 이상의 고득점을 받은 학생들이 많습니다. 필자의 수업에서만 제공했던 그 핵심 노하우를 혼자서 공부하는 수험생들을 위해 이 책에 아낌없이 담았습니다. 저자의 집필 원고를 300명이 넘는 수강생에게 풀어보게 하고, 그들이 준 피드백을 적극 반영하여 실제 시험과 동일한 난이도로 문제를 구성했습니다. 따라서 문제를 풀어 보면 여러분의 점수를 정확하게 가늠해 볼 수 있을 뿐 아니라, 실제 난이도와 출제 의도를 간파해 스스로 적절한 시간 분배와 풀이 요령을 습득할 수 있을 것입니다.

3. 정답, 오답의 이유와 패러프레이징까지 담은 해설집!

이 책을 공부하는 수험생들이 어려움 없이 문제의 의도와 풀이법을 이해하도록 자세한 해설집을 제공합니다. 해설집에는 정답의 이유는 물론 오답의 이유도 담았으며, 특히 파트 7 문제 풀이의 핵심이라고 할 수 있는 패러프레이징까지 제공합니다. 해설집으로도 이해가 안 가는 부분은 카카오톡으로 직접 필자에게 질문할 수 있으니 적극 활용해 보세요.

4. '단어 + 독해 훈련'을 담은 2주 완성용 복습 노트!

파트 7에도 문제를 빠르게 풀 수 있는 다양한 요령과 풀이 기법이 존재하지만 결국 문제 해결의 근본은 독해를 잘 할 수 있는 실력입니다. 이 책은 문제와 해설뿐만 아니라 근본적인 독해 실력이 향상되도록 도와주는 〈독학용 복습 노트〉를 제공합니다. 필자가 수업시간에 나누어 주는 자료와 동일한 형태이므로 충분히 활용해 보세요.

아무쪼록 전국의 모든 토익 수험생들이 필자의 파트 7에 대한 열정을 담은 이 책으로 반드시 목표 점수를 받을 수 있기를 기원합니다.

강진오, 강원기

1

신토익을 완벽히 반영한 국내 유일의 파트 7 실전 전문 교재!'

〈시나공 토익 파트 7 실전문제집 시즌 2〉는 신토익의 최신 경향을 완벽히 반영한 국내 유일의 파트 7 실전 전문 교재입니다. YBM 어학원에서 전국 최다 수강생을 보유하고 있는 저자의 파트 7 핵심 노하우와 자료를 이 한 권의 책에 모두 담았습니다. 또한 300명 이상의 베타테스터들로부터 얻은 피드백을 바탕으로 실제 시험과 동일한 난이도로 문제를 구성하였습니다. 총 12회의 파트 7 모의고사를 풀면서 파트 7에 대한 출제 의도를 파악하고 적절한 시간 배분과 풀이 요령을 습득해 나간다면 파트 7 고득점의 기반을 다질 수 있게 될 것입니다.

2

고난도 지문 '편지, 기사문 100 문제' 추가 제공!

지문 유형 중 가장 어렵고 출제 빈도가 높은 '편지와 기사문'을 추가로 100문제 더 제공합니다. 해석이 쉽지 않아 파트 7의 풀이 시간을 많이 잡아먹는 대표적인 유형입니다. 하지만 출제율이 가장 높으므로 어렵다고 피해서는 안 됩니다. '편지와 기사문'을 100문제 더 풀어보면서 다른 유형보다 강도 높게 훈련하고 정면 돌파해보세요. 제공한 문제를 다 풀면 어려운 문제 때문에 시간이 부족한 문제도 해결되고, 자연스럽게 점수도 향상될 것입니다.

기사문

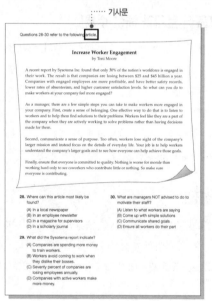

이메일(편지)

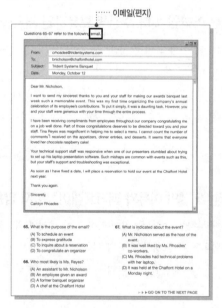

3

패러프레이징 원리를 한눈에 정리할 수 있는 '휴대용 패러프레이징 암기장' 제공!

파트 7에서는 지문의 구문을 패러프레이징한 선지를 고르는 훈련이 상당히 중요합니다. 패러프레이징의 원리를 파악할 수 있도록 따로 모아 정리한 암기장을 들고 다니면서 수시로 암기하세요.

4 정답과 오답의 이유, 패러프레이징까지 정리한 '해설집'과 카카오톡 답변 서비스!

이 책은 혼자서 공부하는 수험생들이 어려움 없이 문제를 풀이하도록 자세한 해설집을 제공합니다. 해설집에는 정답의 이유는 물론 오답의 이유도 담았으며, 특히 파트 7 문제 풀이의 핵심이라고 할 수 있는 패러프레이징까지 제공합니다. 파트 7 한 세트를 50분 안에 풀어본 후 해설집으로 본인이 부족한 부분을 꼼꼼히 체크해 보세요. 틀린 문제를 다시 풀어 보면서, 어떻게 패러프레이징 되어 정답으로 연결되었는지를 파악하는 것이 중요합니다. 만약 해설집으로도 이해가 안 가는 부분이 있으면 카카오톡으로 직접 저자에게 질문할 수 있으니 적극 활용해보세요.

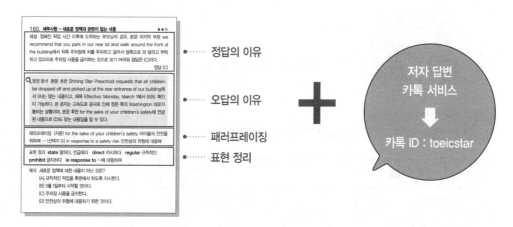

5 단어 + 독해 훈련 + 오답 노트로 구성된 '독학용 복습 노트' 제공!

기본 어휘력과 독해력을 향상시키는 〈독학용 복습 노트〉를 PDF로 제공합니다. 〈독학용 복습 노트〉는 12회분 문제집 분량에 맞추어 2주 완성 프로그램으로 구성되었으며, 각 날짜별로 '복습 단어 + 독해 훈련 + 오답 노트'를 제공합니다. 필자가 수업 시간에 나누어 주는 자료와 동일한 자료이니 독학자들도 충분히 활용해 독해 실력을 단기간에 바짝 향상시키길 바랍니다.

추가 자료 및 MP3 다운로드 방법

1. 홈페이지(gilbut.co.kr)에 접속합니다.(비회원은 회원 가입을 권장합니다.)

gilbut.co.kr에 접속해서
로그인합니다.

2. 상단의 검색창에 〈파트 7 실전문제집 시즌 2〉를 입력합니다.

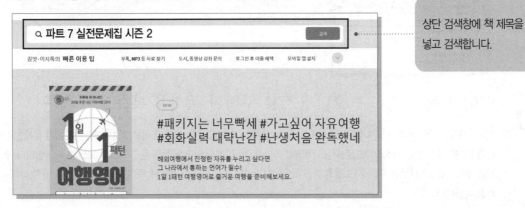

상단 검색창에 책 제목을
넣고 검색합니다.

3. 〈파트 7 실전문제집 시즌 2〉가 검색되면 〈자료실〉을 클릭해서 필요한 자료를 다운로드할 수 있습니다.

〈자료실〉 상자를 클릭해서
자료를 다운로드합니다.

도서 관련 질문하는 방법

1. 시나공 토익 홈페이지(sinagong.gilbut.co.kr/toeic)에 접속해서 상단에 묻고 답하기를 클릭합니다.

〈문고답하기〉를 클릭합니다.

2. 하단에 문의하기를 클릭하고, 〈다른 도서 찾기 ➜ 도서 선택 ➜ 페이지 입력 ➜ 하단 문의하기 클릭 ➜ 문의 내용 입력〉 순으로 문의를 남겨주시면 됩니다. 자주 질문하는 책은 처음에 도서 등록을 해놓으시면 더 간편하게 이용하실 수 있습니다.

〈문의하기〉를 클릭합니다.

3. 길벗이지톡 홈페이지(gilbut.co.kr)에 접속해서 상단에 〈고객센터〉 클릭 후 〈1:1 문의〉를 통해서도 질문하실 수 있습니다.

〈고객센터〉를 클릭한 후 〈1:1문의〉를 클릭합니다.

다른 파트보다 특히 파트 7은 지문 길이가 길고 추론 문제를 풀어야 하기 때문에 너무 어려웠는데요. 이 교재의 문제들을 풀면서 실력이 많이 상승한 것 같아요. 양질의 문제와 더불어 해설집이 매우 꼼꼼해서 혼자 토익 공부하는 수험생에게 최적의 교재가 아닌가 싶습니다. 해설집에는 해석은 물론이고, 지문에 등장한 표현과 선택지의 패러프레이징까지 한눈에 비교할 수 있도록 수록되어 있기 때문에 더욱 더 도움이 많이 되었어요. 문제 풀이 후 해설집을 통해 오답 정리와 표현을 암기하면 복잡한 파트 7도 완전 정복이 가능할 것 같아요. 〈파트 7 실전 문제집 시즌 1〉에 이어 이번 시즌 2 교재도 무척 기대가 돼요.

최자연 (24살, 대학생)

전체적으로 지문과 문제가 깔끔했어요. 자세히 읽지 않으면 놓칠 수 있는 부분들이 있었으나, 억지스러운 문제는 없었어요. 간혹 어떤 문제집들은 어려운 문제라며 심하게 꼬아 놓아 혼란을 주거든요. 그 문제집들과 비교해 볼 때 적극 추천할 만한 교재라고 생각합니다. 특히 정답인 이유에 대한 설명뿐만 아니라 오답의 이유까지 상세하게 설명되어 있어서 해설이 상당히 충실합니다. 본인이 제대로 공부하고자 하는 의욕만 있다면 파트 7 만점을 달성할 수 있는 충분한 교재임이 분명합니다. 앞으로도 좋은 교재 많이 만들어 주세요. 감사합니다.

김지윤 (25살, 대학생)

파트 7은 분량이 워낙 많아 단 1회를 풀어 보는 것도 쉽지 않은 일이었지만, 다 풀고 나니 확실히 독해 실력이 향상된 것을 느낍니다. 토익에서 항상 시간이 부족했는데, 이 책의 6회차쯤 풀 때는 시간도 딱 맞게 풀리더라고요. 역시 많이 풀어 보는 훈련이 중요한가 봐요. 이 책은 해설 또한 너무 자세하고 바람직합니다. 정답의 이유뿐만 아니라 패러프레이징도 제공해서 이해를 돕거든요. 파트 7에서 패러프레이징 표현이 무척 중요하다는 사실을 알았지만 문제를 푸는 과정에서 이렇게까지 도움이 될 줄은 몰랐습니다. 정말 만족스러운 해설집입니다.

곽주연 (24살, 대학생)

토익이 신유형으로 바뀌면서 파트 7이 더욱 더 어려워져 문제집을 좀 꾸준히 풀고 싶었는데요. 시중에 파트 7 실전 문제집이 거의 없는 상황에서 이 책을 보게 되어 무척 반가웠어요. 파트 7이 12회나 담겨 있어서 양적인 면에서 만족스러웠어요. 많은 문제를 푸는 것도 중요하지만 풀이도 중요하겠죠. 그런 점에서 이 책은 해설집도 참 성실합니다. 혼자서도 막힘없이 풀이할 수 있게 해설이 매우 자세하더라고요. 따로 강사의 설명을 들을 필요도 없이 혼자서 공부해도 충분하겠어요. 더군다나 부록으로 수록된 〈패러프레이징 암기장〉과 〈독학용 복습 노트〉도 문제집과 해설집 이외에 많이 도움이 되겠더라구요.

양영희(26살, 대학생)

〈파트 7 실전문제집 시즌 2〉는 독학하는 수험생들이 공부하면 참 편하게끔 구성이 되어 있습니다. 아무래도 RC 중에서는 파트 7이 가장 난이도도 높고 고득점을 위해 비교적 중요한 부분이라, 집중적으로 풀어보면 점수를 올리기 수월할 것 같다는 생각이 들었는데, 실제로 그런 구성으로 짜여 있어서 좋았습니다. 날짜별로 풀어보게끔 계획이 세워져 있는 부분에서 독자에 대한 세심한 배려가 느껴졌고, 특히 파트 7 때문에 고민이 많은 수험생들에게 효과적인 훈련이 되지 않을까 싶습니다. 해설도 자세하게 되어 있다고 느꼈고요. 아무쪼록 토익을 독학하시는 분들께는 더욱 더 강력히 추천해 드리고 싶습니다!

김용준(25살, 대학생)

평소에 파트 7 때문에 고민이 무척 많았는데, 〈시나공 토익 파트 7 실전 문제집 시즌 2〉를 풀면서 파트 7을 집중적으로 공부할 수 있어서 좋았습니다. 파트 7을 풀 때마다 항상 시간에 쫓기는 편이었는데, 여러 번 연습하니 시간 부족 문제도 많이 개선되어서 좋았습니다. 반복학습을 통해서 어느 부분이 부족한지 확실하게 대비할 수 있는 점 또한 주목할 만하다고 생각합니다. 이 교재에서 가장 칭찬할 점은 해설집인데요, 해석과 함께 지문에 등장한 표현과 패러프레이징까지 매우 친절하게 비교가 되어 있습니다. 그리고 해설에서 문제의 정답뿐만 아니라 왜 오답인지에 대해서도 자세하게 설명되어 있어서 혼자서 공부하기에 충분하다고 생각합니다.

박세현(25살, 대학생)

1 TOEIC이란?

TOEIC은 Test Of English for International Communication의 앞 글자들을 따서 만든 용어로서, 영어가 모국 어가 아닌 사람들을 대상으로 하여 언어의 주 기능인 의사소통 능력을 평가하는 시험입니다. 주로 비즈니스와 일상생 활 같은 실용적인 주제들을 주로 다루고 있으며, 듣고 이해하는 Listening 분야와 읽고 파악하는 Reading 분야로 나뉩니다. 이 두 부분은 각각 495점의 배점이 주어지며, 총 만점은 990점입니다. 특히 Listening은 미국뿐만 아니라 영국, 호주의 영어발음까지 섞여 나오기도 합니다.

2 시험의 구성

구성	Part	내용	문항 수	시간	배점
Listening Comprehension	1	올바른 사진 설명 찾기	6	45분	495점
	2	질문에 알맞은 대답 찾기	25		
	3	짧은 대화 내용 찾기	39		
	4	긴 연설문 내용 찾기	30		
Reading Comprehension	5	문법 / 어휘 빈칸 채우기 (문장)	30	75분	495점
	6	문법 / 어휘 빈칸 채우기 (지문)	16		
	7	1개 지문의 주제와 세부사항 찾기	29		
		2개 지문의 주제와 세부사항 찾기	10		
		3개 지문의 주제와 세부사항 찾기	15		
Total		7 Part	200	120분	990점

3 토익 출제분야

토익은 국제적으로 통용되는 비즈니스와 특정 문화에 국한되지 않는 일상생활에 관한 내용을 다룹니다.

비즈니스	일반업무	구매, 영업/판매, 광고, 서비스, 계약, 연구/개발, 인수/합병
	제조	생산 공정, 품질/공장 관리
	인사	채용, 지원, 승진, 퇴직, 급여
	통신	공지, 안내, 회의, 전화, 이메일, 팩스, 회람, 인트라넷, 협조
	재무/회계	투자, 세금 신고, 환급/청구, 은행
	행사	기념일, 행사, 파티, 시상식
일상생활	문화/레저	영화, 공연, 박물관, 여행, 쇼핑, 외식, 캠핑, 스포츠
	구매	주문/예약, 변경/취소, 교환/환불, 배송
	건강	병원 예약, 진료, 의료보험
	생활	고장, 보수, 생활 요금, 일정

4 시험 시간 안내

시간	내용
09:30 ~ 09:45	답안지 배부 및 작성 오리엔테이션
09:45 ~ 09:50	휴식 시간
09:50 ~ 10:05	1차 신분증 검사
10:05 ~ 10:10	문제지 배부 및 파본 확인
10:10 ~ 10:55	LC 시험 진행
10:55 ~ 12:10	RC 시험 진행(2차 신분 확인)

＊아무리 늦어도 9시 50분까지는 입실해야 하며, 고사장의 상황에 따라 위의 시간은 약간 변동될 수 있습니다.

5 토익 접수 방법

접수기간 및 접수처 확인 : TOEIC 위원회 홈페이지 / **응시료** : 44,500원

① 방문 접수

- 해당 회 접수기간에 지정된 접수처에서 응시료를 납부하고, 신청서를 작성한 후 접수합니다.
- 사진(반명함판, 3x4cm) 한 장을 지참합니다.
- 원서 접수시간: 09:00~18:00(점심시간 12:00~13:00)

② 인터넷 접수

해당 회 접수기간에 TOEIC 위원회 홈페이지(www.toeic.co.kr)에서 언제든 등록이 가능합니다. 사진은 jpg 파일로 준비하면 됩니다.

③ 특별 추가 접수

특별 접수기간 내에 인터넷 접수로만 가능하며 응시료가 48,900원입니다.

6 시험 준비 사항

① 규정 신분증

주민등록증, 운전면허증, 공무원증, 여권, 초·중·고생의 경우는 TOEIC 정기시험 신분 확인 증명서, 학생증, 청소년증을 인정합니다. 신분증이 없으면 절대 시험을 볼 수 없습니다. 꼭 챙기세요!

② 필기도구

컴퓨터용 연필(연필심은 굵게 준비해 두면 답안지 작성할 때 편리함), 지우개 ＊사인펜은 사용할 수 없습니다.

7 성적확인 및 성적표 수령

성적은 정해진 성적 발표일 오전 6시부터 토익위원회 홈페이지와 ARS 060-800-0515를 통해 조회할 수 있습니다. 성적표는 선택한 방법으로 수령이 가능하며 최초 발급만 무료입니다.

I 독해의 구성 및 핵심 공략

독해는 총 54문제로 구성되며, Single Passage는 10세트의 지문(29개), Double Passage는 2세트의 지문(10개), Triple Passage는 3세트의 지문(15개)이 나온다. Single Passage는 한 지문에 보통 2~4문제, Double Passage, Triple Passage는 5문제가 출제된다. 보통 단일지문 중에서는 맨 마지막에 출제되는 기사문(article)이, 그리고 이중, 삼중지문에서도 역시 기사문(article)이 난이도가 가장 높기 때문에 이 부분의 문제를 푸는 과정에서 시간 조절에 실패하는 경우가 많으므로 평소에 어려운 지문유형을 틈틈이 훈련해 두어야 한다.

■ 독해 실전 테크닉

❶ 독해를 시작하기 전에 반드시 문제를 먼저 읽고, 무엇을 묻는지를 정확히 파악한다. 글의 상황을 머릿속에 그려보는 것도 좋은 방법이다.

❷ 중요한 것에 중점을 두고 읽는다. 독해의 특성상 중요한 부분과 중요하지 않은 부분이 섞여있으므로 보충 설명에 불과하다고 생각되는 곳은 과감하게 넘어간다. 이것도 시간 안배의 중요한 수단이다. 이처럼 글의 내용 중 먼저 중요한 부분을 집중적으로 이해할 경우 주제를 파악하는 것도 훨씬 쉬워진다.

❸ 모르는 단어에 너무 집착하지 않는다.

❹ 이미 정답을 찾았다면 나머지 지문 내용은 넘어가는 것도 용기이다.

❺ 1분 이상 노력해도 풀리지 않는 문제는 정답으로 가장 근접하게 생각되는 선택지에 표기하고 다음 문제에 집중한다.

❻ 지문을 읽는 동안 항상 글의 주제가 무엇인지를 파악하려고 노력한다.

❼ 강조 표현(only, all, always 등)이 포함된 선택지는 일반적으로 정답일 가능성이 적다.

❽ 시간이 부족할 경우에는 쉬운 지문이나 자신 있는 유형의 문제를 먼저 푸는 것도 좋은 방법이며, 대체적으로 짧은 지문과 광고가 쉽고, 기사가 가장 어렵다. (광고 〈 편지 〈 공지 사항 〈 기사)

❾ 하이라이트나 대문자로 쓰인 부분을 포함해 숫자나 날짜 등에 주목한다.

❿ 지문에 소제목이 있는 경우는 소제목을 그 단락의 주제로 생각하면 된다.

❶ 독해는 글의 흐름을 잘 이해해야 한다.

지문은 대체로 'introduction → main topic → examples → conclusion'의 순서로 진행된다. Introduction 부분이 생략되고 글의 첫머리에 바로 main topic이 오는 경우도 있다. 특히 광고나 팩스

등 지면에 제약을 받는 경우가 그러하다. 대부분 'main topic = conclusion'의 공식이 성립한다. 주제를 문미에 한 번 더 환기시켜주고 싶은 것이 글쓴이의 심정이기 때문이다. 이러한 글의 전체적인 흐름을 묻는 문제가 바로 글의 주제나 목적을 묻는 문제로 출제된다.

■ 글의 주제와 목적을 묻는 문제 유형

Why was the letter sent? 편지를 보낸 이유는?

What is the purpose of this letter/e-mail? 이 편지/이메일의 목적은 무엇인가?

Why was this e-mail written? 이메일이 작성된 이유는?

What does the article mainly discuss? 기사는 주로 무엇을 다루는가?

What is the topic of the article? 기사의 주제는 무엇인가?

■ 풀이 전략

글의 주제와 목적을 묻는 문제는 편지나 이메일의 경우 제목이나 시작 부분을 집중적으로 읽어보도록 한다. 기사문의 경우도 제목을 간과하지 않도록 해야 한다. 난이도가 높은 경우는 글의 흐름을 이해한 후에 정답을 찾게 만드는 경우가 있다. 따라서 독해는 다른 유형의 문제를 먼저 해결한 후 주제와 목적 문제를 나중에 푸는 것도 하나의 방법이다.

Brown's Painting Company would like to be considered for the job of painting the interior and exterior of the headquarters.

브라운 페인팅 사는 본사의 내부 및 외부 페인팅 작업에 참여하고자 합니다.

- -

Q What is the purpose of the e-mail? 이메일의 목적은 무엇인가?

(A) To demand payment 지불을 요청하기 위해

(B) To request a list of company projects 회사 프로젝트의 리스트를 요청하기 위해

(C) To inquire about a business license 사업 면허에 관해 문의하기 위해

(D) To express interest in a contract 계약에 관심을 나타내기 위해

정답 (D)

해설 페인트 작업에 참여하고 싶다는 내용으로 시작하는 이메일로 페인트 공사 계약을 체결하는 것이 목적이므로 (D)가 정답이다.

❷ 독해 문제는 패러프레이징해서 나오는 경우가 많다.

독해 문제는 지문을 다 읽어야 풀 수 있는 문제도 있지만, 특정 문장에 정답이 될만한 결정적인 힌트가 주어져 그 부분만 읽으면 정답을 고를 수 있는 문제도 있다. 두 번째 문제처럼 지문과 문제에 있는 표현이 의미상으로는 같지만 다른 표현으로 패러프레이징되어 나오는 경우가 많다.

The Lincoln Bank Newsletter is issued **every other week**.

링컨 은행 회보는 격주로 발행된다.

Q How often is the newsletter published? 회보는 얼마나 자주 발행되는가?

    (A) Daily 매일

    (B) Biweekly 격주

    (C) Monthly 매월

    (D) Quarterly 분기

정답 (B)

해설 every other week를 biweekly로 바꿔 제시한 경우이며, 정답은 (B)이다.

The subscription form was returned to Mrs. Clark because she **hadn't completed** all the blanks.

그녀가 모든 공란을 채우지 않았기 때문에 구독 신청서가 클라크 씨에게 반송되었다.

Q What was wrong with the subscription form? 구독 신청서에 무엇이 잘못되었는가?

    (A) It had the wrong information. 잘못된 정보가 기재되었다.

    (B) It was incompletely filled in. 완전하게 작성하지 않았다.

    (C) It was not the revised form. 수정된 양식이 아니었다.

    (D) It was partially torn. 일부가 찢어졌다.

정답 (B)

해설 hadn't completed를 incompletely로 바꿔 제시한 경우이며 정답은 (B)이다.

The buyer **was dissatisfied with the sample** and canceled the order immediately.

구매자는 견본품에 만족하지 않았고, 즉시 주문을 취소했다.

Q Why did the customer cancel the order? 구매자는 왜 주문을 취소했는가?

    (A) He didn't have the money to pay for it. 그는 지불할 돈이 없었다.

    (B) The manufacturer couldn't fill it immediately. 구매자가 주문을 바로 이행할 수 없었다.

(C) Another company offered better prices. 다른 회사가 더 나은 가격을 제시하였다.

(D) The customer didn't like the sample. 고객이 샘플을 좋아하지 않았다.

정답 (D)

해설 was dissatisfied with를 didn't like로 바꿔 제시한 경우이며 정답은 (D)이다.

The seminar on January 25 will deal with **anger management** on the job and at home.

1월 25일 세미나는 직장과 가정에서의 분노 관리법을 다룰 것이다.

Q What is the subject of the January 25 session? 1월 25일 과정의 주제는 무엇인가?

(A) Time management 시간 관리

(B) Controlling one's temper 분노 통제

(C) Management positions 관리직

(D) A recent business deal 최근 사업 거래

정답 (B)

해설 anger management를 controlling one's temper로 바꿔 제시한 경우이며 정답은 (B)이다.

---

③ 사실 확인 문제는 시간 관리가 중요하다.

사실 확인 문제란 지문 내용을 올바로 이해했는지를 묻는 문제인데, 특히 NOT이 포함되어 있을 경우 하나씩 대조하며 소거하는 방식을 사용해야 하므로 시간 관리에 특히 유의해야 한다. 이러한 사실 확인 문제는 크게 두 가지 형태로 기억해야 하는데, 지문에서 언급한 내용을 묻는 문제와 언급되지 않은 내용을 묻는 문제 유형이다.

■ **지문에서 언급한 내용을 묻는 문제 유형**

What is **stated** about the project? 프로젝트에 관해 언급된 내용은?

What is **mentioned** in the e-mail? 이메일에서 언급된 내용은?

What is **indicated** in the brochure? 브로셔에서 나타난 내용은?

What is **true** about the event? 행사에 대해 사실인 것은?

■ **지문에서 언급되지 않은 내용을 묻는 문제 유형**

What is NOT mentioned as a **requirement**? 요구사항으로 언급되지 않은 것은?

What is NOT an **advantage** of the product? 제품의 장점이 아닌 것은?

What is NOT a **requirement** for the position?　　　　　　　　직위에 대한 요구 사항이 아닌 것은?

What is NOT included in the **program**?　　　　　　　　　　프로그램에 포함되지 않은 것은?

What is NOT featured in the **exhibition**?　　　　　　　　　전시회에서 다루지 않는 것은?

■ 풀이 전략

위와 같은 질문의 형태는 질문에 언급된 키워드를 기억한 후 지문에서 해당 부분을 찾아 해결해야 한다. 특히 NOT이 언급된 문제는 어렵다기보다 시간이 많이 소요되는 문제 유형이므로 충분한 연습을 해야 한다.

Job Description

Responsibilities include, **but are not limited to** the following.

· Greeting and signing in all facility visitors

· Answering a high volume of incoming calls and transferring calls to departments as necessary

· Sorting received mail and signing for packages

직무 설명

담당 업무는 아래 내용을 포함합니다. 하지만 아래 내용에만 제한되지 않습니다.

· 모든 시설 방문자들의 접대 및 등록

· 많은 전화의 답변 및 필요한 부서로 전화 안내

· 수신 우편물 분리 및 소포 수신 확인

Q What is indicated about the position? 일자리에 관해 나타난 내용은?

(A) It has flexible hours. 근무시간 조절이 가능한 자리이다.

(B) It may include duties that are not listed. 목록에 없는 업무 내용을 포함할 수 있다.

(C) It is available immediately. 즉시 시작 가능하다.

(D) Candidates can apply for it online. 지원자는 온라인으로 지원할 수 있다.

정답 (B)

해설 채용 광고에서 리스트에 없는 업무 내용이 있을 수 있음을 알리는 문제 유형으로 정답은 (B)이다.

④ 난이도가 가장 높은 추론 문제

추론 문제는 지문에 나오는 내용을 통해 정답을 유추해야 하는 문제로 난이도가 아주 높은 문제들이 많다.

■ 추론 문제 유형

What is **suggested** about the event?　　　　　　　　　　행사에 관해 암시하는 것은?

What is **implied** about the meeting?　　　　　　　　　　회의에 관해 암시하는 것은?

What can be **inferred** about the project? 프로젝트에 관해 추론할 수 있는 것은?

Who **most likely** is Mr. Thompson? 톰슨 씨는 누구인가?

When will Ms. Carson **most likely** be in Manila? 카슨 씨는 언제 마닐라에 갈 것인가?

■ **풀이 전략**

위와 같은 질문 유형이 나올 경우 정답을 고르기가 쉽지 않다는 것을 인식하고 문제에 임해야 하며, 따라서 시간이 너무 지체되지 않도록 시간 관리를 잘 해야 한다.

Internships provide in-depth exposure to the Seaside Hotel's operations. Those who complete this training program **may be considered for management positions afterward.**

인턴 과정은 시사이드 호텔 운영에 대해 많은 것을 제공하게 될 것입니다. 교육을 마친 사람들은 이후 매니저 자리에 고려될 수 있습니다.

- -

Q What is suggested about the Seaside Hotel Company?
시사이드 호텔에 관해 암시하는 것은?

(A) It will open new hotels soon. 새로운 호텔을 곧 개장한다.

(B) It is planning a July job fair. 7월 취업박람회를 계획하고 있다.

(C) It does not pay its interns. 인턴들에게는 급여를 지급하지 않는다.

(D) It may hire former interns as managers. 이전 인턴들을 매니저로 고용할 수 있다.

정답 (D)

해설 인턴 과정을 마친 사람들은 향후 매니저 자리에 채용될 수 있음을 추론할 수 있는 문제 유형이며, 정답은 (D)이다.

---

5 신경향 '문장 삽입 문제'는 지시어와 전체적 맥락을 파악해야 한다.

문장 삽입 문제는 Single passage의 2개 지문에서 각 1 문제씩 총 2문제가 나온다. 주어진 문장에서 힌트를 찾고, 지문의 전체적인 맥락을 이해한 다음 문제를 풀어야 한다. 지문의 맥락을 이해하면 무난하게 풀 수 있는 문제들이 대부분이다.

■ **문장 삽입 문제 유형**

In which of the positions marked [1], [2], [3], and [4] does the following sentence best belong? 다음 문장은 [1], [2], [3], [4] 로 표시된 위치 중 어느 곳에 가장 잘 어울리는가?

■ 풀이 전략

1. 지시어(it, that, this), 명사나 대명사(he, they, she), 또는 관사(a, the) 등이 쓰인다면, 그것이 가리키는 것이 앞 맥락에 나와있어야 한다.

2. 주어진 문장의 내용이 지문에서 앞뒤 내용의 연결과 자연스러워야 한다. 즉, 주어진 문장에 application이라는 단어가 있으면, application과 직접적으로 연관된 내용이 앞뒤에 있어야 한다.

Let me take a moment to review your request. — [1] — You would like us to make a large cake to serve all ninety-five guests. — [2] — It will be almond flavored with buttercream icing. You would also like us to decorate it with the floral pattern you provided and to write your company's name across the front. — [3] —. The order will be delivered to the Mihalski Hotel on Saturday, December 3, no later than 3:00 P.M. The contact person there is Derek Turner (555-3403). — [4] —.

당신의 요청을 리뷰 하도록 하겠습니다. — [1] — 당신은 전부 95명의 손님들에게 제공될 큰 케이크를 저희가 만들기를 원하고 있습니다. — [2] — 그것은 버터크림 아이싱과 함께 아몬드 맛일 것입니다. 당신은 또한 당신이 제공한 꽃무늬로 그것을 장식하고 앞쪽에 회사의 이름을 쓰는 것을 원합니다. — [3] — 주문은 12월 3일 토요일, 늦어도 오후 3시까지는 Mihalski 호텔로 배달될 것입니다. 거기서 연락할 사람은 Dereck Turner (555-3403)입니다. — [4] —

Q In which of the positions marked [1], [2], [3], and [4] does the following sentence best belong?

"In addition, your company's logo will be placed on top."

[1], [2], [3], [4] 중 다음 문장이 들어가기에 가장 알맞은 곳은?
"게다가, 당신의 회사의 로고가 맨 위에 놓여질 것입니다."

(A) [1]
(B) [2]
(C) [3]
(D) [4]

정답 (C)

해설 주어진 문장이 "게다가"로 시작하고 있다. 그러므로 주어진 문장은 앞의 내용에 추가적인 정보를 제공함을 알 수 있다. 또한, 회사 로고가 위에 올라간다고 했기 때문에, 제품의 다른 부분에는 어떤 것이 있는지를 설명한 다음에 이 문장이 나올 것을 예상할 수 있다.

---

6 신경향 '의도를 파악하는 문제'는 앞을 살펴 왜 그 말을 했는지 파악한다.

의도를 파악하는 문제는 text message chain과 online chat discussion 지문에서 각각 1문제씩, 총 2문제가 출제된다. 주어진 어구의 진짜 의도를 물어보는 문제이기 때문에, 앞뒤 맥락을 파악해 왜 그 말을 했는지를 파악하는 것이 중요하다.

At 1:34 P.M., what does Ms. Cohn most likely mean when she writes, **"Got it"**?

오후 1시 34분에 Ms. Cohn이 "알겠습니다"라고 했을 때 무엇을 의미하는가?

At 10:08 A.M., why does Mr. Jones write, **"Let me see what I can do"**?

오전 10시 8분에 Mr. Jones가 "내가 무엇을 할 수 있는지 봅시다"라고 말한 이유는 무엇인가?

■ 풀이 전략

전체적인 맥락을 파악하는 것이 중요하긴 하지만, 일반적으로 바로 앞의 내용을 알면 문제의 답을 찾을 수 있는 경우가 대부분이다.

Cramer, Asa (9:39 A.M.) Good news. They can have the meals packaged within half an hour for you to pick up. Will that work for you?

좋은 소식이에요. 당신(Nixon)이 가져가실 수 있도록 30분 안에 도시락을 포장할 수 있어요. 그러면 괜찮을까요?

Nixon, Clarissa (9:41 A.M.) I'm pretty sure. The order form says lunch will be served at noon. I can get back to Scitech by then. Thanks!

그럴 거예요. 주문서에는 점심이 12시에 제공될 거라고 나와있어요. 그때까지 Scitech 사에 돌아갈 수 있어요. 고맙습니다!

- -

Q At 9:41 A.M., what does Ms. Nixon most likely mean when she writes, "I'm pretty sure"? 오전 9시 41분에 Ms. Nixon이 "그럴 거예요"라고 쓴 것은 무엇을 의미하는 것일까?

(A) She believes that Scitech can have lunch later.
그녀는 Scitech 사가 점심을 나중에 먹을 수 있을 거라고 생각한다.

(B) She thinks she has enough time to make the delivery.
그녀는 배달을 하기에 충분한 시간이 있다고 생각한다.

(C) She feels it is important to deliver the items early.
물품을 일찍 배달하는 것이 중요하다고 느낀다.

(D) She is fairly certain the staff can do the packaging.
직원이 포장을 할 수 있다고 전적으로 확신하고 있다.

정답 (B)

해설 이전 문장을 보면, Ms. Nixon이 가져갈 수 있도록 30분 안에 도시락이 준비될 수 있다고 하고, 그게 괜찮은지 물어보고 있다. 그에 대한 답변으로 "I'm pretty sure"라고 하면서 주문서의 시간까지 Scitech 사에 가져가기에 충분한 시간이라고 생각하고 있다.

---

7 삼중지문(Triple Passage)의 연계 문제는 시간과 조건을 파악하라.

삼중지문은 지문을 3개 제시하고, 그에 딸린 5문제를 푸는 형식이다. 삼중지문은 총 3세트로 186~200번에 제시되고, 15문제 중에서 어휘 문제가 2문제 정도 출제된다. 대부분 지문의 순서대로 문제가 나오는데, 주의할 점은 두 지문이나 세 지문을 연계해서 풀어야 하는 문제가 1~2개는 반드시 출제된다는 점이다. 자주 출제되는 삼중지문의 유형을 파악해 각 유형별로 정보가 어떻게 연계되어 출제되는지 알아두면 빨리 문제를 풀 수 있다. 조건에 부합하는 서비스나 제품, 고객이 원하는 장소나 시간과 관련된 문제가 많이 출제된다.

지문 1: 광고 발췌문

Aqua Auto, Inc.

Some of our most popular services
- Basic car wash – we clean the interior and exterior of your vehicle
- Armor Guard™ wax – get extra protection from the elements
- Windshield repair – we seal small chips in the glass
- Super car wash – like the basic car wash but only better

Get 10% off in May. Must present this advertisement at time of service.

Aqua Auto, Inc. 주식회사

저희의 인기 서비스의 일부는 다음과 같습니다.
- 기본 세차 – 차량의 내부와 외부를 청소합니다.
- Armor Guard™ 왁스 – 비바람으로부터 추가적인 보호를 받습니다.
- 앞 유리 수리 – 유리에 난 작은 흠집을 밀봉합니다.
- 슈퍼 세차 – 기본 세차와 같지만 훨씬 좋습니다.

5월에 10% 할인을 받으세요. 이 광고를 서비스 받을 때 보여주어야 합니다.

지문 2: 서비스 신청서 발췌문

My cousin is getting married next week. I will be driving him and his future wife to the reception. We need the vehicle to look absolutely spotless inside and out, so we want your best cleaning service. The vehicle will be parked at my house the day before the wedding.

제 사촌이 다음 주 결혼을 합니다. 사촌과 사촌의 미래 부인을 리셉션까지 데려다 주게 됩니다. 내부와 외부 모두 완벽하게 흠이 없어야 하기 때문에, 귀사의 최고의 세차 서비스를 필요로 합니다. 제 차량은 결혼식 전날 제 집에 주차되어 있을 것입니다.

지문 3: 이메일 발췌문

From: dgrail@aquaauto.com
To: mhoven@jetmail.com
Subject: Your service request for May
Date: May 11

Dear Mr. Hoven,

Thank you for contacting Aqua Auto, Inc. We have added your vehicle to our schedule for the date you requested.

발신: dgrail@aquaauto.com

수신: mhoven@jetmail.com

제목: 귀하의 5월 서비스 요청

일자: 5월 11일

친애하는 Mr. Hoven,

Aqua Auto 주식회사에 연락해주어 감사합니다. 요청하신 날짜에 귀하의 차량을 저희의 세차 스케줄에 추가하였습니다.

Q1 What service does Mr. Hoven request?

Hoven씨가 요청한 서비스는 무엇인가?

(A) Basic car wash

기본 세차

(B) Armor Guard™ wax

Armor Guard™ 왁스

(C) Windshield repair

앞 유리 수리

(D) Super car wash

슈퍼 세차

Q2 What is suggested about Mr. Hoven?

Mr. Hoven에 대해 암시된 것은 무엇인가?

(A) He has utilized mobile car wash services before.

이동식 세차 서비스를 이용해 본 적이 있다.

(B) He recently moved to Carbondale.

Carbondale로 최근 이사했다.

(C) He will park his vehicle in a garage.

차고에 차량을 주차할 것이다.

(D) He will get a discount from Aqua Auto, Inc.

Aqua Auto 주식회사에서 할인을 받을 것이다.

Q1. 정답 (D)

해설 지문 2에서 Mr. Hoven은 신랑과 신부를 태워다 주기 위해 차량의 내부와 외부 모두 깨끗해야 한다고 설명하며, "so we want your best cleaning service"라고 말한다. 따라서, 지문 1에서 회사가 제공하는 가장 깨끗한 세차인 Super Car Wash를 필요로 한다.

Q2. 정답 (D)

해설 지문 3에서 원하는 날짜로 스케줄에 추가했다고 말하고 있고, 이메일의 제목을 보면 "귀하의 5월 서비스 요청"이라고 되어 있으므로 Mr. Hoven은 5월에 서비스를 받을 것이라는 것을 알 수 있다. 또한 지문 1 광고의 "Get 10% off in May."라는 부분을 참고하면 할인을 받는다는 것을 알 수 있다.

광고(Advertisement)

광고는 제품을 광고하기 위한 목적의 신문 광고나 피트니스 센터와 같은 새로운 매장의 오픈 광고, 식료품 매장의 세일 광고, 신입 사원을 채용하기 위한 구인 광고 등 여러 형태로 출제된다.

■ 체크 포인트

(1) 광고 내용을 묻는다.
(2) 광고 대상을 묻는다.
(3) 광고되는 상품의 특징을 묻는다.
(4) 채용 요건을 묻는다.
(5) 담당 업무를 묻는다.

■ 풀이 전략

광고는 소비자 또는 광고 대상자에게 광고 내용을 명확히 알려주며, 내용이 추상적이지 않기 때문에 문제가 까다롭지 않은 편이다.

■ 질문 유형

To whom is this advertisement intended?   이 광고는 누구를 대상으로 하는가?
What is the feature of the product?   제품의 특징은 무엇인가?
What is offered to customers?   고객에게 제공되는 것은 무엇인가?
Who is interested in this advertisement?   이 광고에 관심이 있는 사람은 누구인가?
What is required to receive a discount?   할인받기 위해 무엇이 요구되는가?
What is the advantage of the product?   제품의 장점은 무엇인가?

■ 제품 광고 관련 빈출 어휘

a variety of 다양한	call for reservation 예약 전화를 하다
advertisement 광고	certificate 증명서
advertiser 광고주	characteristic 특징
affordable 저렴한	classified ad 항목별 분류 광고
attractive 매력적인	come up with 생각해내다
available 이용 가능한	complimentary 무료의
be committed to ~에 헌신하다	courtesy 특별 우대
brochure 안내 소책자	customize ~을 주문 제작하다

efficient 효과적인, 능률적인	packaging 포장
elaborate 정교한	patent 특허(권), 특허를 얻다
endorse 승인하다	place an ad 광고를 하다
enhance 향상시키다	potential client 잠재 고객
ensure 보증하다	prestigious 명성 있는
exceptional 특별한, 뛰어난	professional 전문적인
exchange (제품의) 교환	publicity 홍보
exclusive 독점적인	refund 환불
expertise 전문 지식, 기술	replacement 교환
extensive 광범위한	sophisticated 정교한
fabulous 멋진	specialize in ~을 전문으로 하다
family (제품의) 기종, 계열	specialty 전문 분야
fault (제품의) 결함	state-of-the-art 최첨단의
feature 특징; ~을 특징으로 하다	stunning 근사한, 멋진
gift certificate 상품권	toll-free number 수신자 부담 무료전화
hands-on 실제적인	unique 독특한
handy 간편한	upgrade 향상, 업그레이드
incomparable(unparalleled) 견줄 데 없는	versatile 다용도의, 다방면의
outstanding 뛰어난, 미결제의	

■ 구인 광고 관련 빈출 어휘

applicant 지원자	paid vacation 유급휴가
apply for ~에 지원하다	recruit 채용하다
benefit 복리, 혜택; 혜택을 입다	regular job 정규직
commission 판매 수당	reimburse 배상하다, 변제하다
compensation 보수, 급여	resume 이력서
competitive salary 경쟁력 있는 급여	salary history 급여내역서
diploma 졸업증명서, 학위 수여증	submit 제출하다
fringe benefit 부수적 혜택	temporary job 임시직
graduate 대학졸업생, 대학원생	undergraduate 학부생
(help) wanted 구인 광고	vacancy 결원, 공석

❷ 편지와 이메일 (Letter & E-mail)

편지와 이메일은 독해 지문에서 출제 비중이 가장 높다. 자주 등장하는 주제로는 업무 분담, 보고서 마감, 사내행사 등이며, 편지나 이메일을 쓴 목적이나 발신인과 수신인의 정보를 묻기도 한다. 편지글에서는 발신자와 수신자의 주소를 유심히 봐야 하며, 이메일은 견적 요청, 예약 관련, 행사 정보 등을 묻는 문제도 많이 출제된다.

```
┌─────────────────────────────────────┐
│           발신자 회사 정보              │
│           주소/전화번호                │
│                                      │
│  발신인 주소                          │
│  수신인 주소                          │
│                                      │
│  Dear OOO                            │
│  ··································    │
│  ··································    │
│  ··································    │
│  ··································    │
│                                      │
│  서명                                │
│  직위                                │
│                                      │
└─────────────────────────────────────┘
```

※ 위와 같이 발신자의 로고와 정보가 찍힌 편지지를 letterhead라 한다.

■ **체크 포인트**

(1) 편지를 쓴 목적을 묻는다.
(2) 편지의 발신인과 수신인의 정보를 묻는다.
(3) 구체적인 편지 내용을 묻는다.
(4) 첨부 내용과 관련해서 묻는다.

■ **풀이 전략**

(1) 목적을 묻는 문제는 대부분 첫 단락 시작 부분에 위치한다.
(2) 수신인의 주소는 일반적으로 Dear 등으로 시작하는 수신자명 바로 위에 위치한다.
(3) 발신자 정보는 편지 가장 위 로고나 주소 또는 서명 부분에서 찾을 수 있다.
(4) 발신 일자가 있는 경우는 일정과 관련된 문제가 출제될 수 있다.
(5) 첨부 내용과 관련해서는 enclosed, attached, included 등의 단어를 찾아 본다.

■ **질문 유형**

What is the purpose of this letter/e-mail?	이 편지/이메일의 목적은 무엇인가?
Who sent this letter/e-mail?	이 편지/이메일을 보낸 사람은 누구인가?
For whom is this letter/e-mail intended?	이 편지/이메일은 누구를 대상으로 하는가?
What is Mr. Brown asked to do?	브라운 씨는 무엇을 하도록 요청받았나?
What is enclosed with this letter/e-mail?	이 편지/이메일에 무엇이 첨부되었는가?

■ 편지와 이메일 빈출 어휘

accounting department 회계부

administrator 관리자, 경영자, 행정관

advertising department 광고부

affiliate 계열사, 가맹단체, 지부

associate 동료, 공동 경영자

auction 경매

auditor 감사

be all sold out 매진되다

billing department 경리부

board of directors 이사회

branch manager 지점장

brand new 신제품인

bureau 사무국, 지국

business contact 사업인맥

business day 영업일

business line 업종

buying spree 과도한 상품 구입

center business district 중심 상업지역

CEO(Chief Executive Officer) 대표이사

clearance sale 재고처분 세일, 재고 정리

commissary 매점, 구내식당

concession stand (구내) 매점

conglomerate 복합 기업, 대기업

consignment 위탁 판매

construction manager 현장 소장

convenience store 편의점

corporate performance 기업 실적

corporation 법인, 주식회사

cover price 정가

customer service department 고객 서비스부

decision-making 의사 결정

distribution network 판매, 유통망

distributor 판매업자, 유통업자

division (사업) 부문, 부서

do business 거래를 하다

domestic market 국내시장

downsize (규모를) 축소하다

duty-free shop 면세점

emerging market 신흥 시장

enterprise 기업

estimate 견적서

executive 회사의 간부

fill an order 주문을 처리하다

finance division 금융부, 재무부

flea market 벼룩시장

fluctuating 가격 변동이 심한

franchise 특약점

gift certificate 상품권

go bankrupt 파산하다

go out of business 부도나다

headquarters 본사

housekeeping department (호텔의) 관리부

human resource department 인사부

in highest demand 수요가 많은

in stock 재고가 있는

international division 국제부

kiosk 간이건축물

loan department 대출부

maintenance department 관리부

management 경영진

management right 경영권

market climate 시장 분위기

market price 시가

market research 시장조사

market share 시장 점유율

marketable 시장성이 높은

marketing department 마케팅부

mass marketing 대량 판매

monopoly 독점

niche market 틈새시장

non-profit organization 비영리 단체

on the market 판매 중인, 시판 중인

open-air market 노천시장

organization 조직, 기업, 단체

out of stock 품절된
outlet 직영 소매점
overdue 지급 기한이 지난
overseas market 해외시장
parent company 모기업
partnership 합병 회사
personnel department 인사부
place an order 주문하다
price range 가격대
production division 생산부
prospect customer 유망(단골) 손님
public corporation 공기업
purchase 구입하다
purchase order 구입주문서
purchaser 구매자
purchasing power 구매력
R&D division 연구개발부
redeem 상환하다
refund 환불하다
registered brand name 등록 상표
restructure the department 부서를 재편하다

sales figures 판매수치, 매출액
sales promotion 판촉
sales tactics 영업 전략
sales territory 영업구역
sales volume 판매량
shift manager 근무 담당매니저
shipping department 선적부
slash 가격을 대폭 내리다, 깎다
stand 매점, 가판대
store manager 상점 지배인
supervisor 감독, 주임
supplier 납품업체, 공급업체
take an order 주문받다
trade show 전시회, 시사회
trade-in 신제품 구입시 대금의 일부로 사용되는 중고품, 중고품을 대금의 일부로 지급하고 신제품을 사다
turn-over 총매출
upcoming 다가오는
vending machine 자판기
venture business 벤처(모험)기업
vice-president 부사장

③ 공지 사항(Notice, Announcement, Memorandum)

공지 사항은 회사에서 직원들에게 시설 수리, 인사이동 또는 고객을 대상으로 한 행사 안내, 일정 변경 등을 알리는 내용이 주를 이룬다.

■ 체크 포인트

(1) 공지 사항의 주체와 객체를 묻는다.
(2) 지문의 구체적인 내용을 묻는다.
(3) 주의 사항, 요청 사항 등을 묻는다.
(4) 일정에 관한 내용을 묻는다.

■ 풀이 전략

공지 사항은 전달하는 내용이 모호하지 않기 때문에 비교적 쉽게 답을 찾을 수 있다. 일반적으로 공지의 목적은 전반부에, 공지의 내용은 중간에, 당부 사항은 후반부에 배치되므로 공지 사항의 패턴에 익숙해 지도록 노력해야 한다.

▪ 질문 유형

Who issued this notice? ｜ 이 공지 사항을 올린 사람은 누구인가?

For whom is this notice intended? ｜ 이 공지는 누구를 대상으로 하는가?

Which of the following is NOT true? ｜ 아래 내용 중 사실이 아닌 것은?

When will the construction begin? ｜ 공사는 언제 시작되는가?

What are the employees asked to do? ｜ 직원들은 무엇을 하도록 요청받는가?

Where will Mr. Snyder be posted? ｜ 스나이더 씨는 어디로 배치될 것인가?

▪ 공지 사항 관련 빈출 어휘

achieve 성취하다

acknowledge 알리다, 인정하다

address 해결하다, 처리하다

agency 대리점

anniversary 기념일

announce 발표하다

annual 1년의

annual report 연차 보고서

apply 신청하다

approve 승인하다

assembly line 조립 라인

assess 평가하다, 할당하다

auditorium 강당

authorized user 인가된 사용자

carefully 주의하여

caulk 틈을 막는 물건

cause (원인 등을) 야기하다

check out 점검하다, 계산하다

circulation desk 도서관 안내창구

circulation 순환, 유통

collection 수금, 수집

comply with ～에 따르다

confer 협의하다

conserve 보존하다

consumption 소비

corporate 법인의

damage 손해, 손상

defective 결점이 있는

deliver 배달하다

demonstrate 증명하다

designated 지정된

director 관리자

dripping 뚝뚝 떨어짐

drop 하락

drop by 들르다

earn 벌다

effort 노력

electrical wiring 전기 배선

eligible 적격의, 적임자

enclosed 둘러싸인

entity 실재, 본체

exception 제외, 예외

exempt from ～에서 면제받은

experience 경험

experienced 경험 있는

expire 만기가 되다

explore 탐험하다, 탐구하다

extensive 광범위한, 넓은

extra 여분의

fine 벌금

flexible 융통성 있는

former 전의

further 더 나아가

generator 발전기

guarantee 보증하다

housing complex 주택 단지

identification 신분증

implement 실행하다

in person 직접

income 수입

install 설치하다

instruction 교수, 교육

instructor 강사

issue 문제

leisure activity 여가 활동

letterhead 회사로고가 찍힌 편지지

library card 대출 카드

light fixture 조명기구

limit 한계

list 목록을 작성하다

maintenance 유지, 보수

material 재료, 물질

necessary 필요한

note 유의하다

obtain 획득하다

organization 조직, 단체

out of order 고장인

overdue 연체된

policy 정책

practice 연습

prior to ~에 앞서, ~에 먼저

production 생산

range from (범위가) ~에 이르다

rate 비율

reapplication 재신청

reasonable 합리적인

recently 최근에

recur 재발하다

reduction 축소

regulation 규제, 규정

remind 상기하다

reminder 상기시켜 주는 것

replace 대신하다, 바꾸다

request 요구하다

resident 거주자, 주민

retiree 퇴직자

route 길, 배달 구역

satisfy 만족시키다

shift 교대

significant 상당히, 중요한

take measures 조치를 취하다

take over 인계받다

temporarily 일시적으로

tenant 세입자, 임차인

thermostat 온도 조절 장치

tutor 가정교사

ventilation 통풍

written application 신청서

④ 기사문(Article)

독해 문제 중에서 가장 다양한 내용이 등장하며, 따라서 가장 어렵게 느껴지는 부분이기도 하다. 일정한 형식이 없고 난이도 있는 어휘도 자주 등장하는 편이다. 출제 내용으로는 지역 기업 소개, 지역 행사, 서평, 시장 동향, 환경보호 등으로 주제가 다양하다.

■ 체크 포인트

(1) 주제를 묻는 문제가 많이 나온다.

(2) 지문 길이가 길어 사실 확인 문제가 자주 나온다.

(3) 어휘가 난이도 있는 경우가 많아 동의어를 묻는 문제도 자주 제시된다.

(4) 기사 내용과 관련된 추론 문제도 많이 출제된다.

■ 풀이 전략

기사문은 평상시 출제되었던 문제를 실제로 신문기사를 읽듯 많이 읽어 보는 것이 도움이 된다. 아울러 서론–본론–결론을 갖춘 논리적인 글이 많으므로 글의 구성 방식도 잘 살펴봐야 한다. 특히 기사에 제시되는 어휘들은 난이도가 높아 어휘의 중요성이 강조된다. 기사문을 풀 때는 다른 유형보다도 특히 시간 관리를 철저히 해야 한다.

■ 질문 유형

What is the purpose of this article?	이 기사의 목적은?
What is NOT mentioned in the article?	기사에서 언급되지 않은 내용은?
What is suggested about the event?	행사에 대해 암시하는 내용은?
What is stated the article?	기사에서 언급된 내용은?
What is the subject of the article?	기사의 주제는 무엇인가?

■ 기사 관련 빈출 어휘

acid rain 산성비

alert 경계, 경보

analyst 분석가

annual revenue 연간 소득

audit 회계 감사하다

automatic deposit payment 자동 이체

automatic transfer 계좌 이체

bear interest 이자가 붙다

beneficial 유익한

bleach 표백제

blue stock 우량주

bond 채권

bookkeeping 부기

bottom line 순이익

cash flow 현금유동성

checking account 당좌 예금

chemical 화학제품

chemical free vegetable 무공해 채소

clean up 정화하다

commercial bank 상업 은행

common stock 공동 주식

comply with ~에 따르다

confidential access number 비밀 번호

contaminate (방사능, 독가스) 오염시키다

corporate bond 회사채

corporate finance 기업 금융

creditor 대변, 채권자

currency 통화, 지폐

current assets 유동 자산

depletion 고갈

deposit 은행 예금, 보증금

detergent 합성세제

disposable 일회용품

disposable income 가처분 소득

dividend (주식이나 보험금) 이익 배당금

domestic 국내의

downward trend 하락세

draw out cash 현금을 인출하다

earnings 소득

electronic banking 전자 뱅킹

emit 발산하다, 내뿜다

exceed 초과하다, 넘어지다

expenditure 지출

face value 액면가

fertilizer 비료

financial 재무의, 금융상의, 재정적인

financial market 금융 시장

financial statement 재무제표

financier 재정가, 금융업자	overhead 경상비, 총 경비
financing 자금 조달	pesticide 살충제(= insecticide)
fiscal year 회계 연도	pollutant 오염 물질
fluctuating 변동이 심한, 동요하는	pollute 오염시키다
fund 자금, 기금	pollution free 무공해의
fund-raiser 기금 모금운동	prime rate 우대 금리
green effect 온실 효과	private sector 사기업
hazardous 위험한	profit margin 이윤폭
herbicide 제초제	promising 유망한
in the black 흑자인	public sector 공기업
in the red 적자인	recycling 재활용
ingredient 성분, 재료, 원료	remit 돈을 보내다, 송금하다
interest 이자	restrict 제한하다, 금지하다
investment portfolio 투자 목록	reuse 재생하다
investment strategy 투자 전략	saving account 보통 예금
lease 차용 계약(증서)	sector (사업) 부문
lethal 치명적인	securities 유가증권
liabilities 부채(= debt)	sewerage 하수도
litter 종이 쓰레기	stabilize 안정시키다
lucrative 유리한, 돈이 벌리는	statement 내역서, 명세서
make a profit 이윤을 내다	stock broker 주식 중개인
market downturn 시장 침체	stock market 주식 시장
minimize 최소화하다	tax-return (납세를 위한) 소득신고
minimum balance 최저 잔액	taxable 과세 대상
mortgage 담보물(= security)	teller 은행의 창구 직원
negotiate 협상하다	toxic 유독성의
negotiator 협상가	transfer 송금
net income 순이익	waste disposal 쓰레기 처리
oil-spill (해상의) 원유 유출	wasteway 배수구
organic food 유기농 식품	wire transfer 온라인 이체, 송금
overall 전체적으로	withdraw 돈을 인출하다

⑤ 양식(Fax, Schedule, Resume, Chart, Invoice, Bill 등)

여러 가지 비즈니스 양식이 출제된다. 팩스, 일정표, 이력서, 도표, 송장, 공공요금 청구서 등이 출제되므로 각각의 양식에 익숙해져야 한다. 양식은 글의 내용이 적고 비교적 간단하기 때문에 어렵지는 않지만 양식의 구성을 모르면 이를 파악하는데 시간을 낭비할 수 있다.

(1) 일정이나 금액 등 숫자 관련 내용을 많이 묻는다.

(2) 양식을 받을 사람이나 작성자에 관한 정보를 묻는다.

(3) 양식의 각주 사항을 묻는다.

(4) 공공요금(전기요금, 전화요금, 수도요금) 고지서도 등장한다.

■ 풀이 전략

문제를 먼저 읽고 문제에서 요구하는 정보를 찾아가는 방식으로 풀어야 한다. 직장인이 아닌 수험자는 송장이나 도표 상의 비즈니스 용어에 익숙해지도록 해야 한다.

■ 질문 유형

What is true about the invoice?	송장에 대해 사실인 것은?
What is this receipt for?	무엇에 관한 영수증인가?
What is NOT indicated in the form?	양식에 언급되지 않은 것은 무엇인가?
According to the information, what will happen on April 13?	정보에 따르면, 4월 13일에 무슨 일이 있을 것인가?
What is indicated about the Harding City Power Company?	하딩 시 전력회사에 관해 나타난 내용은?
What does the document provide?	서류가 제공하는 것은 무엇인가?
What item was NOT delivered on July 8?	7월 8일에 배달되지 않은 제품은 무엇인가?
How much will the company refund Ms. Ward?	회사는 와드 씨에게 얼마를 환불해 줄 것인가?

■ 양식 관련 빈출 어휘

absent	결석한, 불참한	avoid	피하다
accept	받아들이다	begin	시작하다
additional	추가적인	billing information	요금 정보
adjourn	연기하다	brief	간결한
advertising	광고	budget	예산
ahead	앞쪽에, 앞으로	call off	취소하다
apologize	사과하다	call to order	개회하다, 시작하다
apology	사과	capacity	수용 능력
applicant	신청자	cause	야기하다
as usual	평소와 같이	clearly	뚜렷하게, 명확히
assess	평가하다, 사정하다	compensate	보상하다
assistant	조수, 비서	complaint	불평
assume	가정하다	conference	협의, 회의
attend	참석하다	confirmation	확인, 확정

construction 건설		publisher 출판업자	
consultant 컨설턴트		reach 도달하다	
contact 연락하다		receive 받다	
convenience 편의		reference 참조, 관련	
correctly 바르게, 정확하게		refund 환불하다	
cover 덮다, 지불하다		register 등록하다	
due 지불 기일이 된		reliable 믿을 수 있는	
effort 노력		remainder 나머지	
failure 실패		remaining 남아있는	
get along with ~와 어울리다		remind 상기하다	
handout 유인물, 인쇄물		reschedule 예정을 다시 세우다	
in fact 사실상, 실제로		respondent 응답자	
in full 전부, 전체		response 응답	
in stock 재고로		rest assured ~라고 확신하다	
inconvenience 불편		routine inspection 정기점검	
inquiry 연구, 조사		sales representative 판매사원	
interrupt 중단하다, 방해하다		schedule 예정하다	
invoice 송장		serve 섬기다, 봉사하다	
late-payment fee 연체료		service fee 서비스료	
list 목록에 올리다		sincere 성실한	
minutes 의사록		staff meeting 직원회의	
miscommunicate 잘못 전달하다		strategy 전략	
omit 생략하다, 빠뜨리다		submit 제출하다	
originate 시작하다, 비롯하다		summary 요약	
potential 잠재 가능성		temporarily 일시적으로	
power company 전력회사		thoroughly 철저히	
power usage 전력 사용		urgent 긴급한	
proceeding 진행		washer 똬리쇠, 와셔	
professional 전문적인, 직업적인		water company 식수 공급 회사	
promptly 신속히		wrench 렌치	
propose 제안하다		written permission 서면 허가	

6 문자 메시지와 온라인 대화(Text message chain and online chat discussion)

문자 메시지와 온라인 대화는 주로 각각 1지문씩 총 2문제가 출제된다. 지문에 대화하는 사람의 이름과 시간이 표시되고 서로 구어체로 의견을 교환한다. 난이도는 중하 수준으로 대화의 상황을 이해하면 무난하게 문제를 풀 수 있다.

■ 체크 포인트

(1) 대화가 발생하는 상황, 장소를 묻는다.
(2) 화자의 직업이나 회사의 유형을 묻는다.
(3) 사실 확인, 추론 유형이 나온다.
(4) 화자가 앞으로 해야할 일을 묻는다.
(5) 특정 어구를 말한 의도를 파악하는 문제가 지문당 반드시 1문제씩 나온다.

■ 풀이 전략

대화가 오가는 장소나 화자의 직업을 빨리 파악하는 것이 중요하다. 특정 어구를 파악하는 문제가 반드시 나오기 때문에 전체적인 맥락을 파악하고 해당 문장이 정확히 의도하는 바가 무엇인지 파악한다.

■ 질문 유형

What is suggested about Ms. Holinka? Holinka 씨에 대해 암시하는 내용은?

Where do the writers most likely work? 화자가 대화하는 장소는 어디일까?

What is indicated about the Bleecher Avenue location? Bleecher Avenue 장소에 대해 알 수 있는 것은 무엇인가?

Why did Mr. Phan contact the district manager? Phan 씨가 구역 매니저에게 연락한 이유는?

At 10:08 A.M., why does Mr. Jones write, "Let me see what I can do"?
오전 10시 8분에 Jones 씨가 "제가 무엇을 할 수 있는지 봅시다"라고 쓴 것은 무엇을 의미하나?

What is NOT mentioned about Commercial Custodial? Commercial Custodial에 대해 언급되지 않은 것은?

What does Mr. Shemilt plan to do? Shemilt 씨가 할 일은 무엇인가?

■ 토익 파트 7 중요 구어체 출제 문장

What's up? 무슨 일이야?/요즘 어때?/잘 지냈어?

I guess it can wait. 나중에 해도 돼요.

Do you have a minute? 잠시 시간 좀 내주시겠어요?

Is that it? 그게 다야?

Same here. 나도 마찬가지야.

I'll take care of that. 그건 내가 처리할게.

Thanks for bringing them to my attention.
그것들을 나에게 알려주셔서 감사합니다.

I'm heading there now.
지금 그곳을 향해서 가고 있습니다.

Tomorrow's forecast is calling for storms.
내일 날씨예보는 폭풍우를 예상합니다.

What if I talk to the client?
내가 고객이랑 이야기하면 어떨까?

You've got it. 물론이지. 그렇고 말고.

It's done. 끝마쳤어.

That's a relief. 다행이네요.

You left in such a rush. 당신이 급히 떠났어요.

You raised some good points, though.
그러나 당신은 좋은 점을 제기했습니다.

It would have been perfect.
완벽할 수 있었는데.

It doesn't make sense. 이건 말도 안돼.

Here we go. 여기 있어요. 바로 그거예요.

I'm glad we got that sorted out.
우리가 그것을 해결해서 기쁘다.

I'll get back to you soon.
내가 당신에게 곧 연락할게요.

This is cutting it close.
이렇게 하면 시간을 절약하는 거예요.

What's going on? 무슨 일이야?

Not on such short notice.
급히 공지를 해서 못했어.

I guess it can't be helped. 어쩔 수 없지.

STEP 1

문제집

실전 문제 풀기

먼저 36페이지에 있는 진단테스트로 자신의 실력을 확인한 후 수준에 맞는 학습 스케줄을 짭니다. 학습 스케줄에 따라 TEST 1부터 문제 풀이를 시작하세요. 반드시 55분 안에 문제 풀이와 마킹까지 끝내야 합니다.

STEP 2

해설집

해설 확인하기

문제만 많이 푼다고 실력이 되지는 않습니다. 문제를 풀고 틀린 문제를 확인하지 않는다면 단순히 실력을 평가하는 수준에 불과합니다. 정답의 이유뿐만 아니라, 본인이 고른 오답이 정답이 될 수 없는 이유까지 알아야 합니다. 패러프레이징이 어떻게 되었는지도 반드시 확인해보세요. 패러프레이징이 어떻게 되었는지를 파악하는 게 파트 7에서 정답률을 높이는 핵심이니까요.

STEP 3

독학 노트

필수 단어 암기하기

문제 풀이와 해설 확인이 끝나면, 〈독학용 복습 노트〉에 정리된 필수 단어를 암기하세요. 각 테스트에서 시험에 자주 나오는 단어를 선별해 담았습니다. 이 책에 있는 단어만 확실하게 외워도 시험에 나오는 파트 7 단어는 거의 정복할 수 있습니다.

STEP 4

독학 노트

직독직해 훈련하기

각 테스트의 지문에서 해석이 어려운 문장을 뽑아 정확하게 해석하는 훈련을 하도록 했습니다. 의미 단위로 직독직해하여 빠르게 문장의 뜻을 파악하고, 독해의 포인트가 되는 구문을 집중 훈련하여 근본적인 독해 실력을 기를 수 있게 했습니다.

STEP 5

독학 노트

오답 노트 정리하기

마지막으로 틀린 문제와 모르는 표현, 또는 해석이 잘 안되는 문장을 뽑아 오답 노트를 정리하세요. 많은 수험생이 이미 틀렸던 문제, 몰랐던 단어를 같은 이유로 다시 틀리는 실수를 합니다. 오답 노트에 틀린 문제와 표현을 정리하고, 시험 직전에 한 번 더 보면 짧은 시간에 학습 효과를 제대로 느낄 수 있습니다.

문제집 / 실제 시험에 나오는 핵심 문제만 모았다!

머리말   003

이 책의 특장점   004

〈시나공 토익〉 200% 활용법   006

베타테스터의 한마디   008

토익 시험 소개   010

파트 7 이렇게 공략하라!   012

이 책으로 혼자서 공부하는 방법   034

진단 테스트   036

학습 스케줄   040

TEST 01   041

TEST 02   065

TEST 03   089

TEST 04   113

TEST 05   137

TEST 06   161

TEST 07   185

TEST 08   209

TEST 09   233

TEST 10   257

TEST 11   281

TEST 12   305

Answer Sheet   329

해설집 / 깐깐한 해설로 오답의 이유까지 챙겼다!

TEST 01 정답 및 해설   002

TEST 02 정답 및 해설   015

TEST 03 정답 및 해설   029

TEST 04 정답 및 해설   043

TEST 05 정답 및 해설   056

TEST 06 정답 및 해설   070

TEST 07 정답 및 해설   082

TEST 08 정답 및 해설   096

TEST 09 정답 및 해설   110

TEST 10 정답 및 해설   125

TEST 11 정답 및 해설   138

TEST 12 정답 및 해설   151

다음의 문제를 풀고 본인의 수준에 맞는 일정을 확인한 후 학습하세요.

Questions 1 - 2 refer to the following letter.

Dear Hayley Smith,

We are sad to see you terminating your membership with our company. Before we permanently close the account and delete your user name and password, are there any improvements that you would like to see on our Web site? We would appreciate any input or feedback you would like to share. Thank you.

What are your reasons for terminating your membership?

	I have no time to use the service.
✓	The fees are too expensive.
	I no longer need the service.
	Customer service quality has gone down.
	I have found a better competitor.
	There are too many e-mail messages sent by your company

1. What does Ms. Smith want to do?
   (A) Use a discount voucher
   (B) Inquire about new services
   (C) Change her account information
   (D) Cancel her membership

2. What concerns Ms. Smith?
   (A) The quality of the service has decreased.
   (B) The service is too expensive.
   (C) The company sends too many e-mails.
   (D) The Web site is difficult to use.

New ElectroFone V5 Available Now!

Are you frustrated by slow Internet speeds on your cellular phone? Are you tired of receiving poor service when making a phone call? The ElectroFone V5 could be just what you need. Brought to you by American company Zipstar Corporation, early sales indicate that the V5 model will be a market leader, with over 100,000 units sold within the first two days. — [1] — A spokesman for the company claimed that they expect it to be their fastest-selling item of all time, outperforming all Zipstar cell phone, television, and video recorder products.

The V5 model is available with a gold, silver, or red finish and is one of the lightest phones on the market, weighing only 4 ounces. Its memory card contains space to save 128GB of data, more than any other device currently on the market. — [2] — This allows users to snap over 2,000 photos or record over an hour of video footage. The V5 model also contains a number of exclusive apps, including Predictor, which provides hourly weather updates.

The ElectroFone V5 is competitively priced at $299 on Zipstar's Web site. — [3] — Existing Zipstar customers are able to keep their existing phone numbers when purchasing the new model. Instead of entering the pass code included with their new phone, they should contact customer services at (555) 3939-9223. Upon telling the representative the ID number and password stated on the contract, the old number will become active on the new device. — [4] —

---

3. What is indicated about the Zipstar Corporation?
(A) It is based in Asia.
(B) It was founded twenty years ago.
(C) It has paid for a selection of television advertisements.
(D) It sells a range of electronic items.

4. What is NOT a stated feature of the V5 model?
(A) It contains a built-in flashlight.
(B) It is available in a variety of colors.
(C) It contains some unique applications.
(D) It has a large storage capacity.

5. In which of the positions marked [1], [2], [3], and [4] does the following sentence best belong?

"This figure may be reduced by 20% by entering the code SAVE20 when making a purchase, which will undoubtedly delight customers."

(A) [1]
(B) [2]
(C) [3]
(D) [4]

Culinary Experts of North America(CENA)
Techniques Used in Asian Cooking

Date: Saturday, October 9
Registration Deadline: Monday, October 3
Registration Fee: $200
Venue: Sheraton Center Hotel

Schedule:

7:00 - 8:00	Coffee & Introductions
8:00 - 8:30	Welcome Speech from CENA President Lisa Franklin
8:30 - 10:30	Workshop: A Guide to Asian Flavors and Spices with William Sanders
10:30 - 11:00	Recess
11:00 - 1:00	Workshop: The Art of Curry Making with Sanjay Patel
1:00 - 2:00	Lunch
2:00 - 3:00	Demonstration: The Joys of Asian Desserts with Melanie Bolton
3:00 - 4:30	Movie: 'The History of Asian Foods' - Narrated by Cindy Witherspoon
4:30 - 5:00	Refreshments
5:00 - 6:30	Workshop: Korean and Chinese Dishes with Stacy Kim
6:30 - 8:00	Dinner: A Range of Asian Dishes (Optional - $40 per person)

*Only personal checks and credit cards are accepted.

_ □ X

To:	CENA Members
From:	CENA President, Lisa Franklin <lfranklin@cena.com>
Date:	October 2
Subject:	Experience day - Techniques used in Asian cooking

Dear Culinary enthusiast,

As you are no doubt aware, we are holding our Asian cooking experience day at the Sheraton Center Hotel in Toronto this year. We have a lot of interest in this event, and nearly half of the tickets have already been sold. Thank you for your continued support.

I am writing to inform you of a number of changes made to the schedule of this event. Mr. William Sanders is no longer able to give his workshop 'A Guide to Asian Flavors and Spices' as he has to leave the country to tend to some urgent business. Therefore, his esteemed colleague, Ms. Margaret Hatcher, will lead the workshop in his place. Secondly, due to a booking conflict at the hotel, Ms. Kim's event and Ms. Witherspoon's movie have now switched places on the schedule. So, to clarify, the Korean and Chinese food class will take place at 3 P.M., and the movie will be shown at 5 P.M.

Lastly, due to an increase in the prices of ingredients, the caterers have felt the need to raise the cost of the dinner at the end of the day. It is now priced at $50 per person.

There are still 40 spots available for new customers to register. If you have not done so already and would like to, please call my secretary at (510) 282-4740. We hope to see as many of you as possible on October 9 for what will be a fantastic day.

Lisa Franklin
CENA President

6. According to the notice, when will the event take place?
(A) October 2
(B) October 3
(C) October 9
(D) October 11

7. What is the purpose of the e-mail?
(A) To distribute new work schedules
(B) To inform members of changes to the schedule of an event
(C) To announce that the location of the event has changed
(D) To provide information about discounted accommodation rates

8. What is indicated about the workshop 'A Guide to Asian Flavors and Spices'?
(A) It has been canceled.
(B) It will be led by a different person.
(C) It will be extended in length by one hour.
(D) An extra fee will be charged to attend this course.

9. What time will Ms. Kim's workshop take place?
(A) At 2:00
(B) At 3:00
(C) At 5:00
(D) At 6:30

10. Why is the dinner now more expensive?
(A) The hotel is charging more to provide dinner.
(B) Some top chefs are preparing their best dishes.
(C) The prices of the ingredients have risen.
(D) There will be gourmet food and a show in a hotel-like interior.

정답 1. (D) 2. (B) 3. (D) 4. (A) 5. (C) 6. (C) 7. (B) 8. (B) 9. (B) 10. (C)

학습 스케줄

∷ 초급 레벨 ∷ 일단 어휘량을 늘리고 기본적인 독해 실력을 키우세요! (맞힌 개수 5개 이하)

문장의 뜻을 정확히 파악하기 힘들고 어휘력이 약한 편이라 문제 풀이가 만만치 않겠어요. 실전문제 풀이와 더불어 어휘 암기와 독해 훈련도 게을리하면 안돼요. 하루는 1 세트 문제 풀이를 하고, 다음날에는 틀린 문제를 복습한 후 〈독학 노트〉 하루 분량을 꼭 학습하세요. 〈독학 노트〉의 단어를 외우고, 의미 단위로 해석하는 훈련을 하다보면 기본 어휘력과 독해력이 향상되면서 문제 풀이가 한결 수월해질 거예요.

1일 차	2일 차	3일 차	4일 차	5일 차	6일 차
TEST 1 문제풀이	독학 노트 DAY 1	TEST 2 문제풀이	독학 노트 DAY 2	TEST 3 문제풀이	독학 노트 DAY 3
7일 차	**8일 차**	**9일 차**	**10일 차**	**11일 차**	**12일 차**
TEST 4 문제풀이	독학 노트 DAY 4	TEST 5 문제풀이	독학 노트 DAY 5	TEST 6 문제풀이	독학 노트 DAY 6
13일 차	**14일 차**	**15일 차**	**16일 차**	**17일 차**	**18일 차**
TEST 7 문제풀이	독학 노트 DAY 7	TEST 8 문제풀이	독학 노트 DAY 8	TEST 9 문제풀이	독학 노트 DAY 9
19일 차	**20일 차**	**21일 차**	**22일 차**	**23일 차**	**24일 차**
TEST 10 문제풀이	독학 노트 DAY 10	TEST 11 문제풀이	독학 노트 DAY 11	TEST 12 문제풀이	독학 노트 DAY 12

∷ 중급 레벨 ∷ 문제를 빨리 푸는 스킬을 체득하세요! (맞힌 개수 6개~8개)

독해 실력은 어느정도 있지만 시간이 많이 부족하지 않나요? 정확하고 빠르게 정답을 고르는 스킬을 길러 시간 안에 문제를 다 풀고 정답률도 높여야 해요. 하루에 문제 1 세트 풀이와 〈독학 노트〉 하루 분량을 모두 끝내 보세요. 이 단계에서 중요한 것은 반드시 정해진 시간 안에 문제를 모두 푸는거예요. 12 세트를 풀다보면 스스로 빠르게 정답의 단서를 찾는 법을 체득할 거예요. 아직 완벽히 해석이 되는 단계는 아니므로 〈독학 노트〉도 절대 게을리하지 마세요.

1일 차	2일 차	3일 차	4일 차	5일 차	6일 차
TEST 1 문제풀이 + 독학 노트 DAY 1	TEST 2 문제풀이 + 독학 노트 DAY 2	TEST 3 문제풀이 + 독학 노트 DAY 3	TEST4 문제풀이 + 독학 노트 DAY 4	TEST 5 문제풀이 + 독학 노트 DAY 5	TEST 6 문제풀이 + 독학 노트 DAY 6
7일 차	**8일 차**	**9일 차**	**10일 차**	**11일 차**	**12일 차**
TEST 7 문제풀이 + 독학 노트 DAY 7	TEST 8 문제풀이 + 독학 노트 DAY 8	TEST 9 문제풀이 + 독학 노트 DAY 9	TEST 10 문제풀이 + 독학 노트 DAY 10	TEST 11 문제풀이 + 독학 노트 DAY 11	TEST 12 문제풀이 + 독학 노트 DAY 12

∷ 고급 레벨 ∷ 실전이라고 생각하고 실력을 점검해 보세요! (맞힌 개수 9개 이상)

기본적인 독해 실력과 문제 풀이 스킬이 어느 정도 안정권이군요. 실전이라고 생각하고 문제를 풀면서 자신이 특히 어떤 문제에 약한지 확실히 점검해 보세요. 하루에 2회분을 푼 후 틀린 문제 위주로 정리하며 자신이 어떤 유형이나 함정에 취약한지 점검해 나가면 머지않아 만점도 가능한 수준이에요. 따라서 독학 노트까지 활용할 필요는 없겠어요.

1일 차	2일 차	3일 차	4일 차	5일 차	6일 차
TEST 1, 2 문제풀이	TEST 3, 4 문제풀이	TEST 5, 6 문제풀이	TEST 7, 8 문제풀이	TEST 9, 10 문제풀이	TEST 11, 12 문제풀이

TEST

01

적정 문제 풀이 시간 55분(마킹 포함)

55 min

시작 시간 ___시 ___분	**목표 개수** _____ / 54
종료 시간 ___시 ___분	**실제 개수** _____ / 54

- 반드시 55분 안에 문제 풀이 포함 마킹까지 마쳐야 합니다.
- 실제 시험이라고 생각하고 멈추지 말고 풀어보세요.

- 정답 개수에 5를 곱하면 대략적인 점수가 됩니다.

PART 7

Directions: In this part you will read a selection of texts, such as magazine and newspaper articles, e-mails, and instant messages. Each text or set of texts is followed by several questions. Select the best answer for each question and mark the letter (A), (B), (C), or (D) on your answer sheet.

Questions 147-148 refer to the following e-mail.

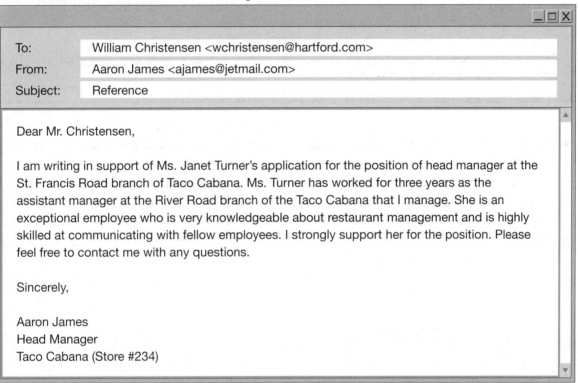

To:	William Christensen <wchristensen@hartford.com>
From:	Aaron James <ajames@jetmail.com>
Subject:	Reference

Dear Mr. Christensen,

I am writing in support of Ms. Janet Turner's application for the position of head manager at the St. Francis Road branch of Taco Cabana. Ms. Turner has worked for three years as the assistant manager at the River Road branch of the Taco Cabana that I manage. She is an exceptional employee who is very knowledgeable about restaurant management and is highly skilled at communicating with fellow employees. I strongly support her for the position. Please feel free to contact me with any questions.

Sincerely,

Aaron James
Head Manager
Taco Cabana (Store #234)

147. Why was this e-mail sent?

(A) To apply for a job opening
(B) To accept a job offer
(C) To recommend a job seeker
(D) To request a reference

148. What is NOT indicated about Ms. Turner?

(A) She has supervisory experience.
(B) She currently works for Mr. James.
(C) She was hired last year.
(D) She knows a lot about running an eatery.

▶ ▶ ▶GO ON TO THE NEXT PAGE

KERMAN "BIG MAX" BICYCLE

SAFETY RECALL

This product is being recalled because of a problem with its adjustable seat mechanism. A number of owners have reported the mechanism becomes loose while the bicycle is in use, resulting in the seat rotating or sliding. The recall is limited to bicycles produced at Kerman's Tenjin plant between March 3 and June 2 and which were sold in the North American market.

Owners of potentially affected bicycles should stop using the bikes immediately. They should contact Kerman at 1-888-476-9032.

149. What is indicated about Big Max bicycles made in Tenjin?

(A) They may have a faulty part.
(B) They were mistakenly sent overseas.
(C) They are missing an information plate.
(D) They were sold without a seat.

150. What are some Big Max owners advised to do?

(A) Return their bikes to stores
(B) Purchase a replacement part
(C) Call the manufacturer
(D) Continue riding their bikes

Questions 151-153 refer to the following article.

Purchasers of certain models of cameras manufactured by JCR, Inc. are being alerted to a potential battery issue. Consumer complaints indicate that the batteries of certain models are unable to hold a charge after only being used a few times. According to JCR, the batteries are designed to be recharged a minimum of fifty times before beginning to lose capacity.

The affected models are those in the J100 and J200 product lines. Customers who purchased any of these models may exchange the camera's original battery at any retailer carrying JCR products or by mailing it back to JCR. Details on the exchange process can be found on the company's Web site. There is no cost to camera owners.

Since news of the problem surfaced, sales of JCR cameras have slumped. The company blames the problem on a supplier. "Customer satisfaction is our first priority," said President Tom Jenkins. "We will do everything to remedy this unfortunate situation, including a redesign of the parts, if needed."

151. What is the article mainly about?

(A) A redesign of a popular camera
(B) A limited-time special offer
(C) A discontinued product line
(D) A flawed component of a product

152. What is indicated about the rechargeable batteries?

(A) They are not working as intended.
(B) They were recently redesigned.
(C) They will be replaced for a fee.
(D) They can be purchased online.

153. What did Mr. Jenkins emphasize about his company?

(A) It strives to make a perfect product.
(B) It makes the best cameras on the market.
(C) It wants customers to be happy with its products.
(D) It will avoid hiring outside suppliers.

▶ ▶ ▶ GO ON TO THE NEXT PAGE

Questions 154-155 refer to the following text message chain.

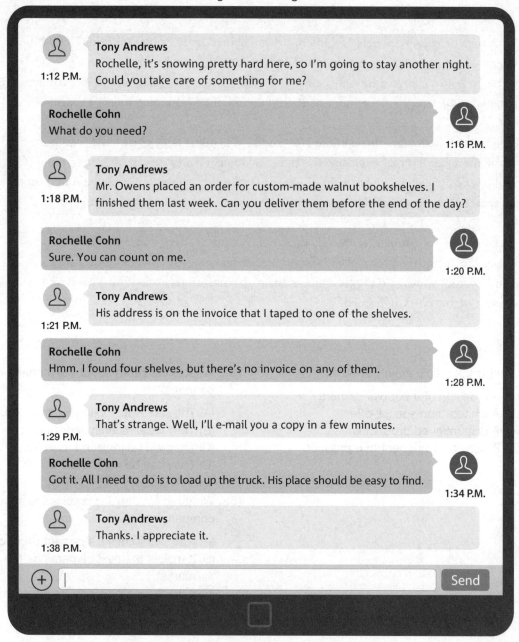

Tony Andrews 1:12 P.M.
Rochelle, it's snowing pretty hard here, so I'm going to stay another night. Could you take care of something for me?

Rochelle Cohn
What do you need?
1:16 P.M.

Tony Andrews 1:18 P.M.
Mr. Owens placed an order for custom-made walnut bookshelves. I finished them last week. Can you deliver them before the end of the day?

Rochelle Cohn
Sure. You can count on me.
1:20 P.M.

Tony Andrews 1:21 P.M.
His address is on the invoice that I taped to one of the shelves.

Rochelle Cohn
Hmm. I found four shelves, but there's no invoice on any of them.
1:28 P.M.

Tony Andrews 1:29 P.M.
That's strange. Well, I'll e-mail you a copy in a few minutes.

Rochelle Cohn
Got it. All I need to do is to load up the truck. His place should be easy to find.
1:34 P.M.

Tony Andrews 1:38 P.M.
Thanks. I appreciate it.

154. Who most likely is Mr. Andrews?

(A) A furniture maker
(B) A truck driver
(C) An office manager
(D) A traveling salesman

155. At 1:34 P.M., what does Ms. Cohn most likely mean when she writes, "Got it"?

(A) She needs to continue searching.
(B) She received the delivery address.
(C) She found the missing invoice.
(D) She understands her duties.

Questions 156-158 refer to the following e-mail.

To: rtomasson@getmail.net

From: gwells@aceappliance.com

Subject: Inspection

Date: March 27

Dear Ms. Tomasson,

I want to let you know that our technician completed his inspection of your Zama 2000 washing machine. He determined that the machine's motor has died. While we could attempt to repair it, we generally find it is less expensive just to install a brand-new motor. — [1] —

During the inspection, the technician also noticed that several of the machine's internal parts were seriously worn and at risk of failure. We could also replace those. Again, you would be responsible for 20% of the cost. — [2] —

Another option is for you simply to purchase a new washing machine. Personally, this is what I would recommend doing. Your current machine is already 15 years old. The average service life for this specific model is nine years. — [3] — If you would like recommendations for potential replacements, I would be happy to discuss them with you.

We patiently await your decision. — [4] —

Sincerely,

George Wells
Ace Appliance Service

---

156. Why did Mr. Wells write to Ms. Tommason?

(A) To suggest a product to a client
(B) To report a problem with an employee
(C) To explain a situation with an appliance
(D) To offer an apology for a mechanical failure

157. What is indicated about Ms. Tommason's washing machine?

(A) It requires two replacement parts.
(B) It lasted longer than most Zama 2000s.
(C) It can be replaced with an identical model.
(D) It was first introduced 15 years ago.

158. In which of the positions marked [1], [2], [3], and [4] does the following sentence best belong?

"Your service contract will cover 80% of the costs."

(A) [1]
(B) [2]
(C) [3]
(D) [4]

▶ ▶ ▶ GO ON TO THE NEXT PAGE

NEW DROP-OFF/PICKUP POLICY

Effective: Monday, March 1

Due to concerns over the increased traffic on Washington Boulevard that has resulted from construction on Highway 45, Shining Star Preschool requests that all children be dropped off and picked up at the rear entrance of our building. Staff will be present every morning from 7:00 until 8:00 to meet children at the rear entrance. In addition, staff will escort children to the rear entrance twice a day at noon and 2:30 P.M. so that parents can pick up their children. Parents arriving after 8:00 A.M. or making a pickup after 2:30 P.M. can still access the building via the main entrance on Washington Boulevard; however, for the sake of your children's safety, we recommend that you park in our rear lot and walk around the front of the building. Please feel free to call me with any questions or concerns at 555-8273.

Sincerely,

Marsha Vernon
Director, Shining Star Preschool

159. For whom is the announcement mainly intended?

(A) Parents
(B) Construction workers
(C) Preschool staff
(D) Students

160. What is NOT stated about the new policy?

(A) It directs regular pickups to the rear entrance.
(B) It will begin on March 1.
(C) It prohibits the use of the parking lot.
(D) It is in response to a safety risk.

Questions 161-163 refer to the following advertisement.

Your Car Is a Reflection of Who You Are!

Give it the care it deserves: Contact Car Care Specialists

We provide a full-service auto wash. We will wash your vehicle at your home or place of business seven days a week. We work hard to make sure your vehicle looks its best.

Here are just a few of our services.

- Full-service exterior wash and hand waxing
- Engine compartment wash
- Interior leather and carpet deep-cleaning and stain treatment
- Minor surface repairs (i.e. paint touchup and scratches)
- Windshield crack repair

Our automated scheduling and payment system make working with us hassle-free. Simply go to www.ccs.com to set up an appointment today.

*A travel fee will be charged for vehicles located outside the following ZIP codes: 88930, 88932, 88941, 88946, and 88948. Current pricing and fee details are posted on our Web site.

161. What is indicated about Car Care Specialists?

(A) It is open for business daily.
(B) It recently changed its prices.
(C) It has five separate locations.
(D) It charges extra to go to clients' homes.

162. What is NOT a service offered by Car Care Specialists?

(A) Washing the outside of a car
(B) Cleaning a car's carpet
(C) Checking a vehicle's oil
(D) Repairing damaged paint

163. According to the advertisement, how can readers schedule a service?

(A) By calling the main number
(B) By visiting a location
(C) By e-mailing a staff member
(D) By visiting a Web site

▷ ▶ ▶ GO ON TO THE NEXT PAGE

Questions 164-167 refer to the following e-mail.

From: Timothy Whitacre

To: John Severin

Subject: Meeting with Alcade

Date: February 8

John,

I just got off the phone with Alcade Promotions. The company has agreed to organize a series of events to promote our newest line of beauty products. Jessica Blackmore, the senior account manager, will plan and coordinate the events. We need to meet with her as soon as possible to start the process. Are you free this Friday at 12:30? I was thinking we could meet for lunch at Winston's.

We need to prepare some preliminary marketing materials before the meeting. Have Tanya Ivers assemble some of the better product photos we took last month. We should also have a summary of the marketing ideas we generated at our last meeting to present to Ms. Blackmore. Maybe Allison Hogan can work with you to prepare that. Finally, get in touch with Richard Pena. He should be able to provide us with some product samples. I understand that the designs for the jars, tubes, and bottles are not ready yet. However, that should not delay us in getting the actual samples to Ms. Blackmore. We can send her the designs later.

Best,

Timothy Whitacre
Marketing Director
Paragon Cosmetics

---

164. What is one reason Mr. Whitacre contacted Mr. Severin?

(A) To propose a project
(B) To reschedule a meeting
(C) To report on a meeting
(D) To make an appointment

165. What is indicated about the product samples?

(A) They will not be available.
(B) They need to be tested.
(C) They were sent to Mr. Whitacre.
(D) Their containers are unfinished.

166. Who most likely is NOT an employee of Paragon Cosmetics?

(A) Jessica Blackmore
(B) Allison Hogan
(C) Richard Pena
(D) Tanya Ivers

167. What does Mr. Whitacre ask Mr. Severin to do?

(A) Obtain the new designs
(B) Send samples to Ms. Blackmore
(C) Generate new marketing ideas
(D) Get ready for a meeting

Questions 168-171 refer to the following announcement.

Bartlett Office Building News   August Issue

Announcements

Recycling: Bartlett management has enacted a new recycling policy that requires all tenants and their employees to recycle. It is the individual duty of each office to sort trash into recyclables and non-recyclables. — [1] — Bins will be provided as follows: blue bins are for plastic, gray bins are for paper, green bins are for aluminum, and black bins are for regular trash. Detailed illustrated charts will be posted throughout the building to help explain the recycling sorting process.

Security: The safety and security of our tenants is our number-one priority at the Bartlett Office Building. The loss of a set of keys to the building's main entrance last month has raised some concerns. — [2] — Since the missing keys were not found, we replaced the locks on all exterior doors. The new locks require the use of swipe cards. Those tenants who have not picked yours up yet, please do so right away. We also ask that you return your old keys to the security office.

Parking Permit: In order to further address security concerns pertaining to our premises, Bartlett management will be issuing parking permits to each office. — [3] — Each person is required to place a permit on the dashboard of his or her car. Cars parked in the building parking lot without a permit will be towed. If you suspect your car has been towed, please call 555-2421. — [4] —

168. What is NOT indicated about the recycling program?

(A) It requires different bins for different types of waste.
(B) It is optional for tenants in the Bartlett Office Building.
(C) It is the first of its kind at the Bartlett Office Building.
(D) It will use graphics to explain how to recycle.

169. What is suggested about the building's tenants?

(A) They must pay for replacement keys.
(B) Some need to show their ID cards.
(C) They like to volunteer with charities.
(D) Some continue to hold useless keys.

170. Why are parking permits being distributed to tenants?

(A) To respond to worries about safety
(B) To keep track of ticketed vehicles
(C) To address overcrowding in parking lots
(D) To raise money for a local charity

171. In which of the positions marked [1], [2], [3], and [4] does the following sentence best belong?

"Please provide the total number of employees present in your office."

(A) [1]
(B) [2]
(C) [3]
(D) [4]

▶ ▶ ▶ GO ON TO THE NEXT PAGE

Questions 172-175 refer to the following online chat discussion.

Paulson, Amber
2:15 P.M.
Sal from Marconi's just called. He isn't going to be able to do our upcoming awards dinner on March 31.

Georgas, Angie
2:16 P.M.
Why not?

Paulson, Amber
2:18 P.M.
He signed a contract for an unusually large wedding that weekend and doesn't have enough additional staff for our event.

Taylor, Ray
2:22 P.M.
Couldn't he still prepare the food? Then we could have some of our own employees take care of serving, cleanup, and such.

Georgas, Angie
2:24 P.M.
That could get really complicated. Someone would have to coordinate, and we are all involved in the ceremony. I think the best course of action is to find another restaurant to do the catering.

Taylor, Ray
2:30 P.M.
It'll be hard to replace Marconi's.

Georgas, Angie
2:34 P.M.
I know. It has catered every event for us for the past ten years or so and always does a great job.

Paulson, Amber
2:38 P.M.
Fortunately, Sal gave me the name of an independent catering company that is operated by one of his chefs. I think we should contact that firm and find out what it can offer us.

Taylor, Ray
2:42 P.M.
It's worth a try. What's the name?

Paulson, Amber
2:45 P.M.
Top Notch Catering. The number is 555-4044.

Taylor, Ray
2:48 P.M.
I will get in touch with it and request a menu before we leave for the day.

Send

172. What most likely is Marconi's?

(A) A restaurant
(B) A grocery store
(C) A culinary school
(D) A banquet hall

173. Why is Marconi's unable to provide the service?

(A) It had to change its menu.
(B) It lacks enough employees.
(C) It is closed on a certain date.
(D) It does not take reservations.

174. At 2:34 P.M., what does Ms. Georgas most likely mean when she writes, "I know"?

(A) It will be impossible to continue with the event.
(B) There is not enough time left to make a change.
(C) It will not be easy to find an equal to Marconi's.
(D) They have no choice but to replace Marconi's.

175. What will Mr. Taylor do later today?

(A) Speak with a potential caterer
(B) Suggest dinner options
(C) Place an order for dinner
(D) Make a change to a menu

▶ ▶ ▶GO ON TO THE NEXT PAGE

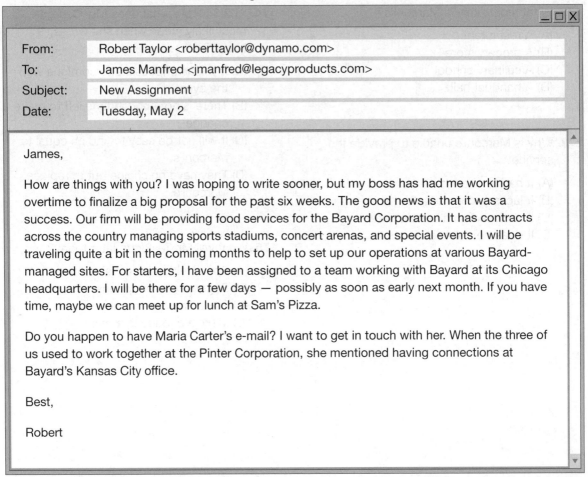

From: Robert Taylor <roberttaylor@dynamo.com>
To: James Manfred <jmanfred@legacyproducts.com>
Subject: New Assignment
Date: Tuesday, May 2

James,

How are things with you? I was hoping to write sooner, but my boss has had me working overtime to finalize a big proposal for the past six weeks. The good news is that it was a success. Our firm will be providing food services for the Bayard Corporation. It has contracts across the country managing sports stadiums, concert arenas, and special events. I will be traveling quite a bit in the coming months to help to set up our operations at various Bayard-managed sites. For starters, I have been assigned to a team working with Bayard at its Chicago headquarters. I will be there for a few days — possibly as soon as early next month. If you have time, maybe we can meet up for lunch at Sam's Pizza.

Do you happen to have Maria Carter's e-mail? I want to get in touch with her. When the three of us used to work together at the Pinter Corporation, she mentioned having connections at Bayard's Kansas City office.

Best,

Robert

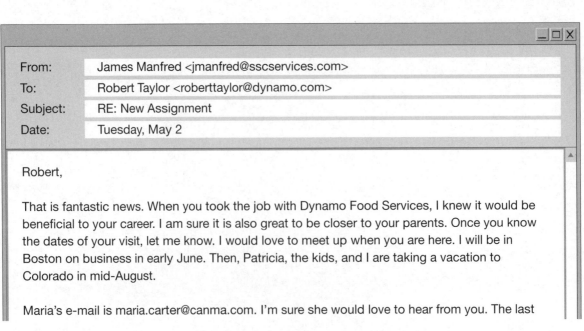

From: James Manfred <jmanfred@sscservices.com>
To: Robert Taylor <roberttaylor@dynamo.com>
Subject: RE: New Assignment
Date: Tuesday, May 2

Robert,

That is fantastic news. When you took the job with Dynamo Food Services, I knew it would be beneficial to your career. I am sure it is also great to be closer to your parents. Once you know the dates of your visit, let me know. I would love to meet up when you are here. I will be in Boston on business in early June. Then, Patricia, the kids, and I are taking a vacation to Colorado in mid-August.

Maria's e-mail is maria.carter@canma.com. I'm sure she would love to hear from you. The last time I heard, she had been promoted to vice president of operations. Good for her!

Cheers,

James

176. What is one purpose of the first e-mail?

(A) To make travel arrangements
(B) To request contact information
(C) To propose a collaboration
(D) To submit a proposal

177. In the first e-mail, the phrase "get in touch with" in paragraph 2, line 1 is closest in meaning to

(A) hire
(B) meet
(C) inform
(D) contact

178. Who is Maria Carter?

(A) Mr. Manfred's boss
(B) An employee at Bayard
(C) A former colleague of Mr. Taylor's
(D) An executive at the Pinter Corporation

179. In the second e-mail, what is indicated about Mr. Manfred?

(A) He might not be able to meet Mr. Taylor.
(B) He often meets with Ms. Carter.
(C) He works for Dynamo Food Services.
(D) He sent an e-mail to Ms. Carter.

180. Where does Mr. Manfred most likely live?

(A) In Boston
(B) In Chicago
(C) In Colorado
(D) In Kansas City

▶ ▶ ▶GO ON TO THE NEXT PAGE

Home Chef

Ship to: Paul Lowman
890 Soma Road
San Angelo, TX 20033

(216) 555-4579
low999@netmail.net

Shipped on: November 13
Order number: 8294043
Ordered on: November 12

Estimated arrival: November 17

SKU #	Description	Color	Quantity	Cost
62007	24" baking pan	black	1	$32.00
62904	Large serving spoon	silver	3	$12.00
63945	18" metal serving tray	silver	1	$18.00
67845	Cloth napkins	brown/orange	15	$16.00
Shipping type: Standard (3-5 days)			Subtotal	$78.00
Payment: credit card/# xxx-xxx-7494			Discount	($0.00)
Coupon code: n/a			Shipping	$4.40
			Tax	$3.90
			Total	$86.30

Thank you for shopping with Home Chef, the nation's largest online kitchen supply retailer. If you are unsatisfied with any item in your order, please return the item within 30 days of the shipping date for a full refund.

Please direct any questions or concerns to our Customer Service Department at info@homechef.com.

```
                                                                    _ □ X
```

From:	Paul Lowman <low999@netmail.net>
To:	Customer Service<info@homechef.com>
Subject:	Order Number 8294043
Date:	Tuesday, November 18

To whom it may concern,

When I arrived home from work this afternoon, I was pleased to find that my order from your company had already been delivered to my home. It was just in time to prepare for the holiday! The tray will look lovely on my table. The pan is large enough to fit the turkey I will prepare.

The only problem is that you sent me five napkins instead of fifteen. I placed the order so that each of my guests and I would have one. This is my first time hosting a Thanksgiving dinner, and my coworkers are attending. I want to make sure everything is perfect. Please send me the missing items as soon as possible!

Sincerely,

Paul Lowman

---

181. What is indicated about Mr. Lowman's order?

(A) He used a coupon.
(B) He lives in an apartment.
(C) He placed it via a Web site.
(D) He paid by check.

182. When did Home Chef send the order to Mr. Lowman?

(A) On November 12
(B) On November 13
(C) On November 17
(D) On November 18

183. What is suggested about Mr. Lowman?

(A) He was at work when the order arrived.
(B) He regularly hosts dinner parties.
(C) He is a vegetarian.
(D) He is a kitchen supply retailer.

184. Which item was missing from Mr. Lowman's order?

(A) 62007
(B) 62904
(C) 63945
(D) 67845

185. How many guests is Mr. Lowman planning to have?

(A) 4
(B) 8
(C) 14
(D) 15

▶ ▶ ▶GO ON TO THE NEXT PAGE

MEMO

From: Jan Albertson
To: All Public Relations Department Staff
RE: Rebranding
Date: Tuesday, July 8

As you may have heard, the proposal to rebrand the company was officially approved at yesterday's board meeting. It was decided that the name change shall be completed as soon as possible. You need to develop a transition plan to ensure that all internal and external communications are ready to be updated. In addition, I would like a team to be formed to create the new company's logo, which will be unveiled to the public at the same time as the official renaming. I look forward to an initial progress report by next Monday, July 14.

Hickox to Get New Name for New Identity

by Veronica Garcia

SEAGRAM (August 12) – As of the last day of this month, Hickox Industrial Manufacturing, Inc. will be no more. The company will announce the official name change to Hickox Technologies during a ceremony at its Seagram headquarters on September 1.

The company's CEO, Jan Albertson, explained, "The new name better reflects the evolution of our company from a major manufacturer to a diversified technology company."

Since taking the top leadership position at Hickox three years ago, Mr. Albertson has aggressively acquired smaller, specialized firms with strong growth potential. He targeted software programmers, robotics designers, and research labs to give Hickox a competitive edge in the twenty-first century economy.

Hickox was founded in 1955 as a designer and manufacturer of precision industrial equipment. It is currently the third largest employer in Bacon County.

From: Ed Norman <edward.norman@getmail.net>

To: Jan Albertson <jan.albertson@hickox.com >

Date: September 2

RE: Congratulations!

Jan,

Sorry, I couldn't make it to yesterday's ceremony. I want to let you know that I really respect all that you have done with the company. When you suggested purchasing Nava Designs four years ago, I disagreed. However, I believed in you enough to petition the board to name you my successor when I retired. I'm glad they did. You were right about Nava Designs and all the other acquisitions. Wishing you continued success!

Regards,

Ed

186. According to the memo, what happened on July 7?

(A) A company publicized a name change.
(B) A transition plan was revised.
(C) A suggestion was accepted.
(D) A gathering was rescheduled.

187. What date was the logo supposed to be made public?

(A) July 8
(B) July 14
(C) September 1
(D) September 2

188. In the article, what is NOT mentioned about Hickox?

(A) The company will open a new headquarters.
(B) The company is located in Bacon County.
(C) The company changed leaders three years ago.
(D) The company has been buying other companies.

189. Why did Mr. Norman write to Mr. Albertson?

(A) To provide an excuse
(B) To criticize a decision
(C) To offer praise
(D) To make a recommendation

190. What most likely was Mr. Norman's former career?

(A) Newspaper reporter
(B) City official
(C) Industrial engineer
(D) Corporate executive

▶ ▶ ▶GO ON TO THE NEXT PAGE

Stay on top of current events with this special offer!

Global Interest magazine has extended a special offer to all Mason-Dixon employees. Subscribe before May 1 and get up to 50% off the regular price. Subscribers will get access to some of the best journalism on the planet. Global Interest is a weekly international news magazine published in print and online. Those who choose digital subscriptions will also get access to the magazine's online archive, which contains over 45 years

Subscriptions	Special Annual Rate
print only	$30
digital only	$50
print + digital	$65
audio version (downloadable)	$75

of exceptional writing. Subscription forms can be obtained at the Human Resources Department on the seventh floor.

To:	Roman Codrescu <rcodrescu@masondixon.com>
From:	Eric Majors <emajcrs@masondixon.com>
Subject:	Global Interest offer
Date:	April 18
Attachment:	subscription_form

Hi, Roman.

I am returning the subscription form for the Global Interest offer. Thanks for taking the time to explain the different subscription options when I picked the form up from your office. I decided to go with the least expensive one that lets me access the older content on its Web site. When I find writers I really appreciate, I like to go back and read their previous articles. I would like to start my subscription as soon as possible. Please let me know the quickest way to do that.

Best,

Eric

Subscriber #9037324

Eric Majors
873 Hope Way

Lincoln, NE 29003

April 29

Dear Mr. Majors,

Thank you for your interest in Global Interest. To start your subscription, we need to receive your payment. Enclosed is a payment card with the amount due. Please return the card with your payment for a one-year subscription. We accept personal checks, credit cards, and bank transfers. Your subscription will be activated within 3-5 business days after your payment is processed.

If you would like to activate your subscription immediately, you can use our online payment option. Just visit www.globalinterst.com and click on the "Manage Subscriptions" tab. There, you will enter your subscriber number. You will be prompted to select a username and a password before submitting your payment information.

Sincerely,

Harris Polanski
Subscriber Services Representative
Global Interest Magazine

191. What is NOT indicated about Global Interest magazine?

(A) It is available in a form for listeners.
(B) It is published on a regular basis.
(C) It is sold in dozens of countries.
(D) It allows readers to see past issues.

192. What is suggested about Mr. Codrescu?

(A) He works on the seventh floor.
(B) He subscribes to Global Interest.
(C) He writes for a news publication.
(D) He is Mr. Polanski's supervisor.

193. How much will Mr. Majors most likely be charged for his subscription to Global Interest?

(A) $30
(B) $50
(C) $65
(D) $75

194. What is suggested about Mr. Majors?

(A) His employer is located in Lincoln.
(B) He will pay for his subscription online.
(C) His job requires him to follow local news.
(D) He works for a media company.

195. Why did Mr. Polanski write the letter?

(A) To recommend a subscription option
(B) To explain a new Web site feature
(C) To request the correction of a payment error
(D) To provide instructions to a new subscriber

▶ ▶ ▶ GO ON TO THE NEXT PAGE

Smart Balance Offers Healthy Meals

By Mark Swenz

Portland, OR (November 18) - Public schools have had to revise their menus to encourage students to eat a more balanced diet. Namely, they have cut down on carbohydrates and refined sugar and replaced them with healthier foods. But have you ever thought about encouraging healthy eating in the workplace?

Privately owned catering company Smart Balance says that employees eating a balanced diet are just as important as it is for students, and that's why it created office-oriented meal plans that include plenty of protein, fruit, and vegetables. Too often, catered food is high in fat and carbohydrates, which can leave employees feeling sluggish.

"Tired employees are not as productive as they can be," said Smart Balance founder Freda Hiens. "In order to have enough energy, employees need to eat a balanced diet." The cost of more balanced meals is often comparable to standard catered fare as well.

Smart Balance, which began in Hiens' own personal kitchen, received funding from investors that topped $500,000. Today, its regular clients include several local corporations such as Maxmay, Chico's, and AdWorld.

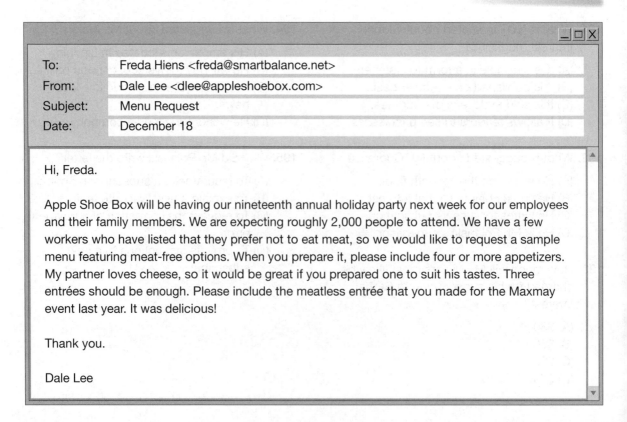

To:	Freda Hiens <freda@smartbalance.net>
From:	Dale Lee <dlee@appleshoebox.com>
Subject:	Menu Request
Date:	December 18

Hi, Freda.

Apple Shoe Box will be having our nineteenth annual holiday party next week for our employees and their family members. We are expecting roughly 2,000 people to attend. We have a few workers who have listed that they prefer not to eat meat, so we would like to request a sample menu featuring meat-free options. When you prepare it, please include four or more appetizers. My partner loves cheese, so it would be great if you prepared one to suit his tastes. Three entrées should be enough. Please include the meatless entrée that you made for the Maxmay event last year. It was delicious!

Thank you.

Dale Lee

Apple Shoe Box
Holiday Party Menu

Appetizers
Sunrise Kale Salad*
Chicken-Bacon Wraps
Spaghetti Squash Cups
Baked Cheese Sticks

Entrées
Wild Rice Stuffed Squash*
Spaghetti with Meatballs
Roasted Chicken
Grilled Fish

*For vegetarian

196. According to the article, what is suggested about Smart Balance's meals?

(A) They help employees stay active at work.
(B) They are tastier than regular meals.
(C) They are easy to prepare.
(D) They are free of fat and carbohydrates.

197. In the e-mail, what is mentioned about the holiday party?

(A) More people are expected this year.
(B) Vegetarian options were available last year.
(C) Employees' spouses are welcome at the event.
(D) All employees are required to attend.

198. What is indicated about Ms. Hiens?

(A) She started her company in her home.
(B) She catered for Mr. Lee in the past.
(C) She will attend the holiday party.
(D) She cooks all the food herself.

199. What dish is most likely for Mr. Lee's partner?

(A) Sunrise Kale Salad
(B) Chicken-Bacon Wrap
(C) Spaghetti Squash Cups
(D) Baked Cheese Sticks

200. What is suggested about Smart Balance's Wild Rice Stuffed Squash?

(A) It was made for a regular customer.
(B) It will not appeal to Mr. Lee.
(C) It is one of the most popular dishes.
(D) It includes some dairy products.

Test 01 정답

147. (C)	**148.** (C)	**149.** (A)	**150.** (C)	**151.** (D)	**152.** (A)
153. (C)	**154.** (A)	**155.** (B)	**156.** (C)	**157.** (B)	**158.** (A)
159. (A)	**160.** (C)	**161.** (A)	**162.** (C)	**163.** (D)	**164.** (D)
165. (D)	**166.** (A)	**167.** (D)	**168.** (B)	**169.** (D)	**170.** (A)
171. (C)	**172.** (A)	**173.** (B)	**174.** (C)	**175.** (A)	**176.** (B)
177. (D)	**178.** (C)	**179.** (A)	**180.** (B)	**181.** (C)	**182.** (B)
183. (A)	**184.** (D)	**185.** (C)	**186.** (C)	**187.** (C)	**188.** (A)
189. (C)	**190.** (D)	**191.** (C)	**192.** (A)	**193.** (B)	**194.** (B)
195. (D)	**196.** (A)	**197.** (C)	**198.** (A)	**199.** (D)	**200.** (A)

TEST

02

적정 문제 풀이 시간 55분(마킹 포함)

55 **min**

시작 시간 ___시 ___분

종료 시간 ___시 ___분

목표 개수 _____ / 54

실제 개수 _____ / 54

• 반드시 55분 안에 문제 풀이 포함 마킹까지 마쳐야 합니다.

• 실제 시험이라고 생각하고 멈추지 말고 풀어보세요.

• 정답 개수에 5를 곱하면 대략적인 점수가 됩니다.

PART 7

Directions: In this part you will read a selection of texts, such as magazine and newspaper articles, e-mails, and instant messages. Each text or set of texts is followed by several questions. Select the best answer for each question and mark the letter (A), (B), (C), or (D) on your answer sheet.

Questions 147-148 refer to the following notice.

With regards to your request to transfer electric service for account 99234, please be advised that the new party is required to continue payment of your monthly service within the same billing cycle beginning and ending on the 5th every month.

After completing the service transfer form, the new responsible party may send service payments by phone or mail. Phone payments can be made by dialing 555-9293 and choosing the payment option. To mail your payment, fill out the pay form attached to each bill and send it to the return address before the due date.

147. For whom is the notice most likely intended?

(A) A bill collector
(B) A utility subscriber
(C) A phone service customer
(D) An electric serviceman

148. What is mentioned about the service transfer?

(A) It must be arranged a month in advance.
(B) A new billing cycle will be assigned.
(C) It will be completed within five business days.
(D) There are two ways to make a payment.

▶ ▶ ▶GO ON TO THE NEXT PAGE

Questions 149-150 refer to the following text message chain.

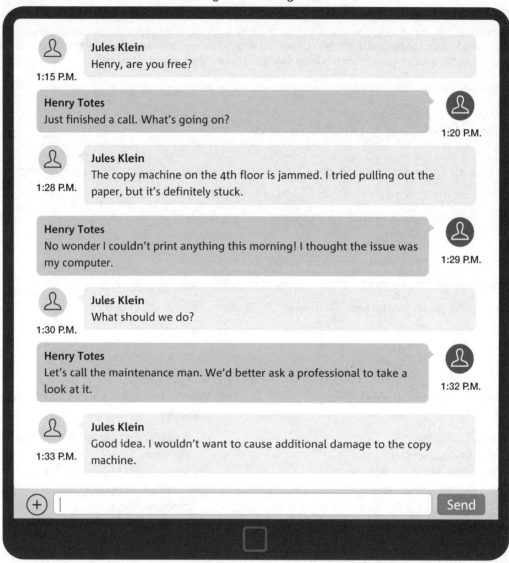

Jules Klein — 1:15 P.M.
Henry, are you free?

Henry Totes — 1:20 P.M.
Just finished a call. What's going on?

Jules Klein — 1:28 P.M.
The copy machine on the 4th floor is jammed. I tried pulling out the paper, but it's definitely stuck.

Henry Totes — 1:29 P.M.
No wonder I couldn't print anything this morning! I thought the issue was my computer.

Jules Klein — 1:30 P.M.
What should we do?

Henry Totes — 1:32 P.M.
Let's call the maintenance man. We'd better ask a professional to take a look at it.

Jules Klein — 1:33 P.M.
Good idea. I wouldn't want to cause additional damage to the copy machine.

Send

149. At 1:32 P.M., what does Mr. Totes most likely mean when he writes, "We'd better ask a professional to take a look at it."?

(A) He will inspect the machine himself.
(B) He suggests ordering a new machine.
(C) He wants Ms. Klein to fix the machine.
(D) He prefers a technician to repair the machine.

150. What is indicated about the copy machine?

(A) It caused Mr. Totes's computer to malfunction.
(B) It ran out of the correct size of paper.
(C) It was broken even before Ms. Klein noticed.
(D) Mr. Totes attempted to fix the machine.

Questions 151-153 refer to the following e-mail.

From: gcharles@bayers.com

To: sallyhu@northon.org

Date: August 12

Subject: Candidate Mary Wiggins

Dear Ms. Hu,

I am writing to recommend you to hire Mary Wiggins for the position of junior editor at Northon. — [1] — Mary was my editorial intern for the past year and worked closely with me on a major editorial project. Her attention to detail is impeccable.

In addition to her editorial skills, her university education makes her a strong candidate for junior editor at Northon. — [2] — When a staff member was uncertain about information presented in a manuscript, Mary buckled down and researched every question until the facts were verified.

Although Mary only finished school last month, I am confident she will be a successful editor. — [3] — I highly recommend Mary Wiggins for your company.

Should you need any further testimony, do not hesitate to call me at (323) 555-4476. I will be happy to talk more about Mary's qualifications. — [4] —

Sincerely,

Gene Charles
Senior Editor
Bayers Books

151. What is the purpose of the e-mail?

(A) To look for a new hire
(B) To endorse a job candidate
(C) To discourage an employee
(D) To admonish a new client

152. What is most likely true about Ms. Wiggins?

(A) She was hired by Mr. Charles.
(B) She recently graduated from college.
(C) She has years of editorial experience.
(D) She enjoys doing scientific research.

153. In which of the positions marked [1], [2], [3], and [4] does the following sentence best belong?

"She is diligent and not afraid to put in the hard work and long hours required for fact-checking."

(A) [1]
(B) [2]
(C) [3]
(D) [4]

▶ ▶ ▶GO ON TO THE NEXT PAGE

Dear business professional,

Professional Star is running a special for headshot photos! Whether you are applying for a new job or just need to spruce up your current business photo, we can shoot and print photos of all styles and sizes.

Use our headshot photos for
• resumes
• business cards
• office photos
• work directories

For photo examples and studio rates, visit our Web site at www.professionalstarphotos.com.

Professional Star's studio is located on Northgate Drive behind Big Apple Dental.

Professional Star
241 Northgate Drive
Warmey, OH 29321

Allen Stone
Cantor Building, Suite B
234 Northgate Drive
Warmey, OH 29322

154. What does the postcard suggest about Mr. Stone?

(A) He has taken headshots before.
(B) He ordered business cards.
(C) He has visited Big Apple Dental before.
(D) He lives close to Professional Star.

155. What is indicated about Professional Star?

(A) It markets services to office workers.
(B) It is hiring new employees.
(C) It works with Big Apple Dental.
(D) It takes children's portraits.

Questions 156-158 refer to the following article.

Subway Protests Will Cause Commuting Delays

SEATTLE (April 1) – The Metropolitan Transport Commission Union has ordered a city-wide strike of all subway employees. This unprecedented action will halt train services during regular operation hours starting next Monday and continuing until the union's demands are met.

Demands such as higher wages and better family benefits are on the long list of improvements subway workers are asking for.

With subways not running, city officials fear major traffic jams and congested commutes. In order to alleviate this, more buses and alternative methods of transportation will be running. Seattle residents are encouraged to go to www.seattlepublictransportation.com to reroute their morning work commutes by using alternative transportation.

As for how long the subway strike will last, union members are preparing for at least a week-long standoff, but the city council has expressed hope of resolving the new contracts before the end of the working day.

156. According to the article, what will happen in Seattle next Monday?

(A) Some roadblocks will be placed on a main street.
(B) A union will meet with the city council about contracts.
(C) A fundraiser will be held for an injured employee.
(D) Subways will be unavailable for work commutes.

157. Why are readers referred to a Web site?

(A) To plan a different way to get to work
(B) To find a list of subway cancelations
(C) To contact the city council about a strike
(D) To map their morning subway commutes

158. What is suggested about the city-wide strike?

(A) It will end by Monday evening.
(B) It is guaranteed to alleviate traffic.
(C) It is taking place for the first time.
(D) It was ordered by the city council.

▶ ▶ ▶GO ON TO THE NEXT PAGE

Questions 159-161 refer to the following Web page.

Furniture> Office> Desks> Reviews

Maple Desk in Mahogany
Average: 4.91 / 5.0 points (42 Reviews)

Sort by: Review Date (newest to oldest)

1. September 30 by Allison Waters in Pittsburgh, PA

Points: *4.5*
Pros: *stable, affordable, attractive*
Cons: *heavy*
How likely are you to recommend this item to a friend? *would recommend*

Review: *When my old and tattered office desk had seen its last days and needed replacing, I knew I wanted to get a famed Maple Desk. I had heard from colleagues that the maple finish of these desks is exquisite, and as I have face-to-face meetings with my clients daily, my desk's appearance played a role in my purchasing decision. The desk is solidly built, so no matter how much paperwork I pile on my desk, I don't have to worry about the desk collapsing. I was also pleasantly surprised by Maple Desk's fair pricing. Given the beautiful composition and popular name, the prices could be a lot higher than they are. Overall, it's a great desk and just a bit hefty in terms of weight. While that made the move a bit of a pain, the loveliness of the desk made up for it.*

Was this review helpful? Vote now.
Yes (11)   No (1)

159. What is indicated about the review?

(A) It awarded the maximum score.
(B) It led 11 people to buy the desk.
(C) It is the most recent one posted.
(D) It was read by 42 reviewers.

160. What is mentioned about the Maple Desk?

(A) It is reasonably priced.
(B) It only comes in one color.
(C) It is carefully handmade.
(D) It includes wheels for moving.

161. What is suggested about Ms. Waters?

(A) Her old desk was a Maple Desk.
(B) Clients sit at her desk regularly.
(C) She was given a budget for the desk.
(D) She is dissatisfied with her new desk.

Questions 162-164 refer to the following advertisement.

Diligent Days Workspace: Office space for the busy body

If you have ever owned your own business, you know how expensive renting an office building can be. Rental prices are through the roof, and the leasing market isn't letting up anytime soon. Work smarter, not harder, we say! Office buildings are a thing of the past. Why waste money on empty space when you can just pay for what you use? We are now introducing an innovative shared office space for working professionals.

The following options are available:

- Desk Rental - When all you need is a desk where you can finish your paperwork, the cheapest option of renting a desk is perfect!
- Standard Room Rental - For professionals who need a bit more room to conduct business or a space to invite clients to, renting a standard room is affordable.
- Deluxe Room Rental - If you're looking for an exclusive personal office feel without the personal office bill, this is your best bet. It is an entirely private office space for rent by the hour.

To reserve a space today, call us at 555-2321. All renters must be over the age of 18 and provide a valid business bureau certificate with the registration number of your company.

162. According to the advertisement, what is an advantage of renting a workspace?

(A) Office buildings provide a personal office feel.
(B) The leasing market is steadily decreasing.
(C) Renters only pay for the space they occupy.
(D) There are no requirements for renting a workspace.

163. What is NOT indicated about Diligent Days Workspace?

(A) There are three types of choices available.
(B) Room rentals are limited to one hour.
(C) Reservations can be made over the phone.
(D) Certain rentals offer complete privacy.

164. According to the advertisement, what should a customer provide?

(A) A copy of a personal ID card
(B) A signed contract for the workspace
(C) Payment in full upon renting a workspace
(D) A certificate and company ID number

▶ ▶ ▶ GO ON TO THE NEXT PAGE

Silverton Technology Searches for Next Big Startup Idea

AUSTIN (July 10) – Giant tech firm Silverton Technology attended the annual Southriver Technology Conference this past Saturday and announced it is looking for the next big startup idea. Silverton will provide funding in the amount of $1.2 million to the winner of its contest.

Small startup companies are encouraged to submit ideas that could change the future of technology. While previous recipients of Silverton funding were all makers of computer hardware, the technology company specified that it hopes to find environmental technology ideas this time around.

"Global warming cannot be ignored anymore," said Silverton President Jennie Hapon. "As leaders in the technology field, it's our responsibility to use our skills to address the world's most pressing problems."

During the panel discussion, Hapon highlighted green projects the company is currently working on, such as solar-powered machinery that purifies rainwater.

"Going green is no longer just a catchy slogan," added Hapon. "It's the drive behind our work."

Silverton Technology was started in 2005 by Hapon and her partner, Jorge Ramon. Within the first year of its founding, the company sold its revolutionary rotary technology and raised $2.5 million dollars. Though its start was in mechanical technology, in recent years, Silverton has shifted toward technology with a social impact.

165. What is suggested about Silverton Technology?

(A) It is engaged in addressing global warming.
(B) It hopes to create a revolutionary rotary technology.
(C) It attends many technology conferences.
(D) It is in search of young technology inventors.

166. In the article, the word "green" in paragraph 4, line 1 is closest in meaning to

(A) new
(B) innovative
(C) environmental
(D) comfortable

167. Who most likely is Jennie Hapon?

(A) A news reporter
(B) A conference organizer
(C) A government employee
(D) An engineer

Questions 168-171 refer to the following online chat discussion.

Gibings, Monica
7:48 A.M.
Good morning. We have a customer inquiry about an order placed on April 2 from the UK. The customer's name is Henry Boare.

Yoo, James
7:51 A.M.
I can't find his name in the order log. What book did he order? We might even have it on hand. Then we could just send him a copy.

Sutter, Ann
7:54 A.M.
I am checking the order backlog in case his slipped through and ended up in the backlog.

Yoo, James
7:55 A.M.
That's a good idea. But since he placed the order last month, let's send it to him as soon as possible. We can worry about what happened later.

Gibings, Monica
8:15 A.M.
The book ID number is 249320. I will ask the customer for his mailing address.

Sutter, Ann
8:16 A.M.
No need! I found his order. The name on the order slip was misspelled as Henry Bore. I'll print the shipping label and send his book out immediately.

Yoo, James
8:17 A.M.
Excellent work, Ann. We should find out why his name was misspelled and if it was a mistake on our end. Monica, please get in touch with the customer and let him know his book is on its way.

Gibings, Monica
8:20 A.M.
Will do. Thank you, Ann and James.

Send

---

168. What kind of company do the writers most likely work for?

(A) A paper store
(B) A bookseller
(C) A delivery company
(D) A call center

169. At 7:51 A.M., what does Mr. Yoo most likely mean when he writes, "We might even have it on hand"?

(A) He thinks the customer likely made a mistake.
(B) He is concerned that the book may be out of stock.
(C) He thinks a copy of the order is on his desk.
(D) He believes the book could be readily available.

170. According to the writers, when will the book be shipped?

(A) In February
(B) In March
(C) In April
(D) In May

171. What will Ms. Gibings probably do next?

(A) Inform the customer his order is being sent
(B) Ask the customer for his mailing address
(C) Search the backlog list for the missing order
(D) Check the inventory to see if the book is available

► ► ►GO ON TO THE NEXT PAGE

JC Property Management
223 Mountain View Road
Singleton, CO 30036

May 2

Mr. Oliver Kern
789 Tumulo Way, Apt 8A
Singleton, CO 30034

Dear Mr. Kern,

Thank you for notifying us of your intent to vacate your apartment on Sunday, June 20. As per your request, we will perform an inspection of the unit on the same day as your departure. The apartment must be completely empty of all belongings and cleaned before an inspection can be conducted. — [1] — You are, of course, welcome to be present.

If the unit is found to be in satisfactory condition, you will be refunded the full amount of your security deposit of $800. However, if any problems, such as damage to the walls or flooring beyond normal wear and tear, are found, the cost of repairs will be deducted from your security deposit. — [2] —

Since we cannot know the condition of the unit until the inspection is completed, we are unable to issue you a check on your departure date. Therefore, we ask that you provide us with a forwarding address where we can send a check. — [3] —

I have tentatively scheduled the inspection for 3:00 P.M. If you need to change the time, please contact my office at 555-9822. — [4] —

Sincerely,

Albert Mohn

172. What is the purpose of the letter?

(A) To issue a warning
(B) To respond to a complaint
(C) To request a payment
(D) To confirm a plan

173. According to the letter, what will happen on June 20?

(A) Apartment 8A will be repainted.
(B) A property's condition will be checked.
(C) Money will be given to Mr. Kern.
(D) A rental payment will be due.

174. In which of the positions marked [1], [2], [3], and [4] does the following sentence best belong?

"If I am not personally able to do it, my assistant Karen will."

(A) [1]
(B) [2]
(C) [3]
(D) [4]

175. What does Mr. Mohn ask Mr. Kern to do?

(A) Provide a mailing address
(B) Hire a professional cleaner
(C) Suggest a different date
(D) Write him a check

▶ ▶ ▶GO ON TO THE NEXT PAGE

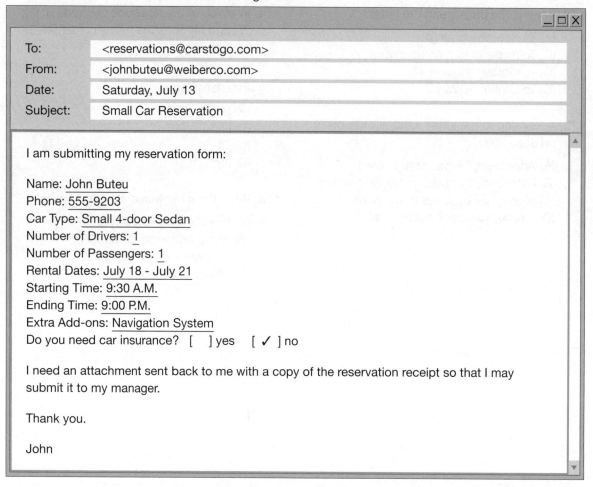

To: <reservations@carstogo.com>
From: <johnbuteu@weiberco.com>
Date: Saturday, July 13
Subject: Small Car Reservation

I am submitting my reservation form:

Name: John Buteu
Phone: 555-9203
Car Type: Small 4-door Sedan
Number of Drivers: 1
Number of Passengers: 1
Rental Dates: July 18 - July 21
Starting Time: 9:30 A.M.
Ending Time: 9:00 P.M.
Extra Add-ons: Navigation System
Do you need car insurance? [   ] yes   [✓] no

I need an attachment sent back to me with a copy of the reservation receipt so that I may submit it to my manager.

Thank you.

John

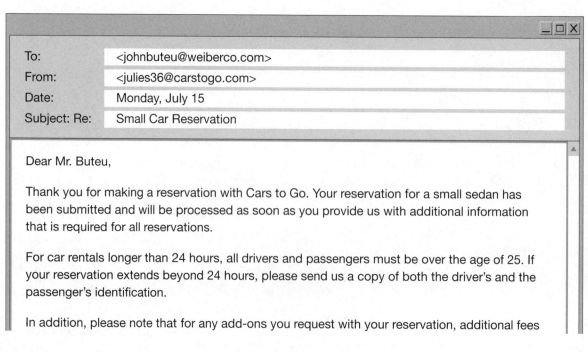

To: <johnbuteu@weiberco.com>
From: <julies36@carstogo.com>
Date: Monday, July 15
Subject: Re: Small Car Reservation

Dear Mr. Buteu,

Thank you for making a reservation with Cars to Go. Your reservation for a small sedan has been submitted and will be processed as soon as you provide us with additional information that is required for all reservations.

For car rentals longer than 24 hours, all drivers and passengers must be over the age of 25. If your reservation extends beyond 24 hours, please send us a copy of both the driver's and the passenger's identification.

In addition, please note that for any add-ons you request with your reservation, additional fees will apply. The prices are as follows:

Map: $5
Gas Card: $10
Navigation System: $25
Baby Seat: $30

For guests who require car insurance through our company, a $200 deposit will be needed at the start of the rental date and will be refunded once the car is safely returned.

To confirm and process your reservation, please send us the required information and your credit card number. For any further inquiries, do not hesitate to contact me directly at my office. My number is 555-1953.

Have a wonderful day,

Julie Soon
Reservations Manager
Cars to Go

176. In the first e-mail, what is suggested about the reservation?

(A) Two people will be riding in the car.
(B) A map is needed during the rental.
(C) The car will be picked up at an airport.
(D) Proof of the reservation is not necessary.

177. What is indicated about Mr. Buteu's reservation?

(A) It was approved by his manager.
(B) It is flexible in terms of what car is needed.
(C) It has not yet been processed.
(D) It will have a rental period of one month.

178. What does Ms. Soon offer Mr. Buteu in her e-mail?

(A) A list of available car features
(B) An extension on the rental period
(C) An upgrade on his car reservation
(D) A number where she can be reached

179. What additional fee will Mr. Buteu be charged?

(A) $5
(B) $10
(C) $25
(D) $30

180. What does Ms. Soon NOT need from Mr. Buteu?

(A) A credit card number
(B) A confirmation of age
(C) A $200 deposit
(D) A copy of his identification

▶ ▶ ▶GO ON TO THE NEXT PAGE

Dougers LLC Monthly Employee Events

Bowling Night – September 1
Five bowling lanes will be reserved for Dougers employees to enjoy. Drink and food specials will be available, too. Contact: David (555-6230)

Taco Tuesday – October 1
A taco buffet will be set up in the employee cafeteria. Come and make your own tacos with toppings including seasoned beef, fajita chicken, cheese, and salsa. Contact: Joe (555-2456)

$1 Movie Tickets – November 1
Purchase deeply discounted movie tickets for you and your family to enjoy. There will be three movie options to choose from, and tickets are good through the month of November. Contact: Sally (555-1232)

Christmas Play – December 1
Join your department for a special holiday outing: The Christmas Carol, a Christmas play, will be showing at the Lelain Theater exclusively for Dougers employees. Contact: Meredith (555-0283)

For more information on any of the monthly employee events, please call the organizers directly.

From:	Jodie Klein <jklein@dougers.com>
To:	Betty Smith <bsmith@dougers.com>
Date:	November 8
Subject:	Christmas Play

Good morning, Betty.

I called Meredith to ask about the Christmas play reservation, and she said that if we require more than 10 tickets, we need to contact the venue and reserve tickets directly.

You and your husband have 3 sons, and my husband and I have 4 children, so our families are quite large. Please reserve the tickets at your convenience. I will wait for your confirmation before telling my family about the event.

We have attended all the previous employee events, and they are spectacular. My children enjoyed the tacos immensely, and we couldn't stop laughing during that hilarious family comedy we saw during movie night. During the bowling event, my kids were able to meet other employees' children, and they remain great friends even to this day. Last year, Dougers organized an overnight summer vacation trip for its employees! I hope the company will do something similar again.

Looking forward to seeing your family,

Jodie

181. What is NOT indicated about the events?

(A) They may require reservations.
(B) They are open to friends of employees.
(C) They are organized by different people.
(D) They are held on the first day of each month.

182. In the e-mail, the word "spectacular" in paragraph 3, line 1 is closest in meaning to

(A) visible
(B) impressive
(C) sudden
(D) expensive

183. What is suggested about Ms. Klein?

(A) She just met Ms. Smith for the first time.
(B) She will attend her first employee event.
(C) She has worked at Dougers for over a year.
(D) She has organized an employee event before.

184. Why did Ms. Klein write to Ms. Smith?

(A) To request that she obtain event tickets
(B) To suggest she contact the event organizer
(C) To inquire about the size of Ms. Smith's family
(D) To ask if Ms. Smith will attend the Christmas play

185. What is suggested about Ms. Klein's children?

(A) They missed the September 1 event.
(B) They were able to see a free movie.
(C) They have been to the Lelain Theater before.
(D) They ate in the Dougers cafeteria.

▶ ▶ ▶GO ON TO THE NEXT PAGE

Questions 186-190 refer to the following Web page, e-mail, and information.

www.healthysnacksdelivery.com

Snack Guilt Free: Healthy Food Options for Your Employees			
Snacks	About Us	Order by Phone	Online Orders

We offer the following delicious, low-calorie snacks for every budget.
All are prepared with fresh natural ingredients.

Fruit Tray

When your sweet tooth needs satiating, fruit is the best option. Don't let your employees get into sugary treats like chocolate and candy. Give them nature's candy instead.

Vegetable Dip

If your employees require a heartier bite for their snack cravings, crisp earthy vegetables such as carrots, broccoli, and celery are the best choice. Delicious dips are included!

Salads

Need a more well-rounded snack to keep your hunger at bay while working all day? Colorful mini-salads include meat-free protein to energize your employees the right way.

Baked Veggie Chips

For those times when your mouth just needs a little distraction from the busy work at hand, bite-sized baked veggie chips are ready to serve and nourish you.

From:	Gale Carter <gc443@ladyred.com>
To:	inquiry@healthysnacksdelivery.com
Date:	July 22
Subject:	Food Allergies and Available Options

Hi,

I run a medium-sized company, with 100 employees including me, located in downtown Portland, Oregon. Among my staff, dietary restrictions vary, and while I would like to offer all my employees healthy options for snacking, it has come to my attention that a few of my workers have food allergies, including both of my personal administrative assistants. Specifically, these employees are gluten-intolerant; therefore, any snacks made with wheat, such as crackers, cannot be served in our office.

Please send me a price listing of all your snacks that fit our requirements.

Sincerely,

Gale

SNACK PRICING – CLIENT: LADY RED

Order Size
150 servings or less (standard price listed)
151 - 300 servings (save 10% off the standard price)
over 300 servings (save 20% off the standard price)

Snacks (Standard Price)
Fruit Tray: $3.00/serving
Vegetable Dip: $3.50/serving
Caesar Salad: $4.50/serving
Tomato Salad: $5.00/serving

To place an order, e-mail us the order size, snacks of choice, method of payment, and delivery date and address.

---

186. According to the Web page, what is true about all of the snack options?

(A) They have a modest caloric content.
(B) They contain real vegetables.
(C) They are easy to customize.
(D) They have fixed prices.

187. What is suggested about the baked veggie chips?

(A) They are currently out of stock.
(B) They must be ordered by phone.
(C) They contain wheat gluten.
(D) They have a lot of calories.

188. What is indicated about Ms. Carter's administrative assistants?

(A) They were recently hired.
(B) They follow a vegetarian diet.
(C) They suggested Healthy Snacks Delivery.
(D) They cannot eat certain crackers.

189. What will Ms. Carter be charged to order one fruit tray servings for all of her employees?

(A) $240
(B) $270
(C) $300
(D) $330

190. What is Lady Red NOT instructed to do to order snacks?

(A) Place a phone call
(B) Specify how it will pay
(C) State the number of servings
(D) Send an e-mail message

▶ ▶ ▶GO ON TO THE NEXT PAGE

Questions 191-195 refer to the following Web page, online form, and e-mail.

| Home | About | Sign Up | Log In |

Protect Your Office After Hours

Who is there to take care of your business after everyone has gone home? There is no need to worry about your office once the doors have closed when you have an Office Security Alarm system in place.

With our alarm system, any motion within your office will trigger a siren and alert the local authorities of an intruder. Prevent burglaries and break-ins for just $9.99 a month for our basic system.

Maybe your business uses high-end technology and sophisticated machinery that require top-notch security and the monitoring of your office after operating hours. For those who desire around-the-clock surveillance, we can set up cameras with live video feeds accessible anytime, anywhere starting at $29.99 a month.

To sign up for one of our security systems today, click here.

www.officesecurityalarm.com/clientaccount   Welcome: Bob Harsey

| Home | About | Register | Log In |

Client Information:
Client: Bob Harsey
Account number: 243560

Payment Information:
Amount: $9.99
Type: Wire Transfer
Frequency: Monthly

Payment is due on the 15th of every month.

Note: For late payments, please pay by phone: 555-2567

```
                                                              _ □ X
┌─────────────────────────────────────────────────────────────────┐
│ From:      bharsey@jaxco.com.                                     │
│ To:        service@officesecurityalarm.com                        │
│ Date:      March 12                                               │
│ Subject:   Account Upgrade                                        │
└─────────────────────────────────────────────────────────────────┘
```

Dear Office Security Alarm,

I am writing to request an upgrade of my Office Security Alarm service. For the past 2 years, I have had your system in my office.

I would like to upgrade my office security, so please e-mail me back to set up an appointment for camera installation. I would like surveillance of my office as well as a camera facing the front door.

I understand that there will be an additional installation fee and an increase in my monthly payment. I just paid this month's bill, so I expect the billing change to take effect next month. Please respond at your earliest convenience.

Sincerely,

Bob Harsey

191. On the Web page, what is mentioned about the company's alarm system?

(A) It uses light to warn intruders.
(B) It is only connected to doors.
(C) It can detect movement.
(D) It comes with free signs.

192. What is true about Office Security Alarm?

(A) Payment is due bi-monthly.
(B) Service fees are negotiable.
(C) One type of service is available.
(D) Late payments are accepted.

193. What is indicated about account #243560?

(A) It has to pay a late fee.
(B) It was billed for the basic system.
(C) It was paid by phone.
(D) It was updated in February.

194. Why did Mr. Harsey send the e-mail?

(A) To review different payment options
(B) To report an error on his account
(C) To make a payment on his account
(D) To schedule the installation of some equipment

195. What is suggested about Mr. Harsey?

(A) He will pay at least $29.99 in April.
(B) He is a new client at Office Security Alarm.
(C) He would like a pricing list sent to him.
(D) He is uncertain about changing his plan.

▶ ▶ ▶GO ON TO THE NEXT PAGE

NOTICE

To: Paperfax LLC
Date: Friday, May 23

This notice is to inform you that the Internet in your area will be changed from a standard Internet service to a new fiber optic system.

All office buildings in the area will be affected. The new service price options are as follows:

• $45/month standard fiber optic
• $55/month high-speed fiber optic
• $65/month ultra-high-speed fiber optic

Be advised that your current Internet service will end at 5:00 P.M. today. The new service will commence on Monday at 7:00 A.M.

For more information, e-mail Josh Bergen: joshb@netservice.com

Sincerely,

Benjamin Mauer
Netservice Incorporated

FROM:	kimberlyhwang@paperfax.net
TO:	joshb@netservice.com
DATE:	Friday, May 23
RE:	Highland Views' Better Business Bureau Complaint

Dear Mr. Bergen,

I received your notice about the Internet being cut off this evening. I am going to file an official complaint against your company with the Highland Views' Better Business Bureau for inadequate notice. You have given us only a few hours to prepare for a complete shutdown of our online capabilities, which will have a negative impact on my business. Plus, I will have to pay more than my current $35-a-month fee.

Will you compensate me for any financial setbacks that occur due to the Internet outage? If you are going to terminate a service that has been in place for years, you must give more advance notice.

Sincerely,

Kimberly Hwang

```
                                                           _ □ X
FROM:     joshb@netservice.com
TO:       kimberlyhwang@paperfax.net
DATE:     Friday, May 23
RE: Re:   Highland Views' Better Business Bureau Complaint
```

Dear Ms. Hwang,

I would like to apologize on behalf of Netservice Incorporated. We acknowledge our mistake of not informing the surrounding businesses of the Internet termination sooner.

We will extend your standard cable Internet access until Sunday at 5:00 P.M. However, we are unable to continue offering our current rates. The new rates mentioned in the notice will apply to all our existing customers as well as new customers.

To make up for our mistake, we will upgrade you to our high-speed fiber optic service for the same price as our standard fiber optic service. Your new service will take effect on the date stated in the notice.

Sincerely,

Josh Bergen

196. What is the purpose of the notice?

(A) To introduce a new building manager
(B) To request a transfer of service
(C) To explain a new technology that is available
(D) To announce the termination of a service

197. What is suggested about Ms. Hwang?

(A) She refuses to switch to the new service.
(B) She has used cable Internet for years.
(C) She is satisfied with Netservice Incorporated.
(D) She wants to upgrade to the fastest option.

198. What will Ms. Hwang most likely pay for the service Mr. Bergen offers her?

(A) $35
(B) $45
(C) $55
(D) $65

199. What is the earliest Ms. Hwang can use the new Internet service?

(A) On Friday
(B) On Saturday
(C) On Sunday
(D) On Monday

200. What does Mr. Bergen apologize for?

(A) Charging higher rates to everyone
(B) Forcing customers to change their Internet services
(C) Upgrading a service over the weekend
(D) Failing to tell customers earlier

Test 02 정답

147. (B)	**148.** (D)	**149.** (D)	**150.** (C)	**151.** (B)	**152.** (B)
153. (B)	**154.** (D)	**155.** (A)	**156.** (D)	**157.** (A)	**158.** (C)
159. (C)	**160.** (A)	**161.** (B)	**162.** (C)	**163.** (B)	**164.** (D)
165. (A)	**166.** (C)	**167.** (D)	**168.** (B)	**169.** (D)	**170.** (D)
171. (A)	**172.** (D)	**173.** (B)	**174.** (A)	**175.** (A)	**176.** (A)
177. (C)	**178.** (D)	**179.** (C)	**180.** (C)	**181.** (B)	**182.** (B)
183. (C)	**184.** (A)	**185.** (D)	**186.** (A)	**187.** (C)	**188.** (D)
189. (C)	**190.** (A)	**191.** (C)	**192.** (D)	**193.** (B)	**194.** (D)
195. (A)	**196.** (D)	**197.** (B)	**198.** (B)	**199.** (D)	**200.** (D)

TEST
03

적정 문제 풀이 시간 55분(마킹 포함)

55
min

시작 시간 ___시 ___분   목표 개수 _____ / 54

종료 시간 ___시 ___분   실제 개수 _____ / 54

- 반드시 55분 안에 문제 풀이 포함 마킹까지 마쳐야 합니다.
- 실제 시험이라고 생각하고 멈추지 말고 풀어보세요.

· 정답 개수에 5를 곱하면 대략적인 점수가 됩니다.

PART 7

Directions: In this part you will read a selection of texts, such as magazine and newspaper articles, e-mails, and instant messages. Each text or set of texts is followed by several questions. Select the best answer for each question and mark the letter (A), (B), (C), or (D) on your answer sheet.

Questions 147-148 refer to the following e-mail.

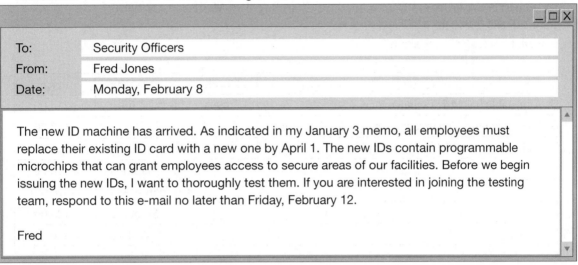

To: Security Officers
From: Fred Jones
Date: Monday, February 8

The new ID machine has arrived. As indicated in my January 3 memo, all employees must replace their existing ID card with a new one by April 1. The new IDs contain programmable microchips that can grant employees access to secure areas of our facilities. Before we begin issuing the new IDs, I want to thoroughly test them. If you are interested in joining the testing team, respond to this e-mail no later than Friday, February 12.

Fred

147. When is the deadline for obtaining a new ID?

(A) January 3
(B) February 8
(C) February 12
(D) April 1

148. What does Mr. Jones ask security officers to do?

(A) Get their IDs immediately
(B) Volunteer to be part of a team
(C) Test their current IDs
(D) Learn how to program microchips

▶ ▶ ▶ GO ON TO THE NEXT PAGE

Snider Manufacturing
2190 Old Farm Road, Lancaster, PA 17570
(717) 555-0293 www.snider.com

Order Number: 290340
Date: June 19
Customer: Frank Proctor, Viviance, Inc., 203 Charming Way, Masterson, IN 29930
Phone: 1-885-293-0403
E-mail: fproctor@viviance.com

Item	Number	Quantity	Price
Adjustable hat with Viviance logo	4994	20	$210.00
Polo shirt with Viviance logo, royal blue (medium)	2394	5	$97.50
Plain front pants, black (medium)	4400	5	$112.50
		Subtotal	$420.00
		Coupon #2940	(-$10.00)
		Shipping	$20.00
		TOTAL	$430.00

Thank you for your purchase.
All of our products come with a 100% satisfaction guarantee.
Visit our Web site for details.

149. What does Snider Manufacturing sell?

(A) Athletic equipment
(B) Footwear
(C) Paint
(D) Workplace uniforms

150. What is indicated about Mr. Proctor?

(A) He did not pay for shipping.
(B) He is a new customer.
(C) He received a discount.
(D) He placed the order online.

Questions 151-152 refer to the following text message chain.

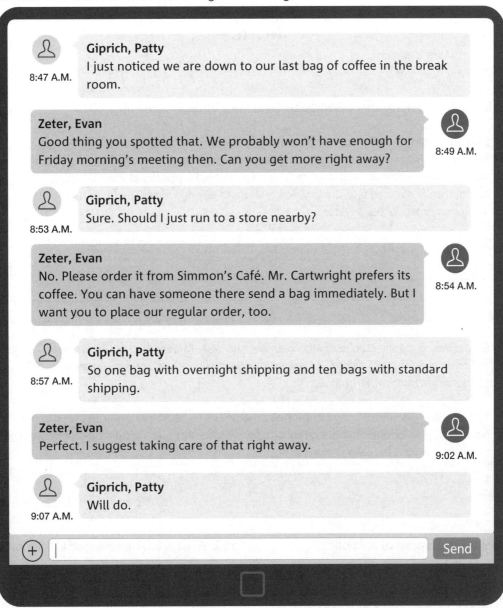

Giprich, Patty
8:47 A.M.
I just noticed we are down to our last bag of coffee in the break room.

Zeter, Evan
8:49 A.M.
Good thing you spotted that. We probably won't have enough for Friday morning's meeting then. Can you get more right away?

Giprich, Patty
8:53 A.M.
Sure. Should I just run to a store nearby?

Zeter, Evan
8:54 A.M.
No. Please order it from Simmon's Café. Mr. Cartwright prefers its coffee. You can have someone there send a bag immediately. But I want you to place our regular order, too.

Giprich, Patty
8:57 A.M.
So one bag with overnight shipping and ten bags with standard shipping.

Zeter, Evan
9:02 A.M.
Perfect. I suggest taking care of that right away.

Giprich, Patty
9:07 A.M.
Will do.

Send

151. What is suggested about the meeting on Friday?

(A) A beverage will be served.
(B) It is being organized by Mr. Zeter.
(C) More people than expected will attend.
(D) It will take place in a break room.

152. At 9:07 A.M., why does Ms. Giprich write, "Will do"?

(A) To state that she will go to the store
(B) To confirm she will place an order
(C) To accept that she will make coffee
(D) To agree to contact Mr. Cartwright

▶ ▶ ▶GO ON TO THE NEXT PAGE

NOTICE

From: Martha Janich
To: All employees

Retirement Plan Open Enrollment through September 30

Current employees who are not participating in the company's voluntary retirement plan are invited to do so during the month of September. Employees who enroll in the plan before the end of the month may choose to have a portion of each paycheck automatically directed into the tax-free retirement savings plan. The table below illustrates potential tax savings.

For each paycheck, if you contribute	You could reduce your taxes by
$100	$10
$250	$25
$500	$50

Employees currently enrolled in the plan are only able to change their investment options during the month of September. To do so, request an investment allotment change form from the HR office.

New employees have 90 days from their date of hire to decide whether to enroll in the retirement plan or other benefit options, after which they must wait until the next open enrollment period to make changes.

153. What is the purpose of the notice?

(A) To announce a change in a retirement plan
(B) To inform employees of an opportunity
(C) To encourage employees to retire soon
(D) To explain a change in the tax law

154. According to the notice, what will happen on October 1?

(A) Some employees will retire.
(B) Employees will receive their paychecks.
(C) New employees may select benefits.
(D) The period for making changes will end.

155. What is NOT mentioned in the notice?

(A) The types of investments available
(B) The way to change investments
(C) The amount employees can save on taxes
(D) The timeframe available for new employees to register

New Classes in the Community Room

Arts and Crafts (September 18 – December 19, $85)

Adults and school-aged children are welcome to join Marylou Baker on Thursdays from 3:00 P.M. to 5:00 P.M. for arts and crafts lessons. Materials provided.

Fitness Dancing (October 1 – December 20, $50)

Move your body to music with professional dance instructor and resident Linda Riley on Friday from 7:00 P.M. to 8:00 P.M. No prior dance experience necessary.

Scrapbooking (September 3 – December 14, free)

Scrapbooking is a great way to share memories. On Saturday mornings from 10:00 A.M. to noon, Evelyn Grayson will share techniques she has learned over the past fourteen years. Materials extra.

Registration and prepayment required. Please call Bethany White at 555-4003. Participation restricted to residents of Greenbrier Condominiums.

156. For whom is the flyer likely intended?

(A) Potential instructors
(B) Property managers
(C) Greenbrier residents
(D) Local artists

157. What is indicated about all the classes?

(A) Participants must pay a fee.
(B) Participants must sign up in advance.
(C) They are open to the public.
(D) They will be offered again in the spring.

▶ ▶ ▶ GO ON TO THE NEXT PAGE

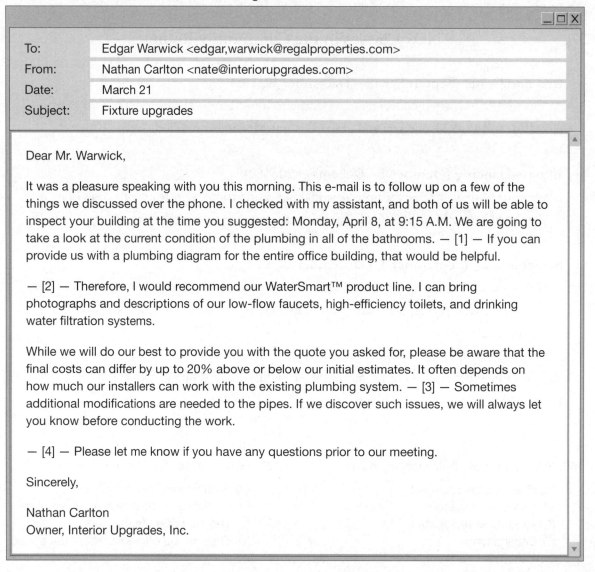

To: Edgar Warwick <edgar,warwick@regalproperties.com>

From: Nathan Carlton <nate@interiorupgrades.com>

Date: March 21

Subject: Fixture upgrades

Dear Mr. Warwick,

It was a pleasure speaking with you this morning. This e-mail is to follow up on a few of the things we discussed over the phone. I checked with my assistant, and both of us will be able to inspect your building at the time you suggested: Monday, April 8, at 9:15 A.M. We are going to take a look at the current condition of the plumbing in all of the bathrooms. — [1] — If you can provide us with a plumbing diagram for the entire office building, that would be helpful.

— [2] — Therefore, I would recommend our WaterSmart™ product line. I can bring photographs and descriptions of our low-flow faucets, high-efficiency toilets, and drinking water filtration systems.

While we will do our best to provide you with the quote you asked for, please be aware that the final costs can differ by up to 20% above or below our initial estimates. It often depends on how much our installers can work with the existing plumbing system. — [3] — Sometimes additional modifications are needed to the pipes. If we discover such issues, we will always let you know before conducting the work.

— [4] — Please let me know if you have any questions prior to our meeting.

Sincerely,

Nathan Carlton
Owner, Interior Upgrades, Inc.

158. What is indicated about Mr. Warwick?

(A) He met with Mr. Carlton on March 21.
(B) He is an Interior Upgrades employee.
(C) He owns an office building.
(D) He requested an estimate of costs.

159. What is Mr. Carlton NOT likely to do on April 8?

(A) Attempt to install high-efficiency toilets
(B) Show pictures about products
(C) Check the condition of existing fixtures
(D) Review a picture of water pipes

160. In which of the positions marked [1], [2], [3], and [4] does the following sentence best belong?

"You mentioned that you want to install water saving fixtures."

(A) [1]
(B) [2]
(C) [3]
(D) [4]

Questions 161-163 refer to the following job announcement.

Campbell Industries is seeking a payroll manager to oversee a team of payroll processes. Applicants must possess a bachelor's degree or higher and have at least 2 years' experience in a similar position with supervisory responsibilities. Certified Payroll Professional(CPP) Certification is required at the time of hiring. Applicants must have a working knowledge of all applicable state and federal payroll laws. Experience in supervising a staff of ten or more employees is preferred. Being bilingual in English and Spanish is a plus.

The payroll manager is responsible for supervising the preparation, processing, and distribution of the payroll. The payroll manager will hire, train, and develop his/her staff. Additional responsibilities include resolving payroll conflicts, developing and improving payroll policies and procedures, and providing support in the event of an internal or external audit.

Headquartered in Dallas, Texas, Campbell Industries is a fast-growing company in the field of fuel extraction, manufacturing, and refining, with a current payroll of 1,250+ employees and contractors. We offer competitive salary and benefits packages.

To apply, please fax or e-mail a cover letter and résumé to Brenda Shannon (308-555-4003 / bshannon@campbell.com).

161. What most likely is Campbell Industries?

(A) An employment agency
(B) A certified academy
(C) A financial institution
(D) An energy company

162. According to the announcement, what does the payroll manager do?

(A) Supervise the payroll staff
(B) Calculate benefits for new hires
(C) Explain benefits packages to employees
(D) Write memos to contractors

163. What is NOT an essential requirement for the position?

(A) The ability to speak two languages
(B) The completion of a college degree
(C) Past experience as a manager
(D) The possession of a professional certification

▶ ▶ ▶ GO ON TO THE NEXT PAGE

Questions 164-167 refer to the following online chat discussion.

Morgan, Kelly 8:48 A.M.	Hi, everyone. I just want to see how things are going with the new digital cameras we got. Have you run into any problems?
Alexander, Herb 8:50 A.M.	Not at all. Mine is easy to use. Takes very good pictures, too. I really like how I can automatically send copies to my e-mail account.
Soto, Ken 8:51 A.M.	Hey, why doesn't my camera do that?
Alexander, Herb 8:52 A.M.	It can. You just have to select the function that tells the camera to send files to a destination via Wi-Fi.
Soto, Ken 8:53 A.M.	Can you tell me how to do that?
Alexander, Herb 8:55 A.M.	It's probably better that I show you. The steps are a little complicated, but once you have it set up, everything should work smoothly. Are you going to be at the departmental meeting tomorrow? I could show you afterward.
Soto, Ken 8:56 A.M.	Sounds good.
Loos, Nancy 8:58 A.M.	I am having a problem downloading photo and video files off the camera and onto my workstation. Can somebody show me how to do it?
Morgan, Kelly 9:01 A.M.	Sure. I had trouble at first, but then I called the Technical Support Desk. David Shandler showed me several ways to do it. The easiest, I think, is to just download a program from the manufacturer's Web site. The program is called File Box. It's easy to install.
Loos, Nancy 9:06 A.M.	I think I can handle that. Thanks, Kelly!

Send

164. What is suggested about Mr. Alexander?

(A) He was the first person to get a camera.
(B) He will teach a workshop on photography.
(C) He prefers to communicate by e-mail.
(D) He is skilled at using his new camera.

165. What will Mr. Soto probably do tomorrow?

(A) Meet with Mr. Alexander
(B) Install software
(C) Give a presentation
(D) Pick up a new camera

166. What is indicated about the new cameras?

(A) They have moderately decent image quality.
(B) They can be programmed to send photos.
(C) They require training to use the basic functions.
(D) They cannot be used to make videos.

167. At 9:06 A.M., what does Ms. Loos most likely mean when she writes, "I think I can handle that"?

(A) She is going to call Technical Support.
(B) She will get help from Mr. Shandler.
(C) She can figure out how to use the camera.
(D) She is confident she can use File Box.

▶ ▶ ▶ GO ON TO THE NEXT PAGE

Announcement

Wednesday, April 18

In January, the Human Resources (HR) Department announced that Cormac Manufacturing would begin the transition to Omega, an electronic timesheet system. — [1] — Since that time, several departments have successfully made the shift. Those changes have resulted in paychecks being issued 35% faster and with 65% fewer errors, freeing up Payroll and HR employees to focus on other tasks.

Electronic timesheets offer many advantages for Cormac Manufacturing employees. Staff members can enter their hours from any location with secure Internet access. This is especially helpful for employees working remotely. — [2] — With Omega, managers can easily prepare reports on individual employees or all hours contributed by multiple employees to a project.

By July 31, the adoption of Omega will be complete. Employees currently using paper timesheets will no longer be able to do so at that time. To help ease those growing pains, we will offer short trainings to interested employees starting next week. These will introduce the basic concepts and functions of Omega. — [3] — In addition, there will be opportunities for individual questions to be addressed.

The forty-five minute Omega workshops are scheduled for Wednesdays and Fridays at 1:00 P.M, 2:00 P.M., and 3:00 P.M. They will be held in the Chancellor Meeting Room in the Chase Building. — [4] — Contact Sherry Greenfield at extension 2029 to reserve a space for you and/or your staff.

168. What is suggested about Omega?

(A) It requires extensive training to use.
(B) It is not currently used by all departments.
(C) It was first adopted by Payroll.
(D) It was released earlier in the year.

169. What is NOT mentioned as a benefit of the electronic timesheet system?

(A) Allowing supervisors to create reports
(B) Reducing the number of mistakes
(C) Saving money for the company
(D) Making it easier for telecommuters

170. What is indicated about the upcoming training sessions?

(A) They will provide information about a software program.
(B) They will be conducted exclusively over the Internet.
(C) They are mandatory for all managers and staff.
(D) They will be offered on six separate occasions.

171. In which of the positions marked [1], [2], [3], and [4] does the following sentence best belong?

"Because seating is limited, advance registration is required."

(A) [1]
(B) [2]
(C) [3]
(D) [4]

CONTACT REQUEST FORM

Please complete this form, and one of our certified financial planners will contact you.

Name: *Charles Horton*
Address: *89 Birch Lane, Sweetham, CT 18930*
Phone Number: *(212) 555-8943*
E-mail: *chorton@quickmail.com*
Employer: *Simmons Products*
Position: *Manager*

How do you prefer to be contacted?

[   ] phone (during normal business hours: Monday – Friday 9:00 A.M. – 5:00 P.M.)
[✓] phone (outside normal business hours)
[   ] e-mail
[   ] mail

How did you first hear about us?

[   ] promotional mailing   [   ] radio   [   ] newspaper   [✓] word of mouth
[   ] other (please specify): _____

Which of the following services are you interested in? (Check all that apply.)

[   ] Tax Management Strategies
[✓] Retirement Planning
[✓] College Savings Plans
[✓] Life, Disability, or Other Insurance Products
[   ] Estate Planning
[   ] Other (please specify) : _____

Comments:

So avoid trying to contact me on Saturday mornings. Weekend afternoons are generally good.

172. What is indicated about Mr. Horton?

(A) He is currently employed.
(B) He is a small business owner.
(C) He does not have an e-mail account.
(D) He works as a financial planner.

173. How did Mr. Horton learn about Pyramid Financial?

(A) He received information in the mail.
(B) Someone told him about it.
(C) He saw an advertisement.
(D) A representative called him.

174. When is Mr. Horton available for a call?

(A) On Monday at 9 A.M.
(B) On Friday at 3 P.M.
(C) On Saturday at 11 A.M.
(D) On Sunday at 1 P.M.

175. What service does NOT interest Mr. Horton?

(A) Saving money for education
(B) Having his tax forms prepared
(C) Preparing to stop working
(D) Obtaining insurance

▶ ▶ ▶ GO ON TO THE NEXT PAGE

From:	Ken Jones <kjones@nativematerials.com>
To:	John Evanston <jevanston@miroctech.com>
Date:	Friday, March 1
Subject:	Analysis Needed

John,

Thanks for coming in to check on the new electron microscope last week. I had a feeling that it needed to be checked since some of the readings I was getting seemed strange. I appreciate your spending the time making the needed adjustments. Everything is running smoothly now.

Do you remember meeting the director of my lab, Roger Wayne, back in November? He has asked me to analyze a sample for a client. Normally, I do work for other departments in the company, and the samples are iron, copper, or other metals. This sample, on the other hand, is a new ceramic material that will be used in industrial applications. That material is outside my expertise. I vaguely recall you saying that you had some experience with ceramics from your former job, so I wonder if you can take a look at it the next time you come to Richmond. This is not urgent.

Best,

Ken Jones
Materials Analyst
Native Materials

From:	John Evanston <jevanston@miroctech.com>
To:	Ken Jones <kjones@nativematerials.com>
Date:	Monday, March 4
Subject: RE:	Analysis Needed

Ken,

I would be happy to lend a hand. You have a good memory. Janus Technology had a ceramics manufacturing program before it was bought out by the Kempthorn Corporation. That was a decade ago, but I have kept up with trends in the field since then, so I can show you how to analyze the samples. I plan to be in your area sometime next month. I don't have the exact dates yet as I may also be attending the NMRC conference in Baltimore around that time. I can let you know as soon as my schedule is finalized.

Cheers,

John

176. According to the first e-mail, why did Mr. Evanston visit Native Materials?

(A) To install a machine
(B) To edit a report
(C) To analyze a sample
(D) To modify equipment

177. In the first e-mail, the word "expertise" in paragraph 2, line 5 is closest in meaning to

(A) department
(B) knowledge
(C) job
(D) company

178. What does Mr. Evanston agree to do?

(A) Provide guidance to Mr. Jones
(B) Send materials to Mr. Jones
(C) Repair a microscope
(D) Meet Mr. Jones's client

179. What is most likely true about Janus Technology?

(A) It purchased another company.
(B) It manufactured metal products.
(C) It used to employ Mr. Evanston.
(D) It was located in Baltimore.

180. What will happen in April?

(A) Mr. Jones will attend a conference.
(B) Mr. Evanston will meet a lab director.
(C) Mr. Jones will receive industrial ceramics.
(D) Mr. Evanston may go to Richmond.

▶ ▶ ▶ GO ON TO THE NEXT PAGE

Katelin Lance
280 Barley Ct.
Penn Hills, PA 15228

Dear Ms. Lance,

We would like to thank you for booking with Enchanted Tours during your recent visit to New Mexico. We hope you enjoyed sampling the local cuisine, touring museums and galleries, and exploring the town of Taos. Our goal is to share the beauty of our state with visitors like you. To help us continue to improve our tour offerings, we would like to ask you to complete a brief survey. Please let us know what we did well and what we could do better. Once you have completed the enclosed survey, please mail it back to us in the envelope provided. We have already taken care of the postage. As a token of our appreciation for your completing the survey, we will send you a hat or T-shirt with our logo. Simply indicate your preference on the survey form.

Sincerely,

David Archuleta

Enchanted Tours

Experience Authentic New Mexico

Horseback Nature Tour
Enjoy the scenic beauty of the Sangre de Cristo Mountains from the back of a horse. Hourly rides to multi-day tours available for riders of all experience levels.

Fly Fishing Camping Trip
Our guides will take you to pristine, hidden mountain streams where native trout are abundant. Camping gear provided.

Jeep Explorer Tour
Experience the rugged wilderness. We will introduce you to the rugged desert landscape of the Bisti Badlands and the sacred ruins of ancient settlements in beautiful Chaco Canyon.

Cultural Tour
Let us show you the cultural wonders of northern New Mexico. Tour historic towns, eat local foods, and watch Pueblo dancers.

To book a standard tour, call 1-888-555-8393.

Additional details and photos are on our Web site at www.enchantedtours.com.
Custom packages available. Contact David at david@enchantedtours.com for details.

181. What is the purpose of the letter?

(A) To solicit feedback from a customer
(B) To return lost objects to a traveler
(C) To confirm travel arrangements
(D) To promote an upcoming tour

182. What is Ms. Lance asked to do?

(A) Confirm her reservation
(B) Return an enclosure
(C) Purchase a stamp
(D) Refer a friend

183. Which activity is NOT mentioned as part of a tour or trip?

(A) Going on brief rides on horses
(B) Riding on an old train
(C) Catching fish in the mountains
(D) Sleeping outdoors

184. Which tour did Ms. Lance most likely take?

(A) Horseback Nature Tour
(B) Fly Fishing Trip
(C) Jeep Explorer Tour
(D) Cultural Tour

185. Why are readers asked to e-mail David?

(A) To reserve a space on a standard tour
(B) To make flight arrangements
(C) To order photos from their trip
(D) To discuss other tour options

▶ ▶ ▶ GO ON TO THE NEXT PAGE

Questions 186-190 refer to the following schedule, e-mail, and notice.

McGuiness Hospital

Weekly schedule for Tuesday, September 1 – Monday, September 8

Security Guard	Shift
Aaron Parsel	Tuesday – Friday 6:30 A.M. – 3:30 P.M.
Ben Rover	Tuesday – Friday 3:30 P.M. – 1:30 A.M.
Dang Ngo	Saturday – Monday 6:30 A.M. – 3:30 P.M.
Harry Liu	Saturday – Monday 3:30 P.M. – 1:30 A.M.

Please contact your manager right away if you cannot make a shift.

To: Ben Rover <brover@mcguiness.com>
From: Ted Newsome <tnewsome@mcguiness.com>
Date: August 19
Subject: Shift Change

Ben,

I appreciate your contacting me in advance about your dental procedure scheduled for Tuesday, September 1. You also mentioned that you may need a day or two to recover. Instead of hiring a temporary replacement for a few days, I have decided to just have you and Harry switch shifts. That way, you will get the time off when you need it, and we will have trusted staff on hand for both shifts. He has agreed to the change.

Please get in touch with Dang Ngo before September 1 to see how he wants to manage the transition between your respective shifts.

If you have any questions, just let me know.

Thanks.

Ted

ADVANCED FIRST-AID TRAINING

All non-medical staff at McGuiness Hospital must complete an advanced first-aid training program, called MedAlert, in October. Even if you have received first-aid certification in the past, you are still required to take the MedAlert training and to pass the test. MedAlert will supplement basic first-aid knowledge by teaching you skills for specific high-risk situations.

To equip you with the tools to better handle these high-risk situations, the Training Department will be offering MedAlert training sessions as follows.

Security Department	Monday, October 5 (7:00 A.M. – 3:00 P.M.)
Maintenance Department	Tuesday, October 6 (7:00 A.M. – 3:00 P.M.)
Custodial Department	Wednesday, October 7 (7:00 A.M. – 3:00 P.M.)
Administrative Department	Thursday, October 8 (7:00 A.M. – 3:00 P.M.)

In addition, if you cannot attend on the date assigned to your department, please contact Fred Veranda at extension 4859. We will attempt to put you in another session. Additional sessions will be added as needed.

TEST 03

186. What is indicated about Mr. Liu?

(A) He is supposed to work on September 1.
(B) He is a new employee.
(C) He recently saw a dentist.
(D) He prefers to work mornings.

187. What is suggested about Mr. Newsome?

(A) He could not find a temporary worker.
(B) He supervises Mr. Rover.
(C) He plans to speak with Mr. Ngo.
(D) He will take a few days off.

188. What does Mr. Newsome ask Mr. Rover to do?

(A) Coordinate with a coworker
(B) Arrive early for his shift
(C) Permanently change shifts
(D) Request time off

189. In the notice, what are employees required to do?

(A) Pass a medical examination
(B) Obtain additional skills
(C) Change their schedules
(D) Reduce risky behavior

190. On what day will Mr. Parsel most likely take the MedAlert training?

(A) October 5
(B) October 6
(C) October 7
(D) October 8

▶ ▶ ▶ GO ON TO THE NEXT PAGE

Sky Air Aims High

Sky Air, a popular low-cost domestic air carrier, is planning to fly to eight new destinations. On May 1, we will begin offering daily flights to the following destinations in the southeastern region: Hammet, Franklin, Pomona, and New Bay. Service to new destinations in the northeastern region will start in June. By the end of the summer, Sky Air will be serving seventy-two airports nationwide. View a map of our current and upcoming locations on our Web site at www.skyair.com.

To celebrate our growth, we are giving away prizes, including airline tickets, meal vouchers, and hotel stays. Anyone can participate by completing an entry form at www.skyair.com up to April 30.

Rockford (June 3) – Rockford-area residents have been waiting five years for the return of a commercial airline service. Currently, only private planes fly into and out of Devon White Municipal Airport in Rockford. That will change tomorrow when Sky Air's first flight out of Rockford's only airport takes off.

"It will be nice to be able to catch a flight to Portland," said Rene Charles, who is looking forward to visiting her sister in Portland. Since Coastal Airlines stopped offering service to Devon White Municipal Airport, Ms. Charles had to drive ten hours to Portland "I'm glad that regular travelers like me can use this airport again."

A press release from the airport's management said that shuttle service to and from downtown Rockford will be offered by the end of the year. In the meantime, there is paid parking at the airport. Taxi service is also available.

Vincent Barone
12 Robin Lane
Rockford

May 3

Dear Mr. Barone,

Congratulations on being selected to receive two meal vouchers! Each can be exchanged for one boxed meal and beverage of your choice.

Simply present the voucher to the flight attendant when placing your in-flight order. The voucher will remain valid for twelve months from today.

Sincerely,

Nancy Gabaldon
Director of Passenger Relations
Sky Air

191. What is mentioned about Sky Air in the announcement?

(A) It is a well-known airline.
(B) It is headquartered in the southeastern region.
(C) It offers service to international airports.
(D It currently flies to over seventy locations.

192. What is implied about Rockford?

(A) It is located along a body of water.
(B) It has a private airport.
(C) It is a major urban area.
(D) It is in the northeastern part of the country.

193. What is suggested about Coastal Airlines?

(A) It used to fly to Hammet and Franklin.
(B) It stopped flying to Rockford five years ago.
(C) It is no longer in business.
(D) It will return to Rockford by the end of the year.

194. What is indicated about Devon White Municipal Airport?

(A) It recently expanded its parking facilities.
(B) It plans to add additional ground transportation.
(C) It intends to build a commercial terminal.
(D) It charges a fee to taxi drivers.

195. What is most likely true about Mr. Barone?

(A) He is a frequent passenger on Sky Air.
(B) He recently moved to Rockford.
(C) He filled out a form on Sky Air's Web site.
(D) He has a trip planned in twelve months.

▶ ▶ ▶ GO ON TO THE NEXT PAGE

Questions 196-200 refer to the following e-mail, Web page, and article.

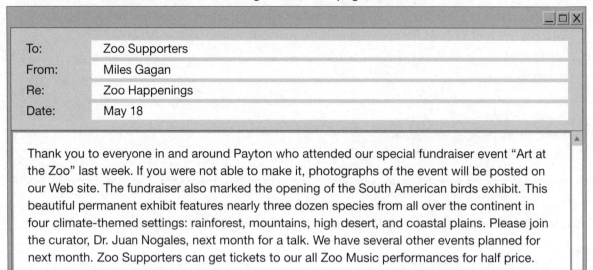

To:	Zoo Supporters
From:	Miles Gagan
Re:	Zoo Happenings
Date:	May 18

Thank you to everyone in and around Payton who attended our special fundraiser event "Art at the Zoo" last week. If you were not able to make it, photographs of the event will be posted on our Web site. The fundraiser also marked the opening of the South American birds exhibit. This beautiful permanent exhibit features nearly three dozen species from all over the continent in four climate-themed settings: rainforest, mountains, high desert, and coastal plains. Please join the curator, Dr. Juan Nogales, next month for a talk. We have several other events planned for next month. Zoo Supporters can get tickets to our all Zoo Music performances for half price.

http://www.paytonzoo.org

Exhibits	Planning a Visit	Events	Become a Supporter

June 4
Grandparents' Day: 9:00 A.M. – 4:30 P.M.
Free admission for grandparents when they come with their grandchildren. Storytelling will take place in the theater.

June 11
Saturday Seminars for Kids: 10:00 A.M. – 11: 30 A.M.
Children can meet the curator of primates, Dr. Wanda Lee, and learn all about monkeys. Games, crafts, and other fun activities are planned. Registration required. Call 3339-7595.

June 23
Zoo Music: 6:00 P.M. – 9:00 P.M.
Return to the zoo after our normal hours and enjoy live music performed by the Colbert Quarter. Bring your own packed dinner or purchase picnic basket meals from our own Wild Animal Café. Click here to buy tickets.

June 26
Special Event: 2:00 P.M. – 4:00 P.M.
Join Dr. Juan Nogales for a lecture. Dr. Nogales will talk about the new exhibit on South American birds.

Flying South at the Zoo
by Michael Kendall

Our local zoo just got better thanks to the opening of the South American birds exhibit. It is clearly a labor of love for curator Juan Nogales. Last Saturday, Dr. Nogales spoke about his journey from a village in Ecuador to Harvard University and how growing up so close to nature instilled in him a fascination with all avian life. If you didn't get a chance to see him speak, you can experience his passion for birds, which comes out in this beautiful and informative exhibit. To find out more, visit www.paytonzoo.org.

196. What is NOT indicated about the South American birds exhibit?

(A) It will remain at the zoo indefinitely.
(B) It opened to the public in May.
(C) It includes different types of birds.
(D) It has been extensively photographed.

197. What is suggested about Zoo Supporters?

(A) They are mostly older people with grandchildren.
(B) They can see the Colbert Quarter at a discount.
(C) They worked as volunteers at the fundraiser event.
(D) They are invited to special events hosted by curators.

198. When did Mr. Kendall visit the zoo?

(A) On June 4
(B) On June 11
(C) On June 23
(D) On June 26

199. What is indicated about the curator of the South American birds exhibit?

(A) He plans to give a second talk soon.
(B) He spent his childhood in Ecuador.
(C) He has collected birds his entire life.
(D) He taught a class on birds at college.

200. What is most likely true about Mr. Kendall?

(A) He is a Zoo Supporter.
(B) He attended "Art at the Zoo."
(C) He interviewed Mr. Nogales.
(D) He lives in the Payton area.

Test 03 정답

147. (D)	**148.** (B)	**149.** (D)	**150.** (C)	**151.** (A)	**152.** (B)
153. (B)	**154.** (D)	**155.** (A)	**156.** (C)	**157.** (B)	**158.** (D)
159. (A)	**160.** (B)	**161.** (D)	**162.** (A)	**163.** (A)	**164.** (D)
165. (A)	**166.** (B)	**167.** (D)	**168.** (B)	**169.** (C)	**170.** (A)
171. (D)	**172.** (A)	**173.** (B)	**174.** (D)	**175.** (B)	**176.** (D)
177. (B)	**178.** (A)	**179.** (C)	**180.** (D)	**181.** (A)	**182.** (B)
183. (B)	**184.** (D)	**185.** (D)	**186.** (A)	**187.** (B)	**188.** (A)
189. (B)	**190.** (A)	**191.** (A)	**192.** (D)	**193.** (B)	**194.** (B)
195. (C)	**196.** (D)	**197.** (B)	**198.** (D)	**199.** (B)	**200.** (D)

TEST
04

55
min

시작 시간 ___시 ___분 　　　　목표 개수 _____ / 54

종료 시간 ___시 ___분 　　　　실제 개수 _____ / 54

- 반드시 55분 안에 문제 풀이 포함 마킹까지 마쳐야 합니다.
- 실제 시험이라고 생각하고 멈추지 말고 풀어보세요.　　　　・ 정답 개수에 5를 곱하면 대략적인 점수가 됩니다.

PART 7

Directions: In this part you will read a selection of texts, such as magazine and newspaper articles, e-mails, and instant messages. Each text or set of texts is followed by several questions. Select the best answer for each question and mark the letter (A), (B), (C), or (D) on your answer sheet.

Questions 147-148 refer to the following e-mail.

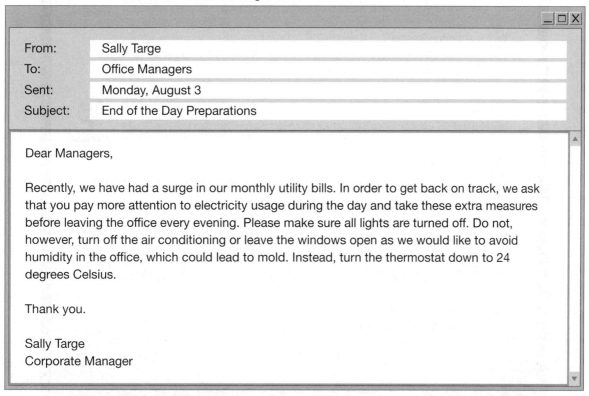

From:	Sally Targe
To:	Office Managers
Sent:	Monday, August 3
Subject:	End of the Day Preparations

Dear Managers,

Recently, we have had a surge in our monthly utility bills. In order to get back on track, we ask that you pay more attention to electricity usage during the day and take these extra measures before leaving the office every evening. Please make sure all lights are turned off. Do not, however, turn off the air conditioning or leave the windows open as we would like to avoid humidity in the office, which could lead to mold. Instead, turn the thermostat down to 24 degrees Celsius.

Thank you.

Sally Targe
Corporate Manager

147. Why did Ms. Targe send the e-mail?

(A) To inquire about ways to save energy
(B) To request recurring actions
(C) To notify employees of a company problem
(D) To ask managers to turn off all the equipment

148. What are employees asked to do?

(A) Turn off the air conditioning during the day
(B) Open the windows when it is too humid
(C) Turn on lights before leaving at night
(D) Lower the office temperature at the end of the day

▶ ▶ ▶GO ON TO THE NEXT PAGE

Questions 149-150 refer to the following text message chain.

Celine Bannel
7:25 A.M.
Can you finish putting together the board meeting packets by 8:55 A.M.? That will give us an extra 5 minutes to set up the conference room.

William Venice
I still need to print the last page of graphs, but I will try my best.
7:36 A.M.

Celine Bannel
7:40 A.M.
I don't think all of the interns are busy. We need the room set up by the time the meeting starts. No delays.

William Venice
I grabbed two interns from Marketing to lend a hand.
7:43 A.M.

Celine Bannel
7:49 A.M.
Message me when you head to the conference room with the completed packets. Thanks.

William Venice
Ms. Bannel, I've got the packets with me in the conference room, now. Setup is almost done.
8:52 A.M.

Celine Bannel
Good. See you soon.
8:53 A.M.

149. What is suggested about the board meeting?

(A) It is about the interns.
(B) It will take 5 minutes.
(C) It will begin at 9:00 A.M.
(D) It has been rescheduled.

150. At 7:40 A.M., why does Ms. Bannel write, "I don't think all of the interns are busy"?

(A) To suggest Mr. Venice ask for help
(B) To criticize Mr. Venice's management style
(C) To report a problem in the office
(D) To invite the interns to attend the meeting

116

HOLTZ Corporation

Supply Request Form

Supplies Needing to be Ordered:
NAME: *Mark Colbert*
DATE: *March 13*
DEPTMENT: *Sales*
EMPLOYEE ID#: *S201343*
SUPPLIES NEEDED: *Dry erase markers*
QUANTITY: *10*
DATE NEEDED BY: *As soon as possible*

SPECIAL INSTRUCTIONS:
We're down to our last marker in the sales room. We have been using markers made by Case, but any brand will do. The important thing is that they have a broad tip and that they be black. Please have the new markers delivered to our cubicle on the 4th floor as soon as they arrive.

DELIVER TO: *Sales Cubicle, 4th floor, Building B*

FOR DEPARTMENT USE ONLY:
Received by: *Anita Jones*   Order Completed: *Yes*
Date and time: *March 13, 9:10 A.M.*   Order Date and time: *March 13, 9:30 A.M.*
Initials: *AJ*   Order Delivered: _____

151. What does Mr. Colbert NOT request on the form?

(A) The markers need to be a specific color.
(B) The markers need to be delivered to him.
(C) The markers need to be ordered quickly.
(D) The markers need to be a specific brand.

152. Who most likely is Anita Jones?

(A) An assistant to Mr. Colbert in Sales
(B) A worker at an office supply store
(C) An employee at the HOLTZ Corporation
(D) A clerk in the HOLTZ Corporation's mailroom

153. What is indicated about the supply order?

(A) It was submitted over the phone to Ms. Jones.
(B) It was completed the same day it was received.
(C) It was processed by two different employees.
(D) It was delivered to Building B in the morning.

▶ ▶ ▶ GO ON TO THE NEXT PAGE

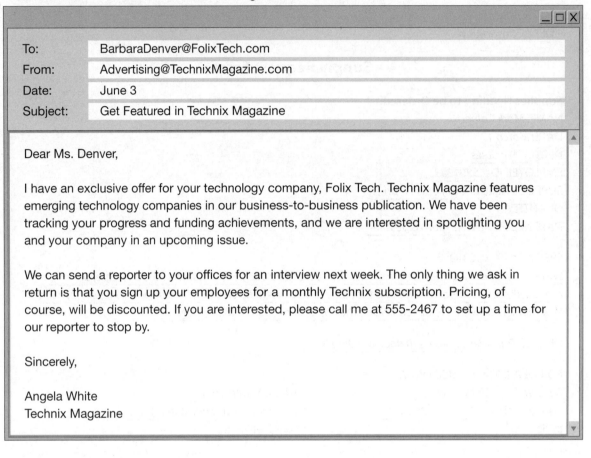

To: BarbaraDenver@FolixTech.com

From: Advertising@TechnixMagazine.com

Date: June 3

Subject: Get Featured in Technix Magazine

Dear Ms. Denver,

I have an exclusive offer for your technology company, Folix Tech. Technix Magazine features emerging technology companies in our business-to-business publication. We have been tracking your progress and funding achievements, and we are interested in spotlighting you and your company in an upcoming issue.

We can send a reporter to your offices for an interview next week. The only thing we ask in return is that you sign up your employees for a monthly Technix subscription. Pricing, of course, will be discounted. If you are interested, please call me at 555-2467 to set up a time for our reporter to stop by.

Sincerely,

Angela White
Technix Magazine

154. What is offered to Ms. Denver?

(A) A free Technix subscription
(B) A refund for employees
(C) A marketing opportunity
(D) A discounted advertisement space

155. What does Ms. White invite Ms. Denver to do?

(A) Review a subscription
(B) Contact her by phone
(C) Offer her a discount
(D) Meet her for an interview

Commercial Actors for Hire:
Highlight Your Company with Professional Acting

We have all seen the cheesy, cheap, and poorly produced commercial videos on television that bring nothing but embarrassment to the company featured. — [1] — Don't fall victim to such bad marketing! Hire skilled professional actors from Ace Acting to really give your commercials spark. Draw in customers and build your business with an enticing commercial.

Ace Acting's actors are handpicked and trained in acting techniques for no less than 6 months. — [2] — Many of our seasoned actors even have certifications from technical workshops in case your commercial requires a specific technique. "Dramatic, humorous, whatever talent you are looking for, we've got it!" says company founder John Lemons.

Ready to scope out our talent pool? — [3] — Stop by the Ace Acting studio to browse through actors' profiles or to meet the talent directly. While there, you can also sit in and observe one of the many acting classes.

Not quite sure what kind of commercial your company wants to make? Take a seat in our gallery viewing room and watch an array of advertisements produced by Ace Acting. — [4] — We can help. Come see us today!

TEST 04

156. What is NOT mentioned about Ace Acting?

(A) It was established by John Lemons.
(B) It doesn't have its own commercial film crew.
(C) It has an archive of commercials.
(D) It teaches acting techniques.

157. In which of the positions marked [1], [2], [3], and [4] does the following sentence best belong?

"We can even tailor a script to your company's needs if you have no ideas."

(A) [1]
(B) [2]
(C) [3]
(D) [4]

158. What is indicated about the actors at Ace Acting?

(A) They are recruited from local theaters.
(B) They are available to meet with potential clients.
(C) They are personally trained by Mr. Lemons.
(D) They are hired for a minimum of six months.

▶ ▶ ▶GO ON TO THE NEXT PAGE

Cleaning Supplies Bulk Delivery

Large buildings require a lot of cleaning, and a lot of cleaning means a large amount of cleaning supplies. If you are an administrator for your company in charge of ordering supplies, this message is for you: Don't waste your company's precious budget on ordering and reordering cleaning supplies. Think bigger. Order in bulk!

Visit our Web site, www.cleaningbulk.com, to see just how heavily discounted our bulk cleaning supplies are. Place the items you need in your cart, and your completed bulk order will be delivered within 48 hours. It's really that easy.

If storage is a concern, we also offer weekly or monthly delivery setups. No supply storage room is necessary. We will only deliver the supplies you need for the period that you set (one week, for example), and you can change the frequency at any time. One of our clients, for example, orders 12 liters of bathroom cleaner to be delivered every 3 weeks.

So what are you waiting for? Order today!

159. According to the information, what is a benefit of ordering in bulk?

(A) Getting high-quality supplies
(B) Finding specialized products
(C) Saving a large amount of time
(D) Reducing business expenses

160. According to the information, when is the latest an order will arrive?

(A) In a few hours
(B) In one day
(C) In two days
(D) In one week

161. What is NOT indicated about the recurring delivery service?

(A) The supplies will be delivered routinely.
(B) Orders can be modified between deliveries.
(C) Customers can set the duration of delivery.
(D) Orders can be made online.

June 31

Dear Friends and Family of Pax Go,

The Pax Go Cosmetics Company is hosting a picnic for friends and family of our employees on Sunday, July 14.

Pax Go focuses on natural, organic skincare and makeup that enhances users' natural beauty and shines a light on the beauty already there. The company was founded by Marlene Kay, who was tired of the message the makeup industry was sending about needing to cover flaws and to appear perfect.

While growing her business, she relied heavily on her family and friends to help brainstorm ideas, create campaigns, fine-tune products, market her makeup, and spread the word. Before long, Pax Go was a thriving entity, and even to this day, 20 years later, Ms. Kay has nothing but gratitude for the family and friends of Pax Go.

"I wouldn't be here today if it weren't for the support of my family and friends, and I think many of our employees feel the same. That is why we host this special event that honors those closest to our company every year," stated Ms. Kay at last year's event.

Please join Pax Go on July 14.

Sincerely,

Hugh Britters
Pax Go Events Coordinator

TEST 04

162. What is the purpose of the letter?

(A) To announce a leadership change
(B) To disclose a mission statement
(C) To detail a new company plan
(D) To offer an invitation to an event

163. In the letter, the word "cover" in paragraph 2, line 3 is closest in meaning to

(A) report
(B) fix
(C) conceal
(D) include

164. What is NOT indicated about Pax Go?

(A) It was started two decades ago.
(B) It holds an annual get-together.
(C) It values family relationships.
(D) It will expand in the near future.

▶ ▶ ▶ GO ON TO THE NEXT PAGE

Citywide Office Safety Training Events
Taught by Philadelphia Police and Firemen's Association

Safe Ladder Use:
Accidents happen at work all the time, and the chances of injury increase tenfold with ladder use. Ensure all your employees know the proper way to use a ladder with our training. We detail a 3-points-of-contact system that eliminates nearly all ladder accidents.

Deescalating Office Aggression:
Tensions can be high in a stressful work setting. Make sure all your employees know how to handle a disgruntled coworker or deescalate a potentially violent argument between staff.

Emergency Fire Drill Practice:
Do your employees know where to go in case a fire breaks out? Is there a safety plan in place? We can help you set up a company-wide escape plan and run fire drills so that everyone is prepared.

Inclement Weather Safety:
What will your office do when facing especially bad weather? With the number of natural disasters on the rise, it is important to carve out an evacuation plan if inclement weather strikes. Schedule this training to ensure employees' safety during weather emergencies.

To schedule one or more of these office safety trainings, visit our Web site at www.paofficesafety. org. Additional courses beyond those listed can be requested.

165. What is suggested about the Philadelphia Police and Firemen's Association?

(A) It accepts donations on its Web site.
(B) It conducts training at various locations.
(C) It offers more than four training events.
(D) It has highly experienced teachers.

166. What is indicated about the citywide office safety training events?

(A) There is a fee to participate.
(B) They are held in all weather conditions.
(C) Participants practice real-life skills.
(D) They can be booked online.

167. What event most likely teaches interpersonal communication skills?

(A) Safe Ladder Use
(B) Deescalating Office Aggression
(C) Emergency Fire Drill Practice
(D) Inclement Weather Safety

Questions 168-171 refer to the following e-mail.

```
_ □ X
```

From:	Alex Micheline (amich@corporatebighall.com)
To:	Wesley Farn (wfarn@farnfinancials.com)
Subject:	Re: Rental Inquiry
Date:	November 19

Dear Mr. Farn,

I received your letter of inquiry regarding renting an event hall for your company's party. — [1] —

According to the form, your requested rental date is December 22, and your list of requirements includes space, chairs, catering, and music. To complete your reservation, please e-mail me back with how many guests you expect and your credit card information. — [2] —

I've attached a menu options list with this e-mail. Choose what appetizer and main entrée you would like served at your party, and we will have our caterer contact you to confirm the menu and serving time. — [3] —

You and your associates may access the venue on Friday, December 21, after 6:00 P.M. in order to drop off any personal supplies you will need and to set up any additional decorations you may have.

I will be on the premises that Friday as well. If you have any questions that day, feel free to come to my office on the 2nd floor, or you may e-mail me at the above address at any time.
— [4] — Please note that the total payment must be paid in cash in full by the day of the event. After receipt of payment, your card will be cleared of the deposit charge.

Alex Micheline
Event Planner
Corporate Big Hall

168. On what day is the Farn Financials event?

(A) Thursday
(B) Friday
(C) Saturday
(D) Sunday

169. What is indicated about the Corporate Big Hall?

(A) It offers a selection of live bands.
(B) It arranges food service for events.
(C) It does not require a deposit for events.
(D) It has worked with Farn Financials before.

170. What does Mr. Micheline ask Mr. Farn to do?

(A) Send the number of attendees
(B) Pay the remainder of a bill
(C) Send invitations to guests
(D) Contact a catering company

171. In which of the positions marked [1], [2], [3], and [4] does the following sentence best belong?

"We will run it for a deposit amount of $100.00 in order to hold the space."

(A) [1]
(B) [2]
(C) [3]
(D) [4]

▶ ▶ ▶ GO ON TO THE NEXT PAGE

Questions 172-175 refer to the following online chat discussion.

Wendy Young 5:01 P.M.
Guys, we need ideas for the upcoming employee outing. Last month, we saw a play, and before that, we had a cultural event. What should we do this month?

Harry Sims 5:03 P.M.
I think a company dinner would be a nice change. We could have a delicious meal for everyone to enjoy and chat over.

Josh Bae 5:05 P.M.
I'm all in for that. Who doesn't like good food and conversation?

Harry Sims 5:06 P.M.
How about if we start by deciding on what kind of food we want? And what about having a theme for the evening?

Wendy Young 5:07 P.M.
Dinner sounds good, but there are a lot of things to consider, and not just the food. We'll need to find a place that has enough space for a big group. Then there is the issue of food allergies and dietary restrictions.

Josh Bae 5:08 P.M.
How about surveying the staff to see what everyone would like to eat and to find out about the food concerns you mentioned?

Harry Sims 5:09 P.M.
Good thinking! I'll research some restaurants nearby and put together a list of possible places. Josh, I'll e-mail it to you in about an hour. You can use that to make the survey.

Josh Bae 5:10 P.M.
Sounds good.

Wendy Young 5:12 P.M.
Since you two have got the ball rolling, I'll step aside until you have the survey results. Let me know, and I'll take care of the actual scheduling.

Send

172. What is most likely true about the cultural event?

(A) Mr. Sims organized it.
(B) It took place at a theater.
(C) Few employees participated.
(D) It was held two months ago.

173. What is suggested about the upcoming employee outing?

(A) A similar event was organized before.
(B) Many people are expected to attend.
(C) Ms. Young will conduct a survey.
(D) Different types of seafood will be served.

174. At 5:05 P.M., what does Mr. Bae most likely mean when he writes, "I'm all in for that"?

(A) He really enjoyed last month's show.
(B) He wants to be in charge of planning.
(C) He likes the suggestion of having dinner.
(D) He prefers that they have food delivered.

175. What is indicated about the survey?

(A) It will be created by Mr. Sims.
(B) It will ask about what people can't eat.
(C) It will be distributed by e-mail.
(D) It will include a list of possible dates.

▶ ▶ ▶ GO ON TO THE NEXT PAGE

For Immediate Release Contact: Adam Shield, 555-2351

Built Train for Commuters

Starting on Monday, June 22, Heinsfield Station will offer bullet train services for commuters to Champagne Station, 125 kilometers away in downtown Heinsfield. The route will run nonstop between the stations, a perk of the recent opening of a large conglomerate, Homeaway Products.

With the opening of Homeaway, 50,000 employees commute to the nearby Champagne station daily. The heavy traffic prompted city officials to open new train routes to alleviate congestion. The bullet train had been tested in Los Angeles and New York with much success and unprecedented speeds. The bullet train features 10 cars with 70 seats in each.

Ticket costs for the bullet train are higher than those for the regular trains, but monthly passes can be purchased by working professionals, who will ride to and from the office every day, at a slight discount. Cars 3 through 5 are for women only to ensure extra measures of safety and comfort for female riders.

https://www.bullettrainusa.org

To leave an inquiry or comment for Champagne Station services, complete the form below:

Name: *Hailey Nirem*
Date: *July 6*
Phone: *555-8261*
E-mail: *hanir@mailnets.com*

Comments:
I cannot tell you how happy my fellow Homeaway colleagues and I are to have the direct bullet train route taking us from home to work and back again. Before the opening of this segment, I was driving a long distance back and forth every day!

But I would like to inform you of a mechanical error that has occurred twice on my way to work, and I worry that it could lead to larger problems. The left-side door on car 4 seems to get stuck halfway through closing every once in a while. There have been moments where riders believe the train will start running with the door partially open! Please send a technician to repair the malfunctioning door. Speed and efficiency are welcomed and appreciated by your riders, but safety is important and key. Thank you for your time.

176. In the press release, what is NOT mentioned about the bullet train?

(A) Commuters can get tickets at a reduced rate.
(B) It travels 125 kilometers one way.
(C) It will offer direct service between two stations.
(D) Passengers can buy tickets on the train.

177. What is the reason the new service is being offered?

(A) It is replacing an outdated train.
(B) It was donated by a major corporation.
(C) It aims to reduce overcrowding.
(D) It was demanded by local commuters.

178. Why did Ms. Nirem visit the Champagne Station Web site?

(A) To change her ticket
(B) To complain about a schedule
(C) To inquire about tickets
(D) To report a problem

179. Where does Ms. Nirem most likely live?

(A) Champagne
(B) Heinsfeld
(C) Los Angeles
(D) New York

180. What is suggested about Ms. Nirem?

(A) She has a monthly unlimited ticket.
(B) She now drives 250 kilometers a day.
(C) She rode in a car restricted to females.
(D) She recently received a job promotion.

▶ ▶ ▶ GO ON TO THE NEXT PAGE

November 4

Edwina Shangles
293 Bener Lane
Boston, MA 23163

Dear Ms. Shangles,

We spoke briefly on the phone last week about the appointment I made to have the holiday decorations put up in my office building. As I mentioned in our conversation, the building is quite large. It is 10 stories high with 2 sets of stairways and 15 offices on each floor.

I would like to remind you to send me a breakdown of the installation day schedule the day prior to the actual setup. I will need to arrange times with the departments on each floor for offices to be vacated in order for the decorating to take place. The affected employees will need somewhere to go during that time. As you may already know, this requires a lot of preplanning and coordination.

I look forward to hearing from you.

Sincerely,

Laura Zeal
Managing Director

Installation Day Schedule

Tuesday, November 28

9:15 A.M. – 9:45 A.M.	Crew arrives and unloads trucks
9:45 A.M. – 10:45 A.M.	Measurements
10:45 A.M. – 11:50 A.M.	Decoration preparation
11:50 A.M. – 2:00 P.M.	Installation: 1st & 2nd floors
2:00 P.M. – 3:00 P.M.	Installation: 3rd floor
3:00 P.M. – 5:00 P.M.	Installation: 4th & 5th floors
5:00 P.M. – 7:00 P.M.	Installation: 6th & 7th floors
7:00 P.M. – 8:00 P.M.	Installation: 8th floor
8:00 P.M. – Finish	Installation: 9th & 10th floors

181. What is the reason Ms. Zeal wrote to Ms. Shangles?

(A) To remind Ms. Shangles of an existing appointment
(B) To schedule a phone conversation
(C) To inquire about an installation payment
(D) To request further information be sent

182. In the letter, the word "vacated" in paragraph 2, line 3 is closest in meaning to

(A) closed
(B) emptied
(C) relaxed
(D) unlocked

183. According to the information, what is true about the planned work?

(A) It will be carried out by Ms. Shambles.
(B) It will begin at the bottom of the building.
(C) It will continue for two days.
(D) It will stop only for meal breaks.

184. How many offices are expected to be decorated by 2:00 P.M.?

(A) 2
(B) 15
(C) 30
(D) 40

185. On what date will the installation day schedule most likely be sent?

(A) November 26
(B) November 27
(C) November 28
(D) November 29

▶ ▶ ▶GO ON TO THE NEXT PAGE

Paid Advertisement

Hypercolor Clarity Print Services

Hypercolor Clarity guarantees crystal-clear printing services for your business. Whether it is a stack of small business cards or a wall-sized advertisement poster, each of your print projects will be handled with care and printed using only the latest technology.

Enjoy an additional 20% discount on services totaling more than $100.00 in the month of March.

April Promotions:
Business cards: 500 cards for $90.00.
Color Brochures: 100 brochures for $75.00.
Posters: 10 posters for $55.00.

For more information, e-mail us at inquiry@hypercolor.com

[_][□][X]

To:	inquiry@hypercolor.com
From:	YeminAsher@soundsori.net
Date:	April 2
Re:	Print Job Order
	Attachment: orderform, manual, poster

Good morning. I saw your advertisement in the Daily Bureau paper and would like to hire your company to prepare our intern manuals. My company will host a large workshop for over 100 interns, so we must prepare a lot of printed materials. These need to be assembled into individual packets.

I also saw on your Web site that posters can be printed for a special price this month. I would like to order 20 posters as well. I would appreciate it if the posters are delivered a week before the manuals since we want to advertise the event beforehand. The completed manuals should be delivered three days ahead of the workshop, which will be held in the last week of April.

I've attached the completed order form from your Web site along with files containing the manuals and poster.

Please confirm that you have received my order. Do not hesitate to contact me if you have any questions.

Thank you.

Yemin

Hypercolor Clarity Printing

Order Form

Name: *Yemin Asher*

Phone Number: *555-0932*

Delivery Date: *April 20 and April 27*

Delivery For: *Yemin Asher, Marketing Department*

Delivery Address: *2914 Segway Lane*

Order Item: *100 printed manuals, 20 posters*

Printed Item Format: *Files attached*

186. In the advertisement, what is NOT indicated about Hypercolor Clarity?

(A) It has promotional prices in April.
(B) It does business only with small companies.
(C) It uses modern printing equipment.
(D) It offers additional discounts to orders.

187. What most likely is true about Mr. Asher?

(A) He will drop off the printed materials at Hypercolor.
(B) He will pay the regular price for the intern manuals.
(C) He designed the event posters himself.
(D) He subscribes to the Daily Bureau.

188. In the e-mail, what does Mr. Asher ask Hypercolor to do?

(A) Review materials for interns
(B) Participate in an event
(C) Design advertisements
(D) Verify receipt of his request

189. When is the intern workshop?

(A) On April 20
(B) On April 24
(C) On April 27
(D) On April 30

190. What is suggested about Mr. Asher's order?

(A) It will be sent to him all together.
(B) It will not be processed.
(C) It will be over $110.00.
(D) It is not his first order.

▶ ▶ ▶GO ON TO THE NEXT PAGE

Grow Your Public Speaking Skills!

Is giving motivational and inspiring speeches part of your job? How about just delivering a concise message to a large group of people? No matter what your title, being able to speak well is an asset for any working professional. Hone that skill with our special speaking series offered by the Better Business Bureau of Willmington. All of the courses run for six weeks and are taught by professional communicator James Mason.

Speaking Series Courses

Speaking 101: Introduction to Public Speaking Thursdays 7:30 P.M. Venue: Garrick Hall	Speaking 102: Intonation and Emotions Tuesdays 6:00 P.M. Venue: Lorie Hall
Speaking 103: Content Creation Fridays 5:30 P.M Venue: James Hall	Speaking 104: Inspire and Motivate Saturdays 10:30 A.M Venue: Kennedy Hall

For price listings and registration, visit us online at www.bbbwillmington.org

Important Dates:

September 1 - 30	Early registration (5% discount)
October 1 - 31	Regular registration
November 1	Classes begin

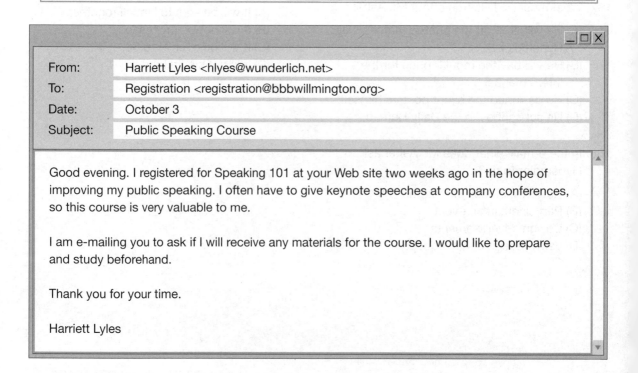

From:	Harriett Lyles <hlyes@wunderlich.net>
To:	Registration <registration@bbbwillmington.org>
Date:	October 3
Subject:	Public Speaking Course

Good evening. I registered for Speaking 101 at your Web site two weeks ago in the hope of improving my public speaking. I often have to give keynote speeches at company conferences, so this course is very valuable to me.

I am e-mailing you to ask if I will receive any materials for the course. I would like to prepare and study beforehand.

Thank you for your time.

Harriett Lyles

Please note that the course listed below will have a later starting date of November 13.

Speaking 101 – Garrick Hall

Books for all classes can be picked up from the campus bookstore on the first day of class. If you would like to purchase books in advance, please e-mail your course instructor to place an expedited order for you. You can find the e-mail address in the campus directory.

191. What is indicated about the speaking courses?

(A) They will end in November.
(B) Large groups are expected to enroll.
(C) Each is held at a different location.
(D) Students completing them will receive certificates.

192. What is suggested about Ms. Lyles?

(A) She is the CEO at her company.
(B) She paid less than the standard tuition.
(C) She has no experience with public speaking.
(D) She will have to miss certain class days.

193. At what time is Ms. Lyles' class scheduled to start?

(A) At 10:30 A.M.
(B) At 5:30 P.M.
(C) At 6:00 P.M.
(D) At 7:30 P.M.

194. What is the purpose of the notice?

(A) To announce schedule adjustments
(B) To notify readers of new courses
(C) To promote a new service for students
(D) To communicate cancelations

195. What will Ms. Lyles most likely do before November 13?

(A) Order materials online
(B) Contact Mr. Mason
(C) E-mail the bookstore
(D) Switch courses

▶ ▶ ▶GO ON TO THE NEXT PAGE

Ventures Hedge Fund: Presidential Election
Date: July 1

New President to Be Chosen by Company Employees

Attention, Ventures Hedge Fund Employees: As you know, our current president will step down at the end of this year for personal reasons. As such, we have decided to take a new democratic approach to our leadership and will hold an election for our new president for the first time.

Please plan to attend the election event in its entirety. You will be able to listen to the nominees' platforms and then vote at the end of the session. The winner will be announced on the spot. His or her name will also be published on our Web site that evening.

Greg Fry, Chairman of the Board
Ventures Hedge Fund

Ventures Hedge Fund: Presidential Election Event

Date: July 31

8:15 A.M.	Meeting Opening
8:25 A.M.	Current President's Address
8:45 A.M.	Nominee Introductions
8:55 A.M.	Nominee Presentations
12:30 P.M.	Lunch
1:30 P.M.	Return to Meeting
1:45 P.M.	Voting
3:00 P.M.	New President's Address

From:	BrandonJiles@ventures.com
To:	MarshaPidjorn@ventures.com
Subject:	Congratulations
Date:	August 1

Marsha,

I want to personally congratulate and welcome you as our new president at Ventures Hedge Fund. You were enthusiastically chosen to lead our group into a bright and prosperous future. I believe our company has made the right choice.

Given your experience with us over the past 12 years and your valuable contributions to our most recent collaborative endeavor, I expect nothing but the best from you. Your first order of presidential business will be to move to the executive office on the 15th floor. Misty Allen will be available to help you with your relocation. I look forward to seeing you at the next board meeting this Tuesday.

Sincerely,

Brandon

196. What is indicated about the Ventures Hedge Fund's presidential election?

(A) It will announce its new president later.
(B) It was not how previous presidents were selected.
(C) It will hold a board meeting about voting.
(D) It is scheduled to be a biannual event.

197. When was the name of the new president made public?

(A) On July 1
(B) On July 30
(C) On July 31
(D) On August 1

198. What is suggested about Ms. Pidjorn?

(A) She was given her first job by Mr. Jiles.
(B) She spoke twice during the election event.
(C) She has worked directly under Mr. Fry.
(D) She helped to count the votes.

199. What is indicated about Mr. Jiles?

(A) He has worked on projects with Ms. Pidjorn before.
(B) He was unable to vote in the election.
(C) He started at the company around a decade ago.
(D) His office will be on the same floor as Mr. Pidjorn's.

200. What does Mr. Jiles expect Ms. Pidjorn to do?

(A) Write a speech for the employees
(B) Help Ms. Allen to relocate
(C) Attend an upcoming gathering
(D) Find someone to move her belongings

Test 04 정답

147. (B)	**148.** (D)	**149.** (C)	**150.** (A)	**151.** (D)	**152.** (C)
153. (B)	**154.** (C)	**155.** (B)	**156.** (B)	**157.** (D)	**158.** (B)
159. (D)	**160.** (C)	**161.** (B)	**162.** (D)	**163.** (C)	**164.** (D)
165. (C)	**166.** (D)	**167.** (B)	**168.** (C)	**169.** (B)	**170.** (A)
171. (B)	**172.** (D)	**173.** (B)	**174.** (C)	**175.** (B)	**176.** (D)
177. (C)	**178.** (D)	**179.** (B)	**180.** (C)	**181.** (D)	**182.** (B)
183. (B)	**184.** (C)	**185.** (B)	**186.** (B)	**187.** (B)	**188.** (D)
189. (D)	**190.** (C)	**191.** (C)	**192.** (B)	**193.** (D)	**194.** (A)
195. (B)	**196.** (B)	**197.** (C)	**198.** (B)	**199.** (A)	**200.** (C)

TEST

05

시작 시간 ___시 ___분

종료 시간 ___시 ___분

목표 개수 _____ / 54

실제 개수 _____ / 54

· 반드시 55분 안에 문제 풀이 포함 마킹까지 마쳐야 합니다.

· 실제 시험이라고 생각하고 멈추지 말고 풀어보세요.

· 정답 개수에 5를 곱하면 대략적인 점수가 됩니다.

PART 7

Directions: In this part you will read a selection of texts, such as magazine and newspaper articles, e-mails, and instant messages. Each text or set of texts is followed by several questions. Select the best answer for each question and mark the letter (A), (B), (C), or (D) on your answer sheet.

Questions 147-148 refer to the following e-mail.

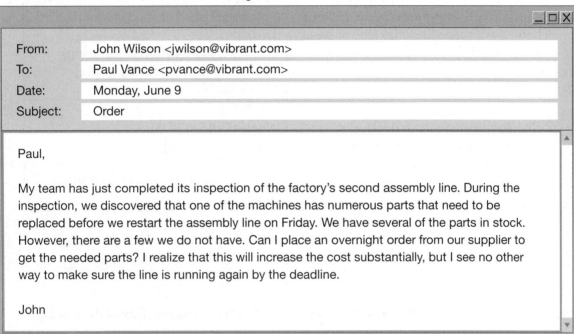

From: John Wilson <jwilson@vibrant.com>
To: Paul Vance <pvance@vibrant.com>
Date: Monday, June 9
Subject: Order

Paul,

My team has just completed its inspection of the factory's second assembly line. During the inspection, we discovered that one of the machines has numerous parts that need to be replaced before we restart the assembly line on Friday. We have several of the parts in stock. However, there are a few we do not have. Can I place an overnight order from our supplier to get the needed parts? I realize that this will increase the cost substantially, but I see no other way to make sure the line is running again by the deadline.

John

147. Why did Mr. Wilson write to Mr. Vance?

(A) To find a repairperson
(B) To request permission
(C) To check on an order
(D) To schedule an inspection

148. What is indicated about Mr. Wilson?

(A) He ordered replacement parts.
(B) He made some necessary repairs.
(C) He finished an examination.
(D) He received a few machine parts.

▶ ▶ ▶ GO ON TO THE NEXT PAGE

Frank's Family Restaurant

October Specials*

Beef Cutlet	Chicken Dinner for Four
A tender beef cutlet cooked to perfection. Topped with mozzarella cheese and our homemade sauce. Includes side of pasta, salad, bread, and soft drink. Just $15.00!	Includes 8 pieces of baked or fried chicken Two sides Bread and salad (choice of dressing) Drinks included (soda, tea, coffee) All for $30.00!
Supreme Pizza	Apple Pie
Choose thin, regular, or thick crust. Three cheeses with pepperoni, sausage, peppers, olives, and onions. Only $10.00!	Whole (8 slices) $8.00 Half (4 slices) $4.50 Slice $1.50 Add a scoop of ice cream for $0.50 per slice!

*Valid from October 1 - 31. Cannot be combined with other offers. Take out or eat in.

149. What is the purpose of the advertisement?

(A) To promote a new menu
(B) To comment on services
(C) To attract customers
(D) To announce an opening

150. What is indicated about the specials?

(A) They are available for one month.
(B) They are only for orders to go.
(C) They can be used with other coupons.
(D) They are limited to four locations.

The National Center for Health and Wellness recommends that teenagers incorporate regular exercise into their weekly routines. According to a survey conducted last year, nearly 45% of teenagers today are overweight. In addition to being socially frowned upon, being overweight can lead to health problems in both the short and long term. Therefore, it is essential that teenagers adopt a healthy diet, get sufficient sleep, and exercise regularly.

Teenagers who regularly exercise report having better skin, stronger muscles and bones, and more energy. Teens can enjoy the benefits of regular exercise by participating in organized sports, by joining a dance or fitness program, or simply by incorporating more walking into their daily routines. For more information on how to help your teenager get and stay fit, visit www.nchw.org.

151. What is the purpose of the information?

(A) To warn about exercising incorrectly
(B) To inform teens of a new program
(C) To demand weight loss programs
(D) To promote healthy practices

152. What is mentioned about teenagers?

(A) They are not taught about dieting.
(B) Most refuse to exercise.
(C) Almost half have weight problems.
(D) They enjoy fitness programs.

153. What is one benefit of exercise for teenagers?

(A) It can help them succeed at sports.
(B) It can improve their school performance.
(C) It can reduce their caloric intake.
(D) It can boost their energy levels.

Questions 154-155 refer to the following memo.

Memo

FROM: Pauline Samuelson
TO: All Store Managers
CC: Penny Bale

Deborah's is launching a new marketing campaign in conjunction with the release of this year's fall fashions. Our advertising and marketing team has designed a series of promotional displays featuring characters from the video ads we are showing on social media and other Web sites. These displays will be shipped to all retail locations in the coming week. Be sure to prominently display them at the front of your stores. We want to draw customers in to browse and purchase clothing from the fall fashion line. If you have any questions, please direct them to my assistant, Penny Bale (pbale@deborahs.com).

154. What are store managers instructed to do?

(A) Submit ideas for social media marketing
(B) Place marketing materials where they are visible
(C) Change the inventory of clothing in the stores
(D) Report on the success of the advertisements

155. What is indicated about the new marketing campaign?

(A) It features real store employees.
(B) It began last week.
(C) It aims to attract younger shoppers.
(D) It includes an online component.

Questions 156-157 refer to the following text message chain.

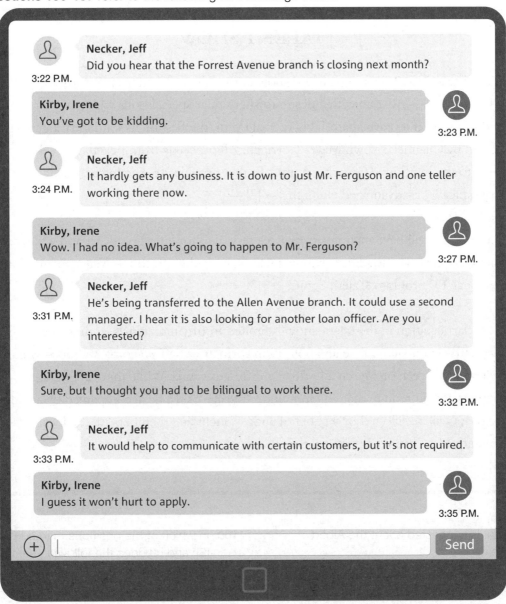

Necker, Jeff
Did you hear that the Forrest Avenue branch is closing next month?
3:22 P.M.

Kirby, Irene
You've got to be kidding.
3:23 P.M.

Necker, Jeff
It hardly gets any business. It is down to just Mr. Ferguson and one teller working there now.
3:24 P.M.

Kirby, Irene
Wow. I had no idea. What's going to happen to Mr. Ferguson?
3:27 P.M.

Necker, Jeff
He's being transferred to the Allen Avenue branch. It could use a second manager. I hear it is also looking for another loan officer. Are you interested?
3:31 P.M.

Kirby, Irene
Sure, but I thought you had to be bilingual to work there.
3:32 P.M.

Necker, Jeff
It would help to communicate with certain customers, but it's not required.
3:33 P.M.

Kirby, Irene
I guess it won't hurt to apply.
3:35 P.M.

Send

156. At 3:23 P.M., why does Ms. Kirby write, "You've got to be kidding"?

(A) She thinks Mr. Necker is funny.
(B) She received unexpected news.
(C) She is worried about losing her job.
(D) She is surprised to hear from Mr. Necker.

157. What is suggested about the Allen Avenue branch?

(A) It was founded by Mr. Ferguson.
(B) It is the bank's newest location.
(C) It has non-English speaking customers.
(D) It is where Mr. Necker currently works.

▶ ▶ ▶ GO ON TO THE NEXT PAGE

TALENT SHOW

Channel 3 television is hosting a talent show at the Albert Theater on Saturday, April 5, at 6:00 P.M. — [1] — Anyone with a desire to share their special skills with a live audience is invited to audition to participate. This special event, the first of its kind in Bridgeport, will be hosted by Channel 3's own Mayra Corrigan. All proceeds from ticket sales will be donated to the Sunflower Center, a nonprofit that provides free acting and dance classes to economically disadvantaged children. — [2] —

All participants will have their performances recorded for later broadcast and will receive a commemorative T-shirt. Three winners will be invited to go to Las Vegas to audition for the national TV program 'Talent Scout.' — [3] —

Because participation in the talent show is limited to fifty individuals, auditions are required. To sign up, complete an application form at www.TV3.com. Auditions will be held during the week of March 24 - 28 at a different venue. While there are no age restrictions, we do require that children under the age of 18 be accompanied by an adult. Participants will be selected by a panel of judges, including members of the local arts community and Channel 3 personalities.
— [4] —

158. What is suggested about the Albert Theater?

(A) It is sponsoring an event for children.
(B) Seating is reserved for fifty people.
(C) Auditions will be held there.
(D) It is located in Bridgeport.

159. What are readers invited to do?

(A) Apply for free classes
(B) Compete for a position
(C) Meet local celebrities
(D) Visit a TV studio

160. In which of the positions marked [1], [2], [3], and [4] does the following sentence best belong?

"Transportation and lodging will be paid for by the show's producer, Miracle Entertainment."

(A) [1]
(B) [2]
(C) [3]
(D) [4]

Summer is almost here!

Stay cool with Polar.

With proper maintenance, modern air-conditioning systems will keep your home cool when the temperature outside rises. Without proper care, chances are that your system could underperform, or even fail, in the middle of a heat wave.

Give Polar Heating and Cooling a call at 555-3033. We can help ensure that you and your family have a comfortable summer.

Basic Air Conditioner Preventive Maintenance Package – Regular $99.99
Now $75*

Includes:
- Complete inspection of air-conditioning unit, vents, and electrical connections
- Cleaning of air-conditioning unit and drain line
- Check thermostat, temperature range, air flow, and air filter
- Lubricate motor
- Free quote and 5% discount for any additional work that may be recommended

For over 30 years, Polar Heating and Cooling has been providing exceptional service to residents of Glendale and the surrounding communities. We are a family-owned, family-operated heating and cooling installation, maintenance, and repair company. We were the first authorized Carbon Furnace and Ice King air-conditioning installer in the Glendale area. All of our work is backed by a one-year warranty.

*Offer good through May 31

Polar Heating and Cooling
879 Harmony Avenue
Glendale, AZ 09830
(218) 555-3033
www.polarheatingcooling.com

161. For whom is this advertisement intended?

(A) Homeowners
(B) Technicians
(C) Business owners
(D) Job seekers

162. What is NOT indicated about Polar Heating and Cooling?

(A) It operates a Web site.
(B) It installs purchases for free.
(C) It can fix broken air-conditioning units.
(D) It opened decades ago.

163. What is indicated about the service being offered?

(A) It is limited to certain brands of air conditioners.
(B) It will have a reduced price in June.
(C) It is covered by a guarantee.
(D) It includes the cost of replacement parts.

▶ ▶ ▶ GO ON TO THE NEXT PAGE

Questions 164-167 refer to the following online chat discussion.

Corinne Evans 11:02 A.M.		The mayor is asking us to do more to attract businesses to the city.
Nate Greely 11:06 A.M.		Well, we have already convinced two dozen companies to relocate here in the first year of the City Vision Program. I'd consider that a success.
Colin Harrison 11:08 A.M.		It's a good first step. But we have only brought in small companies so far.
Deena Sojourner 11:17 A.M.		Right. Those employ only a handful of people. The mayor asked us to think big.
Corinne Evans 11:21 A.M.		Exactly. One of the goals of City Vision is to generate hundreds of good-paying jobs in the city. That means we need to attract large companies. I'm open to suggestions.
Nate Greely 11:25 A.M.		I think we should use tax incentives. Let's reduce taxes and maybe even let businesses operate tax free for a few years.
Corinne Evans 11:26 A.M.		Okay. Nate, go ahead and research tax incentive options for us to discuss at our next meeting. Any other suggestions?
Colin Harrison 11:28 A.M.		Here's an idea. Instead of looking outside, why not invest in people starting businesses here? Give them loans and provide mentorship to help them grow.
Deanne Sojourner 11:32 A.M.		I'm with you, Colin. That's exactly the long-term growth strategy we need.
Corinne Evans 11:40 A.M.		Right now, though, we need more immediate results to keep the mayor happy. See what ideas you can come up with before our meeting with him on Friday.

Send

164. Where do the writers most likely work?

(A) At an online advertising firm
(B) At an industrial engineering company
(C) At an economic development organization
(D) At a commercial real estate agency

165. At 11:08 A.M., why does Mr. Harrison write, "It's a good first step"?

(A) To point out more work needs to be done
(B) To suggest redefining some goals
(C) To change the focus to small companies
(D) To propose extending the program another year

166. What is suggested about Ms. Sojourner?

(A) She has experience running a small business.
(B) She wants more support for local entrepreneurs.
(C) She recently relocated to the city herself.
(D) She knows a lot about lending money.

167. What is implied about the city's mayor?

(A) He was recently elected to his position.
(B) He wants to bring lots of jobs to the city.
(C) He campaigned to reduce taxes for residents.
(D) He hired Mr. Greely to lead the City Vision Project.

▶ ▶ ▶ GO ON TO THE NEXT PAGE

Questions 168-171 refer to the following article.

Today's hospitality industry relies on technology more than ever before. Travelers have come to expect high-speed wireless Internet access at their hotels. They want to be able to book flights and room reservations via their smartphones.

San Francisco's Bayside Hotel has taken technology to a new level. The luxury hotel uses Wi-Fi technology to coordinate everything from stocking refrigerators in rooms to making sure guests have clean towels. Every staff member is issued either a tablet or smartphone so they can communicate instantaneously with the hotel's Digital Management System (DMS).

"We installed the DMS twelve months ago to make it easier for management to monitor hotel supplies," said hotel manager Sam Wayland. "It was soon apparent that we could improve communication and efficiency, so we expanded the system." And they did improve efficiency.

Bayside guests can order room service, request extra towels, and even book a shuttle to the airport via their tablet or smartphone. A new program allows busy business travelers to preorder meals at the hotel's restaurant. They click on a menu and select a dining time, and their food and beverages are served as soon as they take their reserved seat at the restaurant.

While only a handful of hotels worldwide have adopted systems like Bayside's DMS, some industry analysts predict similar systems will become more mainstream by the end of the decade.

168. What is true about the Bayside Hotel?

(A) It only accepts reservations made online.
(B) It first opened a decade ago.
(C) It has the fastest Wi-Fi in the region.
(D) It offers transportation for its guests.

169. What is NOT mentioned about the Bayside Hotel's DMS?

(A) It is the only system of its kind.
(B) It communicates with appliances.
(C) It has been in use for a year.
(D) It is used by hotel employees.

170. According to the article, what can Bayside guests do via their smartphones?

(A) Pay their hotel bill
(B) Set up a checkout time
(C) Check hotel supplies
(D) Order a meal in advance

171. The word "mainstream" in paragraph 5, line 2 is closest in meaning to

(A) expensive
(B) common
(C) efficient
(D) rapid

Questions 172-175 refer to the following e-mail.

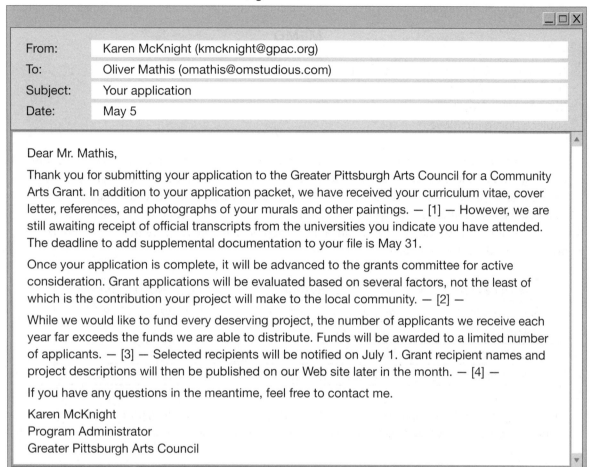

From: Karen McKnight (kmcknight@gpac.org)

To: Oliver Mathis (omathis@omstudious.com)

Subject: Your application

Date: May 5

Dear Mr. Mathis,

Thank you for submitting your application to the Greater Pittsburgh Arts Council for a Community Arts Grant. In addition to your application packet, we have received your curriculum vitae, cover letter, references, and photographs of your murals and other paintings. — [1] — However, we are still awaiting receipt of official transcripts from the universities you indicate you have attended. The deadline to add supplemental documentation to your file is May 31.

Once your application is complete, it will be advanced to the grants committee for active consideration. Grant applications will be evaluated based on several factors, not the least of which is the contribution your project will make to the local community. — [2] —

While we would like to fund every deserving project, the number of applicants we receive each year far exceeds the funds we are able to distribute. Funds will be awarded to a limited number of applicants. — [3] — Selected recipients will be notified on July 1. Grant recipient names and project descriptions will then be published on our Web site later in the month. — [4] —

If you have any questions in the meantime, feel free to contact me.

Karen McKnight
Program Administrator
Greater Pittsburgh Arts Council

172. What is one reason Ms. McKnight wrote to Mr. Mathis?

(A) To ask for an additional reference
(B) To acknowledge receipt of materials
(C) To change a stated deadline
(D) To explain the denial of a request

173. Who most likely is Mr. Mathis?

(A) An author
(B) An educator
(C) A painter
(D) A photographer

174. When will the Greater Pittsburgh Arts Council contact grant awardees?

(A) On May 5
(B) On May 31
(C) On July 1
(D) On July 31

175. In which of the positions marked [1], [2], [3], and [4] does the following sentence best belong?

"For a complete list of evaluative criteria, please visit our Web site at www.gpac.org."

(A) [1]
(B) [2]
(C) [3]
(D) [4]

▶ ▶ ▶ GO ON TO THE NEXT PAGE

MEMO

To: Marketing Department Team Leaders
From: Shawn Schaller
Date: Monday, May 2
Subject: Upcoming Move

I have just received word from Paul Stevens, the project manager overseeing the expansion of our building. He said that our offices are almost complete and that we can begin moving in next week. He has also been able to schedule a crew of movers to assist us. However, because they are already scheduled to assist other departments, they will not be able to move our entire department at once. Therefore, I have assigned each team a different time and date to move their office. Below are the move dates for each team:

Team Leader	Date/Time	New Location
Andrew Cooper	Monday, May 9 / 8:00 A.M	Cubicles 1 - 4
Haley Quinn	Tuesday, May 10 / 9:30 A.M.	Cubicles 9 - 12
Sara Martinez	Wednesday, May 11 / 1:30 P.M	Cubicles 5 - 8
Chloe White	Thursday, May 12 / 11:30 A.M.	Cubicles 13 - 15

Please have your staff members box up their belongings, unplug computers, printers, phones, and other electronic devices and discard unnecessary items before your scheduled move.

If you have any questions or concerns, let me know as soon as possible.

Shawn Schaller

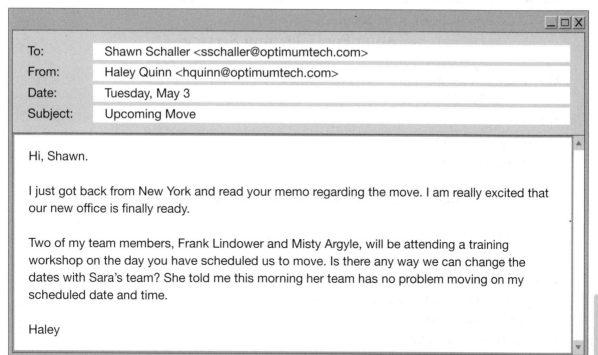

To: Shawn Schaller <sschaller@optimumtech.com>

From: Haley Quinn <hquinn@optimumtech.com>

Date: Tuesday, May 3

Subject: Upcoming Move

Hi, Shawn.

I just got back from New York and read your memo regarding the move. I am really excited that our new office is finally ready.

Two of my team members, Frank Lindower and Misty Argyle, will be attending a training workshop on the day you have scheduled us to move. Is there any way we can change the dates with Sara's team? She told me this morning her team has no problem moving on my scheduled date and time.

Haley

176. What is the purpose of the memo?

(A) To communicate a plan
(B) To announce a new policy
(C) To request movers
(D) To correct an error

177. What is suggested about Mr. Schaller?

(A) He has a supply of moving boxes.
(B) He is a member of Mr. Stevens's crew.
(C) He designed the new office space.
(D) He works in the Marketing Department.

178. What does Mr. Schaller ask the team leaders to do?

(A) Complete preparations prior to moving
(B) Schedule their moves with Ms. Quinn
(C) Decide on office space
(D) Send him a crew of movers

179. What is most likely true about Ms. Martinez?

(A) She used to be on Mr. Quinn's team.
(B) She will lead a workshop.
(C) She recently spoke with Ms. Quinn.
(D) She relocated from New York.

180. On which date will Mr. Lindower be trained?

(A) May 9
(B) May 10
(C) May 11
(D) May 12

▶ ▶ ▶ GO ON TO THE NEXT PAGE

Aqua Pool Cleaning Service

8940 Highway 12, Suite 8
San Esteban, NV 29940
555-3202
david@aquapoolcleaning.com
www.aquapoolcleaning.com

Relax and let us take care of your swimming pool!

Basic and Deluxe cleaning packages available for San Esteban homeowners:

Basic Package: $99/ month*
• 20-point inspection and maintenance
• Test and balance water chemistry
• Test and clean water filter
• Test and adjust pump system

Deluxe Package: $129/month* includes all of the services in the Basic Package plus
• Vacuum pool
• Brush pool walls and tile
• Remove all debris with net

"David and his team have made sure the water in my pool is clean and clear for years. I wouldn't trust anyone else."   *— Betty Herman*

Winner of the 2018 Best Pool Cleaning Service Award   *— The San Esteban Register*

*Price quoted for standard size in-ground swimming pool (70 cubic meters or less) and above-ground pools. Rates for larger in-ground pools and hot tubs available on our Web site.

	_□X
From:	"Penny Martin" pen88@globalmail.com
To:	"Aqua Pool Cleaning" david@aquapoolcleaning.com
Subject:	Service
Date:	Monday, May 21

Dear David,

My husband and I just opened our pool for the summer, and we realized that due to changes in our work schedules, it will be difficult for us to perform all the regular maintenance that our pool needs. My son can help with removing grass and leaves, cleaning the walls, and vacuuming. So we don't need those services from your company. We would like to hire your company to do the other maintenance. The rates posted for a big pool like ours on the Web site are quite reasonable. What is your availability over the next two weeks?

In addition, it wasn't clear on your Web site if your company will help your customers prepare their pools for winter.

Sincerely,

Penny Martin

181. What is indicated about Aqua Pool Cleaning?

(A) It has single rate for pool sizes.
(B) It was founded in 2016.
(C) It has received public recognition.
(D) It has one employee.

182. Why did Ms. Martin write to Aqua Pool Cleaning?

(A) To reschedule a cleaning
(B) To change a service
(C) To contest a billing
(D) To request a service

183. In the e-mail, the word "reasonable" in paragraph 1, line 6 is closest in meaning to

(A) inexpensive
(B) plausible
(C) logical
(D) irrational

184. What is most likely true about the Martins' pool?

(A) It has an attached hot tub.
(B) It is larger than 70 cubic meters.
(C) It has tiles on its sides.
(D) It is an above-ground type.

185. What is suggested about Ms. Martin?

(A) Her husband works for Aqua Pool Cleaning.
(B) She wants the Basic Package.
(C) She will pay over $129 per month.
(D) She keeps her pool open all year.

▶ ▶ ▶GO ON TO THE NEXT PAGE

Questions 186-190 refer to the following Web page, e-mail, and information.

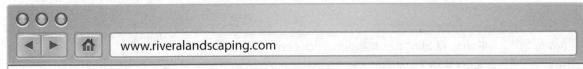

Home	Commercial	Residential	Galleries

Rivera Landscaping

- Proudly serving thousands of clients in Haverford since 1992.
- Winner of over 25 awards.
- Member of the National Association of Landscaping Professionals (NALP) and Haverford Commerce Council (HCC).

Choose Rivera with confidence. We are licensed and insured. Check out samples of our work and customer testimonials on our photo gallery pages. We offer full service landscaping services to residential and commercial clients: design, installation, maintenance, and more. We work on a project-by-project basis as well as offer long-term service contracts.

To set up an appointment for a consultation, contact our Client Services Department at clients@riveralandscaping.com.

From:	clients@riveralandscaping.com
To:	echarleston@gogetter.com
Date:	October 1
Subject: RE:	quote
Attachment:	charleston_5

Dear Mr. Charleston,

It was a pleasure to meet you on Monday to discuss your company's needs. The oak and elm trees lining the driveway are fine specimens. Whoever did the original landscape design knew what they were doing.

Please find attached a quote for the services that we discussed. It is good for one week from the date it was prepared. While quoted rates and prices are carefully prepared, they may change slightly due to unforeseen circumstances. The estimates provided, especially for the wall, should thus be considered rough. We will make every effort to inform you of any unexpected issues and will obtain your permission before completing additional work that will affect the final cost.

Feel free to contact me if you have any questions.

Sincerely,

Michael Ingles

Rivera Landscaping

Quote

Prepared for: Edward Charleston
Prepared on: Tuesday, October 1
Prepared by: Michael Ingles

Services Discussed

►**Routine maintenance: $150 per week***
Includes lawn mowing, watering, and weeding performed on a weekly basis.
Minimum three-month contract required.

►**Irrigation installation: $2,800**
Design and install an automated irrigation system to water trees, beds, and lawns.

►**Tree pruning: $100 per tree**
Normally performed once every year.

*Get 5% off by signing a twelve-month contract

186. In the Web page, what is NOT mentioned about Rivera Landscaping?

(A) It belongs to a business group.
(B) It relocated its business in 1992.
(C) It showcases completed projects.
(D) It provides services to homeowners.

187. According to the e-mail, what can Mr. Charleston expect if extra work needs to be done?

(A) He will be informed before that work starts.
(B) He will need to sign a new contract.
(C) He will be charged at a reduced rate.
(D) He will have to get approval from Mr. Ingles.

188. What is most likely true about Mr. Charleston?

(A) He hired an architectural firm.
(B) He planted two types of trees.
(C) He visited Mr. Ingles' office.
(D) He works in the same area as Mr. Ingles.

189. What is indicated about the routine maintenance service?

(A) Discounts are only available to commercial clients.
(B) Services can be adjusted every week.
(C) Contracts of varying lengths are offered.
(D) Work is directly supervised by Mr. Ingles.

190. When will the quoted prices expire?

(A) On October 8
(B) On October 10
(C) On October 31
(D) On November 1

▶▶▶GO ON TO THE NEXT PAGE

EMPLOYEE BENEFITS OPEN HOUSE

Open to all Link Corporation employees

• New hires can learn about what benefit options are available to them, including:
  Health Insurance, Dental Plan, Vision Plan, Life Insurance, Disability Insurance, Retirement Plan
• Existing employees can make more informed choices about retaining, changing, or canceling
  their benefit options.
• Find out about new health insurance and retirement plan options that are soon to be available.
• Get a heads-up on premium increases for insurance options.
• Retirement specialists will be on hand for those in the latter stages of their careers.

Remember that employees have one chance per year to change their benefit options. The benefit change period is October 1 – October 31. Changes requested at that time will take effect on January 1.

This event will be held in late September. The time, date, and location are to be announced. Check the Link Corporation Web site for updates.

Employee Benefits Open House

Wednesday, September 21
Vincent Building
Link Corporation

Time	Event	Location
9:00 A.M. – 12:00 P.M.	Meeting with representatives from benefit providers	Lobby
12:30 P.M. – 1:30 P.M.	Understanding the benefit enrollment process (Chris Watson, Director of Human Resources, Link Corporation)	Auditorium
2:00 P.M. – 3:30 P.M.	Planning for retirement (Alan Wright, workforce support specialist)	Room 12
4:00 P.M. – 5:00 P.M.	Receiving assistance completing benefit forms (Human Resources staff, Link Corporation)	Room 14

```
                                                                    _ □ X
```

From:	Christina Cartwright <ccartwright@linkcorp.com>
To:	Benjamin Caseman <bcaseman@linkcorp.com>
Re:	Event
Date:	September 22

Ben,

I just want to tell you that I found yesterday's event extremely useful. I now know the difference between life insurance and disability insurance and why I should enroll in both of these options. The benefits representatives were really friendly and answered all of my questions. Moreover, the talk I attended helped me to see why I need to start saving for retirement even though I still have many years ahead of me. I'm just sorry I missed Chris's talk.

I especially want to thank you for helping me fill out the paperwork to make these changes. I will return the forms as soon as the benefit change enrollment period begins.

Sincerely,

Christina Cartwright

191. In the notice, why are employees referred to the company's Web site?

(A) To register for an event
(B) To make an appointment
(C) To request benefit change forms
(D) To get an event schedule

192. What is indicated about the event on the schedule?

(A) It is held in a single structure.
(B) It is open to retired employees.
(C) It features a former Link executive.
(D) It includes a lunch break.

193. At what time can Link Employees most likely talk with the Vision Plan provider?

(A) 9:00 A.M.
(B) 12:30 P.M.
(C) 2:00 P.M.
(D) 4:00 P.M.

194. What location did Ms. Cartwright NOT visit during the event?

(A) The auditorium
(B) The lobby
(C) Room 12
(D) Room 14

195. When does Ms. Cartwright plan to hand in the paperwork to get disability insurance?

(A) On September 23
(B) On October 1
(C) On November 1
(D) On January 1

▶ ▶ ▶ GO ON TO THE NEXT PAGE

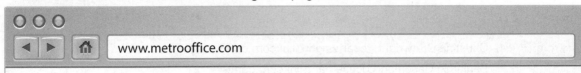

About us | Products | Support | Contact

Metropolitan Office Equipment > Business > Copy Machines

We are an authorized Highmark dealer!

Highmark Digital Copy Machine
45 pages per minute
600 X 600 DPI resolution
Print, copy, scan, and fax functions
USB port

We work exclusively with business clients. All of our copy machines are available for lease or lease with the option to purchase. Machines purchased now come with a twelve-month warranty. If you have any problems, our technicians will travel to your place of business to diagnose and, whenever possible, repair the equipment on site.

Click on this link to get a free quote.

INVOICE

Order # 689434
Taken by: Ned Katz
Date ordered: August 29
Expected delivery date: September 5

Company: Sanford Graphic Designs
Contact person: Eugene Petty
Phone: (610) 555-3034
Ship to: 7124 S. Waverly Street, Shillington, PA 19609
Bill to: same as above

MODEL#	DESCRIPTION	COST
M7894	Highmark Digital Copy Machine	$3,750.00
M8945	Dust cover	$75.00
M0001	Delivery, installation, and calibration	$50.00
M0008	Extended warranty (+12 months)	$200.00

Subtotal: $4,075.00
Tax: $305.00
Total: $4,380.00

Thank you for choosing Metropolitan Office Machines!

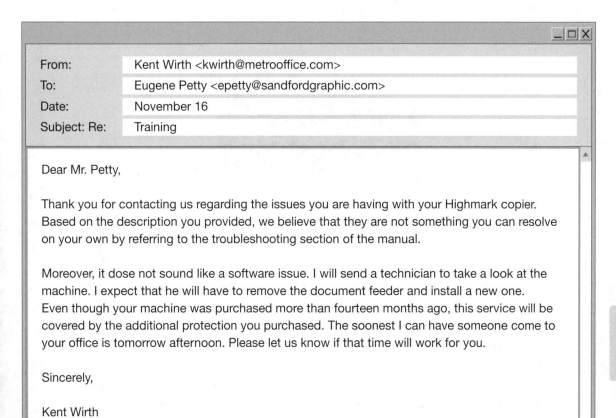

From: Kent Wirth <kwirth@metrooffice.com>

To: Eugene Petty <epetty@sandfordgraphic.com>

Date: November 16

Subject: Re: Training

Dear Mr. Petty,

Thank you for contacting us regarding the issues you are having with your Highmark copier. Based on the description you provided, we believe that they are not something you can resolve on your own by referring to the troubleshooting section of the manual.

Moreover, it dose not sound like a software issue. I will send a technician to take a look at the machine. I expect that he will have to remove the document feeder and install a new one. Even though your machine was purchased more than fourteen months ago, this service will be covered by the additional protection you purchased. The soonest I can have someone come to your office is tomorrow afternoon. Please let us know if that time will work for you.

Sincerely,

Kent Wirth

196. What is NOT indicated about Metropolitan Office Equipment?

(A) It has several retail locations.
(B) It is approved to sell a certain brand.
(C) It rents machines to companies.
(D) It can provide estimates at no cost.

197. What is suggested about product M7894?

(A) It is leased for twelve months.
(B) It was shipped at no extra charge.
(C) It was sold at a discounted price.
(D) It can be used to scan documents.

198. What payment covered the service Mr. Wirth offers to Mr. Petty?

(A) $50.00
(B) $75.00
(C) $200.00
(D) $305.00

199. What does Mr. Wirth think the technician will do for Mr. Petty?

(A) Update the machine's software
(B) Show Mr. Petty how to use the manual
(C) Change the machine's audio settings
(D) Replace a part of the copy machine

200. What does Mr. Wirth ask Mr. Petty to do?

(A) Provide detailed documentation
(B) Confirm a suggested appointment
(C) Refer to official instructions
(D) Make an additional payment

▶ ▶ ▶GO ON TO THE NEXT PAGE

Test 05 정답

147. (B)	**148.** (C)	**149.** (C)	**150.** (A)	**151.** (D)	**152.** (C)
153. (D)	**154.** (B)	**155.** (D)	**156.** (B)	**157.** (C)	**158.** (D)
159. (B)	**160.** (C)	**161.** (A)	**162.** (B)	**163.** (C)	**164.** (C)
165. (A)	**166.** (B)	**167.** (B)	**168.** (D)	**169.** (A)	**170.** (D)
171. (B)	**172.** (B)	**173.** (C)	**174.** (C)	**175.** (B)	**176.** (A)
177. (D)	**178.** (A)	**179.** (C)	**180.** (B)	**181.** (C)	**182.** (D)
183. (A)	**184.** (B)	**185.** (B)	**186.** (B)	**187.** (A)	**188.** (D)
189. (C)	**190.** (A)	**191.** (D)	**192.** (A)	**193.** (A)	**194.** (A)
195. (B)	**196.** (A)	**197.** (D)	**198.** (C)	**199.** (D)	**200.** (B)

TEST

06

시작 시간 ___시 ___분

종료 시간 ___시 ___분

목표 개수 _____ / 54

실제 개수 _____ / 54

• 반드시 55분 안에 문제 풀이 포함 마킹까지 마쳐야 합니다.

• 실제 시험이라고 생각하고 멈추지 말고 풀어보세요.

• 정답 개수에 5를 곱하면 대략적인 점수가 됩니다.

Directions: In this part you will read a selection of texts, such as magazine and newspaper articles, e-mails, and instant messages. Each text or set of texts is followed by several questions. Select the best answer for each question and mark the letter (A), (B), (C), or (D) on your answer sheet.

Questions 147-148 refer to the following form.

www.printedplates.com

Printed Plates

Personalized Dishes for Any Occasion

Name: *Josephine Warner*
E-mail: *jwarner@medicare.org*
Item: *Coffee Mugs*
Color: *White*
Number: *100*
Print description: *Our company logo in navy blue*

Order Specifics:

My company, Medicare, would like 100 white coffee mugs printed with our company logo picture in navy blue to give to our employees as anniversary gifts. Please make sure that the mugs are dishwasher safe as we utilize a high-temperature dishwasher in our office. I understand that expedited delivery will cost an extra $50.00. I'm fine with that since Medicare's anniversary party is this Saturday, and we need these mugs as soon as possible.

147. Why did Ms. Warner complete the form?

(A) To confirm her order
(B) To request information
(C) To change an order
(D) To place an order

148. What does Ms. Warner agree to do?

(A) Pay an additional fee
(B) Add text to the mugs
(C) Change the mug color
(D) Cancel her order

▶ ▶ ▶GO ON TO THE NEXT PAGE

3rd Floor Bathrooms: Water Shutoff

Be advised that next Monday, July 2, the water will be turned off for 3rd floor bathrooms in the Rayburn Office Building.

All restrooms on the 3rd floor will have no water from 1:00 P.M. to 6:00 P.M. as pipes will be repaired. The men's and women's bathrooms can be found on the 1st and 5th floors.

All 3rd floor employees and visitors to the Rayburn Building should not enter the restrooms during the hours listed above.

149. What is mentioned about the repairs?

(A) They will take place in the afternoon.
(B) They will affect only one bathroom.
(C) They are scheduled to last for a few days.
(D) They will be done on three floors.

150. What are readers advised to do during the water shutoff?

(A) Use the bathrooms on the 3rd floor
(B) Work from home
(C) Use alternative restrooms
(D) Drink only bottled water

Winex CEO to Retire at Farewell Dinner

Renowned window design company Winex will bid farewell to its CEO, Leman Rhines, on Saturday, September 30, at the company's annual gala. This year, the event will be held at the Catamount Hotel and will include an eight-course meal and dancing accompanied by a live jazz band.

Rhines joined Winex in 1998. Since then, he has made the company very profitable and revolutionized design technology that is still in use today. Though he has built a legendary career with Winex, Rhines will retire early due to health issues.

The new Winex CEO has not been decided yet, but employees expect an announcement to be made at the dinner. All employees are encouraged to attend to send Mr. Rhines off with jovial well wishes. There is a limit of two tickets per employee. Stop by Human Resources to pick up yours.

151. Where would the article most likely appear?

(A) In a design trade journal
(B) In a finance magazine
(C) In a company newsletter
(D) In a window catalog

152. What is most likely true about Mr. Rhines?

(A) He has attended previous Winex galas.
(B) He is an amateur musician.
(C) He built the company's windows.
(D) He has appointed a successor.

153. How can tickets be obtained?

(A) By calling a hotel
(B) By reserving them online
(C) By asking Mr. Rhines
(D) By getting them in person

TEST 06

▶ ▶ ▶GO ON TO THE NEXT PAGE

Questions 154-155 refer to the following text message chain.

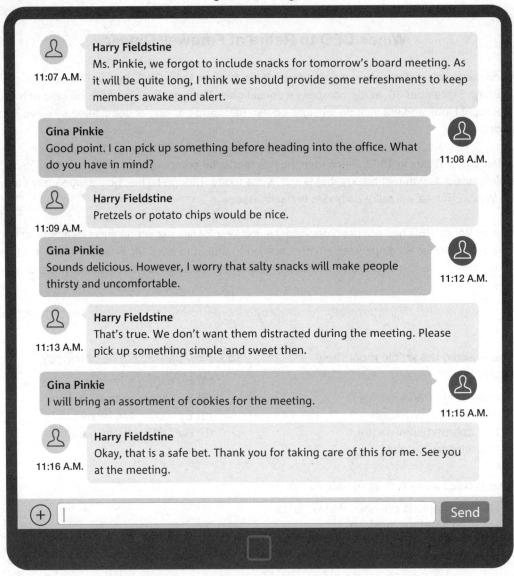

Harry Fieldstine
11:07 A.M.
Ms. Pinkie, we forgot to include snacks for tomorrow's board meeting. As it will be quite long, I think we should provide some refreshments to keep members awake and alert.

Gina Pinkie
Good point. I can pick up something before heading into the office. What do you have in mind?
11:08 A.M.

Harry Fieldstine
11:09 A.M.
Pretzels or potato chips would be nice.

Gina Pinkie
Sounds delicious. However, I worry that salty snacks will make people thirsty and uncomfortable.
11:12 A.M.

Harry Fieldstine
11:13 A.M.
That's true. We don't want them distracted during the meeting. Please pick up something simple and sweet then.

Gina Pinkie
I will bring an assortment of cookies for the meeting.
11:15 A.M.

Harry Fieldstine
11:16 A.M.
Okay, that is a safe bet. Thank you for taking care of this for me. See you at the meeting.

Send

154. What is suggested about Mr. Fieldstine?

(A) He will go out and buy cookies.
(B) He gets distracted when hungry.
(C) He does not like sweet snacks.
(D) He will attend the board meeting.

155. At 11:08 P.M., what does Ms. Pinkie most likely mean when she writes, "What do you have in mind?"

(A) She has some suggestions for snacks.
(B) She would like instructions on what to buy.
(C) She needs directions to the snack store.
(D) She is asking what snacks are in the office.

Questions 156-158 refer to the following e-mail.

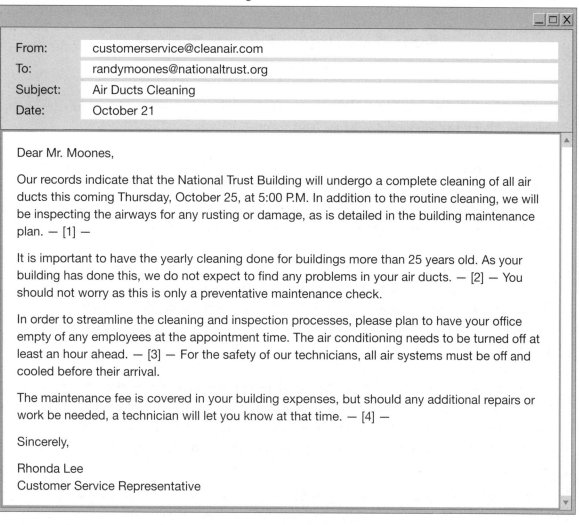

From: customerservice@cleanair.com

To: randymoones@nationaltrust.org

Subject: Air Ducts Cleaning

Date: October 21

Dear Mr. Moones,

Our records indicate that the National Trust Building will undergo a complete cleaning of all air ducts this coming Thursday, October 25, at 5:00 P.M. In addition to the routine cleaning, we will be inspecting the airways for any rusting or damage, as is detailed in the building maintenance plan. — [1] —

It is important to have the yearly cleaning done for buildings more than 25 years old. As your building has done this, we do not expect to find any problems in your air ducts. — [2] — You should not worry as this is only a preventative maintenance check.

In order to streamline the cleaning and inspection processes, please plan to have your office empty of any employees at the appointment time. The air conditioning needs to be turned off at least an hour ahead. — [3] — For the safety of our technicians, all air systems must be off and cooled before their arrival.

The maintenance fee is covered in your building expenses, but should any additional repairs or work be needed, a technician will let you know at that time. — [4] —

Sincerely,

Rhonda Lee
Customer Service Representative

156. Why was the e-mail sent?

(A) To give instructions to a technician
(B) To welcome a new cleaning technician
(C) To notify the recipient of an appointment
(D) To provide a bill for the cleaning services

157. What is indicated about the National Trust Building?

(A) It has monthly cleanings.
(B) It is at least 25 years old.
(C) It will cancel a service.
(D) It is closed after 5:00 P.M.

158. In which of the positions marked [1], [2], [3], and [4] does the following sentence best belong?

"If this is not possible, call us at 555-2833 to reschedule."

(A) [1]
(B) [2]
(C) [3]
(D) [4]

▶ ▶ ▶GO ON TO THE NEXT PAGE

Sonar Technology to Focus on Software

Software of the future

Seattle (March 8) – Startup company, Sonar Technology was once hailed as the future of hardware, but it has announced a change in its focus.

"While we pride ourselves on our skilled engineers," founder Jay Tolina said at this year's Pacific Tech Conference in Seattle, "we know the real moneymaker in the technology field is in creating innovative software." Sonar has raised nearly 100 million dollars in funding and hired over 200 new employees at its new Sunnyvale, California headquarters.

Originally based out of Austin, the company decided to move to the west and it would be a fresh start and a good way to find new talent. More than 1,000 applicants interviewed and fought for one of the new employee spots. Sonar is famous for its employee benefits, including free laundry onsite, an employee gym, and a 24-hour cafeteria with subsidized meals.

"We are still in the early stages of software development, but you can be assured that we have great ideas up our sleeves," hinted Tolina. His appearance at the conference was met with very much excitement among tech fans, who have been buzzing about the big changes at the company. Given all the publicity it has received, Sonar stock is predicted to skyrocket in the near future.

159. What is the article about?

(A) Unexpected changes in leadership
(B) Innovative ways to motivate employees
(C) Collaboration in the software industry
(D) New directions for a company

160. According to the article, where is Mr. Tolina's company based?

(A) Seattle
(B) Sunnyvale
(C) Austin
(D) New York

161. What is suggested about Sonar Technology?

(A) It has received mostly positive publicity.
(B) It will release new software soon.
(C) It currently has two office locations.
(D) It recently laid off 200 new employees.

Maritime Harbor Hotel
New Hope, Maine

May 19

Julie Ramond
221 Wayward Lane
Bridgewater, NJ 23134

Dear Ms. Ramond,

We are pleased that you have chosen to stay with us for two nights at the Maritime Harbor Hotel for your trip to New Hope on June 2. On your online order, you listed that this would be your second stay here. We appreciate your return business and will automatically upgrade your room to a private suite at no additional charge.

While your Express Diamond credit card has been charged for the room deposit in the amount of $200.00, this deposit is only a placeholder and will be returned to you at checkout provided that no damage has been done to the room and the bill is paid in full.

Amenities at our hotel include a fitness center, a health spa, and a 5-star restaurant. Room service and other in-room services can be ordered for additional fees. Should you have any questions regarding your stay with us or any of our hotel facilities, do not hesitate to contact me at (555) 232-8593.

Thank you for choosing the Maritime Harbor Hotel.

Sincerely,

Michelle Harwin
Hotel Concierge

162. Why did Ms. Harwin write to Ms. Ramond?

(A) To request an additional payment
(B) To offer her a free upgrade
(C) To list some new hotel services
(D) To explain a problem with a credit card

163. What is indicated about the Maritime Harbor Hotel?

(A) Exercise facilities are available.
(B) Deposits are nonrefundable.
(C) Room service is included in the room mate.
(D) Shuttle services can be booked.

164. According to the letter, when is Ms. Ramond checking out?

(A) June 2
(B) June 3
(C) June 4
(D) June 5

▶ ▶ ▶ GO ON TO THE NEXT PAGE

Steam-cleaned and Ready to Work

"Dress for success!" It is a popular mantra for a reason. It's the truth! Don't even think about going into work with a wrinkly uniform. You want to make a good impression by looking sharp. We know you are busy juggling work, kids, and your personal life. Who has time to iron their own clothes? Let the professionals at Stanley's get the wrinkles out of your uniform.

How does it work?
Drop off your uniform at one of our 10 convenient locations, and we'll clean and steam-press it for you. Drop off up to 100 items! We'll be happy to clean them all!

How long does it take?
In a rush? No problem. We have express steaming for employees on the clock. Just wait 10 minutes, and you'll look brand new. For drop off, 5 or fewer uniforms can be picked up the very next day!

What does it all cost?
Prices vary based on the state of the uniform.

165. Who most likely is the intended audience for the advertisement?

(A) Job seekers with deadlines
(B) Self-employed designers
(C) Workers with a dress code
(D) Busy homemakers

166. What is indicated about Stanley's?

(A) It offers same-day service.
(B) It has five employees per location.
(C) It can repair damaged uniforms.
(D) It requires appointments.

167. What is NOT mentioned as a service offered by Stanley's?

(A) Bulk drop-off and cleaning
(B) Delivery of cleaned uniforms
(C) Steam-pressing completed in minutes
(D) Removing wrinkles from clothes

Paperworks Print to Open 3 New Locations

By Wendy Stein

July 18

Paperworks Print is the largest self-copy services retailer in Phoenix, Arizona. — [1] — With 7 locations already spread throughout the state, the print shop will soon expand even more with 3 additional locations planned.

Paperworks Print came to be when its founder Kale Logers was a college student four decades ago. He had an urgent deadline to make but nowhere to print his paper. — [2] — After running to his friend's college dorm room to frantically print his assignment, he realized that there was a business idea that could solve his dilemma.

The following month, Logers and his roommates opened their dorm room to other students who needed to print or make copies of papers. They soon offered an assembly line of staplers and other tools that were needed to complete various projects.

Five years later, the first official Paperworks Print shop opened just 2 kilometers from their college campus. Its huge success cleared the way for 6 more stores to open. — [3] —

While Kale Logers has since retired, his successor, Cal Smith, oversees the company. Smith has spearheaded the opening of the most recent stores. — [4] — The new locations have yet to be announced, but many wonder if the print shops will cross state lines and appear beyond the state of Arizona.

168. What is NOT mentioned about Paperworks Print?

(A) It was started in a student's room.
(B) It will soon have a total of 10 locations.
(C) Its new locations are on college campuses.
(D) It is no longer managed by Mr. Logers.

169. What is suggested about Paperworks Print?

(A) It will not make a profit this year.
(B) It used to provide delivery services.
(C) It will force Kale Logers to retire.
(D) It could expand into new states.

170. According to the article, how long did it take to open an official Printworks store?

(A) 2 years
(B) 3 years
(C) 5 years
(D) 7 years

171. In which of the positions marked [1], [2], [3], and [4] does the following sentence best belong?

"The company has become far more profitable than Logers and his roommates could have ever predicted."

(A) [1]
(B) [2]
(C) [3]
(D) [4]

▶ ▶ ▶ GO ON TO THE NEXT PAGE

Questions 172-175 refer to the following online chat discussion.

Joe Garcia 8:25 A.M.		I left my planner on the company shuttle bus this morning. Will someone tell me if they see it?
Jessica Burt 8:26 A.M.		What does your planner look like? I'm on bus number 2 and just passed building B.
Danny Sails 8:29 A.M.		I am on shuttle bus number 9 right now and am headed to building G. Which bus were you on?
Joe Garcia 8:49 A.M.		It's gray leather, and I believe I placed it on the seat beside me toward the front of the bus. Unfortunately, as I was in a hurry, I didn't see the bus number.
Danny Sails 8:55 A.M.		I'm at my desk now. Sorry, Joe, but I did not see any planners on bus number 9.
Jessica Burt 8:58 A.M.		No such luck here. I'll be taking the shuttle home tonight, too. I'll keep an eye out.
Joe Garcia 9:05 A.M.		Thanks for checking. I should probably try our office lost and found.
Danny Sails 9:19 A.M.		Brilliant! Someone probably found it and turned it in.
Jessica Burt 9:25 A.M.		Why didn't I think of that? Good luck!

Send

172

172. What is the online discussion mainly about?

(A) Planning a shuttle bus ride
(B) Locating a misplaced item
(C) Contacting the office lost and found
(D) Comparing shuttle bus numbers

173. At 8:58 A.M., what does Ms. Burt most likely mean when she writes, "I'll keep an eye out"?

(A) She disagrees that the planner was lost.
(B) She will check all of the other shuttles.
(C) She will continue looking for the planner.
(D) She is unsure about what the planner looks like.

174. What does Mr. Garcia mention about the bus he took this morning?

(A) He is unsure what its number is.
(B) He reported the lost item to the driver.
(C) He will take the same one home tonight.
(D) He boarded it later than usual.

175. What does Mr. Sails imply about the planner?

(A) It is still on the bus where Mr. Garcia left it.
(B) An employee placed it in the lost and found.
(C) It will be on the bus he rides home tonight.
(D) It might be on shuttle bus number 9.

▶ ▶ ▶ GO ON TO THE NEXT PAGE

Western Bank Training Seminar

Training Schedule (February 3 - 6)

Monday	Tuesday	Wednesday	Thursday
Check-in 8:00 A.M.	Check-in 8:00 A.M.	Check-in 8:00 A.M.	Check-in 9:00 A.M.
Lunch 1:15 P.M.	Lunch 1:15 P.M.	Lunch 1:15 P.M.	Lunch 1:15 P.M.
Closing Speech Conference Room 1 4:30 P.M.	Closing Speech Conference Room 2 4:30 P.M.	Closing Speech Conference Room 1 4:30 P.M.	Closing Speech Conference Room 5 3:00 P.M.

Business attire is required. Late check-in and leaving early will not be tolerated. You will not receive certification at the end of the training if you do not attend all of the sessions.

Questions? Contact organizer Vladimir Do at vdo@westernbank.com or 555-2827.

From:	Amber Collins
To:	Vladimir Do
Date:	January 29
Subject:	Closing Speaker

Dear Mr. Do,

My name is Amber Collins, and I was asked to speak at your seminar on February 6. I was recruited by your manager, Fred Samber, with whom I attended accounting school a number of years ago. He asked me to speak on the growth of my bank branch as well as our successful loan program.

While I am happy to deliver the closing speech for the seminar, I received the seminar schedule yesterday from you and have a dilemma. I need to be back at my bank branch by 5:00 P.M. in order to shut off our computers and turn on our security system. This task must be done at 5:00 P.M. on the dot every day as it is linked to additional security servers connecting all of the branches.

Unfortunately, my speech will take at least two hours to deliver and cannot be trimmed as the information I am presenting must be given in detail. Perhaps I could start half an hour earlier than scheduled to allow me enough time to return to my branch? Otherwise, I am afraid I must cancel my closing speech if I am unable to be back at my bank by 5:00.

Thank you for your understanding in the matter.

Amber Collins
Branch Manager
Granite Bank

176. What is indicated about the Western Bank Training Seminar schedule?

(A) Participants are expected to arrive on time.
(B) Meal times will vary from day to day.
(C) Closing speeches will be in the same location.
(D) Certificates will be handed out daily.

177. What is the purpose of the e-mail?

(A) To cancel a closing speech
(B) To complain about a policy
(C) To inform Mr. Do of a scheduling conflict
(D) To apologize for coming in early

178. In the e-mail, what is suggested about Granite Bank's security system?

(A) It can sometimes be turned on remotely.
(B) It was recently reset to start at 5:00 P.M.
(C) It can only be activated by a branch manager.
(D) It will be discussed in Ms. Collin's speech.

179. What is indicated about Mr. Samber?

(A) He sent out the itinerary.
(B) He will lead the seminar.
(C) He hired Mr. Do.
(D) He works at Western Bank.

180. At what time does Ms. Collins propose giving her speech?

(A) 2:30 P.M.
(B) 3:00 P.M.
(C) 3:30 P.M.
(D) 4:00 P.M.

▶ ▶ ▶ GO ON TO THE NEXT PAGE

Better Business Trips Planner

Are you in need of planning a company-wide trip but have no time to actually do it? Hire us! We are professional trip planners who have put together more than 50 corporate getaways.

Our mission is to provide a fun and flexible trip itinerary to fit the needs of your employees. We can plan in as much detail or as loosely as your company needs.

Trip Durations:
• Short 1- or 2-hour excursions
• Half-day trips outside the office
• Weekend trips for large groups
• Long trips abroad are possible!

Detailed options:
• Transportation
• Meal plans
• Travel snacks
• Emergency kits

If you are interested in meeting with our planners to discuss an event, stop by our office at:

Better Business Trips Planner
Vera Tealie, Planning Manager
293 Happyway Lane
San Jacinto, CA 13724

A gallery of past trips can be found at www.BetterBusinessTrips.net.

| About Us | Testimonials | Gallery Photos | Frequently Asked Questions |

"My manager asked me to put together a weekend workers' trip in one week for our 5-year anniversary! Without much notice, I had to figure out a way to plan transportation, lodging, sights, and food for 10 people. It seemed impossible until I found Better Business Trips Planner through a blog. I called Vera, and she put me in touch with their weekend trip planner, Jason, and within 24 hours, he e-mailed me a list of options with everything from the bus company prices to the snacks that can be assembled by his team and delivered to us on the day of departure. Three days later, the entire trip was planned and within our company's budget.

My manager was very impressed with "my" quick, hard work. I highly recommend them. Friendly, organized, and prompt, Better Business Trips Planner can't be beat."

Shelly Franks
Bitcoil Software Engineer

181. According to the brochure, what is a benefit of hiring Better Business Trips Planner?

(A) The trip is guaranteed to be a fun time.
(B) It works faster than its competitors.
(C) It is cheaper than self-planning.
(D) It can customize trips for clients.

182. What is NOT indicated bout Better Business Trips Planner?

(A) It arranges short trips.
(B) It can assist with food planning.
(C) It offers multiple price levels.
(D) It can organize a trip in a few days.

183. How did Ms. Franks find out about Better Business Trips Planner?

(A) She was referred by a client.
(B) She read about the company online.
(C) She went to the company's office.
(D) She heard about it from her boss.

184. What is suggested about Ms. Franks?

(A) She spoke with a planning manager.
(B) She had to pay a deposit.
(C) She planned a trip to San Jacinto.
(D) She ordered supplies for emergencies.

185. In the testimonial, the word "beat" in paragraph 2, line 2 is closest in meaning to

(A) abused
(B) outsmarted
(C) surpassed
(D) reduced

▶ ▶ ▶ GO ON TO THE NEXT PAGE

Questions 186-190 refer to the following schedule, notice, and comment form.

Lunch Delivery Schedule

Bermington LLC (Buildings 1 - 8)

Daily Delivery

Building 1	Building 2	Building 3	Building 4
11:25 A.M.	11:35 A.M.	11:45 A.M.	11:55 A.M.
12:50 P.M.	1:00 P.M.	1:15 P.M.	1:25 P.M.
Building 5	Building 6	Building 7	Building 8
12:10 P.M.	12:25 P.M.	12:45 P.M.	12:55 P.M.
1:40 P.M.	1:55 P.M.	2:10 P.M.	2:25 P.M.

Early and late lunch deliveries are available every day to accommodate employee meeting schedules. The daily menu can be found on the Bermington company Web site inside the employee portal.

If you miss your scheduled delivery, you may pick up your lunch in the central cafeteria between the hours of 12:00 P.M. and 3:00 P.M.

NOTICE

Late lunch delivery suspended for summer hours
Posted: May 29

From Monday, June 1, through July 30, late lunch deliveries will not take place in order to cut costs during summer hours. As the company will be operating at half capacity during these months, management has decided to offer just one meal delivery per day. The cafeteria will continue to offer its pickup service at the usual times.

Please leave your comments below:

Date: *July 1*
Name: *Connor Giles*
Department: *Sales, Building 6*
E-mail: *cgiles@bermington.net*

Comment/Question/Suggestion:
During the regular season, the lunch deliveries were always on time. This summer, I've noticed that the meals show up sporadically. Yesterday, I ended my meeting early in line with the usual lunch delivery schedule and planned to attend a second meeting after I ate, but the delivery was 20 minutes late, and because of that, I missed my second meeting. Please look into the delivery delays.

186. What is NOT indicated about the Bermington lunch delivery service?

(A) It has canceled the second delivery indefinitely.
(B) There are two delivery times during most of the year.
(C) Missed deliveries can still be picked up in July.
(D) It takes more than an hour to deliver lunch to eight buildings.

187. What is suggested about Bermington LLC?

(A) It doesn't value employee feedback.
(B) It will do away with lunch delivery.
(C) It has fewer employees in June.
(D) It always works at full capacity.

188. What is most likely true about Mr. Giles?

(A) He is satisfied with the new delivery schedule.
(B) He wants the second delivery to be reinstated right away.
(C) He will leave Bermington LLC soon.
(D) He did not miss meetings due to late deliveries in May.

189. At what time was Mr. Giles supposed to get his lunch?

(A) 12:10 P.M.
(B) 12:25 P.M.
(C) 12:45 P.M.
(D) 1:55 P.M.

190. When is the soonest Mr. Giles could obtain a late lunch delievery?

(A) July 1
(B) July 30
(C) July 31
(D) August 1

▶ ▶ ▶GO ON TO THE NEXT PAGE

Company Badminton Team Tryouts!

3 Levels: Recreational, Intermediate, Competitive

Employees at Sanders Storage Disks are invited to try out for the fall season's badminton league! There will be 3 levels, so everyone can join! Recreational players do not need to try out but can just show up on the first day of practice.

Wednesday Practice (Intermediate, Competitive):	6:30 P.M. – 8:30 P.M.
Thursday Practice (Recreational):	6:30 P.M. – 8:00 P.M.
Matches(All Levels) will be held every Saturday morning:	10:00 A.M.

If you are interested in joining, bring your racket and sneakers to the company gym on Friday, September 13, at 5:30 P.M.

Sanders Company Gym
Badminton Tryouts
5:30 P.M.

Sanders Company

Facilities Booking Form

Name: *Michael Nealers*
E-mail: *michael@sanders.com*
Facility: *Gym*
Reservation Date: *September 13, 5:30 P.M. - 7:30 P.M.*
Event: *Company Badminton Team Tryouts*

To:	Michael Nealers [michael@sanders.com]
From:	Tara Walkins [facilitiesmanager@sanders.com]
Subject:	Gym Reservation Approval
Date:	September 9

Hi, Michael.

We got your form to reserve the company gym for the badminton tryouts. As there are no other reservations at the time you want, your request has been approved.

You may enter the gym to prepare for the event an hour before your scheduled time. However, you need to pick up the keys from me before 3 P.M. the day before your reservation. After that time, I will be out of the office until Monday morning. My office is on the 4th floor of the west wing.

Once you're done with the gym, please make sure to clean up any trash and place all equipment back where you found it. There is an equipment checklist you need to fill out and return with the keys afterward. All gym equipment must be accounted for.

Following the event, return the keys to the drop box outside my office.

Have a great time.

Tara

191. What is indicated about the Sanders Company Badminton Program?

(A) There will be four different teams.
(B) Participation is open to the general public.
(C) Participants must have their own equipment.
(D) There are competitions once a month.

192. What is most likely true about the badminton tryouts?

(A) They are held three times a year.
(B) They are optional for intermediate players.
(C) They entail having a medical examination.
(D) They will last for no more than two hours.

193. When is the earliest Mr. Nealers can set up for the tryouts?

(A) 3:00 P.M.
(B) 4:30 P.M.
(C) 5:15 P.M.
(D) 5:30 P.M.

194. What does Ms. Walkins ask Mr. Nealers do after the tryouts end?

(A) Lock a storage chest
(B) Distribute rackets
(C) Remove garbage
(D) Complete a survey

195. On what day will Ms. Walkins be at work?

(A) September 12
(B) September 13
(C) September 14
(D) September 15

▶ ▶ ▶ GO ON TO THE NEXT PAGE

Office Supply Store

All your office needs in one store!

Weekly Sales*
November 1 - November 7
Black Gel Ink Pens – $1 each

It writes clearly and smoothly. It's the only pen you'll ever need.

November Specials:
• 30% off printer ink refills: black and color
• Buy one box of blank paper and get a second box free!
• Save $30 on a new computer chair with desk purchase.
• LaserJet printer now $89.99! (originally $109.99)

*Weekly sales limit: 5 per customer

Coupon
10% off
Your total purchase over $150.
Expires: November 30, 2017
Valid only at Stelton Street store

Office Supply Store
3520 Stelton Street
555-1532

Date: November 6
Time: 5:15
Purchase: #25163
Cashier: Bob Thornton

Item #	Description	Quantity	Cost
BG201	Black Gel Ink Pens	5	$5.00
LJ0394	LaserJet Printer	1	$89.99
BP2391	Blank Paper	4	$24.00
		Subtotal	$118.99
		Tax	$10.01
		Total	$129.00
		Received	$130.00
		Change	$1.00

Thank you for shopping at Office Supply Store!

```
  _ □ X
```

FROM: Barry Valentino

TO: customersupport@officesupply.com

SUBJECT: Printer Refund

Dear Customer Support,

I purchased a new printer (Item #LJ0394) from your Stelton Street store yesterday. However, once I tried to hook it up to my computer, I was unable to get it to work. At first, I suspected that it was a faulty product. However, a technician at my workplace tested the printer on his computer, and there were no issues. He was able to print a test sheet easily. His conclusion is that it is simply not compatible with the software on my computer. Since all of the current software on my machine is essential for my work and your technical support staff could not offer another solution, I am unable to use the printer.

I made the purchase fewer than 30 days ago, so I am eligible for a refund. I plan to bring the product back to my local store tomorrow.

Sincerely,

Barry V.

TEST 06

196. What is NOT indicated in the advertisement?

(A) Customers can get 10% off all month long.
(B) Customers can buy an unlimited number of $1 gel pens.
(C) The coupon can only be used at one location.
(D) The sale price on the pens ends before the rest of the sale items.

197. What is suggested about purchase #25163?

(A) The customer used a coupon.
(B) The customer did not receive change.
(C) The customer paid with a credit card.
(D) The customer only bought promotional items.

198. In the e-mail, the word "issues" in paragraph 1, line 4 is closest in meaning to

(A) distributions
(B) instructions
(C) problems
(D) results

199. What day does Mr. Valentino plan to go to Office Supply Store?

(A) November 7
(B) November 8
(C) November 10
(D) November 11

200. What is true about the item Mr. Valentino wants to return?

(A) It is a highly rated product.
(B) It will be on sale in December.
(C) It normally costs over $100.
(D) It included a user's manual.

▶ ▶ ▶GO ON TO THE NEXT PAGE

TEST 06 **183**

Test 06 정답

147. (D)	**148.** (A)	**149.** (A)	**150.** (C)	**151.** (C)	**152.** (A)
153. (D)	**154.** (D)	**155.** (B)	**156.** (C)	**157.** (B)	**158.** (C)
159. (D)	**160.** (B)	**161.** (A)	**162.** (B)	**163.** (A)	**164.** (C)
165. (C)	**166.** (A)	**167.** (B)	**168.** (C)	**169.** (D)	**170.** (C)
171. (C)	**172.** (B)	**173.** (C)	**174.** (A)	**175.** (B)	**176.** (A)
177. (C)	**178.** (C)	**179.** (D)	**180.** (A)	**181.** (D)	**182.** (C)
183. (B)	**184.** (A)	**185.** (C)	**186.** (A)	**187.** (C)	**188.** (D)
189. (B)	**190.** (C)	**191.** (C)	**192.** (D)	**193.** (B)	**194.** (C)
195. (A)	**196.** (B)	**197.** (D)	**198.** (C)	**199.** (B)	**200.** (C)

TEST

07

55
min

시작 시간 ___시 ___분   목표 개수 _____ / 54

종료 시간 ___시 ___분   실제 개수 _____ / 54

- 반드시 55분 안에 문제 풀이 포함 마킹까지 마쳐야 합니다.
- 실제 시험이라고 생각하고 멈추지 말고 풀어보세요.

    • 정답 개수에 5를 곱하면 대략적인 점수가 됩니다.

Directions: In this part you will read a selection of texts, such as magazine and newspaper articles, e-mails, and instant messages. Each text or set of texts is followed by several questions. Select the best answer for each question and mark the letter (A), (B), (C), or (D) on your answer sheet.

Questions 147-148 refer to the following flyer.

NOW OPEN!

King's Shoes
New Linford Location!

Campbell Street Shopping Center
2890 Wilson Highway, Suite 23

Open 7 days a week!

We have the largest selection of footwear in the entire state!
Now selling Fast Walk and Racer brand athletic shoes.

Men's, women's, children's,
casual, formal, athletic, specialty, and more

Present this flyer to the cashier and receive a 10% discount.*

*Cannot be combined with other offers or used for online orders.

147. What is indicated about the price reduction?

(A) It can be obtained on weekends.
(B) It is offered at multiple locations.
(C) It is restricted to employees.
(D) It is valid for one month.

148. What is NOT mentioned about King's Shoes?

(A) It has a store in a mall.
(B) It specializes in unusual shoes.
(C) It carries products for kids.
(D) It sells products via the Internet.

▶ ▶ ▶ GO ON TO THE NEXT PAGE

Questions 149-150 refer to the following text message chain.

Farrell, Denise 10:21 A.M.
I was just asked to attend a meeting this afternoon. Could you do me a favor and pick up Mr. Qi from the airport?

Folkman, Owen 10:24 A.M.
Sure. Can you give me his flight information?

Farrell, Denise 10:25 A.M.
He's on National Airlines Flight 894 arriving from Philadelphia at 3:25 P.M. You might want to double-check if it's on time. There is a snowstorm in the Northeast that may cause delays.

Folkman, Owen 10:27 A.M.
Good idea. Anything else?

Farrell, Denise 10:29 A.M.
I booked him a room at the Grand Continental Hotel on 84th Street. Help him check in. I'll arrange for a taxi to bring him to the office in the morning. Pickup's at 8:45. Make sure Mr. Qi understands that.

Folkman, Owen 10:34 A.M.
You can count on me.

149. What is most likely true about Mr. Qi?

(A) He will have dinner with Ms. Farrell.
(B) He made a hotel reservation.
(C) He does not have a driver's license.
(D) He is traveling from Philadelphia.

150. At 10:34 A.M., what does Mr. Folkman most likely mean when he writes "You can count on me"?

(A) He will confirm a hotel reservation.
(B) He will relay information to Mr. Qi.
(C) He will get directions to a hotel.
(D) He will contact a taxi company.

Eric Cardon
89 Blaine Road
Seager, MD 99343

April 16

Dear Mr. Cardon,

This letter provides written confirmation of our phone conversation yesterday. — [1] — You have been offered, and accepted, a part-time position as Cultural Resource Specialist II at Caldera Engineering. The salary for the position is $25,879 for a total of 1,400 hours worked per year. The scheduling of your actual work hours may vary from week to week as determined by your supervisor but may never exceed 32 hours per week. — [2] —

We have scheduled you to start work on Monday, May 3, at 8:30 A.M. Please check in at the front office. Your supervisor, Roger Vance, will need to sign you in and escort you to Security, where you will be fingerprinted and receive an official ID card. — [3] — After that, you will be able to access the building on your own.

All new employees are required to complete an orientation. This will consist of online training modules and a brief meeting with my staff and me. — [4] — We have scheduled your orientation for your first day of work. Please report to my office on the second floor after meeting with Mr. Vance.

We are excited to have you join the team at Caldera Engineering. Feel free to contact me if you have any questions or need assistance.

Sincerely,

Cindy Fergus
Director, Personnel Office
Caldera Engineering

151. What is Mr. Cardon NOT instructed to do on May 3?

(A) Meet with his new manager
(B) Obtain an employee identification card
(C) Enter a section of a building on his own
(D) Speak with employees in Personnel

152. What is suggested about Mr. Cardon?

(A) He has worked with Mr. Vance before.
(B) He prefers to have a full-time position.
(C) He will work five days each week.
(D) He spoke with Ms. Fergus on April 15.

153. In which of the positions marked [1], [2], [3], and [4] does the following sentence best belong?

"You may receive benefits in accordance with your part-time status."

(A) [1]
(B) [2]
(C) [3]
(D) [4]

▶ ▶ ▶GO ON TO THE NEXT PAGE

Questions 154-155 refer to the following article.

Edgewood(April 12) – Sandwich lovers in Edgewood are in for a treat next month. For the first two weeks of May, Sammy's Sandwiches will cut prices on select menu items in half.

The promotional pricing, says company spokesperson Andrew Gilford, is a way for the Philadelphia-based restaurant chain to celebrate its 30th anniversary. "We want to thank our customers for their support over the years," said Gilford.

In addition to the promotional pricing, which will apply to several popular sandwiches, sides, and drinks, Sammy's is offering its customers a chance to win a trip for two to London. Customers can enter to win by posting a photo of themselves with a Sammy's sandwich at a unique location. The winner will be selected at random at the end of the month.

Since opening its first restaurant in Phoenixville, PA, in 1985, Sammy's has spread to 185 locations in 28 states across the country to become one of the nation's most popular sandwich chains.

154. Where was the article probably published?

(A) In a promotional brochure
(B) In a local newspaper
(C) In a restaurant guidebook
(D) In a financial magazine

155. What is indicated about Sammy's?

(A) It has twenty-eight stores nationwide.
(B) It will offer discounts for one month.
(C) It has a partnership with a travel agency.
(D) It was founded decades ago.

Questions 156-157 refer to the following information.

Feeling down? Here are some simple, but effective ways to improve your mood naturally.

Focus on the positive. Some people automatically think about the negative elements in a situation. However, by changing your focus to seeing the positive, you can generate positive feelings in yourself.

Get enough sleep. The average person needs between 7.5 and 8.5 hours of sleep a night. Too much or too little sleep is harmful to the body and can lead to depression.

Eat a balanced diet. People who eat lots of fruits and vegetables are healthier and feel better.

Exercise regularly. Exercise releases endorphins, chemicals in the brain that make us feel good. Just 30 minutes of exercise a day is often enough to improve your mood and overall health.

156. What is NOT mentioned as a way to have a better mood?

(A) Sleep around 8 hours
(B) Move your body daily
(C) Consume nutritious meals
(D) Take medication

157. According to the information, what is a benefit of positive thinking?

(A) Replacing lost sleep
(B) Generating new ideas
(C) Enhancing activities
(D) Creating good emotions

▶ ▶ ▶ GO ON TO THE NEXT PAGE

Memo

TO: Employees, Corrigan Building
FROM: Sara Johnson
SUBJECT: Swipe Cards
DATE: June 8

The installation of new electronic door locks is currently underway. All exterior doors and several interior doors are scheduled to have functioning electronic locking systems on them by June 15. A magnetic swipe card will be needed to enter these doors, which will automatically lock when closed. All other doors will continue to use the existing key locks.

Swipe cards will be available at the security office starting on June 10. To obtain one, return the attached request form to the security office. On the form, please specify which doors you need to open. All cards will be coded to open exterior doors. However, employees may only use their cards to open interior doors they are permitted to access. Requests cannot be processed without a supervisor's signature. Please allow 24 - 48 hours for your request to be processed.

Thank you.

Sara Johnson
Assistant Director, Security
Landis Corporation

158. Why did Ms. Johnson write the memo?

(A) To request feedback from supervisors
(B) To explain upcoming changes
(C) To announce the completion of a project
(D) To report malfunctioning locks

159. What is indicated about the electronic locking system?

(A) It will be installed on all interior doors.
(B) It is scheduled to be tested on June 15.
(C) It requires the use of coded cards.
(D) It will replace all current key locks.

160. What are employees asked to do?

(A) Submit paperwork
(B) Turn in their existing keys
(C) Test the locks on their doors
(D) Obtain identification cards

Musical Fingers

Winter, Spring, Summer, and Fall — Musical Fingers is available all year!

We are currently accepting new students ages 5 - 18.

We would like to invite you to become a part of the Musical Fingers community. Our professionally developed curriculum has been proven to help children develop their guitar skills. Working with beginner through advanced learners, Musical Fingers offers more than just music lessons. We cultivate a broad appreciation for music, creativity, and self-expression. All of our Musical Fingers instructors have completed comprehensive training in the teaching methods first developed by founder and former high school music teacher Mike Parka.

With locations in Camden, Ardmore, Wayne, and Germantown
www.musicalfingers.com
(412) 555-9894

Member of the National Guitar Teaching Association and Society of Music Teachers

161. What is NOT stated about Musical Fingers?

(A) It offers lessons at multiple sites.
(B) It accepts students of varying levels.
(C) It aims to help students become creative.
(D) It offers classes in several instruments.

162. What is suggested about the instructors?

(A) They are trained to work with kids.
(B) They are graduates of Musical Fingers.
(C) They are professional musicians.
(D) They are currently high school students.

163. What is mentioned about Mike Parka?

(A) He only teaches advanced students.
(B) He is an instructor at a public school.
(C) He started a music education program.
(D) He is the leader of a professional group.

▶ ▶ ▶ GO ON TO THE NEXT PAGE

Questions 164-167 refer to the following online chat discussion.

Peck, Allison 8:45 A.M.		I graduated with a degree in computer science two years ago and took my first job in the same small city where I attended college. I am ready for a change to advance my career. My former classmates suggest that I move, but I live with my parents now and think I would miss them. The nearest big city is over four hours away! What should I do?
Johnson, River 9:01 A.M.		Your friends are giving you sound advice. You need to move to where the best technology companies are if you want to seriously advance in your career.
Evans, Nathan 10:10 A.M.		It really depends on your goals.
Johnson, River 11:01 A.M.		But the best jobs are in the big cities.
Evans, Nathan 11:10 A.M.		River, that's a matter of opinion. Good jobs in computer science are available pretty much anywhere. Nowadays, nearly all companies need employees with your background.
Uribe, Iris 11:20 A.M.		Allison, stay close to home if you want. I graduated with the same degree five years ago. My first job was in the area where I grew up. I gained good experience and later moved to the nation's capital.
Johnson, River 12:01 P.M.		Allison, wherever you choose to go, the key is to get your foot in the door with an employer. Use your school's alumni office to network. You might find a great job in another city nearby.
Peck, Allison 1:45 P.M.		Thanks for giving me a lot to consider. I'll let you know what I decide.

164. What is most likely true about Ms. Peck?

(A) She is a mediocre employee.
(B) She is employed at a college.
(C) She did not move to attend school.
(D) She recently visited a former classmate.

165. According to the writers, what is suggested about leading technology companies?

(A) They are located in major urban areas.
(B) Graduates of top schools get hired there.
(C) They prefer to hire young people.
(D) Mr. Evans works for one of them.

166. At 11:10 A.M., why does Mr. Evans write "That's a matter of opinion"?

(A) To provide support for his own opinion
(B) To express agreement mildly
(C) To question the validity of a statement
(D) To criticize a professional judgment

167. What is suggested about Ms. Uribe?

(A) She is currently working in her hometown.
(B) She attended the same school as Ms. Peck.
(C) She is a staff member in an alumni office.
(D) She studied computer science in college.

MEMO

TO: Maintenance Staff
FROM: Karl Urban
DATE: March 16

Due to budgetary restrictions set to take effect next month, our department will be required to adjust our practices concerning the university grounds. While it is essential that they be kept in the best possible condition at all times, it has become necessary to reduce the resources and manpower that we have committed in the past. The following cost-saving measures are to take effect immediately:

- Lawns are to be mowed once every two weeks instead of weekly. The only exception is the university's sports fields, which will continue to be maintained on their current schedule.
- All sprinkler systems will be inspected. Leaks will be repaired, and broken parts will be replaced immediately upon discovery. Unnecessary sprinkler lines will be removed and their parts placed in storage.
- Flowers will no longer be planted in the beds at the library, Chandler Hall, and the dormitories and along Graduate Avenue. Instead, the beds will be covered with decorative crushed stone.
- Maintenance staff members are to limit their use of electrical carts to assigned work tasks. Personal vehicles should be used for all nonofficial uses.

Additional cost-saving measures affecting our other functions will be announced in a July memo. Your continued commitment to the maintenance of the university's facilities and grounds is appreciated during this challenging time. If you have any questions or concerns about these changes, contact me directly at 272-5120.

Sincerely,

Karl Urban
Director of Facilities and Grounds
Paramount University

168. Why did Mr. Urban write the memo?

(A) To criticize some practices
(B) To announce changes
(C) To propose budget cuts
(D) To explain additional tasks

169. The word "only" in paragraph 2, line 1 is closest in meaning to

(A) single
(B) just
(C) mere
(D) simple

170. What does Mr. Urban NOT ask his staff to do?

(A) Replace flowerbeds with ornamental rocks
(B) Plant fewer trees and bushes
(C) Cut grass less frequently
(D) Remove unused water lines

171. What will Mr. Urban most likely do in July?

(A) Obtain a larger budget for next year
(B) Participate in basic grounds keeping
(C) Upgrade his department's vehicles
(D) State other ways to save money

▶ ▶ ▶GO ON TO THE NEXT PAGE

TEST 07

San Andreas Community College
Job Connection Office (JCO)

Employer Recruitment Event

Held the second Thursday of every month.

Thursday, November 10
11:00 A.M. - 2:00 P.M.
Student Resources Building, Daniels Auditorium
Central Campus

Below is just a sampling of the many employers who will be on hand.

• City of San Andreas Police Department has over 200 openings for police officers, service workers, instructors, and office personnel.
• Sally's Bakery is looking for maintenance workers for its 45th Street production facility.
— [1] —
• Guardian Angels is hiring home health aides.

Upcoming Workshops

In addition to our recruitment events, the JCO hosts free workshops open to all members of our community. — [2] — Advance registration is required. All workshops are held at the JCO, which is located on the second floor of the Penner Building on Central Campus. If you would like to participate, visit our Web site at www.sanandreas.edu/jco.

Resume Tune Up
Wednesday, November 2
1:00 P.M. – 5:00 P.M.

Stop by any time during this open workshop and speak with one of our writing tutors. Bring a copy of your résumé, or even just a list of current and prior employment, and we will help you make it even better. — [3] —

Introduction to Health Care Careers
Friday, November 4
12:00 P.M. – 1:00 P.M.

Join us for a lunchtime presentation on one of the largest and fastest growing sectors of our local economy. — [4] — Each year, there are more job openings in health care than there are applicants to fill them. Find out about opportunities for work at hospitals, health clinics, nursing homes, and other similar places. Equally important, learn what steps you need to take to gain the education and skills to be a successful job seeker.

172. What is NOT indicated about the Employer Recruitment Event?

(A) It is organized on a regular basis.
(B) It requires advance registration.
(C) It lasts for a total of three hours.
(D) It is held at an educational institution.

173. According to the flyer, why should readers go to the Job Connection Office's Web site?

(A) To participate in a job fair
(B) To apply for job openings
(C) To contact potential employers
(D) To register for workshops

174. What is suggested about San Andreas?

(A) Its population has declined in recent years.
(B) Local employers only hire college graduates.
(C) Health care is an important part of its economy.
(D) Several large companies are located there.

175. In which of the positions marked [1], [2], [3], and [4] does the following sentence best belong?

"No prior business writing experience is necessary to participate."

(A) [1]
(B) [2]
(C) [3]
(D) [4]

▶ ▶ ▶GO ON TO THE NEXT PAGE

Monet's Garden: A Story of Love and Betrayal

Review by Sam Sheppard
Monday, September 8

When I received a free ticket from the Kaliope Theater inviting me to its first production of the fall season, I put it on my desk and nearly forgot about it. None of the productions in Kaliope's spring or summer seasons was noteworthy. It was a good thing I found the ticket because *Monet's Garden* is quite the opposite. From the moment the curtain opened, I was impressed by the beautiful sets. Although *Monet's Garden* features just five actors, each gave a marvelous performance. The chemistry between Todd Jordan as Monet and Lindsay White as Helene was awesome! Fans of Rene Pilar (and I am one of them) are not going to be disappointed by this production. If the rest of the fall season is as good, then local theater goers are in for a treat!

Kaliope Theater

Fall Season: Special Production

Monet's Garden
By Rene Pilar
Directed by Oliver Preston

Dates: September 5 – 28
Times: Friday and Saturday, 7:30 P.M.; Sunday, 2:00 P.M.
Tickets: $20

Special preview night*: September 4, Thursday, 7:00 P.M.

The Kaliope Theater is very proud to present *Monet's Garden*, the opening production of the fall season and the first at our new location!

Monet's Garden is about French Impressionist painter Claude Monet falling in love with a young female student, Helene. Because he is married, Monet must keep his budding relationship with Helene secret by restricting their meetings to a hidden corner of his garden.

NEW LOCATION! 890 Baker Way, two blocks south of Armadillo Boulevard.

*Invitation-only event for members of the Kaliope Club and the press

176. What is indicated about Mr. Sheppard?

(A) He has never been to the Kaliope Theater.
(B) He likes Ms. Pilar's works.
(C) He had to request another ticket.
(D) He sponsored the production of *Monet's Garden*.

177. In the article, the word "noteworthy" in line 3 is closest in meaning to

(A) enterprising
(B) artistic
(C) remarkable
(D) unattractive

178. What is indicated about the Kaliope Theater?

(A) It has only one production this fall.
(B) It hired a new director.
(C) It recently moved to Baker Way.
(D) It is only open on weekends.

179. In the information, what is NOT mentioned about *Monet's Garden*?

(A) There is an admission fee.
(B) It was written by Rene Pilar.
(C) Club members can get discounted tickets.
(D) It is the first show of the season.

180. When did Mr. Sheppard most likely see the play?

(A) On September 4
(B) On September 5
(C) On September 6
(D) On September 8

▶ ▶ ▶ GO ON TO THE NEXT PAGE

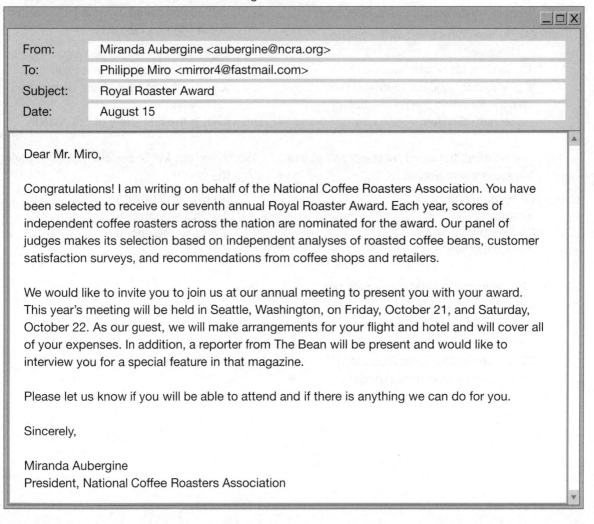

From: Miranda Aubergine <aubergine@ncra.org>
To: Philippe Miro <mirror4@fastmail.com>
Subject: Royal Roaster Award
Date: August 15

Dear Mr. Miro,

Congratulations! I am writing on behalf of the National Coffee Roasters Association. You have been selected to receive our seventh annual Royal Roaster Award. Each year, scores of independent coffee roasters across the nation are nominated for the award. Our panel of judges makes its selection based on independent analyses of roasted coffee beans, customer satisfaction surveys, and recommendations from coffee shops and retailers.

We would like to invite you to join us at our annual meeting to present you with your award. This year's meeting will be held in Seattle, Washington, on Friday, October 21, and Saturday, October 22. As our guest, we will make arrangements for your flight and hotel and will cover all of your expenses. In addition, a reporter from The Bean will be present and would like to interview you for a special feature in that magazine.

Please let us know if you will be able to attend and if there is anything we can do for you.

Sincerely,

Miranda Aubergine
President, National Coffee Roasters Association

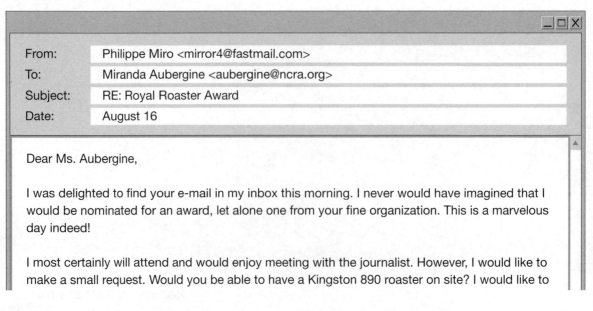

From: Philippe Miro <mirror4@fastmail.com>
To: Miranda Aubergine <aubergine@ncra.org>
Subject: RE: Royal Roaster Award
Date: August 16

Dear Ms. Aubergine,

I was delighted to find your e-mail in my inbox this morning. I never would have imagined that I would be nominated for an award, let alone one from your fine organization. This is a marvelous day indeed!

I most certainly will attend and would enjoy meeting with the journalist. However, I would like to make a small request. Would you be able to have a Kingston 890 roaster on site? I would like to use it at the event to roast a special batch of coffee beans to share with the other attendees. Moreover, I would be happy to demonstrate and discuss my approach to roasting as well. These are, I believe, the best ways in which I can express my appreciation for this award.

Thank you!

Sincerely,

Philippe Miro

181. What is the purpose of the first e-mail?

(A) To accept an application
(B) To make a recommendation
(C) To extend an invitation
(D) To reschedule a meeting

182. What is NOT indicated about the National Coffee Roasters Association?

(A) It has given an award for several years.
(B) It will pay for Mr. Miro's lodging.
(C) It will hold a two-day event.
(D) It operates many retail locations.

183. What does Mr. Miro ask Ms. Aubergine to do?

(A) Obtain equipment for him
(B) Book his flight right away
(C) Invite some other guests
(D) Permit him to join her organization

184. What does Mr. Miro offer to do?

(A) Select an award winner
(B) Give a demonstration
(C) Provide free coffee beans
(D) Write an article

185. What is suggested about Mr. Miro?

(A) He travels with his roasting equipment.
(B) He plans to be in Seattle in October.
(C) He recently created a new product.
(D) He will interview Ms. Aubergine at a conference.

▶ ▶ ▶GO ON TO THE NEXT PAGE

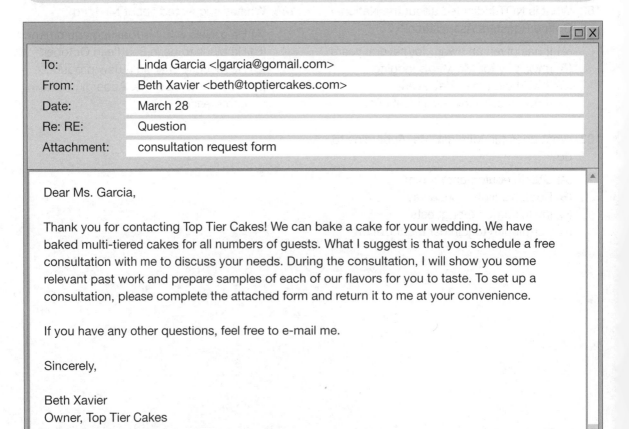

Top Tier Cakes

"A Specialty Cake Company for Your Special Occasion"

Our beautiful and delicious custom cakes will make your event all the more special. We only use the finest natural ingredients — no artificial flavors or colors! All of our cakes are baked with wholesome goodness and decorated with an eye for style. We specialize in handmade tiered cakes for weddings, anniversaries, graduations, and other special occasions. Choose from vanilla, chocolate, or almond. Our talented crew can decorate your cake to your exact specifications. Or let us help you set up a decorating party, where you and your guests transform a cake into a work of art.

Contact us at beth@toptiercakes.com.

To:	Linda Garcia <lgarcia@gomail.com>
From:	Beth Xavier <beth@toptiercakes.com>
Date:	March 28
Re: RE:	Question
Attachment:	consultation request form

Dear Ms. Garcia,

Thank you for contacting Top Tier Cakes! We can bake a cake for your wedding. We have baked multi-tiered cakes for all numbers of guests. What I suggest is that you schedule a free consultation with me to discuss your needs. During the consultation, I will show you some relevant past work and prepare samples of each of our flavors for you to taste. To set up a consultation, please complete the attached form and return it to me at your convenience.

If you have any other questions, feel free to e-mail me.

Sincerely,

Beth Xavier
Owner, Top Tier Cakes

Top Tier Cakes

Order Form

Customer name: *Linda Garcia*
Customer phone number: *(412) 555-6736*
Date(s) needed: *Saturday, May 4*
Order type: [   ] pickup   [✓] delivery
Delivery address: *Singleton Banquet Hall, 88 Oak Way, Buford*

Delivery instructions:
Must be set up no later than 3:00 P.M. Speak with Sharon Tate (555-2030) for
detailed set up instructions. Ms. Tate will be on site to assist.

Cake size: *five tiers, 40cm base, additional cakes for 150 guests*
Cake type: *almond*
Icing type: *white butter cream*

Additional instructions:
Unique decorations requested (see drawing on back), place mini-statue of bride and
groom on top of cake

---

186. What will Ms. Garcia most likely do when she meets with Ms. Xavier?

(A) Attempt to decorate a cake herself
(B) Observe a cake being made
(C) View photographs of graduation cakes
(D) Eat a piece of almond cake

187. What does Ms. Xavier ask Ms. Garcia to do?

(A) Describe an event
(B) Visit a bakery
(C) Meet with an assistant
(D) Submit a document

188. What is most likely true about Ms. Garcia?

(A) She designed the cake decorations herself.
(B) She wants a cake without artificial ingredients.
(C) She will pick up the order herself.
(D) She has done business with Ms. Xavier before.

189. What is suggested about the wedding reception?

(A) It will take place in a hotel.
(B) It will include over 200 guests.
(C) It will be held on a weekend.
(D) It will have live music.

190. What is NOT indicated about the order?

(A) It will be delivered to Buford.
(B) It will include edible decorations.
(C) It is for more than one cake.
(D) It will have multiple layers.

▶ ▶ ▶ GO ON TO THE NEXT PAGE

Notice

To: All tenants
Re: Onsite fitness center proposal

Defined Fitness, the owner of several fitness centers in and around Kensington, is considering opening a new location in the Halcion Building. It would lease 500 square meters of unused retail space on the first floor of our building. Before moving forward with the plan, Defined Fitness would like to hear from you. During the week of February 8 - 14, it will send out a survey to each person working in the Halcion Building. Please complete the survey and place it in the secure box in the lobby no later than February 28.

Sam Rogan, Building Manager

Survey Form

Name (optional): _Colleen Leopardi_
Phone (optional): _555-2903_
Employer: _Banek Designs_

– Are you currently a member of a gym or fitness center?   [ ] yes   [✔] no

– Would you consider joining a fitness center in your building? [✔] yes   [ ] no

– What services would you like a fitness center to provide?
  weight machines, exercise classes, towel and locker rentals

– How frequently do you exercise? _most weekdays_

– What hours do you prefer to exercise?
  [ ] before 8:00 A.M.   [ ] 8:00 A.M. – 11:00 A.M.
  [ ] 11:00 A.M. – 1:00 P.M.   [ ] 1 P.M. – 6:00 P.M.   [✔] after 6:00 P.M.

– Can we contact you with follow-up questions?   [✔] yes   [ ] no

Thank you for your valuable feedback!

To:	Sam Rogan <srogan@halcionbuilding.com>
From:	Penny Ivans <penny.ivans@definedfitness.com>
Subject:	Survey Results
Date:	March 8

Dear Mr. Rogan,

Thank you for your assistance in distributing the survey on schedule. We were surprised at the level of interest. Of the 1,480 surveys we distributed, 1,012 were returned. Based on the overwhelmingly positive feedback we received, we would like to move forward with developing a new location in your building with exercise equipment, classrooms, and locker rooms. Please let me know when you are available to discuss the next steps.

Sincerely,

Penny Ivans

191. According to the notice, what is Defined Fitness thinking about doing?

(A) Purchasing a building
(B) Hiring a surveying company
(C) Relocating its business
(D) Renting an interior area

192. What is suggested about the Halcion Building?

(A) Fewer than 1,500 people work there.
(B) Its entire first floor is vacant.
(C) Management will renovate it in March.
(D) It has security officers in its lobby.

193. What is suggested about the survey?

(A) It was designed by Mr. Rogan.
(B) It was mailed directly to Ms. Ivans.
(C) It was sent out before February 15.
(D) It was conducted online.

194. What is NOT indicated about Ms. Leopardi on the survey form?

(A) She works out on Saturdays.
(B) She volunteered her phone number.
(C) She is not a Defined Fitness member.
(D) She likes to exercise in the evening.

195. What is suggested about Ms. Leopardi?

(A) She used to work for Ms. Ivans.
(B) The services she requested are popular.
(C) She intends to meet with Mr. Rogan.
(D) Her coworkers all want a new gym.

▶ ▶ ▶GO ON TO THE NEXT PAGE

Barkwood(April 15) – Yesterday morning, hundreds of shoppers lined up for the grand opening of Mother Earth Market, a natural food retail chain based out of Boulder, Colorado. Located in the Maiden Creek Shopping Center, this is the first store of its kind in Barkwood.

Natural foods have been growing in popularity over the past decade as consumers become more concerned about the effects of pesticides on their health. Mother Earth Foods only sells pesticide-free produce, most of which has also been certified organic. In addition, a minimum of 25% of meat and dairy products sold in the store must come from nearby farms.

Mother Earth Market in Barkwood is open 8:00 A.M. to 9:00 P.M. daily.

To:	Kelly Giles <kgiles@marveloushoes.com>
From:	Kyle Lowe <klowe@bluemoon.com>
Subject: RE:	Parking Issues
Date:	May 12

Dear Ms. Giles,

Thank you for contacting us regarding the congestion in the parking lot at Maiden Creek. The popularity of the new natural food store has caught everyone off guard. We understand that the parking lot is at full capacity almost every day, especially at peak times. We are working with the new store's management as well as officials from the Barkwood Parking Authority to ensure that each of our tenants, Marvelous Shoes included, has adequate parking for customers. Details of the plan are coming soon.

Sincerely,

Kyle Lowe
Blue Moon Properties

NOTICE

Date: May 29
From: Blue Moon Properties
To: All Tenants at Maiden Creek Shopping Center

In order to address the parking issue and to minimize its impact on your business, we propose the following solutions. First, each tenant will receive a set number of parking spaces reserved exclusively for their customers. These spaces will be located directly in front of each business and clearly marked with signs. Violators will be ticketed by the Barkwood Parking Authority. (Call 555-9303 to report violations.) Second, the city has permitted us to use a vacant lot behind the shopping center for overflow parking. Signs will be posted to inform shoppers.

196. What is implied about Barkwood?

(A) It is located in a rural area.
(B) It only has one health food store.
(C) It has numerous small businesses.
(D) It is close to Boulder, Colorado.

197. What is the reason for the parking problems at Maiden Creek?

(A) Parking spaces were recently removed.
(B) A new tenant demanded extra parking.
(C) A shopping center is under construction.
(D) A new store is drawing more customers than expected.

198. Who most likely is Mr. Lowe?

(A) A retail supervisor
(B) A local official
(C) A property manager
(D) A police officer

199. In the notice, the word "address" in line 1 is closest in meaning to

(A) resolve
(B) elevate
(C) locate
(D) discuss

200. What is suggested about Marvelous Shoes?

(A) Ms. Giles is the store's former owner.
(B) It is located next to Mother Earth Market.
(C) Customers cannot find its new location.
(D) It will get assigned parking spaces.

Test 07 정답

147. (A)	**148.** (B)	**149.** (D)	**150.** (B)	**151.** (C)	**152.** (D)
153. (B)	**154.** (B)	**155.** (D)	**156.** (D)	**157.** (D)	**158.** (B)
159. (C)	**160.** (A)	**161.** (D)	**162.** (A)	**163.** (C)	**164.** (C)
165. (A)	**166.** (C)	**167.** (D)	**168.** (B)	**169.** (A)	**170.** (B)
171. (D)	**172.** (B)	**173.** (D)	**174.** (C)	**175.** (C)	**176.** (B)
177. (C)	**178.** (C)	**179.** (C)	**180.** (A)	**181.** (C)	**182.** (D)
183. (A)	**184.** (B)	**185.** (B)	**186.** (D)	**187.** (D)	**188.** (B)
189. (C)	**190.** (B)	**191.** (D)	**192.** (A)	**193.** (C)	**194.** (A)
195. (B)	**196.** (B)	**197.** (D)	**198.** (C)	**199.** (A)	**200.** (D)

TEST
08

시작 시간 ___시 ___분   목표 개수 _____ / 54

종료 시간 ___시 ___분   실제 개수 _____ / 54

- 반드시 55분 안에 문제 풀이 포함 마킹까지 마쳐야 합니다.
- 실제 시험이라고 생각하고 멈추지 말고 풀어보세요.   - 정답 개수에 5를 곱하면 대략적인 점수가 됩니다.

Directions: In this part you will read a selection of texts, such as magazine and newspaper articles, e-mails, and instant messages. Each text or set of texts is followed by several questions. Select the best answer for each question and mark the letter (A), (B), (C), or (D) on your answer sheet.

Questions 147-148 refer to the following advertisement.

Professional Edits
Say What You Want with the Right Words.

Our services include:

– editing existing content for typos, spelling errors, and grammar problems
– drafting new text for marketing or promotional purposes
– writing engaging blog posts to draw more customers to your Web site

Professional Edits knows that not everyone can major in writing or have an eagle eye for editing, and that is why we have a smart, quick, and diligent staff of writers to help your business out. Whether it's small corrections or creating new content, Professional Edits is here for all your editorial needs.

To see our editorial portfolio, please stop by our office at 3252 Merryway Lane.

147. What is NOT indicated about Professional Edits?

(A) It works for commercial clients.
(B) It charges for each word written.
(C) It can correct writing mistakes.
(D) It can write for online audiences.

148. Why are readers referred to an address?

(A) To receive a free brochure
(B) To write a blog post
(C) To make an appointment
(D) To view writing samples

TEST 08

▶ ▶ ▶GO ON TO THE NEXT PAGE

Paperworks, LLC

For all your paper needs!

Paper			
Basic	Thick	Cardstock	Cardboard
White 500 pieces $50	White/Off-White 300 pieces $75	White/Black 200 pieces $100	White/Brown 100 pieces $150

Ms. Simone, here are the final paper choices for the invitations for your company's event. Please let me know which paper you would like the invitations printed on and specify the color. It will take me a day or two to print them, so it is best to contact me by October 2 at the latest. Then wire the total amount to our bank account: 2342-13282-5232. If you have any questions, please let me know.

Terry Gomez (tgomez@paperwork.net)

149. What is the purpose of the card?

(A) To deny a request
(B) To correct a mistake
(C) To request instructions
(D) To announce a delay

150. What is suggested about the event?

(A) It requires white paper.
(B) It will occur after October 2.
(C) It is organized by Paperworks.
(D) It is for company staff and family.

Questions 151-153 refer to the following article.

Traveling with young children does not need to be a nightmare. In fact, many families successfully travel with their young ones. The secret is in the planning.

Successful traveling families take their time. They arrive early to airports, train stations, and bus terminals to make sure that sufficient time is available for unforeseen emergencies. Arriving early reduces the stress felt by everyone in the family.

Small children have limited attention spans. That's why it is a good idea to pack games, puzzles, coloring books, and other activities that can keep the kids occupied during long car rides or flights. Some parents rely on the portable entertainment available on their tablet computers and smartphones. Whatever you prefer, think ahead about how to keep the kids entertained, and you will have fewer headaches along the way.

Last, but certainly not least, stick to your children's routines as much as possible. If your little boy eats a morning snack every day at 10 A.M., try to make sure that happens regardless of where you are. The same goes for naps, baths, bedtime stories, etc. The more familiar routines remain intact, the more likely your little one will adjust to the new environment with ease.

That said, every child is different, and some deal with new experiences better than others. Nevertheless, planning ahead can make traveling with kids easier.

151. What is the purpose of the article?

(A) To explain the way children should be raised
(B) To give advice on how to travel with children
(C) To encourage traveling by air
(D) To criticize those who don't plan for trips

152. According to the article, why are routines important for children when traveling?

(A) They help kids adapt to changes.
(B) They allow parents to move more slowly.
(C) They ensure kids get enough rest.
(D) They keep children entertained.

153. What is indicated about smartphones?

(A) They are useful for communicating with kids.
(B) They can be used to distract kids.
(C) They are essential for traveling families.
(D) They can help track travel routines.

▶ ▶ ▶ GO ON TO THE NEXT PAGE

Questions 154-155 refer to the following text message chain.

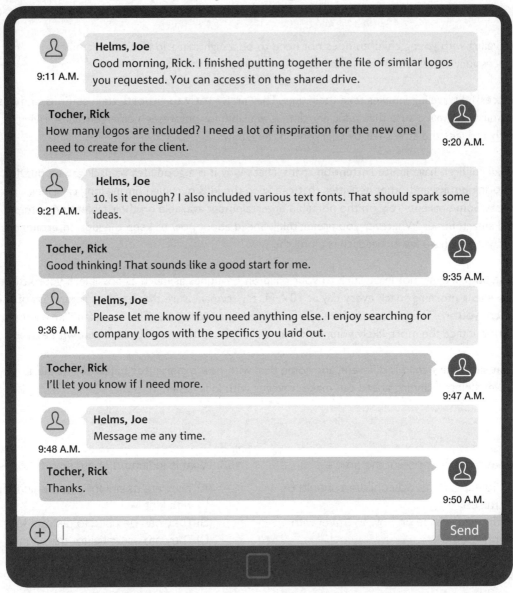

Helms, Joe
9:11 A.M.
Good morning, Rick. I finished putting together the file of similar logos you requested. You can access it on the shared drive.

Tocher, Rick
How many logos are included? I need a lot of inspiration for the new one I need to create for the client.
9:20 A.M.

Helms, Joe
9:21 A.M.
10. Is it enough? I also included various text fonts. That should spark some ideas.

Tocher, Rick
Good thinking! That sounds like a good start for me.
9:35 A.M.

Helms, Joe
9:36 A.M.
Please let me know if you need anything else. I enjoy searching for company logos with the specifics you laid out.

Tocher, Rick
I'll let you know if I need more.
9:47 A.M.

Helms, Joe
9:48 A.M.
Message me any time.

Tocher, Rick
Thanks.
9:50 A.M.

Send

154. What type of business does Mr. Helms most likely work for?

(A) A family restaurant
(B) A graphic design firm
(C) A government office
(D) A clothing store

155. At 9:21 A.M., what does Mr. Helms most likely mean when he writes, "That should spark some ideas"?

(A) He is still collecting logos at the moment.
(B) He wants his ideas to be taken seriously.
(C) He thinks the fonts will inspire Mr. Tocher.
(D) He designed a new font for Mr. Tocher's project.

Better-Tech PowerView Conference

Event name: Better-Tech PowerView Conference
Starting date: January 12   Time: 9:00 A.M.
Ending date: January 13   Time: 5:00 P.M.
Contact person: Sally Gales
Phone: 555-8921
E-mail: sgales@bettertech.com
Registration fee: $100
Attached files: application form, payment instructions

About the event: PowerView presentations are a widely underutilized tool for large and small companies. For users who know the basics of creating a PowerView presentation, this conference will teach you more advanced applications of the software. Plus, you will receive tips and pointers on both the creation of your presentation and also on the presentation delivery. Stand on stage and deliver your speech with confidence, and maximize your marketing strategy with Better-Tech's revolutionary PowerView Conference. The registration deadline for the conference is January 3. Space is limited to 50 participants. Signed applications need to be sent via e-mail to Sally Gales at sgales@bettertech.com. If interest exceeds our expectations, additional space may be opened. Notification of that or other changes will be posted on our Web site on January 4 at www.bettertech.com.

156. What is indicated about the PowerView conference?

(A) It is open only to employees of Better-Tech.
(B) It will teach basic computer skills.
(C) It is directed at software developers.
(D) It will provide information on public speaking.

157. What is NOT required to attend the conference?

(A) Completing an online form
(B) Signing a document
(C) Making a payment
(D) E-mailing a contact person

158. When is the latest application forms can be submitted electronically?

(A) January 3
(B) January 4
(C) January 12
(D) January 13

TEST 08

▶ ▶ ▶GO ON TO THE NEXT PAGE

Questions 159-161 refer to the following letter.

Direct Delivery

Keifer Jones
KJ Law Firm
2214 34th Avenue
Oklahoma City, OK

November 9

Dear Mr. Jones,

Your head administrative assistant, Jessica Klein, is a close acquaintance of mine. — [1] — She mentioned that your law firm is looking for a private delivery service for your practice's confidential paperwork. We understand the private nature of your work and that time is of the essence for legal matters.

My delivery company, Direct Delivery, specializes in small business delivery services. We specifically only do business with small companies so that we can pay attention to detail and not be inundated with work. — [2] —

We can adjust our services to each client's unique needs. For close deliveries, we offer a bike courier service which allows us to avoid traffic jams and to deliver small packages quickly. For larger deliveries or those farther away, we have a van and are happy to pick up packages directly from your office at any time. Our company runs 24 hours a day, 7 days a week. — [3] —

If our services sound like a good fit for the KJ Law Firm, please feel free to call me to discuss contract terms. I would also be happy to stop by your office to have a face-to-face chat about what we can offer you. Please send my regards to Ms. Klein. — [4] —

Sincerely,

Harry Pines
Direct Delivery

159. What is suggested about Direct Delivery?

(A) It has worked with Mr. Jones before.
(B) It is a one-man bike courier service.
(C) It offers customized services to clients.
(D) It will expand in size in the near future.

160. In which of the positions marked [1], [2], [3], and [4] does the following sentence best belong?

"You won't just be another number in a long line of deliveries."

(A) [1]
(B) [2]
(C) [3]
(D) [4]

161. What is NOT indicated about the KJ Law Firm?

(A) It is Ms. Klein's employer.
(B) It has sensitive documents.
(C) It requires timely deliveries.
(D) It uses a large courier service.

Brighten your day
with
Wilson's Office Window Cleaners

Don't put up with mediocre cleaning services that swipe and go. Call Wilson's instead! Our team of professionals has been cleaning skyscrapers for over 20 years. With the latest array of high-tech equipment, there's no window that Wilson's can't reach. Have a small company? Wilson's cleans windows of all sizes. There's no need to have your office view shrouded in a layer of dust. Clean windows are on their way.

Satisfaction guaranteed: If you can't see your reflection in any of your serviced windows, we'll clean it again and give you a free cleaning appointment.

Spotless windows are Wilson's way. Schedule 3 months of weekly cleanings and get a 10% discount. Offer valid until November 30.

Phone number: (713) 555-2152

162. What is true about the discount?

(A) It is limited to three cleanings.
(B) It cannot be used in December.
(C) It requires an annual contract.
(D) It applies only to small offices.

163. In the advertisement, the word "reflection" in paragraph 2, line 1 is closest in meaning to

(A) image
(B) sign
(C) surface
(D) thoughts

164. What is suggested about Wilson's Office Window Cleaners?

(A) The company schedules appointment online.
(B) Its workers are available at any time of the day.
(C) The company has extensive experience.
(D) It is capable of cleaning a variety of surfaces.

TEST 08

▶ ▶ ▶ GO ON TO THE NEXT PAGE

To: Freugers Accounting Department
From: Nancy Digly, IT Manager
Date: February 10
Subject: Accounting Department's New Phones

Be advised that your current Freugers company cell phone will be replaced next week. The company has signed a new 5-year contract with Clearcom Telecoms for all of our phone service. This brings an end to our service contract with our current provider, Green Line Communications.

You should back up any files from your company cell phone that you would like to keep, such as photos, contact phone numbers, and work files. The IT Department suggests that you transfer the files to the extra storage space on the company cloud. Once you receive your new company phones, you can then download the files to the phone from cloud storage. Storing phone data temporarily on the cloud will not affect the total storage you have been allotted.

If you need assistance with the data transfer or need to arrange to pick up your new phone, dial extension 5 on the IT Department phone line to reach me.

Nancy Digly
IT Manager

165. Why was the memo sent?

(A) To explain a new data storage system
(B) To introduce a new employee
(C) To notify employees of a change
(D) To announce an event promotion

166. What is NOT indicated about Freugers?

(A) It will soon have a new service provider.
(B) It recently released a new phone.
(C) It will partner with Clearcom for 5 years.
(D) It gives employees cloud storage.

167. What is suggested about Ms. Digly?

(A) She is in charge of phone distribution.
(B) She will collect all outdated phones.
(C) She prefers to be contacted by e-mail.
(D) She will need assistance with the transfer.

Questions 168-171 refer to the following Web page.

About us	Services	Gallery & Info	Pricing	Contact Us

Upgrade your office decor and present your clients
with your best (building) face!

First impressions matter, and when it comes to business, how your clients feel when they walk into your office will surely decide if they will come again. That is why it is important to keep your office looking good and trendy with the latest styles of today. Trust us. — [1] —

At Office Decorators, we do it all, from painting and adorning bare walls to selecting the best furniture appropriate for the kind of work you do. We offer personal shopping and styling for any professional industry, and we don't stop decorating until your place looks great! Your own style will be put into play. — [2] — Your new office will represent you and what you do.

Stop by our showroom to see signature pieces, including wooden desks and handcrafted chairs on display for rent, as well as an extensive photo gallery of companies we have worked with in the past. — [3] — Gallery hours are Monday to Thursday from 1 P.M. to 4 P.M.

Office Decorators was started by interior designer Pierre Niels. To schedule an exclusive consultation with Pierre, call 555-2164. — [4] — Please be advised that appointments with Pierre require a 5% deposit. All other consultations are free.

---

168. What is a purpose of the Web page?

(A) To introduce a new location
(B) To detail a company's services
(C) To explain a customer review
(D) To recruit new decorators

169. What is NOT mentioned about Office Decorators?

(A) It has special furniture on view.
(B) It has handmade furniture.
(C) It has an architect on staff.
(D) It has examples of past work.

170. What is indicated about Mr. Niels?

(A) He designed the chairs on display.
(B) He is available most afternoons.
(C) He offers a free initial meeting.
(D) He is the founder of the company.

171. In which of the positions marked [1], [2], [3], and [4] does the following sentence best belong?

"Office Decorator's design expertise will transform your workspace right before your eyes."

(A) [1]
(B) [2]
(C) [3]
(D) [4]

▶ ▶ ▶GO ON TO THE NEXT PAGE

Questions 172-175 refer to the following online chat discussion.

Linda Ambers 6:29 A.M.		I'm up early here in Toronto because I have a phone call with the Paris office in two hours. We are trying to land a contract with a major player to market its gourmet food products. I just realized I didn't test the conference room projector. Can someone let me do a test call?
Barbara Summers 6:30 A.M.		I'm still here in the Berlin office working overtime. I can go into our conference room, and you can try to video call me. I'll confirm if I can see the images on your projector.
Linda Ambers 6:32 A.M.		That's fantastic. My call to Paris might end up being a three-way call. Anyone else want to jump in?
Paula Rubio 6:34 A.M.		Morning, Linda. It's Paula from the Mexico office. I can give you a hand.
Linda Ambers 6:36 A.M.		Hi, Paula. Give me a minute to set everything up for a three-way call.
Paula Rubio 6:37 A.M.		Sure. Call my office when you're ready.
Linda Ambers 6:39 A.M.		Barbara, Paula. Can you see my presentation clearly on your end?
Barbara Summers 6:41 A.M.		The images are clear here in Berlin. Your projector seems fine.
Paula Rubio 6:43 A.M.		Clear and crisp. You should be good to go for your Paris meeting. Good luck!

Send

172. What field does Ms. Ambers most likely work in?

(A) Film production
(B) International marketing
(C) Luxury tourism
(D) Technology design

173. At 6:32 A.M., what does Ms. Ambers most likely mean when she writes, "Anyone else want to jump in"?

(A) She is inviting another office to join her meeting later.
(B) She is hoping the projector will work without testing it.
(C) She wants to call Paris early to check the projector.
(D) She needs to test the projector in multiple countries.

174. What does Ms. Rubio do for Ms. Ambers?

(A) Confirms that some equipment is working
(B) Offers to assist with a meeting
(C) Requests that images be sent
(D) Calls her on a personal line

175. What is suggested about Ms. Summers?

(A) She has fixed the projector before.
(B) She will join the Paris call later.
(C) She stayed at the office after closing.
(D) She is traveling for business.

▶ ▶ ▶ GO ON TO THE NEXT PAGE

Replace your office carpet today!

Fantastic Flooring is running an unbeatable September special. We will pull up your existing carpet and replace it with brand-new carpeting for half the usual price — all on the same day! Plus, there's no extra installation fee. Amazing!

Please note wooden or tile flooring can be removed with the same promotion but with an additional labor charge of $500.00 and an additional day of work.

Standard Carpet Removal *Promotion*	$0.00
Beige Carpet	$350.00/room
Brown Carpet	$450.00/room
Navy Carpet	$500.00/room

Only the above colors are part of our September discount event! Prices are as listed for free carpet removal service. If you would like to participate in the promotion but want a different color carpet to be installed, we can offer you free removal plus a 30% discount on the new carpet price.

To schedule an appointment with our installers, please visit www.FantasticFlooring.com. The promotion ends on September 30, but orders must be made by September 20 due to delivery and installation time.

_ □ X

To:	Bernard Derk <customerservice@fantasticflooring.com>
From:	Janice Weggin <jweggin@polytech.com>
Subject:	Reschedule flooring appointment
Date:	September 2

Hello, Bernard.

We spoke on the phone 2 weeks ago when I called to schedule an appointment to have the flooring redone in my one-room office. However, I just saw a flyer for Fantastic Flooring's September pricing and was told by another representative that I could get the special promotional pricing for my order.

Originally, I was scheduled to have my tile floor removed tomorrow and black carpet installed on September 4 at the promotional price. After seeing a sample, I have decided I would like to change the carpet's color to navy. I would also like to reschedule the tile removal for September 6 and the carpet installation for the following day. Please let me know if this will work and e-mail me an updated invoice with the promotional pricing.

Thank you.

Janice Weggin

176. According to the advertisement, what is true about carpet installation?

(A) It must be ordered ten days in advance.
(B) It cannot be done over wooden floors.
(C) It can be completed in a single day.
(D) It requires the labor of two installers.

177. What is suggested about Ms. Weggin?

(A) She had been offered a discount of 30%.
(B) She booked the carpet installation in July.
(C) She will be out of town for a few days.
(D) She made a payment to Mr. Derk.

178. What will Ms. Weggin most likely be charged?

(A) $450.00
(B) $500.00
(C) $950.00
(D) $1,000.00

179. When does Ms. Weggin want the carpet installed?

(A) On September 3
(B) On September 4
(C) On September 6
(D) On September 7

180. What does Ms. Weggin ask Mr. Derk to do?

(A) Supervise an installation
(B) Send her a new bill
(C) Refund a payment
(D) Give her a carpet sample

▶ ▶ ▶ GO ON TO THE NEXT PAGE

Employee Excellence Awards

The Vexus Corporation is currently seeking nominations for our annual Employee Excellence Awards. The Employee Excellence Awards acknowledge employees who make exceptional contributions to the success of the Vexus Corporation.

Nominees:
– must be full-time employees of the Vexus Corporation with at least 2 years at the company
– must have demonstrated excellent performance above their normal duties and responsibilities
– cannot have received a previous Employee Excellence Award

Nominees will be evaluated on their:
– understanding and implementation of the company's mission
– innovation in the workplace
– demonstrated leadership qualities
– relationships with coworkers

To nominate an individual, please send that person's name, employee ID number, and a one-page narrative statement describing why the nominee deserves an Employee Excellence Award. Nominations can be submitted to the HR office or faxed/e-mailed to Benita Kito (555-8930 / bkito@vexus.com).

Nominations must be received by April 15. Awards will be announced in June and presented to the winners at our annual company picnic in July.

To:	Benita Kito <benita.kito@vexus.com>
From:	Robert Wilson <robert.wilson@vexus.com>
Subject:	Nomination
Attachments:	nomination_wells

Dear Benita,

I am writing to nominate Jason Wells (ID# 485003) for an Employee Excellence Award. Jason has worked as a technician in my department for three years. Without being asked by me or the other supervisors, Jason has taken the initiative by reorganizing the testing lab to maximize efficiency and safety. In fact, after implementing his suggested changes, accidents have been reduced by 35% and breakage by 85%. Jason is highly regarded by his colleagues and supervisors. If he continues along this path, it is hard not to see him being promoted to a managerial position in a few years. A statement supporting his nomination is attached. Please contact me with any questions at this e-mail or my direct extension at 3456.

Sincerely,

Robert Wilson
Lead Supervisor
Division of Product Testing

181. How can someone nominate a colleague for an award?

(A) By meeting with someone in HR
(B) By completing an online application
(C) By telling person's supervisor
(D) By submitting a written statement

182. What is indicated about the Employee Excellence Awards?

(A) They are given once a year.
(B) They are given to employees of the HR office.
(C) They are given at a special awards dinner.
(D) They are given in autumn.

183. What is NOT required of nominees?

(A) A recommendation by a colleague
(B) Exceptional job performance
(C) More than 2 years of working at Vexus
(D) An award-winning experience

184. In the e-mail, the word "implementing" in line 4 is closest in meaning to

(A) performing
(B) evaluating
(C) noticing
(D) confusing

185. What is suggested about Mr. Wells?

(A) He is training for management.
(B) He is good at multitasking.
(C) He works full time at Vexus.
(D) He was hired by Mr. Wilson.

▶ ▶ ▶ GO ON TO THE NEXT PAGE

MEMO

To: Teams A and B
From: Hayley Narco, Managing Director
Date: March 2

Please note the weekend trip for employees of Directco Deliveries has been moved from March 23 to March 30. This is due to the unseasonably cold weather.

The trip itinerary remains the same, and everyone should be on the bus by 9:00 A.M. The bus will be waiting, and names will be called and checked at 9:05 A.M. As managing time is important, I ask that no one be late; if you know you will be late, please send me a message.

Hayley

Meeting Agenda: Departure Day
Date: Friday, March 30 *Note the change*
Departure Time: 9:00 A.M.
Attendees: Directco Teams A and B

Check-in	8:30 - 9:00 A.M.	Meeting Point: Delivery Dock #8 Please check in with Hayley.
Bus Roll Call	9:05 A.M.	Please be seated on your assigned bus.
Restroom Break	11:15 A.M.	15-minute break
Lunch	1:00 P.M.	Team Lunches
Arrival	3:45 P.M.	We will arrive at Yosemite Park. Listen for cabin assignments.
Dinner	6:15 P.M.	Team Dinners Pick up tomorrow's agenda at dinner.

Contact Hayley Narco for any questions: hnarco@directco.com

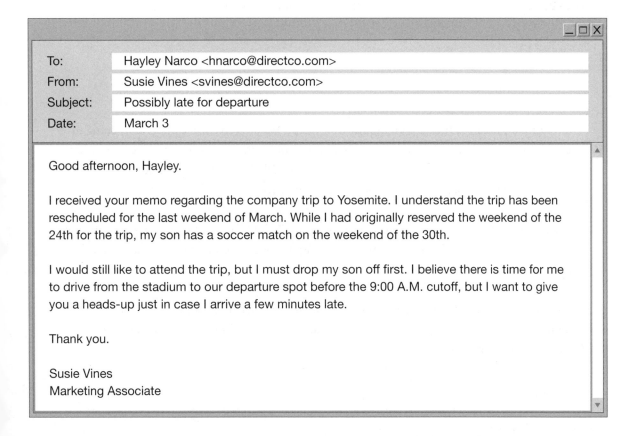

To: Hayley Narco <hnarco@directco.com>

From: Susie Vines <svines@directco.com>

Subject: Possibly late for departure

Date: March 3

Good afternoon, Hayley.

I received your memo regarding the company trip to Yosemite. I understand the trip has been rescheduled for the last weekend of March. While I had originally reserved the weekend of the 24th for the trip, my son has a soccer match on the weekend of the 30th.

I would still like to attend the trip, but I must drop my son off first. I believe there is time for me to drive from the stadium to our departure spot before the 9:00 A.M. cutoff, but I want to give you a heads-up just in case I arrive a few minutes late.

Thank you.

Susie Vines
Marketing Associate

186. In the memo, what is NOT mentioned about the weekend trip?

(A) It has been organized for two teams.
(B) Directco will pay for food and lodging.
(C) Directco arranged transportation for employees.
(D) The departure date has been modified.

187. What is suggested about Ms. Narco?

(A) She works in marketing.
(B) She has been to Yosemite.
(C) She will not go on the trip.
(D) She will arrive by 8:30 A.M.

188. What is the purpose of Ms. Vines' e-mail?

(A) To respond to a request
(B) To ask to join a different trip
(C) To make an announcement
(D) To cancel her trip plans

189. What does Ms. Vines say she plans to do on March 30?

(A) Attend a soccer game
(B) Board the bus at the stadium
(C) Go to Delivery Dock #8
(D) Lead Team A on a trip

190. In the e-mail, the word "cutoff" in paragraph 2, line 2 is closest in meaning to

(A) reduction
(B) deadline
(C) restriction
(D) departure

▶ ▶ ▶GO ON TO THE NEXT PAGE

October 13

Dear Ms. Moore,

Our company, Halifax, Inc., is looking for new talent. While we've listed the job opening in various online outlets and job boards, we're hoping your temporary employment agency has some good candidates on hand. My counterpart at Signal Design recommended your company after having a great experience working with you.

We need a software engineer who has worked in the IT field for at least 10 years. The person should be proficient in all major computer languages as well as competent in diagnosing IT problems.

As for school experience, we are not too concerned about what school was attended. Please send us the resumes of any candidates who fit the above description. We would like to interview as soon as possible.

Sincerely,

Teddy Gershwin

MEMO

FROM: Julie Moore, Staffing Director
TO: All Solid Staffing Talent
DATE: October 14
RE: Looking for Software Engineer

Halifax, Inc. is looking to hire a seasoned software engineer. If you've got more than 10 years under your belt, take a look at the attached guidelines for the application process and let me know if you would be interested in interviewing with them.

Once you've prepared your application, contact Ben Turner. He will be your point of connection with the client. Good luck!

Solid Staffing

Job Application Guidelines:
Updated: October 14

- Prepare a resume listing all your past work experience. It should also list your skills, education, and achievements. Submit that directly to us, and we will forward it to the employer.

- Practice your answers for any questions that may be asked during the interview. You can find a list of commonly asked questions on our Web site for your own use.

- Pick a professional, conservative outfit to wear for your interview. Neat hair and makeup are advised. Wear comfortable but clean shoes and minimal jewelry.

- When you are offered to interview with the employer, be sure to arrive early. You want to make a good impression. Double-check your interview schedule time and date.

To schedule a face-to-face mock interview with one of our interns, contact the Staffing Director at 555-3120. There is no charge for this service.

191. Who most likely is Mr. Gershwin?

(A) A software engineer
(B) A hiring manager
(C) A professional interpreter
(D) A staffing agency owner

192. What is suggested about Signal Design?

(A) It found employees for Ms. Moore.
(B) It advertised job openings on the Internet.
(C) It was satisfied with Solid Staffing.
(D) It is the former employer of Mr. Turner.

193. What should job seekers do if they want to practice interviewing in person?

(A) Apply for an internship
(B) Stop by Solid Staffing
(C) Pay a fee
(D) Call Ms. Moore

194. What will Mr. Turner most likely do?

(A) Conduct practice interviews
(B) Introduce clients to Ms. Moore
(C) Send resumes to Halifax
(D) Prepare job postings

195. What advice is NOT given to job applicants?

(A) They should bring a resume to the interview.
(B) They should rehearse their answers.
(C) They should dress appropriately.
(D) They should be punctual to the interview.

▶ ▶ ▶GO ON TO THE NEXT PAGE

Aqua Auto, Inc.

Mobile Car Wash Service

We go to your home or place of work and wash your vehicle on site.
Proudly serving residents of Carbondale for the past 25 years.

Some of our most popular services:
- Basic car wash – clean the interior and exterior of your vehicle
- Armor Guard™ wax – get extra protection from the elements
- Windshield repair – seal small chips in the glass
- Super car wash – like the basic car wash but only better

For details on these and other services, including pricing, visit www.aquaauto.com. You can also schedule service there.

Get 10% off in May. Must present this advertisement at time of service. Limit one discount per vehicle.

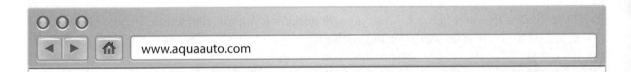

www.aquaauto.com

Service Request Form

Name: *Michael Hoven*
Phone: *(512) 555-6743*
E-mail: *mhoven@jetmail.com*
Date(s) services needed: *Friday, May 18*
Location where vehicle will be serviced: *787 Harper Lane, Carbondale*

Vehicle type: *Sedan*
Make/model: *Hanata Edge*
Color: *black*
License plate#: *HJT 619*

What service(s) do you need?
My cousin is getting married next week. I will be driving him and his future wife to the reception. We need the vehicle to look absolutely spotless inside and out, so we want your best cleaning service. The vehicle will be parked at my house the day before the wedding.

Credit card number (required for reservations): *XXX-XXXX-XXXX-7840*

Note: Your credit card will not be billed until completion of the requested service(s).

Thank you for your submission. A representative will be in touch with you in the next 24 hours.

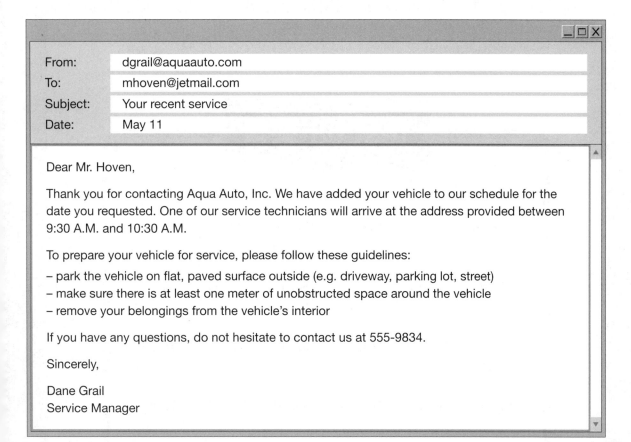

From: dgrail@aquaauto.com
To: mhoven@jetmail.com
Subject: Your recent service
Date: May 11

Dear Mr. Hoven,

Thank you for contacting Aqua Auto, Inc. We have added your vehicle to our schedule for the date you requested. One of our service technicians will arrive at the address provided between 9:30 A.M. and 10:30 A.M.

To prepare your vehicle for service, please follow these guidelines:

– park the vehicle on flat, paved surface outside (e.g. driveway, parking lot, street)
– make sure there is at least one meter of unobstructed space around the vehicle
– remove your belongings from the vehicle's interior

If you have any questions, do not hesitate to contact us at 555-9834.

Sincerely,

Dane Grail
Service Manager

---

196. What is NOT indicated about Aqua Auto, Inc.?

(A) It requires a full payment in advance.
(B) It has been in business for decades.
(C) It gives tips for preservice preparations.
(D) It has not advertised all of its services.

197. What service does Mr. Hoven request?

(A) Basic car wash
(B) Armor Guard™ wax
(C) Windshield repair
(D) Super car wash

198. What is suggested about Mr. Hoven?

(A) He has utilized mobile car wash services before.
(B) He recently moved to Carbondale.
(C) He will park his vehicle in a garage.
(D) He will get a discount from Aqua Auto, Inc.

199. What is scheduled to happen on May 18?

(A) Mr. Hoven will be getting married.
(B) A technician will go to Mr. Hoven's home.
(C) Mr. Hoven will take his car to Aqua Auto, Inc.
(D) A bill will be sent to Mr. Hoven.

200. What does Mr. Grail ask Mr. Hoven to do?

(A) Confirm an appointment by phone
(B) Provide measurements of his vehicle
(C) Empty his car before a service is provided
(D) Place a request for a parking permit

▶ ▶ ▶GO ON TO THE NEXT PAGE

Test 08 정답

147. (B)	**148.** (D)	**149.** (C)	**150.** (B)	**151.** (B)	**152.** (A)
153. (B)	**154.** (B)	**155.** (C)	**156.** (D)	**157.** (A)	**158.** (A)
159. (C)	**160.** (B)	**161.** (D)	**162.** (B)	**163.** (A)	**164.** (C)
165. (C)	**166.** (B)	**167.** (A)	**168.** (B)	**169.** (C)	**170.** (D)
171. (A)	**172.** (B)	**173.** (D)	**174.** (A)	**175.** (C)	**176.** (C)
177. (A)	**178.** (D)	**179.** (D)	**180.** (B)	**181.** (D)	**182.** (A)
183. (D)	**184.** (A)	**185.** (C)	**186.** (B)	**187.** (D)	**188.** (A)
189. (C)	**190.** (B)	**191.** (B)	**192.** (C)	**193.** (D)	**194.** (C)
195. (A)	**196.** (A)	**197.** (D)	**198.** (D)	**199.** (B)	**200.** (C)

TEST
09

55 min

시작 시간 ___시 ___분	목표 개수 _____ / 54
종료 시간 ___시 ___분	실제 개수 _____ / 54

- 반드시 55분 안에 문제 풀이 포함 마킹까지 마쳐야 합니다.
- 실제 시험이라고 생각하고 멈추지 말고 풀어보세요.

- 정답 개수에 5를 곱하면 대략적인 점수가 됩니다.

Directions: In this part you will read a selection of texts, such as magazine and newspaper articles, e-mails, and instant messages. Each text or set of texts is followed by several questions. Select the best answer for each question and mark the letter (A), (B), (C), or (D) on your answer sheet.

Questions 147-148 refer to the following invitation.

Celebrate Community at Weston Park!

Saturday, May 6, 1:00 P.M. to 8:00 P.M.

After 6 months of closure for renovations, Weston Park will once again be open to the public! Join Mayor Tom Stafford and members of the local community to celebrate. Check out the new walking and biking trails, the improved athletic fields, and the city's newest swimming pool.

Live music performed by
Shirley Winston, Alex's Band of Fools, and The Jokers Wild

Face painting, jugglers, and games for the kids

Local caterers will be selling food next to the picnic pavilion.

Call Ted Flinders for details at 555-3020.

147. What is the purpose of the event?

(A) To reopen a recreational area
(B) To welcome a new local leader
(C) To plan changes to a park
(D) To hold an athletic competition

148. What most likely is The Jokers Wild?

(A) A food vendor
(B) A comedy troupe
(C) A music group
(D) A sports team

▶ ▶ ▶GO ON TO THE NEXT PAGE

Questions 149-151 refer to the following job advertisement.

Carter and Case is seeking a graphic designer to create e-mail marketing materials along with occasional newspaper and magazine ads. This position in our Dartmore office also involves helping to launch e-mail marketing campaigns. Most of the time, the graphic designer will use Plato software to create graphic-rich automated e-mails. This is a part-time position with flexible hours and the potential for some work to be completed from home.

Applicants must have a bachelor's degree in graphic design or a related field. Strong multitasking and organizational skills required. Must be detail oriented. Experience using Plato, Insight, and other standard graphic design software is a must.

Founded in 1909, Carter and Case provides advertising and marketing solutions to companies in 26 countries.

Send your resume and a cover letter to Shawn Livermore at slivermore@ carterandcase.com.

149. According to the advertisement, what will the graphic designer do?

(A) Communicate with multiple offices
(B) Prepare online videos
(C) Make advertisements
(D) Obtain training in new software programs

150. What is suggested about Carter and Case?

(A) Its headquarters is in Dartmore.
(B) It is a leader in online marketing.
(C) It does not have full-time positions.
(D) It has international clients.

151. What is NOT required of applicants for this position?

(A) Being able to do multiple tasks
(B) Having earned a college degree
(C) Completing a professional writing course
(D) Being attentive to details

Questions 152-153 refer to the following text message chain.

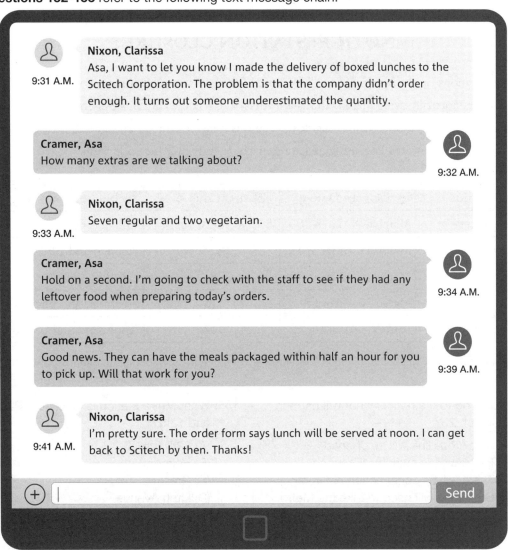

Nixon, Clarissa
9:31 A.M.
Asa, I want to let you know I made the delivery of boxed lunches to the Scitech Corporation. The problem is that the company didn't order enough. It turns out someone underestimated the quantity.

Cramer, Asa
How many extras are we talking about?
9:32 A.M.

Nixon, Clarissa
9:33 A.M.
Seven regular and two vegetarian.

Cramer, Asa
Hold on a second. I'm going to check with the staff to see if they had any leftover food when preparing today's orders.
9:34 A.M.

Cramer, Asa
Good news. They can have the meals packaged within half an hour for you to pick up. Will that work for you?
9:39 A.M.

Nixon, Clarissa
9:41 A.M.
I'm pretty sure. The order form says lunch will be served at noon. I can get back to Scitech by then. Thanks!

152. Where does Mr. Cramer most likely work?

(A) A packaging manufacturer
(B) A grocery store
(C) A technology company
(D) A catering company

153. At 9:41 A.M., what does Ms. Nixon most likely mean when she writes, "I'm pretty sure"?

(A) She believes that Scitech can have lunch later.
(B) She thinks she has enough time to make the delivery.
(C) She feels it is important to deliver the items early.
(D) She is fairly certain the staff can do the packaging.

▶ ▶ ▶GO ON TO THE NEXT PAGE

||||||||||||||||||||||||||||||||||||||||||||||||||||||||||||||||||||||||||||||||||||||||||||||||||||||||||||||||||||||||||||||||||||||

NOTICE: STATION CLOSURES

Several stations on the North Line will be closed for renovations beginning next month. Customers normally using these stations are advised to use the City Bus System. Metro Pass holders may obtain a free bus pass at closed stations good for the duration of the closure. To do so, insert your Metro Pass into a ticketing machine and enter the code 5668.

Station	Closure Dates	Nearest Bus Line	Nearest Bus Stop
89th Street	March 2 – March 10	84B	89th and Ellis
Belmont	March 11 – March 15	82C	Pullman and 12th
Greely	March 16 – March 29	78	Oak and Main
Fitch Avenue	March 30 – April 8	116	Freemont and Fitch
Woolworth Road	April 9 – April 16	14A	Woolworth and Franklin

||||||||||||||||||||||||||||||||||||||||||||||||||||||||||||||||||||||||||||||||||||||||||||||||||||||||||||||||||||||||||||||||||||||

154. According to the notice, what will happen on March 20?

(A) A new bus line will be opened.
(B) Fitch Avenue station will reopen.
(C) There will be construction at Greely.
(D) Bus riders will need to take the Metro.

155. What Metro station is closest to Pullman and 12th?

(A) 89th Street
(B) Belmont
(C) Greely
(D) Fitch Avenue

To:	Karen Grisham <kgrisham@getmail.net>
From:	Customer Service <custserve@zephyrcomputers.com>
Date:	October 12
Subject:	Your order

Thank you for choosing Zephyr Computers, the nation's largest online supplier of computer hardware. Items currently in stock ship within 48 hours. Your order can be tracked by visiting www.instantshipment.com/zephyr and entering your tracking number.

Tracking number: 78-90454-0430
Order number: HJ9300430
Date: October 12
Customer name: Karen Grisham
Billing address: 1920 Whitney Avenue, New Haven, CT 06501
Shipping address: (as above)
Purchase details: Kayman USB drive, 16MB
Status: in stock
Amount: $8.99 (w/free shipping*)
Billed to credit card number ending in 3940

Unopened items can be returned within 30 days of date of purchase for a full refund. Go to www.zephyrcomputers.com for our complete return policy.

*Special offer

156. What is true about Ms. Grisham's order?

(A) It was placed on October 10.
(B) It will be shipped to Zephyr Computers.
(C) It includes a free gift item.
(D) It should ship no later than October 14.

157. What is suggested about Zephyr Computers?

(A) It does not charge for shipping.
(B) It sells its products at many retail stores.
(C) It designs computer programs.
(D) It accepts payment by credit card.

TEST 09

▶ ▶ ▶ GO ON TO THE NEXT PAGE

```
                                                                    _ □ X
```

From:	Robert Navarro <rnavarro@diynetwork.com>
To:	Lena Rivers <lrivers@getmail.net>
Date:	November 2
Subject: Re:	My Order

Dear Ms. Rivers,

I am writing to let you know that one of the items (PM48994) from your order (#13849) is currently out of stock. — [1] — The other items have just been sent to you. We anticipate having the missing item in stock within 5-7 days. — [2] — As soon as it arrives at our warehouse, it will be sent directly to you via overnight shipping at no extra charge to you. Once the item ships, you will receive a notification and tracking number at this e-mail address.

— [3] — If you are not fully pleased with any purchase, return it within 30 days, and we will give you your money back. No questions asked. To learn more about our return and exchange policies, visit www.diynetwork.com.

To thank you for choosing DIY Network, we would like to offer you a 10% discount on your next order. — [4] — Simply use coupon code GET10 when you check out. The code can be used only one time.

Please let us know if you have any questions.

Sincerely,

Robert Navarro

158. Why did Mr. Navarro send the e-mail?

(A) To explain a delivery delay
(B) To request an additional payment
(C) To offer a replacement item
(D) To confirm receipt of a backorder

159. What is most likely true about Ms. Rivers?

(A) She will have to pay additional shipping costs.
(B) She will get a discount for item PM48994.
(C) She will get a refund for the missing item.
(D) She will receive two separate shipments.

160. In which of the positions marked [1], [2], [3], and [4] does the following sentence best belong?

"DIY Network values customer satisfaction."

(A) [1]
(B) [2]
(C) [3]
(D) [4]

May 14

Colin Hayes
793 Coulter Pace
Minneapolis, MN 55423

Dear Mr. Hayes,

I am pleased to inform you that the Gruber Corporation has agreed to hire you as a junior electrical engineer. Your official starting date is Monday, May 28. On that date, please report to your supervisor, David McGrath, in the Product Testing Department at 8:30 A.M. After meeting with Mr. McGrath, you need to see me to sign your contract. Please bring a valid proof of identification and your social security card. The mandatory new employee orientation is scheduled for Tuesday, June 5, from 8:30 A.M. to 4:30 P.M.

This is a twelve-month contract position renewable annually based on performance. The salary is $48,750 and will be paid bi-weekly. As a full-time position, it is eligible for standard company benefits: health insurance, dental insurance, vision plan, life insurance, retirement plan, paid vacation, paid sick leave, educational reimbursement, etc. You will receive additional details regarding the benefits package during the orientation. You will have 60 days from your starting date to enroll in some or all of the options.

If you have any questions about the position, please feel free to contact me at 224-8940.

Sincerely,

Mayra Greene
Assistant Director
Personnel Office

161. What is the purpose of the letter?

(A) To announce a promotion
(B) To modify an employment contract
(C) To make a job offer
(D) To recommend an employee

162. What is NOT mentioned about the benefits package?

(A) It is available to employees working full time.
(B) It will be explained on June 5.
(C) It includes insurance for a vehicle.
(D) It has a deadline for signing up.

163. What is suggested about Mr. Hayes?

(A) He completed an online application.
(B) He will be paid once a month.
(C) He must leave after working one year.
(D) He will go to the personnel office on Monday.

TEST 09

▶ ▶ ▶GO ON TO THE NEXT PAGE

Questions 164-167 refer to the online chat discussion.

Don Shemilt 8:52 A.M.	We have five weeks left before the contract with our office building's cleaning service expires. Paul Owens says he is satisfied with the company and plans to renew the contract, but he wants to hear your opinions.
Noah Morgan 8:54 A.M.	I know that we have only been working with Commercial Custodial for about six months, but the work crew used some pretty strong-smelling cleaners one time.
Betty Freidman 8:56 A.M.	That was a standard commercial cleaning product. After we told them that it was irritating some employees, they switched to a less pungent product. I have actually found them quite accommodating.
Noah Morgan 8:57 A.M.	Now that you mention it, they were responsive when one of my staff members asked them to do some extra dusting.
Betty Freidman 9:02 A.M.	We have a lot of new employees on the third floor. They sometimes forget to put recyclable materials in the correct waste disposal bin. Commercial Custodial has never complained about the extra work involved in correcting those mistakes.
Don Shemilt 9:07 A.M.	This is all very helpful. Thanks. How are things going on the fourth floor?
Jocelyn Rich 9:08 A.M.	No complaints for any one up here. The office space is cleaned regularly. When I stay late, I chat with one of the cleaning ladies. She is very friendly and seems to take her job seriously.
Don Shemilt 9:11 A.M.	Sounds like everyone is satisfied. I'll relay that to Paul.

Send

164. What is NOT mentioned about Commercial Custodial?

(A) It changed its cleaning chemicals.
(B) Its contract might be extended.
(C) It sorted trash properly.
(D) It has a lot of new staff members.

165. At 9:07 A.M., what does Mr. Shemilt most likely mean when he writes, "This is all very helpful"?

(A) He really likes the work the cleaners have done.
(B) He appreciates the feedback from the writers.
(C) He wants to train Mr. Friedman's staff.
(D) He is changing his opinion about Commercial Custodial.

166. What is indicated about Ms. Rich?

(A) She works overtime every day.
(B) She works in Mr. Shemilt's office.
(C) She is generally a serious person.
(D) She works on the fourth floor.

167. What does Mr. Shemilt plan to do?

(A) Share the responses with Mr. Owens
(B) Recommend hiring a new company
(C) Report problems to his manager
(D) Speak with the head of Commercial Custodial

▶ ▶ ▶GO ON TO THE NEXT PAGE

Masterson Whiteboards

Masterson is a global leader in the dry-erase and wet-erase whiteboard market. All of our whiteboard products are designed for durability and ease of use. Our products are used daily in corporations, universities, and hospitals around the world.

Masterson whiteboards are constructed of a scratch-resistant surface with a durable fiberglass backing and are housed in a lightweight but sturdy aluminum frame. Whiteboards can be ordered with or without a magnetic layer. In addition to standard sizes, Masterson can produce customized whiteboards to meet customer specifications. All of our whiteboard products can be easily mounted horizontally or vertically on most wall surfaces by using our adjustable mounting system. In addition, many of our standard-sized whiteboards can be mounted on our folding stands.

For best results, Masterson advises that only official Masterson products be used with our whiteboards. We manufacture a complete line of wet-erase and dry-erase markers in twelve colors and five sizes. In addition, we produce erasers, cleaning solutions, and surface restorations kits.

A complete list of our whiteboards and related products, along with their technical specifications and photographs, can be found on our Web site (www.masterson.com). To place an order, call our sales representatives at 1-888-456-0940.

168. What is the information mainly about?

(A) A new presentation technology
(B) The importance of an international company
(C) An overview of a company's products
(D) The process for placing an order

169. What is indicated about Masterson?

(A) It sells more than just whiteboards.
(B) It can mount whiteboards for customers.
(C) It offers lifetime warranties on its products.
(D) It has offices in many different countries.

170. What is mentioned about Masterson's Web site?

(A) It explains installation procedures.
(B) It provides pictures of its products.
(C) It gives directions to the company.
(D) It receives feedback from customers.

171. In the information, the word "housed" in paragraph 2, line 2 is closest in meaning to

(A) manufactured
(B) delivered
(C) completed
(D) placed

Questions 172-175 refer to the following article.

TARNTON (March 3) – For almost fifty years, residents of the Oak Park neighborhood have turned to Harrison Hardware for their home maintenance needs. People have been saying that it was going to shut its doors, but owner Tom Carrol has finally stated publically that the business will be moving to a new part of the city this summer.

"I love Oak Park," said Mr. Carrol. "My best customers are my neighbors." The neighborhood has seen dozens of small businesses close in the past five years. — [1] — The closures have left stretches of several streets in the heart of the community empty. "We are the last business on our section of Ivy Street," explained Mr. Carrol. "Shoppers aren't coming from other parts of the city anymore, and that's hurting business. It's our loyal local customers keeping us afloat."

— [2] — He says he is getting ready to retire in the next few years. "I learned this business from my father, and now I am ready to pass it on to my son-in-law, Alex Romansky."

While a new location has not yet been announced, Mr. Carrol says he is looking at buildings nearby since he lives in Oak Park. "Alex is helping me with this transition," added Mr. Carrol. — [3] — "This is a big step for him, and I hope it prepares him to take over when I am finally ready to sell."

In addition, Harrison Hardware plans to invest more in the online side of its business, which it launched last year. — [4] — The expectation is that the new store will handle more online sales while still offering exceptional service to its local customers.

172. What is the article mainly about?

(A) A rise in Internet commerce
(B) A business preparing to relocate
(C) A city's plan for growth
(D) A neighborhood in decline

173. What is indicated about Oak Park?

(A) It is where Mr. Carrol will move.
(B) It has fewer stores than in the past.
(C) It no longer has a demand for hardware.
(D) It is not a popular tourist attraction.

174. What is suggested about Mr. Romansky?

(A) He has lived his whole life in Tarnton.
(B) He is the head manager at Harrison Hardware.
(C) He is considering buying Harrison Hardware.
(D) He recently started working with Mr. Carrol.

175. In which of the positions marked [1], [2], [3], and [4] does the following sentence best belong?

"It's not just economics that has driven Mr. Carrol's decision."

(A) [1]
(B) [2]
(C) [3]
(D) [4]

▶ ▶ ▶ GO ON TO THE NEXT PAGE

Draft

Plant a Tree for the Future!

The Green City Initiative would like to invite you to attend our twelfth annual Arbor Day celebration in Glendale's Gateway Park on Saturday, April 18, from 11 A.M. to 4 P.M. This fun and educational event features speakers, workshops, games, and live performances. Dozens of local vendors will be on hand selling food, art, clothing, and more. Everyone attending will receive a free pine or oak sapling, which can be planted in a special area of the park or at home. Sponsored by several area businesses and community groups, this family-friendly event is free and open to the public. For more information, visit www.greencity.org.

From:	Andrew Gates <agates@greencity.org>
To:	Mayra Olivas <molivas@jetmail.net>
Date:	March 27
Subject:	Performers

Mayra,

I just reviewed the announcement you drafted for this year's Arbor Day event. Everything looks fine. I will send it to the printer tomorrow.

Before our April 2 planning meeting, can you call the performers and verify their schedules? We want the correct information on the Web site.

Performer	Time	Location
Jugglers	all day	Wandering
Face Painting	all day	Picnic Area
Storytellers	12:45 P.M.	Dawson Creek Stage
Irish Dancers	1:00 P.M.	Bandstand
The Soda Crackers	2:15 P.M.	Dawson Creek Stage
Dan's Big Band	3:00 P.M.	Bandstand

I really appreciate all the hard work you and the other volunteers have put into helping me organize this year's event. I'm looking forward to meeting all of your families at the event.

Thanks.

Andrew

176. What will be given away at the Arbor Day celebration?

(A) Tickets
(B) Food
(C) Trees
(D) Money

177. What is NOT mentioned about the celebration?

(A) It has been held in the past.
(B) It has local sponsors.
(C) Tickets can be purchased online.
(D) Food can be bought there.

178. What is the purpose of the e-mail?

(A) To delegate tasks to a volunteer
(B) To place an order for printing
(C) To communicate a schedule change
(D) To inquire about availability

179. In the e-mail, the word "drafted" in paragraph 1, line 1 is closest in meaning to

(A) advertised
(B) wrote
(C) reported
(D) performed

180. When will Mr. Gates meet Ms. Olivas's family?

(A) On March 27
(B) On March 28
(C) On April 2
(D) On April 18

▶ ▶ ▶ GO ON TO THE NEXT PAGE

Questions 181-185 refer to the following e-mail and schedule.

_ □ X

FROM:	Kalib Schwan (kalib.schwan@luckman.com)
TO:	Sales Team (salesteam@luckman.com)
SUBJECT:	Upcoming Retreat
DATE:	March 19
ATTACHMENT:	schedule

Greetings!

I am sure that all of you are as excited as I am about the upcoming retreat at Whispering Pines. This will be our first time to hold the event at this location; however, Sam Richards attended an event there last year and spoke very highly of the facilities and staff.

Gary Bane in Transportation has agreed to provide us with company vans and cars. I urge you to sign up as a driver or passenger as soon as possible. Signup sheets are on my desk. Drivers have to provide a copy of their driver's license to Gary before they can receive keys.

The weather can be cool in the mountains this time of year. So everyone is advised to bring warm clothing, especially hats and gloves for the rope course. Dress is casual for both days. I am told comfortable walking shoes are a good idea. Whispering Pines has walking trails and gardens you can enjoy in your free time.

Please review the attached schedule and print a copy for our trip. If you have any questions, contact our company's event coordinator, Paul Orpheus, at 555-6998.

I look forward to seeing you all at the retreat!

Sincerely,

Kalib

Sales Team Annual Retreat

March 26 – 27
Whispering Pines Convention Center and Hotel
Conestoga, PA 19040

Friday, March 26
11:00 A.M.   Assemble in Room 180 for Lodging Assignments*
11:30 A.M.   Depart Luckman Headquarters
1:00 P.M.   Arrive Whispering Pines

1:30 P.M.	Lunch and Welcome
2:30 P.M.	Team Orientations
4:30 P.M.	Unscheduled Time
6:30 P.M.	Dinner

Saturday, March 27

8:00 A.M.	Breakfast
8:45 A.M.	Tour of Grounds
9:00 A.M.	Training Seminar
10:00 A.M.	Team Exercises
11:30 A.M.	Rope Course
12:30 P.M.	Lunch
1:30 P.M.	Team A Presentation
2:15 P.M.	Team B Presentation
3:00 P.M.	Break
3:15 P.M.	Team C Presentation
4:00 P.M.	Closing Remarks
4:30 P.M.	Depart Whispering Pines
6:00 P.M.	Arrive Luckman Headquarters

*Private rooms not available. Doubles only.

181. What are sales team members advised to do?

(A) Bring electronic devices
(B) Prepare for wet weather
(C) Wear business attire
(D) Travel in company vehicles

182. Who will most likely go to Conestoga in March?

(A) Kalib Schwan
(B) Sam Richards
(C) Gary Bane
(D) Paul Orpheus

183. What is suggested about the schedule?

(A) Employees can choose their teams.
(B) Employees will help prepare food.
(C) Employees have to share hotel rooms.
(D) Employees will remain indoors for the entire event.

184. When will employees most likely be able to explore the gardens?

(A) On Friday at 1:00 P.M.
(B) On Friday at 4:30 P.M.
(C) On Saturday at 9:00 A.M.
(D) On Saturday at 11:30 A.M.

185. What is NOT indicated about the retreat?

(A) It will take place over two days.
(B) It features an evening tour.
(C) It is held every year.
(D) It has scheduled meals.

▶ ▶ ▶ GO ON TO THE NEXT PAGE

http://www.alpahemployment.com/home/aboutus

| Home | Job Seekers | Employers | Resources |

Alpha Employment Agency

We were founded in 1995 and have become the largest employment agency serving clients in the greater Marston area for decades. We fill an average of 2,000 positions a year in health care, manufacturing, transportation, retail, office, and other settings.

Looking for a job?
We are here to help. Complete our online application and upload supporting documentation onto our secure Web site. We will notify you as soon as positions you qualify for become available. There is no charge for this service.

Looking for employees?
Provide us with your needs, and we will only send applicants meeting your minimum qualifications. We will send their application materials and set up the interviews. We will bill you only if you agree to hire a candidate referred by us.

STAFFING REQUEST FORM

POSITION

Job title: *Airport Shuttle Bus Driver*
Position type: [✓] temporary [ ] part-time [ ] full-time
Hours: *6:00 A.M. – 1:00 P.M., Tuesday through Friday*
Education/Credentials: *High school diploma or higher; commercial driver's license preferred*
Experience: *Three months in the same or related position*
Duties: *Pick up and drop off passengers at correct destinations; load and unload passengers' luggage (up to 100 kilograms); communicate with parking lot crew at airport; keep accurate daily activity log and submit weekly*
Location: *Franklin*
Other Information: *Position may be made permanent after a three-month review; benefits available at that time*
How did you hear about us? *Saw advertisement in Franklin Register*

EMPLOYER

Company: *Jetside Airport Parking*
Contact: *Molly Ringer*
Phone: *(410) 555-2903*
Email: *molly.ringer@jetsideparking.com*

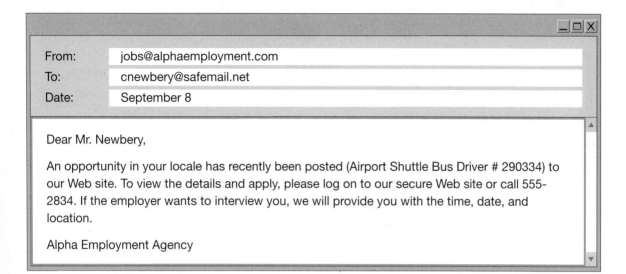

From: jobs@alphaemployment.com
To: cnewbery@safemail.net
Date: September 8

Dear Mr. Newbery,

An opportunity in your locale has recently been posted (Airport Shuttle Bus Driver # 290334) to our Web site. To view the details and apply, please log on to our secure Web site or call 555-2834. If the employer wants to interview you, we will provide you with the time, date, and location.

Alpha Employment Agency

---

186. What is NOT mentioned about the Alpha Employment Agency?

(A) It prefers to work directly with hiring managers.
(B) It places workers in a variety of industries.
(C) It collects information from job seekers.
(D) It has been operating for many years.

187. What is indicated about the shuttle bus driver position?

(A) It entails coordinating with airport employees.
(B) It involves working on weekends.
(C) It offers health insurance benefits right away.
(D) It requires obtaining a special license.

188. What is suggested about Ms. Ringer?

(A) She will certainly hire Mr. Newbery.
(B) She will receive adequately skilled applicants.
(C) She will contact job applicants personally.
(D) She will conduct phone interviews.

189. Why did Alpha contact Mr. Newbery?

(A) To confirm receipt of an application
(B) To tell him about a job opening
(C) To schedule an interview
(D) To remind him to submit a document

190. What is most likely NOT true about Mr. Newberry?

(A) He is able to work mornings.
(B) He paid Alpha Employment.
(C) He can lift heavy bags.
(D) He lives in Franklin.

▶ ▶ ▶GO ON TO THE NEXT PAGE

MEMO

To: All Sales Department Staff Members
From: Gordon Mosher, Vice President of Sales
Date: April 10

Next month, TrackPro, the company that makes our new inventory software, will be in Williamsport. Its experienced trainers are coming all the way from the company's headquarters in Jefferson City to lead a one-day workshop. I was able to get TrackPro to hold four spaces in the workshop for Sigma employees. Other local companies will be sending select employees as well.

Sigma will cover all fees for the training and reimburse travel expenses. Those chosen to attend must give a presentation about Numera at the next department meeting.

If you would like to be considered for the workshop, send me a letter listing your qualifications. The letter should also explain how the department will benefit by investing in your skills. Send it to me by April 20. The names of the attendees will be announced on May 1.

Numera Training

Date: Friday, May 23
Time: 8:00 A.M. – 4:30 P.M,
Location: Williamsport Convention Center, Room 205

8:00 A.M.	Welcome (Presenter: Doug Popovich)
8:15 A.M.	Mastering the basics of Numera (Presenter: Tim Song)
10:00 A.M.	Using Numera's advanced functions (Presenter: Jill Yen)
11:45 A.M.	LUNCH BREAK (Lunch included)
12:15 P.M.	Addressing hardware/software conflicts issues (Presenter: Norma Lee)
2:30 P.M.	Creating customized reports (Presenter: Doug Popovich)
4:00 P.M.	Q&A (All presenters)

Participants will receive an official certificate of completion from TrackPro.

To:	Betina Richards <brichards@wagogo.com>
From:	Kim Jordan <kjordan@sigmatechnologies.com>
Date:	Tuesday, May 27

Dear Betina,

It was nice to meet you at the Numera workshop last week. I was surprised that you and your colleagues at Wagogo are having some of the same issues with the software that we experience at Sigma.

The presentation by Ms. Yen was extremely useful. I like that she taught us how to adjust the view when checking product availability. I followed her directions, but I can't remember how to save the changes. I wonder if you took notes on that detail. If so, could you tell me how to do it?

Best,

Kim

191. In the memo, the word "hold" in paragraph 1, line 3 is closest in meaning to

(A) grasp
(B) host
(C) own
(D) reserve

192. What is suggested about Mr. Song?

(A) He was recently hired by TrackPro.
(B) He traveled for the May 23 training.
(C) He organizes workshops for TrackPro.
(D) He distributed notes to participants.

193. Why did Ms. Jordan send the e-mail?

(A) To schedule a meeting
(B) To provide feedback
(C) To ask for assistance
(D) To recommend some training

194. What is implied about Ms. Jordan?

(A) She wrote to Mr. Mosher.
(B) She led a workshop.
(C) She is a sales manager.
(D) She used to work at Wagogo.

195. At what time did Ms. Richards most likely learn about making adjustments to the view in Numera?

(A) At 8:15 A.M.
(B) At 10:00 A.M.
(C) At 12:15 P.M.
(D) At 2:30 P.M.

▶ ▶ ▶ GO ON TO THE NEXT PAGE

http://www.dominorecords.com/

Domino Records				
ABOUT US	ARTISTS	NEWS	SHOP	SUBSCRIBE

Domino Records

Domino Records began when Chuck Miller started recording local musicians in 1943 in his small studio in Queens, New York. We have since grown into one of the largest and best-known jazz labels in the world. With main offices in New York, London, and Tokyo, we are now at the forefront of bringing great music from the jazz tradition and beyond to customers in 26 countries. Artists who have chosen Domino include Sam Harris, The Golden Trio, and Skip Tracer. We signed world-famous vocalist Betty Raygun in June. In addition to our new releases, we maintain a catalog of original recordings going back to our founding days, many of which are still available for purchase.

Easton Times   Wednesday, December 1

Bright Lights, Betty Raygun

Her voice has been described as smooth as silk, and, as any serious jazz fan knows, Betty Raygun always sings with passion. This is evident, once again, on her newest recording 'Bright Lights' with her new company. Despite the title, the eight songs on this album touch on themes of loss, longing, and regret. Perhaps she was recalling her years spent in Paris as a young music student. This album will appeal both to her diehard fans and many who are not yet familiar with her earlier work. That crossover appeal may help explain her decision to go on tour with hip-hop artists To Go Bros. They will hit the road in January for twenty-two stops across the country. — *Shawn Price*

From:	Ed O'Neal
To:	Kate Magus
Date:	December 2
Subject:	New Music

Kate,

Yesterday, I read a review about a jazz singer named Betty Raygun. She is touring soon with one of my favorite bands. That made me curious, so I downloaded one of her tracks, "Downtown", for free at www.soundvoyage.com. The song is amazing! I suggest you check it out. All of the other songs on her new album are just as good. If you like what you hear, maybe we could buy her new CD and play it for our customers in the coffee shop.

Ed

196. What is mentioned about Domino Records?

(A) It only records jazz musicians.
(B) It moved its headquarters.
(C) It was founded by Mr. Miller.
(D) It only sells music online.

197. What is most likely true about 'Bright Lights'?

(A) It was produced in Tokyo.
(B) It was released on Domino.
(C) It is Ms. Raygun's debut album.
(D) It is considered a hip-hop album.

198. What is NOT indicated about Ms. Raygun?

(A) She studied in Paris.
(B) She is an acclaimed artist.
(C) She will be traveling next year.
(D) She has recorded eight albums.

199. What is suggested about Mr. O'Neal?

(A) He is a fan of To Go Bros.
(B) He has seen Ms. Raygun live.
(C) He subscribed to Easton Times in December.
(D) He plans to open a coffee shop.

200. What is one reason Mr. O'Neal sent the e-mail to Ms. Magus?

(A) To order a music recording
(B) To tell about a new Web site
(C) To promote an upcoming tour
(D) To recommend a song

▶ ▶ ▶GO ON TO THE NEXT PAGE

Test 09 정답

147. (A)	**148.** (C)	**149.** (C)	**150.** (D)	**151.** (C)	**152.** (D)
153. (B)	**154.** (C)	**155.** (B)	**156.** (D)	**157.** (D)	**158.** (A)
159. (D)	**160.** (C)	**161.** (C)	**162.** (C)	**163.** (D)	**164.** (D)
165. (B)	**166.** (D)	**167.** (A)	**168.** (C)	**169.** (A)	**170.** (B)
171. (D)	**172.** (B)	**173.** (B)	**174.** (C)	**175.** (B)	**176.** (C)
177. (C)	**178.** (A)	**179.** (B)	**180.** (D)	**181.** (D)	**182.** (A)
183. (C)	**184.** (B)	**185.** (B)	**186.** (A)	**187.** (A)	**188.** (B)
189. (B)	**190.** (B)	**191.** (D)	**192.** (B)	**193.** (C)	**194.** (A)
195. (B)	**196.** (C)	**197.** (B)	**198.** (D)	**199.** (A)	**200.** (D)

TEST

10

| 시작 시간 ___시 ___분 | 목표 개수 _____ / 54 |
| 종료 시간 ___시 ___분 | 실제 개수 _____ / 54 |

· 반드시 55분 안에 문제 풀이 포함 마킹까지 마쳐야 합니다.

· 실제 시험이라고 생각하고 멈추지 말고 풀어보세요.

· 정답 개수에 5를 곱하면 대략적인 점수가 됩니다.

Directions: In this part you will read a selection of texts, such as magazine and newspaper articles, e-mails, and instant messages. Each text or set of texts is followed by several questions. Select the best answer for each question and mark the letter (A), (B), (C), or (D) on your answer sheet.

Questions 147-148 refer to the following announcement.

Shipley's is coming to Branford!

"Fresh Produce, Great Food"

Join us on Monday, July 1, for the grand opening of our newest location
at 478 State Street in Branford, CT.

The first 50 customers will receive a free reusable shopping bag!

Grand Opening Specials (June 1 – June 7)

Sweet white peaches $0.99/lb
Jumbo seedless watermelons only $3.99 each
Juicy tangerines $0.79/lb
Granola (select varieties) $1.99/lb
Dried fruit and nut mixes $2.99 and up

Parking is available along State Street and in the lot behind the store.

147. What will happen on July 1?

(A) Vegetables will be sold at a discount.
(B) Sale items will no longer be available.
(C) A store will open at a new location.
(D) A new parking lot will open.

148. What is indicated about Shipley's?

(A) It specializes in gourmet foods.
(B) It has gifts for some customers.
(C) It has other stores in Branford.
(D) It is currently hiring employees.

▶ ▶ ▶GO ON TO THE NEXT PAGE

Even with today's high levels of unemployment, some professions are in high demand. Nursing is a prime example. Since 1999, the demand for nurses has spiked as the population has, on average, grown older. In the meantime, fewer people entering the field have resulted in shortages of nurses at some hospitals and medical facilities. In fact, employers frequently offer cash bonuses of $2,000 or more to attract new hires. Training to enter the field can be completed in as little as 3 to 6 months for nursing assistant positions.

149. According to the article, what is one cause of the nurse shortage?

(A) The demand for nurses is decreasing.
(B) Not enough people are becoming nurses.
(C) Few people will accept the low pay.
(D) Many experienced nurses are retiring.

150. What is needed to become a nursing assistant?

(A) Finishing several months of study
(B) Getting sponsorship from a medical facility
(C) Earning a college degree
(D) Obtaining a specialized license

Questions 151-152 refer to the following text message chain.

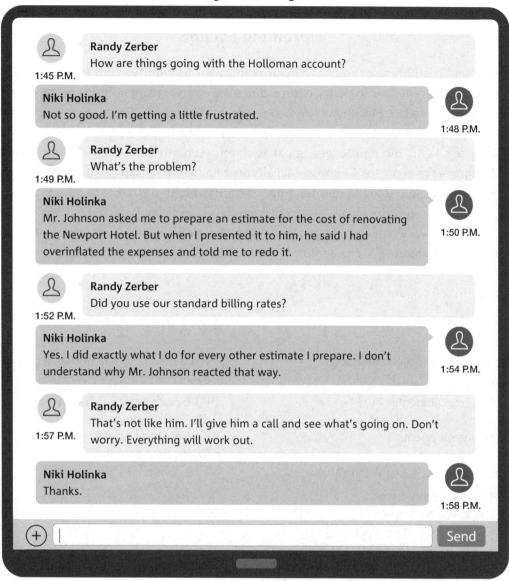

Randy Zerber 1:45 P.M.
How are things going with the Holloman account?

Niki Holinka 1:48 P.M.
Not so good. I'm getting a little frustrated.

Randy Zerber 1:49 P.M.
What's the problem?

Niki Holinka 1:50 P.M.
Mr. Johnson asked me to prepare an estimate for the cost of renovating the Newport Hotel. But when I presented it to him, he said I had overinflated the expenses and told me to redo it.

Randy Zerber 1:52 P.M.
Did you use our standard billing rates?

Niki Holinka 1:54 P.M.
Yes. I did exactly what I do for every other estimate I prepare. I don't understand why Mr. Johnson reacted that way.

Randy Zerber 1:57 P.M.
That's not like him. I'll give him a call and see what's going on. Don't worry. Everything will work out.

Niki Holinka 1:58 P.M.
Thanks.

Send

151. What is suggested about Ms. Holinka?

(A) She made a mistake in her calculations.
(B) She has worked with Holloman before.
(C) She prepared a quote in the regular way.
(D) She turned in her estimate late.

152. At 1:57 P.M., what does Mr. Zerber most likely mean when he writes, "That's not like him"?

(A) He thinks Mr. Johnson was acting strangely.
(B) He suspects Mr. Johnson does not like the project.
(C) He thinks Mr. Johnson disapproves of his work.
(D) He believes Mr. Johnson was being reasonable.

▶ ▶ ▶ GO ON TO THE NEXT PAGE

Upcoming Events

Happy New Year! Many of you have made resolutions to improve your health. Whether it is to lose ten pounds or to exercise three times a week, we want to help you reach your goal. Joins us for a free Health and Wellness Fair on Wednesday, February 8, from 11:00 A.M. to 3:00 P.M. in the 2nd floor atrium. Learn about the health and wellness resources available to all Dili, Inc. employees. Speak with representatives from Blue Star insurance, St. Margaret's hospital, Total Fitness, Mega Nutrition, Sarah's Natural Foods, and more. Get a health checkup (blood pressure, pulse, height, weight, BMI). Learn how to cook simple, delicious, healthy meals. Students from the Gates School of Culinary Arts will be giving lessons every half hour. Register to win a visit to the Bamboo Spa, dinner for two at Manny's, and more. For more information, call Sherry Wilson at 555-3112.

We hope to see you there!

153. For whom is this event intended?

(A) Healthcare workers
(B) Potential students
(C) Employees at Dili, Inc.
(D) Insurance agents

154. Who most likely is Ms. Wilson?

(A) The newsletter editor
(B) The event organizer
(C) A nurse at St. Margaret's
(D) An employee at the Bamboo Spa

155. What is NOT mentioned as a part of the event?

(A) Blood pressure checks
(B) A prize drawing
(C) Cooking classes
(D) Product samples

Questions 156-157 refer to the following receipt.

Gordon's
78 Mithos Road
Edgewood, NM 89943
(505) 555-5673

Date: July 28
Register #: 4
Cashier: Jason Smith

Item Code	Description	Quantity	Price
05642	Jump rope	1	$5.00
29045	Exercise shorts	2	$26.00
03434	Runner's tank-top	3	$30.00
54455	Sneakers (clearance)	1	$85.00

Subtotal: $146.00
Tax: $10.22
Total: $156.22
Paid: $160.00
Change: ($3.78)

Thank you for shopping at Gordon's!

Items may be returned for store credit within 30 days with a receipt.
*No returns on clearance items.

156. What is Gordon's?

(A) A convenience store
(B) A shoe store
(C) A sporting goods store
(D) A fitness center

157. What is NOT indicated on the receipt?

(A) The customer used a coupon.
(B) The customer was served by Mr. Smith.
(C) The sneakers cannot be returned.
(D) The customer received some money.

▶ ▶ ▶GO ON TO THE NEXT PAGE

From:	Lionel Opher <lionel@excelcatering.com>
To:	Kim Reininger <kim.reininger@hopesprings.com>
Subject:	Installation Contract
Date:	March 2

Dear Ms. Reininger,

It was a pleasure speaking with you yesterday. The plans you have for your company's upcoming awards banquet are quite impressive. — [1] — I'm sure your colleagues will enjoy it. I want to let you know that I talked with my partner and that we would be more than happy to prepare the custom-made desserts for your event.

Let me take a moment to review your request. You would like us to make a large cake to serve all ninety-five guests. It will be almond flavored with buttercream icing. You would also like us to decorate it with the floral pattern you provided and to write your company's name across the front. — [2] —

The order will be delivered to the Mihalski Hotel on Saturday, December 3, no later than 3:00 P.M. The contact person there is Derek Turner (555-3403). — [3] —

Please let me know if the above information is correct or if any changes need to be made. — [4] —

Sincerely,

Lionel Opher

---

158. Why was the e-mail sent?

(A) To accept an invitation
(B) To reschedule a delivery
(C) To confirm a request
(D) To place an order

159. What is NOT indicated about Ms. Reininger's event?

(A) It will include her coworkers.
(B) It will be held at a restaurant.
(C) It will have fewer than 100 attendees.
(D) It will take place on a weekend.

160. In which of the positions marked [1], [2], [3], and [4] does the following sentence best belong?

"In addition, your company's logo will be placed on top."

(A) [1]
(B) [2]
(C) [3]
(D) [4]

Questions 161-163 refer to the following letter.

King Heating Oil
894 Green Street
Baltimore, MD 21231

March 7

Susan Miller
2894 Reisterstown Road
Owings Mills, MD 21283

Dear Ms. Miller,

I am writing to inform you that the payment you sent on March 3 was received. However, the amount sent was less than the balance due for the heating oil delivered to your home on February 19. We received your payment of $159.65 toward the balance of $195.65. If you wish to avoid a late fee of $25, please pay the remaining balance of $36.00 by March 15. Payments may be made at our administrative office, sent by mail, or posted via our secure Web site at www.kingheatingoil.com. We accept credit cards, personal checks, money orders, and electronic funds transfers (EFT) from valid bank accounts. As of January 1 this year, we no longer accept cash payments.

If you have any questions or concerns about this matter, feel free to contact me.

Sincerely,

Fred Parker
Account Technician
(410) 555-0367
fparker@kingheatingoil.com

161. What is the purpose of the letter?

(A) To refund money
(B) To make an inquiry
(C) To negotiate a price
(D) To request a payment

162. How much was the total cost of the heating oil?

(A) $25.00
(B) $36.00
(C) $159.65
(D) $195.65

163. What is suggested about King Heating Oil?

(A) It delivered the wrong amount of oil.
(B) It used to let customers pay with cash.
(C) It has several locations in Baltimore.
(D) It sent Ms. Miller an incorrect bill.

▶ ▶ ▶GO ON TO THE NEXT PAGE

TEST 10

Questions 164-167 refer to the following online chat discussion.

🔵	**Tom Jones** 9:48 A.M.	I just got the quarterly figures from district headquarters. Our new menu and promotions have driven sales through the roof! I'm sure all of you have been quite busy. Can you give me a short report on each location?
🔵	**Lynn Westerberg** 9:49 A.M.	Busy is an understatement. We have seen sales increase by 125% this past month. Thank goodness I hired a new cook and two servers a few weeks back.
🔵	**Tom Jones** 9:52 A.M.	That's great for Bleecher Avenue! How about 98th Street?
🔵	**Josh Phan** 9:53A.M.	Like Lynn, we've been super busy. Our main issue is that we keep running low on supplies. I have had to use my own money to buy flour, oil, and a few other things.
🔵	**Vijay Rao** 9:55 A.M.	I hope you have been getting reimbursed for that.
🔵	**Josh Phan** 9:58 A.M.	I put in a request, but I am still waiting for approval from our district manager. He said he would get back to me in two weeks.
🔵	**Vijay Rao** 10:01 A.M.	Maybe we could send you some of our extra supplies. Things aren't as busy at Oliver Road as at your location.
🔵	**Josh Phan** 10:04 A.M.	I'd be up for that.
🔵	**Lynn Westerberg** 10:06 A.M.	That's only a temporary solution. You really need a bigger budget.
🔵	**Josh Phan** 10:07 A.M.	I'm not sure district headquarters would authorize that even if I asked them.
🔵	**Tom Jones** 10:08 A.M.	Let me see what I can do.

164. Where do the writers most likely work?

(A) At a food distributor
(B) At a warehouse
(C) At a restaurant chain
(D) At a factory cafeteria

165. What is indicated about the Bleecher Avenue location?

(A) Its customers are very loyal.
(B) It recently hired additional employees.
(C) Its employees are dissatisfied.
(D) It still needs additional supplies.

166. Why did Mr. Phan contact the district manager?

(A) To propose a reassignment
(B) To place an order for food
(C) To ask for repayment
(D) To file a complaint

167. At 10:08 A.M., why does Mr. Jones write, "Let me see what I can do"?

(A) To offer to work at the 98th Street location
(B) To encourage Mr. Phan to speak with a manager
(C) To suggest he can pick up supplies
(D) To offer to help obtain more money

Memo

To: All Building Operations Employees
From: Leonard Piot
Date: January 15
Subject: Annual Performance Evaluations

Starting next week, I will begin scheduling annual performance evaluations. As in the past, evaluations will be done one on one with me and will take between thirty minutes and an hour to complete, depending on the responsibilities of the individual employee. Evaluations will begin next month and continue through April. I will make every effort to schedule evaluations to minimize disruptions in each section. However, supervisors should prepare for temporary staff absences.

Please be aware that some changes have been made to this year's performance evaluation process. Employees are now required to submit documentation for all training completed during the period under evaluation and for any new certifications or licenses obtained. In addition, several new criteria have been added to the performance evaluation form. Details of these are explained in an online training module.

Employees are strongly advised to view the online training module developed by the Human Resources (HR) Department to assist in preparing for their review. Click on the "Online Trainings" link. The "Annual Performance Evaluation Preparation Training" module can be found there.

All employees at the Viro Corporation are required to participate in a performance evaluation annually. If you have any questions about the company policy, contact Michael Parker in HR at extension 478.

---

168. What is the purpose of the memo?

(A) To confirm an evaluation
(B) To explain a process
(C) To introduce a new Web site
(D) To schedule meetings

169. The word "documentation" in paragraph 2, line 2 is closest in meaning to

(A) records
(B) videos
(C) notices
(D) permission

170. What is NOT indicated about the performance evaluations?

(A) They differ from last year.
(B) They take an hour or less.
(C) They include an online exam.
(D) They will commence in February.

171. What is suggested about Mr. Piot?

(A) He developed new performance evaluation procedures.
(B) He will meet with all of the employees in his department.
(C) He has already had his performance evaluated.
(D) He works for the Human Resources Department.

▶ ▶ ▶ GO ON TO THE NEXT PAGE

http://www.vacationguide.com

Based on your search criteria and profile, we recommend the following:

If you are planning a visit to Bright Mountain National Park, consider renting a cabin in Grizzly Gulch. — [1] —. There, you can stay in a rustic cabin deep in the forest to experience nature at its best. All twenty-eight cabins are tastefully decorated and offer modern amenities like fully equipped kitchens, adjustable heating and cooling units, satellite TV, and Wi-Fi. Most cabins also have covered porches if you prefer to sit outside to take in the views and to watch the wildlife. Lodging options for single guests to parties of a dozen or more are available.

The cabins are privately owned and managed by the town of Grizzly Gulch. Unlike cabins run by the park itself, you are able to make reservations up to three months in advance.
— [2] —. Please be aware, however, that a sizable deposit is required. Moreover, it is not refundable in the event of a cancelation.

The Grizzly Gulch cabins are twelve miles outside the park's southern entrance, making it very convenient for visitors interested in exploring that section of the park. — [3] —. It's a suitable jumping-off point for visiting the northern half of the park as well, but be prepared for a considerable drive before you actually reach the most popular sights there.

If you choose to stay at the Grizzly Gulch cabins, be prepared to either make your own food or to eat out. — [4] —. This is strictly a do-it-yourself option, but a very pleasant one nonetheless.

148 readers found this review useful

172. What is a purpose of the Web page?

(A) To promote a local sight
(B) To evaluate a lodging option
(C) To request customer feedback
(D) To criticize a hotel company

173. What is NOT mentioned about the Grizzly Gulch cabins?

(A) They are located in a national park.
(B) They have cooking facilities.
(C) They are run by a municipality.
(D) They can accommodate groups.

174. What is suggested about Bright Mountain National Park?

(A) It takes reservations for camping.
(B) It has two famous sights.
(C) It has multiple entrances.
(D) It requires a refundable deposit.

175. In which of the positions marked [1], [2], [3], and [4] does the following sentence best belong?

"No meals are included."

(A) [1]
(B) [2]
(C) [3]
(D) [4]

▶ ▶ ▶ GO ON TO THE NEXT PAGE

```
_ □ X
```

From:	Sandra Magsaysay <smagsaysay@pacificair.com>
To:	Alan Hao <alan.hao@coastaindustries.com>
Date:	October 18
Subject:	Your Membership

Dear Mr. Hao,

Thank you for enrolling in the Pacific Airlines frequent flyer club. Your account has been credited for all flights booked under your name in the current calendar year.

Member Number: 8300-534-9920
Preferred Flight Class: Business
Miles Flown: 27,000

Your Coastal Industries employee credit card (XXX-XXXX-3893) has been charged $19.99 for the one-time enrollment fee. If you wish to upgrade your membership level at any time, additional miles can be purchased at our Web site.

You should receive your membership card in the mail within 3-4 weeks. In the meantime, please print a copy of this e-mail. Use it as proof of membership when checking in and passing through airport security screenings.

If you have any questions, please contact our customer care line at 1-888-555-3000 or visit www.pacificair.com/frequentflyers.

Sincerely,

Sandra Magsaysay
Member Services

Pacific Airlines Frequent Flyer Club

We appreciate customer loyalty. As a way of saying thank you to our most loyal customers, we offer frequent flyer benefits at four levels.

Eligibility	Diamond	Platinum	Gold	Premier
Minimum miles flown*	40,000	30,000	20,000	10,000
Benefits				
Priority boarding	✓	✓	✓	✓
Earn bonus miles on travel-related purchases	✓	✓	✓	✓
Complimentary Wi-Fi	✓	✓	✓	

Access to VIP lounge	✓	✓	✓	
Can check in up to 3 bags	✓	✓		
Complimentary upgrades**	✓			

*Calculated based on current calendar year (January 1 – December 31)
**Based on availability at boarding time.

Pacific Airlines allows frequent flyer club members to upgrade their level by purchasing additional miles.

Miles Needed	Purchase fee
1 – 1,000	$179
1,001 – 2,000	$329
2,001 – 3,000	$479
3,001 – 4,000	$629
3,001 – 5,000	$779

176. What is suggested about Mr. Hao?

(A) He frequently flies to Asia.
(B) He renewed his membership.
(C) He is a first-time flyer on Pacific Airlines.
(D) He will receive his card in November.

177. What is Mr. Hao instructed to do?

(A) Use a copy of the e-mail to check in
(B) Register with airport security
(C) Upgrade his level immediately
(D) Make a credit card payment

178. What is indicated about the frequent flyer club membership levels?

(A) They are restricted to business and first-class flyers.
(B) Their benefits can only be applied at certain airports.
(C) They are based on the number of miles flown this year.
(D) They must be purchased before the start of the year.

179. What benefit is NOT currently available to Mr. Hao?

(A) Priority boarding
(B) Complimentary Wi-Fi
(C) Access to the VIP lounge
(D) Checking in three bags

180. How much must Mr. Hao pay to upgrade to the next membership level?

(A) $179.00
(B) $329.00
(C) $479.00
(D) $629.00

▶ ▶ ▶GO ON TO THE NEXT PAGE

TEST 10

Questions 181-185 refer to the following advertisement and e-mail.

Get Your Computer Checked by a Pro
Computer Pros, LLC.

Complete Computer Tune-Up Now $49.99 (Reg. 74.99)

Our Complete Tune-Up Includes:

• Scan for and remove viruses, spyware, and malware
• Clean up registry and remove unnecessary files and programs
• Scan and check hard drive (and defragment if needed)
• Streamline computer's startup and shutdown
• Update firewalls, antivirus software, and security programs (and install free versions when applicable)

You must mention this advertisement when scheduling your service to receive this rate.
Cannot be combined with other ads, coupons, or special offers.
Discount applicable for residential service only.
Offer expires November 30.

Ask us about this month's hardware and software deals!
We have laptops, USB drives, and more on sale!

help@computerpros.com
1-888-555-4040

To:	Computer Pros <help@computerpros.com>
FROM:	Allison Parker <aparker@topmail.com>
SUBJECT:	Service Appointment
Date:	Monday, November 14

Hi,

I would like to schedule a tune-up for my home computer at your special advertised rate. It is a two-year-old PC that, up until recently, had been hassle free. Sometime in September, I started to notice that my computer was slower than usual. Programs took a long time to open and close. A friend suggested that I run a free virus-removal program called SunClean. That seemed to help for a while at least, but then the computer started running slower again. To give you an example, it used to take less than 2 minutes for the computer to boot up or shut down. It now takes 5 minutes or longer! I am available to have my computer checked any morning this week before 10 A.M.

I would also like to know if you are offering any discounts on external hard drives this month. I am looking for a 500GB model that I can set up to back up files on my computer.

Thanks.

Allison Parker

181. What information is NOT included in the advertisement?

(A) The normal price of a service
(B) Contact information for a company
(C) Restrictions placed on an offer
(D) The types of computers serviced

182. What is indicated about the Complete Computer Tune-Up?

(A) It includes an inspection of other hardware.
(B) It can be used for mobile devices.
(C) It includes optional software installation.
(D) It will no longer be available in December.

183. What is true about Ms. Parker's computer?

(A) It was repaired by a friend.
(B) It is no longer working.
(C) It is unable to shut down.
(D) It has reduced performance.

184. In the e-mail, the phrase "hassle free" in paragraph 1, line 2 is closest in meaning to

(A) convenient
(B) up to date
(C) problematic
(D) complex

185. What is suggested about Ms. Parker?

(A) She works in the afternoon.
(B) She will be charged $49.99.
(C) Her computer lacks a hard drive.
(D) SunClean damaged her computer.

► ► ►GO ON TO THE NEXT PAGE

Questions 186-190 refer to following Web page, schedule, and e-mail.

HOME	EXHIBITS	CALENDAR	CONTACT US

Located in Waterbury, the Janus Museum of Art has some of the finest collections of North American art in the entire region. The museum was founded in 1898 by Herbert Janus to make his family's collection of art available for the public to enjoy.

Rotunda: Information Desk, Ticketing, Portraits
East Wing: Early American Art, American Modernism
West Wing: European Art, Asian Art, African Art
Annex: Sculpture Collection, Temporary Exhibits

Hours: Monday – Friday, 11:00 A.M. – 4:00 P.M. and Saturday, noon to 5:00 P.M.
Admission: $5, free for children under 5 years old

Janus Museum of Art

CALENDAR

August 7
Art Talk: "Watercolors: Past and Present" by Dr. Amanda Gaines
Pierce Auditorium 3:00 P.M.

August 11
Exhibit Opening: "Contemporary Urban Painters"
Annex: 1:00 P.M.

August 15
Art Talk: "Landscapes in Different Artistic Traditions" by Devon Roland
Pierce Auditorium: 3:00 P.M.

August 22
Meet the Artist: Jan Jansen, featured in "Contemporary Urban Painters"
Pierce Auditorium: 2:30 P.M.

Guided tours of select galleries are offered on a weekly basis and are included in the price of admission. Tours meet at the information desk and last approximately 50 minutes.

Tuesdays, 10 A.M.	European Art Gallery
Wednesday, 2 P.M.	Asian and African Art Galleries
Fridays, 1 P.M.	Sculpture Gallery
Saturdays, noon	American Art Galleries

Questions/Comments:
Contact our outreach and events coordinator, Paula Garcia (pgarcia@janus.org)

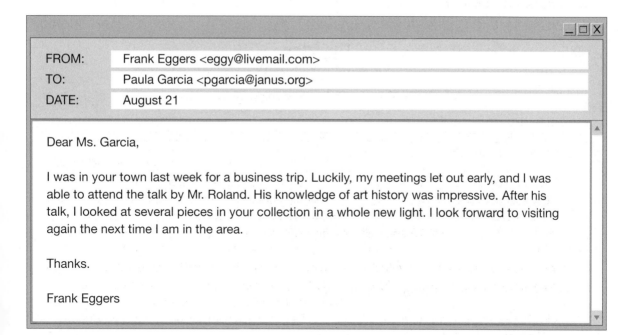

FROM: Frank Eggers <eggy@livemail.com>
TO: Paula Garcia <pgarcia@janus.org>
DATE: August 21

Dear Ms. Garcia,

I was in your town last week for a business trip. Luckily, my meetings let out early, and I was able to attend the talk by Mr. Roland. His knowledge of art history was impressive. After his talk, I looked at several pieces in your collection in a whole new light. I look forward to visiting again the next time I am in the area.

Thanks.

Frank Eggers

186. What is indicated about the museum?

(A) It offers discounts to seniors.
(B) It is open six days a week.
(C) It has a movie theater.
(D) It was founded by a famous artist.

187. What is true about the Saturday guided tour?

(A) It visits the museum's east wing.
(B) It is led by a museum curator.
(C) It is more than an hour long.
(D) It requires advance registration.

188. What is suggested about Ms. Garcia?

(A) She will lead a tour on Friday.
(B) She began working as a sculptor.
(C) Her work is displayed in the annex.
(D) She is a member of the museum's staff.

189. On what date did Mr. Eggers visit the museum?

(A) August 7
(B) August 11
(C) August 15
(D) August 22

190. In the e-mail, the word "light" in line 3 is closest in meaning to

(A) brightness
(B) gleam
(C) manner
(D) vision

▶ ▶ ▶ GO ON TO THE NEXT PAGE

TEST 10

The Edge

www.theedge.com

The Premier Online Shopping Club!

March Deals

Get 10% off any item of your choice.*	Download select music for up to 35% off our already low prices.
Buy one pair of Ace or Mile athletic shoes and get a second for half price.	Get a free The Edge key chain with any single purchase of $100 or more.**

The Edge is a members-only online shopping club. New offers every month. Join now and take advantage of these great deals. In addition, new members get free shipping on their first order (not applicable to returning members). Membership costs just $2 a month!***

Go to TheEdge.com to start shopping now!

*Applicable to a single transaction in March. Cannot be combined with any other offers or coupons.
**Limit one per customer.
***When you sign up for a three-month trial membership.

_ □ X

FROM:	Customer Service <custserv@theedge.com>
TO:	Norman Greer <norm.greer@ezmail.com>
DATE:	March 12

Dear Mr. Greer,

Welcome to The Edge! You are now part of an elite group of shoppers who have access to some of the best deals on the Web.

Thank you for signing up for a three-month trial membership. Your member number is 2890338. You can begin shopping right away. To take advantage of this month's specials, visit www.theedge.com. There, you need to create an account before you can make your first purchase. Simply enter your member number. Then, choose a username and password.

If at the end of your trial membership, you decide The Edge is for you, do nothing, and we will bill your credit card each month. After the trial period, you can cancel your membership at any time by contacting us. No questions asked.

We welcome member feedback. Feel free to drop us a line at custserv@theedge.com.

Sincerely,

The Edge

www.theedge.com

Order #: YU8495
Date: Friday, March 15
Member No.: 2890338

Ship to: Norman Greer
         222 Lily Lane
         Canton, OH 39034
Phone: (808) 555-9303

Shopping Cart

Quantity	Code	Item	Unit Price	Total
1	63343	Ace "Tiger" Sneakers	$58.00	$58.00
1	59856	Ace "Puma" Sneakers	$50.00	$25.00
1	35935	Rigo athletic shorts	$14.25	$14.25
1	90698	Rigo athletic top	$17.99	$17.99

Total: $115.24 billed to credit card ending in 7934

Your order has been processed. It will ship within the next 24 hours. Orders can be tracked at www.theedge.com/tracking.

Thank you for your purchase!

---

191. What is NOT mentioned in the advertisement?

(A) The specials are good for one month.
(B) New members can get discounted music.
(C) Coupon codes must be used when ordering.
(D) A one-time discount on anything is being offered.

192. What is Mr. Greer able to do in June?

(A) Obtain free shipping
(B) Receive a special coupon
(C) Request a refund of fees
(D) Terminate his membership

193. What is suggested about Mr. Greer?

(A) He was billed $6 for his membership.
(B) He provided suggestions via e-mail.
(C) He does all of his shopping online.
(D) He was formerly a member of The Edge.

194. What did Mr. Greer most likely do before making his March 15 purchase?

(A) He chose a new number.
(B) He contacted customer service.
(C) He set up an online account.
(D) He tracked a product.

195. What is most likely true about order YU8495?

(A) It was billed for shipping.
(B) It is eligible for a free gift.
(C) It included a 35% discount.
(D) It will arrive in a day.

▶ ▶ ▶GO ON TO THE NEXT PAGE

Online Training Now Available!
Desanti Corporation

The Desanti Corporation wants to ensure all of our employees have the most up-to-date knowledge and skills. That's why we have contracted with NetLearn to develop a series of online training modules. The first series will become available this fall.

Each training module focuses on a specific topic of utility in today's fast-changing workplace. Freed from the constraints of classrooms and instructors, the courses can be completed by employees at their own pace.

Sign up on the Talent Development Team's Web site: https://www.desanti.com/talentdevelopment.

Online Training Modules
Desanti Corporation

Group 1

OT 101: New Employee Orientation
This online course is a required follow-up to the face-to-face orientation session to introduce the company's Web site and Web-based programs. Only open to new hires.

OT 203: Leveraging Digital Technology
This hands-on course teaches you how to make the most of your smartphone or other digital devices. Learn ways to better manage time, communicate professionally, and more.

OT 301: Digital Security *
Learn company policy related to all matters digital: file storage, electronic communication, data transfer, and so forth.

OT 403: Staying Healthy in Cold and Flu Season
This module will teach you practical ways to protect yourself and others against illness.

*Either the online version or the classroom version of this training must be completed by all employees by December 31

Group 1 Training modules are available from September 10 to December 31. Employees will receive a certificate upon successful completion.

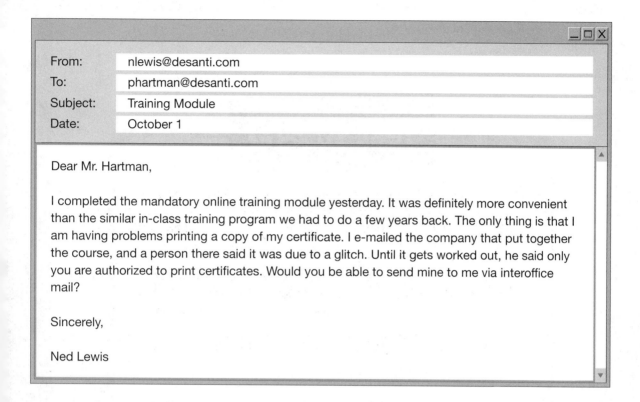

From: nlewis@desanti.com
To: phartman@desanti.com
Subject: Training Module
Date: October 1

Dear Mr. Hartman,

I completed the mandatory online training module yesterday. It was definitely more convenient than the similar in-class training program we had to do a few years back. The only thing is that I am having problems printing a copy of my certificate. I e-mailed the company that put together the course, and a person there said it was due to a glitch. Until it gets worked out, he said only you are authorized to print certificates. Would you be able to send mine to me via interoffice mail?

Sincerely,

Ned Lewis

196. In the announcement, why are readers referred to a Web site?

(A) To provide suggestions for training
(B) To reserve seats for an event
(C) To participate in an online survey
(D) To register for courses in a series

197. What is indicated about the training modules?

(A) They take several months to complete.
(B) Two of them teach about data entry.
(C) One is restricted to certain staff members.
(D) They are only available online.

198. Why did Mr. Lewis write to Mr. Hartman?

(A) To register for another course
(B) To request a copy of a document
(C) To complain about a company
(D) To report an inaccessible course

199. Which training module did Mr. Lewis finish?

(A) OT 101
(B) OT 203
(C) OT 301
(D) OT 403

200. What is suggested about Mr. Lewis?

(A) He contacted NetLearn.
(B) He works in Mr. Hartman's department.
(C) He is a new employee.
(D) He is a software engineer.

▶ ▶ ▶GO ON TO THE NEXT PAGE

Test 10 정답

147. (C)	**148.** (B)	**149.** (B)	**150.** (A)	**151.** (C)	**152.** (A)
153. (C)	**154.** (B)	**155.** (D)	**156.** (C)	**157.** (A)	**158.** (C)
159. (B)	**160.** (B)	**161.** (D)	**162.** (D)	**163.** (B)	**164.** (C)
165. (B)	**166.** (C)	**167.** (D)	**168.** (B)	**169.** (A)	**170.** (C)
171. (B)	**172.** (B)	**173.** (A)	**174.** (C)	**175.** (D)	**176.** (D)
177. (A)	**178.** (C)	**179.** (D)	**180.** (C)	**181.** (D)	**182.** (C)
183. (D)	**184.** (A)	**185.** (B)	**186.** (B)	**187.** (A)	**188.** (D)
189. (C)	**190.** (C)	**191.** (C)	**192.** (D)	**193.** (A)	**194.** (C)
195. (B)	**196.** (D)	**197.** (C)	**198.** (B)	**199.** (C)	**200.** (A)

TEST

11

55 min

시작 시간 ___시 ___분   목표 개수 _____ / 54

종료 시간 ___시 ___분   실제 개수 _____ / 54

- 반드시 55분 안에 문제 풀이 포함 마킹까지 마쳐야 합니다.
- 실제 시험이라고 생각하고 멈추지 말고 풀어보세요.   · 정답 개수에 5를 곱하면 대략적인 점수가 됩니다.

PART 7

Directions: In this part you will read a selection of texts, such as magazine and newspaper articles, e-mails, and instant messages. Each text or set of texts is followed by several questions. Select the best answer for each question and mark the letter (A), (B), (C), or (D) on your answer sheet.

Questions 147-148 refer to the following e-mail.

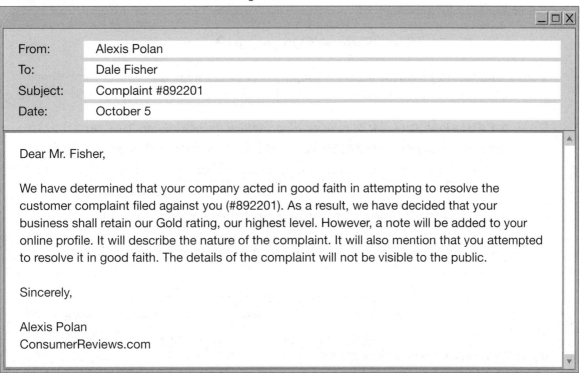

From:	Alexis Polan
To:	Dale Fisher
Subject:	Complaint #892201
Date:	October 5

Dear Mr. Fisher,

We have determined that your company acted in good faith in attempting to resolve the customer complaint filed against you (#892201). As a result, we have decided that your business shall retain our Gold rating, our highest level. However, a note will be added to your online profile. It will describe the nature of the complaint. It will also mention that you attempted to resolve it in good faith. The details of the complaint will not be visible to the public.

Sincerely,

Alexis Polan
ConsumerReviews.com

147. Why is Ms. Polan contacting Mr. Fisher?

(A) To alert him about a complaint
(B) To report a status upgrade
(C) To request additional information
(D) To explain the results of a decision

148. What is suggested about Mr. Fisher's company?

(A) It prepares product reviews for Ms. Polan.
(B) It tried to respond to an unhappy customer.
(C) It has received many complaints from customers.
(D) It only conducts business online.

▶ ▶ ▶ GO ON TO THE NEXT PAGE

Grover Towers

We currently have one-and two-bedroom apartments for rent
ranging from 70 to 90 square meters in area!

Choose from monthly or annual lease options.

$800 a month and up!
Reasonable security deposits.

Located minutes away from the highway, Grover Towers is in a quiet residential neighborhood.
Tenants can walk to a park, a shopping center, a bank, and a library.

Parking is available for all tenants at no additional charge in our gated lot.
Coin-operated washer and dryers are located on the ground floor.

The building manager is on site 24 hours a day to provide assistance.

Photographs and floor plans can be viewed at www.grovertowers.com.

Call the building manager at 555-0303 to set up a free tour.

149. What is NOT indicated about Grover Towers?

(A) It offers appliances in its apartments.
(B) It rents out different-sized units.
(C) It is located near shopping.
(D) It charges an $800 security deposit to all tenants.

150. According to the advertisement, how can a prospective tenant see an apartment?

(A) By making a phone call
(B) By filling out an online form
(C) By sending an e-mail
(D) By stopping by an office

Questions 151-152 refer to the following text message chain.

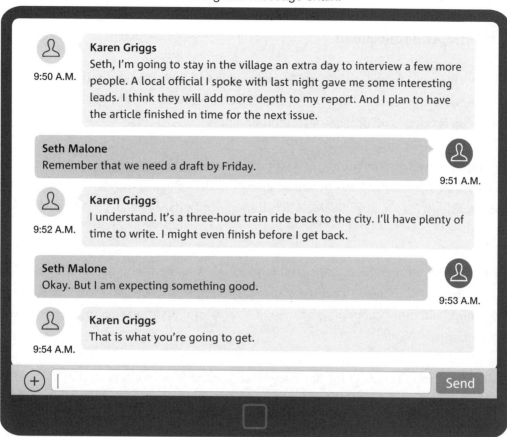

151. What type of business does Ms. Griggs most likely work for?

(A) An advertising firm
(B) A travel agency
(C) A magazine
(D A railway

152. At 9:52 A.M., what does Ms. Griggs imply when she writes, "I'll have plenty of time to write"?

(A) She plans to work while traveling.
(B) She will work overtime if needed.
(C) She thinks the deadline can be extended.
(D) She is almost finished writing.

▶ ▶ ▶ GO ON TO THE NEXT PAGE

Conference Announcement

The Association of Professional Sports Photographers (APSP) plans to hold its sixty-second annual conference on May 7-9 at the Manatee Hotel in Naples, Florida. APSP membership is open to all professional photographers.

Photography clinics, presentations, and workshops will be held during the conference. An annual lifetime membership award will be given to Mitch Bullard during the membership dinner on Friday, May 8, at 6:00 P.M. After dinner, Mr. Bullard will give a talk about his career.

Registration opens for APSP members on January 31. Members who register before March 1 will receive a 10% discount. Visit www.apsp.org to register. There, you can also find a list of workshops and other happenings, a map of Naples, and reviews of recommended hotels and restaurants in Naples.

A limited number of rooms at the Manatee Hotel are available at a special APSP group rate. Reservations can be made by calling 1-888-555-1277.

153. What is NOT indicated about Mr. Bullard?

(A) He will be in Florida in May.
(B) He will lead a workshop.
(C) He has worked as a photographer.
(D) He will speak in the evening.

154. According to the announcement, what can readers do on the association's Web site?

(A) Find a list of members' names
(B) Book a hotel room
(C) Read about conference activities
(D) Join the association

Questions 155-157 refer to the following newsletter article.

Employee Spotlight: Anna Ferguson   May Issue
by Miranda Chen

Last month, I sat down with Anna Ferguson and asked her a few questions about her job. If you have contacted Document Services, a team within the Corporate Communications Department, you may have worked with Anna. She is the senior-most member of the team of three document production specialists supervised by Maria Tate. Anna focuses on document formatting and layout while the other members of the team, Cara Bailey and Trish Landis, handle graphic design and other tasks. If you need help with proofreading or basic editing, Anna is the person to turn to.

Anna joined Lighthouse Enterprises eight years ago as an intern in the Sales Department and was hired by the Communications Department six months later. After two years, she returned to school to earn a master's degree thanks to financial support from the company. Her commitment to quality has made her stand out. Last year, Anna was given an employee excellence award.

155. What is suggested about Cara Baily?

(A) She was hired before Anna Ferguson.
(B) She mostly checks for spelling errors.
(C) She works under Maria Tate's direction.
(D) She used to work in the Sales Department.

156. What is indicated about Miranda Chen?

(A) She is the editor of a newspaper.
(B) She works in a group of three employees.
(C) She needed help to write a press release.
(D) She interviewed Anna Ferguson in April.

157. What is NOT mentioned about Lighthouse Enterprises?

(A) It offered an apprenticeship in the past.
(B) It helped pay for an employee's education.
(C) It has a reputation for selling high-quality products.
(D) It recognized the work of Ms. Ferguson.

▶ ▶ ▶ GO ON TO THE NEXT PAGE

Questions 158-160 refer to the following letter.

August 8

Gerhard Essen
Camello Corporation
1209 Merrimack Road
Manchester, NH03101

Dear Mr. Essen,

I work for a bicycle messenger service in New York City. Every week, I ride hundreds of kilometers on my bike. — [1] —. As you can imagine, my tires take quite a beating.

When I started doing this work five years ago, I bought my first Camello 500 tires. Now, nearly everyone at my company uses them. The soft rubber provides an excellent grip on city streets whether they are wet, dry, hot, or cold. — [2] —. They are also reasonably priced for being such high-performance tires.

About a year or so ago, my coworkers and I noticed that our Camello tires were wearing out faster than normal. — [3] —. The rubber is not a durable as it used to be. It also feels stiffer.

As a loyal customer, I would like to know what happened to the quality of your tires. — [4] —. Please bring back the original Camello 500s as soon as possible.

I look forward to your response.

Sincerely,

Gabe Aspen

---

158. What is suggested about Mr. Aspen?

(A) He founded a company five years ago.
(B) He used to live in New York City.
(C) He competes in bike races.
(D) He rides his bike in a variety of conditions.

159. What complaint does Mr. Aspen have with the Camello tires?

(A) They are now too expensive.
(B) They have become less robust.
(C) They are dwindling in popularity.
(D) They are no longer available.

160. In which of the positions marked [1], [2], [3], and [4] does the following sentence best belong?

"Not only that, but we are also experiencing more punctures and tears."

(A) [1]
(B) [2]
(C) [3]
(D) [4]

Questions 161-164 refer to the following online chat discussion.

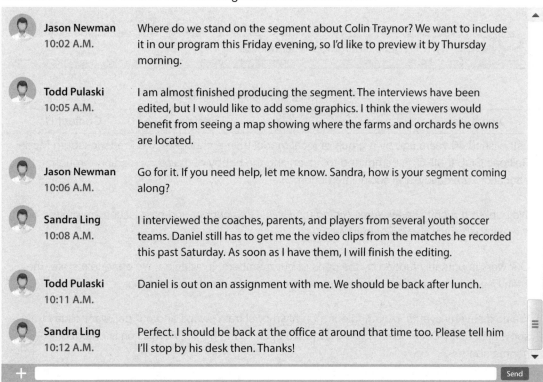

Jason Newman 10:02 A.M.	Where do we stand on the segment about Colin Traynor? We want to include it in our program this Friday evening, so I'd like to preview it by Thursday morning.
Todd Pulaski 10:05 A.M.	I am almost finished producing the segment. The interviews have been edited, but I would like to add some graphics. I think the viewers would benefit from seeing a map showing where the farms and orchards he owns are located.
Jason Newman 10:06 A.M.	Go for it. If you need help, let me know. Sandra, how is your segment coming along?
Sandra Ling 10:08 A.M.	I interviewed the coaches, parents, and players from several youth soccer teams. Daniel still has to get me the video clips from the matches he recorded this past Saturday. As soon as I have them, I will finish the editing.
Todd Pulaski 10:11 A.M.	Daniel is out on an assignment with me. We should be back after lunch.
Sandra Ling 10:12 A.M.	Perfect. I should be back at the office at around that time too. Please tell him I'll stop by his desk then. Thanks!

161. Where most likely do the speakers work?

(A) At a TV station
(B) At a newspaper
(C) At a radio station
(D) At a sports magazine

162. What is indicated about Mr. Traynor?

(A) He has agricultural land.
(B) He will meet Mr. Newman on Thursday.
(C) He had an interview with Ms. Ling.
(D) He is a journalist.

163. At 10:06 A.M., why does Mr. Newman write, "Go for it"?

(A) To permit Mr. Pulaski to take time off
(B) To voice approval of an idea
(C) To request additional interviews
(D) To encourage Mr. Pulaski to visit more than one place

164. What does Ms. Ling say she will do later today?

(A) Have lunch with a friend
(B) Conduct some interviews
(C) Go out on an assignment
(D) Meet with a colleague

▶ ▶ ▶GO ON TO THE NEXT PAGE

Questions 165-167 refer to the following Web page.

www.FredericksburgModelRailroad.net

Fredericksburg Model Railroad Club

About Us	Join	Events	Contact Us

Established 46 years ago by a group of local model train enthusiasts, the Fredericksburg Model Railroad Club (FMRC) is committed to advancing the hobby of model railroading through education, advocacy, and social interaction.

We publish a monthly newsletter, *Riding the Rails*. Both current and past issues are posted on the members-only section of our Web site.

Our work is primarily funded by the dues of our members. In addition, we operate a store, the Train Depot, where anyone can buy model trains, books, posters, and more.

We hold several events, including our monthly model train swaps and our popular holiday train show held every December. These events are open to the public. Admission is charged to nonmembers.

Individual Memberships

Apprentice $5/year
- A reduced-rate membership just for youths (ages 18 and under)
- Attend all of our events for free
- Receive *Riding the Rails*

Supporter $20/year
- Get all the benefits of Apprentice plus receive 10% off all model trains, supplies, and more sold at theTrain Depot.

Conductor $50/year
- Get all the benefits of Supporter. Plus, we will post your name on our Web site.

Engineer $100/year
- Get all the benefits of Conductor plus two tickets to the Train Museum in Baltimore.

Businesses Sponsorships
Would you like to become a sponsor? Sponsors will have their businesses featured in our newsletter and at our events. Contact Pat Gaston at 555-8101 for more information.

165. What is true about the Fredericksburg Model Railroad Club?

(A) It operates its own museum.
(B) It has been around for decades.
(C) It has branches in several localities.
(D) It raises money by selling tickets for train rides.

166. What is NOT indicated about individuals with Conductor memberships?

(A) They will receive a publication every month.
(B) They can get reduced prices at the club's store.
(C) They will be acknowledged online.
(D) They must be younger than a certain age.

167. According to the Web page, what are nonmembers able to do?

(A) Purchase model trains
(B) Obtain a discount
(C) Read past articles online
(D) Attend events for free

▶ ▶ ▶ GO ON TO THE NEXT PAGE

Questions 168-171 refer to the following e-mail.

```
                                                                    _ □ X
From:        Owen Medan <owen.medan@labova.com>
To:          Henry Chinaski <hchinaski@dreamland.com>
Subject:     Round Two
Date:        January 27
```

Dear Mr. Chinaski,

Congratulations! You passed the initial screening interview at the Labova Corporation. As a result, you will advance to the second round of our hiring process.

Candidates who advance to the second round are invited to return to our offices to take a skills test. The test is administered via a computer and takes approximately two hours. If you get above the minimum score for the test, we will forward your test results and application materials to a department manager. If the manager is interested in you, he or she will invite you back for a final interview. If you are not invited back at this time, your application will remain active for the next 6 months.

Nearly 75% of all applicants who pass our skills test are eventually hired and stay with the company for over ten years. In fact, we have some of the lowest turnover rates in the industry. This is due to our careful screening as well as our generous salaries and benefits.

Please call me at 555-1122 to set up a time to take the skills test.

Sincerely,

Owen Medan

168. What is the purpose of the e-mail?

(A) To offer a job to an applicant
(B) To arrange an employment interview
(C) To request additional documentation
(D) To explain the next steps in a procedure

169. What is suggested about Mr. Chinaski?

(A) He has visited the Labova Corporation before.
(B) He has spoken with a department manager.
(C) He was first interviewed over six months ago.
(D) He is currently employed at Mr. Medan's company.

170. What is indicated about the Labova Corporation?

(A) It has the highest-paying jobs in the industry.
(B) It offers online training opportunities.
(C) It retains many of its new hires.
(D) It now offers even more benefits.

171. What does Mr. Medan ask Mr. Chinaski to do?

(A) Call a manager
(B) Complete an online form
(C) Attend an initial interview
(D) Schedule an exam

Questions 172-175 refer to the following memo.

MEMO

FROM: David Gresh, Facilities Manager
TO: All Employees
DATE: May 3
SUBJECT: Fitness Center

The company opened a fitness center on the fifth floor of our building four years ago. The facilities are free for use by any employee. Initially, we scheduled the fitness center to be open from Monday through Friday from 7:00 A.M. to 9:00 A.M. and from 5:00 P.M. to 7:00 P.M. —[1]—. However, due to requests from employees, we changed the hours to 7:00 A.M. to 7:00 P.M. for a three-month trial period. Because the new hours have been so popular, we have decided to make them our new regular hours. Thanks to support from our new vice president, we will soon be able to keep the fitness center open on Saturday and Sunday mornings as well. —[2]—. The exact hours will be announced before this change takes effect next month.

I would also like to inform you that the fitness center is going to be enlarged. Starting next week, we will remove all the items in the storage room next door. —[3]—. That will give us almost twice the amount of space. With more room, we can purchase some new exercise machines and weights. Work is expected to be completed by the end of the month. Until that happens, use of a portion of the existing exercise facility will be restricted. —[4]—.

172. What change to the fitness center was made in response to employee comments?

(A) Its hours were extended.
(B) Its fees were reduced.
(C) Its location was moved.
(D) Its weights were upgraded.

173. According to the memo, why is the company planning to install new equipment?

(A) Employees requested it.
(B) Existing equipment was outdated.
(C) Additional space will become available.
(D) The equipment was on sale.

174. What is most likely true about the fitness center in June?

(A) It will be closed for construction.
(B) It will be open on weekends.
(C) It will feature new posted information.
(D) It will try out new daytime hours.

175. In which of the positions marked [1], [2], [3], and [4] does the following sentence best belong?

"The wall between the two rooms will be torn down."

(A) [1]
(B) [2]
(C) [3]
(D) [4]

▶ ▶ ▶ GO ON TO THE NEXT PAGE

High Plains Engineering

www.highplainsengineering.com

We offer unpaid internships for students in their final year of their bachelor's degree program at an accredited college or university. We accept applicants interested in working on one of our teams in the following fields: environmental engineering, civil engineering, surveying, and project management. Internships are held in either the fall or the spring and can last from six to twelve weeks, depending on the schedule of the participant. Interns are expected to contribute to existing projects. Moreover, they must commit to working two days a week at our offices for between six and eight hours per day. Applications are due by May 31 for internships starting in September and by October 31 for internships starting in January.

To apply, download an application packet from our Web site. After filling out the application form, applicants must submit it by mail along with a letter of interest, copies of their transcripts, and three reference letters from current or former professors or supervisors.

To:	Civil Engineering Team <allcivil@highplainsengineering.com>
From:	Eldon Charlie <echarlie@highplainsengineering.com>
Date:	December 8
Subject:	Internship
Attachment:	letter

Dear All,

Kyle Richardson would like to start an internship with us in January. He has expressed interest in working on a highway construction project. He has excelled in his coursework. In addition, he has worked two summers as a surveyor's assistant, so he has some relevant experience. I strongly recommend we select him.

Attached is his letter of interest. Please take a look at it and let me know if you think he would be a good fit for our team. If so, which project would you recommend assigning him to? We will discuss his application at our next team meeting on December 15.

Thanks,

Eldon

176. According to the information, what must interns be able to do?

(A) Participate in weekly meetings
(B) Come to the workplace twice a week
(C) Propose a project idea
(D) Work for at least twelve weeks

177. What is indicated about the internship applications?

(A) They must be submitted by one of two deadlines.
(B) They require proof of graduation.
(C) They can be completed online.
(D) They require payment of a fee.

178. What is the purpose of the e-mail?

(A) To ask for feedback about an applicant
(B) To schedule a team meeting
(C) To propose a project for Mr. Richardson
(D) To request a starting date for an internship

179. In the information, the word "fields" in paragraph 1, line 3, is closest in meaning to

(A) agricultural areas
(B) outdoor spaces
(C) subjects
(D) worksites

180. What is most likely true about Mr. Richardson?

(A) He took courses in surveying.
(B) He has not earned a bachelor's degree yet.
(C) He will receive a salary as an intern.
(D) He is studying environmental engineering.

▶ ▶ ▶GO ON TO THE NEXT PAGE

Event Room Rentals

The Cherry Hills Community Center Great Room is available for rent by nonprofit groups and other members of the community. The Great Room can hold up to 100 people and can be rented for talks, trainings, performances, classes, parties, and more.

Rates:
$20 for up to 1 hour
$60 for up to 4 hours
$100 for up to 8 hours
$150 for more than 8 hours

A limited number of tables and chairs are available for use in the Great Room. Event organizers can rent additional furniture from Peterson Rentals (555-9332). Peterson Rentals has worked with us for many years and offers reasonable rates. It will take care of the delivery, setup, and teardown.

The Cherry Hills Community Center is open from Monday through Friday from 9 A.M. to 8 P.M. and on Saturday and Sunday from 10 A.M. to 5 P.M. Events held outside our normal business hours will require a staff member to be present to unlock and lock the community center. An additional fee will be charged for this service.

Community Center Event Reservation Form

Today's date: June 7

Event Name: Beginning Tai Chi Class
Organizer's Name: Juliette Masetta
Group: Soto Martial Arts
Phone: 555-0033
E-mail: julie@sotomartialarts.com

Room Requested: Great Room
Date: Monday (eight weeks: July 9 – August 17)
Hours: 6:00 P.M. – 6:50 P.M.
Number of Attendees: unknown

Additional Requirements/Instructions: I have spoken with Beverly Varney about offering an opportunity for members of the community to learn about and experience the health benefits of tai chi exercises. She has permitted me to charge participants $5 per class. We need all of the furniture either removed from the room or placed along the south wall so that we can have enough floor space.

One of our staff members will contact you within 48 hours from the time we receive your request.

181. What is indicated about the Great Room?

(A) It is only available on weekdays.
(B) It cannot be rented by individuals.
(C) It requires all furniture to be rented.
(D) It can be used for birthday celebrations.

182. What must organizers do to use the Great Room after 8:00 P.M.?

(A) Pay for the rental in advance
(B) Request a key for the door
(C) Hire a security guard
(D) Make an extra payment

183. What type of event is Ms. Masetta organizing?

(A) A health fair
(B) A fitness class
(C) A demonstration
(D) A lecture series

184. How much will Ms. Masetta most likely be charged per week for her event?

(A) $20
(B) $60
(C) $100
(D) $150

185. What is suggested about Ms. Masetta?

(A) She will not contact Peterson Rentals.
(B) She is trying to raise money for a charitable group.
(C) She is a community center employee.
(D) She will be contacted by Ms. Varney on July 9.

▶ ▶ ▶ GO ON TO THE NEXT PAGE

The Association of Library and Information Science Professionals (ALISP) will hold its thirty-fifth annual conference at the Great Western Convention Center in Denver, Colorado, from April 18 to April 22. All current ALISP members are invited to attend. *This year, Heritage Tours will be taking groups to visit local historical sites.

Register for the conference at www.alisp.org/conference. Practicing professionals can receive a "Presenter" discount by giving a presentation, by leading a workshop, or by participating in a panel discussion.

Registration Fees:
 Student $150
 Professional $400
 Presenter $300
 Retiree $250

The event is only for ALISP members. To join ALISP, visit our Web site at www.alisp.org. Our members include students as well as practicing library and information science professionals working at universities and corporate institutions.

ALISP ANNUAL CONFERENCE
REGISTRATION FORM

Name: Kelsey Walton
Title: Associate Librarian
Organization: McManus Medical Center
Registration type: Professional
Phone: (412) 555-7718
E-mail: k.walton@mcmanus.org
Payment type: credit card (ending in 5653)
Will you be presenting? [ ] yes [x] no
If so, please describe the topic of your presentation/talk/panel: _____

Please review your registration form before clicking on the "Submit" button below. Once your registration has been processed, a confirmation will be sent to the e-mail address above. If you have any problems, contact our technical support office at 1-888-555-7830.

[SUBMIT]

	⊟□✕
From:	Kelsey Walton <k.walton@mcmanus.org>
To:	Brenda Pierce <b.pierce@hoffman.edu>
Date:	April 27
Subject:	Conference

Brenda,

It was great catching up with you in Denver. It's hard to believe that ten years have passed since we worked together at the Sinclair Corporation. I'm so glad we were able to go on a Heritage Tours excursion together with some of our former colleagues.

I really enjoyed your talk about the cloud-based storage systems that your university is using. We are looking to install a similar system at my workplace. When you have a chance, could you kindly e-mail me the outline of your presentation?

Best,

Kelsey

186. What is NOT indicated about the ALISP conference?

(A) It will run for five days.
(B) It is only open to people who have joined the group.
(C) It offers free registration for locals.
(D) It was first held over three decades ago.

187. How much did Ms. Walton pay to register for the conference?

(A) $150
(B) $250
(C) $300
(D) $400

188. What is suggested about Ms. Pierce?

(A) She designed a computer network.
(B) She works at a software company.
(C) She received a reduced registration rate.
(D) She used to supervise Ms. Walton.

189. What did Ms. Walton most likely do in Denver?

(A) She visited cultural attractions.
(B) She led a training event.
(C) She gave a history lecture.
(D) She got a new job.

190. What does Ms. Walton ask Ms. Pierce to do?

(A) Give a talk at her company
(B) Help set up new technology
(C) Recommend a system
(D) Send some information

▶ ▶ ▶ GO ON TO THE NEXT PAGE

H&R Building Supplies
78 Allen Street
Salish, WA78331
(608) 555-1249
www.hrbuildingsupplies.com

We are the largest supplier of lumber, bricks, concrete, and other construction materials in the Wasatch Valley.

Sign up for a business account with us. It's easy! Just give us a call and speak with someone in the Accounting Department. You will be given a username and a password which you can use to access our secure Web site. There, you can search our current inventory, make purchases, track your orders, and schedule pickups and deliveries. Plus, with an existing account, billing is a cinch!

We can deliver your order directly to you. Rates are per truckload and are based on the distance from our warehouse to your job site.

Distance	Rate
0-20km	$150
21-40km	$200
41-80km	$350
81-200km	$500

ORDER FORM -- H&R Building Supplies

Customer Information
Account Number: 89532
Name: *Kenny Barlow*
Company: *Drummond Construction*
Phone: *(608) 555-1832*
E-mail: *kbarlow@drummond.com*

Order Information

Item #	Description	Quantity
4893	framing lumber	100
3322	cinder blocks	500
7873	mortar	20
2921	plywood sheets	40

Delivery Information
Date: *Friday, July 12*
Address: *170 Coburn Road, Andersville, WA*
Size: *one truckload*
Charges: *$200*

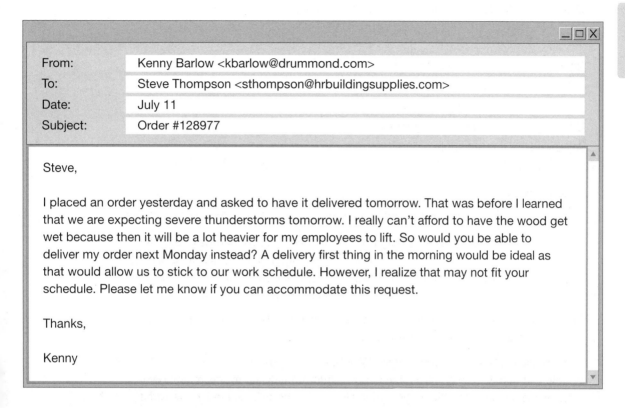

From: Kenny Barlow <kbarlow@drummond.com>

To: Steve Thompson <sthompson@hrbuildingsupplies.com>

Date: July 11

Subject: Order #128977

Steve,

I placed an order yesterday and asked to have it delivered tomorrow. That was before I learned that we are expecting severe thunderstorms tomorrow. I really can't afford to have the wood get wet because then it will be a lot heavier for my employees to lift. So would you be able to deliver my order next Monday instead? A delivery first thing in the morning would be ideal as that would allow us to stick to our work schedule. However, I realize that may not fit your schedule. Please let me know if you can accommodate this request.

Thanks,

Kenny

---

191. According to the information, how can a customer find out what products are currently available at H&R Building Supplies?

(A) By logging on to a Web site
(B) By calling a sales associate
(C) By visiting a warehouse
(D) By sending an e-mail

192. What is the most likely distance from H&R's storage facility to Andersville?

(A) 0-20km
(B) 21-40km
(C) 41-80km
(D) 81-200km

193. Why does Mr. Barlow want to reschedule a delivery?

(A) His work deadline has been moved up.
(B) He has recalculated the amount of supplies needed.
(C) He is concerned about the weather.
(D) He needs to find additional workers.

194. On what day did Mr. Barlow write the e-mail?

(A) Monday
(B) Thursday
(C) Friday
(D) Saturday

195. What does Mr. Barlow indicate he is aware of?

(A) He has to pay an additional fee.
(B) He waited too long to make his request.
(C) His appeal might not be accepted.
(D) His e-mail might not be read by Mr. Thompson.

▶ ▶ ▶GO ON TO THE NEXT PAGE

Questions 196-200 refer to the following e-mails and schedule.

From:	Carla Jensen <cjens@bixtechnologies.com>
To:	Alex Rondeaux <arond@bixtechnologies.com>
Date:	March 7
Subject:	Travel Arrangements
Attachment:	Schedule

Dear Mr. Rondeaux,

I have made the following flight reservations on Sunshine Airlines(reservation #7883).:

Monday, June 6   Flight 1622   Departing Albuquerque at 9:03 A.M.
Arriving in Minneapolis at 12:45 P.M.
Thursday, June 9   Flight 788   Departing Minneapolis at 5:23 P.M.
Arriving in Albuquerque at 8:09 P.M.

You can view your electronic ticket on the airline's Web site. Simply give your reservation number and show a photo ID when you check in.

I also booked you a single room at the Winchester Hotel(reservation #HJ763). The hotel's shuttle can take you to and from the airport. Unfortunately, no rooms meeting your requirements were available at the Logan Hotel. Your hotel is located in the same part of the town as the Logan. So there are plenty of theaters, restaurants, and coffee shops within walking distance.

Finally, I set up meetings with some potential buyers in Minneapolis(see attached schedule).

If there is anything else I can help you with, please let me know.

Sincerely,

Carla Jensen
Travel Office
Bix Technologies

Meeting Schedule

June 6
2:30 P.M. Sam Harrison (Gleeson Corporation)

June 7
9:30 A.M. Tracy Ericson (STX, Inc.)
1:30 P.M. Devon White (Lighthouse Medical Supply)

June 8
9:45 A.M. Paul Corby (Haberstam Ltd.)
2:00 P.M. Elaine Shew (St. Vincent Hospital)

June 9
10:30 A.M. Patricia Linklater (CRX Transportation)

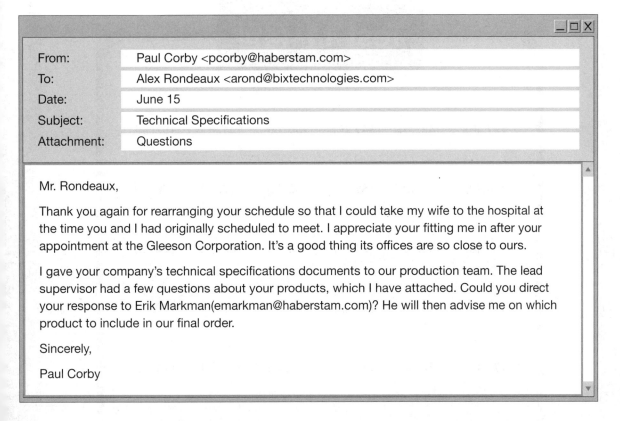

From:	Paul Corby <pcorby@haberstam.com>
To:	Alex Rondeaux <arond@bixtechnologies.com>
Date:	June 15
Subject:	Technical Specifications
Attachment:	Questions

Mr. Rondeaux,

Thank you again for rearranging your schedule so that I could take my wife to the hospital at the time you and I had originally scheduled to meet. I appreciate your fitting me in after your appointment at the Gleeson Corporation. It's a good thing its offices are so close to ours.

I gave your company's technical specifications documents to our production team. The lead supervisor had a few questions about your products, which I have attached. Could you direct your response to Erik Markman(emarkman@haberstam.com)? He will then advise me on which product to include in our final order.

Sincerely,

Paul Corby

196. What is mentioned about Mr. Rondeaux's travel arrangements?

(A) He has a layover on his return flight.
(B) His initial flight leaves in the morning.
(C) He needs to print his ticket.
(D) He must take a taxi to his hotel.

197. What is indicated about the Winchester Hotel?

(A) It only books reservations online.
(B) It serves meals to guests.
(C) It is near entertainment venues.
(D) It has meeting rooms for guests.

198. When did Mr. Corby meet Mr. Rondeaux?

(A) On June 6
(B) On June 7
(C) On June 8
(D) On June 9

199. What is suggested about Ms. Ericson?

(A) She had to change her appointment.
(B) She is an existing Bix Technologies customer.
(C) She met Mr. Rondeaux at his hotel.
(D) She works in Minneapolis.

200. What does Mr. Corby want Mr. Rondeaux to do?

(A) Give him a suggestion
(B) Send a technical document
(C) Provide some answers
(D) Meet with a colleague

▶ ▶ ▶ GO ON TO THE NEXT PAGE

Test 11 정답

147. (D)	**148.** (B)	**149.** (D)	**150.** (A)	**151.** (C)	**152.** (A)
153. (B)	**154.** (C)	**155.** (C)	**156.** (D)	**157.** (C)	**158.** (D)
159. (B)	**160.** (C)	**161.** (A)	**162.** (A)	**163.** (B)	**164.** (D)
165. (B)	**166.** (D)	**167.** (A)	**168.** (D)	**169.** (A)	**170.** (C)
171. (D)	**172.** (A)	**173.** (C)	**174.** (B)	**175.** (C)	**176.** (B)
177. (A)	**178.** (A)	**179.** (C)	**180.** (B)	**181.** (D)	**182.** (D)
183. (B)	**184.** (A)	**185.** (A)	**186.** (C)	**187.** (D)	**188.** (C)
189. (A)	**190.** (D)	**191.** (A)	**192.** (B)	**193.** (C)	**194.** (B)
195. (C)	**196.** (B)	**197.** (C)	**198.** (A)	**199.** (D)	**200.** (C)

TEST
12

55
min

시작 시간 ___시 ___분   목표 개수 _____ / 54

종료 시간 ___시 ___분   실제 개수 _____ / 54

- 반드시 55분 안에 문제 풀이 포함 마킹까지 마쳐야 합니다.
- 실제 시험이라고 생각하고 멈추지 말고 풀어보세요.   · 정답 개수에 5를 곱하면 대략적인 점수가 됩니다.

PART 7

Directions: In this part you will read a selection of texts, such as magazine and newspaper articles, e-mails, and instant messages. Each text or set of texts is followed by several questions. Select the best answer for each question and mark the letter (A), (B), (C), or (D) on your answer sheet.

Questions 147-148 refer to the following article.

Professional News

The Society of Certified Optometrists (SCO) held its ninth annual conference at the Mac Douglas Convention Center in New Orleans, Louisiana. This year's event, which took place from May 3 to May 5, drew over four hundred and fifty attendees from all over the country.

Dr. Frieda Olsen, the president of the Sampson College of Optometry, gave a keynote address entitled "Envisioning the Future of Optometry." The event also included 24 talks, 18 professional development workshops, and 5 panel discussions. Over eighty vendors from leading companies were on site to showcase new products.

Current SCO members can access copies of speeches, presentations, and workshop notes at www.sco.org.

---

147. What is NOT mentioned about the conference?

(A) It has been held for almost ten years.
(B) It included product representatives.
(C) It has workshops for college students.
(D) It took place over three days.

148. According to the article, how can SCO members read the text of Dr. Olsen's speech?

(A) By signing up for a newsletter
(B) By writing to the Sampson College of Optometry
(C) By ordering a copy from SCO
(D) By going to a Web site

▶ ▶ ▶ GO ON TO THE NEXT PAGE

Questions 149-150 refer to the following text message chain.

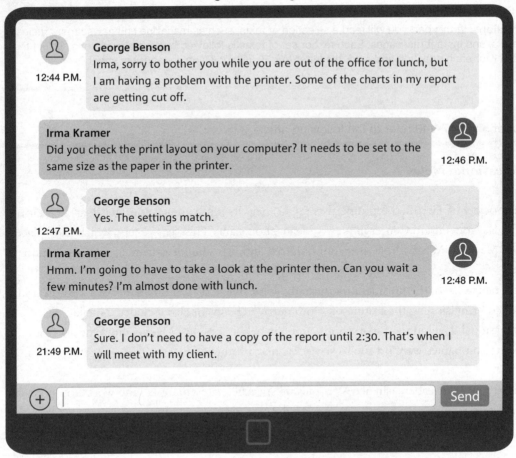

George Benson
12:44 P.M.
Irma, sorry to bother you while you are out of the office for lunch, but I am having a problem with the printer. Some of the charts in my report are getting cut off.

Irma Kramer
Did you check the print layout on your computer? It needs to be set to the same size as the paper in the printer.
12:46 P.M.

George Benson
12:47 P.M.
Yes. The settings match.

Irma Kramer
Hmm. I'm going to have to take a look at the printer then. Can you wait a few minutes? I'm almost done with lunch.
12:48 P.M.

George Benson
21:49 P.M.
Sure. I don't need to have a copy of the report until 2:30. That's when I will meet with my client.

Send

149. What is Mr. Benson trying to do?

(A) Obtain a paper version of report
(B) Connect his computer to a printer
(C) Change the content of a chart
(D) Repair a broken printer

150. At 12:48 P.M., what does Ms. Kramer imply when she writes, "Can you wait a few minutes"?

(A) She is not sure what to do right now.
(B) She will return to the office soon.
(C) She needs time to change the print layout.
(D) She thinks Mr. Benson is impatient.

308

Questions 151-152 refer to the following notice.

Dear customers,

The Shore Bird will be closed from December 22 to January 31 for renovations. With additional customers coming to Casey Beach every summer during tourist season, we have decided to expand.

Another dining room, which can be reserved for private parties, will be added to the back of the restaurant. We also plan to double the size of our outdoor setting areas so more diners can enjoy the sounds of the ocean and feel the sea breezes. We're renovating the kitchen and replacing our stoves, ranges, and refrigerators with more energy-efficient models.

But don't worry. We have every intention of keeping our award-winning menu.

Mark your calendars for our grand reopening on February 1. All of our classic entrées will be 10% off.

Sincerely,

Andrea D'Abrosso

151. What is indicated about the Shore Bird?
(A) It is moving to a new location.
(B) It will no longer be open in December.
(C) It was purchased by Ms. D'Abrosso two years ago.
(D) It will be adding a space for private dining.

152. What will happen on February 1?
(A) An award will be given.
(B) A new menu will debut.
(C) A private party will be held.
(D) A discount will be offered.

▶ ▶ ▶ GO ON TO THE NEXT PAGE

From: Greg Miller <gmiller@furniturewarehouse.com>
To: All Sales Employees <sales@furniturewarehouse.com>
Subject: Announcement – Sales Contest!
Date: April 18

Once again, we are gearing up for our sales season here at Furniture Warehouse. To get things started early this year, we would like to announce a sales contest. Sales associates working at any one of our nine stores in the Dallas-Fort Worth area are invited to participate.

Participants will be assigned a partner, thus forming a team. Teams will receive points for their combined sales. The team with the highest number of points at the end of the contest will be declared the winner. First prize is $250 for each partner. Second prize is two certificates for a meal at Stetson Steakhouse. Third prize is two pairs of movie tickets.

The contest officially begins at 9:00 A.M. on May 1 and ends at 5:00 P.M. on May 30. Only actual sales receipts and signed sales contracts submitted by the deadline will be counted.

To sign up, contact David Bacon at dbacon@furniturewarehouse.com.

---

153. What is mentioned about Furniture Warehouse?

(A) It will have a large sale next month.
(B) It has more than one location.
(C) It has sales contests each year.
(D) It plans on hiring additional employees.

154. What is NOT true about the contest?

(A) The top sales team will be awarded cash.
(B) Employees should send an e-mail to register.
(C) It takes place over one month.
(D) All sales associates are required to compete.

Questions 155-157 refer to the following information.

Delta Materials

Delta Materials is a stainless steel manufacturer headquartered in Montreal, Canada. We design a range of stainless steel alloys for use in specialized applications. Our alloys are used by manufacturers in the aerospace, automotive, and medical device industries. Delta products are sold to customers in 17 countries, with the North American market accounting for nearly 60% of all of our sales.

Delta Materials employs over 600 individuals worldwide, with 400 in Canada alone. In addition to our main offices and production facility in Montreal, we have distribution centers in Vancouver, British Columbia, and Detroit, Michigan. We have sales representatives based in several major cities in Europe, Asia, and South America.

Delta Materials has been led by CEO George McClelland since 2013. Under Mr. McClelland's leadership, Delta has focused on customizing orders for its clients. Mr. McClelland has also increased employee training through a program called Enhance. Since the program was launched two years ago, productivity has increased by 50%.

155. What type of company would most likely be a customer of Delta Materials?

(A) A travel agency
(B) A car manufacturer
(C) A dental clinic
(D) A furniture maker

156. What is indicated about Delta Materials?

(A) It was founded in 2013.
(B) It has offices in 17 countries.
(C) It does a lot of business in North America.
(D) It has three distribution centers.

157. According to the information, what did Delta Materials do two years ago?

(A) Selected a new leader
(B) Increased employee salaries
(C) Hired additional staff
(D) Created a worker training initiative

▶ ▶ ▶ GO ON TO THE NEXT PAGE

MEMO

From: Carlton Farmer
To: All Employees
Date: May 3
Subject: Store Relocation

Three months ago, our landlord announced that he planned to sell our building. He has found a buyer, but that individual plans to convert the building into a restaurant. As a result, we will be forced to relocate. I have been working with agents at Empire Realty. They found a two-story building property close to the university for us. The rent is slightly higher than here, but there is heavy pedestrian traffic in the area. — [1] —.

I was able to negotiate with the new owner to let us stay here until June 30. Our lease at the new location starts on June 15. — [2] —. To reduce the amount of inventory we have to move, we are going to have a two-week sale starting on June 1. I would like to start moving the remaining inventory, display racks, and signage to our new building at 7117 Davis Avenue starting on the first day of our new lease.

All employees are required to help prepare for our upcoming sale. — [3] —. Working during the two-week move, however, is voluntary. — [4] —. Let me know your preference.

---

158. What is indicated about the property at 7117 Davis Avenue?

(A) It used to be an eatery.
(B) It is located in a busy area.
(C) It is across the street from a school.
(D) It has two entrances.

159. What does Mr. Farmer plan to do on June 15?

(A) Begin transporting things to the new location
(B) Hire a professional moving company
(C) Negotiate a deal with a real estate company
(D) Sign a lease with a new landlord

160. In which of the positions marked [1], [2], [3], and [4] does the following sentence best belong?

"If you choose to work at that time, you will be paid your regular rate."

(A) [1]
(B) [2]
(C) [3]
(D) [4]

Questions 161-163 refer to the following advertisement.

Fallstaff Theater

The oldest theater in East St. Louis

This year marks our 100th anniversary. To celebrate, we will be offering free music performances, plays, lectures, and film showings all year long.

Kicking off the celebration are four of the best-known films by Paolo Grimaldi. Mr. Grimaldi was born to Italian immigrant parents not far from the Fallstaff. After graduating from Central High School, he moved to Hollywood, California, and found a work as a camera operator, sound engineer, and actor before making his own films. His films explore existential themes and often draw on experiences from his own life.

Husbands and Wives (1956) Saturday, January 8 2:00 P.M.	*The Long Walk Home* (1958) Saturday, January 15 7:00 P.M.
Finding Faith (1955) Saturday, January 22 2:00 P.M.	*Open and Closed* (1960) Friday, January 28 6:00 P.M.

Free popcorn and drinks will be provided at each showing. Arrive early to get the best seats.
For tickets, stop by the box office or visit www.fallstafftheater.org.

---

161. What is NOT mentioned about the Fallstaff Theater?

(A) It is located in East St. Louis.
(B) It will offer events over the next twelve months.
(C) It was founded by Mr. Grimaldi.
(D) It opened a century ago.

162. What is indicated about Mr. Grimaldi?

(A) He was born in Hollywood.
(B) He made several movies.
(C) He studied to be an actor.
(D) He spent time in Italy.

163. What will most likely happen at the Fallstaff Theater on January 8?

(A) Refreshments will be served.
(B) A director will give a talk about his life.
(C) A theater will reopen.
(D) Tickets will not be available for purchase online.

▶ ▶ ▶ GO ON TO THE NEXT PAGE

Questions 164-167 refer to the following online chat discussion.

Shelia Cotter 1:23 P.M.		I just had lunch with Rachel Simmons, a representative from Luxa. She wants to know if we are interested in selling its products. What do you think?
Elaine Nguyen 1:24 P.M.		Luxa? I thought its shampoos and conditioners were only sold to beauty salons.
Shelia Cotter 1:25 P.M.		Currently, only licensed salons can buy its products. But Luxa has created a new line of products for sale in department stores.
Nancy Saba 1:27 P.M.		My stylist uses its products. I really like the results. They leave my hair feeling healthy and shiny. I say we go for it.
Elaine Nguyen 1:28 P.M.		Wait a minute. What makes Luxa think it can break into the retail shampoo market?
Shelia Cotter 1:29 P.M.		It has done a lot of product testing. Consumer focus groups were given samples of its new shampoos and conditioners to try, and they responded very favorably. Plus, it is counting on its brand name to drive sales.
Elaine Nguyen 1:31 P.M.		What about pricing?
Shelia Cotter 1:32 P.M.		Luxa products are expected to cost a bit more than those of its main competitors. For a 450ml bottle, the leading brand's shampoo sells for about $9.50. Luxa's retail shampoo will be $10.25.
Nancy Saba 1:33 P.M.		That's nothing. I doubt consumers will even notice. They will focus on the brand name.
Shelia Cotter 1:34 P.M.		Nancy, that was my conclusion, too. Let me give Rachel a call and let her know.

Send

164. Where most likely do the speakers work?

(A) At a department store
(B) At a cosmetics manufacturer
(C) At a beauty salon
(D) At a grocery store

165. What is indicated about the new line of Luxa products?

(A) They are used by stylists.
(B) They are currently sold in only a few stores.
(C) They were well received by some consumers.
(D) They will be sold at a discount.

166. At 1:33 P.M., what does Ms. Saba mean when she writes, "That's nothing"?

(A) She is not impressed with Luxa's brand name.
(B) She believes that Luxa should charge a lot more.
(C) She sees little profit to be gained by selling Luxa products.
(D) She thinks the price difference is insignificant.

167. What will Ms. Cotter probably do next?

(A) Cancel an order
(B) Distribute product samples
(C) Contact a salesperson
(D) Speak with consumers

▶ ▶ ▶ GO ON TO THE NEXT PAGE

New Brinn Book On the Way
by Jennifer Andres
February 7

Rumors that Karl Brinn has been working on a new novel have been verified. Brinn's publisher, Brickhouse Books, confirmed yesterday that it plans to release his newest novel, *Light and Darkness*, sometime next month. The novel is set in Brinn's hometown of Bainbridge, Connecticut, and tells the story of a young man's coming of age.

Since he published his first novel twenty-two years ago, Brinn has gained millions of fans worldwide. His best-selling novel, *Kim's Game*, has been translated into 12 different languages.

The press release from Brickhouse Books came out just one day after Brinn appeared on a local radio program in New York hosted by his longtime friend, Dale Carradine. During the live interview, Brinn hinted at his new book. The timing of the interview and press release was the topic of much speculation on social media.

Brinn has studiously avoided public appearances and rarely reveals information about his personal life. However, while conversing with Carradine on the radio, he shared a story about his time in the Navy. While on leave in San Francisco, he attended a classical music concert. That night, Brinn explained, he decided to become a writer.

168. What is indicated about *Light and Darkness*?

(A) It is Mr. Brinn's twenty-third novel.
(B) It is about Mr. Brinn's youth.
(C) It was written in Connecticut.
(D) It will go on sale in March.

169. What is suggested about Mr. Brinn's earlier novels?

(A) They were published by Brickhouse Books.
(B) They have been sold in multiple countries.
(C) They take place in cities around the world.
(D) They are based on Mr. Brinn's life experiences.

170. When was Mr. Brinn interviewed by Mr. Carradine?

(A) On February 4
(B) On February 5
(C) On February 6
(D) On February 7

171. What was discussed during the radio interview?

(A) Mr. Brinn's lifelong love of classical music
(B) Why Mr. Brinn is such a private person
(C) An experience that changed Mr. Brinn's life
(D) The reason Mr. Brinn joined the military

Questions 172-175 refer to the following article.

Downtown Office Building Opens

HAYWOOD (October 3) – A new office building owned by CKY Properties opened on Monday. The 20-story Santos Building claims its place among the tallest buildings in the urban skyline.

Designed by renowned local architectural firm Seagrams, the Santos Building evokes the styling of the Art Deco movement. Its sweeping lines and sculpted features are reminiscent of skyscrapers built in New York and Chicago during the 1920s. — [1] —. At the same time, it incorporates state-of-the-art features, such as passive air circulation, so that it will require less energy to heat and cool. In fact, Seagrams predicts its utility bills will be 45% lower than similar-sized buildings in the city. "At the request of our clients, we installed photovoltaic panels on the roof," explained Marc Cassidy of Seagrams. "My team and I incorporated them in our final architectural designs, so they not only generate electricity for the building but also improve the building's appearance." — [2] —.

Prior to opening, CKY Properties had already signed contracts with nineteen tenants. — [3] —. Excluding the latter, the current occupancy rate is around 65%. In contrast, it normally takes up to twelve months for the owners of new buildings to rent out the majority of their available office space. — [4] —.

---

172. What is true about the Santos Building?

(A) It was built in the 1920s.
(B) It is the highest building in the city.
(C) It will make all the electricity it needs.
(D) It is designed to be energy-efficient.

173. Who most likely is Mr. Cassidy?

(A) An office manager
(B) A property owner
(C) A building designer
(D) A real estate agent

174. What is suggested about CKY Properties?

(A) It requires tenants to sign a one-year contract.
(B) It will be completely rented out soon.
(C) It is filling up faster than usual.
(D) It houses over sixty businesses.

175. In which of the positions marked [1], [2], [3], and [4] does the following sentence best belong?

"Two more are currently in the review process."

(A) [1]
(B) [2]
(C [3]
(D) [4]

▶ ▶ ▶ GO ON TO THE NEXT PAGE

Questions 176-180 refer to the following e-mail and information.

From:	Wendy Brooks <wendy.brooks@ana.org>
To:	Patricia Hui <p.hui@achievingexcellence.com>
Subject:	June 3
Date:	ANA Conference

Dear Patricia,

It was a pleasure catching up with you this morning. I just want to thank you again for agreeing to speak at our annual conference in Atlanta in November. Our members would be very interested in hearing about your work designing state-of-the-art computer networks for universities in Africa and South America.

This e-mail confirms what we discussed over the phone. You will give a fifty-minute talk in the afternoon or evening of the second day of the conference. The exact time will be provided to you once it has been determined. The ANA will cover the costs of your airfare and lodging. In addition, we will pay your speaking fee of $2,000.

My assistant, Tamara Keller, will contact you in the coming weeks. She is responsible for making travel arrangements for all of our guest speakers. She will pick you up when you arrive and bring you to the conference.

If you have any questions or concerns, don't hesitate to reach out to me.

Sincerely,

Wendy

Association of Network Analysts (ANA)
17th Annual Conference
Bascomb Convention Center
Atlanta, Georgia
November 6 – November 9

The ANA Annual Conference is the nation's largest gathering of computer network analysts. Our members work in a variety of industries as well as at government agencies and nonprofit organizations. The conference features hundreds of presentations, workshops, displays, and guest speakers.

Registration opens on July 1 and ends on October 31. Save 10% if you register before August 15. Only active ANA members can attend the conference, so be sure to renew your membership before registering.

Members traveling from out of town can receive special rates at the Kenworth Hotel. To find out more about this offer, visit our Web site at www.ana.org. There, you can also find which roads to take to get to the conference, recommended restaurants nearby, and a list of things to do in Atlanta. An online conference program will also be posted as soon as it becomes available.

176. Who most likely is Ms. Hui?

(A) A government administrator
(B) A technology expert
(C) A college instructor
(D) A travel writer

177. What is suggested about Ms. Keller?

(A) She has worked with Ms. Hui before.
(B) She will meet Ms. Hui at the airport.
(C) She is the main conference organizer.
(D) She will give a talk at the conference.

178. When will Ms. Hui give her talk?

(A) On November 6
(B) On November 7
(C) On November 8
(D) On November 9

179. According to the information, how can conference attendees get a discount?

(A) By filling out an online form
(B) By agreeing to give a talk
(C) By renewing their membership
(D) By registering before a deadline

180. According to the information, what is NOT currently listed on the ANA Web site?

(A) Instructions for getting lodging discounts
(B) Driving directions to the convention center
(C) A list of workshops being offered
(D) Suggested places to eat

▶ ▶ ▶GO ON TO THE NEXT PAGE

From: Electronics Outlet <orders@electronicsoutlet.com>
To: Sam Rayburn <samr12@adventurouslife.com>
Date: August 13
Subject: Your Electronics Outlet Order Confirmation (#12843)

Thanks for your order!

Your order ID # is 12843

Billing address	**Shipping address**
Sam Rayburn	Sam Rayburn
118 Howe Street	118 Howe Street
Lincoln, NE68501	Lincoln, NE68501

Your order contains

Cart Items	SKU #	Qty.	Item Price	Item Total
Tobashi 8700 laptop computer	TB2934	1	$550.00	$550.00
Extra battery for Tobashi 8700	TB7494	1	$50.00	$50.00
Singha USB drive, 32GB	SH1323	2	$15.00	$30.00
Singha wireless headphones	SH8995	1	$24.00	$24.00

Subtotal $654.00
Tax $32.70
Shipping $12.75
Grand Total $699.45

Billed to credit card xxxx-xxxx-xxxx-3472

Orders typically ship within 48 hours of being placed. However, when an item is out of stock, a shipment may be delayed. Check the status of your order, including its estimated date of arrival, at www.electronicsoutlet.com. For questions about your order, please contact us at orders@electronicsoutlet.com.

From:	Electronics Outlet <orders@electronicsoutlet.com>
To:	Sam Rayburn <samr12@adventurouslife.com>
Date:	August 14
Subject:	Your Request

Dear Mr. Rayburn,

Thank you for contacting us regarding your order. Your request was forwarded to me. I have made the following changes. Item SH8995 has been replaced with item SH8999. Shipping has been changed from standard to express. Your order should now arrive in 2-3 business days rather than in 5-7 business days. The estimated delivery date is now August 16. The order will now be shipped to your place of work instead of your home. We have also included instructions that your signature is required upon delivery.

As a result of the above changes, your order now comes to $705.65. An updated invoice will be e-mailed to you shortly. Please let me know if you have any additional questions or concerns.

Sincerely,

Veronica Tiller
Customer Service Representative
Electronics Outlet

181. According to the invoice, what can customers do on the company's Web site?

(A) Find out when an order will be delivered
(B) Make changes to an existing order
(C) Communicate with customer service
(D) Order items that are out of stock

182. Which item did Mr. Rayburn decide NOT to buy?

(A) The battery
(B) The headphones
(C) The laptop
(D) The USB drive

183. What did Mr. Rayburn request in his e-mail?

(A) He would like to receive free shipping.
(B) He would like to send the order to another person.
(C) He would like the order to arrive earlier.
(D) He would like to pay with a different credit card.

184. What is suggested about Mr. Rayburn?

(A) He used a gift card with his order.
(B) He lives on Howe Street.
(C) He works for Electronics Outlet.
(D) He will move soon.

185. In the e-mail, the phrase "comes to" in paragraph 2, line 1, is closest in meaning to

(A) arrives at
(B) combines
(C) increases to
(D) totals

▶ ▶ ▶GO ON TO THE NEXT PAGE

Petstore.com

Pamper your pets with Petstore.com.

We carry over 1,000 brands of food, toys, treats, and accessories
for dogs, cats, birds, fish, and exotic pets.

If you order $50 or more, we will deliver your order directly
to your home or business at no charge.*

Special Offer

Get $25 off your next order of $100 or more

Enter the following coupon code:

J7434BH1

Valid: March 1 to March 31

Standard Shipping only (3-5 business days). A fee will be charged to upgrade to Express Shipping (1-2 business days). Addresses outside the United States will be charged our international shipping rates.

https://www.petstore.com

ORDER NUMBER: M78331   DATE: March 18

Customer Information
Name: Jessica D'Francesca
Address: 37 Penn Avenue, Apartment 8, New York City, NY, USA
Phone: (412) 555-8933
E-mail: jessica20@megafac.net

ORDER SUMMARY

Product Number	Product Description	Quantity	Price
F6733	Homer Dog Food, 13.5kg bag	2	$64.00
A3034	Chew Toy, 3 count	1	$5.50
A5237	Dog Bed, medium	1	$22.25
F1223	Dog Treats, 24 count bag	2	$19.00

SUBTOTAL: $110.75

Coupon Code: J7434BH1

<Back Change Cart Pay Now Next >

To:	Pet Store <custserv@petstore.com>
From:	Jessica D'Francesca <jessica20@megafac.net>
RE:	My Order
Date:	April 2

As the new owner of a golden retriever puppy named Goldie, I am still learning the best way to help her get what she needs. When I received your advertisement in the mail, I thought I would give your company a try. I am glad I did. Shopping on your Web site was so easy. My order arrived within the timeframe you promised. Goldie loves the food, treats, and chew toys. While initially uninterested in the new bed, she is slowly getting used to it. You should be getting an order soon from my sister, who first told me about your company. She was over the other day, and I let her dogs try some of the treats, which they loved!

Sincerely,

Jessica D'Francesca

186. What is NOT mentioned about Petstore. com in the advertisement?

(A) It sells edible items for a variety of animals.
(B) It offers free shipping on certain orders.
(C) It carries only the most popular brands.
(D) It ships to customers in multiple countries.

187. What is suggested about order M78331?

(A) It will be delivered in fewer than 3 days.
(B) It will be charged sales tax.
(C) It is eligible for a discount.
(D) It required a payment for delivery.

188. What is suggested about Ms. D'Francesca?

(A) She has more than one pet.
(B) She ordered from Petstore.com before.
(C) She rarely shops on the Internet.
(D) She lives in an urban area.

189. Why did Ms. D'Francesca write the e-mail?

(A) To welcome a new customer
(B) To express satisfaction with an order
(C) To complain about a product
(D) To inquire about a delivery delay

190. Which product will Ms. D'Francesca's sister most likely order?

(A) A3034
(B) A5237
(C) F1223
(D) F6733

▶ ▶ ▶GO ON TO THE NEXT PAGE

Questions 191-195 refer to the following Web sites and e-mail.

http://www.hdc.com

HUNTINGTON DINING CLUB			
HOME PAGE	ABOUT US	LOG IN	MEMBERSHIP

Best Burgers in Huntington
by Sally Twinning
Posted: Tuesday, August 7

Each week, I focus on a different part of town, style of food, or theme. This week, it's burgers. Whenever I am downtown, I eat at Sammy's Café. For just $7, you can get a hamburger with fries and a drink. If you are looking for something a little fancier in the same area, try Harris Grill. Its bacon avocado burger is delicious. One of my favorite places for lunch, and not just because it is close to my office, is Allison's. There, you can get an award-winning burger with sweet potato fries for just $8. Arrive early because it gets busy! The best burgers in town, however, are found at Main Street Diner.

Members can log in to read this and all of our other reviews.

http://www.hdc.com

HUNTINGTON DINING CLUB			
HOME PAGE	ABOUT US	LOG IN	MEMBERSHIP

MEMBERSHIP FORM

Become a member of the Huntington Dining Club and save. We'll send you a membership card, which entitles you to 5% off at any restaurant reviewed on our Web site. In addition, you'll get special offers in your inbox every Thursday.

Date: August 8
Name: Jennifer Landis
Phone: (412) 555-7393
E-mail: jennytenny@aimhigh.net
Annual Membership Fee: $50
Payment Type: Credit card ending in 6283

SUBMIT PAYMENT

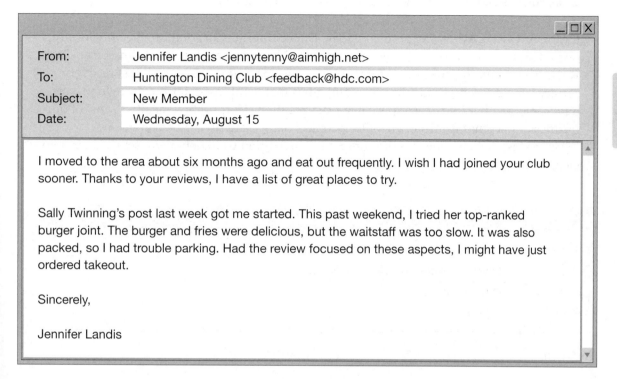

From: Jennifer Landis <jennytenny@aimhigh.net>

To: Huntington Dining Club <feedback@hdc.com>

Subject: New Member

Date: Wednesday, August 15

I moved to the area about six months ago and eat out frequently. I wish I had joined your club sooner. Thanks to your reviews, I have a list of great places to try.

Sally Twinning's post last week got me started. This past weekend, I tried her top-ranked burger joint. The burger and fries were delicious, but the waitstaff was too slow. It was also packed, so I had trouble parking. Had the review focused on these aspects, I might have just ordered takeout.

Sincerely,

Jennifer Landis

191. Who most likely is Sally Twinning?

(A) A blogger
(B) A chef
(C) A membership coordinator
(D) An office manager

192. What is suggested about Allison's?

(A) It is located in the central business district.
(B) All hamburgers sold there come with a side dish.
(C) Ms. Twinning eats there on a weekly basis.
(D) Huntington Dining Club members can get a discount there.

193. What is indicated about Ms. Landis?

(A) She is not comfortable parking her car.
(B) She has lived in Huntington for less than a year.
(C) She recently renewed her membership.
(D) She regularly orders takeout for dinner.

194. Where did Ms. Landis recently eat?

(A) Allison's
(B) Harris Grill
(C) Main Street Diner
(D) Sammy's Café

195. What did Ms. Landis enjoy about her recent dining experience?

(A) The speed of the service
(B) The price of her meal
(C) The mood of the restaurant
(D) The taste of the food

▶ ▶ ▶ GO ON TO THE NEXT PAGE

CAPE GIRARDEAU — (September 11) The Data Solutions Corporation, the only locally owned and operated data storage solutions provider, celebrated its third anniversary last week. The company offers data storage solutions, cloud computing, and data recovery services. In addition, it consults with companies that want to establish their own private data centers rather than lease space in a Data Solutions Corporation facility. "Most of our business still comes from storing other people's data," said owner Benjamin Ochs. "Starting last year, however, more companies have hired us to help them set up their own storage facilities."

_ □ X

From:	Greg Towner <greg@bullionfinancial.com>
To:	Owen Wissler <owen@bullionfinancial.com>
Subject:	Data Storage
Date:	October 8

Owen,

I just had lunch with Richard Deacon, the assistant director of IT at Accenture. During our conversation, the topic of data security came up. Richard recommended the Data Solutions Corporation, which his company has contracted with since it first started offering its services. Prior to that, Accenture used Mega Storage, which is our current provider.

Richard said that while the larger national companies often have lower rates, they are unable to provide the personalized attention that his company gets from the Data Solutions Corporation.

Richard put me in touch with the account manager at Data Solutions. The quote she gave me over the phone is within our budget and offers more services than we are currently receiving. I would like to discuss it with you in person. What would be a good time for you?

Best,

Greg

October 28

Owen Wissler
Bullion Financial Advisors
1212 State Street
Cape Girardeau, MO63703

Dear Mr. Wissler:

Thank you for choosing the Data Solutions Corporation to provide long-term data storage for your company, Bullion Financial Advisors.

As part of our agreement, you will receive designated space in our servers. In addition, our technical support staff will oversee the migration of your data from your existing provider to our servers. The full details of this agreement can be found in the attached service contract. Please review it carefully and return a signed copy to me.

If you have any questions, feel free to contact me at 555-7070 or paula@datasolutions.com.

Sincerely,

Paula Ochs
Account Manager
Data Solutions Corporation

196. According to the article, what is true about the Data Solutions Corporation?

(A) It bought out all of its local competitors.
(B) It sells computer hardware to local companies.
(C) Its consulting business has been growing over the last year.
(D) It owns multiple private data centers.

197. What is most likely true about Accenture?

(A) It is owned by Mr. Deacon.
(B) It is a national company.
(C) It has its own private data storage facility.
(D) It hired the Data Solutions Corporation three years ago.

198. Why did Mr. Towner write to Mr. Wissler?

(A) To introduce a contact
(B) To respond to a request
(C) To criticize a current service provider
(D) To request a face-to-face meeting

199. What is indicated about Mr. Towner?

(A) He spoke with Ms. Ochs.
(B) He is Mr. Wissler's supervisor.
(C) He is in charge of a budget.
(D) He used to work at Accenture.

200. In the letter, the word "full" in paragraph 2, line 3, is closest in meaning to

(A) additional
(B) complete
(C) large
(D) numerous

147. (C)	**148.** (D)	**149.** (A)	**150.** (B)	**151.** (D)	**152.** (D)
153. (B)	**154.** (D)	**155.** (B)	**156.** (C)	**157.** (D)	**158.** (B)
159. (A)	**160.** (D)	**161.** (C)	**162.** (B)	**163.** (A)	**164.** (A)
165. (C)	**166.** (D)	**167.** (C)	**168.** (D)	**169.** (B)	**170.** (B)
171. (C)	**172.** (D)	**173.** (C)	**174.** (C)	**175.** (C)	**176.** (B)
177. (B)	**178.** (B)	**179.** (D)	**180.** (C)	**181.** (A)	**182.** (B)
183. (C)	**184.** (B)	**185.** (D)	**186.** (C)	**187.** (C)	**188.** (D)
189. (B)	**190.** (C)	**191.** (A)	**192.** (D)	**193.** (B)	**194.** (C)
195. (D)	**196.** (C)	**197.** (D)	**198.** (D)	**199.** (A)	**200.** (B)

Test 2

READING (Part V ~ VII)

NO.	ANSWER	NO.	ANSWER	NO.	ANSWER	NO.	ANSWER
	A B C D		A B C D	147	ⓐ ⓑ ⓒ ⓓ	161	ⓐ ⓑ ⓒ ⓓ
				148	ⓐ ⓑ ⓒ ⓓ	162	ⓐ ⓑ ⓒ ⓓ
				149	ⓐ ⓑ ⓒ ⓓ	163	ⓐ ⓑ ⓒ ⓓ
				150	ⓐ ⓑ ⓒ ⓓ	164	ⓐ ⓑ ⓒ ⓓ
				151	ⓐ ⓑ ⓒ ⓓ	165	ⓐ ⓑ ⓒ ⓓ
				152	ⓐ ⓑ ⓒ ⓓ	166	ⓐ ⓑ ⓒ ⓓ
				153	ⓐ ⓑ ⓒ ⓓ	167	ⓐ ⓑ ⓒ ⓓ
				154	ⓐ ⓑ ⓒ ⓓ	168	ⓐ ⓑ ⓒ ⓓ
				155	ⓐ ⓑ ⓒ ⓓ	169	ⓐ ⓑ ⓒ ⓓ
				156	ⓐ ⓑ ⓒ ⓓ	170	ⓐ ⓑ ⓒ ⓓ
				157	ⓐ ⓑ ⓒ ⓓ	171	ⓐ ⓑ ⓒ ⓓ
				158	ⓐ ⓑ ⓒ ⓓ	172	ⓐ ⓑ ⓒ ⓓ
				159	ⓐ ⓑ ⓒ ⓓ	173	ⓐ ⓑ ⓒ ⓓ
				160	ⓐ ⓑ ⓒ ⓓ	174	ⓐ ⓑ ⓒ ⓓ
						175	ⓐ ⓑ ⓒ ⓓ
						176	ⓐ ⓑ ⓒ ⓓ
						177	ⓐ ⓑ ⓒ ⓓ
						178	ⓐ ⓑ ⓒ ⓓ
						179	ⓐ ⓑ ⓒ ⓓ
						180	ⓐ ⓑ ⓒ ⓓ

NO.	ANSWER
181	ⓐ ⓑ ⓒ ⓓ
182	ⓐ ⓑ ⓒ ⓓ
183	ⓐ ⓑ ⓒ ⓓ
184	ⓐ ⓑ ⓒ ⓓ
185	ⓐ ⓑ ⓒ ⓓ
186	ⓐ ⓑ ⓒ ⓓ
187	ⓐ ⓑ ⓒ ⓓ
188	ⓐ ⓑ ⓒ ⓓ
189	ⓐ ⓑ ⓒ ⓓ
190	ⓐ ⓑ ⓒ ⓓ
191	ⓐ ⓑ ⓒ ⓓ
192	ⓐ ⓑ ⓒ ⓓ
193	ⓐ ⓑ ⓒ ⓓ
194	ⓐ ⓑ ⓒ ⓓ
195	ⓐ ⓑ ⓒ ⓓ
196	ⓐ ⓑ ⓒ ⓓ
197	ⓐ ⓑ ⓒ ⓓ
198	ⓐ ⓑ ⓒ ⓓ
199	ⓐ ⓑ ⓒ ⓓ
200	ⓐ ⓑ ⓒ ⓓ

Test 1

READING (Part V ~ VII)

NO.	ANSWER	NO.	ANSWER	NO.	ANSWER	NO.	ANSWER
	A B C D		A B C D	147	ⓐ ⓑ ⓒ ⓓ	161	ⓐ ⓑ ⓒ ⓓ
				148	ⓐ ⓑ ⓒ ⓓ	162	ⓐ ⓑ ⓒ ⓓ
				149	ⓐ ⓑ ⓒ ⓓ	163	ⓐ ⓑ ⓒ ⓓ
				150	ⓐ ⓑ ⓒ ⓓ	164	ⓐ ⓑ ⓒ ⓓ
				151	ⓐ ⓑ ⓒ ⓓ	165	ⓐ ⓑ ⓒ ⓓ
				152	ⓐ ⓑ ⓒ ⓓ	166	ⓐ ⓑ ⓒ ⓓ
				153	ⓐ ⓑ ⓒ ⓓ	167	ⓐ ⓑ ⓒ ⓓ
				154	ⓐ ⓑ ⓒ ⓓ	168	ⓐ ⓑ ⓒ ⓓ
				155	ⓐ ⓑ ⓒ ⓓ	169	ⓐ ⓑ ⓒ ⓓ
				156	ⓐ ⓑ ⓒ ⓓ	170	ⓐ ⓑ ⓒ ⓓ
				157	ⓐ ⓑ ⓒ ⓓ	171	ⓐ ⓑ ⓒ ⓓ
				158	ⓐ ⓑ ⓒ ⓓ	172	ⓐ ⓑ ⓒ ⓓ
				159	ⓐ ⓑ ⓒ ⓓ	173	ⓐ ⓑ ⓒ ⓓ
				160	ⓐ ⓑ ⓒ ⓓ	174	ⓐ ⓑ ⓒ ⓓ
						175	ⓐ ⓑ ⓒ ⓓ
						176	ⓐ ⓑ ⓒ ⓓ
						177	ⓐ ⓑ ⓒ ⓓ
						178	ⓐ ⓑ ⓒ ⓓ
						179	ⓐ ⓑ ⓒ ⓓ
						180	ⓐ ⓑ ⓒ ⓓ

NO.	ANSWER
181	ⓐ ⓑ ⓒ ⓓ
182	ⓐ ⓑ ⓒ ⓓ
183	ⓐ ⓑ ⓒ ⓓ
184	ⓐ ⓑ ⓒ ⓓ
185	ⓐ ⓑ ⓒ ⓓ
186	ⓐ ⓑ ⓒ ⓓ
187	ⓐ ⓑ ⓒ ⓓ
188	ⓐ ⓑ ⓒ ⓓ
189	ⓐ ⓑ ⓒ ⓓ
190	ⓐ ⓑ ⓒ ⓓ
191	ⓐ ⓑ ⓒ ⓓ
192	ⓐ ⓑ ⓒ ⓓ
193	ⓐ ⓑ ⓒ ⓓ
194	ⓐ ⓑ ⓒ ⓓ
195	ⓐ ⓑ ⓒ ⓓ
196	ⓐ ⓑ ⓒ ⓓ
197	ⓐ ⓑ ⓒ ⓓ
198	ⓐ ⓑ ⓒ ⓓ
199	ⓐ ⓑ ⓒ ⓓ
200	ⓐ ⓑ ⓒ ⓓ

Test 4

READING (Part V ~ VII)

NO.	ANSWER A B C D	NO.	ANSWER A B C D	NO.	ANSWER A B C D	NO.	ANSWER A B C D
		147	a b c d	161	a b c d	181	a b c d
		148	a b c d	162	a b c d	182	a b c d
		149	a b c d	163	a b c d	183	a b c d
		150	a b c d	164	a b c d	184	a b c d
		151	a b c d	165	a b c d	185	a b c d
		152	a b c d	166	a b c d	186	a b c d
		153	a b c d	167	a b c d	187	a b c d
		154	a b c d	168	a b c d	188	a b c d
		155	a b c d	169	a b c d	189	a b c d
		156	a b c d	170	a b c d	190	a b c d
		157	a b c d	171	a b c d	191	a b c d
		158	a b c d	172	a b c d	192	a b c d
		159	a b c d	173	a b c d	193	a b c d
		160	a b c d	174	a b c d	194	a b c d
				175	a b c d	195	a b c d
				176	a b c d	196	a b c d
				177	a b c d	197	a b c d
				178	a b c d	198	a b c d
				179	a b c d	199	a b c d
				180	a b c d	200	a b c d

Test 3

READING (Part V ~ VII)

NO.	ANSWER A B C D	NO.	ANSWER A B C D	NO.	ANSWER A B C D	NO.	ANSWER A B C D
		147	a b c d	161	a b c d	181	a b c d
		148	a b c d	162	a b c d	182	a b c d
		149	a b c d	163	a b c d	183	a b c d
		150	a b c d	164	a b c d	184	a b c d
		151	a b c d	165	a b c d	185	a b c d
		152	a b c d	166	a b c d	186	a b c d
		153	a b c d	167	a b c d	187	a b c d
		154	a b c d	168	a b c d	188	a b c d
		155	a b c d	169	a b c d	189	a b c d
		156	a b c d	170	a b c d	190	a b c d
		157	a b c d	171	a b c d	191	a b c d
		158	a b c d	172	a b c d	192	a b c d
		159	a b c d	173	a b c d	193	a b c d
		160	a b c d	174	a b c d	194	a b c d
				175	a b c d	195	a b c d
				176	a b c d	196	a b c d
				177	a b c d	197	a b c d
				178	a b c d	198	a b c d
				179	a b c d	199	a b c d
				180	a b c d	200	a b c d

Test 5

READING (Part V ~ VII)

NO.	ANSWER				NO.	ANSWER				NO.	ANSWER				NO.	ANSWER				NO.	ANSWER			
	A	B	C	D		A	B	C	D		A	B	C	D		A	B	C	D		A	B	C	D
															161	a	b	c	d	181	a	b	c	d
															162	a	b	c	d	182	a	b	c	d
															163	a	b	c	d	183	a	b	c	d
															164	a	b	c	d	184	a	b	c	d
															165	a	b	c	d	185	a	b	c	d
															166	a	b	c	d	186	a	b	c	d
										147	a	b	c	d	167	a	b	c	d	187	a	b	c	d
										148	a	b	c	d	168	a	b	c	d	188	a	b	c	d
										149	a	b	c	d	169	a	b	c	d	189	a	b	c	d
										150	a	b	c	d	170	a	b	c	d	190	a	b	c	d
										151	a	b	c	d	171	a	b	c	d	191	a	b	c	d
										152	a	b	c	d	172	a	b	c	d	192	a	b	c	d
										153	a	b	c	d	173	a	b	c	d	193	a	b	c	d
										154	a	b	c	d	174	a	b	c	d	194	a	b	c	d
										155	a	b	c	d	175	a	b	c	d	195	a	b	c	d
										156	a	b	c	d	176	a	b	c	d	196	a	b	c	d
										157	a	b	c	d	177	a	b	c	d	197	a	b	c	d
										158	a	b	c	d	178	a	b	c	d	198	a	b	c	d
										159	a	b	c	d	179	a	b	c	d	199	a	b	c	d
										160	a	b	c	d	180	a	b	c	d	200	a	b	c	d

Test 6

READING (Part V ~ VII)

NO.	ANSWER				NO.	ANSWER				NO.	ANSWER				NO.	ANSWER				NO.	ANSWER			
	A	B	C	D		A	B	C	D		A	B	C	D		A	B	C	D		A	B	C	D
															161	a	b	c	d	181	a	b	c	d
															162	a	b	c	d	182	a	b	c	d
															163	a	b	c	d	183	a	b	c	d
															164	a	b	c	d	184	a	b	c	d
															165	a	b	c	d	185	a	b	c	d
															166	a	b	c	d	186	a	b	c	d
										147	a	b	c	d	167	a	b	c	d	187	a	b	c	d
										148	a	b	c	d	168	a	b	c	d	188	a	b	c	d
										149	a	b	c	d	169	a	b	c	d	189	a	b	c	d
										150	a	b	c	d	170	a	b	c	d	190	a	b	c	d
										151	a	b	c	d	171	a	b	c	d	191	a	b	c	d
										152	a	b	c	d	172	a	b	c	d	192	a	b	c	d
										153	a	b	c	d	173	a	b	c	d	193	a	b	c	d
										154	a	b	c	d	174	a	b	c	d	194	a	b	c	d
										155	a	b	c	d	175	a	b	c	d	195	a	b	c	d
										156	a	b	c	d	176	a	b	c	d	196	a	b	c	d
										157	a	b	c	d	177	a	b	c	d	197	a	b	c	d
										158	a	b	c	d	178	a	b	c	d	198	a	b	c	d
										159	a	b	c	d	179	a	b	c	d	199	a	b	c	d
										160	a	b	c	d	180	a	b	c	d	200	a	b	c	d

Test 8

READING (Part V ~ VII)

NO.	ANSWER A B C D	NO.	ANSWER A B C D	NO.	ANSWER A B C D	NO.	ANSWER A B C D
		147	Ⓐ Ⓑ Ⓒ Ⓓ	161	Ⓐ Ⓑ Ⓒ Ⓓ	181	Ⓐ Ⓑ Ⓒ Ⓓ
		148	Ⓐ Ⓑ Ⓒ Ⓓ	162	Ⓐ Ⓑ Ⓒ Ⓓ	182	Ⓐ Ⓑ Ⓒ Ⓓ
		149	Ⓐ Ⓑ Ⓒ Ⓓ	163	Ⓐ Ⓑ Ⓒ Ⓓ	183	Ⓐ Ⓑ Ⓒ Ⓓ
		150	Ⓐ Ⓑ Ⓒ Ⓓ	164	Ⓐ Ⓑ Ⓒ Ⓓ	184	Ⓐ Ⓑ Ⓒ Ⓓ
		151	Ⓐ Ⓑ Ⓒ Ⓓ	165	Ⓐ Ⓑ Ⓒ Ⓓ	185	Ⓐ Ⓑ Ⓒ Ⓓ
		152	Ⓐ Ⓑ Ⓒ Ⓓ	166	Ⓐ Ⓑ Ⓒ Ⓓ	186	Ⓐ Ⓑ Ⓒ Ⓓ
		153	Ⓐ Ⓑ Ⓒ Ⓓ	167	Ⓐ Ⓑ Ⓒ Ⓓ	187	Ⓐ Ⓑ Ⓒ Ⓓ
		154	Ⓐ Ⓑ Ⓒ Ⓓ	168	Ⓐ Ⓑ Ⓒ Ⓓ	188	Ⓐ Ⓑ Ⓒ Ⓓ
		155	Ⓐ Ⓑ Ⓒ Ⓓ	169	Ⓐ Ⓑ Ⓒ Ⓓ	189	Ⓐ Ⓑ Ⓒ Ⓓ
		156	Ⓐ Ⓑ Ⓒ Ⓓ	170	Ⓐ Ⓑ Ⓒ Ⓓ	190	Ⓐ Ⓑ Ⓒ Ⓓ
		157	Ⓐ Ⓑ Ⓒ Ⓓ	171	Ⓐ Ⓑ Ⓒ Ⓓ	191	Ⓐ Ⓑ Ⓒ Ⓓ
		158	Ⓐ Ⓑ Ⓒ Ⓓ	172	Ⓐ Ⓑ Ⓒ Ⓓ	192	Ⓐ Ⓑ Ⓒ Ⓓ
		159	Ⓐ Ⓑ Ⓒ Ⓓ	173	Ⓐ Ⓑ Ⓒ Ⓓ	193	Ⓐ Ⓑ Ⓒ Ⓓ
		160	Ⓐ Ⓑ Ⓒ Ⓓ	174	Ⓐ Ⓑ Ⓒ Ⓓ	194	Ⓐ Ⓑ Ⓒ Ⓓ
				175	Ⓐ Ⓑ Ⓒ Ⓓ	195	Ⓐ Ⓑ Ⓒ Ⓓ
				176	Ⓐ Ⓑ Ⓒ Ⓓ	196	Ⓐ Ⓑ Ⓒ Ⓓ
				177	Ⓐ Ⓑ Ⓒ Ⓓ	197	Ⓐ Ⓑ Ⓒ Ⓓ
				178	Ⓐ Ⓑ Ⓒ Ⓓ	198	Ⓐ Ⓑ Ⓒ Ⓓ
				179	Ⓐ Ⓑ Ⓒ Ⓓ	199	Ⓐ Ⓑ Ⓒ Ⓓ
				180	Ⓐ Ⓑ Ⓒ Ⓓ	200	Ⓐ Ⓑ Ⓒ Ⓓ

Test 7

READING (Part V ~ VII)

NO.	ANSWER A B C D	NO.	ANSWER A B C D	NO.	ANSWER A B C D	NO.	ANSWER A B C D
		147	Ⓐ Ⓑ Ⓒ Ⓓ	161	Ⓐ Ⓑ Ⓒ Ⓓ	181	Ⓐ Ⓑ Ⓒ Ⓓ
		148	Ⓐ Ⓑ Ⓒ Ⓓ	162	Ⓐ Ⓑ Ⓒ Ⓓ	182	Ⓐ Ⓑ Ⓒ Ⓓ
		149	Ⓐ Ⓑ Ⓒ Ⓓ	163	Ⓐ Ⓑ Ⓒ Ⓓ	183	Ⓐ Ⓑ Ⓒ Ⓓ
		150	Ⓐ Ⓑ Ⓒ Ⓓ	164	Ⓐ Ⓑ Ⓒ Ⓓ	184	Ⓐ Ⓑ Ⓒ Ⓓ
		151	Ⓐ Ⓑ Ⓒ Ⓓ	165	Ⓐ Ⓑ Ⓒ Ⓓ	185	Ⓐ Ⓑ Ⓒ Ⓓ
		152	Ⓐ Ⓑ Ⓒ Ⓓ	166	Ⓐ Ⓑ Ⓒ Ⓓ	186	Ⓐ Ⓑ Ⓒ Ⓓ
		153	Ⓐ Ⓑ Ⓒ Ⓓ	167	Ⓐ Ⓑ Ⓒ Ⓓ	187	Ⓐ Ⓑ Ⓒ Ⓓ
		154	Ⓐ Ⓑ Ⓒ Ⓓ	168	Ⓐ Ⓑ Ⓒ Ⓓ	188	Ⓐ Ⓑ Ⓒ Ⓓ
		155	Ⓐ Ⓑ Ⓒ Ⓓ	169	Ⓐ Ⓑ Ⓒ Ⓓ	189	Ⓐ Ⓑ Ⓒ Ⓓ
		156	Ⓐ Ⓑ Ⓒ Ⓓ	170	Ⓐ Ⓑ Ⓒ Ⓓ	190	Ⓐ Ⓑ Ⓒ Ⓓ
		157	Ⓐ Ⓑ Ⓒ Ⓓ	171	Ⓐ Ⓑ Ⓒ Ⓓ	191	Ⓐ Ⓑ Ⓒ Ⓓ
		158	Ⓐ Ⓑ Ⓒ Ⓓ	172	Ⓐ Ⓑ Ⓒ Ⓓ	192	Ⓐ Ⓑ Ⓒ Ⓓ
		159	Ⓐ Ⓑ Ⓒ Ⓓ	173	Ⓐ Ⓑ Ⓒ Ⓓ	193	Ⓐ Ⓑ Ⓒ Ⓓ
		160	Ⓐ Ⓑ Ⓒ Ⓓ	174	Ⓐ Ⓑ Ⓒ Ⓓ	194	Ⓐ Ⓑ Ⓒ Ⓓ
				175	Ⓐ Ⓑ Ⓒ Ⓓ	195	Ⓐ Ⓑ Ⓒ Ⓓ
				176	Ⓐ Ⓑ Ⓒ Ⓓ	196	Ⓐ Ⓑ Ⓒ Ⓓ
				177	Ⓐ Ⓑ Ⓒ Ⓓ	197	Ⓐ Ⓑ Ⓒ Ⓓ
				178	Ⓐ Ⓑ Ⓒ Ⓓ	198	Ⓐ Ⓑ Ⓒ Ⓓ
				179	Ⓐ Ⓑ Ⓒ Ⓓ	199	Ⓐ Ⓑ Ⓒ Ⓓ
				180	Ⓐ Ⓑ Ⓒ Ⓓ	200	Ⓐ Ⓑ Ⓒ Ⓓ

Test 10

READING (Part V ~ VII)

NO.	ANSWER	NO.	ANSWER	NO.	ANSWER	NO.	ANSWER
	A B C D		A B C D		A B C D		A B C D
		147	ⓐ ⓑ ⓒ ⓓ	161	ⓐ ⓑ ⓒ ⓓ	181	ⓐ ⓑ ⓒ ⓓ
		148	ⓐ ⓑ ⓒ ⓓ	162	ⓐ ⓑ ⓒ ⓓ	182	ⓐ ⓑ ⓒ ⓓ
		149	ⓐ ⓑ ⓒ ⓓ	163	ⓐ ⓑ ⓒ ⓓ	183	ⓐ ⓑ ⓒ ⓓ
		150	ⓐ ⓑ ⓒ ⓓ	164	ⓐ ⓑ ⓒ ⓓ	184	ⓐ ⓑ ⓒ ⓓ
		151	ⓐ ⓑ ⓒ ⓓ	165	ⓐ ⓑ ⓒ ⓓ	185	ⓐ ⓑ ⓒ ⓓ
		152	ⓐ ⓑ ⓒ ⓓ	166	ⓐ ⓑ ⓒ ⓓ	186	ⓐ ⓑ ⓒ ⓓ
		153	ⓐ ⓑ ⓒ ⓓ	167	ⓐ ⓑ ⓒ ⓓ	187	ⓐ ⓑ ⓒ ⓓ
		154	ⓐ ⓑ ⓒ ⓓ	168	ⓐ ⓑ ⓒ ⓓ	188	ⓐ ⓑ ⓒ ⓓ
		155	ⓐ ⓑ ⓒ ⓓ	169	ⓐ ⓑ ⓒ ⓓ	189	ⓐ ⓑ ⓒ ⓓ
		156	ⓐ ⓑ ⓒ ⓓ	170	ⓐ ⓑ ⓒ ⓓ	190	ⓐ ⓑ ⓒ ⓓ
		157	ⓐ ⓑ ⓒ ⓓ	171	ⓐ ⓑ ⓒ ⓓ	191	ⓐ ⓑ ⓒ ⓓ
		158	ⓐ ⓑ ⓒ ⓓ	172	ⓐ ⓑ ⓒ ⓓ	192	ⓐ ⓑ ⓒ ⓓ
		159	ⓐ ⓑ ⓒ ⓓ	173	ⓐ ⓑ ⓒ ⓓ	193	ⓐ ⓑ ⓒ ⓓ
		160	ⓐ ⓑ ⓒ ⓓ	174	ⓐ ⓑ ⓒ ⓓ	194	ⓐ ⓑ ⓒ ⓓ
				175	ⓐ ⓑ ⓒ ⓓ	195	ⓐ ⓑ ⓒ ⓓ
				176	ⓐ ⓑ ⓒ ⓓ	196	ⓐ ⓑ ⓒ ⓓ
				177	ⓐ ⓑ ⓒ ⓓ	197	ⓐ ⓑ ⓒ ⓓ
				178	ⓐ ⓑ ⓒ ⓓ	198	ⓐ ⓑ ⓒ ⓓ
				179	ⓐ ⓑ ⓒ ⓓ	199	ⓐ ⓑ ⓒ ⓓ
				180	ⓐ ⓑ ⓒ ⓓ	200	ⓐ ⓑ ⓒ ⓓ

Test 9

READING (Part V ~ VII)

NO.	ANSWER	NO.	ANSWER	NO.	ANSWER	NO.	ANSWER
	A B C D		A B C D		A B C D		A B C D
		147	ⓐ ⓑ ⓒ ⓓ	161	ⓐ ⓑ ⓒ ⓓ	181	ⓐ ⓑ ⓒ ⓓ
		148	ⓐ ⓑ ⓒ ⓓ	162	ⓐ ⓑ ⓒ ⓓ	182	ⓐ ⓑ ⓒ ⓓ
		149	ⓐ ⓑ ⓒ ⓓ	163	ⓐ ⓑ ⓒ ⓓ	183	ⓐ ⓑ ⓒ ⓓ
		150	ⓐ ⓑ ⓒ ⓓ	164	ⓐ ⓑ ⓒ ⓓ	184	ⓐ ⓑ ⓒ ⓓ
		151	ⓐ ⓑ ⓒ ⓓ	165	ⓐ ⓑ ⓒ ⓓ	185	ⓐ ⓑ ⓒ ⓓ
		152	ⓐ ⓑ ⓒ ⓓ	166	ⓐ ⓑ ⓒ ⓓ	186	ⓐ ⓑ ⓒ ⓓ
		153	ⓐ ⓑ ⓒ ⓓ	167	ⓐ ⓑ ⓒ ⓓ	187	ⓐ ⓑ ⓒ ⓓ
		154	ⓐ ⓑ ⓒ ⓓ	168	ⓐ ⓑ ⓒ ⓓ	188	ⓐ ⓑ ⓒ ⓓ
		155	ⓐ ⓑ ⓒ ⓓ	169	ⓐ ⓑ ⓒ ⓓ	189	ⓐ ⓑ ⓒ ⓓ
		156	ⓐ ⓑ ⓒ ⓓ	170	ⓐ ⓑ ⓒ ⓓ	190	ⓐ ⓑ ⓒ ⓓ
		157	ⓐ ⓑ ⓒ ⓓ	171	ⓐ ⓑ ⓒ ⓓ	191	ⓐ ⓑ ⓒ ⓓ
		158	ⓐ ⓑ ⓒ ⓓ	172	ⓐ ⓑ ⓒ ⓓ	192	ⓐ ⓑ ⓒ ⓓ
		159	ⓐ ⓑ ⓒ ⓓ	173	ⓐ ⓑ ⓒ ⓓ	193	ⓐ ⓑ ⓒ ⓓ
		160	ⓐ ⓑ ⓒ ⓓ	174	ⓐ ⓑ ⓒ ⓓ	194	ⓐ ⓑ ⓒ ⓓ
				175	ⓐ ⓑ ⓒ ⓓ	195	ⓐ ⓑ ⓒ ⓓ
				176	ⓐ ⓑ ⓒ ⓓ	196	ⓐ ⓑ ⓒ ⓓ
				177	ⓐ ⓑ ⓒ ⓓ	197	ⓐ ⓑ ⓒ ⓓ
				178	ⓐ ⓑ ⓒ ⓓ	198	ⓐ ⓑ ⓒ ⓓ
				179	ⓐ ⓑ ⓒ ⓓ	199	ⓐ ⓑ ⓒ ⓓ
				180	ⓐ ⓑ ⓒ ⓓ	200	ⓐ ⓑ ⓒ ⓓ

Test 12

READING (Part V ~ VII)

NO.	ANSWER	NO.	ANSWER	NO.	ANSWER
	A B C D		A B C D		A B C D
		147	ⓐ ⓑ ⓒ ⓓ	161	ⓐ ⓑ ⓒ ⓓ	181	ⓐ ⓑ ⓒ ⓓ
		148	ⓐ ⓑ ⓒ ⓓ	162	ⓐ ⓑ ⓒ ⓓ	182	ⓐ ⓑ ⓒ ⓓ
		149	ⓐ ⓑ ⓒ ⓓ	163	ⓐ ⓑ ⓒ ⓓ	183	ⓐ ⓑ ⓒ ⓓ
		150	ⓐ ⓑ ⓒ ⓓ	164	ⓐ ⓑ ⓒ ⓓ	184	ⓐ ⓑ ⓒ ⓓ
		151	ⓐ ⓑ ⓒ ⓓ	165	ⓐ ⓑ ⓒ ⓓ	185	ⓐ ⓑ ⓒ ⓓ
		152	ⓐ ⓑ ⓒ ⓓ	166	ⓐ ⓑ ⓒ ⓓ	186	ⓐ ⓑ ⓒ ⓓ
		153	ⓐ ⓑ ⓒ ⓓ	167	ⓐ ⓑ ⓒ ⓓ	187	ⓐ ⓑ ⓒ ⓓ
		154	ⓐ ⓑ ⓒ ⓓ	168	ⓐ ⓑ ⓒ ⓓ	188	ⓐ ⓑ ⓒ ⓓ
		155	ⓐ ⓑ ⓒ ⓓ	169	ⓐ ⓑ ⓒ ⓓ	189	ⓐ ⓑ ⓒ ⓓ
		156	ⓐ ⓑ ⓒ ⓓ	170	ⓐ ⓑ ⓒ ⓓ	190	ⓐ ⓑ ⓒ ⓓ
		157	ⓐ ⓑ ⓒ ⓓ	171	ⓐ ⓑ ⓒ ⓓ	191	ⓐ ⓑ ⓒ ⓓ
		158	ⓐ ⓑ ⓒ ⓓ	172	ⓐ ⓑ ⓒ ⓓ	192	ⓐ ⓑ ⓒ ⓓ
		159	ⓐ ⓑ ⓒ ⓓ	173	ⓐ ⓑ ⓒ ⓓ	193	ⓐ ⓑ ⓒ ⓓ
		160	ⓐ ⓑ ⓒ ⓓ	174	ⓐ ⓑ ⓒ ⓓ	194	ⓐ ⓑ ⓒ ⓓ
				175	ⓐ ⓑ ⓒ ⓓ	195	ⓐ ⓑ ⓒ ⓓ
				176	ⓐ ⓑ ⓒ ⓓ	196	ⓐ ⓑ ⓒ ⓓ
				177	ⓐ ⓑ ⓒ ⓓ	197	ⓐ ⓑ ⓒ ⓓ
				178	ⓐ ⓑ ⓒ ⓓ	198	ⓐ ⓑ ⓒ ⓓ
				179	ⓐ ⓑ ⓒ ⓓ	199	ⓐ ⓑ ⓒ ⓓ
				180	ⓐ ⓑ ⓒ ⓓ	200	ⓐ ⓑ ⓒ ⓓ

Test 11

READING (Part V ~ VII)

NO.	ANSWER	NO.	ANSWER	NO.	ANSWER
	A B C D		A B C D		A B C D
		147	ⓐ ⓑ ⓒ ⓓ	161	ⓐ ⓑ ⓒ ⓓ	181	ⓐ ⓑ ⓒ ⓓ
		148	ⓐ ⓑ ⓒ ⓓ	162	ⓐ ⓑ ⓒ ⓓ	182	ⓐ ⓑ ⓒ ⓓ
		149	ⓐ ⓑ ⓒ ⓓ	163	ⓐ ⓑ ⓒ ⓓ	183	ⓐ ⓑ ⓒ ⓓ
		150	ⓐ ⓑ ⓒ ⓓ	164	ⓐ ⓑ ⓒ ⓓ	184	ⓐ ⓑ ⓒ ⓓ
		151	ⓐ ⓑ ⓒ ⓓ	165	ⓐ ⓑ ⓒ ⓓ	185	ⓐ ⓑ ⓒ ⓓ
		152	ⓐ ⓑ ⓒ ⓓ	166	ⓐ ⓑ ⓒ ⓓ	186	ⓐ ⓑ ⓒ ⓓ
		153	ⓐ ⓑ ⓒ ⓓ	167	ⓐ ⓑ ⓒ ⓓ	187	ⓐ ⓑ ⓒ ⓓ
		154	ⓐ ⓑ ⓒ ⓓ	168	ⓐ ⓑ ⓒ ⓓ	188	ⓐ ⓑ ⓒ ⓓ
		155	ⓐ ⓑ ⓒ ⓓ	169	ⓐ ⓑ ⓒ ⓓ	189	ⓐ ⓑ ⓒ ⓓ
		156	ⓐ ⓑ ⓒ ⓓ	170	ⓐ ⓑ ⓒ ⓓ	190	ⓐ ⓑ ⓒ ⓓ
		157	ⓐ ⓑ ⓒ ⓓ	171	ⓐ ⓑ ⓒ ⓓ	191	ⓐ ⓑ ⓒ ⓓ
		158	ⓐ ⓑ ⓒ ⓓ	172	ⓐ ⓑ ⓒ ⓓ	192	ⓐ ⓑ ⓒ ⓓ
		159	ⓐ ⓑ ⓒ ⓓ	173	ⓐ ⓑ ⓒ ⓓ	193	ⓐ ⓑ ⓒ ⓓ
		160	ⓐ ⓑ ⓒ ⓓ	174	ⓐ ⓑ ⓒ ⓓ	194	ⓐ ⓑ ⓒ ⓓ
				175	ⓐ ⓑ ⓒ ⓓ	195	ⓐ ⓑ ⓒ ⓓ
				176	ⓐ ⓑ ⓒ ⓓ	196	ⓐ ⓑ ⓒ ⓓ
				177	ⓐ ⓑ ⓒ ⓓ	197	ⓐ ⓑ ⓒ ⓓ
				178	ⓐ ⓑ ⓒ ⓓ	198	ⓐ ⓑ ⓒ ⓓ
				179	ⓐ ⓑ ⓒ ⓓ	199	ⓐ ⓑ ⓒ ⓓ
				180	ⓐ ⓑ ⓒ ⓓ	200	ⓐ ⓑ ⓒ ⓓ

딱 750점이 필요한 당신을 위한 책!

시나공 혼자서 끝내는 토익

750 완벽대비
김병기, 이관우 지음 | 728쪽 | 21,000원

········ 빈출 문제 유형 + 실전 모의고사 3회로 750점 달성! ········

 초보자도 이해하기 쉬운 친절한 단계별 해설집

 주요 LC 문제 받아쓰기 훈련

 파트 5 핵심 문제 문장분석 훈련

 파트 7 어려운 문장 직독직해 훈련

 MP3 5종 세트

- 실전용 MP3
- 1.2 배속 MP3
- 고사장용 MP3
- 받아쓰기용 MP3
- 영국 | 호주 발음 MP3

권장하는 점수대	400	500	600	700	800	900

이 책의 난이도	쉬움	비슷함	어려움

시험에 나오는 것만 공부한다!

시나공 토익

실전 문제 **12회분!** +
고난도 **100문제!**

7

파트

YBM 전국 수강생 수 1위 초초강추
강진오, 강원기 지음

실전문제집 시즌2

✻ **자세한 해설집!** + **패러프레이징 암기장**

정답
&
해설집

✻ **저자 카카오톡 1:1 관리**

독학용 복습 노트 제공 www.gilbut.co.kr

길벗
이지:톡

시험에 나오는 것만 공부한다!

시나공 토익

7

파트 실전문제집 시즌2

강진오, 강원기 지음

정답 & 해설집

길벗
이지:톡

문제 147-148번은 다음 이메일을 참조하시오.

Mr. Christensen 님께,

¹⁴⁷저는 Taco Cabana의 St. Francis Road 지점 지점장 직에 지원한 Ms. Janet Turner를 위해 이 글을 씁니다. ^{148(A), (B), (C)}Ms. Turner는 제가 관리하는 Taco Cabana의 River Road 지점에서 3년 간 부지점장으로 근무해 왔습니다. ^{148(D)}그녀는 레스토랑 경영에 관한 많은 지식을 갖추고 있으며, 동료 직원들과의 의사소통에도 매우 뛰어난 직원입니다. 저는 그 자리에 지원한 그녀를 적극 추천합니다. 궁금한 사항이 있으면 언제든지 연락 바랍니다.

Aaron James
지점장
Taco Cabana (Store #234)

표현 정리 reference 추천서 in support of ~을 지지해 application 지원 head manager 지점장 branch 지점, 지사 manage 관리하다 exceptional 훌륭한, 특출한 knowledgeable 많이 아는 highly 매우 be skilled at ~에 능하다 communicate 의사 소통하다 fellow employee 직장 동료 strongly 적극, 강력히

147. 주제 - 이메일을 보낸 목적 ★☆☆

해설 이메일 본문 첫 번째 문장 'I am writing in support of Ms. Janet Turner's application for the position of head manager at the St. Francis Road branch of Taco Cabana.'에서 지원자인 Ms. Janet Turner를 지지하기 위해 글을 쓴다고 밝혔으므로 정답은 (C)이다. 정답 (C)

표현 정리 job opening (직장의) 빈 자리 job offer 일자리 제의 job seeker 구직자 request 요청하다

해석 이메일을 보낸 이유는?
(A) 일자리에 지원하기 위해
(B) 일자리 제안을 받아들이기 위해
(C) 구직자를 추천하기 위해
(D) 추천서를 요청하기 위해

148. 세부사항 - Ms. Turner와 관련된 내용 ★★☆

해설 'Ms. Turner has worked for three years as the assistant manager at the River Road branch of the Taco Cabana that I manage.'에서 3년 간 River Road 지점에서 일했다고 했으므로 작년에 채용된 것은 사실이 아니며, 따라서 정답은 (C)이다. 정답 (C)

🔍 함정 분석 'Ms. Turner has worked for three years as the assistant manager at the River Road branch of the Taco Cabana that I manage.'에서 부지점장으로 일했기 때문에 (A)의 관리직 경험은 맞는 내용이고, 시제 상으로도 현재완료형을 사용해 과거부터 지금까지 Mr. James와 일하고 있음을 알 수 있어 (B) 역시 맞는 내용이다. She is an exceptional employee who is very knowledgeable about restaurant management를 통해 음식점 운영에 대한 많은 지식을 갖고 있음을 역시 알 수 있으므로 (D)도 맞는 내용이다.

패러프레이징 |지문| Ms. Turner has worked for three years as the assistant manager Turner 씨는 부지점장으로 3년 일해 왔다 → |선택지 A| She has supervisory experience 그녀는 관리직 경험이 있다
|지문| She is an exceptional employee who is very knowledgeable about restaurant management 그녀는 음식점 운영에 관해 많이 알고 있는 특출 난 직원이다 → |선택지 D| She knows a lot about running an eatery 그

녀는 음식점 운영에 대하여 많이 안다

표현 정리 supervisory 관리 상의 currently 현재 eatery 음식점

해석 Ms. Turner에 관해 언급된 내용이 아닌 것은?
(A) 그녀는 관리직 경험이 있다.
(B) 그녀는 현재 Mr. James를 위해 일한다.
(C) 그녀는 작년에 채용됐다.
(D) 그녀는 음식점 운영에 대해 많이 안다.

문제 149-150번은 다음 안내를 참조하시오.

KERMAN "BIG MAX" 자전거

안전 리콜

¹⁴⁹이 제품은 조절 가능한 안장에 발생한 결함으로 리콜을 실시하고 있습니다. 많은 소유주들이 자전거를 이용하는 도중에 안장이 헐거워져, 그 결과 회전하고 미끄러진다고 보고했습니다. 이번 리콜은 Kerman의 Tenjin 공장에서 3월 3일에서 6월 2일 사이에 생산돼 북아메리카 시장에서 판매된 자전거들로 제한됩니다.

¹⁵⁰이러한 결함을 가진 자전거 소유주들은 즉시 자전거 이용을 중지하고, Kerman 1-888-476-9032로 연락하시기 바랍니다.

표현 정리 recall 회수하다, 리콜하다 adjustable 조절 가능한 mechanism 기계 장치 a number of 다수의 loose 헐거워진, 느슨한 in use 사용 중인 result in 그 결과 ~가 되다 rotating 회전하는 sliding 미끄러져 움직이는 potentially 잠재적으로 affect 영향을 미치다 immediately 즉시

149. 세부사항 - Big Max 자전거에 관한 내용 ★☆☆

해설 첫 번째 문장 'This product is being recalled because of a problem with its adjustable seat mechanism.'을 통해 조절 가능한 안장에 결함이 있음을 알 수 있으므로 정답은 (A)이다. 정답 (A)

패러프레이징 |지문| a problem with its adjustable seat mechanism 조절 가능한 안장 장치의 문제점 → |선택지 A| a faulty part 결함이 있는 부품

표현 정리 faulty 결함이 있는 mistakenly 잘못하여, 실수로 overseas 해외로

해석 Tenjin에서 생산된 Big Max 자전거에 대해 언급된 내용은?
(A) 결함이 있는 부품을 갖고 있다.
(B) 실수로 해외로 보내졌다.
(C) 정보판이 빠져 있다.
(D) 안장이 없이 팔렸다.

150. 세부사항 - Big Max의 소유주들이 해야 할 일 ★☆☆

해설 두 번째 단락에 소유주들이 해야 할 내용이 언급되어 있다. 'Owners of potentially affected bicycles should stop using the bikes immediately. They should contact Kerman at 1-888-476-9032.'에서 즉시 이용을 멈추고, Kerman 사로 연락하라고 했으므로 정답은 (C)이다. 정답 (C)

표현 정리 return 반품하다, 돌려주다 replacement part 대체 부품 manufacturer 제조사

해석 Big Max의 소유주들이 하도록 조언받은 것은?
(A) 그들의 자전거를 매장에 반품한다.
(B) 대체 부품을 구입한다.
(C) 제조사에 전화한다.
(D) 그들의 자전거를 계속 사용한다.

문제 151-153번은 다음 기사를 참조하시오.

> ¹⁵¹JCR 사가 제조한 특정 카메라 모델의 구매자들 사이에 배터리에 문제가 있다는 내용이 확산되고 있다. ¹⁵²구매자들의 불만에 의하면 특정 모델의 배터리는 불과 몇 차례 사용한 후에 충전이 제대로 되지 않는다고 한다. JCR에 따르면, 배터리는 성능이 감소하기 전까지 최소 50회 재충전이 가능하도록 디자인되었다.
>
> 여기에 해당되는 모델들로는 J100과 J200이 있다. 이 모델 제품을 구입한 고객들은 JCR 제품을 판매하는 매장에서 카메라 배터리를 교환하거나, JCR로 우편 발송을 해서 교환할 수 있다. 교환 과정의 세부사항들은 회사 웹사이트에서 찾아 볼 수 있다. 카메라 구매자들에게 비용이 부과되지는 않는다.
>
> 이에 관한 뉴스가 보도된 이후, JCR 카메라 판매가 급감했다. 회사는 이 문제의 원인이 공급자에게 있다고 본다. ¹⁵³"고객 만족이 우리의 최우선이다."라고 회장인 Tom Jenkins는 말했다. "우리는 이 문제를 해결하기 위해 부품들을 재설계하는 것을 포함한 모든 조치를 취할 것이다."

표현 정리 purchaser 구매자 manufacture 제조하다 alert 알리다 potential 잠재적인 complaint 불평 hold a charge 충전하다 capacity 용량, 성능 retailer 소매점 surface 수면으로 부상하다 slump 급감하다 blame 탓하다, ~때문으로 보다 supplier 공급자 satisfaction 만족 priority 우선 사항 remedy 바로잡다 unfortunate 유감스러운 redesign 재설계

151. 주제 – 기사의 주제 ★☆☆

해설 첫 번째 단락 첫 번째 문장 'Purchasers of certain models of cameras manufactured by JCR, Inc. are being alerted to a potential battery issue.'를 통해 기사의 내용이 특정 카메라 모델의 배터리 문제에 관한 것임을 알 수 있으므로 정답은 (D)이다. **정답 (D)**

패러프레이징 |지문| a potential battery issue 잠재적인 배터리 문제 → |선택지 D| a flawed component of a product 제품의 결함이 있는 부품

표현 정리 special offer 특가 판매 discontinued 중단된 flawed 결함이 있는 component 부품

해석 기사의 주된 내용은?
(A) 인기 있는 카메라의 재설계
(B) 제한된 기간의 특가 판매
(C) 중단된 생산 라인
(D) 제품의 결함이 있는 부품

152. 세부사항 – 재충전되는 배터리에 관한 내용 ★☆☆

해설 첫 번째 단락, 두 번째 문장 이후의 내용 'Consumer complaints indicate that the batteries of certain models are unable to hold a charge after only being used a few times. According to JCR, the batteries are designed to be recharged a minimum of fifty times before beginning to lose capacity.'를 보면 애초에는 최소 50회 이상 재충전이 가능하도록 설계된 제품인데, 몇 회 충전을 한 이후에는 재충전이 되지 않는다고 소비자들이 불만을 제기했으므로 (A)가 정답임을 알 수 있다. **정답 (A)**

표현 정리 rechargeable 재충전되는 as intended 계획대로, 본래 의도대로 replace 대체하다

해석 재충전 배터리에 관해 언급된 내용은?
(A) 본래의 기능을 하지 않는다.
(B) 최근에 재설계되었다.
(C) 수수료를 내면 교체 받을 수 있다.
(D) 온라인으로 구입할 수 있다.

153. 세부사항 – Mr. Jenkins가 회사에 대해 강조한 내용 ★☆☆

해설 마지막 단락 '"Customer satisfaction is our first priority," said President Tom Jenkins.'에서 Tom Jenkins는 고객 만족이 최우선이라고 했으므로 (C)가 정답에 가장 가깝다고 볼 수 있다. **정답 (C)**

패러프레이징 |지문| Customer satisfaction is our first priority 고객 만족이 우리의 최우선이다 → |선택지 C| want customers to be happy with its products 회사 제품에 대해 고객들이 만족하길 원한다

표현 정리 strive 분투하다, 노력하다 avoid 피하다

해석 Mr. Jenkins가 그의 회사에 대해 강조한 것은?
(A) 완벽한 제품을 만들기 위해 노력한다.
(B) 시장에서 최고의 카메라를 만든다.
(C) 고객들이 회사 제품에 만족하기를 바란다.
(D) 외부 공급자를 고용하는 것을 피할 것이다.

문제 154-155번은 다음 문자 메시지 내용을 참조하시오.

> **Tony Andrews** Rochelle, 여기 눈이 꽤 많이 내리고 있어요. 그래서 하룻밤 더 머물러야 할 것 같아요. 나 대신 처리해 줄 일이 있어요.　오후 1시 12분
>
> **Rochelle Cohn** 뭔데요?　오후 1시 16분
>
> ¹⁵⁴**Tony Andrews** Mr. Owens이 주문 제작 월넛 책장을 주문했어요. 내가 지난주에 그 일을 마쳤어요. 퇴근 전에 그것들을 배달해 줄 수 있나요?　오후 1시 18분
>
> **Rochelle Cohn** 물론이죠. 제게 맡겨도 됩니다.　오후 1시 20분
>
> **Tony Andrews** 그의 주소는 책장 중 하나에 붙여놓은 송장에 있어요.　오후 1시 21분
>
> **Rochelle Cohn** 흠. 네 개의 책장 어디에도 송장이 보이지 않는데요.　오후 1시 28분
>
> **Tony Andrews** 그거 이상하네요. ¹⁵⁵몇 분 후에 복사본을 이메일로 보낼게요.　오후 1시 29분
>
> **Rochelle Cohn** ¹⁵⁵받았어요. 트럭에 싣기만 하면 되고, 그의 집은 찾기 쉬울 거예요.　오후 1시 34분
>
> **Tony Andrews** 고마워요.　오후 1시 38분

표현 정리 take care of ~을 처리하다 place an order 주문하다 custom-made 주문 제작한 walnut 호두, 호두나무 deliver 배달하다 count on ~을 믿다 invoice 송장, 계산서 tape 테이프로 붙이다 load up ~에 싣다

154. 유추 – Mr. Andrews의 직업 ★☆☆

해설 'Tony Andrews (1:18 P.M.): Mr. Owens placed an order for custom-made walnut bookshelves. I finished them last week.'에서 Andrews는 Mr. Owens로부터 주문받은 책장 제작을 지난주에 마쳤다고 하면서 배송을 부탁하고 있으므로 그의 직업은 가구 제조업자임을 알 수 있어 정답은 (A)이다. **정답 (A)**

해석 Mr. Andrews는 누구인가?
(A) 가구 제조자
(B) 트럭 운전자
(C) 사무실 관리자
(D) 외판원

155. 의도 파악하기 ★☆☆

해설 송장을 찾을 수 없다는 Cohn의 메시지에, 오후 1시 29분에 Andrews가 'Well, I'll e-mail you a copy in a few minutes.'라며 주소를 바로 보내겠다

고 했고, 오후 1시 34분에 Cohn이 'Got it, All I need to do is to load up the truck.'이라고 했으므로 정답은 (B)임을 짐작할 수 있다. 참고로 대화 중에 언급되는 'Got it.'은 종종 상대방이 말한 내용을 이해했다는 내용으로도 자주 사용된다는 점을 알아 두자.

정답 (B)

해석 Ms. Cohn이 오후 1시 34분에 "받았어요."라고 한 말의 의미는 무엇인가?
(A) 그녀는 검색을 계속하는 것이 필요하다.
(B) 그녀는 배송 주소를 받았다.
(C) 그녀는 잃어버린 송장을 찾았다.
(D) 그녀는 그녀의 의무를 이해한다.

문제 156-158번은 다음 이메일을 참조하시오.

수신: rtomasson@getmail.net
발신: gwells@aceappliance.com
제목: 점검
날짜: 3월 27일

Ms. Tomasson 님께,

156저희 담당 기술자가 귀하의 Zama 2000 세탁기의 점검을 마쳤음을 알려드립니다. 그는 세탁기 모터에 이상이 있는 것으로 결론 내렸습니다. 저희가 그것을 수리할 수도 있지만, 일반적으로는 모터를 새것으로 교체하는 것이 비용이 적게 드는 경우도 있음을 알려드립니다. 158계약에 따라 비용의 80퍼센트는 보장을 받게 됩니다.

점검 중에, 담당 기술자는 세탁기의 여러 내부 부품들이 심하게 닳아 고장이 날 가능성이 크다는 점 또한 발견했습니다. 저희는 그것들도 교체할 수 있습니다. 158다시 한 번, 귀하는 비용의 20퍼센트를 부담하시면 됩니다.

귀하가 취할 수 있는 또 하나의 선택은 세탁기를 새것으로 구입하시는 것입니다. 개인적으로는 그렇게 하실 것을 추천합니다. 157현재 사용하고 계신 귀하의 세탁기는 이미 15년이 되었습니다. 이 모델의 평균 사용 시간은 9년입니다. 교체 가능한 부품에 대한 추천을 원하실 경우, 귀하와 함께 기꺼이 상의하겠습니다.

귀하의 결정을 기다리겠습니다.

George Wells
Ace 기기 서비스

표현 정리 technician 기술자 inspection 점검 determine 결론짓다, 알아내다 attempt 시도하다 repair 수리하다 generally 일반적으로, 대개 install 설치하다 brand-new 신제품인 internal 내부의 seriously 심하게 worn 해진, 닳은 at risk of ~의 위험에 처한 replace 대체하다 be responsible for ~에 책임이 있다 simply 간단히 recommend 추천하다 current 기존의 average 평균의 service life 사용 기간 specific model 특정 모델 potential 가능성이 있는, 잠재적인 replacement 교체 discuss 상의하다 patiently 인내심 있게, 끈기 있게 await 기다리다 appliance (가정용) 기기

156. 주제 – Mr. Wells가 이메일을 작성한 목적 ★☆☆
해설 본문 첫 번째 문장 'I want to let you know that our technician completed his inspection of your Zama 2000 washing machine. He determined that the machine's motor has died.'에서 세탁기에 대한 점검을 실시했고, 그 결과 모터에 이상이 있음을 발견했다는 내용을 알리는 이메일이므로 정답은 (C)이다.
정답 (C)

표현 정리 offer an apology 사과하다 mechanical failure 기계적 결함

해석 Mr. Wells가 Ms. Tommason에게 이메일을 보낸 이유는?
(A) 고객에게 제품을 제안하기 위해
(B) 직원에 관한 문제를 보고하기 위해
(C) 기기에 대한 상황을 설명하기 위해

(D) 기계적 결합에 대해 사과하기 위해

157. 세부사항 – Ms. Tommason의 세탁기에 관한 내용 ★★☆
해설 세 번째 단락 'Your current machine is already 15 years old. The average service life for this specific model is nine years.'에서 모델의 평균 사용 기간이 9년인데, 이미 15년을 사용했다고 했으므로 Ms. Tommason의 세탁기는 평균 사용 연한이 지났음을 알 수 있어 정답은 (B)이다.
정답 (B)

🔍 **함정 분석** 'Your current machine is already 15 years old.'를 통해 세탁기를 사용한지 이미 15년이 됐음을 알 수는 있지만, 세탁기가 15년 전에 처음 도입되었는지의 여부는 확인할 수 없으므로 (D)는 오답이다.

표현 정리 last 지속되다 identical 동일한

해석 Ms. Tommason의 세탁기에 관해 언급된 내용은?
(A) 두 개의 교체 부품이 필요하다.
(B) 대부분의 Zama 2000 제품보다 오래 사용했다.
(C) 동일 모델로 대체될 수 있다.
(D) 15년 전에 처음 도입되었다.

158. 문장 위치 찾기 ★☆☆
해설 두 번째 단락 마지막 문장 'Again, you would be responsible for 20% of the cost.'에서 '다시'라는 표현이 언급된 것으로 보아, 본 문장 앞에서 이미 서비스 비용에 대한 언급이 있었음을 짐작할 수 있다. 따라서 첫 번째 단락 마지막 부분 'While we could attempt to repair it, we generally find it is less expensive just to install a brand-new motor.'에서 새 모터를 설치하는 것이 저렴하다고 한 문장 뒤인 [1]에 본 문장이 들어가는 것이 가장 적합하다고 볼 수 있으므로 정답은 (A)이다.
정답 (A)

표현 정리 contract 계약 cover 보장하다

해석 [1], [2], [3], [4] 중 다음 문장이 들어가기에 가장 적합한 곳은?

"계약에 따라 비용의 80퍼센트는 보장을 받게 됩니다."
(A) [1]
(B) [2]
(C) [3]
(D) [4]

문제 159-160번은 다음 안내 사항을 참조하시오.

새로운 내려주기/태우기 정책

160(B)시행: 3월 1일, 월요일

45번 고속도로의 공사로 인해 Washington 대로의 교통량이 증가해 사고가 발생할 염려가 있어, 159,160(A)Shining Star 유치원은 모든 아이들이 건물 후문에서 내려지고 태워져야 한다는 것을 요청 드립니다. 직원들은 매일 아침 7시부터 8시까지 후문에서 아이들을 만날 것입니다. 또한, 부모님이 아이를 태워갈 수 있도록 하루에 두 차례, 정오와 오후 2시 30분에 직원들이 아이들을 후문으로 인도할 것입니다. 오전 8시 이후에 도착하거나 오후 2시 30분 이후에 아이를 태우러 오실 부모님들은 Washington 대로 쪽 정문을 통해 건물로 접근하실 수 있습니다만, 160(D)아이들의 안전을 위해 160(C)뒤쪽 주차장에 주차하시고 건물 앞으로 걸어올 것을 조언 드립니다. 궁금한 사항은 555-8273로 전화 주시기 바랍니다.

Marsha Vernon
원장, Shining Star 유치원

표현 정리 drop-off 내려주기, 하차 pickup 태우기 effective 시행되는, 효력을 갖는 concerns 염려, 우려 traffic 교통량 boulevard 대로, 큰 길 result from ~이 원인이다 construction 공사 preschool 유치원 request 요청하다 rear entrance 후문 present 동석하는, 참여하는

in addition 또한, 게다가   access 접근하다   for the sake of ~을 위해
lot 주차장, 공터

159. 주제 – 안내 사항의 대상   ★☆☆

해설 'Shining Star Preschool requests that all children be dropped off and picked up at the rear entrance of our building.'의 내용을 보면 학부모들이 아이들을 내려주고, 태워갈 때 후문을 이용해 줄 것을 요청하는 내용임을 알 수 있으므로 정답은 (A)이다.   정답 (A)

해석 누구를 대상으로 한 안내 사항인가?
　　(A) 부모들
　　(B) 공사 현장 근로자들
　　(C) 유치원 직원들
　　(D) 학생들

160. 세부사항 – 새로운 정책과 관련이 없는 내용   ★★☆

해설 정해진 픽업 시간 이후에 도착하는 부모님의 경우, 본문 마지막 부분 'we recommend that you park in our rear lot and walk around the front of the building'에서 뒤쪽 주차장에 차를 주차하고 걸어서 앞쪽으로 와 달라고 부탁하고 있으므로 주차장 사용을 아예 금지하는 것으로 보기 어려워 정답은 (C)이다.   정답 (C)

🔍함정 분석 본문 초반 'Shining Star Preschool requests that all children be dropped off and picked up at the rear entrance of our building'에서 (A)는 맞는 내용이고, 제목 'Effective: Monday, March 1'에서 (B)도 확인이 가능하다. 본 공지는 고속도로 공사로 인해 정문 쪽의 Washington 대로가 붐비는 상황이며, 본문 후반 'for the sake of your children's safety'에 언급된 내용으로 (D)도 맞는 내용임을 알 수 있다.

패러프레이징 |지문| for the sake of your children's safety 아이들의 안전을 위하여 → |선택지 D| in response to a safety risk 안전상의 위험에 대응해

표현 정리 state 말하다, 언급하다   direct 지시하다   regular 규칙적인
prohibit 금지하다   in response to ~에 대응하여

해석 새로운 정책에 대한 내용이 아닌 것은?
　　(A) 규칙적인 픽업을 후문에서 하도록 지시한다.
　　(B) 3월 1일부터 시작할 것이다.
　　(C) 주차장 사용을 금지한다.
　　(D) 안전상의 위험에 대응하기 위한 것이다.

문제 161-163번은 다음 광고를 참조하시오.

귀하의 차량이 곧 귀하의 모습입니다!

당신의 차를 돌봐주세요: Car Care Specialists로 연락주세요.

저희는 전체적인 자동 세차 서비스를 제공합니다. ¹⁶¹ **저희는 귀하의 차량을 가정 또는 직장에서 일주일 내내 세차해 드릴 것입니다.** 저희는 귀하의 차량이 최고가 되도록 확실하게 해 드립니다.

다음은 저희가 제공해 드리는 서비스 내용입니다.

- ¹⁶²⁽ᴬ⁾ **전체적인 외부 세차와 손 왁싱**
- 엔진 칸 세척
- 내부 가죽과 ¹⁶²⁽ᴮ⁾ **카펫 클리닝과 얼룩 해결**
- ¹⁶²⁽ᴰ⁾ **가벼운 표면 수리 (페인트 손질과 긁힌 자국 등)**
- 금 간 앞 유리 보수

저희의 자동화된 일정 관리와 결제 시스템은 저희 업체 이용을 편리하게 해 줍니다. ¹⁶³ **오늘 저희와 일정을 정하기 위해 www.ccs.com을 방문해 주십시오.**

다음 우편번호 88930, 88932, 88941, 88946, 88948 이외의 지역에 위치한

차량들에 한해서는 출장비가 부과될 것입니다. 현 서비스 가격과 비용에 관한 상세 내용은 저희 웹사이트에 공지되어 있습니다.

표현 정리 reflection 반영   deserve ~을 받을 만하다   specialist 전문가   vehicle 차량   make sure 확실하게 하다   exterior 외부   compartment 칸   interior 내부   leather 가죽   stain 얼룩   treatment 처치   minor 가벼운   surface 표면   repair 수리, 보수   i.e. 즉(라틴어 id est에서)   touchup 손질   scratch 긁힌 자국   windshield 차량의 앞 유리, 바람막이   crack 금   automated 자동의   hassle-free 편리한   set up an appointment 약속을 정하다   travel fee 출장비   charge 부과하다   ZIP code 우편번호   post 공고하다, 올리다

161. 세부사항 – Car Care Specialists에 관한 내용   ★★☆

해설 첫 번째 단락 'We will wash your vehicle at your home or place of business seven days a week.'에서 일주일 내내 영업을 한다고 했으므로 정답은 (A)이다.   정답 (A)

🔍함정 분석 마지막 단락 'A travel fee will be charged for vehicles located outside the following ZIP codes: 88930, 88932, 88941, 88946, and 88948.'에서 추가 비용을 부과하는 것은 특정 우편번호 밖의 지역으로 갈 때만 해당되므로 (D)를 정답으로 고르지 않도록 주의해야 한다.

패러프레이징 |지문| business seven days a week 일주일 중 7일 영업 → |선택지 A| business daily 매일 영업

표현 정리 recently 최근에   location 지점   charge 부과하다   extra 추가의

해석 Car Care Specialists에 관해 언급된 내용은?
　　(A) 매일 영업한다.
　　(B) 최근 가격을 변경했다.
　　(C) 다섯 곳에 지점을 두고 있다.
　　(D) 고객의 집까지 가는데 추가 비용을 부과한다.(무조건의 의미)

162. 세부사항 – Car Care Specialists가 제공하는 서비스가 아닌 것   ★★☆

해설 두 번째 단락 'Full-service exterior wash and hand waxing'에서 (A)가, 'carpet deep-cleaning'에서 (B)가, 'Minor surface repairs (i.e. paint touchup and scratches)'에서 (D)가 확인되지만, 차량의 오일을 체크해 준다는 내용은 언급되지 않았으므로 정답은 (C)이다.   정답 (C)

패러프레이징 |지문| Full-service exterior wash 외부 세차 서비스 → |선택지 A| Washing the outside of a car 차량의 외부를 세차하는 것
|지문| Interior leather and carpet deep-cleaning 내부 가죽과 카펫 청소 → |선택지 B| Cleaning a car's carpet 차의 카펫을 청소하는 것
|지문| Minor surface repairs 가벼운 표면 수리 → |선택지 D| Repairing damaged paint 벗겨진 페인트를 보수하는 것

해석 Car Care Specialists가 제공하는 서비스가 아닌 것은?
　　(A) 차량 외부 세차
　　(B) 차량 카펫 청소
　　(C) 차량 오일 확인
　　(D) 훼손된 페인트 보수

163. 세부사항 – 서비스 일정을 잡을 수 있는 방법   ★☆☆

해설 세 번째 단락 'Simply go to www.ccs.com to set up an appointment today.'에서 오늘 약속을 잡기 위해 웹사이트를 방문해 줄 것을 요청했으므로 정답은 (D)이다.   정답 (D)

표현 정리 main number 대표 전화 번호

해석 광고에 따르면, 독자들은 어떻게 서비스 일정을 잡을 수 있나?
　　(A) 대표 전화 번호로 전화를 해서

(B) 지점을 방문해서
(C) 직원에게 이메일을 보내서
(D) 웹사이트를 방문해서

문제 164-167번은 다음 이메일을 참조하시오.

발신: Timothy Whitacre
수신: John Severin
제목: Alcade와의 회의
날짜: 2월 8일

John,

166방금 Alcade Promotions와 통화했습니다. 그쪽 회사에서 우리 회사 최신 화장품을 홍보하기 위한 행사들을 준비하는 것에 동의했습니다. 선임 고객 매니저인 Jessica Blackmore가 행사를 계획하고, 준비할 것입니다. 우리는 이 절차를 시작하기 위해 가능한 빨리 그녀를 만날 필요가 있습니다. 164이번 주 금요일 12시 30분에 시간 있나요? Winston's에서 만나 점심을 같이 할까 합니다.

167그녀와 회의를 하기 전에 몇 가지 사전 마케팅 자료를 준비할 필요가 있을 것 같습니다. Tanya Ivers에게 우리가 지난 달에 촬영한 사진들 중에서 좋은 것으로 몇 장 준비하도록 해 주세요. 또한 우리가 지난 미팅에서 도출해 낸 마케팅 아이디어를 간략하게 준비해 Ms. Blackmore에게 보여줄 수 있도록 준비해야 합니다. 아마도 Allison Hogan이 당신을 도와 그것을 준비할 수 있을 것입니다. 마지막으로, Richard Pena와 연락하십시오. 그가 우리에게 몇 가지 샘플 제품을 제공해 줄 수 있을 것입니다. 165물론 용기, 튜브, 병들의 디자인이 아직 준비되지 않은 것을 알고 있습니다. 하지만, 그렇다고 해서 Ms. Blackmore에게 실제 샘플을 제공하는 것이 지체돼서는 안 됩니다. 디자인들은 나중에 그녀에게 보내면 됩니다.

Timothy Whitacre
마케팅 부장
Paragon 화장품

표현 정리 get off the phone 통화를 마치다 organize 준비하다 a series of 일련의 promote 홍보하다 beauty products 미용 제품 coordinate 준비하다, 조직화하다 preliminary 예비의 assemble 모으다 summary 요약 generate 만들어 내다, 도출해 내다 get in touch with ~와 연락하다 provide A with B A에게 B를 제공하다 jar 단지, 용기, 병 cosmetics 화장품

164. 주제 - Mr. Whitacre가 연락한 이유 ★★☆
해설 첫 번째 단락 마지막 부분 'Are you free this Friday at 12:30? I was thinking we could meet for lunch at Winston's.'에서 이번 주 금요일에 만나 점심을 하자고 제안하고 있으므로 정답은 (D)이다. **정답 (D)**

🔍 **함정 분석** 새로운 화장품 제품의 홍보를 할 업체가 결정되기는 했지만, 그 업체와의 회의 일정은 아직 정해지지 않았으므로 회의 일정을 재조정하기 위해서라는 (B)와 회의에 관해 보고하기 위해서라는 내용의 (C)는 오답이다.

표현 정리 propose 제안하다 make an appointment 약속을 정하다

해석 Mr. Whitacre가 Mr. Severin에게 연락한 이유는?
(A) 프로젝트를 제안하기 위해
(B) 회의 일정을 다시 정하기 위해
(C) 회의에 관해 보고하기 위해
(D) 약속을 정하기 위해

165. 세부사항 - 제품 샘플에 대한 내용 ★☆☆
해설 두 번째 단락, 후반 'I understand that the designs for the jars, tubes, and bottles are not ready yet.'의 내용을 보면 화장품을 담을 용기의 디자인

이 아직 완성되지 않았음을 알 수 있으므로 정답은 (D)이다. **정답 (D)**

패러프레이징 |지문| the designs for the jars, tubes, and bottles are not ready yet 용기, 튜브, 병들의 디자인이 아직 준비되지 않았다 → |선택지 D| containers are unfinished 용기가 미완성이다

표현 정리 container 용기, 컨테이너 unfinished 완료되지 않은, 끝나지 않은

해석 제품 샘플에 관해 언급된 내용은?
(A) 그것들은 사용 가능하지 않을 것이다.
(B) 그것들은 테스트가 필요하다.
(C) 그것들은 Mr. Whitacre에게 보내졌다.
(D) 그것들의 용기는 완료되지 않았다.

166. 유추 - Paragon 화장품 직원이 아닌 사람 ★★☆
해설 첫 번째 단락, 'I just got off the phone with Alcade Promotions. The company has agreed to organize a series of events to promote our newest line of beauty products. Jessica Blackmore, the senior account manager, will plan and coordinate the events.'에서 Jessica Blackmore는 Paragon 화장품을 홍보해 줄 홍보회사인 Alcade Promotions의 선임 매니저임을 알 수 있으므로 정답은 (A)이다. **정답 (A)**

🔍 **함정 분석** 두 번째 단락 'We should also have a summary of the marketing ideas we generated at our last meeting to present to Ms. Blackmore. Maybe Allison Hogan can work with you to prepare that.'에서 Allison Hogan은 마케팅 아이디어의 요약 작업을 준비하는 일을 도와 줄 동료이고, 'He should be able to provide us with some product samples.'에서 Richard Pena는 샘플을 제공해 줄 동료이다. 마지막으로, 'Have Tanya Ivers assemble some of the better product photos we took last month.'에서 Tanya Ivers는 제품 사진을 준비해 줄 동료임을 알 수 있다.

해석 Paragon 화장품의 직원이 아닌 사람은?
(A) Jessica Blackmore
(B) Allison Hogan
(C) Richard Pena
(D) Tanya Ivers

167. 세부사항 - Mr. Whitacre가 Mr. Severin에게 요청한 일 ★★☆
해설 두 번째 단락, 'We need to prepare some preliminary marketing materials before the meeting.'에서 회의에 앞서 사전 자료를 준비해야 할 필요가 있다고 했으므로 정답은 (D)이다. **정답 (D)**

🔍 **함정 분석** 두 번째 단락 'I understand that the designs for the jars, tubes, and bottles are not ready yet.'를 통해 아직 디자인이 완성되지 않았음을 알 수 있고, 'However, that should not delay us in getting the actual samples to Ms. Blackmore.'에서 Ms. Blackmore에게 샘플을 제공한다는 말은 향후 Ms. Blackmore와 있을 회의에 가져갈 샘플을 준비해야 한다는 내용이지, 지금 보내야 한다는 것은 아니며, 'We should also have a summary of the marketing ideas we generated at our last meeting to present to Ms. Blackmore.'를 통해 지난 회의에서 이미 마케팅 아이디어가 도출되었음을 알 수 있으므로 (A), (B), (C)는 오답이다.

패러프레이징 |지문| assemble some of the better product photos 더 나은 제품 사진을 모아 놓기 → |선택지 D| Gather images of products 제품의 이미지를 모으기

표현 정리 obtain 얻다 generate 도출해 내다, 만들어내다

해석 Mr. Whitacre가 Mr. Severin에게 요청한 것은?
(A) 새로운 디자인을 입수한다.
(B) Ms. Blackmore에게 샘플을 보낸다.

6

(C) 새로운 마케팅 아이디어를 생각해 낸다.
(D) 회의를 준비하다.

문제 168-171번은 다음 발표를 참조하시오.

Bartlett 사무실 건물 뉴스   8월호

공지 사항

168(C)재활용: Bartlett 관리부는 모든 입주자와 그들의 직원들이 재활용해야 한다는 새로운 재활용 정책을 수립했습니다. 168(B)쓰레기를 재활용할 수 있는 것과 그렇지 않은 것으로 분류하는 일은 각 사무실의 개별 의무입니다. 168(A)쓰레기통은 다음과 같이 제공될 것입니다: 파란색 쓰레기통은 플라스틱을 위한 것이고, 회색 쓰레기통은 종이를 위한 것, 녹색 쓰레기통은 알루미늄을 위한 것, 그리고 검은색 쓰레기통은 일반 쓰레기를 위한 것입니다. 168(D)구체적인 도표가 재활용 분류 과정을 설명하는 것을 돕기 위해 건물 도처에 게시될 것입니다.

보안: 세입자의 안전과 보안은 Bartlett 사무실 건물의 최우선 사항입니다. 지난 달 건물의 정문 열쇠 한 세트를 분실한 것이 몇 가지 우려를 낳았습니다. 잃어버린 열쇠들을 찾지 못했기 때문에, 저희는 모든 외부 문들의 자물쇠를 교체했습니다. 새로운 자물쇠는 카드를 갖다 대야 문이 열리는 구조입니다. 169아직 자신의 카드를 수령하지 않으신 입주자께서는 즉각 수령해 가시기 바랍니다. 또한 이전 열쇠들을 경비실에 반납해 주실 것을 요청합니다.

주차 허가: 170저희 건물과 관련된 보안 문제를 강화하기 위해, Bartlett 관리부는 각 사무실에 주차 허가증을 발급할 예정입니다. 171여러분의 사무실에 근무하는 전체 직원 수를 제출해 주시기 바랍니다. 입주자께서는 허가증을 그들의 차량 계기판 위에 위치해 둬야 합니다. 허가증 없이 건물 주차장에 주차한 차량에 대해서는 견인 조치를 할 것입니다. 만약 차량이 견인되었다고 의심되면, 555-2421로 전화 주시기 바랍니다.

표현 정리 issue (잡지, 신문 같은 정기 간행물의) 호   **management** 관리부, 경영   **enact** (법을) 제정하다   **tenant** 세입자   **sort** 분류하다   **trash** 쓰레기   **recyclable** 재활용할 수 있는   **bin** 쓰레기통   **as follows** 다음과 같이   **illustrate** 분명히 보여주다   **chart** 도표   **throughout** 도처에   **priority** 우선 사항   **loss** 분실   **raise** 일으키다   **exterior** 외부의   **swipe** (전자 카드를 인식기에) 대다[읽히다]   **right away** 즉각   **further** 좀 더, 더 나아가   **address** (문제, 상황 등에 대해) 고심하다[다루다]   **pertain to** ~와 관련 있다   **premises** 구내, 부지, 지역   **permit** 허가증   **dashboard** 계기판   **tow** 견인하다   **suspect** 의심하다

168. 세부사항 – 재활용 프로그램에 관한 내용이 아닌 것   ★★☆
해설 첫 번째 단락 'It is the individual duty of each office to sort trash into recyclables and non-recyclables.'에서 쓰레기를 분류하는 것은 각 사무실의 의무라고 했으므로 세입자들 모두가 의무적으로 해야 하는 일임을 짐작할 수 있어 정답은 (B)이다.   **정답 (B)**

🔍**함정 분석** 첫 번째 단락, 'Bins will be provided as follows: blue bins are for plastic, gray bins are for paper, green bins are for aluminum, and black bins are for regular trash.'에서 (A)를, 'Bartlett management has enacted a new recycling policy that requires all tenants and their employees to recycle.'에서 (C)를, 그리고 'Detailed Illustrated charts will be posted throughout the building to help explain the recycling sorting process.'에서 (D)를 각각 확인할 수 있다.

패러프레이징 |지문| blue bins are for plastic, gray bins are for paper ~ 파란색 쓰레기통은 플라스틱을 위한 것이고, 회색 쓰레기통은 종이를 위한 것 ~ → |선택지 A| require different bins for different types of waste 여러 종류의 쓰레기를 위해 다른 쓰레기통들이 필요하다
|지문| have enacted a new recycling policy 새로운 재활용 정책이 시행되

다 → |선택지 C| be the first of its kind 최초로 시행되는 것이다
|지문| Detailed Illustrated charts will be posted ~ to help explain the recycling sorting process 재활용 절차를 설명하기 위해 도표가 게시될 것이다 → |선택지 D| will use graphics to explain how to recycle 재활용하는 방법을 설명하기 위하여 도표를 사용할 것이다

표현 정리 **require** 요구하다, 필요로 하다   **waste** 쓰레기   **optional** 선택적인

해석 재활용 프로그램에 관해 언급된 내용이 아닌 것은?
(A) 다른 종류의 쓰레기를 위한 각기 다른 쓰레기통이 필요하다.
(B) Bartlett 사무실 건물의 입주자들에게 (의무가 아니라) 선택적이다.
(C) Bartlett 사무실 건물에서 처음 시행되는 것이다.
(D) 재활용하는 방법을 설명하기 위하여 도표를 사용할 것이다.

169. 유추 – 건물 세입자들에 관한 내용   ★☆☆
해설 두 번째 단락 후반 'Those tenants who have not picked yours up yet, please do so right away. We also ask that you return your old keys to the security office.'에서 새로 교체한 출입문 열쇠를 아직 수령하지 않은 사람들은 수령을 한 후, 이전 열쇠를 반납해 달라고 한 내용을 통해 아직 이전 열쇠를 소지하고 있는 세입자가 있음을 유추할 수 있으므로 정답은 (D)이다.   **정답 (D)**

🔍**함정 분석** 마지막 단락에서 Jolly Jingles가 어린이 자선단체를 위한 기금 모금을 위해 행사를 열 예정이라고 한 것과, 건물 세입자들이 자원봉사를 좋아하는 것과는 관계가 없는 내용이므로 (C)를 답으로 고르지 않도록 한다.

표현 정리 **replacement** 대체   **ID card** 신분증   **volunteer** 자원하다   **useless** 소용없는, 못쓰는

해석 건물 세입자들에 관해 암시된 내용은?
(A) 그들은 대체 열쇠를 위해 돈을 지불해야 한다.
(B) 신분증을 제시해야 하는 사람들도 있다.
(C) 그들은 자선단체들에 자원하는 것을 좋아한다.
(D) 못쓰는 열쇠를 아직 보유하고 있는 사람들이 있다.

170. 세부사항 – 세입자들에게 주차 허가증을 발급하는 이유   ★☆☆
해설 세 번째 단락, 'In order to further address security concerns pertaining to our premises, Bartlett management will be issuing parking permits to each office.'에서 안전상의 문제를 다루기 위해 각 사무실에 주차 허가증을 발급할 것이라고 했으므로 정답은 (A)이다.   **정답 (A)**

패러프레이징 |지문| In order to further address security concerns 보안 관련 문제를 다루기 위해 → |선택지 A| To respond to worries about safety 안전에 대한 걱정에 대응하기 위해

표현 정리 **distribute** 나누어 주다   **respond** 대응하다   **keep track of** ~을 기록하다   **ticketed** 범칙금이 부과된   **address** 다루다, 고심하다   **overcrowding** 과잉 수용, 과밀   **raise** 모금하다

해석 세입자들에게 주차 허가증이 발급되는 이유는?
(A) 안전에 대한 우려에 대응하기 위해
(B) 범칙금이 부과된 차량을 기록하기 위해
(C) 주차장 내 과잉 수용 문제를 관리하기 위해
(D) 지역 자선단체를 위한 기금을 마련하기 위해

171. 문장 위치 찾기   ★☆☆
해설 세 번째 단락, 'In order to further address security concerns pertaining to our premises, Bartlett management will be issuing parking permits to each office.'에서 건물 보안 사항을 강화하기 위해 각 사무실에 주차 허가증을 발급할 것이라고 했고, 'Each person is required to place a permit on the dashboard of his or her car.'에서 각 입주자는 허가증을 그들의 차량 계기판 위에 위치해 두라고 한 내용을 통해 문맥상 그 사이에는 'Please provide

the total number of employees present in your office.'가 들어가는 것이 가장 적절하다. 따라서 정답은 (C)가 된다. **정답 (C)**

해석 [1], [2], [3], [4] 중 다음 문장이 들어가기에 가장 알맞은 위치는?

"여러분의 사무실에 근무하는 전체 직원 수를 제출해 주시기 바랍니다."
(A) [1]
(B) [2]
(C) [3]
(D) [4]

문제 172-175번은 다음 온라인 채팅을 참조하시오.

Paulson, Amber	Marconi's의 Sal과 방금 통화했는데, 그는 3월 31일에 있을 우리 시상식 만찬을 담당할 수 없을 거라고 하는군요.	오후 2시 15분
Georgas, Angie	왜 안 된대요?	오후 2시 16분
Paulson, Amber	173그는 그 주말에 규모가 매우 큰 결혼식에 음식을 공급하는 계약에 서명했고, 우리 행사를 위한 충분한 직원을 보유하고 있지 않아요.	오후 2시 18분
Taylor, Ray	음식도 준비할 수 없다고 하던가요? 그렇다면 우리 직원들에게 서빙, 청소 등을 하도록 할 수 있을 겁니다.	오후 2시 22분
Georgas, Angie	그럴 경우 일이 복잡해 질 거예요. 누군가 준비를 해야 하는데, 우리 모두 행사에 참석해요. 172최선의 방법은 음식을 공급해 줄 다른 음식점을 찾는 것이라고 생각해요.	오후 2시 24분
Taylor, Ray	174Marconi's를 대체하기는 힘들 거예요.	오후 2시 30분
Georgas, Angie	저도 알아요. 172그들은 지난 10년 동안 있었던 우리의 모든 행사에 음식을 공급했고, 항상 훌륭하게 일을 합니다.	오후 2시 34분
Paulson, Amber	다행히도 Sal이 그의 요리사 중 한 명이 운영하는 별도의 다른 케이터링 회사 이름을 저에게 알려줬어요. 저는 우리가 그 회사에 연락해 우리에게 음식을 제공할 수 있는지 알아봐야 한다고 생각해요.	오후 2시 38분
Taylor, Ray	연락해 봐도 괜찮을 것 같아요. 이름이 뭐죠?	오후 2시 42분
Paulson, Amber	Top Notch Catering입니다. 번호는 555-4044번이고요.	오후 2시 45분
Taylor, Ray	175제가 그들에게 연락해 퇴근 전에 메뉴를 요청할게요.	오후 2시 48분

표현 정리 upcoming 다가오는 awards dinner 시상식 만찬 contract 계약 unusually 대단히 additional 별도의, 추가의 and such 등등 get complicated 복잡해지다 coordinate 준비하다 a course of action 행동 방침 catering 음식 공급 cater 음식을 공급하다 independent 독립적인, 별도의 operate 운영하다 find out 알아내다 worth a try 시도해 볼 가치가 있다 get in touch 연락을 취하다

172. 유추 – Marconi's의 업종 ★☆☆
해설 Angie Georgas가 오후 2시 24분에 보낸 메시지, 'I think the best course of action is to find another restaurant to do the catering.'에서 또 다른 음식점이라는 말이 언급되었고, 오후 2시 34분에 보낸 메시지 'It has catered every event for us for the past ten years or so and always does a great job.'에서 Marconi's가 행사 때마다 좋은 음식을 제공해 주었다고 했고, 이어지는 내용에서도 catering에 관한 내용이 언급되었으므로 정답은 (A) 이다. **정답 (A)**

표현 정리 culinary 요리의 banquet 연회

해석 Marconi's는 무엇인가?

(A) 음식점
(B) 식료품점
(C) 요리 학교
(D) 연회장

173. 세부사항 – Marconi's가 서비스를 제공할 수 없는 이유 ★☆☆
해설 Amber Paulson은 오후 2시 18분에 보낸 메시지 'He signed a contract for an unusually large wedding that weekend and doesn't have enough additional staff for our event.'에서 Marconi's가 그 주말에 매우 큰 결혼식에 음식을 제공하기로 계약을 맺은 관계로 인력이 부족하다고 했으므로 정답은 (B)이다. **정답 (B)**

패러프레이징 |지문| don't have enough additional staff 충분한 추가 직원이 없다 → |선택지 B| It lacks enough employees 직원이 충분하지 않다

표현 정리 lack 부족하다 take reservations 예약을 받다

해석 왜 Marconi's는 서비스를 제공할 수 없나?

(A) 그들의 메뉴를 바꿔야만 했다.
(B) 직원이 충분하지 않다.
(C) 특정 날짜에 문을 닫는다.
(D) 예약을 받지 않는다.

174. 의도 파악하기 ★★☆
해설 Ray Taylor가 오후 2시 30분에 보낸 메시지 'It'll be hard to replace Marconi's.'에서 음식점을 대체하는 것이 어려울 것이라고 말하자, Angie Georgas가 'I know.'라고 했는데, 이는 Marconi's만한 음식점을 찾는 것이 어렵다는 내용에 동의하는 의미로 볼 수 있으므로 정답은 (C)이다. **정답 (C)**

표현 정리 impossible 불가능한 make a change ~을 변경하다 have no choice but to ~할 수밖에 없다

해석 오후 2시 34분에 Ms. Georgas가 "저도 알아요."라고 한 말의 의미는?

(A) 행사를 계속하는 것은 불가능할 것이다.
(B) 변경할 만큼 충분한 시간이 없다.
(C) Marconi's와 대등한 곳을 찾는 것이 쉽지 않을 것이다.
(D) Marconi's를 대체하는 것 외에 다른 방법이 없다.

175. 세부사항 – Mr. Taylor가 오늘 할 일 ★☆☆
해설 마지막 메시지에서 Mr. Taylor는 'I will get in touch with it and request a menu before we leave for the day.'라고 했는데, 이는 Mr. Paulson이 앞서 알려준 전화 번호로 연락해 메뉴를 요청하겠다는 의미이므로 (A)가 가장 적절한 정답이다. **정답 (A)**

표현 정리 place an order 주문하다

해석 Mr. Taylor가 오늘 늦게 할 일은?

(A) 잠재적인 음식 공급 업체와 대화를 한다.
(B) 저녁 만찬 옵션을 제시한다.
(C) 저녁 식사를 주문한다.
(D) 메뉴를 변경한다.

문제 176-180번은 다음 이메일들을 참조하시오.

발신: Robert Taylor <roberttaylor@dynamo.com>
수신: James Manfred <jmanfred@legacyproducts.com>
제목: 새로운 임무
날짜: 5월 2일, 화요일

James,

잘 지내죠? 좀 더 일찍 이메일을 보내고 싶었지만, 저의 상사가 지난 6주 동안 큰 제안서를 마무리짓기 위해 초과 근무를 시켰습니다. 좋은 소식은 그것이 성공했다는 것입니다. 저희 회사는 Bayard 사에 음식 서비스를 제공하

게 될 것입니다. Bayard 사는 계약을 맺고 전국 각지에서 운동 경기장, 콘서트 장, 특별한 행사들을 운영하는 회사입니다. 저는 Bayard 사가 관리하는 여러 장소에서 우리 사업을 수립하는 것을 돕기 위해 향후 수 개월 동안 많은 여행을 하게 될 것입니다. **180**먼저, 저는 시카고에 있는 Bayard 본사에서 일할 팀에 배정되었습니다. **179**저는 며칠 동안 – 아마 빠르면 다음 달 초에는 그곳에 있을 것입니다. 시간이 있다면, Sam's Pizza에서 만나 점심을 먹을 수 있을 것입니다.

176,177혹시 Maria Carter의 이메일 주소를 갖고 있나요? 그녀와 연락하고 싶거든요. **178**우리 세 명이 Pinter Corporation에서 함께 근무할 때, 그녀가 Bayard의 Kansas 사무실에 알고 지내는 사람이 있다고 했거든요.

Robert

표현 정리 assignment 임무, 과제 overtime 초과 근무 finalize 마무리짓다 proposal 제안서 success 성공 firm 회사 corporation 기업 contract 계약 quite a bit 꽤 많은 for starters 우선, 먼저 assign 배정하다 headquarters 본사 possibly 아마 get in touch with ~와 연락을 취하다 used to (과거에) ~했다

발신: James Manfred 〈jmanfred@sscservices.com〉
수신: Robert Taylor 〈roberttaylor@dynamo.com〉
제목: RE: 새로운 임무
날짜: 5월 2일, 화요일

Robert,

정말 놀라운 뉴스군요. 당신이 Dynamo Food Services에 취직했을 때, 저는 그것이 당신의 경력에 유익할 것이라는 것을 알았어요. 저는 당신이 부모님과 가까이 있는 것도 또한 좋은 일이라고 생각합니다. 방문할 날짜를 알게 되면, 저에게 알려주세요. 당신이 이곳에 오면 만나고 싶습니다. **179**저는 6월 초에 Boston에 출장을 갈 예정입니다. 그런 다음, Patricia와 아이들, 그리고 저는 8월 중순에 Colorado로 휴가를 갈 것입니다.

Maria의 이메일은 maria.carter@canma.com입니다. 저는 그녀가 당신 소식을 들으면 좋아할 거라고 확신합니다. 지난 번에 그녀가 회사 경영 담당 부사장으로 승진했다는 소식을 들었습니다. 그녀에게는 잘 된 일이죠!

James

표현 정리 fantastic 놀라운, 환상적인 take the job 취직하다 beneficial 유익한 take a vacation 휴가를 가다 promote 승진하다 vice president 부사장

176. 주제 – 첫 번째 이메일의 목적 ★★☆
해설 첫 번째 이메일, 두 번째 단락에서 'Do you happen to have Maria Carter's e-mail? I want to get in touch with her.'를 통해 Maria Carter의 이메일 주소를 요청하고 있음을 알 수 있으므로 정답은 (B)이다. **정답 (B)**

🔍**함정 분석** 첫 번째 단락에서 자신의 출장 정보를 알리며 'If you have time, maybe we can meet up for lunch at Sam's Pizza.'에서 시간이 되면 점심식사를 함께 하자는 말을 했지만, 그것이 여행 준비와 직접 관련이 있다고 보기는 어려워 (A)는 오답이다.

패러프레이징 |지문| e-mail 이메일 → |선택지 B| contact information 연락처 정보

표현 정리 arrangements 준비 collaboration 공동 작업 submit 제출하다

해석 첫 번째 이메일의 목적 중 하나는 무엇인가?
(A) 여행 준비를 하기 위해
(B) 연락처 정보를 요청하기 위해
(C) 공동 작업을 제안하기 위해

(D) 제안서를 제출하기 위해

177. 동의어 ★☆☆
해설 두 번째 단락, 'Do you happen to have Maria Carter's e-mail? I want to get in touch with her.'에서 Maria Cater의 이메일 주소를 물으면서, 그녀와 연락하고 싶다고 했으므로 '연락하다'라는 의미를 가진 (D) contact가 정답이다. **정답 (D)**

해석 첫 번째 이메일, 두 번째 단락, 첫 번째 줄의 "get in touch with"와 의미가 가장 가까운 것은?
(A) 고용하다
(B) 만나다
(C) 알리다
(D) 연락하다

178. 세부사항 – Maria Cater와의 관계 ★★☆
해설 첫 번째 이메일, 두 번째 단락에서 Maria Cater와 연락하고 싶다는 의사를 밝힌 후, When the three of us used to work together at the Pinter Corporation이라고 말한 내용을 통해 메일을 보낸 Robert Taylor와 메일을 받을 James Manfred, 그리고 Maria Cater가 Pinter Corporation에서 함께 근무한 사실을 알 수 있으므로 Mr. Taylor의 이전 직장 동료라는 (C)가 정답임을 알 수 있다. **정답 (C)**

🔍**함정 분석** 첫 번째 이메일 마지막 문장 she mentioned having connections at Bayard's Kansas City office에서 Bayard의 Kansas 지사에 아는 사람이 있다고 언급했을 뿐, Bayard의 직원인지는 알 수 없으므로 (B)는 오답이다. 두 번째 이메일, 두 번째 단락에서 이메일 주소를 전달하면서 언급한 'The last time I heard, she had been promoted to vice president of operations.'에서 경영 담당 부사장으로 승진했다고 했지만 지금도 Pinter Corporation에서 일하는지 여부는 알 수 없으므로 (D)도 정답이 될 수 없다.

표현 정리 colleague 동료 executive 고위 간부

해석 Maria Cater는 누구인가?
(A) Mr. Manfred의 상사
(B) Bayard 사의 직원
(C) Mr. Taylor의 이전 직장 동료
(D) Pinter Corporation의 경영 간부

179. 연계 문제 – Mr. Manfred에 대한 내용 ★★☆
해설 첫 번째 이메일에서 이메일을 보내는 Robert Taylor가 'I will be there for a few days – possibly as soon as early next month. If you have time, maybe we can meet up for lunch at Sam's Pizza.'에서 다음 달 초, 즉 6월 초에 시카고에서 만나 점심을 하자고 했는데, 두 번째 이메일, 첫 번째 단락 후반에서 Mr. Manfred가 'I will be in Boston on business in early June.'이라며 6월 초에 업무 차 보스턴에 있을지도 모른다고 했으므로 정답은 (A)가 된다. **정답 (A)**

🔍**함정 분석** 두 번째 이메일 두 번째 단락 'The last time I heard, she had been promoted to vice president of operations.'에서 소식을 들은 적이 있다는 것은 알 수 있지만, Ms. Carter와 자주 만나는 지는 확인이 불가하므로 (B)는 오답이다. 두 번째 이메일, 첫 번째 단락 When you took the job with Dynamo Food Services에서 Mr. Taylor가 Dynamo Food Services에 근무하고 있음을 알 수 있지만, Mr. Manfred도 같은 회사에 근무하는지는 알 수 없으므로 (C) 역시 오답이다.

해석 두 번째 이메일에서 Mr. Manfred에 대해 알 수 있는 내용은?
(A) 그는 Mr. Taylor를 만날 수 없을 지도 모른다.
(B) 그는 자주 Ms. Carter를 만난다.
(C) 그는 Dynamo Food Services를 위해 일한다.

(D) 그는 Ms. Carter에게 이메일을 보냈다.

180. 세부사항 – Mr. Manfred가 사는 곳 ★☆☆

해설 Robert Taylor가 보낸 첫 번째 이메일, 'For starters, I have been assigned to a team working with Bayard at its Chicago headquarters. I will be there for a few days — possibly as soon as early next month.'에서 Bayard 본사가 있는 시카고에 근무하게 되어 그곳에 갈 것이라고 했고, 이어 'If you have time, maybe we can meet up for lunch at Sam's Pizza.'에서 시간이 되면 점심식사를 함께 하자는 제안을 하고 있으므로, Mr. Manfred가 사는 곳은 Chicago임을 유추할 수 있어 정답은 (B)이다. **정답 (B)**

해석 Mr. Manfred가 사는 곳은?
(A) Boston
(B) Chicago
(C) Colorado
(D) Kansas City

문제 181-185번은 다음 송장과 이메일을 참조하시오.

Home Chef

수신인: Paul Lowman   (216) 555-4579
890 소마 로드   low999@netmail.net
산 안젤로, 텍사스 20033

182출하일: 11월 13일   도착 예정일: 11월 17일

주문 번호: 8294043
주문일: 11월 12일

SKU #	품목	색상	수량	가격
62007	24" 베이킹 팬	검은색	1	32,00달러
62904	큰 서빙 스푼	은색	3	12,00달러
63945	18" 금속 서빙 쟁반	은색	1	18,00달러
18467845	천 냅킨	갈색/오렌지색	15	16,00달러

배송 형태: 표준 (3-5일)	소계 78,00달러
지불: 신용카드/# xxx-xxx-7494	할인 (0,00달러)
쿠폰 코드: n/a	배송비 4,40달러
	세금 3,90달러
	총 86,30달러

181전국에서 가장 큰 온라인 주방 용품 소매상인 Home Chef를 이용해 주셔서 감사합니다. 주문 제품에 불만이 있을 경우, 전액 환불을 위해 배송 일 기준으로 30일 이내에 제품을 반품해 주십시오.

궁금 사항은 저희 고객 서비스 info@homechef.com로 연락 바랍니다.

표현 정리 estimated 추정의, 추측의   SKU 재고 관리 코드(Stock Keeping Unit)   description 설명, 종류   quantity 수량   cloth 천   subtotal 소계   retailer 소매상   be unsatisfied with ~에 만족하지 않다   return 반품하다   refund 환불

발신: Paul Lowman 〈low999@netmail.net〉
수신: 고객 서비스 〈info@homechef.com〉
제목: 주문 번호 8294043
날짜: 11월 18일, 화요일

관계자 분께,

183오늘 오후 직장에서 집에 도착했을 때, 제가 주문한 제품이 이미 집으로 배달된 것을 발견하고 기뻤습니다. 연휴를 준비하기에 딱 맞게 도착했습니다! 쟁반은 제 탁자에서 사랑스러워 보일 것입니다. 팬은 제가 준비할 칠면조에 맞을 만큼 충분히 큽니다.

184, 185유일한 문제는 15개 대신 5개의 냅킨을 보내주셨다는 것입니다. 저

의 손님들과 제가 하나씩 가질 수 있도록 주문했습니다. 이번이 처음으로 제가 추수감사절 저녁 만찬을 주최하는 것이며, 저의 동료들이 참석할 예정입니다. 저는 모든 것을 완벽하게 준비하길 원합니다. 빠진 물건들을 가능한 빨리 저에게 보내주시기 바랍니다!

Paul Lowman

표현 정리 in time 시간에 맞춰   look lovely 멋져 보이다   fit 맞다, 적합하다   instead of ~대신   place the order 주문하다   host 주최하다   Thanksgiving 추수감사절   coworker 동료   attend 참석하다

181. 세부사항 – Mr. Lowman의 주문에 관한 내용 ★★☆

해설 송장 후반 내용 'Thank you for shopping with Home Chef, the nation's largest online kitchen supply retailer.'에서 전국에서 가장 규모가 큰 온라인 주방용품 소매점이라고 했으므로, 주문 역시 온라인으로 이루어졌음을 짐작할 수 있어 정답은 (C)이다. **정답 (C)**

🔍**함정 분석** 송장의 내용의 Coupon code: n/a(not applicable: 해당 없음, 이용 안함)를 통해 쿠폰 사용 내용이 없으므로 (A)는 오답이다. 지불은 Payment: credit card/# xxx-xxx-7494를 통해 신용카드로 지불되었음을 알 수 있으므로 (D)도 오답이다.

표현 정리 pay by ~로 지불하다   check 수표

해석 Mr. Lowman의 주문에 대해 언급된 내용은?
(A) 그는 쿠폰을 사용했다.
(B) 그는 아파트에서 살고 있다.
(C) 그는 웹사이트를 통해 주문했다.
(D) 그는 수표로 지불했다.

182. 세부사항 – Home Chef가 Mr. Lowman에게 물품을 보낸 날짜 ★☆☆

해설 송장의 Shipped on: November 13를 통해 배송일은 11월 13일임을 알 수 있어 정답은 (B)이다. **정답 (B)**

해석 Home Chef가 Mr. Lowman에게 주문품을 보낸 것은 언제인가?
(A) 11월 12일
(B) 11월 13일
(C) 11월 17일
(D) 11월 18일

183. 유추 – Mr. Lowman에 관한 암시 내용 ★★☆

해설 이메일 첫 번째 단락, 'When I arrived home from work this afternoon, I was pleased to find that my order from your company had already been delivered to my home.'에서 퇴근했을 때, 물품이 도착한 것을 보고 기뻤다고 했으므로, 주문이 도착했을 당시에는 직장에 있었음을 유추할 수 있어 정답은 (A)이다. **정답 (A)**

🔍**함정 분석** 이메일 두 번째 단락, 'This is my first time hosting a Thanksgiving dinner'에서 처음으로 추수감사절 저녁 만찬을 주최한다고 했으므로 (B)는 오답이다.

표현 정리 regularly 정기적으로   vegetarian 채식주의자

해석 Mr. Lowman에 대해 암시할 수 있는 것은?
(A) 주문이 도착했을 때 직장에 있었다.
(B) 그는 정기적으로 저녁 파티를 주최한다.
(C) 그는 채식주의자이다.
(D) 그는 주방용품 소매업자이다.

184. 연계 문제 – Mr. Lowman의 주문에서 빠진 물품 ★☆☆

해설 이메일 두 번째 단락 첫 번째 문장, 'The only problem is that you sent me five napkins instead of fifteen.'에서 냅킨이 빠진 것을 알 수 있는데, 송장

내용에서 냅킨을 찾으면 67845: Cloth napkins을 확인할 수 있으므로 정답은 (D)이다. 정답 (D)

해석 Mr. Lowman의 주문에서 빠진 물품은?
　　(A) 62007
　　(B) 62904
　　(C) 63945
　　(D) 67845

185. 세부사항 – Mr. Lowman이 초대할 손님의 수 ★★☆
해설 이메일 두 번째 단락, 'The only problem is that you sent me five napkins instead of fifteen.'을 통해 원래 주문한 냅킨은 15개라는 사실을 알 수 있고, 이어지는 문장 'I placed the order so that each of my guests and I would have one.'에서 각 손님들과 자신이 하나씩 가질 수 있도록 주문했다고 했으므로 손님의 수는 14명임을 알 수 있어 정답은 (C)이다. 정답 (C)

해석 Mr. Lowman은 몇 명의 손님을 초대할 계획인가?
　　(A) 4
　　(B) 8
　　(C) 14
　　(D) 15

문제 186-190번은 다음 회람, 기사, 그리고 이메일을 참조하시오.

회람

발신: Jan Albertson
수신: 모든 홍보 부서 직원
RE: 리브랜딩
186 날짜: 7월 8일, 화요일

186 들으신 바와 같이, 회사 브랜드를 교체하자는 제안이 어제 이사회에서 공식 승인되었습니다. 브랜드 교체는 가능한 빨리 완료하기로 결정했습니다. 여러분들은 모든 대내외적인 의사소통이 업데이트될 수 있도록 할 이행 계획서를 준비해야 합니다. 덧붙여, **187** 저는 공식 브랜드 교체와 동시에 발표할 회사 로고를 제작할 팀이 구성되었으면 합니다. 저는 7월 14일인 다음 주 월요일까지 초기 진행 보고서를 기대합니다.

표현 정리 **public relations** 홍보 **rebranding** 브랜드 이미지 쇄신(회사명을 바꾸는 것 등) **proposal** 제안 **officially** 공식적으로 **approve** 승인하다 **board meeting** 이사회 **transition plan** 이행 계획 **ensure** 보장하다 **internal and external** 대내외적인 **update** 갱신하다 **in addition** 덧붙여, 또한 **unveil** 공개하다 **renaming** 개명 **look forward to** ~을 기대하다 **initial progress** 초기 진행 과정

새로운 정체성을 위해 새로 이름을 얻게 된 Hickox
Veronica Garcia

SEAGRAM (8월 12일) – 이번 달 말을 기해 Hickox Industrial Manufacturing 사는 더 이상 존재하지 않을 것이다. **187,188(A)** 회사 측은 9월 1일 Seagram 본사에서 기념식을 열어 사명을 Hickox Technologies로 공식 변경하는 내용을 발표할 예정이다.

190 회사 CEO인 Jan Albertson은 "새로운 이름이 제조업체에서 다양화된 기술회사로의 진화를 더욱 잘 반영한다."고 설명했다.

188(C),(D) 3년 전 Hickox의 최고 지도자 자리에 오른 이래, Mr. Albertson은 성장 잠재력이 큰 소규모, 전문성이 있는 회사들을 공격적으로 인수해 왔다. 그는 21세기 경제 시대에 Hickox에 경쟁 우위를 가져다 줄 소프트웨어 프로그래머, 로봇 공학 디자이너, 연구소들을 인수 대상으로 삼았다.

Hickox는 1955년에 정밀 산업 장비의 설계 및 제조사로 설립되었으며,

188(B) 현재는 Bacon County에서 세 번째로 큰 회사이다.

표현 정리 **identity** 정체성 **as of** ~일자로 **headquarters** 본사 **reflect** 반영하다 **evolution** 진화 **manufacturer** 제조사 **diversified** 다각적인, 다양화된 **aggressively** 공격적으로 **acquire** 인수하다, 얻다 **specialized** 전문화된 **growth potential** 성장 잠재력 **target** 목표로 삼다 **competitive edge** 경쟁 우위 **found** 설립하다 **precision** 정밀 **currently** 현재

발신: Ed Norman ⟨edward.norman@getmail.net⟩
수신: Jan Albertson ⟨jan.albertson@hickox.com⟩
날짜: 9월 2일
RE: 축하합니다!

Jan,

어제 기념식에 참석하지 못해 미안합니다. **189** 나는 당신이 회사와 함께 이루어 낸 모든 것에 대해 진심으로 존경합니다. 4년 전 Nava Designs를 인수할 것을 당신이 제안했을 때, 나는 동의하지 않았습니다. **190** 그러나, 내가 은퇴할 때 나의 후임자로 당신을 지명할 것을 이사회에 천거할 만큼 당신을 충분히 믿었습니다. 나는 그들이 당신을 최고 경영자로 임명한 것이 기쁩니다. **189** Nava Designs를 비롯한 모든 다른 인수 건에 대한 당신의 생각이 옳았습니다. 계속해서 번영하기를 바랍니다!

Ed

표현 정리 **make it to** ~에 참석하다 **petition** 탄원하다 **the board** 이사회 **name** 지명하다, 임명하다 **successor** 후임자 **retire** 은퇴하다 **acquisitions** 인수

186. 세부사항 – 7월 7일에 발생한 일 ★☆☆
해설 메모의 첫 번째 문장 'As you may have heard, the proposal to rebrand the company was officially approved at yesterday's board meeting.'을 보면, 어제 이사회에서 회사 브랜드를 쇄신하자는 제안이 승인되었다고 했고, 메모를 작성한 날짜를 보면 July 8으로 되어 있으므로, 이사회는 7월 7일에 개최되었다는 것을 알 수 있다. 지문의 the proposal을 A suggestion으로, approved를 accepted로 바꾼 (C)가 정답이 된다. 정답 (C)

표현 정리 **publicize** 알리다, 광고하다 **transition** 이행, 과도, 전환 **revise** 수정하다, 변경하다 **gathering** 모임

해석 메모에 따르면, 7월 7일에 무엇이 발생했는가?
　　(A) 회사가 이름 변경을 발표했다.
　　(B) 전환 계획이 수정되었다.
　　(C) 제안이 받아들여졌다.
　　(D) 모임 일정이 변경되었다.

187. 연계 문제 – 로고가 발표될 날짜 ★☆☆
해설 첫 번째 지문 후반부, 'I would like a team to be formed to create a new company's logo, which will be unveiled to the public at the same time as the official renaming.'에서 새로운 로고와 회사 명이 동시에 발표될 것임을 알 수 있었고, 두 번째 지문, 두 번째 문장, 'The company will announce the official name change to Hickox Technologies during a ceremony at its Seagram headquarters on September 1.'에서 9월 1일에 새 회사 명을 발표할 예정이라고 했으므로 정답은 (C)이다. 정답 (C)

표현 정리 **make public** 공표하다

해석 로고가 발표될 날짜는?
　　(A) 7월 8일
　　(B) 7월 14일
　　(C) 9월 1일
　　(D) 9월 2일

188. 세부사항 – Hickox에 관한 내용이 아닌 것 ★★☆

해설 기사문 'The company will announce the official name change to Hickox Technologies during a ceremony at its Seagram headquarters on September 1.'에서 Seagram에 본사가 있음을 알 수 있고, 이후 본사를 새로 옮긴다는 말은 언급되지 않아 정답은 (A)이다. **정답 (A)**

🔍 **함정 분석** 기사문 마지막 단락 'It is currently the third largest employer in Bacon County.'를 통해 Bacon City에 회사가 위치해 있음을 알 수 있어 (B)는 맞는 내용이고, 세 번째 단락 'Since taking the top leadership position at Hickox three years ago, Mr. Albertson has aggressively acquired smaller, specialized firms with strong growth potential.'에서 3년 전에 리더십에 변동이 있었고, 또 다른 회사들을 공격적으로 인수해 왔다는 사실을 알 수 있으므로 (C)와 (D) 역시 맞는 내용이다.

패러프레이징 |지문| has aggressively acquired smaller, specialized firms 작은, 전문화된 회사를 공격적으로 인수해 왔다 → |선택지 D| has been buying other companies 다른 회사들을 인수해 왔다

해석 기사에서, Hickox에 대해 언급된 내용이 아닌 것은?
(A) 회사는 새로운 본사를 열 것이다.
(B) 회사는 Bacon County에 위치해 있다.
(C) 회사는 3년 전에 리더들을 교체했다.
(D) 회사는 다른 회사들을 인수해 왔다.

189. 주제 – Mr. Norman이 이메일을 보낸 이유 ★★☆

해설 이메일 두 번째 문장, 'I want to let you know that I really respect all that you have done with the company.'를 통해 Mr. Albertson이 이룬 업적을 칭찬했고, 후반 부분 'You were right about Nava Designs and all the other acquisitions.'에서는 칭찬을 받을 만한 사례를 들고 있으므로 정답은 (C)이다. **정답 (C)**

🔍 **함정 분석** 이메일을 시작하면서 'Sorry I couldn't make it to yesterday's ceremony.'라며 어제 행사에 참석하지 못한 것에 대해 사과를 했지만 변명으로 보이지는 않고, 또 사과가 이메일의 목적으로 보이지는 않아 (A)는 오답이다.

표현 정리 excuse 변명 criticize 비판하다 praise 칭찬하다 make a recommendation 추천하다

해석 Mr. Norman이 Mr. Albertson에게 이메일을 보낸 이유는?
(A) 변명을 하기 위해
(B) 결정을 비판하기 위해
(C) 칭찬하기 위해
(D) 추천을 하기 위해

190. 연계 문제 – Mr. Norman의 이전 경력 ★☆☆

해설 두 번째 지문인 신문 기사를 통해 Jan Albertson은 회사의 CEO임을 알 수 있는데, 세 번째 지문인 이메일 'However, I believed in you enough to petition the board to name you my successor when I retired.'에서 자신이 은퇴하면서 Mr. Albertson을 후임자로 천거했다고 했으므로 Mr. Norman은 전직 CEO였음을 알 수 있어 정답은 (D)이다. **정답 (D)**

표현 정리 corporate 회사의 executive 고위 간부

해석 Mr. Norman의 이전 경력은?
(A) 신문 기자
(B) 시 공무원
(C) 산업 엔지니어
(D) 최고 경영자

문제 191-195번은 다음 발표, 이메일, 그리고 편지를 참조하시오.

이 특가 제공과 함께 시사 상식의 정상에 머무르세요!

Global Interest 잡지가 전 Mason-Dixon 직원들에게 특별가 구독을 제공합니다. 5월 1일 이전에 구독하시고 정가의 50%까지 할인을 받으세요. 구독자들은 지구상 최고의 언론이 제공하는 기사를 읽어볼 수 있습니다. **191**Global Interest는 인쇄와 온라인 상에 출간되는 주간 국제 뉴스 잡지입니다. 디지털 구독을 선택하는 사람들은 45년 이상 된 기사들이 수록된 온라인 기록 보관소에 접근할 수 있습니다. **192**구독 신청서는 7층에 있는 인사과에서 구할 수 있습니다.

구독	연중 특별가
인쇄물만	30달러
193디지털만	50달러
인쇄물+디지털	65달러
오디오 버전 (다운로드 가능)	75달러

표현 정리 current events 시사 special offer 특가 제공 extend 뻗치다, 연장하다 subscribe 구독하다 up to ~까지 subscriber 구독자 get access 접근하다 journalism 언론 weekly 주간의 in print 인쇄된 subscription 구독 archive 기록 보관소 contain 포함하다 exceptional 훌륭한 obtain 얻다 human resources department 인사과

수신: Roman Codrescu 〈rcodrescu@masondixon.com〉
발신: Eric Majors 〈emajcrs@masondixon.com〉
제목: Global Interest 제공
날짜: 4월 18일
첨부: 구독_신청서

안녕하세요, Roman.

Global Interest 구독에 필요한 구독 신청서를 보냅니다. **192**당신의 사무실에서 신청서를 가져갈 때 시간을 할애해 다른 구독 옵션들에 대해 설명해 줘서 고마워요. **193**저는 웹사이트를 통해 보다 오래된 기사들에 접근이 가능한 가장 저렴한 것을 구독하기로 결정했습니다. 제가 정말 좋아하는 작가를 발견한 후, 과거로 돌아가 그들의 이전 기사들을 보는 것을 좋아합니다. **194**가능한 빨리 구독을 시작하고 싶습니다. 그것을 가능하게 해 줄 가장 빠른 방법을 알려주세요.

Eric

표현 정리 subscription form 구독 신청서 appreciate 인정하다 previous 이전의

구독자 #9037324

Eric Majors
873 Hope Way
Lincoln, NE 29003

4월 29일

Mr. Majors 님께,

Global Interest에 대한 귀하의 관심에 감사 드립니다. **195**구독을 시작하려면, 귀하가 구독료를 결제해야 합니다. 동봉된 것은 지불 금액이 포함된 결재 카드입니다. 1년 구독을 위해 금액과 함께 카드를 보내주시기 바랍니다. 저희는 개인 수표, 신용카드, 은행 이체도 받습니다. 귀하의 구독은 결제가 확인된 후, 3~5일의 영업일 이내에 가능하게 될 것입니다.

195만약 즉시 구독을 원한다면, 저희 온라인 결제 옵션을 이용하실 수 있습

니다. www.globalinterst.com으로 방문하셔서 "구독 처리" 표시를 클릭해 주십시오. 그런 다음 귀하의 구독자 번호를 입력하십시오. 귀하의 결제 정보를 제출하기 전에 사용자 이름과 비밀번호를 입력하도록 요청 받을 것입니다.

Harris Polanski
구독자 서비스 대표
Global Interest 잡지

표현 정리 **payment card** 결제 카드 **amount due** 결제 금액, 지불액 **accept** 받아들이다 **bank transfer** 은행 이체 **activate** 활성화시키다 **prompt** 요청하다, 유도하다 **username** 사용자 이름 **password** 비밀번호 **submit** 제출하다 **representative** 대표

191. 세부사항 – Global Interest 잡지에 대한 내용이 아닌 것 ★☆☆

해설 첫 번째 지문, 'Global Interest is a weekly international news magazine published in print and online.'에서 국제 뉴스 잡지라는 내용은 언급되었지만 수십 개 국에서 판매가 되는지는 언급되지 않았으므로 정답은 (C)이다. **정답 (C)**

🔍 **함정 분석** (A)의 경우는 첫 번째 지문의 도표를 보면 audio version이 75달러에 구매 가능하기 때문에, 읽는 것이 아니고 듣기를 원하는 사람들 역시 구독이 가능함을 알 수 있다.

표현 정리 **on a regular basis** 정기적으로 **dozens of** 수십의, 많은

해석 Global Interest 잡지에 대해 언급되지 않은 것은?
(A) 청취자들을 위한 형태로 이용 가능하다.
(B) 정기적으로 출판된다.
(C) 수십 개 국에서 판매된다.
(D) 독자들이 지난 호를 보도록 허락한다.

192. 연계 문제 – Mr. Codrescu에 대한 내용 ★☆☆

해설 Mr. Codrescu는 두 번째 지문인 이메일 수신자이다. Eric Majors가 보낸 이메일, 'Thanks for taking the time to explain the different subscription options when I picked the form up from your office'를 통해 구독 신청서를 받으러 갔을 때 도움 준 것에 대해 Mr. Codrescu에게 고마움을 표했는데, 첫 번째 지문 마지막 문장 'Subscription forms can be obtained at the Human Resources Department on the seventh floor.'에서 신청서는 7층 인사과에서 받아갈 수 있다고 했으므로 Mr. Codrescu는 잡지 구독과 관련된 업무를 돕는 인사과 직원이라고 추측할 수 있어 정답은 (A)이다. **정답 (A)**

표현 정리 **publication** 출판, 출판물

해석 Mr. Codrescu에 대해 암시된 것은?
(A) 그는 7층에서 근무한다.
(B) 그는 Global Interest를 구독한다.
(C) 그는 뉴스 출판물에 기고한다.
(D) 그는 Mr. Polanski의 상사이다.

193. 연계 문제 – Mr. Majors의 구독료 ★☆☆

해설 이메일에서 Mr. Majors는 인터넷에서 정보를 이용할 수 있는 것 중에서 가장 저렴한 것을 원한다고 했으므로, 첫 번째 지문의 도표에서 digital 형태로 된 것 중에서 가장 낮은 가격을 찾으면 $50임을 알 수 있으므로 정답은 (B)이다. **정답 (B)**

해석 Mr. Majors는 Global Interest 구독을 위해 얼마를 결제할 것인가?
(A) 30달러
(B) 50달러
(C) 65달러
(D) 75달러

194. 연계 문제 – Mr. Majors에 대한 내용 ★★☆

해설 Mr. Majors는 이메일, 'I would like to start my subscription as soon as possible.'에서 가능한 빨리 구독하기를 원한다는 의사를 나타냈고, 편지 두 번째 단락, 첫 번째 문장 'If you would like to activate your subscription immediately, you can use our online payment option.'에서 즉시 구독을 원하는 경우, 온라인으로 결제할 수 있다는 정보가 있으므로, Mr. Majors는 구독료를 온라인으로 결제할 것임을 유추할 수 있어 정답은 (B)이다. **정답 (B)**

🔍 **함정 분석** 발표문의 'Global Interest is a weekly international news magazine published in print and online.'에서 Global Interest는 국제 뉴스를 다루는 잡지라는 것을 알 수 있으므로 본 잡지의 구독을 원하는 Mr. Majors가 지역 뉴스를 잘 알아야 하는 직업을 가지고 있는지에 대해서는 알 수 없어 (C)는 오답이다.

해석 Mr. Majors에 대해 암시된 것은?
(A) 그의 회사는 Lincoln에 위치해 있다.
(B) 그는 그의 구독료를 온라인으로 지불할 것이다.
(C) 그의 직업은 그가 지역 뉴스에 익숙할 것을 요구한다.
(D) 그는 미디어 회사를 위해 일한다.

195. 세부사항 – Mr. Polanski가 편지를 작성한 이유 ★☆☆

해설 편지의 시작부분을 보면, 'To start your subscription, we need to receive your payment.'라고 되어 있으므로, 새로운 구독자에게 쓰는 편지라는 것을 알 수 있고, 그 이하 내용에서 구독료를 지불하는 방법에 대해서 상세하게 설명하고 있다. 두 번째 단락에서 즉시 구독을 활성화하기를 원한다면 'If you would like to activate your subscription immediately, you can use our online payment option.'이라고 하며, 온라인으로 지불할 수도 있다는 설명을 이어가고 있다. 그러므로 새로운 구독자에게 지침(설명)을 제공하기 위해서 편지를 작성했다는 것을 알 수 있다. **정답 (D)**

표현 정리 **recommend** 추천하다 **subscription** 구독 **feature** 특징, 특색 **payment** 지불 **instructions** 설명, 지시, 지침

해석 Mr. Polanski가 편지를 쓴 이유는?
(A) 구독 옵션을 추천하기 위해
(B) 웹사이트 특징을 설명하기 위해
(C) 지불 오류의 수정을 요청하기 위해
(D) 새로운 구독자에게 지침을 제공하기 위해

문제 196-200번은 다음 기사, 이메일, 그리고 회람을 참조하시오.

건강한 음식을 제공하는 Smart Balance
Mark Swenz

포틀랜드, 오레건 (11월 18일) – 공립학교들은 학생들이 보다 균형 잡힌 식사를 하도록 격려하기 위해 메뉴들을 교체해야 했다. 즉, 그들은 탄수화물과 정제된 설탕을 줄이고, 보다 건강한 음식으로 대체했다. 하지만 직장에서 건강한 음식을 권장하는 것에 대해 여러분은 생각해 본 적이 있는가?

민간 음식 업체인 Smart Balance는 균형 잡힌 식사를 하는 직원들이 학생들 못지않게 중요하며, 그것이 그들이 고단백질, 과일과 채소를 포함하는 회사원들 위주의 식단표를 만든 이유라고 말한다. 많은 경우에, 배달 음식은 직원들을 나른하게 만드는 지방과 탄수화물 함량이 높다.

"피곤한 직원들은 생산성을 발휘하지 못한다."고 Smart Balance 창업자인 Freda Hiens는 말했다. 196"충분한 에너지를 공급받기 위해, 직원들은 균형 잡힌 식사를 해야 한다." 균형 잡힌 음식의 비용은 종종 표준으로 공급된 음식의 비용과 비교할 만하다.

198Hiens가 자신의 주방에서 시작한 Smart Balance는 투자자들로부터 500,000달러 이상의 자금을 유치했다. 200현재, 이 회사의 정규 고객들은 Maxmay, Chico's, AdWorld와 같은 여러 현지 기업들을 포함한다.

표현 정리 public school 공립학교 revise 변경하다, 교체하다 **namely** 즉 cut down on ~을 줄이다 **carbohydrate** 탄수화물 **refined** 정제된 **workplace** 직장 **privately owned** 개인이 소유한 catering 음식 공급 oriented ~을 지향하는 **protein** 단백질 **sluggish** 나른한, 부진한 **productive** 생산적인 **comparable** 비교할 만한 **investor** 투자자 **top** 능가하다, 더 낫다 **corporation** 기업

수신: Freda Hiens 〈freda@smartbalance.net〉
발신: Dale Lee 〈dlee@appleshoebox.com〉
제목: 메뉴 요청
날짜: 12월 18일

안녕하세요, Freda.

197Apple Shoe Box가 다음 주에 직원들과 그들의 가족을 위한 19회 연례 휴일 파티를 가질 예정입니다. 대략 2,000여 명의 직원이 참석할 것이라고 생각합니다. 저희는 고기를 먹지 않는 것을 선호하는 직원들이 있는 관계로 고기가 들어가지 않는 샘플 메뉴를 요청합니다. 그것을 준비할 때, 4개 이상의 전채 요리를 포함시켜 주시기 바랍니다. 199저희 파트너는 치즈를 좋아하고, 그래서 그의 입맛에 맞춘 하나를 준비해 주신다면 좋을 것입니다. 3개의 주요리는 충분할 겁니다. 200작년에 Maxmay 행사를 위해 만들었던 고기가 들어가지 않은 주요리를 포함시켜 주십시오. 그것은 맛있었습니다!

Dale Lee

표현 정리 feature 특징으로 하다, 포함하다 appetizer 전채 요리 entrée 주요리 meatless 고기가 없는

Apple Shoe Box
휴일 파티 메뉴

전채 요리
Sunrise 케일 샐러드*
치킨-베이컨 말이
스파게티 호박 컵
구운 치즈 스틱

주요리
쌀을 채운 호박*
미트볼 스파게티
구운 치킨
그릴에 구운 생선

*채식주의자 용

표현 정리 squash 호박 stuff 채우다 vegetarian 채식주의자

196. 유추 - Smart Balance의 음식에 관한 내용 ★★☆
해설 기사 세 번째 단락, 두 번째 문장 'In order to have enough energy, employees need to eat a balanced diet.'는 Smart Balance 창업자인 Freda Hiens의 인터뷰 내용으로 균형 잡힌 식사가 직원들에게 충분한 에너지를 공급해 생산성을 높여준다고 말하고 있다. 민간 음식 공급 업체인 Smart Balance가 균형 잡힌 식단을 제공함으로써 직원들이 활력을 유지할 수 있게 돕는다고 할 수 있으므로 정답은 (A)이다. 정답 (A)

🔍 **함정 분석** 기사 첫 번째 단락은 공립학교에서 균형 잡힌 식단을 도입했고, 이러한 식단이 직장에도 적용될 수 있음을 언급하고 있다. 'Namely, they have cut down on carbohydrates and refined sugar and replaced them with healthier foods.'를 통해 탄수화물과 정제된 설탕을 줄여 더 건강한 식단을 만드는 것을 알 수 있지만, 지방과 탄수화물이 아예 들어가지 않는 것인지 또는 Smart Balance가 지방과 탄수화물이 함유되지 않은 식사를 제공하는지를 알 수 있는 것은 아니므로 (D)는 오답이다.

패러프레이징 |지문| have enough energy 충분한 에너지를 갖는다 → |선택지 A| stay active 활동적인 상태를 유지하다

표현 정리 active 활동적인 tasty 맛있는 be free of ~에서 자유롭다, ~이 없다

해설 기사에서, Smart Balance의 음식에 관해 암시된 것은?
(A) 직원들이 직장에서 활력을 유지하도록 돕는다.
(B) 일반 식사보다 더 맛있다.
(C) 준비하기 쉽다.
(D) 지방과 탄수화물이 없다.

197. 세부사항 - 파티에 관한 내용 ★☆☆
해설 이메일의 첫 번째 문장을 보면, 'Apple Shoe Box will be having our nineteenth annual holiday party next week for our employees and their family members.'라고 하며, 파티를 여는 대상은 직원들과 그들의 가족이라고 되어 있고, 직원들의 spouses는 가족의 일원이므로 (C)가 정답이 된다. 정답 (C)

표현 정리 vegetrain 채식의, 채식주의자 spouse 배우자

해설 이메일에서 휴일 파티에 관해 언급된 것은?
(A) 올해 더 많은 사람들이 참석할 것이라고 기대된다.
(B) 채식 옵션이 작년에 있었다.
(C) 직원들의 배우자들이 행사에 환영받는다.
(D) 모든 직원들은 참여해야 한다.

198. 세부사항 - Ms. Hiens에 관한 내용 ★★☆
해설 기사문 마지막 단락, 'Smart Balance, which began in Hiens' own personal kitchen, received funding from investors that topped $500,000.'에서 Smart Balance 창업자인 Hiens는 자신의 집 부엌에서 회사를 시작했음을 알 수 있으므로 정답은 (A)이다. 정답 (A)

🔍 **함정 분석** 두 번째 지문인 이메일을 보낸 Mr. Lee는 본인의 회사 Apple Shoe Box의 휴일 파티에 필요한 음식을 요청하고 있다. 'Please include the meatless entrée that you made for the Maxmay event last year.'에서 작년에 있었던 Maxmay 행사에 제공했던 메뉴에 대해 언급하고 있지만, 그것은 Maxmay라는 회사를 위해서 제공된 것이기 때문에 (B)는 오답이다.

패러프레이징 |지문| Smart Balance, which began in Hiens' own personal kitchen Smart Balance는 Hiens의 집 부엌에서 시작했다 → |선택지 A| She started her company in her home 그녀는 그녀의 집에서 회사를 시작했다

해설 Ms. Hiens에 관해 나타난 내용은?
(A) 그녀는 그녀의 집에서 회사를 시작했다.
(B) 그녀는 과거에 Mr. Lee를 위해 음식을 제공한 적이 있다.
(C) 그녀는 휴일 파티에 참석할 것이다.
(D) 그녀는 모든 음식을 자신이 요리한다.

199. 연계 문제 - Mr. Lee의 파트너를 위한 요리 ★★☆
해설 이메일에서 Mr. Lee는 'When you prepare it, please include four or more appetizers.'라고 하며, 4개 이상의 전채 요리를 포함시켜 달라고 한 뒤, 'My partner loves cheese, so it would be great if you prepared one to suit his tastes.'에서 파트너가 치즈를 좋아하며, 그의 입맛을 맞출 수 있는 메뉴를 준비해 달라고 부탁하고 있으므로 전채에 포함된 구운 치즈 스틱이 이 조건에 맞는다고 볼 수 있어 정답은 (D)이다. 정답 (D)

해설 Mr. Lee의 파트너를 위한 요리는 무엇인가?
(A) Sunrise 케일 샐러드
(B) 치킨-베이컨 말이
(C) 스파게티 호박 컵
(D) 구운 치즈 스틱

200. 연계 문제 – 쌀을 채운 호박에 관한 내용 ★★★

해설 세 번째 지문인 메뉴 리스트를 보면 Wild Rice Stuffed Squash*는 채식주의자를 위한 메뉴인데, 두 번째 지문에서 Mr. Lee가 'Please include the meatless entrée that you made for the Maxmay event last year.'라고 한 말을 통해 이 메뉴는 작년에도 Maxmay 행사를 위해 제공되었던 요리임을 알 수 있다. 또한 첫 지문의 마지막 문장 'Today, its regular clients include several local corporations such as Maxmay, Chico's, and AdWorld.'에서 Maxmay는 Smart Balance의 단골 고객 중 한 곳임을 알 수 있으므로 정답은 (A)이다. 정답 (A)

🔍 **함정 분석** 이메일에서 Mr. Lee가 Wild Rice Stuffed Squash에 관해 구체적으로 언급하고 있는 것으로 보아 관심을 끌지 않는다고 볼 수 없으므로 (B)는 오답이다. 하지만 이 메뉴가 가장 인기 있는 메뉴 중 하나인지는 알 수 없으므로 (C)도 오답이다.

패러프레이징 |지문| regular clients 단골 고객 → |선택지 A| regular customer 단골 고객

표현 정리 regular customer 단골 고객 dairy product 유제품

해석 Smart Balance의 쌀을 채운 호박에 관해 암시된 내용은?
(A) 단골 고객을 위해 만들어진 적이 있다.
(B) Mr. Lee의 관심을 끌지 않을 것이다.
(C) 가장 인기 있는 메뉴 중 하나이다.
(D) 유제품을 포함한다.

Test 02
Part 7

문제 147-148번은 다음 공지 사항을 참조하시오.

> [147]99234번 계정의 전기 공급 서비스 이전 요청과 관련해서, 새로운 당사자는 매월 5일에 시작되어 종료되는 전기 요금 납부 기간 내에 월 요금을 납부해야 한다는 것을 참고하시기 바랍니다.
>
> [148]서비스 이전 절차를 완료한 후에, 새로운 당사자는 전화 또는 우편으로 요금을 납부할 수 있습니다. 전화로 납부하려면 555-9293으로 전화해 납부 옵션을 선택하면 됩니다. 우편으로 납부하는 경우 청구서에 첨부된 양식을 작성해 반송 주소로 만기일 전에 제출하면 됩니다.

표현 정리 with regards to ~와 관련해 request 요청 transfer 이전하다 account 고객 계정 be advised that ~임을 숙지하다 party (소속, 계약 등의) 당사자 payment 납부, 지금 monthly 월간의 within ~ 이내에 billing cycle 납부 주기 transfer form 이전 양식 responsible 책임있는 dial 전화를 걸다 fill out a form 서식을 작성하다 attached 부착된, 첨부된 return address 반송 주소 due date 만기일

147. 유추 – 공지 대상 ★☆☆

해설 첫 번째 문장 'With regards to your request to transfer electric service for account 99234' 내용을 통해 공지 대상자는 전에 전기 공급에 대해 문의한 적이 있음을 짐작할 수 있다. 또한 'please be advised that the new party is required to continue payment of your monthly service within the same billing cycle beginning and ending on the 5th every month'를 통해서도 결제 기간 내에 전기 요금을 납부해야 하는 사람이 누구인지를 짐작할 수 있으므로 정답은 (B)이다. 정답 (B)

표현 정리 bill collector 수금원 utility (수도, 전기, 가스 같은) 공익 사업 subscriber 가입자

해석 공지 대상은 누구인가?
(A) 수금원
(B) 유틸리티 가입자
(C) 전화 서비스 고객
(D) 전기 서비스 기사

148. 세부사항 – 서비스 이전에 대한 내용 ★★☆

해설 'After completing the service transfer form, the new responsible party may send service payments by phone or mail.'에서 새로운 당사자가 전화 또는 우편을 통해 서비스 요금을 납부할 수 있다고 했고, 이어지는 내용에서도 납부 방법에 대한 부연 설명이 이어지고 있으므로 정답은 (D)이다. 정답 (D)

🔍 **함정 분석** 첫 번째 단락에서 납부 주기에 대해 언급했지만, 새로운 납부 주기에 대해서는 언급되지 않았기 때문에 혼동 보기인 (B)는 오답이다.

패러프레이징 |지문| service payments by phone or mail 전화 혹은 우편으로의 납부액 지불 → |선택지 D| two ways to make a payment 두가지의 납부 방법

표현 정리 arrange 처리하다, 정하다 in advance 미리, 사전에 business days 영업일 make a payment 납부하다

해석 서비스 이전에 대해 언급된 것은?
(A) 한 달 전에 처리되어야 한다.
(B) 새로운 납부 기간이 정해질 것이다.
(C) 업무일 기준 5일 이내에 완료될 것이다.
(D) 두 가지의 납부 방법이 있다.

문제 149-150번은 다음 문자 메시지 내용을 참조하시오.

Jules Klein	Henry, 시간 있어요?	오후 1시 15분
Henry Totes	방금 전화 통화 끝났어요. 무슨 일이에요?	오후 1시 20분
Jules Klein	4층에 있는 복사기에 종이가 걸렸어요. 종이를 빼보려고 했지만 완전히 막혔어요.	오후 1시 28분
Henry Totes	150오늘 아침에 프린트가 안 된 이유가 있었군요! 내 컴퓨터에 문제가 있다고 생각했거든요.	오후 1시 29분
Jules Klein	어떻게 해야 하죠?	오후 1시 30분
Henry Totes	149수리 기사에게 전화를 하죠. 전문가가 살펴보도록 하는 게 좋을 것 같아요.	오후 1시 32분
Jules Klein	좋은 생각이에요. 복사기가 더 망가지게 하고 싶진 않아요.	오후 1시 33분

표현 정리 copy machine 복사기 jammed (막히거나 걸려) 꼼짝 하지 않는 pull out 당겨 꺼내다 definitely 분명히 stuck 막힌 no wonder ~하는 것도 당연하다, ~할 만하다 issue 문제 maintenance man 정비공, 수리 기사 had better (~하는 것이) 좋을 것이다 professional 전문직 종사자 take a look at ~을 살펴보다 cause ~을 초래하다 additional damage 부가적 손상

149. 의도 파악하기 ★☆☆
해설 Henry Totes가 오후 1시 32분에 보낸 문자 'Let's call the maintenance man. We'd better ask a professional to take a look at it.'에서 수리 기사를 불러 복사기를 살펴보게 하자고 제안하고 있으므로 정답은 기술자가 기계를 고치도록 한다는 내용의 (D)이다. 정답 (D)

표현 정리 inspect 점검하다 order 주문하다 fix 고치다 prefer 선호하다 technician 기술자 repair 수리하다

해석 Mr. Totes가 오후 1시 32분에 "전문가가 살펴보도록 하는 게 좋을 것 같아요."라고 말한 의미는 무엇인가?
(A) 스스로 기계를 점검할 것이다.
(B) 새로운 기계를 주문할 것을 제안한다.
(C) Ms. Klein이 기계를 고치기를 원한다.
(D) 기술자가 기계를 고치는 것을 선호한다.

150. 세부사항 – 복사기에 대한 내용 ★★☆
해설 Jules Klein이 메시지를 보내 복사기에 문제가 있다고 말하자, Henry Totes가 'No wonder I couldn't print anything this morning! I thought the issue was my computer.'라고 말했는데, 이 내용을 통해 복사기는 이미 고장이 나 있었음을 알 수 있으므로 정답은 (C)이다. 정답 (C)

🔍 함정 분석 Mr. Totes의 컴퓨터는 복사기로 인해 제대로 작동하지 않는 것이 아니므로 (A)는 오답이다. Mr. Totes는 오전에 출력할 수 없었던 것을 본인의 컴퓨터 문제로 생각했을 뿐, 복사기의 문제라고 생각하지는 못했으므로 고치려는 시도를 했다고 볼 수 없어 (D)도 오답이다.

표현 정리 indicate 나타내다 cause 초래하다 malfunction 제대로 작동하지 않다 run out of ~이 떨어지다, 바닥나다 correct 맞는, 정확한 be broken 부서지다, 고장 나다 notice 의식하다, 알다 attempt 시도하다

해석 복사기에 관해 언급된 내용은 무엇인가?
(A) Mr. Totes의 컴퓨터가 오작동하도록 만들었다.
(B) 복사 용지가 모두 떨어졌다.
(C) Ms. Klein이 알아채기 전에도 고장 나 있었다.
(D) Mr. Totes는 기계를 고치려고 시도했다.

문제 151-153번은 다음 이메일을 참조하시오.

발신: gcharles@bayers.com
수신: sallyhu@northon.org
날짜: 8월 12일
제목: Candidate Mary Wiggins

Ms. Hu 님께,

151저는 Northon의 보조 편집자 자리에 Mary Wiggins를 추천하고자 글을 씁니다. Mary는 지난 1년간 저희 인턴으로 근무했으며, 중요한 편집 프로젝트에서 저와 함께 밀접하게 작업했습니다. 그녀의 세부적인 것에 주의를 기울이는 능력은 흠잡을 데가 없습니다.

152그녀의 편집 능력 외에도, 대학 교육은 그녀가 Northon의 보조 편집자 후보가 되는데 충분한 자격을 제공합니다. 153그녀는 근면하고, 열심히 일하며, 사실 확인을 위해 장시간 노력하는 것을 마다 하지 않습니다. 저희 직원이 원고에 나온 정보에 대해 잘 모를 때에도 Mary는 그 일에 매달려, 사실이 확인될 때까지 모든 질문들을 조사했습니다.

152Mary는 지난 달에 학교를 갓 졸업했지만, 저는 그녀가 성공적인 편집자가 될 것임을 확신합니다. 귀사에 Mary Wiggins를 적극 추천하는 바입니다.

추가적인 진술이 필요할 경우, 주저하지 마시고 (323) 555-4476로 전화 주시기 바랍니다. Mary의 자격에 대해 기꺼이 말씀드릴 수 있습니다.

Gene Charles
선임 편집자
Bayers Books

표현 정리 candidate 후보자 recommend 추천하다 hire 고용하다 junior editor 보조 편집자 editorial 편집의, 편집과 관련된 closely 밀접하게, 친밀하게 attention 주의, 관심 detail 세부 사항들 impeccable 흠잡을 데 없는 in addition to ~에 더하여 staff 직원 uncertain 확신이 없는, 잘 모르는 present 제출하다 manuscript 원고 buckle down ~에 착수하다 research 조사하다 verify 확인하다 confident 확신하는 successful 성공적인 highly 적극적으로 testimony 증언, 진술 hesitate 망설이다 qualification 자격

151. 주제 – 이메일의 목적 ★★☆
해설 첫 문장 'I am writing to recommend you hire Mary Wiggins for the position of junior editor at Northon.'에서 Mary Wiggins를 보조 편집자 자리에 추천하고 있음을 알 수 있고, 이어지는 문장에서도 Mary Wiggins의 업무 능력을 칭찬하고 있음을 알 수 있으므로 정답은 (B)이다. 정답 (B)

표현 정리 look for ~을 찾다, 구하다 new hire 신규 채용자 endorse 지지하다, 보증하다 job candidate 입사 지원자 discourage 좌절시키다 admonish 책망하다, (강력히) 충고하다 client 의뢰인, 고객

해석 이메일의 목적은 무엇인가?
(A) 신입 직원을 찾기 위해
(B) 입사 지원자를 보증하기 위해
(C) 종업원을 좌절시키기 위해
(D) 새로운 고객을 책망하기 위해

152. 세부사항 – Ms. Wiggins에 대한 사실 내용 ★★☆
해설 두 번째 단락 'In addition to her editorial skills, her university education makes her a strong candidate for junior editor at Northon.'에서 대학 교육을 받았다는 사실과 세 번째 단락 'Although Mary only finished school last month'를 통해 지난 달에 대학을 졸업했음을 알 수 있으므로 정답은 (B)이다. 정답 (B)

16

표현 정리 **recently** 최근에 **graduate from** ~을 졸업하다 **experience** 경험 **scientific** 과학적인

해석 Ms. Wiggins에 대한 사실 내용은?
(A) 그녀는 Mr. Charles에 의해 고용되었다.
(B) 그녀는 최근 대학을 졸업했다.
(C) 그녀는 수 년 간의 편집 경력을 가지고 있다.
(D) 그녀는 과학적인 조사를 하는 것을 즐긴다.

153. 문장 위치 찾기 ★★☆

해설 주어진 문장 "She is diligent and not afraid to put in the hard work and long hours required for fact-checking."은 인턴으로 일하면서 원고 작성을 위해 조사 작업을 완수했다는 의미를 강조하기 위해 제시된 내용으로 글의 내용을 매끄럽게 이어줄 뿐만 아니라 추천의 메시지를 강하게 전달하고 있으므로 정답은 (B)이다. 정답 (B)

표현 정리 **diligent** 근면한 **long hours** 장시간 **fact-checking** 사실 확인

해석 [1], [2], [3], [4] 중 다음 문장이 들어가기에 가장 적합한 곳은?

"그녀는 근면하고, 열심히 일을 하며, 사실 확인을 위해 장시간 노력하는 것을 두려워하지 않습니다."

(A) [1]
(B) [2]
(C) [3]
(D) [4]

문제 154-155번은 다음 엽서 내용을 참조하시오.

비즈니스 전문가 분께,	Professional Star
	241 노스게이트
Professional Star는 얼굴 사진에 대한 특별 행사를 실시합니다! 155새로운 일자리에 지원하든, 기존의 명함을 꾸미는데 필요하든, 모든 스타일과 크기의 사진들을 촬영해 인화해 드릴 수 있습니다.	드라이브 워메이, 오하이오 29321
저희 얼굴 사진을 다음의 용도로 사용하십시오.	
• 이력서	
• 명함	
• 사무실 사진	
• 작업 안내 책자	
사진 샘플과 촬영 비용은 저희 웹사이트 www.professionalstarphotos.com을 방문해 확인하십시오.	Allen Stone 캔톤 건물, 스위트 B
Professional Star 스튜디오는 Big Apple Dental 뒷편 Northgate Drive에 위치해 있습니다.	154234 노스게이트 드라이브 워메이, 오하이오 29322

표현 정리 **professional** 전문가 **run** 제공하다 **headshot photo** 얼굴 **apply for** ~에 지원하다 **spruce up** (~을) 단장하다 **current** 현재의, 기존의 **shoot** 촬영하다 **business card** 명함 **work directory** 작업

안내책자 **rate** 요금

154. 유추 – Mr. Stone에 대한 유추 내용 ★☆☆

해설 Professional Star라는 사진 전문 업체가 Allen Stone이라는 사람에게 보낸 엽서이다. 주로 해당 업체의 주력 사업과 상세한 정보 제공을 위한 웹사이트 주소, 실제 위치를 언급한다. Mr. Stone의 개인 정보는 주소 이외에 드러난 점이 없으며, 이를 통해 해당 업체와 같은 Northgate Drive에 살고 있다는 것을 알 수 있으므로 정답은 (D)이다. 정답 (D)

해석 이 엽서가 Mr. Stone에 대해 암시하는 것은?
(A) 그는 전에 얼굴 사진을 찍은 적이 있다.
(B) 그는 명함을 주문했다.
(C) 그는 Big Apple Dental을 방문한 적이 있다.
(D) 그는 Professional Star 가까이 산다.

155. 세부사항 – Professional Star에 대한 내용 ★★☆

해설 본문 내용 'Whether you are applying for a new job or just need to spruce up your current business photo'를 통해 Professional Star'는 사무실에 근무하는 사람들을 대상으로 인물 사진을 촬영하는 일을 주로 하고 있음을 알 수 있으므로 정답은 (A)이다. 정답 (A)

표현 정리 **indicate** 나타내다 **market** (상품을) 내놓다 **office worker** 사무직 근로자 **hire** 고용하다 **employee** 종업원 **portrait** 인물 사진

해석 Professional Star에 대해 언급된 내용은?
(A) 사무직 근로자들을 대상으로 서비스를 제공한다.
(B) 새로운 직원을 고용할 것이다.
(C) Big Apple Dental과 함께 일한다.
(D) 아이들의 인물 사진을 찍는다.

문제 156-158번은 다음 기사를 참조하시오.

지하철 시위로 출근길 지연 예상

SEATTLE (4월 1일) – 시 교통 노동조합은 전 지하철 종사자들에게 시 전 지역에서의 총 파업을 명령했다. 156, 158이 전례 없는 조치는 다음 주 월요일에 시작해 노동조합의 요구가 수용될 때까지 정기 운행 시간 동안 열차 서비스를 마비시킬 것임에 틀림없다.

높은 임금과 가족 복지혜택 같은 요구들이 지하철 노동자들의 요구 목록에 포함되어 있다.

지하철이 운행되지 않으면서, 시 공무원들은 큰 교통 체증과 혼잡한 출근길을 우려하고 있다. 이를 완화하기 위해 많은 버스와 대안 교통 수단들이 운행될 것이다. 157시애틀 거주자들은 www.seattlepublictransportation.com을 방문해 대안 운송 수단을 알아 보고, 그들의 오전 출근길 경로를 변경할 것을 권유받고 있다.

지하철 파업이 얼마 동안 지속될 것인지에 대해서, 조합원들은 적어도 일주일의 교착 상태를 예상하고 있으나, 시 의회는 근무 시간이 끝나기 전에 새로운 합의가 성사될 수 있기를 원한다고 말했다.

표현 정리 protest 시위 commute 통근 city-wide 전 도시의 strike 파업 employee 종업원, 직원 unprecedented 전례 없는 halt 중단시키다 regular 정기적인 operation hours 운행 시간 demand 요구 wage 임금 benefit 혜택 improvement 개선 city official 시 공무원 traffic jam 교통 체증 congest 혼잡하게 하다 in order to ~을 위해서 alleviate 완화하다 alternative 대체 가능한 resident 거주자, 주민 reroute 경로를 변경하다 as for ~에 관해 말하면 last 지속되다 standoff (회담 등의) 교착 상태 city council 시 의회 resolve 해결하다 contract 계약 working day 근무 시간대

156. 세부사항 – 다음 주 월요일에 시애틀에서 일어날 일 ★★☆

해설 첫 번째 단락 'This unprecedented action will halt train services during regular operation hours starting next Monday and continuing until the union's demands are met.'에서 다음 주 월요일부터 열차 서비스가 중단될 예정임을 알 수 있으므로 (D)가 정답이다. 정답 (D)

함정 분석 새로운 계약에 합의하기 위해 시 의회가 조합원들과 만나길 기대한 다는 내용이 있긴 하지만 이 만남이 월요일에 있을 지는 알 수 없으므로 (B)는 오답이다.

패러프레이징 |지문| This unprecedented action will halt train services 이 전례 없는 조치는 기차 서비스를 중단시킬 것이다 → |선택지 D| subways will be unavailable 지하철 이용이 불가능하다

표현 정리 according to ~에 따르면 roadblock 바리케이트 be placed on ~에 놓이다 fundraiser 모금 행사 injured 부상을 입은 unavailable 이용할 수 없는

해석 기사에 따르면, 다음 주 월요일에 시애틀에서 일어날 일은 무엇인가?
(A) 중심가에 바리케이트가 놓여질 것이다.
(B) 노동조합은 계약을 위해 시 의회와 만날 것이다.
(C) 부상을 입은 직원을 위해 모금행사가 열릴 것이다.
(D) 지하철이 출근자들에게 이용 가능하지 않을 것이다.

157. 세부사항 – 웹사이트를 알려준 이유 ★☆☆

해설 세 번째 단락 'Seattle residents are encouraged to go to www.seattlepublictransportation.com to reroute their morning work commutes by using alternative transportation.'에서 출근길 대안 교통 수단을 알아보게 하기 위해 웹사이트를 방문하도록 공지했음을 알 수 있으므로 정답은 (A)이다. 정답 (A)

함정 분석 웹사이트 방문은 지하철을 대신할 교통수단을 보여주기 위함일 뿐, 지하철에 관한 정보를 주는 것은 아니므로 (D)는 오답이다.

패러프레이징 |지문| morning work commutes by using alternative transportation 대체 운송수단을 이용한 출근 → |선택지 A| a different way to get to work 직장에 가는 다른 방법

표현 정리 get to work 일하러 가다 cancelation 취소 contact 연락하다 map (배치, 구조 등에 관한 정보를) 보여주다, 지도를 만들다

해석 독자들에게 웹사이트를 방문하도록 고지한 이유는?
(A) 직장에 가는 다른 방법을 알아보도록 하기 위해
(B) 지하철 운행 취소 목록을 찾기 위해
(C) 파업에 대해 시 의회에 연락하기 위해
(D) 그들의 아침 지하철 통근 정보를 보여주기 위해

158. 유추 – 전 도시에 걸친 파업에 대한 내용 ★★☆

해설 첫 번째 단락 'This unprecedented action will halt train services during regular operation hours starting next Monday and continuing until the union's demands are met.'에서 이 파업이 전례가 없는 일이라고 했으므로 (C)가 가장 가까운 정답이다. 정답 (C)

함정 분석 시 의회는 노동조합과의 회의를 통해 업무 시간 내에 파업이 종료되기를 원하지만 그것이 월요일 저녁까지 끝날 것인지는 알 수 없으므로 (A)는 오답이다. 세 번째 단락 'With subways not running, city officials fear major traffic jams and congested commutes.'에서 시 공무원들은 지하철 운행 중단으로 인한 교통체증과 혼잡한 출근길을 우려하고 있으므로 (B)도 정답으로 보기 어렵다. 또한 이 파업은 시 의회의 명령이 아니라 The Metropolitan Transport Commission Union이 주도하고 있으므로 (D) 역시 오답이다.

표현 정리 be guaranteed to 결국 ~하게 될 것이다 take place 일어나다

해석 전 도시에 걸친 파업에 대해 암시된 것은?
(A) 월요일 저녁까지 끝날 것이다.
(B) 교통량을 완화시켜 줄 것이다.
(C) 처음으로 일어나는 것이다.
(D) 시 의회의 명령을 받은 것이다.

문제 159–161번은 다음 웹 페이지를 참조하시오.

---

http://www.mapledesks.com

가구 〉 사무실 〉 책상 〉 리뷰

적갈색 Maple Desk
평균: 4.91 / 5.0점 (42 리뷰)

159 분류: 리뷰 날짜 (최신 순)

1. 9월 30일 펜실베니아주 피츠버그에 거주하는 Allison Waters
점수: *4.5*
장점: *안정적, 적당한 가격, 매력적*
단점: *무거움*
이 제품을 친구에게 추천하시겠습니까? *추천할 것이다*

리뷰: 오래되고 다 망가진 사무실 책상의 수명이 다해 교체가 필요해졌을 때, 저는 유명 Maple Desk를 갖고 싶다는 것을 알게 되었습니다. 동료로부터 단풍나무로 마감된 이 책상이 매우 아름답다는 말을 들었고, 161매일 고객과 대면 미팅을 하기 때문에, 제 책상의 외관이 구매 결정을 하는데 한몫 했습니다. 책상은 튼튼하게 만들어져 아무리 많은 서류 뭉치를 쌓아 두어도 책상이 무너지는 것을 걱정할 필요가 없습니다. 160또한 Maple Desk의 적정 가격에 기분 좋게 놀랐습니다. 아름다운 구성과 명성을 보았을 때, 가격이 훨씬 높을 수도 있다고 봅니다. 종합적으로, 훌륭한 책상으로 무게 면에서 약간 크고 무거운 감이 있습니다. 이동하는 데 약간 어려움이 있지만, 책상의 사랑스러움이 그것을 보상합니다.

이 리뷰가 도움이 되셨습니까? 지금 투표하세요.
네 (11) 아니오 (1)

표현 정리 maple 단풍나무 mahogany 적갈색 sort by ~에 따라 분류하다 newest to oldest 최신 순으로 pros 장점, 찬성 cons 단점, 반대 stable 안정적인 affordable (가격이) 알맞은 attractive 매력적인 recommend 추천하다 tattered 다 망가진 replacing 대체, 교체 famed 유명한 colleague 동료 exquisite 정교한, 매우 아름다운 face-to-face 마주보는, 대면하는 appearance 모습 play a role 역할을 하다 purchasing 구매 solidly 튼튼하게 paperwork 서류 작업 pile (물건을) 쌓다 collapsing 붕괴 pleasantly 기분 좋게 fair 공정한 composition 구성 overall 종합적인 hefty 장대한; 크고 무거운 in terms of ~면에서 loveliness 사랑스러움 make up for ~을 보상하다

159. 세부사항 – 리뷰에 대한 내용 ★★★

해설 Sort by: Review Date (newest to oldest) 다음에 '1. 9월 30일'로 웹페이지가 시작된 것을 보면, 이 웹페이지의 내용은 최신 리뷰 순으로 보여진 것임을 알

수 있으므로 정답은 (C)이다.　　　　　　　　　　정답 (C)

🔍 **함정 분석** 4.5점(5.0 만점 중)을 줬고, 평균이 4.91이므로, 최고 점수를 준 것은 아니므로 (A)는 오답이다. 11명은 리뷰가 도움이 되었다고 투표한 사람이므로 (B)도 오답이다. 42명은 리뷰를 한 인원 수이지 조회 수로 보기는 어려우므로 (D)도 오답이다.

표현 정리 award 수여하다　maximum score 최고 점수　post (웹사이트에 정보, 사진을) 올리다

해석 리뷰에 관해 알 수 있는 것은?
(A) 최고 점수를 줬다.
(B) 11명이 그 책상을 사도록 이끌었다.
(C) 가장 최근에 올려진 리뷰이다.
(D) 42명이 조회했다.

160. 세부사항 – Maple Desk에 대한 내용　　★★☆
해설 Review 내용 중 중반 부분 'I was also pleasantly surprised by Maple Desk's fair pricing.'에서 공정한 가격이 책정되었음을 알 수 있고, 'Given the beautiful composition and popular name, the prices could be a lot higher than they are.'에서는 구성과 명성을 고려했을 때, 더 높은 가격이 책정될 수도 있었다는 의견을 피력했으므로 (A)가 정답이다.　정답 (A)

🔍 **함정 분석** 해당 리뷰가 적갈색의 책상을 다루고 있지만, 이것이 유일한 색상인지 알 수 없으므로 (B)는 오답이다. 유일한 단점으로 지적된 것이 무게인데, 이것으로 보아 이동성을 위해 바퀴를 장착한 것으로 보기는 어려워 (D) 또한 오답이다.

패러프레이징 |지문| fair pricing 공정한 가격 책정 → |선택지 A| be reasonably priced 합리적으로 가격이 책정되다

표현 정리 reasonably 합리적으로　priced 값이 붙은　handmade 손으로 만든　wheel 바퀴

해석 Maple Desk에 대해 언급된 내용은?
(A) 합리적으로 가격이 책정되었다.
(B) 한 가지 색상으로 나온다.
(C) 주의 깊게 수제로 만들어졌다.
(D) 이동에 필요한 바퀴가 포함되었다.

161. 유추 – Ms. Waters에 대한 암시 내용　　★★☆
해설 Review 중반, 'as I have face-to-face meetings with my clients daily, my desk's appearance played a role in my purchasing decision.'에서 고객들과 매일 대면 미팅을 진행하는데, 책상의 모습이 구매 결정을 하는데 역할을 했다고 했으므로 정답은 (B)이다.　정답 (B)

패러프레이징 |지문| I have face-to-face meetings with my clients daily 고객들과 매일 대면 미팅을 진행한다 → |선택지 B| clients sit at her desk regularly 고객들이 정기적으로 그녀의 책상에 둘러앉는다

표현 정리 sit at ~에 둘러앉다　regularly 정기적으로　budget 예산　be dissatisfied with ~에 만족하지 않다

해석 Ms. Waters에 대해 암시된 내용은?
(A) 그녀의 예전 책상은 Maple Desk였다.
(B) 고객들이 정기적으로 그녀의 책상에 둘러앉는다.
(C) 책상을 위한 예산이 주어졌다.
(D) 새 책상에 대해 만족하지 못한다.

문제 162-164번은 다음 광고를 참조하시오.

> **Dillgent Days 작업 공간: 바쁜 단체를 위한 사무 공간**
>
> 자신의 사업체를 소유하고 있는 분이라면, 사무실 임대 비용이 얼마나 비싼지 알고 계실 것입니다. 임대 비용은 지나치게 비싸고, 임대 시장은 곧 약해질 것으로 보이지 않습니다. 더 열심히 일하기보다는 좀 더 효율적으로 일하십시오! 사무실 건물은 과거의 산물입니다. **162사용하는 것에 대한 지불만 하면 될 뿐, 왜 빈 공간에 돈을 낭비하십니까?** 전문직 종사자들을 위한 획기적인 사무 공간 공유를 소개합니다.
>
> **163(A)아래의 옵션들이 이용 가능합니다:**
>
> • 책상 임대 – 문서 업무를 마칠 책상만 필요할 때, 책상만 임대하는 가장 저렴한 옵션이 가장 좋습니다!
> • 스탠다드 룸 임대 – 업무를 수행할 약간 더 넓은 공간, 또는 고객을 초대하기 위한 공간이 필요한 전문가들을 위해서는 스탠다드 방 임대가 알맞습니다.
> • 디럭스 룸 임대 – 만약 개별 사무실 사용료가 없는 개인 전용 사무실 느낌을 찾고 계시다면, 이것이 가장 확실한 방법입니다. **163(D)전적으로 시간제로 운영되는 개별 사무실입니다.**
>
> **163(C)오늘 공간을 예약하기 위해 555-2321로 전화 주시기 바랍니다.** **164모든 임차인들은 18세 이상이어야 하며, 회사 등록 번호와 함께 유효한 사업자등록증을 제출해야 합니다.**

표현 정리 workspace 작업 공간　body 단체, 조직　own 소유하다　expensive 비싼　renting 임대차　rental price 임대 가격　through the roof (가격이 지나치게) 비싼　leasing market 임대 시장　let up 약해지다　waste 낭비하다　innovative 획기적인　office space 사무 공간　professional 전문직 종사자　available 이용할 수 있는　paperwork 문서 업무　conduct (특정한 활동을) 하다　affordable (가격이) 알맞은　exclusive 전용의　best bet 가장 안전하고 확실한 수단　entirely 전적으로　by the hour 시간제로　reserve 예약하다　renter 세입자, 임차인　valid 유효한　business bureau certificate 사업자등록증　registration 등록

162. 세부사항 – 작업 공간을 임대하는 것의 이점　　★★☆
해설 첫 번째 단락 'Why waste money on empty space when you can just pay for what you use?'에서 사무실의 빈 공간을 낭비하는 것에 대한 의문을 제기한 후, 이어지는 내용에서 책상만 임대하는 것부터 사무실을 임대하는 옵션에 따른 차등 가격 지불에 이르기까지의 다양한 정보를 제공하고 있으므로 정답은 (C)이다.　정답 (C)

🔍 **함정 분석** 'Deluxe Room Rental - If you're looking for an exclusive personal office feel without the personal office bill, this is your best bet.'에서 개인 사무실 느낌을 제공하는 것은 디럭스 룸 임대에만 해당하므로 (A)는 오답이다. 'All renters must be over the age of 18 and provide a valid business bureau certificate with the registration number of your company.'에서 임차인들은 18세 이상으로 사업자등록증을 제시해야 하는 필요조건이 있으므로 (D) 또한 오답이다.

패러프레이징 |지문| pay for what you use 사용한 것에 대해서만 지불하다 → |선택지 C| pay for the space they occupy 차지한 공간만큼 비용을 지불하다

표현 정리 according to ~에 따르면　advertisement 광고　advantage 이점　steadily 꾸준히　decreasing 감소하는　occupy 차지하다　requirement 필요 조건

해석 광고에 따르면, 작업 공간을 임대하는 것의 이점은 무엇인가?
(A) 사무실 건물들이 개인 사무실 느낌을 제공한다.
(B) 임대 시장이 꾸준히 줄고 있다.
(C) 임차인들은 그들이 차지하는 공간만큼만 비용을 지불한다.
(D) 작업 공간을 임대하기 위한 필요 조건이 없다.

163. 세부사항 – 작업 공간에 대한 내용이 아닌 것 ★☆☆

해설 옵션은 Desk / Standard Room / Deluxe Room 세 가지 타입으로 제공되며, 'To reserve a space today, call us at 555-2321.'을 통해 전화로 예약이 가능함을 알 수 있다. 또한 디럭스 룸 임대 내용 중 'It is an entirely private office space for rent by the hour.'를 통해 완전한 개인 사무실을 시간 단위로 임대가 가능하다는 것을 알 수 있으므로 정답은 (B)이다.　　　　정답 (B)

표현 정리 over the phone 전화로

해설 Diligent Days 작업 공간에 대해 언급되지 않은 것은?
(A) 세 가지 타입의 선택 사항이 이용 가능하다.
(B) 방 임대는 한 시간으로 제한되어 있다.
(C) 예약은 전화 상으로 가능하다.
(D) 특정 임대는 완전한 프라이버시를 제공한다.

164. 세부사항 – 고객이 제공해야 하는 것 ★☆☆

해설 임대를 하기 위해 고객이 제출해야 하는 것은 'All renters must be over the age of 18 and provide a valid business bureau certificate with the registration number of your company.'에서 사업자등록증 번호와 등록증이므로 정답은 (D)이다.　　　　정답 (D)

패러프레이징 |지문| the registration number of your company 회사의 등록 번호 → company ID number 사업자 등록 번호

표현 정리 ID card 신분증　contract 계약　payment in full 전액 지불 certificate 증명서

해설 광고에 따르면, 고객이 제공해야 하는 것은 무엇인가?
(A) 신분증 복사본
(B) 작업 공간을 위한 서명된 계약서
(C) 사무실 임대 시 전액 지불
(D) 증명서와 사업자 등록 번호

문제 165-167번은 다음 기사를 참조하시오.

Silverton Technology, 미래의 거대한 창업 아이디어를 찾다

AUSTIN (7월 10일) – 거대 기술 회사 Silverton Technology가 지난 토요일 매년 열리는 Southriver Technology 컨퍼런스에 참석해 새로운 거대한 창업 아이디어를 찾고 있다고 밝혔다. Silverton은 대회 우승자에게 120만 달러에 상당하는 액수의 자금을 제공할 것이다.

소규모 창업 회사들은 기술의 미래를 바꿀 아이디어를 제시하도록 권유받는다. 전에 Silverton의 자금을 지원받았던 이들이 모두가 컴퓨터 하드웨어를 만드는 사람들이었던 반면에, 166Silverton은 이번에는 환경 기술 아이디어를 찾기를 원한다는 것을 구체적으로 명시했다.

165"지구 온난화는 더 이상 무시할 수 없습니다."라고 Silverton의 회장인 Jennie Hapon이 말했다. "기술 분야의 리더로서, 세계의 가장 긴급한 문제들을 다루는데 우리의 기술을 사용하는 것은 우리의 책임입니다."

패널 토론 중에, Hapon은 태양 동력을 이용해 빗물을 정화하는 기계와 같이, 회사가 현재 작업 중인 친환경 프로젝트에 대해서 강조했다.

"친환경은 더 이상 외치기 좋은 구호가 아니며, 우리의 일 이면에 있는 추진력이다."라고 Hapon은 말했다.

167Silverton Technology는 2005년에 Hapon과 그녀의 파트너인 Jorge Ramon에 의해 시작되었다. 설립 첫 해 동안, 회사는 혁명적인 회전 기술을 팔아 250만 달러를 벌어들였다. 기계 기술로 시작했으나 최근 Silverton은 사회적 영향력을 가진 기술로 이동했다.

표현 정리 search for ～를 찾다　startup 창업　tech firm 기술 회사 attend 참석하다　annual 연례의　announce 발표하다　look for ～를 찾다　provide funding 자금을 제공하다　amount 양　submit

제출하다　previous 이전의　recipient 수령인　specify (구체적으로) 명시하다　environmental 환경의　global warming 지구 온난화　ignore 무시하다　field 분야　responsibility 책임　address (문제, 상황 등을) 고심하다, 다루다　pressing 긴급한　highlight 강조하다　currently 현재　solar-powered 태양을 동력으로 이용하는　purify 정화하다　go green 친환경이 되다　catchy slogan 기억하기 쉬운 구호　drive 추진력, (조직적인) 운동　founding 설립　revolutionary 혁명적인　rotary 회전하는　raise 모금하다, 모으다　in recent years 최근에　shift toward ～로 이동하다　social impact 사회적 영향

165. 유추 – 실버튼 기술에 대한 내용 ★★★

해설 세 번째 단락 "'Global warming cannot be ignored anymore," said Silverton President Jennie Hapon. "As leaders in the technology field, it's our responsibility to use our skills to address the world's most pressing problems.'"에서 지구 온난화 문제를 책임감을 갖고 해결해야 한다는 내용을 통해 (A)가 정답임을 알 수 있다.　　　　정답 (A)

🔍함정 분석 마지막 단락 'Within the first year of its founding, the company sold its revolutionary rotary technology and raised $2.5 million dollars.'에서 Silverton Technology는 이미 회전 기술을 통해 막대한 부를 창출했으므로 (B)는 오답이다. 그리고 첫 단락 'Giant tech firm Silverton Technology attended the annual Southriver Technology Conference this past Saturday'에서 Silverton Technology가 컨퍼런스에 참석했음을 알 수 있지만 많은 기술 컨퍼런스에 참석했다는 내용은 언급되지 않아 (C)도 오답이다. 두 번째 단락 후반 'the technology company specified that it hopes to find environmental technology ideas this time around'에서 환경 기술 아이디어를 공모할 뿐, 젊은 인재를 찾고 있는 것은 아니므로 (D)도 오답이다.

표현 정리 be engaged in ～에 종사하다, 관여하다　in search of ～을 찾아서　inventor 발명가

해설 Silverton Technology에 관해 암시된 것은 무엇인가?
(A) 지구 온난화를 다루는데 관여한다.
(B) 혁명적 회전 과학을 만들기를 희망한다.
(C) 많은 기술 컨퍼런스에 참여한다.
(D) 젊은 기술 발명가를 찾고 있다.

166. 동의어 ★★☆

해설 go green은 '친환경이 되다'라는 의미를 갖는다. 따라서 green은 '환경'을 의미한다고 볼 수 있다. 또한 두 번째 단락 후반 'the technology company specified that it hopes to find environmental technology ideas this time around'를 통해 이 기업이 찾고 있는 것이 환경 기술임을 알 수 있으므로 정답은 (C)이다.　　　　정답 (C)

표현 정리 innovative 획기적인

해설 기사에서, 네 번째 단락, 첫 번째 줄의 "green"과 의미가 가장 가까운 것은?
(A) 새로운
(B) 획기적인
(C) 환경적인
(D) 안락한

167. 유추 – Jennie Hapon의 직업 ★☆☆

해설 세 번째 단락에 처음 등장한 Jennie Hopon은 Silverton의 회장이다. 마지막 단락 'Silverton Technology was started in 2005 by Hapon and her partner, Jorge Ramon.'에서 2005년에 Silverton Technology를 창업했고, 'Within the first year of its founding, the company sold its revolutionary rotary technology and raised $2.5 million dollars.'에서 창업 첫 해에 혁명적 회전 기술을 통해 막대한 돈을 벌었으며, 'Though its start was in mechanical technology'를 통해 Jennie Hapon은 엔지니어일 가능성이 높아 정답은 (D)이다.　　　　정답 (D)

표현 정리 organizer 주최자 engineer 기술자

해설 Jennie Hapon은 누구인가?
(A) 뉴스 리포터
(B) 컨퍼런스 주최자
(C) 공무원
(D) 엔지니어

문제 168-171번은 다음 온라인 채팅을 참조하시오.

Gibings, Monica 안녕하세요. 168영국에서 4월 2일에 받은 주문에 대한 고객 문의가 들어왔어요. 고객님의 성함은 Henry Boare입니다.
오전 7시 48분

Yoo, James 주문 기록 상에서 이름을 찾을 수가 없네요. 168, 169어떤 책을 주문했나요? 우리가 그 책을 보유하고 있을 수도 있어요. 그렇다면 지금 책을 보내드릴 수 있을 텐데요.
오전 7시 51분

Sutter, Ann 제가 그분의 주문이 빠져 잔고 처리되었을 경우를 대비해 잔고 목록을 찾아보겠습니다.
오전 7시 54분

Yoo, James 좋은 생각이에요. 170하지만 지난 달에 주문하셨기 때문에, 가능한 빨리 보내드리는 것으로 하죠. 무슨 일이 생긴 건지는 나중에 걱정해도 될 것 같아요.
오전 7시 55분

Gibings, Monica 책의 ID 번호는 249320입니다. 고객께 우편 주소를 여쭤보겠습니다.
오전 8시 15분

Sutter, Ann 필요하지 않을 것 같아요! 주문 내역을 찾았습니다. 주문서 상의 고객님 성함이 Henry Bore로 철자가 틀렸네요. 배송표 출력해서 즉시 책을 보내도록 하겠습니다.
오전 8시 16분

Yoo, James Ann, 잘 하셨어요. 왜 철자가 틀렸고, 우리 측의 실수인지 알아내야 합니다. 171Monica, 고객님께 연락을 취하고, 책이 배송 중이라고 알려주세요.
오전 8시 17분

Gibings, Monica 그렇게 하겠습니다. Ann과 James, 고마워요.
오전 8시 20분

표현 정리 customer inquiry 고객 문의 place an order 주문하다 log 기록 backlog 밀린 일, 잔고 in case 경우에 대비해 slip through ~을 지나가다, 빠져나가다 end up 결국 (어떤 처지에) 처하게 되다 happen 일어나다 mailing address 우편 주소 order slip 주문서 misspell 철자가 틀리다 locate ~를 찾아내다 shipping label 배송표 immediately 즉시 find out 알아내다 on our end 우리 측에서 hopefully 바라건대 prevent 방지하다 get in touch 연락을 취하다

168. 유추 – 채팅자들이 일하는 회사 업종 ★★☆
해설 Monica의 글 'We have a customer inquiry about an order placed on April 2 from the UK.'을 통해 고객 주문에 대한 서비스를 제공하는 회사임을 유추할 수 있고, James의 질문 'What book did he order?'를 통해 주문한 물품이 책이라는 것을 알 수 있으므로 정답은 (B)이다.
정답 (B)

🔍함정 분석 Monica는 고객 문의를, Ann은 주문 내역을, 그리고 James는 책임자 위치에 있음을 유추할 수 있으므로 단순 콜센터라고 보기는 어려워 (D)는 오답이며, 대화 후반에서 James가 Monica에게 'please get in touch with the customer and let him know his book is on its way'에서 고객에게 연락을 취해 곧 배송될 것이라고 통보하라고 했지만, 전반적인 대화 내용은 배송이 아니고 책 주문에 관한 것이므로 (C) 배송 업체로 보기는 어렵다.

해설 채팅자들이 일하는 회사로 가장 적합한 곳은?
(A) 종이 판매 상점
(B) 서점
(C) 배송 업체
(D) 콜센터

169. 의도 파악하기 ★★☆
해설 Mr. Yoo가 'What book did he order? We might even have it on hand. Then we could just send him a copy.'에서 질문 내용의 앞의 '그가 주문한 책이 무엇인지?'를 묻는 내용이고, 뒤의 내용은 '그렇다면 그에게 책을 보낼 수 있다.'는 내용이므로 (D)가 가장 적절한 정답이다.
정답 (D)

표현 정리 make a mistake 실수하다 concerned 걱정하는 out of stock 품절인, 떨어진 readily 쉽게 available 구할 수 있는

해설 Mr. Yoo가 오전 7시 51분에 보낸 내용 중 "우리가 그 책을 보유하고 있을 수도 있어요."가 의미하는 것은?
(A) 고객이 실수했을 것 같다고 생각한다.
(B) 재고가 없는 지도 모른다고 걱정한다.
(C) 그의 책상 위에 주문 복사본이 있다고 생각한다.
(D) 책을 쉽게 구할 수 있을 수도 있다고 믿는다.

170. 세부사항 – 책 발송일 ★★☆
해설 Monica가 보낸 메시지 'We have a customer inquiry about an order placed on April 2 from the UK,'에서 처음 주문이 이루어진 시점이 4월 2일이라고 했는데, James가 오전 7시 55분에 보낸 메시지 'But since he placed the order last month, let's send it to him as soon as possible.'에서 지난 달에 주문 받았기 때문에 가능한 빨리 배송할 것을 제안하고 있으므로 배송될 시기는 5월이고, 따라서 정답은 (D)이다.
정답 (D)

해설 채팅자들에 따르면, 책은 언제 발송될 것인가?
(A) 2월
(B) 3월
(C) 4월
(D) 5월

171. 세부사항 – Ms. Gibings가 다음에 할 일 ★★☆
해설 James는 오전 8시 17분에 Monica에게 'Monica, please get in touch with the customer and let him know his book is on its way,'라고 하며 고객에게 책이 배송 중임을 통보하라고 지시했으므로 (A)가 정답이다.
정답 (A)

패러프레이징 |지문| let him know his book is on its way 그의 책이 배송 중이라고 알리다 → |선택지 A| Inform the customer his order is being sent 주문 물품이 배송되었음을 알리다

표현 정리 inform 알리다 inventory 재고

해설 Ms. Gibings가 다음 할 일은?
(A) 고객에게 주문 물품이 배송될 것임을 알린다.
(B) 고객에게 우편 주소를 묻는다.
(C) 빠진 주문을 찾기 위해 잔고 목록을 검색한다.
(D) 책을 구할 수 있을지 재고를 확인한다.

문제 172-175번은 다음 편지를 참조하시오.

JC Property Management
223 Mountain View Road
Singleton, CO 30036

5월 2일

Mr. Oliver Kern
789 Tumulo Way, Apt 8A
Singleton, CO 30034

Mr. Kern 님께,

1736월 20일 일요일에 아파트를 비우겠다는 의사를 전해 주신 점 감사 드립니다. 요청하신 대로, 떠나시는 날짜에 점검을 실시하도록 하겠습니다. 모든 물건들은 완전히 비워져야 하며, 점검이 이루어지기 전에 청소가 완료돼야

합니다. **174**제가 직접 하지 못하는 경우, 저의 보조원인 Karen이 담당할 것입니다. 물론 점검하는 자리에 함께 하시는 것도 환영합니다.

해당 세대가 만족스러운 상태인 것이 확인되면, 임대 보증금 800달러 전액 환불될 것입니다. 그러나 벽이나 바닥에 일상적인 사용에 의한 마모를 넘는 손상과 같은 문제가 발견되는 경우, 임대 보증금에서 수리비가 공제될 것입니다.

점검이 완료되기까지 아파트 상태를 알 수 없기 때문에, 떠나시는 날짜에 수표를 발행할 수 없습니다. **175**그러므로, 저희가 수표를 보낼 새 주소를 알려 주시기 바랍니다.

172잠정적으로 오후 3시에 점검 일정을 잡았습니다. 시간을 변경해야 한다면 저희 사무실 555-9822로 연락 주십시오.

Albert Mohn

표현 정리 notify 알리다　intent 의도　vacate 비우다　as per ~에 따라　request 요청　perform 이행하다　inspection 점검　unit (아파트 같은 공동 주택 내의) 한 가구　departure 출발　completely 완전히　belongings 소지품　conduct 실행하다　present 참석한　satisfactory 만족스러운　refund 환불하다　security deposit 임대 보증금　wear and tear 손상　deduct 공제하다, 차감하다　issue a check 수표를 발행하다　departure date 떠나는 날, 출발일　forwarding address 새 주소　tentatively 잠정적으로　schedule 일정을 잡다　contact 연락하다

172. 주제 – 편지의 목적　★☆☆

해설 마지막 단락 'I have tentatively scheduled the inspection for 3:00 P.M. If you need to change the time, please contact my office at 555-9822.'에서 잠정적인 스케줄을 정했으며, 시간 변경을 원하는 경우 연락해 달라고 했으므로 편지의 목적은 (D)가 가장 적절하다고 볼 수 있다. **정답 (D)**

표현 정리 issue a warning 경고하다　respond 응답하다　complaint 불평, 불만　request 요청하다　payment 지불　confirm 확인하다

해석 편지의 목적은?
(A) 경고하기 위해
(B) 불만에 답변하기 위해
(C) 지불을 요청하기 위해
(D) 계획을 확인하기 위해

173. 세부사항 – 6월 20일에 일어날 일　★★☆

해설 본문 서두 'Thank you for notifying us of your intent to vacate your apartment on Sunday, June 20. As per your request, we will perform an inspection of the unit on the same day as your departure.'에서 Mr. Kern이 6월 20일에 집을 비울 예정이고, 같은 날짜에 점검이 이루어질 것이라는 사실을 알 수 있으므로 정답은 (B)이다. **정답 (B)**

🔍 **함정 분석** 세 번째 단락 'Since we cannot know the condition of the unit until the inspection is completed, we are unable to issue you a check on your departure date.'의 내용은 아파트를 비우는 날에 임대 보증금 지불이 어렵다는 내용이므로 Mr. Kern에게 그날 돈이 전달될 것이라고 한 (C)는 오답이다.

패러프레이징 |지문| will perform an inspection of the unit 아파트 점검을 실시할 것이다 → |선택지 B| a property's condition will be checked 건물의 상태가 점검될 것이다

표현 정리 repaint 다시 칠하다　property 재산　rental payment 임대료　due 지불해야 하는

해석 편지에 따르면, 6월 20일에 일어날 일은?
(A) 8A 아파트는 페인트칠을 다시 할 것이다.
(B) 건물의 상태를 점검할 것이다.

22

(C) Mr. Kern에게 돈이 전달될 것이다.
(D) 임대료를 지불해야 할 것이다.

174. 문장 위치 찾기　★★☆

해설 본인이 직접 점검을 못하는 경우, 보조원이 대신 진행할 것이라는 내용이므로, 점검 이행에 대한 세부 내용(즉, 실행 날짜와 청소 등 기대되는 상황, 세입자 출석 가능)을 다루는 첫 단락에 들어가는 것이 적합해 정답은 (A)이다. **정답 (A)**

표현 정리 personally 직접　assistant 보조원

해석 [1], [2], [3], [4] 중 다음 문장이 들어가기에 가장 알맞은 곳은?

"제가 직접 하지 못하는 경우, 저의 보조원인 Karen이 담당할 것입니다."
(A) [1]
(B) [2]
(C) [3]
(D) [4]

175. 세부사항 – Mr. Mohn이 부탁한 것　★☆☆

해설 Mr. Mohn은 세 번째 단락에서 아파트 점검이 완료될 때까지는 수표 발급이 어렵다는 것을 설명한 후, 'Therefore, we ask that you provide us with a forwarding address where we can send a check.'에서 수표를 받을 새 주소를 알려달라고 요청하고 있으므로 정답은 (A)이다. **정답 (A)**

패러프레이징 |지문| a forwarding address (이전 주소로 온 우편물을 다시 보낼) 새 주소 → |선택지 A| a mailing address 우편 주소

표현 정리 hire 고용하다　professional cleaner 전문 청소부　write a check 수표를 쓰다

해석 Mr. Mohn이 Mr. Kern에게 부탁한 것은?
(A) 우편 주소를 제공해 달라고
(B) 전문 청소부를 고용하라고
(C) 다른 날짜를 제시해 달라고
(D) 그에게 수표를 발행해 달라고

문제 176-180번은 다음 이메일들을 참조하시오.

수신: 〈reservations@carstogo.com〉
발신: 〈johnbuteu@weiberco.com〉
날짜: 7월 13일 토요일
제목: 소형차 예약

예약 서류를 제출합니다.

이름: John Buteu
전화번호: 555-9203
차종: 소형차 4-door 세단
176운전자 수: 1
승객 수: 1
대여 날짜: July 18 – July 21
시작 시간: 오전 9시 30분
종료 시간: 오전 9시
179추가 기능: 내비게이션 시스템
180차량 보험이 필요하십니까? [　] 네　[✓] 아니오
저희 관리자에게 제출할 수 있도록 첨부 파일로 예약 영수증을 받는 것이 필요합니다.

감사합니다.

John

표현 정리 submit 제출하다　reservation form 예약 신청서　passenger 승객　add-on 부가물　insurance 보험　attachment 첨부 파일[서류]

receipt 영수증

수신: 〈johnbuteu@weiberco.com〉
발신: 〈julies36@carstogo.com〉
날짜: 7월 15일, 월요일
제목: Re: 소형차 예약

Mr. Buteu 님께,

Cars To Go에 예약해 주셔서 감사드립니다. 177소형 세단 예약 건은 접수되었으며, 예약에 필요한 모든 추가 정보를 저희 쪽에 제출해 주시는 대로 처리될 것입니다.

24시간 이상 차량을 대여하려면, 모든 운전자와 승객이 25세 이상이어야 합니다. 24시간 이상 예약을 하셨다면 운전자와 승객 모두의 신분증 사본을 보내 주시기 바랍니다.

또한, 예약과 함께 요청하시는 부가서비스에 대해서는 추가 비용이 적용된다는 점을 유의해 주십시오. 가격은 다음과 같습니다:

지도: 5달러
선불 연료 카드: 10달러
179내비게이션 시스템: 25달러
아기용 좌석: 30달러

180저희 회사를 통해 자동차 보험을 요청하시는 고객님들을 위해, 200달러 보증금이 대여 시작일에 필요하며 차를 안전하게 반납하실 때 환불될 것입니다.

예약 확인과 처리에 필요한 필수 정보와 신용카드 번호를 보내 주십시오. 궁금한 사항은 주저하지 마시고 바로 제 사무실로 연락해 주십시오. 178제 번호는 555-1953입니다.

멋진 하루 보내시길 바랍니다.

Julie Soon
예약 매니저
Cars To Go

표현 정리 make a reservation 예약하다   process 처리하다   additional 추가의   require 필요로하다, 요구하다   identification 신분 증명   note 주목하다   fee 요금   apply 신청하다   as follows 다음과 같이   deposit 보증금   refund 환불하다   confirm 확인하다   required information 필수 정보   inquiry 문의   hesitate 망설이다   directly 바로

176. 유추 – 예약에 관한 내용   ★★☆
해설 첫 번째 메일에 기입된 'Number of Drivers: 1 / Number of Passengers: 1'에서 운전자와 승객 수가 각각 한 명이므로 두 사람이 탑승할 것이라고 한 (A)가 정답이다.   정답 (A)

🔍**함정 분석** Extra Add-ons: Navigation System으로 보아 지도는 필요없음을 알 수 있으므로 (B)는 오답이고, 마지막 문장 'I need an attachment sent back to me with a copy of the reservation receipt so that I may submit it to my manager.'에서 예약을 확인할 수 있는 예약 증명서를 요구하고 있으므로 (D)도 오답이다.

표현 정리 pick up 가져가다, 얻다   proof 증명   necessary 필요한

해석 첫 이메일에서, 예약에 관해 암시된 내용은?
　(A) 두 사람이 차에 탑승할 것이다.
　(B) 대여 중에 지도가 필요하다.
　(C) 공항에서 차를 가져갈 것이다.
　(D) 예약 증명서가 필요하지 않다.

177. 세부사항 – Mr. Buteu의 예약에 관한 내용   ★★☆
해설 두 번째 이메일 첫 단락 'Your reservation for a small sedan has

been submitted and will be processed as soon as you provide us with additional information that is required for all reservations.'에서 필요한 추가 정보를 제공한 뒤에 예약이 처리될 것이라는 내용이 있으므로 Mr. Buteu의 예약은 아직 처리되지 않았다고 한 (C)가 정답이다.   정답 (C)

🔍**함정 분석** 첫 번째 이메일 마지막 문장 'I need an attachment sent back to me with a copy of the reservation receipt so that I may submit it to my manager.'에서 관리자에게 제출할 예약 증명서를 요구하고 있으므로 승인이 이루어졌는지는 아직 알 수 없어 (A)는 오답이다. 첫 번째 이메일 'Car Type: Small 4-door Sedan'에서 필요한 차종이 언급되었고, 두 번째 이메일에서도 동일 차종에 대한 예약이 접수되었다고 했으므로 (B) 역시 오답이다. 첫 번째 이메일에서 밝힌 대여 기간은 'Rental Dates: July 18 - July 21'으로 4일간이므로 (D)도 오답이다.

표현 정리 approve 승인하다   flexible 융통성이 있는   in terms of ~면에서   period 기간

해석 Mr. Buteu의 예약에 관해 언급된 내용은?
　(A) 그의 관리자에 의해 승인받았다.
　(B) 필요한 차량에 대한 융통성이 있다.
　(C) 아직 처리되지 않았다.
　(D) 대여 기간이 한 달이다.

178. 세부사항 – 이메일에서 Ms. Soon이 제공한 것   ★★★
해설 Ms. Soon이 보낸 두 번째 이메일 후반 'My number is 555-1953.'에서 전화 번호를 알려 주면서, 'For any further inquiries, do not hesitate to contact me directly at my office.'에서 추가 문의 사항이 있으면 연락하라고 했으므로 정답은 (D)이다.   정답 (D)

표현 정리 feature 특징   extension 연장   reach (특히 전화로) 연락하다

해석 이메일에서 Ms. Soon이 Mr. Buteu에게 제공한 것은?
　(A) 이용 가능한 차량의 특징 목록
　(B) 대여 기간의 연장
　(C) 예약 차량의 업그레이드
　(D) 연락 가능한 번호

179. 연계 문제 – Mr. Buteu에게 청구될 추가 비용   ★☆☆
해설 Mr. Buteu는 첫 번째 이메일에서 추가 서비스로 'Extra Add-ons: Navigation System' 즉, 내비게이션만을 요청했는데, 두 번째 이메일에서 Navigation System 비용은 25달러임을 알 수 있으므로 정답은 (C) $25이다.   정답 (C)

표현 정리 additional fee 추가 비용   charge 청구하다

해석 얼마의 추가 비용이 Mr. Buteu에게 청구될 것인가?
　(A) 5달러
　(B) 10달러
　(C) 25달러
　(D) 30달러

180. 연계 문제 – Mr. Soon이 Mr. Buteu로부터 필요로 하지 않은 것 ★★☆
해설 두 번째 이메일, 다섯 번째 단락 'For guests who require car insurance through our company, a $200 deposit will be needed at the start of the rental date and will be refunded once the car is safely returned.'에서와 같이 보증금 $200가 필요한 경우는 Cars To Go를 통해 차량 보험을 제공받는 경우인데, 첫 번째 이메일 'Do you need car insurance? [ ] yes [✓] no'에서 보험이 필요없다고 체크했으므로 보증금을 지불할 필요가 없어 정답은 (C)이다.   정답 (C)

해석 Ms. Soon이 Mr. Buteu로부터 필요로 하지 않는 것은?
　(A) 신용카드 번호
　(B) 나이 확인

TEST 02

정답 및 해설 _ 23

(C) 200달러 보증금
(D) 신분증 사본

문제 181-185번은 다음 공지과 이메일을 참조하시오.

Dougers LLC 월례 직원 행사

181(D)볼링의 밤 – 9월 1일
다섯 개의 볼링 레인이 Dougers 직원들이 즐길 수 있게 예약될 것입니다. 음료와 음식도 이용 가능합니다. 연락처: 181(C)David (555-6230)

타코 화요일 – 10월 1일
185타코 부페가 직원 식당에 준비될 것입니다. 오셔서 양념을 한 소고기, 파히타 닭고기, 치즈, 살사, 그 이상을 포함한 토핑들로 자신의 타코를 만들어 보세요. 연락처: Joe (555-2456)

1달러 영화 티켓 – 11월 1일
여러분과 여러분 가족들이 즐길 수 있도록 대폭 할인된 영화 티켓을 구매하세요. 세 편의 영화 중에서 고를 수 있으며, 티켓은 11월까지 사용할 수 있습니다. 연락처: Sally (555-1232)

크리스마스 연극 – 12월 1일
특별한 휴일 나들이를 위해 여러분의 부서에 참여하세요. 크리스마스 연극인 The Christmas Carol이 Lelain 극장에서 Dougers 직원들만을 위해 독점 공연됩니다. 연락처: Meredith (555-0283)

월례 직원 행사에 대해 추가 정보가 필요한 분들은 주최자들에게 바로 연락 주십시오.

표현 정리 set up 준비하다, 설치하다 seasoned 양념을 한 purchase 구입하다 deeply 크게 through the month 월말까지 department 부서 holiday outing 휴일 나들이 exclusively 독점적으로 organizer 주최자

발신: Jodie Klein 〈jklein@dougers.com〉
수신: Betty Smith 〈bsmith@dougers.com〉
날짜: 11월 8일
제목: 크리스마스 연극

Betty, 좋은 아침입니다.

Meredith에게 전화해 크리스마스 연극 예약에 대해 문의했더니, 181(A)10매 이상의 티켓이 필요한 경우에는 극장에 연락해 직접 예약해야 한다고 하더군요.

당신과 당신의 남편은 3명의 아들이 있고, 내 남편과 나는 4명의 아이들이 있으니까, 우리 가족은 식구가 꽤 많네요. 184편리한 시간에 티켓을 예약하세요. 저희 가족에게 이 행사에 대해 말하기 전에 당신의 확인을 기다리겠습니다.

182우리는 이전에 있었던 모든 직원 행사에 참여했고, 그것들은 너무 멋졌습니다. 185저희 아이들은 타코를 대단히 즐겼고, 우리는 영화의 밤 동안 관람했던 웃긴 가족 코미디를 보면서 웃음을 멈출 수가 없었어요. 볼링 행사 동안, 저희 아이들은 다른 직원의 자녀들을 만날 수 있었고, 지금까지도 여전히 좋은 친구 관계를 유지하고 있습니다. 183지난 해, Dougers가 직원들을 위한 하룻밤 동안의 여름 휴가 여행을 준비했었죠! 회사가 이와 비슷한 행사를 다시 했으면 해요.

당신의 가족을 볼 수 있길 기대하며,

Jodie

표현 정리 venue 장소 at one's convenience 편리한 시간에 spectacular 장관을 이루는; 극적인 immensely 대단히 hilarious 아주

재미있는 remain 유지하다 organize 준비하다 overnight 하룻밤 동안의 look forward to -ing ~을 기대하다

181. 세부사항 – 행사에 관한 내용이 아닌 것 ★★☆
해설 공지 사항의 제목 Dougers LLC Monthly Employee Events를 통해 월례 행사인 동시에, 직원들을 대상으로 하는 행사임을 알 수 있으므로 정답은 (B)이다. **정답 (B)**

🔍**함정 분석** 이메일 첫 번째 단락, 'I called Meredith to ask about the Christmas play reservation'에서 예약을 필요로 하는 행사도 있으므로 (A)는 확인이 되고, 각 행사를 담당하는 사람이 다르므로 (C) 역시 확인 가능하고, 각 행사는 9월에서 12월까지 매달 1일에 있으므로 (D)도 확인이 된다.

패러프레이징 |지문| monthly Employee Events 월례 직원 행사 → |선택지 D| held on each month 매달 열린다

표현 정리 require 필요로 하다 be held 열리다

해석 행사에 대해 언급된 내용이 아닌 것은?
(A) 예약이 필요할 수도 있다.
(B) 직원들의 친구들에게도 열려 있다.
(C) 각 행사는 다른 사람들에 의해 준비된다.
(D) 매 달 첫 번째 날에 열린다.

182. 동의어 ★★☆
해설 spectacular는 '장관을 이루는, 극적인'이라는 뜻을 갖고 있는데, 'We have attended all the previous employee events, and they are spectacular.'에서 spectacular는 '인상적인'이라는 의미를 가진 impressive와 문맥상 가장 가깝다고 볼 수 있으므로 정답은 (B)이다. **정답 (B)**

표현 정리 visible 보이는 impressive 인상적인 sudden 갑작스러운 expensive 값 비싼

해석 이메일 세 번째 단락. 첫 번째 줄의 "spectacular"와 의미가 가장 가까운 것은?
(A) 보이는
(B) 인상적인
(C) 갑작스러운
(D) 비싼

183. 유추 – Ms. Klein에 대한 암시 내용 ★★★
해설 Jodie Klein은 이메일을 작성한 사람으로, 이메일 세 번째 단락 후반 'Last year, Dougers organized an overnight summer vacation trip for its employees! I hope the company will do something similar again.'에서 작년 여름 휴가 여행에 대해 언급한 것으로 보아 그녀는 Dougers에서 1년 이상 일해 왔음을 유추할 수 있으므로 정답은 (C)이다. **정답 (C)**

🔍**함정 분석** 가족 구성원에 대해서 알고 있고, 함께 연극을 관람하러 갈 계획인 것으로 보아. Smith와 처음 만났다고 볼 수 없으므로 (A)는 오답이다. 또한 이메일 세 번째 단락 'We have attended all the previous employee events, and they are spectacular.'에서 공지된 모든 행사에 참석했음을 알 수 있으므로 (B)도 오답이다. 작년 직원을 위한 행사가 있긴 했지만 그것을 Ms. klein이 준비했다는 것은 알 수 없으므로 (D)도 오답이다.

해석 Ms. Klein에 대해 암시된 내용은?
(A) Ms. Smith와는 처음 만났다.
(B) 처음으로 직원 행사에 참여할 것이다.
(C) 1년 이상 Dougers에서 일해 왔다.
(D) 전에 직원 행사를 준비한 적이 있다.

184. 주제 – Ms. Klein이 이메일을 보낸 이유 ★★☆
해설 Ms. Klein은 이메일 서두에서 크리스마스 연극에 관해 담당자인 Meredith

에게 문의했다는 사실을 언급한 후, 두 번째 단락 'Please reserve the tickets at your convenience.'에서 편리한 시간에 티켓을 예약하라고 했으므로 (A)가 정답이다. **정답 (A)**

패러프레이징 |지문| Please reserve the tickets 티켓을 예약해 주세요 → |선택지 A| request that she obtain event tickets 그녀가 행사 티켓을 얻도록 요청하다

표현 정리 obtain 얻다　inquire 문의하다

해석 Ms. Klein이 Ms. Smith에게 이메일을 보낸 이유는?
(A) 행사 티켓을 구할 것을 요청하기 위해
(B) 행사 주최자에게 연락하도록 제안하기 위해
(C) Ms. Smith의 가족 규모에 대해 질문하기 위해
(D) Ms. Smith가 크리스마스 연극에 참석할 것인지 묻기 위해

185. 연계 문제 – Ms. Klein의 아이들에 대한 암시 내용 ★★☆

해설 첫 번째 지문의 타코 행사에 대한 공지 내용 'A taco buffet will be set up in the employee cafeteria.'에서 타코 부페가 직원 식당에 준비될 것이라고 했는데, Jodie Klein의 이메일 마지막 단락 'My children enjoyed the tacos immensely'에서 자녀들이 타코를 매우 즐겼다고 했으므로 (D)가 정답임을 알 수 있다. **정답 (D)**

🔍 **함정 분석** 'During the bowling event, my kids were able to meet other employees' children, and they remain great friends even to this day.'에서 9월 1일에 열린 볼링 행사에 참석했음을 알 수 있으므로 (A) 는 오답, 영화는 '$1 Movie Tickets - November 1'과 'Purchase deeply discounted movie tickets for you and your family to enjoy.'에서 무료 가 아니라는 사실을 알 수 있으므로 (B)도 오답이다.

해석 Ms. Klein의 아이들에 대해 암시된 내용은?
(A) 9월 1일에 열린 행사를 놓쳤다.
(B) 무료 영화를 볼 수 있었다.
(C) Lelain 극장에 전에 가 본 적이 있다.
(D) Dougers 식당에서 음식을 먹었다.

문제 186-190번은 다음 웹페이지와 이메일, 그리고 정보를 참조하시오.

---

www.healthysnacksdelivery.com

죄책감 없는 간식: 여러분의 직원들을 위한 건강한 음식 옵션

| 간식 | 우리에 대해서 | 전화 주문 | 온라인 주문 |

186우리는 모든 예산에 대해 다음과 같은 맛있는 저칼로리 간식을 제공 합니다. 모든 간식은 신선한 천연 재료로 준비되어 있습니다.

과일 쟁반
단것을 좋아하는 여러분의 입맛을 만족시켜야 할 때, 과일은 최고의 선택 입니다. 여러분의 직원들이 초콜렛과 사탕과 같은 단것을 먹게 하지 말 고, 대신 천연 사탕을 주십시오.

채소 소스
여러분의 직원들이 스낵에 대한 갈망으로 푸짐한 한입 거리를 필요로 한 다면, 당근, 브로콜리, 그리고 샐러리와 같은 아삭아삭하고 땅에서 자란 채소들이 가장 좋은 선택입니다. 맛있는 소스가 포함되어 있어요!

샐러드
온 종일 일하는 동안 배고픔이 느껴지지 않게 풍성한 간식이 필요하십니 까? 화려한 색깔의 미니 샐러드는 육류가 없는 단백질을 포함하고 있으 며, 여러분의 직원들을 올바른 방식으로 활기차게 해 줄 것입니다.

구운 채소 칩
바쁜 업무로부터 벗어나 약간의 입맛을 돋울 필요가 있을 때, 한입 크기 의 구운 채소 칩이 준비되어 영양소를 공급합니다.

표현 정리 guilt free 죄책감 없는　low-calorie 저열량　ingredient 재료　tray 쟁반　sweet tooth 단 것을 좋아함　satiate 실컷 만족시키다　sugary treat 설탕이 든 음식　instead 대신에　dip 소스　heartier 더 푸짐한　a bite 한 입　craving 갈망　crisp 아삭아삭한　earthy 땅의　well-rounded 풍성한, 균형이 잡힌, 포괄적인　keep ~ at bay ~을 가까이 못 오게 하다　meat-free 고기 없는　protein 단백질　energize 활기를 북돋우다　distraction 집중을 방해하는 것; 머리를 식히게 해 주는 것　at hand 가까이 (있는)　bite-sized 한 입 크기의　nourish 영양분을 공급하다

발신: Gale Carter 〈gc443@ladyred.com〉
수신: inquiry@healthysnacksdelivery.com
날짜: 7월 22일
제목: 음식 알레르기와 가능한 옵션들

안녕하세요.

189저는 100명의 직원들과 함께 오레건주, 포틀랜드 시내에서 작은 중소기 업을 운영하고 있습니다. 저희 직원들은 서로 다양한 식성을 갖고 있고, 모든 직원에게 간식으로 건강한 옵션들을 제공하길 원하지만, 저의 비서 둘을 포 함하는 일부 직원들이 음식 알레르기를 갖고 있는 것이 제 관심을 끌었습니다. **187, 188**특별히, 이 직원들은 글루텐 과민증이고, 따라서 크래커와 같이 밀 로 만들어진 것은 저희 사무실에서 제공될 수 없습니다.

저희의 요구 사항에 맞는 간식들의 가격 목록을 보내주시기 바랍니다.

Gale

표현 정리 allergy 알레르기　available 이용 가능한　dietary restriction 식사 제한　vary 서로 다르다, 다양하다　offer 제공하다　snacking 군것질 come to one's attention 관심을 갖게 되다　administrative assistant 비서　specifically 특별히　gluten-intolerant 글루텐 과민증　wheat 밀 fit 맞다　requirement 필요 조건, 요구 조건

간식 가격 – 고객: LADY RED

주문 크기
150인분 미만 (제시된 기준 가격)
151 – 300인분 (기준 가격에서 10퍼센트 할인)
300인분 이상 (기준 가격에서 20퍼센트 할인)

간식 (기준 가격)
189과일 쟁반: 3달러 / 1인당
채소 소스: 3.5달러 / 1인당
시저 샐러드: 4.5달러 / 1인당
토마토 샐러드: 5달러 / 1인당

190주문하기 위해 주문 크기, 선택한 스낵, 지불 방법, 배송 일자와 주소를 이메일로 보내주시기 바랍니다.

표현 정리 place an order 주문하다　method 방식　delivery 배송

186. 세부사항 – 모든 간식 옵션에 관한 내용 ★☆☆

해설 웹 페이지의 첫 번째 문장에 있는, 'We offer the following delicious, low-calorie snacks for every budget.'에서 맛있는 저칼로리 간식을 제공한 다고 되어 있다. 따라서 지문의 low-calorie를 modest로 바꾼 (A)가 정답이 된 다. **정답 (A)**

🔍 **함정 분석** Fruit Tray에는 과일이 포함되어 있고, 야채는 없기 때문에 (B)는 정답이 될 수 없다. 또한 고객이 원하는 바대로 간식을 바꾼다거나 가격에 대 한 언급이 웹 페이지에는 나와 있지 않기 때문에 (C), (D)도 답이 될 수 없다.

표현 정리 modest 크지 않은, 보통의　content 내용물　customize 주문 제작하다, 원하는 대로 바꾸다　fixed 고정된, 정해진

해석 웹 페이지에 따르면, 모든 간식 옵션에 대해 사실인 것은?
(A) 많지 않은 칼로리 함량을 가지고 있다.
(B) 진짜 야채를 포함하고 있다.
(C) 고객이 원하는 대로 바꾸기 쉽다.
(D) 고정된 가격이다.

187. 연계 문제 – 구운 채소 칩에 관한 내용 ★★★
해설 웹페이지에는 4가지 스낵 종류가 언급되어 있는데, 그 중 하나가 Baked Beggie Chips이다. 그리고 이메일 후반 'Specifically, these employees are gluten-intolerant; therefore, any snacks made with wheat, such as crackers, cannot be served in our office.'에서 글루텐을 함유하고 있는 wheat으로 만들어진 스낵은 안된다고 했다. 마지막 지문 LADY RED에 제시된 스낵을 보면, 웹페이지에 나와 있는 4가지 스낵 중 Baked Beggie Chips만 빠져 있기 때문에 이 스낵이 글루텐을 포함하고 있음을 추론할 수 있으므로 정답은 (C)이다. 정답 (C)

🔍 함정 분석 품절되었다는 말은 언급이 없으므로 (A)는 오답이다. 세 번째 지문 마지막 문장 'To place an order, e-mail us the order size, snacks of choice, method of payment, and delivery date and address.'에서 이메일로 주문해 달라고 부탁하고 있기 때문에 전화로 주문해야 한다는 (B)도 오답이다. 웹페이지에 제시된 4가지 스낵 모두 Low-Calorie Snacks로 분류되어 있으므로 많은 열량을 가지고 있다고 보기도 어려워 (D)도 오답이다.

표현 정리 out of stock 품절된, 떨어진   contain 포함하다

해석 구운 채소 칩에 대해 암시된 것은?
(A) 현재 품절되었다.
(B) 전화로 주문해야 한다.
(C) 밀 글루텐을 포함한다.
(D) 많은 열량을 갖고 있다.

188. 세부사항 – Ms. Carter의 비서들에 관한 내용 ★☆☆
해설 Gale Carter의 이메일 중반에서 두 명의 비서를 포함한 직원들이 음식 알레르기가 있다고 한 후, 이어 'Specifically, these employees are gluten-intolerant; therefore, any snacks made with wheat, such as crackers, cannot be served in our office.'에서 이들 직원들이 모두 글루텐 과민증이 있어, 밀이 포함된 스낵, 즉 크래커를 사무실에 제공할 수 없다고 했으므로 정답은 (D)이다. 정답 (D)

해석 Ms. Carter의 행정 비서들에 관해 언급된 내용은?
(A) 최근에 고용되었다.
(B) 채식주의자 식단을 따른다.
(C) Healthy Snacks Delivery를 제안했다.
(D) 특정 크래커를 먹지 못한다.

189. 연계 문제 – Ms. Carter가 지불해야 하는 주문 금액 ★★☆
해설 Ms. Carter의 이메일 'I run a medium-sized company, with 100 employees including me'에서 자신을 포함해 100명의 직원이 일하고 있다고 했는데, 세 번째 지문 '150 servings or less (standard price listed)'에서 150명분 이하는 기준 요금이 청구되므로 1인 당 3달러인 과일 쟁반을 100명의 직원에게 공급하기 위해서는 총 300달러가 필요하므로 정답은 (C)이다. 정답 (C)

해석 Ms. Carter가 그녀의 모든 직원들을 위한 과일 쟁반을 주문하기 위해 청구 받을 금액은?
(A) 240달러
(B) 270달러
(C) 300달러
(D) 330달러

190. 세부사항 – Lady Red가 지시 받지 않은 사항 ★★★
해설 정보문 마지막 문장 'To place an order, e-mail us the order size, snacks of choice, method of payment, and delivery date and address.'

에서 (C) 주문할 양과 (B) 지불 방법 등을 (D) 이메일 메시지로 보내라고 했지만 전화를 걸어 달라는 내용은 없으므로 정답은 (A)이다. 정답 (A)

패러프레이징 |지문 method of payment 주문 방법 → |선택지 B| how it will pay 어떻게 주문할지
|지문 the order size 주문할 양 → |선택지 C| the number of servings 서빙할 숫자

표현 정리 specify 명시하다   state 말하다   a number of 다수의

해석 Lady Red가 간식을 주문할 때 하도록 지시받지 않은 것은?
(A) 전화를 한다.
(B) 어떻게 지불할지 명시한다.
(C) 주문할 양을 말한다.
(D) 이메일 메시지를 보낸다.

문제 191-195번은 다음 웹페이지, 온라인 청구서, 그리고 이메일을 참조하시오.

www.officesecurityalarm.com			
홈	대하여	등록	로그인

근무 시간 후에 여러분의 사무실을 지키세요.

모두 집으로 돌아간 이후에 당신의 사업체를 돌보는 사람이 있습니까? Office Security Alarm을 설치하시면 문이 닫힌 후에도 여러분의 사무실을 걱정할 필요가 없습니다.

저희 알람 시스템을 설치하면, 191사무실의 어떠한 움직임에도 사이렌을 울려 관계 당국에 침입자를 알립니다. 193저희 기본 시스템을 위한 월 9.99달러만으로 빈집털이범과 침입을 방지하십시오.

191여러분의 사업체는 영업시간 후에도 최고의 보안과 사무실 감시를 필요로 하는 첨단 기술과 정교한 기계를 이용할 수도 있습니다. 195밤과 낮을 가리지 않고 감시를 원하시는 분들을 위해 저희는 언제, 어디서든 접근 가능한 실시간 비디오 카메라를 월 29.99달러부터 시작하는 비용으로 설치해 드릴 수 있습니다.

오늘 보안 시스템에 가입하기 원하신다면, 이곳을 클릭하세요.

표현 정리 after hours 근무 시간 후에   take care of ~을 돌보다   in place 제자리에   motion 움직임   trigger 촉발시키다   alert 알리다, 경보를 발하다   intruder 침입자   burglary 빈집털이, 도둑   break-in 침입   high-end 고급의   sophisticated 정교한   top-notch 아주 뛰어난, 최고의   monitoring 감시   operating hours 영업 시간   desire 바라다   around-the-clock 24시간 내내 [밤낮으로]   surveillance 감시   set up 설치하다   live video feeds 실시간 비디오 촬영   accessible 접근 가능한   at anytime 언제라도   sign up for ~에 등록하다, 신청하다

www.officesecurityalarm.com/clientaccount			
		환영합니다: Bob Harsey	
홈	대하여	등록	로그인

고객 정보
고객: Bob Harsey
계정 번호: 243560

지불 정보
193금액: 9.99달러
형태: 전신 송금
빈도: 월 단위

지불은 매달 15일이 마감일입니다.

192주의: 체납 시에는 전화 555-2567로 전화해 납부해 주십시오.

표현 정리 **wire transfer** 전신 송금 **frequency** 빈도 **payment** 납부, 지불 **be due** (기간이) ~이다

> 발신: bharsey@jaxco.com,
> 수신: service@officesecurityalarm.com
> 날짜: 3월 12일
> 제목: 계정 업그레이드
>
> Office Security Alarm 귀하,
>
> 저희 사무실에 설치된 Office Security Alarm 서비스의 업그레이드를 요청하기 위해 메일을 보냅니다. 지난 2년 동안, 저희 사무실에 여러분의 시스템을 사용했습니다.
>
> **194. 195.** 저희 사무실 보안을 업그레이드하기를 원하므로 카메라 설치를 위한 약속을 정하기 위해 이메일에 답장해 주시기 바랍니다. 현관 쪽으로 설치된 카메라뿐 아니라 사무실 감시도 원합니다.
>
> 추가 설치 비용과 매달 내는 비용이 증가할 것이라는 것은 알고 있습니다. 이번 달 분을 방금 납부했으며, 청구서 요금 변화가 다음 달부터 반영되기를 기대합니다. 가급적 빨리 편하실 때 답변 주십시오.
>
> Bob Harsey

표현 정리 **set up an appointment** 약속을 정하다 **installation** 설치 **as well as** ~뿐 아니라 **face** ~을 향하다 **billing** 청구서 발부 **take effect** 효력을 나타내다 **respond** 답변하다 **at one's earliest convenience** 편리한 시간에

191. 세부사항 – 알람 시스템에 관한 내용 ★☆☆

해설 웹 페이지의 두 번째 단락에 있는, 'With our alarm system, any motion within your office will trigger a siren and alert the local authorities of an intruder.'를 통해 알 수 있듯이 사무실의 어떤 움직임도 사이렌이 울리도록 한다고 되어 있기 때문에 움직임을 감지한다는 (C)가 정답이 된다. 정답 (C)

표현 정리 **detect** 발견하다, 감지하다

해설 웹 페이지에서, 그 회사의 알람 시스템에 대해 언급된 것은?
(A) 침입자에게 경고를 하기 위해 빛을 사용한다.
(B) 문에만 연결이 되어 있다.
(C) 움직임을 감지할 수 있다.
(D) 표지판이 무료로 제공된다.

192. 세부사항 – Office Security Alarm에 관한 사실 내용 ★☆☆

해설 두 번째 지문 마지막 문장 'Note: For late payments, please pay by phone: 555-2567.'에서 체납 시에는 전화를 해 납부해 달라고 했으므로 체납이 용인된다고 볼 수 있어 정답은 (D)이다. 정답 (D)

표현 정리 **bi-monthly** 두 달에 한 번씩 **negotiable** 절충 가능한 **late payment** 체납 **accepted** 용인된

해설 Office Security Alarm에 관한 사실 내용은?
(A) 비용은 두 달에 한 번 납부한다.
(B) 서비스 비용은 절충 가능하다.
(C) 한 종류의 서비스 타입이 가능하다.
(D) 체납은 용인된다.

193. 연계 문제 – #243560에 관한 내용 ★★☆

해설 먼저 계정 #243560은 두 번째 지문에서 Bob Harsey의 계정임을 알 수 있으며, 납부 정보 Amount: $9.99에서 지불한 비용이 9.99달러였다. 그런데 첫 지문 두 번째 단락 'Prevent burglaries and break-ins for just $9.99 a month for our basic system.'에서 기본 시스템이 월 9.99달러로 서비스되고 있는 것으로 보아 Bob Harsey는 기본 서비스를 사용해 왔음을 알 수 있으므로 정답은 (B)이다. 정답 (B)

표현 정리 **late fee** 연체료 **bill** (요금을) 청구하다

해설 계정 #243560에 관해 언급된 내용은?
(A) 연체료를 지불해야 한다.
(B) 기본 시스템에 대한 청구서를 받았다.
(C) 전화로 납부했다.
(D) 2월에 업데이트했다.

194. 주제 – Mr. Harsey가 이메일을 보낸 이유 ★★☆

해설 Mr. Harsey가 보낸 이메일 두 번째 단락 'I would like to upgrade my office security, so please e-mail me back to set up an appointment for camera installation.'에서 카메라 장비 설치를 위한 일정을 잡고 싶으니 이메일 답장을 보내 달라고 요청하고 있으므로 이메일을 보낸 목적은 (D) 장비 설치 일정을 잡기 위해서이다. 정답 (D)

패러프레이징 |지문| to set up an appointment for camera installation 카메라 설치를 위한 약속을 잡기 위해 → |선택지 D| To schedule the installation of some equipment 장비 설치 일정을 잡기 위해

표현 정리 **make a payment** 납부하다, 지불하다 **equipment** 장비

해설 Mr. Harsey가 이메일을 보낸 이유는 무엇인가?
(A) 다른 지불 옵션을 검토하기 위해
(B) 그의 계정에 나타난 오류를 보고하기 위해
(C) 그의 계정에 대한 돈을 납부하기 위해
(D) 장비 설치 일정을 잡기 위해

195. 연계 문제 – Mr. Harsey에 관한 암시 내용 ★★★

해설 첫 번째와 두 번째 지문을 통해 Mr. Harsey가 기본 요금 9.99달러만 내면 되는 기본 시스템을 이용해 왔음을 알 수 있었는데, 세 번째 지문 두 번째 단락 'I would like to upgrade my office security, so please e-mail me back to set up an appointment for camera installation.'에서 보안을 업그레이드해서 촬영이 가능한 카메라 설치를 원한다고 했다. 그런데 첫 번째 지문, 세 번째 단락 'we can set up cameras with live video feeds accessible anytime, anywhere starting at $29.99 a month'에서 실시간 비디오 촬영이 가능한 카메라를 설치할 경우 월 최소 비용이 29.99달러라고 했으므로 정답은 (A)가 된다. 정답 (A)

표현 정리 **at least** 적어도 **uncertain** 확신이 없는, 불분명한

해설 Mr. Harsey에 관해 암시된 내용은?
(A) 그는 4월에 적어도 29.99달러를 지불할 것이다.
(B) 그는 Office Security Alarm의 신규 고객이다.
(C) 그는 가격 목록을 받기를 원한다.
(D) 그는 그의 계획을 변경할지 확신하지 못한다.

문제 196-200번은 다음 공지, 그리고 이메일들을 참조하시오.

> ### 공지
>
> 수신: Paperfax LLC
> 날짜: 5월 23일, 금요일
>
> 여러분 지역의 인터넷이 표준 인터넷 서비스에서 새로운 고속 광섬유 시스템으로 전환됨을 알려드리기 위한 공지입니다.
>
> 지역에 위치한 전 사무실 건물들이 영향을 받을 예정이며, 새로운 서비스 가격은 다음과 같습니다:
>
> • **198** 45달러/월 표준 광섬유
> • 55달러/월 고속 광섬유
> • 65달러/월 초고속 광섬유
>
> **196** 기존 서비스는 오늘 오후 5시에 종료됨을 참고하시기 바라며, **199** 새로운 서비스는 월요일, 오전 7시에 시작됩니다.

추가 정보는Josh Bergen: joshb@netservice.com로 이메일 부탁 드립니다.

Benjamin Mauer
Netservice 주식회사

표현 정리 notice 공지, 고지 fiber optic 광섬유(의) affect 영향을 미치다
ultra-high-speed 초고속의 commence 시작되다

발신: kimberlyhwang@paperfax.net
수신: joshb@netservice.com
날짜: 5월 23일, 금요일
RE: Highland Views' Better Business Bureau 불만 사항

Mr. Bergen 님께,

오늘 저녁 인터넷 서비스가 중단될 예정이라는 공지를 받았습니다. 귀사의 부적절한 공지에 대한 공식 항의를 Highland Views' Better Business Bureau 측에 제기할 예정입니다. 귀사는 우리가 인터넷 서비스 중단에 대비할 시간을 고작 몇 시간 주었습니다. 이것이 저희 사업에 부정적인 영향을 끼칠 수 있는 일인데도 말입니다. 199게다가 현재 매월 납부하고 있는 35달러보다 더 많은 사용료를 내야 합니다.

인터넷 차단으로 인한 재정적 손실을 보상해 줄 수 있나요? 197수년간 제공된 서비스를 중단할 계획이었다면 좀더 일찍 사전 통고를 했어야 합니다.

Kimberly Hwang

표현 정리 complaint 불만 cut off 중단시키다 file a complaint 항의를
제기하다 inadequate 부적당한 shutdown 정지 capability 능력, 힘
negative 부정적인 impact 영향 compensate 보상하다 setbacks
차질 due to ~때문에 outage 정전, 단수, 중단 terminate 끝내다,
종료하다 advance notice 사전 통고

발신: joshb@netservice.com
수신: kimberlyhwang@paperfax.net
날짜: 5월 23일, 금요일
RE: Re: Highland Views' Better Business Bureau 불만 사항

Ms. Hwang 님께,

Netservice 주식회사를 대표해 사과 드립니다. 200인터넷 중단을 좀 더 일찍 주변 업체들에게 공지하지 못한 실수를 인정합니다.

귀하의 표준 케이블 인터넷 접속을 일요일 오후 5시까지 연장할 것입니다. 그러나 현재의 요금을 계속 제공할 수는 없습니다. 통지서에 언급된 새로운 요금은 기존 고객뿐 아니라 신규 고객에게도 적용됩니다.

우리의 실수를 보충하기 위해, 198표준 광섬유 서비스와 동일한 가격으로 고속 광섬유 서비스로 업그레이드해드리겠습니다. 귀하의 새로운 서비스는 통지서에 명시된 날짜에 효력이 발생합니다.

Josh Bergen

표현 정리 on behalf of ~을 대신하여 acknowledge 인정하다
surrounding 주변의 termination 종료 extend 연장하다 existing
기존의 make up for 보상하다, 만회하다 take effect 효력이 발생하다

196. 주제 – 공지의 목적 ★★☆
해설 첫 번째 지문 'Be advised that your current Internet service will end at 5:00 P.M. today.'에서 기존 서비스가 중단될 예정임을 알리고 있으므로 정답은 (D)이다. 　　　　　　　　　　　　　　　　　　　　　　정답 (D)

함정 분석 공지 사항 'This notice is to inform you that the Internet in your area will be changed from the standard Internet service to the new high-speed fiber optic system.'에서 새로운 고속 광섬유 서비스로의 전환을 공지하고 있고, 'Be advised that your current Internet service will end at 5:00 P.M. today. New service will commence on Monday at 7:00 A.M.'에서는 기존 서비스를 종료하고, 새로운 서비스를 시작할 것이라고 했으므로 (B) 서비스 이전 요청으로 보기는 어렵다.

패러프레이징 |지문 Internet service will end 인터넷 서비스가 종료되다 → |선택지 D| the termination of a service 서비스의 종료

표현 정리 transfer 이동 announce 발표하다, 알리다

해석 공지의 목적은?
(A) 새로운 빌딩 관리자를 소개하기 위해
(B) 서비스 이전을 요청하기 위해
(C) 이용 가능한 새로운 기술을 설명하기 위해
(D) 서비스 중단을 알리기 위해

197. 유추 – Ms. Hwang에 관한 암시 내용 ★★☆
해설 두 번째 지문의 마지막 문장 'If you are going to terminate a service that has been in place for years, you must give more advance notice.'에서 수년간 서비스를 이용해 왔음을 짐작할 수 있으므로 정답은 (B)이다.
　　　　　　　　　　　　　　　　　　　　　　정답 (B)

함정 분석 Ms. Hwang이 서비스 전환을 거절한다는 내용은 언급되지 않았으므로 (A)는 오답이다. 그리고 갑작스런 서비스 전환에 항의하는 것으로 보아 Netservice 사에 만족하고 있다고 보기도 어려워 (C)도 오답이다.

표현 정리 refuse 거절하다 switch 전환하다 be satisfied with ~에
만족하다

해석 Ms. Hwang에 관해 암시된 내용은?
(A) 새로운 서비스로 전환하기를 거절한다.
(B) 수년간 케이블 인터넷을 이용해 왔다.
(C) Netservice 사에 만족하고 있다.
(D) 가장 빠른 옵션으로 업그레이드하기를 원한다.

198. 연계 문제 – Ms. Hwang이 지불할 금액 ★☆☆
해설 Mr. Bergen은 세 번째 지문에 있는, 'To make up for our mistake, we will upgrade you to our high-speed fiber optic service for the same price as our standard fiber optic service.'를 통해 알 수 있듯이, Ms. Hwang이 표준 광섬유 서비스 가격으로 고속 광섬유 서비스를 이용할 수 있다고 했다. 첫 번째 지문에서 표준 광섬유 가격을 보면 '$45/month standard fiber optic'이라고 되어 있으므로 정답은 (B)가 된다. 　　　정답 (B)

함정 분석 두 번째 지문 'I will have to pay more than my current $35-a-month fee.'에서 곧 중단될 서비스에 대한 비용이 35달러임을 알 수 있으므로 (A)는 오답이다.

해석 Mr. Bergen이 제공할 서비스에 대해 Ms. Hwang이 지불할 금액은 얼마인가?
(A) 35달러
(B) 45달러
(C) 55달러
(D) 65달러

199. 세부사항 – Ms. Hwang이 인터넷을 이용할 수 있는 시점 ★★☆
해설 첫 번째 지문 세 번째 단락 'The new service will commence on Monday at 7:00 A.M.'에 언급된 것처럼 새로운 인터넷 서비스는 월요일, 오전 7시부터 시작되므로 정답은 (D)이다. 　　　　　　정답 (D)

함정 분석 세 번째 지문, 두 번째 단락에 언급된 'We will extend your standard cable Internet access until Sunday at 5:00 P.M.'은 현재 사용하고 있는 표준 케이블을 이용해 인터넷을 사용할 수 있는 시간을 일요일, 오후 5시까지 연장시켜주겠다는 뜻일 뿐, 새로운 인터넷 서비스를 처음 이용할 수 있는 시간이 아니므로 (C) 일요일은 오답이다.

해석 Ms. Hwang이 새로운 인터넷 서비스를 이용할 수 있는 가장 이른 때는 언제인가?
(A) 금요일
(B) 토요일
(C) 일요일
(D) 월요일

200. 세부사항 – Mr. Bergen이 사과하는 내용 ★☆☆

해설 마지막 지문의 첫 번째 단락에 있는, 'We acknowledge our mistake of not informing the surrounding businesses of the Internet termination sooner.'를 통해 알 수 있듯이 좀 더 일찍 공지하지 못한 것에 대해 사과하고 있다고 했으므로 정답은 (D)가 된다. 정답 (D)

표현 정리 charge (요금을) 청구하다

해석 Mr. Bergen은 무엇에 대해 사과를 하는가?
(A) 모든 사람에게 더 높은 요금을 부과하는 것
(B) 기존 고객들이 인터넷 서비스를 바꾸도록 강요하는 것
(C) 주말에 걸쳐서 서비스를 업그레이드하는 것
(D) 고객들에게 보다 일찍 말하지 못한 것

Test 03
Part 7

문제 147-148번은 다음 이메일을 참조하시오.

수신: 보안 담당자
발신: Fred Jones
날짜: 2월 8일, 월요일

새로운 아이디 기기가 도착하였습니다. 147 1월 3일 제 메모에 언급된 바와 같이, 전 직원들은 4월 1일까지 기존 아이디 카드를 새 아이디 카드로 교체해야 합니다. 새 아이디에는 직원들이 회사 보안 구역 접근을 허용해 줄 수 있는 프로그램이 가능한 마이크로 칩이 부착돼 있습니다. 새 아이디를 발급하기 전에 철저한 테스트를 하려고 합니다. 148 테스트 팀에 합류하는데 관심이 있다면 늦어도 2월 12일, 금요일까지 이메일로 답변해 주시기 바랍니다.

Fred

표현 정리 security officer 보안 담당자, 경비원 arrive 도착하다 indicate 나타내다, 표시하다 employee 직원 replace A with B A를 B로 교체하다 existing 기존의, 현재 사용되는 contain ~이 들어있다, 포함하다 programmable 프로그램 작동이 가능한 grant 부여하다, 주다 access 입장, 접근 secure area 보안 구역 facility 시설 issue 발급하다 thoroughly 철저하게 be interested in ~에 관심이 있다 join 합류하다 respond to ~에 답하다 no later than 늦어도 ~까지는

147. 세부사항 – 새 아이디 발급 마감일 ★☆☆

해설 이메일 첫 번째 줄 'As indicated in my January 3 memo, all employees must replace their existing ID card with a new one by April 1.'에서 기존 아이디를 새 아이디로 4월 1일까지 교체해야 한다고 했으므로 정답은 (D)이다. 정답 (D)

표현 정리 deadline 마감일 obtain 얻다

해석 새 아이디를 받기 위한 마감일은 언제인가?
(A) 1월 3일
(B) 2월 8일
(C) 2월 12일
(D) 4월 1일

148. 세부사항 – Mr. Jones가 보안 담당자들에게 요청한 일 ★☆☆

해설 이메일 후반 'If you are interested in joining the testing team, respond to this e-mail no later than Friday, February 12.'에서 테스트 팀 합류에 관심이 있으면 지원해 달라고 요청하고 있으므로 정답은 (B)이다. 정답 (B)

패러프레이징 |지문| If you are interested in joining the testing team, respond to this e-mail 테스트 팀에 합류하는데 관심이 있다면 이메일에 답해 주세요 → |선택지 B| Volunteer to be part of a team 팀 합류에 지원하다

표현 정리 immediately 즉시 volunteer 지원하다 current 현재의, 기존의

해석 Mr. Jones가 보안 담당자들에게 요청한 것은 무엇인가?
(A) 아이디를 즉시 발급받으라고
(B) 팀 합류에 지원하라고
(C) 기존 아이디를 테스트하라고
(D) 마이크로칩 프로그램을 작동하는 법을 배우라고

문제 149-150번은 다음 송장을 참조하시오.

Snider Manufacturing

2190 Old Farm Road, Lancaster, PA 17570

(717) 555-0293 www.snider.com

주문 번호: 290340

날짜: 6월 19일

149고객: Frank Proctor, Viviance, Inc., 203 Charming Way, Masterson, IN 29930

전화번호: 1-885-293-0403

이메일: fproctor@viviance.com

품목	번호	수량	가격
149Viviance 로고를 넣은 조정 가능한 모자	4994	20	210달러
149Viviance 로고를 넣은 폴로 셔츠, 감청색 (중간 사이즈)	2394	5	97.5달러
무늬 없고 주름 없는 바지, 검정색(중간 사이즈)	4400	5	112.5달러
		소계	420달러
150쿠폰 번호 2940			(-10)달러
		배송비	20달러
		합계	430달러

구매해 주셔서 감사합니다.

저희 회사의 모든 제품은 100% 만족을 보장합니다.

자세한 내용은 저희 웹사이트를 방문해 확인하세요.

표현 정리 manufacturing 제조업 adjustable 조정 가능한 royal blue 감청색 plain 무늬 없는 front pant 주름 없는 바지 quantity 수량 subtotal 소계 shipping 배송 purchase 구매 satisfaction 만족 guarantee 보장

149. 세부사항 – Snider Manufacturing의 판매 제품 ★☆☆

해설 송장 주문 정보 'Customer: Frank Proctor, Viviance, Inc., 203 Charming Way, Masterson, IN 29930'에서 고객은 Viviance Inc.에 근무하는 사람이며, 그가 주문한 품목을 보면 회사 로고를 넣은 모자와 셔츠 등임을 알 수 있으므로 정답은 (D)이다. 정답 (D)

표현 정리 athletic equipment 운동 장비 footwear 신발 workplace 직장

해석 Snider Manufacturing이 판매하는 것은?
(A) 운동 장비
(B) 신발
(C) 페인트
(D) 직장 유니폼

150. 세부사항 – Mr. Proctor에 관한 내용 ★★☆

해설 송장 내용을 보면 #2940 쿠폰으로 (-$10.00)의 할인을 받았음을 알 수 있으므로 정답은 (C)이다. 정답 (C)

🔍함정 분석 배송비 20달러를 지불하였으므로 (A)는 틀린 내용이다. (B), (D)는 송장을 보고 확인 가능한 내용이 아니므로 답이 될 수 없다.

표현 정리 indicate 나타내다 shipping 배송 receive 받다 discount 할인 place an[the] order 주문을 하다 online 온라인으로

해석 Mr. Proctor에 대해서 언급된 내용은?
(A) 그는 배송비를 지불하지 않았다.
(B) 그는 신규 고객이다.
(C) 그는 할인을 받았다.
(D) 그는 온라인으로 주문을 했다.

문제 151-152번은 다음 문자 메시지 내용을 참조하시오.

Giprich, Patty 휴게실에 커피가 한 봉지밖에 남지 않았다는 것을 방금 알았어요. 오전 8시 47분

Zeter, Evan 발견해서 다행이네요. 151그러면 금요일 아침 회의에 사용할 양이 부족할 수 있겠네요. 지금 바로 더 구입할 수 있나요? 오전 8시 49분

Giprich, Patty 물론입니다. 그럼 근처에 있는 상점에 가 볼까요? 오전 8시 53분

Zeter, Evan 아니오. Simmon 카페에서 주문해 주세요. Mr. Cartwright는 그곳의 커피를 선호합니다. 커피 한 봉지를 바로 시키실 수 있어요. 그런데 정규 주문도 같이 해 주면 좋겠네요. 오전 8시 54분

Giprich, Patty 그러면 다음 날 도착 배송으로 한 봉지, 그리고 표준 배송으로 열 봉지를 시키겠군요. 오전 8시 57분

Zeter, Evan 정확해요. 지금 당장 처리해 주세요. 오전 9시 2분

Giprich, Patty 152그렇게 하겠습니다. 오전 9시 7분

표현 정리 notice 알아채다 break room 휴게실 spot 알아채다, 발견하다 probably 아마도 enough 충분한 meeting 회의 right away 즉시 nearby 인근에 place an order 주문하다 prefer 선호하다 immediately 즉시 regular 정기적인 overnight 밤 사이에, 하룻밤 동안 overnight shipping 익일 배송 take care of ~을 처리하다

151. 유추 – 금요일 회의에 대한 내용 ★★☆

해설 오전 8시 47분 'I just noticed we are down to our last bag of coffee in the break room.'에서 Ms. Giprich가 커피가 한 봉지밖에 남지 않은 것을 알게 됐다고 하자, Mr. Zeter가 'We probably won't have enough for Friday morning's meeting then.'이라고 답한 내용으로 보아 금요일 회의에 커피가 제공될 것이라는 것을 유추할 수 있으므로 정답은 (A)이다. 정답 (A)

🔍함정 분석 금요일에 있을 회의에 커피가 제공된다는 사실 이외에는 누가 주관하는지, 얼마나 많은 사람들이 참석할 것인지, 회의가 어디서 열리는지에 대한 정보는 나와 있지 않으므로 (B), (C), (D)는 오답이다.

표현 정리 beverage 음료 organize 주관하다, 준비하다 expected 예상된 attend 참석하다 take place 열리다, 일어나다

해석 금요일 회의에 관해 암시된 내용은?
(A) 음료가 제공될 것이다.
(B) Mr. Zeter가 주관한다.
(C) 예상보다 더 많은 사람들이 참석할 것이다.
(D) 휴게실에서 열릴 것이다.

152. 의도 파악하기 ★☆☆

해설 오전 9시 2분에 'Perfect. I suggest taking care of that right away.'라는 Mr. Zeter의 말에 Ms. Giprich가 'Will do.'라고 했으므로, 이는 그녀가 커피를 주문하겠다는 것을 확인하는 말이므로 정답은 (B)이다. 정답 (B)

표현 정리 state 말하다 confirm 확인하다 accept 인정하다, 받아들이다 agree 동의하다 contact 연락하다

해석 오전 9시 7분에 Ms. Giprich가 "그렇게 하겠습니다."라고 한 이유는 무엇인가?
(A) 그녀가 상점에 갈 것이라는 것을 말하기 위해
(B) 그녀가 주문을 할 것이라는 것을 확인하기 위해
(C) 그녀가 커피를 만들 것이라는 것을 인정하기 위해
(D) Mr. Cartwright에게 연락하는 것에 동의하기 위해

문제 153-155번은 다음 공지 사항을 참조하시오.

공지

발신: Martha Janich
수신: 전 직원

9월 30일까지 퇴직금 적립 계획 등록

153회사의 자발적인 퇴직금 적립 계획에 참여하지 않은 직원들은 9월 한 달 동안 참여하시기 바랍니다. 9월말 전에 이 계획에 등록하시는 직원들은 각 급여의 일부가 자동적으로 비과세 퇴직 연금 제도에 바로 적립될 수 있도록 선택하실 수도 있습니다. 아래의 표는 잠재적인 세금 감면액을 보여줍니다.

각 급여당 내는 금액	155(C)세금 감면액
100달러	10달러
250달러	25달러
500달러	50달러

154현재 이 계획에 등록하신 직원들은 9월 한 달 동안에만 투자 옵션을 변경하실 수 있습니다. 그렇게 하기 위해서는, 155(B)인사부에 투자 할당 변경 양식을 요청하십시오.

155(D)신입 직원들은 고용 날짜로부터 90일 간 퇴직금 적립 계획 또는 다른 복리후생 옵션 등록 여부를 결정하실 수 있으며, 그 기간이 지난 후에 변경을 하려면 다음 등록 기간까지 기다려야 합니다.

표현 정리 notice 공지, 공고문 retirement plan 개인 퇴직금 적립 계획 enrollment 등록 current 현재의, 기존의 participate in ~에 참여하다 voluntary 자발적인 enroll in ~에 등록하다 portion 일부 paycheck 급여 automatically 자동적으로 direct ~로 보내다 tax-free 비과세 retirement savings plan 퇴직 적립 계획 illustrate 보여주다 potential 잠재적인 contribute 돈을 내다, 기여하다 reduce 줄이다 request 요청하다 investment 투자 allotment 할당, 배당 form 양식 HR Office 인사부 hire 고용하다 decide 결정하다 benefit 복리후생 period 기간

153. 주제 – 공지의 목적 ★☆☆

해설 공지 첫 번째 줄 'Current employees who are not participating in the company's voluntary retirement plan are invited to do so during the month of September.'에서 9월 한 달 동안 퇴직금 적립 계획에 참여할 수 있는 기회가 있다는 것을 알려주고 있으므로 정답은 (B)이다. **정답 (B)**

표현 정리 purpose 목적 announce 발표하다 inform A of B A에게 B를 알리다 opportunity 기회 encourage 장려하다, 권하다 explain 설명하다 tax law 세법

해석 공지의 목적은 무엇인가?
(A) 퇴직금 적립 계획의 변경 사항을 발표하기 위해
(B) 직원들에게 기회에 대해 알려주기 위해
(C) 직원들에게 조기 은퇴를 장려하기 위해
(D) 세법의 변경 사항을 설명하기 위해

154. 세부사항 – 10월 1일에 발생할 일 ★☆☆

해설 공지의 표 아래 'Employees currently enrolled in the plan are only able to change their investment options during the month of September.'에서 투자 옵션이 9월 한 달 동안만 가능하다는 것을 알려주고 있으므로 10월 1일에는 그 변경 기간이 끝난다는 것을 알 수 있다. **정답 (D)**

표현 정리 according to ~에 따르면 retire 은퇴하다 select 선택하다 benefit 혜택

해석 공지에 따르면, 10월 1일에 무슨 일이 있을 것인가?
(A) 일부 직원들이 은퇴할 것이다.
(B) 직원들은 급여를 받을 것이다.

(C) 신입 직원들은 복리후생 제도를 선택할 수도 있다.
(D) 변경 기간이 끝날 것이다.

155. 세부사항 – 공지에 대한 내용이 아닌 것 ★★☆

해설 두 번째 단락 'Employees currently enrolled in the plan are only able to change their investment options during the month of September. To do so, request an investment allotment change form from the HR office.'에서 투자 옵션 변경이 가능하며, 그렇게 하려면 투자 할당 변경 양식을 작성하라고 알려주고 있지만, 가능한 투자 유형에 대해서는 언급하지 않았으므로 정답은 (A)이다. **정답 (A)**

🔍**함정 분석** 두 번째 단락 'To do so, request an investment allotment change form from the HR office.'에서 투자를 변경하는 방법을 알려주고 있으므로 (B)는 맞고, 표 You could reduce your taxes by에서 세금 감면액을 명시하고 있으므로 (C) 역시 확인 가능하고, 마지막 단락 'New employees have 90 days from their date of hire to decide whether to enroll in the retirement plan or other benefit options'에서 신입 직원들에게 90일 동안 결정할 기간이 주어진다는 것을 알 수 있으므로 (D) 역시 사실이다.

패러프레이징 |지문| investment options 투자 옵션 → |선택지 A| types of investments 투자 유형

표현 정리 mention 언급하다 type 유형 amount 양, 금액 timeframe 기간

해석 공지에 언급되지 않은 것은?
(A) 가능한 투자 유형
(B) 투자 변경 방법
(C) 직원들의 세금 절약 금액
(D) 신입 직원들이 등록할 수 있는 기간

문제 156-157번은 다음 전단을 참조하시오.

커뮤니티 룸의 새로운 수업

공예 (9월 18일 – 12월 19일, 85달러)
성인과 취학 연령의 어린이는 목요일 오후 3시부터 5시에 Marylou Baker 공예 수업에 참가하는 것을 환영합니다. 수업 재료는 제공됩니다.

피트니스 댄스 (10월 1일 – 12월 20일, 50달러)
금요일 오후 7시부터 8시에 전문 댄스 강사이자 주민인 Linda Riley와 함께 음악에 맞춰 춤을 춰 보세요. 사전 댄스 경험이 없어도 됩니다.

스크랩북 만들기 (9월 3일 – 12월 14일, 무료)
스크랩북 만들기는 추억을 공유하는 훌륭한 방법입니다. 토요일 오전 10시부터 정오까지, Evelyn Grayson이 지난 14년 동안 배워 온 기술을 공유할 것입니다. 재료는 별도입니다.

157등록 및 선불이 요구됩니다. Bethany White에게 555-4003으로 전화 주시기 바랍니다. 156참여는 Greenbrier Condominiums 주민들로 제한됩니다.

표현 정리 arts and crafts 공예 school-aged 취학 연령 material 재료 provide 제공하다 professional 전문적인 instructor 강사 resident 주민 prior 사전의 experience 경험 necessary 필요한 scrapbooking 스크랩북 만들기 share 공유하다 registration 등록 prepayment 선불 require 필요하다 participation 참여 restrict to ~로 제한하다

156. 주제 – 전단지의 대상 ★☆☆

해설 전단지 하단 'Participation restricted to residents of Greenbrier Condominiums.'에서 Greendbrier Condominiums 주민들로 참여가 제한된

다고 했으므로 정답은 (C)이다.　　　　　　　정답 (C)

표현 정리 flyer 전단지　intend for ~를 위해 의도되다　potential 잠재적인　instructor 강사　property manager 부동산 관리자　resident 거주민　local 지역의

해석 이 전단지의 대상은 누구인가?
(A) 잠재적인 강사들
(B) 부동산 관리자들
(C) Greenbrier 주민들
(D) 지역 예술가들

157. 세부사항 – 수업에 대한 내용　★★☆
해설 전단지 하단 'Registration and prepayment required.'에서 사전 등록과 수강료 납부가 요구되므로 정답은 (B)이다.　　　　　　정답 (B)

🔍 **함정 분석** 'Scrapbooking (September 3 – December 14, free)'에서 스크랩북 만들기는 무료이므로 (A)는 오답이며, 'Participation restricted to residents of Greenbrier Condominiums.'에서 Greenbrier Condominiums 주민들에게만 개방된다고 했으므로 (C) 역시 틀린 내용이다. (D)의 내용은 전단지에서 확인할 수 없다.

패러프레이징 |지문| Registration and prepayment required 등록과 선결제가 요구된다 → |선택지 B| must sign up in advance 미리 등록해야만 한다

표현 정리 participant 참가자　pay a fee 요금을 지불하다　sign up 등록하다　in advance 미리, 사전에　public 대중　offer 제공하다

해석 모든 수업에 관해 언급된 내용은?
(A) 참가자들은 반드시 요금을 지불해야 한다.
(B) 참가자들은 사전에 등록을 해야 한다.
(C) 수업은 대중(모든 사람)에게 개방되어 있다.
(D) 수업은 봄에 다시 열릴 것이다.

문제 158-160번은 다음 이메일을 참조하시오.

수신: Edgar Warwick 〈edgar.warwick@regalproperties.com〉
발신: Nathan Carlton 〈nate@interiorupgrades.com〉
날짜: 3월 21일
제목: 고정 세간 업그레이드

Mr. Warwick 님께,

158(A)오늘 오전에 귀하와 대화를 나눌 수 있어서 반가웠습니다. 이 이메일은 저희가 통화로 논의한 것에 더해 몇 가지 사항에 대한 후속 내용입니다. 158(B)제 비서에게 확인해 보았는데, 저희 둘 모두 귀하가 제안한 4월 8일, 월요일, 오전 9시 15분에 귀하의 건물을 점검할 수 있을 것 같습니다. 159(C)저희는 화장실에 있는 모든 배관 상태를 살펴 볼 예정입니다. 159(D)저희에게 건물 전체 배관 도표를 제공해 주시면 도움이 되겠습니다.

160귀하께서는 물 절약 고정 장치를 설치하고 싶다고 하셨습니다. 그러므로 저희의 WaterSmart™ 제품을 추천해 드립니다. 159(B)제가 저희 저수량 수도꼭지, 고효율 변기, 식수 여과 시스템의 사진과 설명서를 지참하겠습니다.

158저희는 귀하가 요청하신 견적 가격을 제공하고자 최선을 다하겠지만, 최종 비용은 처음 추정 금액에서 상하 20퍼센트까지 달라질 수 있다는 점을 참고해 주시기 바랍니다. 이는 종종 저희 설치 관리자가 기존 배관 시스템으로 얼마나 작업할 수 있는지에 달려 있습니다. 파이프에 추가적인 변경이 필요할 때도 있습니다. 만약 그런 문제들이 발견된다면, 저희는 작업을 시행하기 전에 항상 귀하께 알려드릴 것입니다.

혹시 궁금한 내용이 있으면, 저희가 만나기 전에 알려 주시기 바랍니다.

Nathan Carlton
Interior Upgrades, Inc. 사장

표현 정리 fixture 고정 세간(욕조, 변기 등과 같이 이사 때 이동할 수 없는 세간)　follow up 후속 조치　discuss 논의하다　assistant 보조, 비서　inspect 점검하다　take a look at ~을 살펴보다　current 기존의, 현재의　plumbing 배관　diagram 도표　entire 전체의　helpful 도움이 되는　therefore 그러므로, 그래서　description 설명　low-flow 저수량　faucet 수도꼭지　high-efficiency 고효율　filtration 여과　quote 견적　differ 다르다　up to ~까지　initial 최초의, 초기의　estimate 견적, 추정치　depend on ~에 달려있다　installer 설치 관리자　existing 기존의　additional 추가적인　modification 변경, 수정　discover 발견하다　issue 문제　conduct 시행하다　prior to ~에 앞서

158. 세부사항 – Mr. Warwick에 대한 내용　★★☆
해설 세 번째 단락 'While we will do our best to provide you with the quote you asked for, please be aware that the final costs can differ by up to 20% above or below our initial estimates.'에서 Mr. Warwick이 비용 견적서를 요청했음을 알 수 있으므로 정답은 (D)이다.　정답 (D)

🔍 **함정 분석** 첫 번째 단락 'It was a pleasure speaking with you this morning. This e-mail is to follow up on a few of the things we discussed over the phone.'에서 통화를 했음을 알 수 있으므로 (A)는 오답이고, 이어 'I checked with my assistant, and both of us will be able to inspect your building at the time you suggested: Monday, April 8, at 9:15 A.M.'에서 Mr. Warwick은 직원이 아니라 사무실 건물 점검을 요청한 고객이어서 (B) 역시 오답이다. 마지막으로 그가 사무실 건물을 소유하고 있는지는 알 수 없다.

패러프레이징 |지문| the quote you asked for 당신이 요청한 견적 → |선택지 D| an estimate of costs 비용 견적서

표현 정리 employee 직원　request 요청하다　estimate 견적서, 추정치　cost 비용

해석 Mr. Warwick에 관해 언급된 내용은?
(A) 그는 3월 21일 Mr. Carlton과 만났다.
(B) 그는 Interior Upgrades 직원이다.
(C) 그는 사무실 건물을 소유하고 있다.
(D) 그는 비용 견적서를 요청했다.

159. 유추 – Mr. Carlton이 4월 8일에 할 일이 아닌 것　★☆☆
해설 두 번째 단락 'I can bring photographs and descriptions of our low-flow faucets, high-efficiency toilets, and drinking water filtration systems.'에서 고효율 변기 사진과 설명서를 가져가겠다고 했을 뿐, 설치하겠다고는 하지 않았으므로 정답은 (A)이다.　　정답 (A)

표현 정리 attempt 시도하다　install 설치하다　high-efficiency 고효율　fixture 고정 세간　review 검토하다

해석 Mr. Carlton이 4월 8일에 하지 않을 일은?
(A) 고효율 변기 설치를 시도한다.
(B) 제품 관련 사진을 보여준다.
(C) 기존 고정 세간 상태를 확인한다.
(D) 수도관 사진을 검토한다.

160. 문장 위치 찾기　★★☆
해설 두 번째 단락 'Therefore, I would recommend our WaterSmart™ product line. I can bring photographs and descriptions of our low-flow faucets, high-efficiency toilets, and drinking water filtration systems.'에서 제품을 추천한 후에 저수량 수도꼭지, 고효율 변기, 식수 여과 시스템의 사진과 설명서를 지참해 가겠다고 했으므로, 바로 앞에 고객이 언급한 말이 나오는 것이 문맥상 적합해 정답은 (B)가 된다.　　정답 (B)

표현 정리 mention 언급하다　install 설치하다　water saving fixtures 물 절약 장치

해석 [1], [2], [3] , [4] 중 다음 문장이 들어가기에 가장 적절한 곳은?

"귀하께서는 물 절약 고정 장치를 설치하고 싶다고 하셨습니다."

(A) [1]
(B) [2]
(C) [3]
(D) [4]

문제 161-163번은 다음 구직 공고를 참조하시오.

162Campbell Industries에서 급여 팀을 감독할 관리자를 찾고 있습니다. 163(B),(C),(D)지원자는 반드시 학사 또는 그 이상의 학위 소지자여야 하며, 이와 유사한 직종에서 최소한 2년 간의 근무 경험이 있어야 합니다. 채용 시에는 공인 급여대장 전문 자격증(CPP)이 요구됩니다. 지원자는 해당 주 및 연방 급여법에 관한 실용적 지식을 갖추고 있어야 합니다. 10명 이상의 직원을 감독했던 경험이 있는 분을 선호하며, 163영어와 스페인어 두 가지 언어 능통자는 우대합니다.

관리자는 급여 준비, 진행 및 분배를 책임지게 됩니다. 관리자는 직원을 고용해 교육하고 발전시켜야 합니다. 부가적인 책임 사항으로는 급여 문제 해결, 급여 정책과 절차 개발 및 개선과 내부 또는 외부 회계 감사 시 지원하는 일을 포함합니다.

161텍사스, 댈러스에 본사를 둔 Campbell Industries는 연료 추출, 제조 및 정제 분야에서 빠르게 성장하고 있는 회사이며, 현재 1,250명이 넘는 직원과 계약자들에게 급여를 제공하고 있습니다. 저희는 경쟁력 있는 급여 및 복리후생 제도를 제공합니다.

지원을 위해서는 자기 소개서 및 이력서를 Brenda Shannon에게 팩스 또는 이메일로 보내 주시기 바랍니다(308-555-4003 / bshannon@campbell.com).

표현 정리 payroll 급여 oversee 감독하다 process 과정, 절차 applicant 지원자 possess 소지하다 bachelor's degree 학사 학위 supervisory 감독의, 관리의 responsibility 책임 certified 공인의 certification 자격증 hiring 채용 working knowledge 실용적 지식 applicable 해당되는 federal 연방의 supervise 감독하다 prefer 선호하다 bilingual 두 개 언어를 할 줄 아는 responsible for ~에 책임이 있는 preparation 준비 distribution 분배 train 교육시키다 develop 성장시키다 additional 추가적인 include 포함하다 resolve 해결하다 conflict 갈등 improve 개선하다 procedure 절차 provide 제공하다 internal 내부의 external 외부의 audit 회계 감사 headquartered in ~에 본사를 둔 field 분야 fuel extraction 연료 추출 manufacturing 제조업 refining 정제 contractor 계약업자 competitive 경쟁력 있는 salary 급여 benefits package 복리후생 제도 apply 신청하다, 지원하다 cover letter 자기소개서 resume 이력서

161. 유추 – Campbell Industries의 업종 ★☆☆

해설 세 번째 단락 'Campbell Industries is a fast-growing company in the field of fuel extraction, manufacturing, and refining, with a current payroll of 1,250+ employees and contractors.'에서 Campbell Industries는 연료 추출, 제조 및 정제를 전문으로 하는 회사라고 했으므로 에너지 회사임을 알 수 있어 정답은 (D)이다. 정답 (D)

표현 정리 employment agency 직업 소개소 certified 인증된 financial institution 금융 기관

해석 Campbell Industries는 무엇을 하는 곳인가?
(A) 직업소개소
(B) 인증된 아카데미
(C) 금융 기관
(D) 에너지 회사

162. 세부사항 – 급여 관리자가 할 일 ★☆☆

해설 첫 번째 단락 'Campbell Industries is seeking a payroll manager to oversee a team of payroll processes.'에서 경리 팀을 감독할 관리자를 찾는다고 했으므로 (A)가 정답이다. 정답 (A)

패러프레이징 |지문| oversee a team of payroll processes 급여 지급 팀을 감독하다 → |선택지 A| supervise the payroll staff 급여 팀 직원을 감독하다

표현 정리 announcement 공지, 발표 calculate 산정하다, 계산하다 benefit 혜택, 이점

해설 공지에 따르면 급여 관리자가 하는 일은?
(A) 경리 직원을 감독한다.
(B) 신입 직원을 위한 복리후생을 산정한다.
(C) 직원들에게 복리후생 제도를 설명한다.
(D) 계약업자들에게 메모를 보낸다.

163. 세부사항 – 관리자의 필수 지원 요건이 아닌 것 ★★☆

해설 첫 번째 단락 마지막 문장 'Being bilingual in English and Spanish is a plus.'에서 두 개의 언어를 구사할 수 있는 지원자는 우대한다고 했을 뿐, 지원에 반드시 필요한 조건이 아니므로 정답은 (A)이다. 정답 (A)

🔍 함정 분석 첫 단락 'Applicants must possess a bachelor's degree or higher and have at least 2 years' experience in a similar position with supervisory responsibilities.'에서 지원자는 학사 학위를 소지해야 하며, 관리자로서 2년 이상의 경력이 있어야 한다고 했고, 이어서 'Certified Payroll Professional (CPP) Certification is required at the time of hiring.'에서는 전문 자격증이 요구된다고 했다.

패러프레이징 |지문| a bachelor's degree 학사 학위 → |선택지 B| a college degree 학사 학위

|지문| 2 years' experience in a similar position with supervisory responsibilities 관리 책임이 있는 2년 이상의 경력 → |선택지 C| Past experience as a manager 관리자로서의 과거 경력

표현 정리 requirement 필요 요건 completion 수료, 완료 college degree 학사 학위 possession 소지

해석 관리자 직의 필수 필요 요건이 아닌 것은?
(A) 두 가지 언어를 구사할 수 있는 능력
(B) 학사 학위 수료
(C) 관리자로서의 과거 경력
(D) 전문 자격증 소지

문제 164-167번은 다음 온라인 채팅을 참조하시오.

Morgan, Kelly 여러분, 안녕하세요. 우리가 구매한 새 디지털 카메라가 어떤지 알고 싶어서요. 어떤 문제점이라도 발견됐나요? 오전 8시 48분

Alexander, Herb 164전혀 없어요. 내 것은 정말 사용하기 쉬워요. 사진도 정말 잘 나오고요. 166사진 복사본을 자동으로 제 이메일 계정에 보낼 수 있어서 정말 마음에 들어요. 오전 8시 50분

Soto, Ken 그런데, 왜 내 카메라는 그 기능이 없죠? 오전 8시 51분

Alexander, Herb 있어요. 와이파이로 파일을 목적지로 보내도록 하는 기능을 선택하기만 하면 돼요. 오전 8시 52분

Soto, Ken 어떻게 하는지 알려줄래요? 오전 8시 53분

Alexander, Herb 165내가 직접 보여주는 게 나을 것 같네요. 과정은 약간 복잡하지만, 한 번 설정해 놓으면 모든 게 순조롭게 작동될 거예요. 내일 부서 회의에 참석할 예정인가요? 회의 후에 보여줄 수 있어요. 오전 8시 55분

Soto, Ken 좋아요. 오전 8시 56분

Loos, Nancy   저는 카메라에서 사진과 동영상 파일을 다운로드해서 제 워크스테이션에 옮기는데 어려움을 겪고 있어요. 어떻게 하는지 누가 보여줄 수 있나요?   오전 8시 58분

Morgan, Kelly   그럴게요. 저도 처음에 문제가 있어서 기술 지원 데스크에 전화했거든요. Davis Shandler가 몇 가지 방법을 알려줬어요. 내 생각에 가장 쉬운 방법은 제조업체 웹사이트에서 프로그램을 다운로드하는 거예요. **167프로그램은 File Box이고, 설치하기는 쉬워요.**   오전 9시 1분

Loos, Nancy   할 수 있을 것 같아요. 고마워요, Kelly!   오전 9시 6분

표현 정리 run into ~를 만나다, 겪다 **not at all** 전혀 아닌 **automatically** 자동으로 **account** 계정 **select** 선택하다 **function** 기능 **destination** 목적지 **via** ~을 매개로, ~을 통해 **probably** 아마도 **step** 단계, 과정 **complicated** 복잡한 **set up** 설정하다 **smoothly** 순조롭게 **afterward** 후에 **workstation** 워크스테이션, 개인 단말 장치 **technical support** 기술 지원 **several** 몇몇의 **manufacturer** 제조업체 **install** 설치하다

164. 유추 – Mr. Alexander에 관한 암시 내용   ★★☆

해설 Mr. Alexander가 오전 8시 50분에 보낸 'Not at all. Mine is easy to use. Takes very good pictures, too. I really like how I can automatically send copies to my e-mail account.'에서 새 디지털 카메라 사용이 정말 쉽고, 기능이 마음에 든다고 한 내용으로 보아 그가 카메라 사용에 능숙함을 짐작할 수 있으므로 (D)가 정답이다.   정답 (D)

표현 정리 photography 사진(술) **prefer to** ~하는 것을 선호하다 **communicate** 연락을 주고 받다, 의사소통하다 **be skilled at** ~에 능숙하다

해석 Mr. Alexander에 관해 암시된 내용은?
(A) 그는 카메라를 얻은 첫 번째 사람이다.
(B) 그는 사진술에 관한 워크숍을 가르칠 것이다.
(C) 그는 이메일을 통해 연락을 주고 받는 것을 선호한다.
(D) 그는 새 카메라 사용에 능숙하다.

165. 유추 – Mr. Soto가 내일 할 일   ★☆☆

해설 오전 8시 53분에 Mr. Soto가 보낸 메시지 'Can you tell me how to do that?'에서 사용 방법을 알려 달라고 하자, Mr. Alexander가 'It's probably better that I show you. ~. Are you going to be at the departmental meeting tomorrow? I could show you afterward.'에서 내일 부서 회의 끝나고 직접 보여주겠다고 했으므로 정답은 (A)이다.   정답 (A)

표현 정리 install 설치하다 **presentation** 발표 **pick up** 집다, 받다

해석 Mr. Soto는 내일 무엇을 할 것인가?
(A) Mr. Alexander와 만난다.
(B) 소프트웨어를 설치한다.
(C) 프레젠테이션을 한다.
(D) 새로운 카메라를 받는다.

166. 세부사항 – 새 카메라에 관한 내용   ★★☆

해설 오전 8시 50분에 Mr. Alexander가 보낸 메시지 'I really like how I can automatically send copies to my e-mail account.'에서 새 카메라로 사진을 자동으로 자신의 이메일 계정으로 보낼 수 있다고 했으므로 정답은 (B)이다.   정답 (B)

🔍 **함정 분석** (A)의 화질에 대한 이야기는 채팅 창에 나오지 않는다. 오전 8시 50분 'Mine is really easy to use.'에서 알 수 있듯이 카메라 사용은 정말 쉽다고 했으므로 (C)는 맞지 않다. 오전 8시 58분에 Ms. Loos는 동영상 파일에 대해 언급했으므로 (D)도 옳지 않다

패러프레이징 |지문| automatically send copies to my e-mail account 사진을 자동으로 자신의 이메일 계정으로 보낼 수 있다 → |선택지 B| be

programmed to send photos 사진을 전송하도록 프로그램되다

표현 정리 moderately 적당히 **decent** 괜찮은 **program** 프로그램하다 **require** 필요하다 **basic** 기본의 **function** 기능 **video** 동영상

해석 새 카메라에 관해 언급된 내용은?
(A) 적당히 괜찮은 화질을 갖고 있다.
(B) 사진을 전송하도록 프로그램될 수 있다.
(C) 기본 기능을 사용하는데 교육이 필요하다.
(D) 동영상을 만드는데 사용될 수 없다.

167. 의도 파악하기   ★★☆

해설 오전 9시 1분에 보낸 메시지 'The program is called File Box. It's easy to install.'에서 Ms. Morgan은 File Box 프로그램 설치가 쉽다고 하자, Ms. Loos가 'I think I can handle that.'이라고 했는데, 이는 그녀가 프로그램을 설치해 사용법을 스스로 알아낼 수 있음을 확신하는 것으로 볼 수 있으므로 (D)가 정답이다.   정답 (D)

표현 정리 figure out ~을 알아내다, 이해하다 **confident** 자신감 있는, 확신하는

해석 오전 9시 6분에 Ms. Loos가 "제가 할 수 있을 것 같아요"라고 한 내용의 의미는 무엇인가?
(A) 그녀는 기술 지원 팀에 전화를 할 예정이다.
(B) 그녀는 Mr. Shandler로부터 도움을 받을 것이다.
(C) 그녀는 카메라 사용법을 알아낼 수 있다.
(D) 그녀는 자신이 File Box를 사용할 수 있을 것으로 확신한다.

문제 168-171번은 다음 공지 사항을 참조하시오.

> **공지**
>
> 4월 18일, 수요일
>
> 인사부는 1월에 Cormac Manufacturing이 전자 근무 시간 기록표인 Omega로 시스템 전환을 할 것이라고 발표한 적이 있습니다. **168그 후로** 여러 부서들이 변화에 성공적으로 적응했습니다. **169(B)이러한** 변화로 인해 급여 제공 절차가 35퍼센트 빨라졌으며, 오류는 65퍼센트 감소해, 급여 담당 및 인사부 직원들이 다른 업무에 주력할 수 있게 되었습니다.
>
> 전자 근무 시간 기록표는 Cormac Manufacturing 직원들에게 많은 이점을 제공합니다. **169(D)특히 원거리 근무를 하는 직원들에게 도움이 됩니다. 169(A)Omega** 사용으로 관리자는 각각의 직원은 물론, 다수의 직원들이 프로젝트에 투입된 시간에 대한 보고서를 쉽게 준비할 수 있게 되었습니다.
>
> 7월 31일까지 Omega 채택이 완료될 예정입니다. 현재 종이 근무 시간 기록표를 사용하고 있는 직원은 그때는 더 이상 그렇게 할 수 없습니다. 일부 관리자와 직원들이 전환 시점에 어려움을 겪을 수도 있습니다. **170그러한 과도기적인 어려움을** 줄이기 위해, 관심 있는 직원들을 대상으로 다음 주부터 단기 교육을 제공하려고 합니다. Omega의 기본적인 개념과 기능이 소개될 것입니다. 또한, 개별 질문들에 대해 답변할 기회가 있을 것입니다.
>
> 45분 간의 Omega 워크숍은 매주 수요일과 금요일 오후 1시, 2시, 3시로 예정되어 있습니다. Chase 건물에 있는 Chancellor 회의실에서 열릴 예정입니다. **171좌석이 제한되어 있으므로,** 사전 등록이 요구됩니다. 본인과 본인 직원들의 자리를 예약하려면 내선번호 2029로 Sherry Greenfield에게 연락을 주시기 바랍니다.

표현 정리 human resources department 인사부 **announce** 발표하다 **transition to** ~로의 전환 **timesheet** 근무 시간 기록표 **since that time** 그 후로 **shift** 변화 **result in** ~을 낳다, 야기하다 **paycheck** 급료 **issue** 발급하다 **free up** 해방하다, 해소하다 **payroll** 급여 대장 **focus on** ~에 초점을 맞추다 **task** 일, 과업 **offer** 제공하다 **advantage** 이점 **secure** 안전한 **remotely** 멀리서 **prepare** 준비하다 **individual** 개인의

contribute 기여하다 multiple 다수의 adoption 채택, 선정 complete 완료하다 currently 현재 no longer 더 이상 ~이 아닌 at that time 그때 ease 편해지다 growing pain 성장통 function 기능 in addition 게다가 address (문제, 상황에 대해) 고심하다, 다루다 extension 내선번호 reserve 예약하다 tutorial 사용 지침서 post 게시하다

168. 유추 – Omega에 관한 암시 내용 ★★☆

해설 첫 번째 단락 'Since that time, several departments have successfully made the shift.'에서 몇몇 부서에서만 변화가 이루어졌다고 한 것으로 보아 아직 모든 부서가 사용하고 있는 것은 아님을 알 수 있으므로 정답은 (B)가 된다. **정답 (B)**

표현 정리 require 요구하다 extensive 집중적인, 광범위한 currently 현재 adopt 채택하다 payroll 급여 대장 release 공개하다

해설 Omega에 관해 암시된 내용은?
(A) 사용을 위해 집중적인 교육이 요구된다.
(B) 현재 모든 부서에서 사용되는 것은 아니다.
(C) 처음에 급여 담당 부서에 의해 채택되었다.
(D) 올해 초에 도입되었다.

169. 세부사항 – 전자 기록 시스템의 이점이 아닌 것 ★★★

해설 본문에서 전자 근무 시간 기록표 시스템을 채택한 후에 나타나는 여러 이점에 대해 언급했지만, 회사가 비용을 절약하게 해 준다는 내용은 언급되지 않았으므로 정답은 (C)이다. **정답 (C)**

🔍 **함정 분석** 두 번째 단락 'With Omega, managers can easily prepare reports on individual employees or all hours contributed by multiple employees to a project.'에서 (A)를, 첫 번째 단락 'Those changes have resulted in paychecks being issued 35% faster and with 65% fewer errors, freeing up Payroll and HR employees to focus on other tasks.'에서 (B)를, 그리고 두 번째 단락 'This is especially helpful for employees working remotely.'에서 (D)를 확인할 수 있다.

패러프레이징 |지문| managers can easily prepare reports 관리자가 쉽게 보고서를 작성한다 → |선택지 A| allowing supervisors to create reports 관리자가 보고서를 만들도록 한다
|지문| with 65% fewer errors 65% 적은 에러 → |선택지 B| reducing the number of mistakes 실수의 횟수를 줄인다
|지문| be helpful for employees working remotely 직원들이 멀리서 근무하는데 도움이 되다 → |선택지 D| making it easier for telecommuters 재택근무자들을 용이하게 하다

표현 정리 benefit 혜택 supervisor 관리자 reduce 감소하다 telecommuter 재택 근무자

해설 전자 근무 시간 기록표 시스템의 이점으로 언급된 것이 아닌 것은?
(A) 관리자가 보고서를 작성할 수 있게 허용한다.
(B) 오류 횟수를 줄여준다.
(C) 회사에 비용을 절약해 준다.
(D) 재택 근무자에게 용이하다.

170. 세부사항 – 곧 있을 교육에 대한 암시 내용 ★★☆

해설 세 번째 단락 'To help ease those growing pains, we will offer short trainings to interested employees starting next week. These will introduce the basic concepts and functions of Omega.'에서 관심이 있는 직원들을 대상으로 다음 주부터 단기 교육을 실시할 예정이며, Omega의 기본적인 개념과 기능이 소개될 것이라고 했으므로 (A)가 정답이다. **정답 (A)**

패러프레이징 |지문| introduce the basic concepts and functions of Omega 오메가에 대한 기본 개념과 기능을 설명한다 → |선택지 A| provide information about a software program 소프트웨어 프로그램에 대한 정보를 제공한다

표현 정리 upcoming 곧 있을, 다가오는 exclusively 독점적으로, 전적으로 mandatory 의무적인 on separate occasion ~차례에 걸쳐

해설 곧 있을 교육에 관해 언급된 것은?
(A) 소프트웨어 프로그램에 관한 정보를 제공할 것이다.
(B) 전적으로 인터넷을 통해 시행될 것이다.
(C) 모든 관리자와 직원들에게 참석이 의무적이다.
(D) 여섯 차례에 걸쳐 제공될 것이다.

171. 문장 위치 찾기 ★★☆

해설 주어진 문장은 좌석이 제한되어 있으니 사전 등록을 하라는 내용인데, 본문에서 [4]번 바로 뒤에서 자리 예약에 관한 내용이 언급되고 있으므로 [4]번 자리에 주어진 문장이 들어가는 것이 적절하여 정답은 (D)이다. **정답 (D)**

표현 정리 advanc registration 사전 등록 require 요구하다

해설 [1], [2], [3], [4] 중 다음 문장이 들어가기에 가장 적절한 곳은?
"좌석이 제한되어 있으므로, 사전 등록이 요구됩니다."
(A) [1]
(B) [2]
(C) [3]
(D) [4]

문제 172-175번은 다음 서식을 참조하시오.

연락 신청서

양식을 작성해 주시면 저희 공인 자산 관리자 중 한 분이 고객님께 연락을 드릴 것입니다.

성명: *Charles Horton*
주소: *89 Birch Lane, Sweetham, CT 18930*
전화번호: *(212) 555-8943*
이메일 주소: *chorton@quickmail.com*
172 고용주: *Simmons Products*
직위: *관리자*

어떻게 연락을 받기를 선호하십니까?
[ ] 전화 (일반 업무 시간: 월 – 금 오전 9시 – 오후 5시)
174 [✓] 전화 (업무 시간 외)
[ ] 이메일
[ ] 우편

저희에 관해 처음 어떻게 알게 되셨습니까?
[ ] 홍보 우편물   [ ] 라디오   [ ] 신문   **173 [✓] 입소문**
[ ] 기타 (자세히 설명해 주십시오.): _____

다음 서비스 중 무엇에 관심이 있으십니까? (해당 항목에 모두 체크해 주세요.)
175 [ ] 세무 관리 전략
[✓] 은퇴 계획
[✓] 학자금 저축 계획
[✓] 생명, 상해 또는 기타 보험 상품
[ ] 부동산 계획
[ ] 기타 (자세히 설명해 주십시오.) : _____

의견:
토요일 오전에 연락하는 것은 피해주세요. **174** *대개 주말 오후는 괜찮습니다.*

표현 정리 contact 연락 request form 신청서 complete 완료하다 certified 공인된 financial planner 자산 관리사 prefer 선호하다 normal business hour 일반 업무 시간 outside ~외에 promotional 홍보의 word of mouth 구전, 입소문 specify 명시하다, 구체화하다

apply 해당되다 tax management 세무 관리 strategy 전략, 방안 retirement 은퇴 life insurance 생명 보험 disability insurance 상해 보험 estate 부동산 consulting 상담 comment 의견 avoid 피하다 generally 보통, 대개

172. 세부사항 – Mr. Horton에 관한 내용 ★★☆

해설 Mr. Horton이 양식에 기입한 내용 중 'Employer: Simmons Products, Position: Manager'에서 그가 현재 Simmons Products의 Manager로 근무하고 있음을 알 수 있으므로 (A)가 정답이다. 정답 (A)

표현 정리 currently 현재 employ 고용하다 financial planner 자산 관리사

해석 Mr. Horton에 관해 언급된 내용은?
(A) 그는 현재 고용되었다.
(B) 그는 소규모 사업주이다.
(C) 그는 이메일 계정을 갖고 있지 않다.
(D) 그는 자산 관리자로 일한다.

173. 세부사항 – Mr. Horton이 Pyramid Financial을 알게 된 계기 ★☆☆

해설 Mr. Horton이 Pyramid Financial을 알게 된 계기를 묻는 문제로, 본문 중간 'How did you first hear about us?'에서 word of mouth에 체크를 했으므로 정답은 (B)임을 짐작할 수 있다. 정답 (B)

패러프레이징 |지문| word of mouth 구두의, 구전의 → |선택지 B| Someone told him 누군가 그에게 말해주다

표현 정리 advertisement 광고 representative 직원, 대리인, 대표

해석 Mr. Horton은 Pyramid Financial에 대해 어떻게 알게 되었는가?
(A) 우편으로 정보를 받았다.
(B) 누군가가 그에게 말해줬다.
(C) 광고를 보았다.
(D) 한 직원이 그에게 전화를 걸었다.

174. 세부사항 – Mr. Horton과 통화가 가능한 시간 ★☆☆

해설 신청서에서 일반 업무 시간을 제외한 모든 시간에 통화가 가능하다고 했는데, 후반 의견란에서 토요일 오전에 종종 사무실에 출근하므로 이때는 피해달라고 했고, 'Weekend afternoons are generally good.'에서 주말 오후에는 대개 통화가 가능하다고 했으므로 정답은 (D)이다. 정답 (D)

🔍 함정 분석 Mr. Horton은 '[✓] phone (outside normal business hours)'에 체크를 했으므로 업무 시간: 월 – 금, 오전 9시 – 오후 5시에는 전화 통화가 불가능하다. 또한 의견란 'I occasionally go into the office on Saturday mornings. So avoid trying to contact me at that time. Weekend afternoons are generally good.'에서 토요일 오전에 사무실에 나가므로 연락을 피해달라고 했으므로 토요일 오전도 통화가 가능하지 않다는 것을 알 수 있다.

표현 정리 available 시간이 있는

해석 Mr. Horton은 언제 전화 통화가 가능한가?
(A) 월요일, 오전 9시
(B) 금요일, 오후 3시
(C) 토요일, 오전 11시
(D) 일요일, 오후 1시

175. 세부사항 – Mr. Horton의 관심을 끌지 못하는 서비스 ★☆☆

해설 Mr. Horton은 Tax Management Strategies에 체크를 하지 않았으므로 그가 세금 서류를 맡기는 것에는 관심이 없음을 알 수 있어 정답은 (B)다. 정답 (B)

패러프레이징 |지문| College Savings Plans 대학 등록금 저축 계획 → |선택지 A| Saving money for education 교육을 위한 저축 계획

|지문| Retirement Planning 은퇴 계획 → |선택지 C| Preparing to stop working 일 중단에 대한 대비

표현 정리 tax form 세무 서류 prepare 준비하다 obtain 얻다, 취득하다 insurance 보험

해석 Mr. Horton은 어떤 서비스에 관심이 없는가?
(A) 교육을 위한 저축
(B) 그의 세무 서류를 준비하게 하는 것
(C) 일을 그만하기 위한 준비
(D) 보험 가입하기

문제 176-180번은 다음 이메일들을 참조하시오.

발신: Ken Jones ⟨kjones@nativematerials.com⟩
수신: John Evanston ⟨jevanston@miroctech.com⟩
날짜: 3월 1일, 금요일
제목: 분석 필요

John,

지난주에 와서 새 전자 현미경을 살펴봐 줘서 고마워요. 제가 살펴보던 자료가 이상해 보여 문제가 있는 것은 아닌지 확인해 봐야 할 것 같다고 느꼈습니다. 176시간을 내 필요한 조정을 해 줘서 감사합니다. 지금은 모든 게 순조롭게 잘 움직이고 있습니다.

지난 11월에 제 연구실 책임자인 Roger Wayne 씨를 만난 것을 기억하나요? 그분이 저에게 어떤 분이 의뢰한 샘플의 분석을 요청했습니다. 저는 보통 사내에서 다른 부서들을 위해 일하며, 샘플들은 철이나 구리, 또는 다른 금속류가 대부분입니다. 반면에 이번 샘플은 산업용으로 사용될 새로운 세라믹 재료입니다. 177그 재료는 저의 전문 분야가 아닙니다. 179,180당신이 이전 직장에서 세라믹을 다룬 경험이 있다고 말했던 것이 기억나서, 혹시 다음번에 Richmond를 방문할 때 살펴봐 줄 수 있는지 궁금합니다. 긴급한 사항은 아닙니다.

Ken Jones
재료 분석가
Native Materials

표현 정리 analysis 분석 check on ~을 살펴보다 electron microscope 전자 현미경 have a feeling ~한 느낌을 갖다 appreciate 고마워하다 adjustment 수정, 조정 smoothly 순조롭게 director 책임자, 감독관 lab 연구실 analyze 분석하다 normally 보통 iron 철 copper 구리 metal 금속 on the other hand 반면에 ceramic 세라믹, 도자기 industrial application 산업용 outside 바깥쪽 expertise 전문 기술 vaguely 희미하게 recall 기억해 내다 former 이전의 take a look at ~을 보다 urgent 긴급한

발신: John Evanston ⟨jevanston@miroctech.com⟩
수신: Ken Jones ⟨kjones@nativematerials.com⟩
날짜: 3월 4일, 월요일
제목: RE: 분석 필요

Ken,

제가 기꺼이 도와 줄게요. 기억력이 좋네요. 179Janus Technology는 Kempthorn Corporation에 매각되기 전까지 세라믹 제조 프로그램을 보유하고 있었어요. 178그 일이 10년 전 일이긴 하지만, 그 후로도 그 분야의 동향을 계속 살펴와왔기 때문에 어떻게 샘플을 분석하는지 제가 도와줄 수 있을 것 같습니다. 180다음 달에 내가 그 지역에 갈 예정인데, 그때쯤 내가 Baltimore에 있는 NMRC 회의에 참석할지도 몰라 아직 정확한 날짜는 알려주기 어렵습니다. 내 일정이 확정되는 대로 알려줄게요.

John

표현 정리 lend a hand 도움을 주다　buy out 구매하다, 인수하다　decade 10년　keep up with 시류를 따르다, ~에 뒤지지 않다　trend 동향　field 분야　exact 정확한　attend 참석하다　around that time 그때쯤에　finalize 확정하다, 마무리 짓다

176. 세부사항 – Mr. Evanston의 방문 이유　★☆☆

해설 첫 번째 이메일, 첫 번째 문장 'Thanks for coming in to check on the new electron microscope last week.'에서 Mr. Evanston이 지난주 Native Materials를 방문해 전자 현미경을 확인했고, 세 번째 문장 'I appreciate your spending the time making the needed adjustments.'에서 장비를 조정해 줬음을 알 수 있으므로 정답은 (D)이다.　**정답 (D)**

패러프레이징 |지문| make the needed adjustments 필요한 조정을 하다 → |선택지 D| modify equipment 장비를 고치다

표현 정리 according to ~에 따르면　install 설치하다　machine 기기, 기계　edit 수정하다　analyze 분석하다　modify 수정하다　equipment 장비, 용품

해설 첫 번째 이메일에 따르면, Mr. Evanston이 Native Materials를 방문했던 이유는?
(A) 기기를 설치하기 위해
(B) 보고서를 수정하기 위해
(C) 샘플을 분석하기 위해
(D) 장비를 고치기 위해

177. 동의어　★★☆

해설 명사 expertise는 '전문 기술, 전문 지식'의 의미이므로 정답은 (B)이다.　**정답 (B)**

표현 정리 expertise 전문 기술　department 부서　knowledge 지식

해설 첫 번째 이메일, 두 번째 단락, 다섯 번째 줄의 "expertise"와 의미가 가장 가까운 것은?
(A) 부서
(B) 지식
(C) 직업
(D) 회사

178. 세부사항 – Mr. Evanston이 동의한 내용　★☆☆

해설 두 번째 이메일 'That was a decade ago, but I have kept up with trends in the field since then, so I can show you how to analyze the samples.'에서 Mr. Evanston은 Mr. Jones에게 샘플 분석 방법을 보여줄 수 있다고 했으므로 지도를 해 주겠다는 내용의 (A)가 정답이다.　**정답 (A)**

패러프레이징 |지문| show you how to analyze the samples 샘플 분석하는 방법을 보여주다 → |선택지 A| provide guidance 지도해 주다

표현 정리 guidance 지도, 안내　material 재료, 자료　repair 수리하다　microscope 현미경

해설 Mr. Evanston이 하기로 동의한 것은 무엇인가?
(A) Mr. Jones에게 지도를 해 준다.
(B) Mr. Jones에게 재료를 보낸다.
(C) 현미경을 수리한다.
(D) Mr. Jones의 의뢰인을 만난다.

179. 연계 문제 – Janus Technology에 대한 내용　★★☆

해설 첫 번째 이메일, 두 번째 단락 'I vaguely recall you saying that you had some experience with ceramics from your former job, ~.'에서 Mr. Evanston이 이전 직장에서 세라믹 관련 일을 했음을 알 수 있었는데, 두 번째 이메일, 'Janus Technology had a ceramics manufacturing program before it was bought out by the Kempthorn Corporation.'에서 Janus Technology가 세라믹 제조 프로그램을 보유했었다고 말했다. 따라서 Mr. Evanston의 이전 직장이 Janus Technology임을 유추할 수 있으므로 정답은 (C)이다.　**정답 (C)**

🔍 **함정 분석** 두 번째 이메일 'Janus Technology had a ceramics manufacturing program before it was bought out by the Kempthorn Corporation.'에서 Janus Technology가 (A) 다른 회사를 인수한 것이 아니라 다른 회사에 매각되었음을 알 수 있고, (B) 금속 제품을 제조한 것이 아니라 세라믹을 제조했음을 알 수 있다. (D) Baltimore는 이 회사가 있던 장소가 아니라 Mr. Evanston이 4월에 참석할 NMRC 회의가 열릴 장소이다.

표현 정리 purchase 매입하다; 매입　manufacture 제조하다　metal product 금속 제품　employ 고용하다　be located in ~에 위치하다

해설 Janus Technology에 대한 사실 내용은?
(A) 다른 회사를 인수했다.
(B) 금속 제품을 제조했다.
(C) Mr. Evanston을 고용했다.
(D) Baltimore에 자리 잡고 있었다.

180. 연계 문제 – 4월에 있을 일　★☆☆

해설 두 사람이 주고 받은 이메일은 3월 초에 작성된 것이다. 첫 번째 이메일 후반 'so I wonder if you can take a look at it the next time you come to Richmond.'에서 Mr. Jones가 있는 지역은 Richmond임을 알 수 있고, 두 번째 이메일 'I plan to be in your area sometime next month.'에서 Mr. Evanston이 다음 달에 Richmond에 갈 것이라고 했으므로 정답은 (D)이다.　**정답 (D)**

표현 정리 lab director 연구실 실장　receive 받다　industrial 산업, 공업의

해설 4월에 어떤 일이 있을 것인가?
(A) Mr. Jones가 회의에 참석할 것이다.
(B) Mr. Evanston은 연구실 실장을 만날 것이다.
(C) Mr. Jones는 공업용 세라믹을 받을 것이다.
(D) Mr. Evanston은 아마 Richmond에 갈 것이다.

문제 181-185번은 다음 편지와 정보를 참조하시오.

Katelin Lance
280 Barley Ct.
Penn Hills, PA 15228

Ms. Lance 님께,

최근 고객님께서 뉴멕시코를 방문하는데 저희 Enchanted Tours를 이용해 주셔서 감사합니다. **184**지역 요리 맛보기, 박물관 및 갤러리 관람, Taos 마을 답사를 통해 즐거운 시간을 보내셨기를 바랍니다. 저희 목표는 고객님과 같은 방문객들과 우리 주의 아름다움을 공유하는 것입니다. **181**저희가 제공해 드리는 투어를 향상시키는데 도움이 될 수 있도록 간단한 설문지를 완성해 주시기 바랍니다. 저희의 좋았던 점이나 개선할 부분에 대해 말씀해 주십시오. **182**동봉된 설문지 작성이 완료되면, 제공해 드린 봉투에 넣어 회신해 주시기 바랍니다. 우편 요금은 저희가 이미 처리해 놓았습니다. 설문지를 작성해 주신 것에 대한 저희의 감사 표시로 저희 회사 로고가 있는 모자 또는 티셔츠를 보내 드리겠습니다. 설문지에 어떤 것을 선호하시는지를 표시만 해 주시면 됩니다.

David Archuleta

표현 정리 book 예약하다　sampling 맛보는 것　cuisine 요리　museum 박물관　explore 탐험; 답사하다　improve 개선시키다　offering 제공된

것 brief 간단한 complete 완성하다 enclosed 동봉된 take care of
~을 처리하다 postage 우편 요금 as a token of appreciation 감사의
표시로 indicate 나타내다 preference 선호

매력적인 여행

진정한 뉴멕시코 경험

말을 타고 하는 자연 관광

말을 타며 Sangre de Cristo 산의 풍치를 즐기세요. 183(A)모든 단계의 말
타기 경험을 시간당 또는 며칠 단위로 하실 수 있습니다.

제물 낚시 캠핑 여행

183(C),(D)저희 가이드가 자연산 송어가 풍부한 오염되지 않은, 숨겨진 산
속의 개울로 여러분을 안내할 것입니다. 캠핑 장비는 제공됩니다.

지프차 탐험 관광

험준한 황야를 체험하세요. Bisti Badlands의 험한 사막 풍경과 아름다운
Chaco Canyon에 있는 고대 원주민 거주지의 신성한 유적을 소개해 드립
니다.

문화 관광

184뉴멕시코 북부의 문화적 경이로움을 보여 드립니다. 역사적인 마을을 여
행하고, 지역 음식을 맛보며 푸에블로족의 춤을 감상합니다.

표준 관광을 예약하시려면, 1–888–555–8393로 연락하시기 바랍니다.

좀더 상세한 내용 및 사진은 저희 웹사이트 www.enchantedtours.com
에서 확인하실 수 있습니다. 185맞춤 패키지도 가능합니다. 자세한 사항은
david@enchantedtours.com 이메일 주소로 David에게 연락하십시
오.

표현 정리 **enchanted** 황홀한, 매력적인 **authentic** 정통의 **horseback**
말을 타고 하는 **scenic beauty** 풍치, 경치 **hourly** 시간당, 매시간으로
multi-day 여러 날의 **fly fishing** 제물 낚시 **pristine** 자연 그대로의,
오염되지 않은 **mountain stream** 산 속의 개울 **native trout** 자연산 송어
abundant 풍부한 **camping gear** 캠핑 장비 **rugged** 험한, 바위투성이의
wilderness 황야 **desert** 사막 **landscape** 풍경 **scared** 신성한 **ruin**
유적 **ancient** 고대의 **settlement** 거주지 **cultural** 문화적인 **wonder**
경이 **northern** 북쪽의; 북부 **historic** 역사적인 **additional** 추가의
custom 맞춤의, 주문 제작한

181. 주제 – 편지의 목적   ★☆☆

해설 편지 'To help us continue to improve our tour offerings, we would
like to ask you to complete a brief survey. Please let us know what we
did well and what we could do better.'에서 고객에게 서비스의 좋았던 점이
나 개선할 사항에 대한 짧은 설문 조사를 요청하고 있으므로 정답은 (A)이다.
정답 (A)

표현 정리 **purpose** 목적 **solicit** 간청, 요청하다 **feedback** 피드백,
반응, 의견 **lost object** 잃어버린 물건 **confirm** 확인하다 **travel
arrangement** 여행 계획 **promote** 홍보하다 **upcoming** 다가오는

해설 편지의 목적은 무엇인가?
(A) 고객으로부터 피드백을 얻기 위해
(B) 여행객에게 잃어버린 물건을 돌려주기 위해
(C) 여행 계획을 확인하기 위해
(D) 다가오는 투어를 홍보하기 위해

182. 세부사항 – Ms. Lance가 요청받은 일   ★☆☆

해설 편지 'Once you have completed the enclosed survey, please mail
it back to us in the envelope provided.'에서 동봉된 설문 조사를 마치면 제
공된 봉투에 넣어 회신해 달라고 했으므로 정답은 (B)이다.   정답 (B)

표현 정리 **reservation** 예약 **return** 돌려보내다, 회신하다 **enclosure**

동봉된 것 **purchase** 구매하다 **stamp** 우표 **refer** 알아보도록 하다

해설 Ms. Lance는 무엇을 하도록 요청받았나?
(A) 자신의 예약을 확인하라고
(B) 동봉된 것을 회신하라고
(C) 우표를 구입하라고
(D) 친구를 추천하라고

183. 세부사항 – 관광 또는 여행 활동이 아닌 것   ★★☆

해설 두 번째 지문 Enchanted Tours 사의 정보를 보면 말 타고 하는 자연 관
광, 산으로 낚시 캠핑 가기, 지프차 타고 황야로 탐험하는 여행을 포함한 문화 관
광이 소개되고 있지만, 오래된 기차 타기에 대해서는 언급되지 않았으므로 정답은
(B)이다.   정답 (B)

🔍 함정 분석 두 번째 지문 첫 번째 단락 'Hourly rides to multi-day tours
available for riders of all experience levels.'에서 시간당으로 짧게 말
을 탈 수 있다고 해서 (A)가 확인되고, 두 번째 단락 'Our guides will take
you to pristine, hidden mountain streams where native trout are
abundant. Camping gear provided.'에서 송어가 풍부한 산으로 안내된다
고 해 (C)가 확인되고, 캠핑 장비가 제공된다는 것을 통해 야외 취침이 가능하
다는 (D)를 확인할 수 있다.

표현 정리 **activity** 활동 **brief** 짧은 **ride** 타다, 승마하다 **outdoor** 야외의

해설 관광 또는 여행의 일부로 언급되지 않은 활동은?
(A) 짧은 시간 말 타러 가기
(B) 오래된 기차 타기
(C) 산에서 물고기 잡기
(D) 야외에서 취침하기

184. 연계 문제 – Ms. Lance가 선택한 투어   ★☆☆

해설 첫 번째 지문 'We hope you enjoyed sampling the local cuisine,
touring museums and galleries, and exploring the town of Taos.'와 두
번째 지문 Cultural Tour 항목이 같으므로 Ms. Lance는 문화 관광을 선택했음
을 유추할 수 있어 정답은 (D)이다.   정답 (D)

표현 정리 **horseback** 말을 타고 하는 **fly fishing** 제물 낚시 **explorer**
탐험가

해설 Ms. Lance는 어떤 투어를 했나?
(A) 말을 타고 하는 자연 관광
(B) 제물 낚시 여행
(C) 지프차 탐험 관광
(D) 문화 관광

185. 세부사항 – David에게 메일을 보내야 하는 이유   ★☆☆

해설 두 번째 지문 후반 'Custom packages available. Contact David at
david@enchantedtours.com for details.'에서 맞춤용 패키지 상품도 이용할
수 있다고 하면서 자세한 사항은 이메일로 연락하라고 했으므로 (D)가 정답이다.
정답 (D)

표현 정리 **reserve** 예약하다 **make a flight arrangement** 비행편을
예약하다 **discuss** 의논하다

해설 독자들이 David에게 이메일을 보내도록 요청받은 이유는?
(A) 표준 관광 자리 예약을 위해
(B) 비행편을 예약하기 위해
(C) 여행에서 찍은 사진을 주문하기 위해
(D) 다른 관광 옵션을 의논하기 위해

문제 186-190번은 다음 일정, 이메일, 그리고 공지를 참조하시오.

맥기네스 병원

9월 1일 화요일 - 9월 8일 월요일의 주간 일정표

190 경비원	근무 시간
Aaron Parsel	화요일 - 금요일, 오전 6시 30분 - 오후 3시 30분
187(B) Ben Rover	화요일 - 금요일, 오후 3시 30분 - 오전 1시 30분
187(C) Dang Ngo	토요일 - 월요일, 오전 6시 30분 - 오후 3시 30분
186 Harry Liu	토요일 - 월요일, 오후 3시 30분 - 오전 1시 30분

187 근무를 할 수 없는 경우에는 관리자에게 즉시 보고하세요.

표현 정리 weekly schedule 주간 일정표 security guard 경비원 shift 근무 시간 contact 접촉하다, 연락하다 make a shift 근무하다

수신: Ben Rover <brover@mcguiness.com>
발신: Ted Newsome <tnewsome@mcguiness.com>
날짜: 8월 19일
제목: 근무 시간 변경

Ben,

187(D) 9월 1일 화요일로 예정된 당신의 치과 진료에 대해 미리 알려줘서 고마워요. 회복하는데 하루나 이틀이 필요할 수 있다고 했어요. 187(A) 며칠 동안 임시로 대체할 사람을 고용하는 대신, 당신과 Harry의 근무 시간을 바꾸기로 했어요. 그렇게 하면 필요할 때 회사를 쉴 수 있고, 신뢰할 만한 직원이 근무 시간을 채울 수 있습니다. 186 Harry는 근무 시간 변경에 동의했어요. 187(C) 각각의 근무시간 사이에 그가 어떻게 전환조정을 하길 바라는지 알아보기 위해 9월 1일 전에 188 Dang Ngo에게 연락해보세요.

질문이 있으면 알려주세요.

Ted

표현 정리 dental procedure 치과 진료 recover 회복하다 instead of ~하는 대신 hire 고용하다 temporary replacement 임시 후임자 get the time off 회사를 쉬다 trusted 신뢰할 만한 on hand 출석하여, 그 자리에 있는 coordinate with ~와 협력하다 get in touch with ~와 연락하다 transition 변경, 전환

상급 응급치료 교육

189 McGuiness Hospital의 모든 비 의료 직원들은 10월에 MedAlert라고 불리는 상급 응급치료 교육 프로그램을 이수해야 합니다. 과거에 응급치료 수료증을 받았다 해도, MedAlert 교육을 받고 시험에 통과해야 합니다. MedAlert는 구체적인 고위험 상황에 대한 대처 기술을 여러분에게 교육시킴으로써 기본적인 응급 치료 지식을 보충해 줄 것입니다.

고위험 상황에 대한 대처 방법을 갖추게 하기 위해 훈련부는 MedAlert 교육 과정을 다음과 같이 제공합니다.

190 보안부   10월 5일, 월요일 (오전 7시 - 오후 3시)
관리부   10월 6일, 화요일 (오전 7시 - 오후 3시)
청소부   10월 7일, 수요일 (오전 7시 - 오후 3시)
행정부   10월 8일, 목요일 (오전 7시 - 오후 3시)

더불어, 여러분 부서에 배정된 날짜에 참석하지 못할 경우에는 내선번호 4859로 Fred Veranda에게 연락 주세요. 다음 세션에 배정해 드리도록 해보겠습니다. 추가적인 교육은 필요할 경우에 추가될 것입니다.

표현 정리 non-medical 비 의료의 complete 완수하다, 이수하다 advanced 상급의, 고급의 first aid 응급치료 certification 수료증 supplement 보충하다 specific 구체적인 high-risk 고위험의 equip

---

A with B A에게 B를 갖추게 하다 handle 처리하다 as follows 다음과 같이 security department 보안부 maintenance department 관리부 custodial department 청소부 administrative department 행정부 in addition 게다가, 또한 assign 배정하다 extension 내선번호 attempt to + 동사 ~을 시도하다, 노력하다 additional 추가적인 add 더하다, 추가하다 as needed 필요할 경우

186. 연계 문제 – Mr. Liu에 관한 내용 ★★☆

해설 근무 일정표에서 Mr. Liu는 'Saturday – Monday 3:30 P.M. - 1:30 A.M.'에 근무를 하기로 되어 있다. 또한 이메일에 보면, Mr. Rover와 Mr. Liu의 근무시간을 바꾸고, Mr. Liu는 그 변경에 동의했다고 되어 있다. 그러므로 Mr. Liu는 Mr. Rover의 근무시간인 9월 1일에 일을 한다는 것을 확인할 수 있으므로 정답은 (A)이다. 정답 (A)

표현 정리 be supposed to ~하기로 되어 있다 new employee 신입 직원 prefer 선호하다

해석 Mr. Liu에 관해 언급된 내용은?
(A) 그는 9월 1일에 근무하기로 되어 있다.
(B) 그는 신입 직원이다.
(C) 그는 최근 치과 진료를 받았다.
(D) 그는 오전 근무를 선호한다.

187. 연계 문제 – Mr. Newsome에 대한 내용 ★★☆

해설 첫 번째 지문, 마지막 문장 'Please contact your manager right away if you cannot make a shift.'와 두 번째 지문, 첫 번째 문장 'I appreciate your contacting me in advance about your dental procedure scheduled for Tuesday, September 1.'를 비교해 보면, 이메일을 보낸 Mr. Newsome은 Mr. Rover의 관리자라는 것을 알 수 있기 때문에, 정답은 (B)이다. 정답 (B)

🔍 함정 분석 이메일 첫 번째 단락 'Instead of hiring a temporary replacement for a few days, I have decided to just have you and Harry switch shifts.'에서 임시 근로자를 구하는 대신 동료와 근무 시간을 바꾸기로 했으므로 (A)는 틀린 내용, 이메일 두 번째 단락 'Since you usually coordinate with Aaron, you also need to get in touch with Dang before September 1 to see how he wants to manage the transition between shifts.'에서 Mr. Newsome은 Mr. Rover에게 Mr. Dang과 대화해 보라고 알려줄 뿐, Mr. Ngo와 직접 대화를 할 거라는 내용은 없으므로 (C) 역시 틀린 내용, 이메일 첫 번째 단락 'You also mentioned that you may need a day or two to recover. Instead of hiring a temporary replacement for a few days,~ .'에서 회사를 며칠 쉴 사람은 Mr. Rover임을 확인할 수 있다.

표현 정리 temporary worker 임시 근로자 supervise 감독하다 take a few days off 며칠 쉬다

해석 Mr. Newsome에 대해 암시된 것은?
(A) 그는 임시 근로자를 구할 수 없었다.
(B) 그는 Mr. Rover를 감독한다.
(C) 그는 Mr. Ngo와 대화할 계획이다.
(D) 그는 며칠 쉴 것이다.

188. 세부사항 – Mr. Newsome이 Mr. Rover에게 요청한 사항 ★☆☆

해설 이메일 지문의 두 번째 단락에 있는, 'Please get in touch with Dang Ngo before September 1 to see how he wants to manage the transition between your respective shifts.'에서 근무시간 변경을 위해서 Mr. Ngo와 연락을 해보라고 했기 때문에, get in touch with를 coordinate으로 바꾼 (A)가 정답이 된다. 정답 (A)

표현 정리 coordinate 조정하다 coworker 동료, 함께 일하는 사람 permanently 영원히 time off 일시적 중단, 휴식

해석 Mr. Newsome이 Mr. Rover에게 요청한 것은?
(A) 동료와 조정하기
(B) 근무시간에 일찍 도착하기
(C) 근무시간을 영원히 바꾸기
(D) 휴식시간을 요청하기

189. 세부사항 – 직원들이 요청 받는 일　★☆☆
해설 공지 첫 번째 단락 'All non-medical staff at McGuiness Hospital must complete an advanced first-aid training program, called MedAlert, in October.'에서 응급치료 교육을 이수해야 한다고 했으므로 (B)가 정답이다.
정답 (B)

표현 정리 medical examination 건강 검진 obtain 획득하다 additional 추가적인 reduce 줄이다 risky 위험한 behavior 행동

해석 공지에서 직원들은 무엇을 하도록 요청받는가?
(A) 건강 검진에 통과하라고
(B) 추가 기술을 익히라고
(C) 일정을 변경하라고
(D) 위험한 행동을 줄이라고

190. 연계 문제 – Mr. Parse이 MedAlert 교육을 받을 날짜　★★☆
해설 근무 일정표를 보면 Mr. Parsel은 경비원이므로 보안부 소속임을 알 수 있는데, 이를 공지에서 확인해 보면 10월 5일에 교육이 예정돼 있음을 알 수 있으므로 정답은 (A)이다.
정답 (A)

표현 정리 take a training 교육을 받다

해석 Mr. Parsel은 언제 MedAlert 교육을 받을 것인가?
(A) 10월 5일
(B) 10월 6일
(C) 10월 7일
(D) 10월 8일

문제 191-195번은 다음 발표, 기사, 그리고 편지를 참조하시오.

> #### Sky Air, 목표를 높이 세우다
>
> 대중적인 국내 저가 항공사인 Sky Air는 8곳의 새로운 목적지에 취항할 계획을 갖고 있습니다. 우리는 5월 1일에 동남부 지역에 있는 다음과 같은 목적지에 매일 항공편을 제공할 것입니다: Hammet, Franklin, Pomona, 및 New Bay. ¹⁹²동북부 지역의 새로운 목적지로 가는 서비스는 6월에 시작할 것입니다. 여름이 끝날 무렵 Sky Air는 전국 72개 공항에서 운항하게 됩니다. 저희 웹 사이트 www.skyair.com에서 현재 및 향후 목적지의 지도를 보십시오.
>
> 항공사의 성장을 축하하기 위해, 저희는 비행기표, 식권 및 호텔 숙박권과 같은 상품을 증정하고 있습니다. ¹⁹⁵저희 웹사이트(www.skyair.com)에 방문하셔서 늦어도 4월 30일까지 참가 신청서를 작성해 주시면 누구나 참여하실 수 있습니다.

표현 정리 popular 대중적인, 인기 있는 low-cost 저가의 domestic air carrier 국내 항공사 destination 목적지 the southeastern region 동남부 지역 flight 항공편, 비행 celebrate 축하하다, 기념하다 give away 증정하다 prize 상품 airline ticket 비행기표 meal voucher 식권 participate 참여하다 complete an entry form 신청서를 작성하다

> ¹⁹²Rockford (6월 3일) – ¹⁹³⁽ᴮ⁾Rockford 지역 주민들은 민간 항공사 서비스를 5년 동안 기다려왔다. 현재 개인 전용기만이 Rockford의 Devon White Municipal Airport에 취항하고 있다. ¹⁹³⁽ᴰ⁾이러한 상황은 Sky Air의 첫 항공편이 Rockford의 유일한 공항을 이륙하게 되는 ¹⁹²내일이면 바뀌게 될 것이다.

"Portland으로 가는 비행기를 탈 수 있다면 좋을 것입니다."라고 Portland에 사는 여동생을 방문하고 싶어하는 Rene Charles는 말했다. Costal Airlines가 Devon White Municipal Airport로 가는 항공 서비스 제공을 중단한 이후 ¹⁹³⁽ᴬ⁾Ms. Charles는 Portland까지 10시간을 운전해 가야만 했다. "저와 같은 일반 여행객들이 이 공항을 다시 이용할 수 있게 되어 기쁩니다."

¹⁹⁴이 공항 관리공단 측이 발표한 언론 보도에 따르면 Rockford 다운타운을 운행하는 셔틀버스 서비스가 올해 말이면 제공될 거라고 한다. 또한 공항에는 유료 주차가 가능하다. 물론 택시 서비스도 이용 가능하다.

표현 정리 resident 주민 commercial airline 민간 항공사 private plane 개인 전용기 take off 이륙하다 catch a flight to ~행 비행기를 타다 look forward to -ing ~을 기대하다 regular traveler 일반 여행객 press release 언론 in the meantime 한편 paid parking 유료 주차 available 이용 가능한

> Vincent Barone
> 12 Robin Lane
> Rockford
>
> 5월 3일
>
> Mr. Barone 님께,
>
> ¹⁹⁵2장의 식권을 받을 수 있게 선정되신 것을 축하 드립니다! 각 식권은 본인이 선택한 도시락 한 개와 음료수와 교환될 수 있습니다.
>
> ¹⁹⁵기내 주문을 하실 때 식권을 승무원에게 보여주시기만 하면 됩니다. 식권은 오늘부터 12개월 동안 유효합니다.
>
> Nancy Gabaldon
> Director of Passenger Relations
> Sky Air

표현 정리 exchange 교환하다 boxed meal 도시락 of one's choice 자기가 고른, 스스로 선택한 simply 그저 present 제시하다, 보여주다 flight attendant 승무원 place an order 주문하다 in-flight 기내의 remain valid 유효하다

191. 세부사항 – Sky Air에 관한 내용　★☆☆
해설 공고의 첫 번째 문장인 'Sky Air, a popular low-cost domestic air carrier, is planning to fly to eight new destinations.'에서 popular라는 단어를 사용했기 때문에 이 단어를 well-known이라는 동의어로 표현한 (A)가 정답이 된다.
정답 (A)

표현 정리 well-known 잘 알려진, 유명한 be headquartered in ~에 본부를 두고 있다

해석 공고에서 Sky Air에 관해 언급된 것은?
(A) 잘 알려진 항공사다.
(B) 동남부 지역에 본사가 있다.
(C) 국제 공항에 취항하고 있다.
(D) 현재 70여 군데 이상 항공편을 운행하고 있다.

192. 연계문제 – Rockford에 대한 내용　★☆☆
해설 공고의 첫 번째 단락의 'Service to new destinations in the northeastern region will start in June.'에서 동북부 지역으로 가는 서비스는 6월에 선보일 거라고 하였으며, 6월 3일 Rockford 기사에서 'That will change tomorrow when Sky Air's first flight out of Rockford's only airport takes off.'에서 항공 서비스가 내일이면 시작된다고 하였으므로 Rockford는 미국의 동북부 지역이라는 것을 유추할 수 있다.
정답 (D)

표현 정리 locate 위치하다 a body of water 수역(물줄기) private

40

airport 민간 공항　major 주요한　urban area 도시지역

해석 Rockford에 대해 유추할 수 있는 것은?
　(A) 수역을 따라 위치해 있다.
　(B) 민간 공항이 있다.
　(C) 주요 도시 지역이다.
　(D) 미국의 동북부 지역에 있다.

193. 유추 – Coastal Airlines에 대한 내용　★★☆

해설 기사 첫 번째 단락 첫 번째 줄 'Rockford-area residents have been waiting five years for the return of a commercial airline service.'에서 Rockford 주민들이 민간 항공 서비스를 5년 동안 기다려왔다고 했으므로 (B)가 정답임을 유추할 수 있다.　**정답 (B)**

🔍**함정 분석** 기사의 두 번째 단락에서, 'Since Coastal Airlines stopped offering service to Devon White Municipal Airport, Ms. Charles had to drive ten hours to Portland.'를 통해 이 항공사는 Portland로 가는 비행편을 제공했다는 사실만 알 수 있을 뿐이다. Rockford 지역에서 6월 3일자로 내보낸 기사에서는 내일부터 Sky Air의 서비스가 시작된다고 하며, Coastal Airlines에 관한 내용이 아니므로 (D)도 맞지 않는 내용이다.

표현 정리 used to + 동사 (과거에) ~했다　stop -ing ~하는 것을 그만두다
no longer 더 이상 ~이 아닌　in business 사업을 하는

해석 Coastal Airlines에 대해 암시된 내용은?
　(A) Hammet과 Franklin으로 비행했다.
　(B) 5년 전에 Rockford로 비행하는 것을 중단했다.
　(C) 더 이상 운영하지 않는다.
　(D) 올해 말까지 Rockford로 돌아올 것이다.

194. 세부사항 – Devon White Municipal Airport에 대한 내용　★☆☆

해설 기사 세 번째 단락 'A press release from the airport's management said that shuttle service to and from downtown Rockford will be offered by the end of the year.'에서 Devon White Municipal Airport가 위치한 Rockford를 운행하는 셔틀버스 서비스가 제공될 것이라고 했으므로 (B)가 정답이다.　**정답 (B)**

패러프레이징 |지문| shuttle service ~ will be offered 셔틀버스 서비스가 제공될 것이다 → |선택지 B| add additional ground transportation 추가적인 지상 교통을 제공하다

표현 정리 expand 확장하다　parking facility 주차 시설　add 더하다, 포함시키다　ground transportation 지상 교통　charge A to B B에게 A를 청구하다　fee 요금

해석 Devon White Municipal Airport에 대해 언급된 것은?
　(A) 최근에 주차 시설을 확장했다.
　(B) 추가적인 지상 교통 시스템을 포함시킬 계획이다.
　(C) 상업 터미널을 지으려고 한다.
　(D) 택시 운전사들에게 요금을 청구한다.

195. 연계 문제 – Mr. Barone에 대한 사실 내용　★☆☆

해설 첫 번째 지문 마지막 단락 'Anyone can participate by completing an entry form at www.skyair.com up to April 30.'에서 항공사 웹사이트를 방문해 참가 신청서를 작성하면 누구나 참여 가능하다고 했는데, 세 번째 지문 'Congratulations on being selected to receive two meal vouchers!'에서 Mr. Barone이 선정되었다고 말한 것으로 보아 그가 신청서를 작성했음을 알 수 있으므로 정답은 (C)가 된다.　**정답 (C)**

패러프레이징 |지문| complete an entry form 참가 신청서를 작성하다 → |선택지 C| fill out a form 양식을 작성하다

표현 정리 frequent passenger 단골 승객　fill out a form 양식을

작성하다

해석 Mr. Barone에 대한 사실 내용은?
　(A) 그는 Sky Air의 단골 승객이다.
　(B) 그는 최근에 Rockford로 이사했다.
　(C) 그는 Sky Air의 웹사이트에 있는 양식을 작성했다.
　(D) 그는 12개월 후에 여행을 갈 계획이다.

문제 196-200번은 다음 이메일, 웹페이지, 그리고 기사를 참조하시오.

수신: 동물원 후원자
발신: Miles Gagan
Re: 동물원 행사
날짜: 5월 18일

196(B), 200 지난주 열린 특별 기금모금 행사인 "Art at the Zoo"에 참석해 주셨던 Payton 주변에 계시는 모든 분들께 감사 드립니다. 참석하지 못한 분들을 위해 행사 사진을 저희 웹사이트에 올릴 것입니다. 본 기금모금 행사는 또한 남미 조류 전시회의 개관을 기념하였습니다. **196(A), (C)** 아름답고 영구적인 이 전시회는 4개의 기후(열대 우림, 산지, 고지대 사막 및 해안 평야)를 테마로 한 배경으로, 전 대륙에서 출품된 36종에 달하는 새들이 전시됩니다. 다음 달에 Dr. Juan Nogales 큐레이터의 강연에 참석해 주세요. 다음 달로 예정된 여러 개의 다른 행사들도 있습니다. **197** 동물원 서포터들은 저희가 진행하는 모든 동물원 음악회 관람 티켓을 반값에 구입하실 수 있습니다.

표현 정리 attend 참석하다　fundraiser (기금) 모금행사　in and around 주변에　make it 도착하다, 참석하다　post 올리다, 게시하다　mark 기념하다　exhibit 전시회　permanent 영구적인　feature 등장하다　species 종　continent 대륙　climate-themed 기후를 테마로 한　setting 배경　rainforest 열대 우림　high desert 고지대 사막　coastal plains 해안 평야　curator 큐레이터, 관장　performance 공연　for half price 절반 가격에, 반값에

http://www.paytonzoo.org			
전시회	방문 계획	이벤트	서포터 되기

6월 4일
조부모님의 날: 오전 9시 – 오후 4시 30분
손주들과 함께 오신 조부모님들은 무료 입장이며, 극장에서 스토리텔링이 있을 것입니다.

6월 11일
어린이들을 위한 토요 세미나: 오전 10시 – 오전 11시 30분
어린이는 영장류 큐레이터인 Dr. Wanda Lee를 만나 원숭이에 관한 모든 것을 배울 수 있습니다. 게임, 공예 및 다른 재미난 활동이 준비돼 있습니다. 등록이 필요하며, 3339-7595로 전화주세요.

6월 23일
동물원 음악회: 오후 6시 – 오후 9시
197 업무 시간 후에 동물원으로 오셔서 Colbert Quarter가 공연하는 라이브 음악을 즐기세요. 저녁식사를 준비해 오거나 저희 Wild Animal Cafe에서 소풍 바구니용 식사를 구입하세요. 티켓 구매를 위해 여기를 클릭하세요.

198 **6월 26일**
특별 행사: 오후 2시 – 오후 4시
Dr. Juan Nogales의 강연을 들어보세요. Dr. Nogales는 새롭게 선보이는 남미 조류 전시회에 대한 이야기를 해 주실 겁니다.

표현 정리 free admission 무료 입장　grandparents 조부모

grandchildren 손주들　take place 열리다, 발생하다　primates 영장류
crafts 공예　registration 등록　normal hours 업무 시간　picnic
basket meals 소풍 바구니용 식사

동물원에서 남미로의 여행
Michael Kendall

200저희 지역 동물원은 남미 조류 전시회 개관 덕분에 좋아졌다. 이는 분명
히 Juan Nogales 큐레이터가 좋아서 하는 작업이다. **198,199**지난 토요
일에 Dr. Nogales는 에콰도르의 한 마을에서 하버드 대학까지 오게 된 그
의 여정과 자연을 가까이하며 성장한 덕분에 모든 조류에 매혹될 수 있었다
는 이야기를 전했다. 그의 이야기를 들을 기회가 없었다면, 조류에 대한 그의
열정을 이 아름답고 유익한 전시회에서 경험할 수 있다. 더 자세한 정보는
www.paytonzoo.org를 방문하면 알 수 있다.

표현 정리 get better 더 좋아지다　**thanks to** ~덕분에　**clearly** 분명히
labor of love 자진해서 좋아서 하는 작업　**journey** 여정　**instill**
주입시키다, 불어넣다　**fascination** 매혹　**avian life** 조류　**passion** 열정
informative 유익한

196. 세부사항 – 남미 조류 전시회에 대한 내용　★★☆
해설 Mr. Gagan이 동물원 서포터들에게 보낸 이메일에서 남미 조류 전시회에
대한 내용이 언급되었다. 그 내용에 사진 촬영에 대한 이야기는 없으므로 (D)가
정답이다.　　정답 (D)

🔍 **함정 분석 이메일** 'This beautiful permanent exhibit ~.'에서 전시회는
영구적인 것이므로 (A)는 맞다. 이메일은 5월 18일에 보내졌는데, 'Thank
you to everyone in and around Payton who attended our special
fundraiser event "Art at the Zoo" last week.'에서 특별 기금모금 행사가
지난주에 열렸다고 했으므로 (B) 역시 맞다. 또한 'This beautiful permanent
exhibit features nearly three dozen species ~ .'에서 알 수 있듯이 36종
에 달하는 다양한 종류의 새들이 전시되므로 (C)의 내용도 맞다.

패러프레이징 |지문| permanent exhibit 영구적인 전시회 → **|선택지 A|**
remain ~ indefinitely 무기한으로 남아있다
|지문| three dozen species 36종의 → **|선택지 C|** different types of 다양한
종류의

표현 정리 remain 남아 있다　**indefinitely** 무기한으로　**extensively**
광범위하게　**photograph** 사진 촬영하다

해석 남미 조류 전시회에 대해 언급되지 않은 것은?
　(A) 동물원에 무기한으로 남아 있을 것이다.
　(B) 5월에 대중에 공개되었다.
　(C) 다양한 유형의 새들을 포함한다.
　(D) 광범위하게 사진 촬영되었다.

197. 연계 문제 – 동물원 후원자들에 대한 내용　★★☆
해설 이메일 마지막 줄 'Zoo Supporters can get tickets to our all Zoo
Music performances for half price.'에서 동물원 서포터들은 동물원 음악
회 티켓을 반값에 구할 수 있음을 알 수 있는데, 동물원 웹페이지에서 Colbert
Quarter가 언급된 6월 23일 행사를 보면, 그가 뮤지션임을 확인할 수 있으므로
정답은 (B)이다.　　정답 (B)

표현 정리 mostly 대부분, 주로　**at a discount** 할인가에　**collect**
donations 기부금을 모금하다　**host** 개최하다

해석 동물원 후원자들에 대해 암시된 것은?
　(A) 대부분 손주들이 있는 노인들이다.
　(B) Colbert Quarter를 할인가에 볼 수 있다.
　(C) 기금 마련 행사에서 자원봉사자로 일했다.
　(D) 큐레이터들이 주최하는 특별 행사에 초대를 받았다.

198. 연계 문제 – Mr. Kendall이 동물원을 방문한 날　★☆☆
해설 Mr. Kendall은 세 번째 지문인 기사 작성자이다. 지문 중반 'Last
Saturday, Dr. Nogales spoke about his journey from a village in
Ecuador to Harvard University and how growing up so close to nature
instilled in him a fascination with all avian life.'에서 Dr. Nogales가 강연을
한 날에 Mr. Kendall이 동물원을 방문했음을 짐작할 수 있는데, 두 번째 지문에
서 Dr. Nogales가 출연하는 행사 날짜를 찾아 보면 6월 26일이라는 것이 확인되
어 정답은 (D)이다.　　정답 (D)

해석 Mr. Kendall은 언제 동물원을 방문했나?
　(A) 6월 4일
　(B) 6월 11일
　(C) 6월 23일
　(D) 6월 26일

199. 세부사항 – 큐레이터에 대한 내용　★★☆
해설 기사 'Last Saturday, Dr. Nogales spoke about his journey from a
village in Ecuador to Harvard University and how growing up so close
to nature instilled in him a fascination with all avian life.'에서 남미 조류 전
시회의 큐레이터인 Dr. Nogales는 그의 어린 시절을 Ecuador에서 보냈음을 알
수 있으므로 (B)가 정답이다.　　정답 (B)

패러프레이징 |지문| his journey from a village in Ecuador to Harvard
University Ecuador의 한 마을에서 Harvard 대학까지 온 그의 여정 → **|선택
지 B|** spend his childhood in Ecuador 그의 어린 시절을 Ecuador에서 보내
다

표현 정리 give a talk 강연하다　**childhood** 어린 시절　**collect** 수집하다

해석 남미 조류 전시회의 큐레이터에 대해 언급된 내용은?
　(A) 그는 두 번째 강연을 할 계획이 있다.
　(B) 그는 어린 시절을 Ecuador에서 보냈다.
　(C) 그는 평생 새들을 수집해 왔다.
　(D) 그는 대학에서 새들에 대한 강의를 했다.

200. 연계 문제 – Mr. Kendall에 대한 사실 내용　★★☆
해설 Mr. Kendall은 기사를 작성한 기자이다. 기사 첫 번째 줄 'Our local zoo
just got better thanks to the opening of the South American birds
exhibit.'에서 '우리 지역 동물원'이라고 했는데, 지역은 이메일 첫 번째줄 'Thank
you to everyone in and around Payton who attended our special
fundraiser event "Art at the Zoo" last week.'에서 Payton을 의미한다고 볼
수 있으므로 (D)가 정답이다.　　정답 (D)

표현 정리 attend 참석하다　**interview** 인터뷰하다

해석 Mr. Kendall에 대한 사실 내용은?
　(A) 그는 동물원 서포터이다.
　(B) 그는 "Art at the Zoo"에 참석했다.
　(C) 그는 Mr. Nogales를 인터뷰했다.
　(D) 그는 Payton 지역에서 산다.

(B) 너무 습할 때 창문을 열라고
(C) 퇴근 전에 조명을 켜라고
(D) 일과가 끝난 후 사무실 온도를 낮추라고

문제 147-148번은 다음 이메일을 참조하시오.

발신: Sally Targe
수신: Office Managers
발송: 8월 3일, 월요일
제목: 하루를 마감하는 준비

관리자분 께,

최근 공과금이 급증했습니다. 147정상으로 돌리기 위해, 낮 시간 동안의 전기 사용에 더욱 유의해 주시고, 매일 저녁 퇴근 전에 추가 조치를 취해 줄 것을 부탁 드립니다. 모든 조명을 끄는 것을 확실해 주시기 바랍니다. 그러나 사무실 내의 습도를 피해 곰팡이가 생기는 것을 방지하고자 하니 에어컨을 끄거나 창문을 열어 놓지는 말아 주세요. 148대신, 온도 조절 장치를 섭씨 24도로 낮춰주십시오.

Sally Targe
회사 관리자

표현 정리 surge 급증, 폭등 monthly utility bills 공과금(전기, 가스, 수도 요금) get back on track 정상으로 돌아오다 pay attention to ~에 유의하다 electricity 전기 usage 사용 take measures 조치를 취하다 make sure 확실히 하다 turn off 끄다 avoid 피하다 humidity 습기 lead to ~로 이어지다 mold 곰팡이 슬다 thermostat 온도 조절 장치 turn down to ~로 낮추다 Celsius 섭씨

---

147. 주제 – 이메일의 목적 ★★☆

해설 두 번째 문장 'In order to get back on track, we ask that you pay more attention to electricity usage during the day and take these extra measures before leaving the office every evening.'을 통해 Ms. Targe는 전기 요금이 폭등한 것을 걱정하면서 낮 시간뿐 아니라 퇴근 시에도 주의를 기울여 달라고 부탁하고 있으므로 (B)가 가장 적절한 정답이다. **정답 (B)**

🔍 **함정 분석** 'Recently, we have had a surge in our monthly utility bills.'에서 최근 발생한 문제를 언급하면서 시작하지만 직원들에게 문제 해결을 위해 부탁하는 내용이 포함되어 있어 (C)가 답이 되기에는 충분하지 않고, Do not, however, turn off the air conditioning에서 모든 장비를 꺼 달라고 요청한 것은 아니므로 (D) 역시 오답이다.

표현 정리 inquire 알아보다, 문의하다 save 절약하다 recurring 반복하는 notify 알리다 equipment 장비

해석 Ms. Targe가 이메일을 보낸 이유는?
(A) 에너지를 절약하는 방법들에 대해 알아보기 위해
(B) 반복되는 행동을 요청하기 위해
(C) 회사 문제를 직원들에게 알리기 위해
(D) 관리자들에게 모든 장비들을 꺼 달라고 요청하기 위해

---

148. 세부사항 – 직원들이 부탁받은 일 ★☆☆

해설 이메일 마지막 문장 'Instead, turn the thermostat down to 24 degrees Celsius.'에서 온도 조절 장치를 24도로 내려줄 것을 요청하고 있음을 알 수 있으므로 정답은 (D)이다. **정답 (D)**

패러프레이징 |지문| turn the thermostat down 온도 조절 장치를 낮추다 → |선택지 D| lower the office temperature 사무실 온도를 낮추다

표현 정리 humid 습한

해석 직원들이 부탁받은 일은 무엇인가?
(A) 낮 동안 에어컨을 끄라고

문제 149-150번은 다음 문자 메시지를 참조하시오.

Celine Bannel 149이사회 회의 자료집 준비를 오전 8시 55분까지 끝낼 수 있나요? 그러면 회의실을 준비하는데 5분의 여유가 더 생기거든요.
오전 7시 25분

William Venice 아직 마지막 도표를 출력하는 일이 남았지만, 최선을 다 하겠습니다.
오전 7시 36분

Celine Bannel 모든 인턴이 바쁠 것 같지는 않아요. 회의 시작 전에 회의실이 준비돼야 해요. 늦어서는 안 돼요.
오전 7시 40분

William Venice 150일을 도와 줄 두 명의 인턴을 마케팅부에서 데려왔어요.
오전 7시 43분

Celine Bannel 완성된 자료집과 함께 회의실로 갈 때, 메시지 보내줘요. 고마워요.
오전 7시 49분

William Venice Ms. Bannel, 자료집을 갖고 지금 회의실에 왔습니다. 준비는 거의 다 되었습니다.
오전 8시 52분

Celine Bannel 좋습니다. 곧 봐요.
오전 8시 53분

표현 정리 put together 준비하다 board meeting 이사회 회의 packets 자료집 set up 세팅하다, 준비하다 conference room 회의실 delay 지연 grab 붙잡다 lend a hand 일손을 돕다 head to ~로 향하다 completed 완성된

---

149. 유추 – 중역 회의에 대한 내용 ★☆☆

해설 Celine Bannel이 오전 7시 25분에 보낸 메시지 'Can you finish putting together the board meeting packets by 8:55 A.M.? That will give us an extra 5 minutes to set up the conference room.'에서 오전 8시 55분까지 자료 준비를 마치면 5분 동안 회의실 준비를 할 수 있을 것이라고 했으므로 회의는 9시에 열릴 예정임을 알 수 있어 정답은 (C)이다. **정답 (C)**

표현 정리 reschedule 일정을 변경하다

해석 이사회 회의에 관해 암시된 것은?
(A) 인턴들에 대한 것이다.
(B) 5분이 소요될 것이다.
(C) 오전 9시에 시작할 것이다.
(D) 일정이 변경되었다.

---

150. 의도 파악하기 ★☆☆

해설 Ms. Bannel이 'I don't think all of the interns are busy. We need the room set up by the time the meeting starts. No delays.'라고 한 말은 곧 바쁘지 않은 인턴도 있을지 모르니 그들에게 도움을 요청하라는 의미로 볼 수 있는데, 이는 이어지는 Mr. Venice의 답변 'I grabbed two interns from Marketing to lend a hand.'에서 도움을 받기 위해 인턴을 데려왔다고 한 말을 통해서도 알 수 있으므로 정답은 (A)이다. **정답 (A)**

표현 정리 criticize 비판하다 attend 참석하다

해석 Ms. Bannel이 오전 7시 40분에 보낸 메시지에서 '모든 인턴이 바쁘지는 않을 것이라고 한 이유는?
(A) Mr. Venice가 도움을 요청하도록 제안하기 위해
(B) Mr. Venice의 관리 스타일을 비판하기 위해
(C) 사무실에 생긴 문제를 보고하기 위해
(D) 인턴들을 회의에 참석하도록 초대하기 위해

문제 151-153번은 다음 양식을 참조하시오.

HOLTZ Corporation

비품 청구서

주문되어야 하는 필요 물품:

이름: *Mark Colbert*

날짜: *3월 13일*

부서: *판매부*

직원 ID#: *S201343*

필요 물품: *화이트 보드 마커*

수량: *10*

151필요 시기: *가능한 한 빨리*

특별 지시:

매장에 마커가 하나밖에 남아 있지 않습니다. 151*Case에 의해 생산된 마커를 사용하고 있지만 어떤 브랜드라도 괜찮습니다. 넓적한 끝을 가진 검은색 마커라는 것이 중요합니다. 4층 저희 방에 도착하는 즉시 배달될 수 있도록 부탁 드립니다.*

배달 장소: *빌딩 B 4층, 판매부*

해당 부서에서만 사용:

152수령자: *Anita Jones*   완료된 주문: *Yes*

153일시: *3월 13일, 오전 9시 10분*   주문 일시: *3월 13일, 오전 9시 30분*

머리글자: *AJ*   배달된 주문: _____

표현 정리 **supply request** 비품 청구 **dry erase marker** 화이트 보드 마커 **instruction** 지시 **be down to** ~밖에 남지 않다 **sales room** 매장 **tip** 끝 **deliver** 배달하다 **cubicle** 좁은 방 **initials** 머리글자

151. 세부사항 – Mr. Colbert가 서류상 요청하지 않은 것 ★★☆

해설 SPECIAL INSTRUCTIONS의 내용 중에 'We have been using markers made by Case, but any brand will do.'에서 현재는 Case 사가 생산한 마커를 사용하고 있지만 어떤 브랜드도 상관 없다고 했기 때문에 특정 브랜드를 요구하고 있지 않다고 볼 수 있으므로 정답은 (D)이다.   정답 (D)

🔍 **함정 분석** 'The important thing is that they have a broad tip and that they be black.'에서 검은색을 주문하라고 했으므로 (A)는 언급되었고, 'Please have the new markers delivered to our cubicle on the 4th floor as soon as they arrive.'에서 부서로 배달을 요청하고 있으므로 (B)도 확인된다. 'DATE NEEDED BY: As soon as possible'에서 가능한 한 빨리 필요하다고 했으므로 (C) 역시 맞는 내용이다.

표현 정리 **specific** 특정한

해석 Mr. Colbert가 양식에서 요청하지 않은 것은?
(A) 마커는 특정 색일 필요가 있다.
(B) 마커는 그에게 배달될 필요가 있다.
(C) 마커는 빨리 주문될 필요가 있다.
(D) 마커는 특정 브랜드일 필요가 있다.

152. 유추 – Anita Jones의 직업 ★★☆

해설 Anita Jones는 양식 후반 'Received by: Anita Jones'에서 비품 청구서를 처리한 사람이라는 것을 알 수 있고, 양식 상단에 보면, 이 양식이 HOLTZ Corporation에서 사용하는 것임을 알 수 있으므로 HOLTZ 직원이 맞아 정답은 (C)이다.   정답 (C)

표현 정리 **assistant** 조수 **office supply** 사무용품 **clerk** 직원 **mailroom** 우편물실

해석 Anita Jones는 누구인가?
(A) 판매부 내 Mr. Colbert의 조수

(B) 사무용품 매장 직원
(C) HOLTZ Corporation의 직원
(D) HOLTZ Corporation 우편물실 직원

153. 세부사항 – 비품 주문에 대한 내용 ★★☆

해설 'Date and time: March 13 9:10 A.M.'에서 비품 청구서가 처리된 일시는 3월 13일 오전 9시 10분이고, 'Order Date and time: March 13 9:30 A.M.'을 보면 주문이 이루어진 일시 역시 3월 13일 오전 9시 30분으로 서류가 접수된 날과 주문된 날이 같은 날임을 확인할 수 있어 정답은 (B)이다.   정답 (B)

🔍 **함정 분석** SUPPLY REQUEST FORM으로 비품 청구가 이루어졌으므로 전화로 제출되었다고 보기 어려워 (A)는 오답이다. 신청자인 Mark Colbert와 서류를 수리한 Anita Jones가 문서상에 나타나지만 비품 주문 과정에 신청자가 관여했다고 보기는 어려우므로 (C)도 오답이다. 'Order Delivered: _____'가 공란으로 남아있는 것으로 보아 아직 배달이 되지 않았으므로 아침에 배달이 되었다는 (D)는 오답이다.

표현 정리 **submit** 제출하다 **over the phone** 전화로 **process** 처리하다

해석 비품 주문에 관해 언급된 내용은?
(A) 그것은 전화로 Ms. Jones에게 제출되었다.
(B) 그것은 수리된 날과 같은 날에 완료되었다.
(C) 그것은 두 명의 다른 직원들에 의해 처리되었다.
(D) 그것은 오전에 건물 B로 배달되었다.

문제 154-155번은 다음 이메일을 참조하시오.

수신: BarbaraDenver@FolixTech.com

발신: Advertising@TechnixMagazine.com

날짜: 6월 3일

제목: Technix Magazine에 특집 수록

Ms. Denver 님께,

저희는 기술회사인 Folix Tech만을 위한 특별 제안을 하고자 합니다. Technix Magazine은 B2B 관련 기사로 최근 부상하는 기술 회사에 관한 특집을 준비하고 있습니다. 154저희는 귀사의 발전과 재정 성취에 관해 추적해 왔고, 귀하와 귀사를 다음 호에서 집중 조명하는데 관심이 있습니다.

저희는 다음 주에 인터뷰를 위해 귀 사무실로 기자를 보낼 수 있습니다. 대신 저희가 부탁 드리고자 하는 것은 귀사의 직원들이 월간 잡지인 Technix를 구독하는 것입니다. 가격 책정은, 물론, 할인될 것입니다. 만약 관심이 있으시다면, 155저희 기자가 방문할 수 있도록 시간을 정하기 위해 555-2467로 전화 주시기 바랍니다.

Angela White

Technix Magazine

표현 정리 **get featured in** ~에 특집으로 실리다 **exclusive offer** 특별 제안, 독점 제안 **feature** 특집으로 다루다 **emerging** 부상하는, 최근 생겨난 **business-to-business** 기업 간의, B2B **publication** 기사, 출판 **track** 추적하다 **progress** 진전, 발전 **funding** 자금, 재정 **achievement** 성취 **be interested in** ~에 흥미가 있다 **spotlight** 집중 조명하다 **upcoming issue** 다음 호 **in return** 대신에 **sign up for** ~에 등록하다, 신청하다 **monthly** 월간의, 매달의 **subscription** 구독 **pricing** 가격 책정 **discounted** 할인된 **set up a time** 시간을 정하다 **stop by** 잠시 들르다

154. 세부사항 – Ms. Denver에게 제안된 내용 ★☆☆

해설 첫 번째 단락, 마지막 문장 'We have been tracking your progress and funding achievements, and we are interested in spotlighting you and your company in an upcoming issue.'에서 Folix Tech를 Technix Magazine에서 집중 조명하고 싶다고 했는데, 이는 Ms. Denver의 입장에서는

회사를 홍보할 수 있는 기회가 주어졌다고 볼 수 있으므로 정답은 (C)이다.

정답 (C)

표현 정리 refund 환불 opportunity 기회

해석 Ms. Denver에게 제안된 것은?
(A) Technix의 무료 구독
(B) 직원들을 위한 환불
(C) 마케팅 기회
(D) 할인된 광고 공간

155. 세부사항 – Ms. White가 Ms. Denver에게 요청한 것 ★☆☆

해설 마지막 문장 'If you are interested, please call me at 555-2467 to set up a time for our reporter to stop by.'에서 관심이 있다면 취재를 위한 시간을 정할 수 있도록 전화해 달라고 했으므로 정답은 (B)이다.

정답 (B)

해석 Ms. White가 Ms. Denver에게 하도록 요청한 것은?
(A) 구독을 검토하라고
(B) 전화로 연락하라고
(C) 그녀에게 할인을 제공해 달라고
(D) 인터뷰를 위해 그녀를 만나 달라고

문제 156-158번은 다음 브로슈어를 참조하시오.

> **채용 가능한 광고 배우들:**
> **당신의 회사를 전문 연기로 강조하세요.**
>
> 우리 모두는 광고에 나온 회사에 오직 당혹감만을 안겨 주는 저급하고, 값싸며, 형편없이 제작된 광고 영상을 텔레비전에서 본 적이 있습니다. 그런 나쁜 마케팅에 희생되지 마십시오! 여러분의 광고에 진정한 불꽃이 튈 수 있도록 Ace Acting으로부터 숙련된 전문 배우를 고용하십시오. 유혹적인 광고로 고객을 끌고, 여러분의 사업을 키우십시오.
>
> Ace Acting의 엄선된 배우들은 6개월 이상 연기 기술을 익혔습니다. 경험이 풍부한 저희 배우들은 여러분의 광고가 특정 기술을 요구할 것에 대비해 기술 워크숍으로부터 자격증을 취득했습니다. 156(A)"드라마틱하고 유머가 있는, 여러분이 찾는 모든 인재들을 저희가 보유하고 있습니다!"라고 회사 창립자인 John Lemons은 말했습니다.
>
> 저희 유능한 배우들에 대해 자세히 알아 볼 준비가 되셨습니까? 158배우들의 프로필을 읽거나 직접 배우를 만나기 위해 Ace Acting 스튜디오에 들러주십시오. 156(D)머무시는 동안, 많은 연기 수업들 중 한 가지를 볼 수 있습니다.
>
> 귀사가 어떤 종류의 광고를 만들어야 할지 확신이 없으신가요? 156(C)저희 갤러리 필름 슬라이드실에 앉아 제작한 광고들을 보십시오. 157만약 아이디어가 없으시다면 저희는 귀사의 필요에 맞는 대본을 준비할 수 있습니다. 저희가 도와드릴 수 있습니다. 오늘 저희를 만나러 오십시오!

표현 정리 commercial actor 광고 배우 highlight 강조하다 professional 전문적인 cheesy 저급한 poorly 형편없이 commercial video 광고 영상 nothing but 오직 embarrassment 당혹감 fall victim 희생되다 skilled 숙련된, 노련한 spark 불꽃 build business 사업을 육성하다 enticing 유혹적인 handpicked 엄선한 no less than 자그마치 seasoned 경험 많은, 노련한 certification 증명 in case 경우에 대비해 scope out ~을 자세히 살피다 talent pool 인재 자원 stop by 잠시 들르다 browse through ~을 훑어보다 directly 직접 observe ~을 보다 take a seat 자리에 앉다 viewing room 필름 슬라이드실 array 모음

156. 세부사항 – Ace Acting에 관한 내용이 아닌 것 ★★☆

해설 마지막 단락 'Take a seat in our gallery viewing room and watch

an array of advertisements produced by Ace Acting.'에서 Ace Acting이 제작한 광고에 대한 언급이 있는 것으로 보아 광고 제작하는 직원이 있는 것을 알 수 있으므로 정답은 (B)다

정답 (B)

🔍 **함정 분석** 두 번째 단락 후반 '"Dramatic, humorous, whatever talent you are looking for, we've got it!" says company founder John Lemons.'에서 설립자 John Lemons에 대한 내용을 찾을 수 있으므로 (A)는 사실, 마지막 단락 'Take a seat in our gallery viewing room and watch an array of advertisements produced by Ace Acting.'에서 (C)도 사실임을 알 수 있고, 세 번째 단락 'While there, you can also sit in and observe one of the many acting classes.'에서 스튜디오에서 연기 수업이 이루어진다는 사실을 알 수 있으므로 (D)도 사실이다.

패러프레이징 |지문| company founder John Lemons 회사 창립자 John Lemons → |선택지 A| established by John Lemons John Lemons에 의해 설립되다
|지문| an array of advertisements 광고들의 집합소 → |선택지 C| an archive of commercials 광고 기록 보관소

표현 정리 establish 설립하다 crew 팀 archive 기록 보관소

해석 Ace Acting에 관해 언급되지 않은 것은?
(A) John Lemons에 의해 설립되었다.
(B) 자체적으로 광고를 제작하는 직원들이 없다.
(C) 광고 기록 보관소를 갖추고 있다.
(D) 연기 기술을 가르친다.

157. 문장 위치 찾기 ★★☆

해설 앞의 세 단락에서는 Ace Acting이 보유한 배우에 대해 다뤘고, 마지막 단락에서는 광고 내용에 대한 도움이 필요한 경우 Ace Acting 측에서 제공할 수 있는 도움에 대해 언급하고 있다. 주어진 문장 앞 'Not quite sure what kind of commercial your company wants to make?'에서 어떤 광고를 만들어야 할지 확신이 서지 않느냐고 묻는 내용으로 시작된 마지막 단락에 주어진 문장이 들어가는 것이 가장 적절하다고 볼 수 있으므로 정답은 (D)이다.

정답 (D)

표현 정리 tailor 맞추다, 조정하다 script 대본

해석 [1], [2], [3], [4] 중 다음 문장이 들어가기에 가장 알맞은 곳은?

"만약 아이디어가 없으시다면 저희는 귀사의 필요에 맞는 대본을 준비할 수 있습니다."
(A) [1]
(B) [2]
(C) [3]
(D) [4]

158. 세부사항 – Ace Acting의 배우들에 대한 내용 ★☆☆

해설 세 번째 단락 'Stop by the Ace Acting studio to browse through actors' profiles or to meet the talent directly.'에서 배우들의 프로필뿐 아니라 직접 배우들을 만날 수 있다고 했으므로 정답은 (B)이다.

정답 (B)

표현 정리 recruit 채용하다 potential 잠재적인

해석 Ace Acting의 배우들에 대해 알 수 있는 것은?
(A) 그들은 지역 극장으로부터 채용된다.
(B) 그들은 잠재적인 고객과 만나는 것이 가능하다.
(C) 그들은 개인적으로 Mr. Lemons에 의해 훈련받는다.
(D) 그들은 최고 6개월 동안 고용된다.

문제 159-161번은 다음 정보를 참조하시오.

청소용품 대량 배달

큰 건물들은 많은 청소를 필요로 하고, 많은 청소는 많은 양의 청소용품을 의미합니다. 만약 여러분이 회사를 위해 용품을 주문하는 업무를 맡고 있는 관리자라면, 이 메시지는 당신을 위한 것입니다: 159여러분 회사의 청소용품을 주문하고 재주문하는데 귀중한 예산을 낭비하지 마십시오. 더 크게 생각하십시오. 대량으로 구입하세요!

161(D)저희 웹사이트 www.cleaningbulk.com을 방문해 저희 대량의 청소용품이 얼마나 할인되는 지를 보십시오. 160필요하신 물품을 카트에 넣으시면, 완료된 대량 주문이 48시간 이내에 배달될 것입니다. 정말 간단한 일입니다.

161(A)만약 보관이 걱정이라면, 저희는 또한 주 또는 월별 배달 일정을 제시합니다. 용품 보관실이 필요하지 않습니다. 161(C)저희는 오직 필요로 하는 물품을 설정하신 기간(예를 들어, 일주일)을 위해 배달하며, 언제라도 빈도를 변경하실 수 있습니다. 예를 들어, 저희 고객 중 한 회사는 화장실 청소제 12리터가 3주마다 배달되도록 주문합니다.

그렇다면 무엇을 기다리고 계십니까? 오늘 주문하세요!

표현 정리 cleaning supplies 청소용품 bulk 큰 규모[양] delivery 배달 require 필요하다 administrator 관리자 in charge of ~을 맡아, 책임지고 waste 낭비하다 precious 귀중한 budget 예산 in bulk 대량으로 heavily 심하게 place 놓다, 두다 storage 보관 concern 걱정 necessary 필요한 period 기간 frequency 빈도 at any time 언제라도

159. 세부사항 – 대량 주문의 이점 ★☆☆

해설 첫 번째 단락 후반 'Don't waste your company's precious budget on ordering and reordering cleaning supplies.'에서 대량 주문을 통해 회사 예산을 낭비하지 말 것을 권유하고 있으므로 본 정보에서 알 수 있는 대량 주문의 이점은 (D)라고 할 수 있다. **정답 (D)**

패러프레이징 |지문| don't waste your company's precious budget 회사의 귀중한 자원을 낭비하지 마라 → |선택지 D| reduce business expenses 사업 비용을 아껴라

표현 정리 high-quality 고품질의 specialized 전문화된 amount 양 reduce 줄이다 expense 비용

해석 정보에 따르면, 대량 주문의 이점은 무엇인가?
(A) 고품질의 용품을 얻는 것
(B) 전문화된 제품을 찾는 것
(C) 많은 양의 시간을 아끼는 것
(D) 운영비를 줄이는 것

160. 세부사항 – 주문이 도착하는 가장 늦은 때 ★☆☆

해설 두 번째 단락, 마지막 문장 'Place the items you need in your cart, and your completed bulk order will be delivered within 48 hours.'에서 주문을 완료하면, 48시간, 즉 늦어도 이틀 안에 배송이 될 것이라고 했으므로 정답은 (C)이다. **정답 (C)**

해석 정보에 따르면, 가장 최근의 주문은 언제까지 도착하는가?
(A) 몇 시간 안에
(B) 하루 안에
(C) 이틀 안에
(D) 일주일 안에

161. 세부사항 – 배달 서비스에 대한 내용이 아닌 것 ★★★

해설 배달 중 주문 내용 변경 사항에 대해서는 언급된 내용이 없으므로 정답은 (B)이다. 본문에서 변경 가능한 것으로 언급된 것은 배달 기간과 빈도뿐이다.

정답 (B)

🔍**함정 분석** 세 번째 단락, 첫 번째 문장 'If storage is a concern, we also offer weekly or monthly delivery setups. No supply storage room is necessary.'에서 (A)가 확인되고, 이어서 'We will only deliver the supplies you need for the period that you set (one week, for example), and you can change the frequency at any time.'에서 (C)도 확인되었다. 두 번째 단락 'Visit our Web site, www.cleaningbulk.com'을 통해 역시 온라인으로 주문이 가능하다는 것을 알 수 있으므로 (D)도 확인이 가능하다.

패러프레이징 |지문| offer weekly or monthly delivery setups 주간 또는 월간으로 정기적인 배달을 제공한다 → |선택지 A| be delivered routinely 정기적으로 배달된다

|지문| deliver the supplies you need for the period that you set 필요로 하는 물품을 정한 기간에 맞춰 배달한다 → |선택지 C| customers can set the duration of delivery 고객들은 배달 기간을 설정할 수 있다

표현 정리 recurring 되풀이되는 routinely 일상적으로, 정례적으로 modify 수정하다 duration 기간

해석 반복되는 배달 서비스에 관해 언급된 것이 아닌 것은?
(A) 용품들은 정기적으로 배달될 것이다.
(B) 배송 중에 주문이 변경될 수 있다.
(C) 고객들은 배달 기간을 설정할 수 있다.
(D) 주문은 온라인 상에서 이루어질 수 있다.

문제 162-164번은 다음 편지를 참조하시오.

6월 31일

Pax Go의 친구들과 가족 여러분께,

162Pax Go 화장품 회사는 7월 14일 일요일에 직원 가족과 친구들을 위해 야유회를 주최할 예정입니다.

Pax Go는 고객님 본연의 아름다움을 향상시키고, 이미 타고난 아름다움을 빛나게 해 주는 자연적, 유기농 피부 관리와 메이크업에 초점을 맞추고 있습니다. 163본사는 결점을 덮고, 완벽해 보일 필요성에 대한 메시지를 전달하는 메이크업 산업에 싫증을 느낀 Marlene Kay에 의해 설립되었습니다.

사업을 성장시키는 과정에서 그녀는 아이디어 내는 것을 돕고, 캠페인을 하고, 제품을 세심하게 조정하고, 화장품을 출시하고, 소문을 확산시키는데 가족과 친구들의 도움을 크게 받았습니다. 164(A)곧 Pax Go는 번창하는 기업이 되었고, 심지어 20년이 지난 지금도 Ms. Kay는 Pax Go의 가족과 친구들에게 고마운 마음을 갖고 있습니다.

164(C)"나의 가족과 친구들의 지원이 아니었다면, 나는 오늘 이곳에 있지 않았을 것입니다. 그리고 우리 직원 대부분 그렇게 느낄 것이라고 생각합니다. 164(B)그것이 바로 우리 회사에 가장 가까운 분들을 존경하는 마음으로 이런 특별한 행사를 매년 주최하는 이유입니다."라고 Ms. Kay는 작년 행사에서 말했다.

1627월 14일에 Pax Go 행사에 함께 해 주십시오.

Hugh Britters
Pax Go 행사 코디네이터

표현 정리 cosmetics 화장품 host 주최하다 focus on ~에 초점을 맞추다 organic 유기농의 enhance 향상시키다 be tired of ~에 싫증이 나다 flaw 결점 rely on ~에 의존하다 create 창조하다, 만들다 campaign 캠페인, 활동 fine-tune 미세 조정을 하다 market (상품을) 내놓다 spread the word 말을 퍼뜨리다 before long 오래지 않아 thriving 번창하는 entity 독립체, 기업 nothing but 오직 gratitude

46

162. 주제 – 편지의 목적　★☆☆

해설 첫 번째 문장 'The Pax Go Cosmetics Company is hosting a picnic for friends and family of our employees on Sunday, July 14.'에서 7월에 있을 행사를 알리고 있고, 마지막 문장에서는 함께 해 줄 것을 권유하고 있으므로 정답가 (D)이다.　정답 (D)

표현 정리 disclose 밝히다　mission statement (기업, 조직의) 강령 detail 상세히 알리다

해석 편지의 목적은?
(A) 리더십의 변화를 발표하기 위해
(B) 강령을 발표하기 위해
(C) 새로운 회사 계획을 상세히 알리기 위해
(D) 행사에 초대하기 위해

163. 동의어　★☆☆

해설 두 번째 단락 'The company was founded by Marlene Kay, who was tired of the message the makeup industry was sending about needing to cover flaws and to appear perfect.'에서 문장에 포함된 cover는 '결점'이라는 뜻을 가진 flaws와 함께 쓰여 '결점을 덮다, 감추다'의 의미에 가깝게 사용되었으므로 정답은 (C)이다.　정답 (C)

표현 정리 conceal 감추다, 숨기다

해석 편지 두 번째 단락, 세 번째 줄의 "cover"와 의미가 가장 가까운 것은?
(A) 알리다
(B) 고정시키다
(C) 감추다
(D) 포함하다

164. 세부사항 – Pax Go에 관한 내용이 아닌 것　★☆☆

해설 세 번째 단락 'Before long, Pax Go was a thriving entity, and even to this day, 20 years later'를 통해 설립 이후 오래되지 않아 큰 회사로 성장했고, 20년이 지난 지금도 그렇다는 것을 알 수 있지만, 가까운 미래에 확장될 가능성에 대한 언급은 찾을 수 없으므로 정답은 (D)이다.　정답 (D)

패러프레이징 │지문│ 20 years 20년 → │선택지 A│ two decades 20년 │지문│ host this special event ~ every year 매년 이 특별 행사를 연다 → │선택지 B│ hold an annual get-together 매년 함께 모이는 파티를 연다

표현 정리 decade 10년　hold 열다　get-together (비격식적인) 모임, 파티 value 가치있게 생각하다　expand 확대되다, 확장시키다

해석 Pax Go에 관해 언급된 내용이 아닌 것은?
(A) 20년 전에 시작되었다.
(B) 매년 함께 모이는 파티를 연다.
(C) 가족 관계를 가치있게 생각한다.
(D) 가까운 미래에 확장할 것이다.

문제 165-167번은 다음 광고를 참조하시오.

전 도시 사무실 안전 훈련 행사
Philadelphia 경찰과 소방 협회 주최

안전 사다리 사용:
사고는 항상 근무 중에 발생하고, 사다리를 사용할 경우 부상 가능성이 10배 증가합니다. 여러분의 모든 직원들이 사다리를 사용하는 적절한 방법을 저희 교육을 통해 반드시 알 수 있도록 하십시오. 저희가 거의 모든 사다리 사고를 없앨 세 단계의 접촉점 시스템을 상세히 알려드리겠습니다.

167 사무실 내 공격성 줄이기:
스트레스가 많은 환경에서는 긴장감이 높아질 수 있습니다. **모든 직원이**

불만을 가진 동료를 다루는 방법과 직원들 사이에 잠재적으로 발생할 수 있는 폭력 사태를 줄일 수 있는 방법을 숙지하시기 바랍니다.

비상 소방 훈련 연습:
화재가 발생할 경우 직원들이 어디로 가야 하는지 알고 있나요? 안전 계획은 마련되어 있나요? 저희는 모든 사람들이 준비될 수 있도록 회사 전체의 대피 계획을 세우고 소방 훈련을 실행하는 것을 도울 수 있습니다.

궂은 날씨 안전:
특별히 날씨가 나쁜 날 여러분의 사무실은 무엇을 할 건가요? 자연재해 발생 빈도가 증가세에 있는 요즘, 궂은 날씨에 대비해 대피 계획을 세우는 것이 중요합니다. 비상 날씨에 직원의 안전을 보장하기 위해 이 훈련의 일정을 잡으시기 바랍니다.

166 한 가지 또는 그 이상의 사무실 안전 훈련 일정을 잡으시려면, 웹사이트 www.paofficesafety.org에 방문해 주십시오. 165 나열된 항목 이외의 과정들도 등록이 가능합니다.

표현 정리 citywide 도시 전체의　association 협회　ladder 사다리　at work 근무 중　all the time 언제나, 항상　injury 부상　increase 증가하다　ten-fold 10배의　ensure 반드시 ~하게 하다　proper 적절한　detail 상세히 알리다　point of contact 접촉점　eliminate 없애다　nearly 거의　de-escalate 단계적으로 줄이다　aggression 공격성　tension 긴장　stressful 스트레스가 많은　setting 환경　make sure (~을) 확실히 하다　handle 다루다　disgruntled 불만스러워하는　coworker 동료 potentially 잠재적으로　violent 폭력적인　emergency 비상　fire drill 소방 훈련　in case (~할) 경우에 대비해　break out 발생하다　in place 제자리에　company-wide 회사 전반의　escape 탈출하다　inclement 궂은　face 직면하다　on the rise 증가세에, 오름세에　carve out 노력하여 얻다　evacuation 대피　strike (재난, 질병 등이 갑자기) 발생하다　ensure 보장하다　beyond ~넘어, ~외에

165. 유추 – 경찰과 소방 협회에 대한 내용　★★☆

해설 본문 마지막 문장 'Additional courses beyond those listed can be requested.'에서 광고에 언급된 네 가지 훈련 외에 추가 과정을 요청하는 것도 가능하다고 했으므로 4개 이상의 훈련을 제공한다고 볼 수 있어 정답은 (C)이다.　정답 (C)

표현 정리 donation 기부　conduct (특정한 활동을) 하다　various 다양한 highly 많이, 고도로

해석 Philadelphia 경찰과 소방 협회에 관해 제시된 내용은?
(A) 그들의 웹사이트 상에서 기부를 받는다.
(B) 다양한 장소에서 훈련을 한다.
(C) 4개 이상의 훈련 행사를 제공한다.
(D) 고도로 훈련된 교육관들을 보유하고 있다.

166. 세부사항 – 사무실 안전 훈련 행사에 대한 내용　★☆☆

해설 마지막 단락 'To schedule one or more of these office safety trainings, visit our Web site www.paofficesafety.org.'에서 안전 훈련 일정을 잡기 위해 웹사이트를 방문할 것을 권하고 있으므로 온라인 예약이 가능해 정답은 (D)이다.　정답 (D)

패러프레이징 │지문│ To schedule ~, visit our Web site 일정을 잡기 위해서는 웹사이트를 방문하라 → │선택지 D│ can be booked online 온라인으로 예약할 수 있다

표현 정리 participate 참가하다　participant 참가자　real-life 실생활

해석 전 도시 사무실 안전 훈련 행사에 대해 언급된 내용은?
(A) 참가를 위한 요금이 있다.
(B) 그것들은 모든 날씨 상황 속에서 열린다.
(C) 참가자들은 실생활에 필요한 기술들을 연습한다.
(D) 온라인으로 예약할 수 있다.

167. 세부사항 – 대인 관계와 관련된 의사소통 기술을 가르치는 행사 ★☆☆

해설 두 번째 행사 'Deescalating Office Aggression'은 다른 훈련과는 달리 'Make sure all your employees know how to handle a disgruntled coworker or deescalate a potentially violent argument between staff.'에서처럼 동료를 대하는 방법이나 논쟁을 줄이는 방법을 가르치는 대인 관계와 관련된 기술을 다룬다는 것을 알 수 있으므로 정답은 (B)이다.　　　정답 (B)

표현 정리 interpersonal 대인 관계와 관련된

해석 어떤 행사가 대인 관계와 관련된 의사소통 기술을 가르치는가?
　　　(A) 안전한 사다리 사용
　　　(B) 사무실 내 공격성 줄이기
　　　(C) 비상 소방 훈련 연습
　　　(D) 궂은 날씨 안전

문제 168-171번은 다음 이메일을 참조하시오.

발신: Alex Micheline (amich@corporatebighall.com)
수신: Wesley Farn (wfarn@farnfinancials.com)
제목: Re: 임대 문의
날짜: 11월 19일

Mr. Farn 님께,

귀사의 파티에 필요한 이벤트 홀 대여에 관해 문의하는 편지를 받았습니다.

서식에 따르면, 요청하신 대여 일은 12월 22일이고, 필요 목록은 장소, 의자, 음식 공급과 음악입니다. **170,171예약을 마치기 위해, 참석 예상 인원과 신용카드 정보를 이메일로 보내주시기 바랍니다. 저희는 장소를 확보하기 위해 100달러의 보증금을 카드에 부과할 것입니다.**

이 이메일에 메뉴 옵션을 첨부합니다. **169어떤 종류의 전체 요리와 주요리가 파티에 제공되기를 원하는지 선택해 주시면, 메뉴와 제공 시간을 확인하도록 저희 음식 공급자가 연락드릴 수 있도록 하겠습니다.**

168귀하와 귀하의 동료분들은 필요한 개인 물품을 가져다 놓고, 추가적인 장식을 설치하기 위해 본 장소를 12월 21일, 금요일, 오후 6시 이후에 이용하실 수 있습니다.

저도 금요일에 현장에 있을 것입니다. 만약 그날 질문이 있으면, 2층에 있는 제 사무실로 찾아오시거나 위에 있는 주소로 언제든 이메일 주시기 바랍니다. 총 금액은 행사 당일까지 현금으로 지불돼야 한다는 점 참고하시기 바랍니다. 결제 이후, 카드에 보증금 청구한 것이 취소될 것입니다.

Alex Micheline
행사 플래너
Corporate Big Hall

표현 정리 inquiry 문의　regarding ~에 관해　form 서식, 양식　request 요청하다　requirement 필요(한 것)　catering 음식 공급　reservation 예약　expect 예상하다　attach 첨부하다　appetizer 전채(요리)　entrée 주 요리　caterer 음식 공급자　confirm 확인해 주다　associate 동료　access 이용하다　drop off 갖다 놓다　additional 추가의　premises 구내　above 위에　note 주목하다　in full 전부　receipt 수령　clear A of B A에서 B를 치우다(본문에서는 카드로 청구한 보증금 내역을 취소한다는 의미)　deposit 보증금

---

168. 세부사항 – Farn Financials 행사 요일 ★☆☆

해설 두 번째 단락 'According to the form, your requested rental date is December 22'에서 행사 일은 12월 22일인데, 다섯 번째 단락 'You and your associates may access the venue on Friday, December 21, after 6:00 P.M.'에서 행사 전 날이 금요일이고, 따라서 행사 당일은 토요일이라는 것을 알 수 있으므로 정답은 (C) 토요일이다.　　　정답 (C)

해석 Farn Financials 행사는 무슨 요일에 열리는가?
　　　(A) 목요일
　　　(B) 금요일
　　　(C) 토요일
　　　(D) 일요일

---

169. 세부사항 – Corporate Big Hall에 대한 내용 ★☆☆

해설 세 번째 단락 'Choose what appetizer and main entrée you would like served at your party, and we will have our caterer contact you to confirm the menu and serving time.'에서 전채와 메인 요리를 선택해 주면 음식 공급 업체로 하여금 연락하도록 해 메뉴와 제공 시간을 확인하겠다고 했으므로 정답은 (B)이다.　　　정답 (B)

표현 정리 selection 선택　arrange 마련하다, 준비하다

해석 Corporate Big Hall에 관해 언급된 내용은?
　　　(A) 엄선한 라이브 밴드를 제공한다.
　　　(B) 행사들을 위한 음식 서비스를 준비한다.
　　　(C) 행사를 위한 보증금을 요청하지 않는다.
　　　(D) 전에 Farn Financials의 행사를 치러본 적이 있다.

---

170. 세부사항 – Mr. Micheilne이 Mr. Farn에 요청한 일 ★★☆

해설 두 번째 단락 'To complete your reservation, please e-mail me back with how many guests you expect and your credit card information.'에서 참석 인원 수와 신용카드 정보를 요청하고 있으므로 정답은 (A)이다.　정답 (A)

🔍 **함정 분석** 마지막 단락 'Please note that the total payment must be paid in cash in full by the day of the event.'에서 행사 당일까지 총 금액을 현금으로 결제해 달라고 했기 때문에 (B)는 오답이다. 세 번째 단락 'and we will have our caterer contact you to confirm the menu and serving time'에서 Corporate Big Hall의 음식 공급 담당자가 연락을 취할 것이기 때문에 음식 공급 업체에 따로 연락할 필요는 없으므로 (D)도 오답이다.

표현 정리 attendee 참석자　remainder 나머지　bill 계산서　catering company 음식 공급 업체

해석 Mr. Micheline이 Mr. Farn에게 하도록 요청한 것은?
　　　(A) 참석자들의 인원 수를 보내라고
　　　(B) 계산서의 나머지를 지불해 달라고
　　　(C) 손님들에게 초대장을 보내라고
　　　(D) 음식 공급 업체에게 연락하라고

---

171. 문장 위치 찾기 ★★☆

해설 주어진 문장은 장소를 예약하기 위해 필요한 보증금 100달러를 신용카드로 청구할 것이라는 내용이다. 이에 관한 내용은 두 번째와 마지막 단락에서 찾을 수 있는데, 주어진 문장 "We will run it for a deposit amount of $100.00 in order to hold the space."에서 밑줄 친 it이 받는 단어는 신용카드로, 예약을 하는 과정과 관련이 있는 [2]에 들어가야 가장 자연스럽다. [4]에 들어가게 되면, it이 바로 앞 문장에 있는 the above address를 받게 돼 문맥이 통하지 않는다. 따라서 정답은 (B)이다.　　　정답 (B)

해석 [1], [2], [3], [4] 중 다음 문장이 들어가기에 가장 적절한 곳은?

"저희는 장소를 확보하기 위해 100달러의 보증금을 부과할 것입니다."

　　　(A) [1]
　　　(B) [2]
　　　(C) [3]
　　　(D) [4]

문제 172-175번은 다음 온라인 채팅을 참조하시오.

> **Wendy Young** 여러분, 우리는 다가오는 직원 야유회를 위한 아이디어가 필요합니다. **172**지난 달에 함께 연극을 봤고, 그 전에는 문화 행사를 가졌어요. 이번 달에는 무엇을 해야 할까요? 오후 5시 1분
>
> **Harry Sims** 제 생각에는 회사 만찬이 좋은 변화가 될 수 있을 것 같아요. 모든 사람이 즐기고 이야기 나누는 맛있는 식사요. 오후 5시 3분
>
> **Josh Bae** **174**전적으로 동의해요. 누가 좋은 음식과 대화를 좋아하지 않겠어요? 오후 5시 5분
>
> **Harry Sims** 어떤 종류의 음식을 원하는지 결정하는 것으로 시작하면 어때요? 그리고 저녁을 위한 주제를 정하면 어떨까요? 오후 5시 6분
>
> **Wendy Young** 저녁 식사는 좋은 생각이네요. 하지만 단지 음식만이 아니라 고려해야 할 사항들이 많습니다. **173**대규모 인원을 위한 공간을 갖춘 장소를 찾는 것이 필요할 거예요. 그리고 나서 음식 알레르기와 식단 문제가 있구요. 오후 5시 7분
>
> **Josh Bae** **175**직원들이 무엇을 먹기 원하는 지와 언급하신 음식과 관련된 우려에 대해 알 수 있도록 조사를 해 보면 어떨까요? 오후 5시 8분
>
> **Harry Sims** 좋은 생각이에요! 근처에 있는 음식점들을 알아보고, 가능한 장소 목록을 만들게요. Josh, 내가 대략 한 시간 안에 이메일로 보낼게요. 그것을 당신이 조사하는 데 사용할 수 있을 거예요. 오후 5시 9분
>
> **Josh Bae** 좋은 생각입니다. 오후 5시 10분
>
> **Wendy Young** 두 분이 일을 시작했기 때문에, 조사 결과를 얻기까지는 옆으로 비켜 있을 게요. 알려주면 실제 일정은 내가 맡을게요. 오후 5시 12분

표현 정리 upcoming 다가오는 outing 야유회 dietary restriction 식사 제한 survey 조사하다 find out 알아내다 concern 우려 nearby 근처에 put together 만들다 make a survey 조사하다 get the ball rolling 일을 시작하다 step aside 옆으로 비키다

172. 세부사항 – 문화 행사에 대한 내용 ★☆☆
해설 이번 달 직원 야유회 내용을 결정하기 위한 온라인 채팅 내용이다. Wendy Young이 오후 5시 1분에 보낸 메시지 'Last month, we saw a play, and before that, we had a cultural event.'에서 지난 달 연극 관람을 했고, 그 전에는 문화 행사를 가졌다고 했으므로 두 달 전에 문화 행사가 있었음을 알 수 있어 정답은 (D)이다. 정답 (D)

표현 정리 organize 준비하다 take place 발행하다, 일어나다

해석 문화 행사에 대한 사실 내용은?
(A) Mr. Sims가 준비했다.
(B) 극장에서 개최되었다.
(C) 참석한 직원이 거의 없었다.
(D) 2개월 전에 열렸다.

173. 유추 – 직원 야유회에 대한 내용 ★★☆
해설 Wendy Young이 오후 5시 3분에 보낸 메시지 'We'll need to find a place that has enough space for a big group.'은 대규모 인원을 위한 공간 확보에 대해 언급하고 있으므로 다음 직원 야유회에 많은 사람이 참석할 것을 예상할 수 있어 정답은 (B)이다. 정답 (B)

🔍 **함정 분석** Harry Sims가 오후 5시 3분에 보낸 메시지 'I think a company dinner would be a nice change.'에서 저녁 식사가 좋은 변화를 불러올 것이라고 한 내용을 통해 이전에는 이와 비슷한 행사는 없었다는 것을 유추할 수 있으므로 (A)는 오답이다. Harry Sims가 오후 5시 9분에 보낸 메시지 'You can use that to make the survey.'에서 실제 조사를 할 사람은 Josh Bae이므로 (C) 역시 오답이다.

해석 다가오는 직원 야유회에 관해 암시된 내용은?

(A) 이전에 비슷한 행사가 준비되었다.
(B) 많은 사람들이 참석할 것으로 예상된다.
(C) Ms. Young은 조사를 실시할 것이다.
(D) 다른 형태의 해산물이 제공될 것이다.

174. 의도 파악하기 ★☆☆
해설 저녁 식사를 제안한 Harry Sims의 의견에 'Who doesn't like good food and conversation?'이라고 한 내용으로 보아, 앞의 내용 'I'm all in for that.'은 전적으로 동의하고 있다는 의미로 볼 수 있으므로 정답은 (C)이다. 정답 (C)

표현 정리 in charge of ~을 담당해서

해석 Mr. Bae가 오후 5시 5분에 보낸 메시지 'I'm all in for that.'가 의미하는 것은?
(A) 그는 정말로 지난 달의 쇼를 즐겼다.
(B) 그는 계획하는 것을 담당하기를 원한다.
(C) 그는 저녁 식사 제안을 좋아한다.
(D) 그는 음식이 배달되도록 하는 것을 선호한다.

175. 세부사항 – 조사에 대한 내용 ★☆☆
해설 Josh Bae가 오후 5시 8분에 보낸 메시지 'How about surveying the staff to see what everyone would like to eat and to find out about the food concerns you mentioned?'에서 사람들이 원하는 메뉴를 비롯해, Wendy Young이 언급한 음식 알레르기와 식단 제한에 대해서 알아보자고 했으므로 참석자들이 먹을 수 없는 음식에 대해서도 질문을 할 것으로 짐작해 정답은 (B)이다. 정답 (B)

표현 정리 distribute 배포하다, 분배하다

해석 조사에 관해 언급된 내용은?
(A) 조사는 Mr. Sims에 의해 이루어질 것이다.
(B) 조사는 사람들이 먹을 수 없는 것에 대해 물을 것이다.
(C) 이메일로 배포될 것이다.
(D) 가능한 날짜의 목록을 포함할 것이다.

문제 176-180번은 다음 보도 자료와 웹페이지를 참조하시오.

> 보도 자료를 위한 연락처: Adam Shield, 555-2351
>
> **통근자들을 위한 고속 열차**
>
> **176(B),(C),179**6월 22일, 월요일부터 Heinsfield 역은 Heinsfield 시내에서 125킬로미터 떨어진 Champagne 역까지 통근자들을 수송하기 위해 고속 열차 서비스를 제공한다. 이 노선은 최근 대기업인 Homeaway Products의 준공을 기념해 두 역 사이를 논스톱으로 운행할 것이다.
>
> **177**Homeaway의 업무 시작과 함께, 50,000명의 직원들이 인근 Champagne 역으로 매일 통근한다. 극심한 교통 정체가 시 당국으로 하여금 혼잡을 완화시키기 위한 새 열차 노선을 신설하도록 하는 원인이 됐다. 고속 열차는 Los Angeles와 New York에서 많은 성공과 전례 없는 속도로 시범 운영되었다. 고속 열차는 각각 70개의 좌석을 갖춘 10개의 객차로 구성되어 있다.
>
> 고속 열차를 위한 티켓 가격은 일반 기차에 비해 비싸지만, **176(A)**매일 출퇴근하는 직장인들은 할인 가격으로 월 정기권을 구입할 수 있다. **180**3번에서 5번까지의 객차는 별도의 안전과 안락함을 위해 여성 전용칸으로 정해졌다.

표현 정리 immediate 즉각적인 release 방출 bullet train 고속열차 commuter 통근자 route 경로, 노선 perk 특전 conglomerate 대기업 prompt 촉발시키다 alleviate 완화하다 congestion 혼잡 unprecedented 전례 없는 feature 포함하다 regular 보통의 monthly pass 한 달 정기권 at a discount 할인으로 slight 약간의 ensure 보장하다 comfort 편안 female 여성 malfunctioning 제대로 기능하지

https://www.bullettrainusa.org

Champagne Station 서비스에 대한 문의나 의견을 남기시려면, 아래 서식을 작성해 주십시오:

이름: *Hailey Nirem*
날짜: *7월 6일*
전화: *555-8261*
이메일: *hanir@mailnets.com*

논평:
179 *저를 비롯한 Homeaway 동료들은 집과 직장을 오갈 수 있는 직행 고속 열차를 이용할 수 있게 돼 말할 수 없이 행복합니다. 이 열차가 개통되기 전에는 매일 왕복 장거리 운전을 해야 했습니다!*

178 *그러나 출근길에 두 번 발생한 기계적 결함에 대한 문제를 전달하고 싶고, 그것이 더 큰 문제들로 이어질까 걱정됩니다. 180 4번 객실의 왼쪽 문이 닫힐 때 가끔 반쯤 끼는 것 같습니다. 열차 문의 일부가 열린 채 달리는 느낌을 탑승자들이 가진 적이 있습니다. 제대로 작동하지 않는 문을 수리하기 위해 기술자를 보내주십시오. 속도와 효율성은 탑승자들에 의해 환영과 감사를 받지만 안전도 중요한 핵심 사항입니다. 시간 내 주셔서 감사합니다.*

표현 정리 inquiry 문의 colleague 동료 segment 부분 back and forth 왕복으로 mechanical 기계와 관련된 lead to ~로 이어지다 get stuck 꼼짝 못하게 되다 every once in a while 가끔 partially 부분적으로

176. 세부사항 – 고속열차에 대한 내용이 아닌 것 ★★☆
해설 티켓 구입처에 대한 언급은 본문에서 찾을 수 없으므로 정답은 (D)이다.
정답 (D)

🔍함정 분석 보도 자료 마지막 단락 'but monthly passes can be purchased by working professionals, who will ride to and from the office every day, at a slight discount'에 (A)가 확인되고, 보도 자료 첫 문장 'Heinsfield Station will offer bullet train services for commuters to Champagne Station, 125 kilometers away in downtown Heinsfield.'에서 (B)도 확인된다. 이어서 'The route will run nonstop between the stations'에서 두 역 사이를 직행으로 운행할 예정임을 알 수 있으므로 (C)도 맞다.

패러프레이징 |지문| who will ride to and from the office every day 매일 사무실로 오고 갈 때 탑승하는 직장인들 → |선택지 A| Commuters 통근자들 |지문| at a slight discount 할인된 가격으로 → |선택지 A| at a reduced rate 할인된 요금으로
|지문| 125 kilometers 125 킬로미터 → |선택지 B| 125 kilometers one way 편도로 125 킬로미터
|지문| run nonstop between the stations 두 역 사이를 멈추지 않고 운행하다 → |선택지 C| offer direct service between two stations 두 역 사이의 직통 서비스를 제공하다

표현 정리 press release 보도 자료 reduced rate 할인 요금 one way 편도 passenger 승객

해설 보도 자료에서 고속 열차에 대해 언급되지 않은 것은?
(A) 통근자들은 할인 요금으로 티켓을 구할 수 있다.
(B) 편도로 125킬로미터를 운행한다.
(C) 두 역 사이의 직행 서비스를 제공할 것이다.
(D) 승객들은 기차에서 티켓을 구입할 수 있다.

177. 세부사항 – 새로운 서비스가 제공되는 원인 ★☆☆
해설 보도 자료 두 번째 단락 'With the opening of Homeaway, 50,000 employees commute to the nearby Champagne station daily. The heavy traffic prompted city officials to open new train routes to alleviate congestion.'에서 5만 명의 대기업 직원들이 매일 출근함으로써 교통 체증이 발생해 이를 완화하기 위해 열차 노선을 신설했다고 했으므로 정답은 (C)이다.
정답 (C)

패러프레이징 |지문| to alleviate congestion 교통 혼잡을 완화시키기 위해 → |선택지 C| to reduce overcrowding 과밀 사태를 줄이기 위해

표현 정리 replace 대체하다 outdated 구식인 donate 기부하다 corporation 기업 aim 목표하다 reduce 줄이다 overcrowding 초만원, 과잉 수용 demand 요구하다

해설 새로운 서비스가 제공되는 원인은 무엇인가?
(A) 구식 열차를 대체한다.
(B) 대기업이 기부했다.
(C) 교통 체증을 줄이는 것을 목표로 한다.
(D) 지역 통근자들이 요구했다.

178. 세부사항 – Ms. Nirem이 웹사이트를 방문한 이유 ★☆☆
해설 두 번째 지문, 두 번째 단락 'But I would like to inform you of a mechanical error that has occurred twice on my way to work, and I worry that it could lead to larger problems.'에서 기계적인 결함에 대해 알리고 싶다고 했으므로 (D)가 정답이다.
정답 (D)

해설 Ms. Nirem이 Champagne 역 웹사이트를 방문한 이유는?
(A) 그녀의 티켓을 바꾸기 위해
(B) 스케줄에 대해 이의를 제기하기 위해
(C) 티켓에 대해 문의하기 위해
(D) 문제점을 보고하기 위해

179. 연계 문제 – Ms. Nirem이 사는 곳 ★☆☆
해설 두 번째 지문 'I cannot tell you how happy my fellow Homeaway colleagues and I are to have the direct bullet train route taking us from home to work and back again.'에서 Ms. Nirem은 Homeaway에 근무하는 직원으로 고속 열차를 이용해 출근하고 있음을 알 수 있는데, 첫 지문에서 열차는 Heinsfield 역에서 Homeaway Products가 위치한 Champagne 역까지 운행한다고 했으므로 Ms. Nirem은 Heinsfield에 거주한다고 볼 수 있어 정답은 (B)이다.
정답 (B)

해설 Ms. Nirem이 사는 곳은?
(A) Champagne
(B) Heinsfield
(C) Los Angeles
(D) New York

180. 연계 문제 – Ms. Nirem에 대한 내용 ★☆☆
해설 Ms. Nirem은 두 번째 지문을 작성한 사람이며, 두 번째 단락 'The left-side door on car 4 seems to get stuck halfway through closing every once in a while'을 통해 4번 객실에 탑승했음을 알 수 있는데, 보도 자료 마지막 문장 'Cars 3 through 5 are for women only to ensure extra measures of safety and comfort for female riders.'에서 3번에서 5번 객차는 여성 전용칸으로 지정되었다고 했으므로 정답은 (C)이다.
정답 (C)

표현 정리 unlimited 무제한의 ride in ~에 타다 restricted 제한된 job promotion 승진

해설 Ms. Nirem에 관해 암시된 내용은?
(A) 그녀는 월 무제한 티켓을 갖고 있다.
(B) 그녀는 지금 하루에 250킬로미터를 운전한다.
(C) 그녀는 여성 전용 객차를 탔다.

(D) 그녀는 최근 승진했다.

문제 181-185번은 다음 편지와 정보를 참조하시오.

11월 4일

Edwina Shangles
293 Bener Lane
Boston, MA 23163

Ms. Shangles 님께,

제 사무실 건물에 연휴 장식을 하는 문제로 잡았던 약속에 관해 지난주 간단한 대화를 나눴죠? 대화 중 언급한 것처럼, 건물이 꽤 높은데, **184**각 층에 2개의 계단과 15개의 사무실이 있는 10층 건물입니다.

181,185설치일 하루 전에 당일 일정표를 보내주셨으면 합니다. **182**장식을 설치하는 작업을 하려면 각 층의 부서들이 사무실을 비울 시간을 잡아야 하니까요. 해당 직원들은 그 시간 동안 근무할 장소가 필요합니다. 아시겠지만, 이것은 많은 사전 계획과 조율이 필요합니다.

연락을 기대합니다.

Laura Zeal
상무이사

표현 정리 **briefly** 간단히 **put up** 달다 **stairways** 계단 **breakdown** 명세 **installation** 설치 **prior to** ~이전에 **setup** 설치 **arrange times** 시간을 잡다 **vacate** 비우다 **take place** 일어나다 **affected** 영향을 받은, 해당되는 **preplanning** 사전 계획 **coordination** 조율 **look forward to** ~을 기대하다

설치 당일 일정표	
18511월 28일, 화요일	
오전 9시 15분 - 오전 9시 45분	직원 도착 후 트럭에서 짐 하역
오전 9시 45분 - 오전 10시 45분	측량
오전 10시 45분 - 오전 11시 50분	장식 준비
오전 11시 50분 - 오후 2시	**184**설치: 1층과 2층
오후 2시 - 오후 3시	설치: 3층
오후 3시 - 오후 5시	설치: 4층과 5층
오후 5시 - 오후 7시	설치: 6층과 7층
오후 7시 - 오후 8시	설치: 8층
오후 8시 - Finish	설치: 9층과 10층

표현 정리 **unload** (짐을) 내리다 **measurement** 측량 **preparation** 준비

181. 주제 - Ms. Zeal이 글을 쓴 목적 ★☆☆
해설 Ms. Zeal은 편지 두번째 단락 'I would like to remind you to send me a breakdown of the installation day schedule the day prior to the actual setup.'에서 설치 당일의 상세 일정표를 보내줄 것을 요청하고 있으므로 정답은 (D)이다. 정답 (D)

표현 정리 **existing** 기존의 **further** 추가의

해석 Ms. Zeal이 Ms. Shangles에게 편지를 보낸 이유는?
(A) Ms. Shangles에게 기존 약속을 상기시켜 주려고
(B) 전화 통화 일정을 잡기 위해
(C) 설치비에 대해 문의하기 위해
(D) 추가 정보를 보내달라고 요청하기 위해

182. 동의어 ★★☆
해설 두 번째 단락 'I will need to arrange times with the departments on each floor for offices to be vacated in order for the decorating to take

place.'에서 vacated는 '비워진'의 의미를 갖고 있다. 따라서 이와 비슷한 단어로는 (B)가 적절하다. 정답 (B)

해석 편지에서 두 번째 단락, 세 번째 줄의 "vacated"와 의미가 가장 가까운 것은?
(A) 닫힌
(B) 비워진
(C) 편안한
(D) 잠겨 있지 않은

183. 세부사항 - 계획된 일정에 대한 사실 내용 ★☆☆
해설 일정표를 살펴 보면 작업 순서가 하층에서 상층으로 진행될 것임을 알 수 있으므로 정답은 (B)이다. 정답 (B)

표현 정리 **carry out** 수행하다 **bottom** 맨 아래 **meal break** 식사 휴식시간

해석 정보에 따르면, 계획된 작업에 대한 사실 내용은?
(A) Ms. Shambels에 의해 진행될 것이다.
(B) 건물의 맨 아래 층에서 시작할 것이다.
(C) 이틀 동안 계속될 것이다.
(D) 식사 시간에만 쉴 것이다.

184. 연계 문제 - 오후 2시까지 장식될 사무실 수 ★★☆
해설 두 번째 지문인 일정표에 따르면 오전 11시 50분부터 시작되는 장식물 설치는 오후 2시까지 1, 2층을 완료할 예정이다. 그런데 편지 첫 번째 단락 후반 내용에서 각 층에 15개의 사무실이 있다고 했으므로 2시까지 30개의 사무실에 장식을 완료할 수 있음을 알 수 있어 정답은 (C)이다. 정답 (C)

해석 오후 2시까지 몇 개의 사무실이 장식될 것으로 예상되는가?
(A) 2
(B) 15
(C) 30
(D) 40

185. 연계 문제 - 설치 당일의 일정표가 보내질 날짜 ★★☆
해설 편지 두 번째 단락 'I would like to remind you to send me a breakdown of the installation day schedule the day prior to the actual setup.'에서 하루 전까지 일정표를 보내달라고 했는데, 일정표를 보면 설치일은 Tuesday, November 28일임을 알 수 있다. 따라서 일정표는 하루 전인 11월 27일에 보내진다고 볼 수 있으므로 정답은 (B)이다. 정답 (B)

해석 설치 당일 일정표가 보내질 날짜는 언제인가?
(A) 11월 26일
(B) 11월 27일
(C) 11월 28일
(D) 11월 29일

문제 186-190번은 다음 광고와 이메일, 그리고 양식을 참조하시오.

유료 광고

Hypercolor Clarity Print 서비스

Hypercolor Clarity는 귀 기업을 위한 아주 확실한 인쇄 서비스를 보장합니다. 그것이 작은 명함이든, 아니면 벽 크기만 한 광고 포스터든, **186(C)**귀하의 모든 인쇄물은 주의 깊게 다뤄지고, 오직 최신 기술을 사용해 인쇄될 것입니다.

186(D)3월에 총액 100달러 이상에 적용되는 20퍼센트 할인을 추가로 받으세요.

186(A),1874월 프로모션:

명함: 500장에 90달러
컬러 소책자: 100장에 75달러
190 포스터: 10장에 55달러

자세한 정보는 inquiry@hypercolor.com으로 이메일을 보내주십시오.

표현 정리 guarantee 보장하다 crystal-clear 아주 명확한 a stack of 뭉치, 무더기 business card 명함 wall-sized 벽 크기의 handle 다루다 with care 주의 깊게 latest 최신의 brochure 소책자

수신: inquiry@hypercolor.com
발신: YeminAsher@soundsori.net
날짜: 4월 2일
Re: 프린트물 주문
첨부: 매뉴얼, 포스터

안녕하세요. Daily Bureau를 통해 광고를 보았고, 저희 인턴 매뉴얼을 준비하기 위해 귀사를 이용하려고 합니다. 저희 회사는 100명 이상의 인턴들을 위한 대형 워크숍을 주최할 예정이며, 따라서 많은 양의 인쇄 자료들을 준비해야 합니다. 이것들은 개별적인 꾸러미로 모아질 필요가 없습니다.

저는 또한 이번 달에 포스터를 특별가로 인쇄할 수 있다는 사실을 귀사의 웹사이트에서 봤습니다. 20매의 포스터를 주문하고 싶습니다. 저희가 행사를 사전에 광고하고자 하기 때문에 포스터가 매뉴얼보다 일주일 먼저 배달된다면 감사하겠습니다. **189 완성된 매뉴얼은 4월 마지막 주에 열릴 워크숍 3일 전에 배달되면 됩니다.**

웹사이트에서 작성된 주문서를 매뉴얼과 포스터가 포함된 파일에 덧붙여 첨부합니다.

188 저의 주문을 받으셨는지 확인해 주시기 바랍니다. 질문이 있으면 망설이지 마시고 연락 주십시오.

Yemin

표현 정리 order form 주문서 hire 고용하다 materials 자료 assemble 모으다, 취합하다 packet 꾸러미 beforehand ~전에 미리 ahead of ~에 앞서 attach 첨부하다 contain 포함하다 along with ~와 함께

Hypercolor Clarity Printing

주문서

이름: *Yemin Asher*
전화번호: *555–0932*
189 배송 일자: *4월 20일과 4월 27일*
수신인: *Yemin Asher, Marketing Department*
배송지: *2914 Segway Lane*
190 주문 물품: 인쇄된 매뉴얼 100부, 포스터 20장
인쇄 물품 형식: *첨부된 파일들*

---

186. 세부사항 – Hypercolor Clarity에 관해 언급된 내용이 아닌 것 ★★★

해설 (A)는 첫 번째 지문 세 번째 단락 April Promotions에서 4월 프로모션 행사가가 적용되는 품목이 있음을 확인할 수 있고, (C)는 첫 단락 'each of your print projects will be handled with care and printed using only the latest technology'에서 최신 기술을 사용해 인쇄가 이루어지는 것을 알 수 있고, (D)는 두 번째 단락 'Enjoy an additional 20% discount on services totaling more than $100.00 in the month of March.'에서 추가 할인이 적용됨을 알 수 있지만, (B) 소규모 기업들만을 상대로 사업을 한다는 내용은 언급되지 않아 정답이다. 정답 (B)

패러프레이징 |지문| be printed using only the latest technology 최신 기술을 사용해 인쇄되다 → |선택지 C| use modern printing equipment 현대적인

장비를 사용한다

표현 정리 promotional 홍보의 do business 사업을 하다 modern 현대적인 equipment 장비

해석 광고에서, Hypercolor Clarity에 대해 언급되지 않은 것은?
(A) 4월에 홍보 가격이 있다.
(B) 작은 회사들만을 상대로 사업을 한다.
(C) 현대적인 인쇄 장비를 사용한다.
(D) 주문에 추가 할인을 제공한다.

187. 연계 문제 – Mr. Asher에 대한 사실 내용 ★★☆

해설 Mr. Asher는 두 번째 지문인 이메일 작성자로, 4월에 사용할 인턴 매뉴얼과 포스터 인쇄를 주문하고 있다. 그런데 첫 번째 지문 April Promotions 항목에 매뉴얼은 포함되지 않기 때문에 정상가를 적용 받는다고 볼 수 있으므로 정답은 (B)이다. 정답 (B)

🔍 **함정 분석** Mr. Asher가 보낸 이메일, 첫 번째 단락 'Good morning. I saw your advertisement in the Daily Bureau paper and would like to hire your company to prepare our intern manuals.'에서 Daily Bureau에 실린 광고를 본 후, 자신의 회사 인턴 매뉴얼 인쇄를 맡기고 싶다고 했지만 Mr. Asher가 이 신문을 구독하는 지는 알 수 없으므로 (D)는 오답이다.

표현 정리 drop off ~에 갖다 놓다 regular 정상의, 보통의 subscribe 구독하다

해석 Mr. Asher에 대한 사실 내용은?
(A) 그는 Hypercolor에 인쇄된 자료들을 갖다 놓을 것이다.
(B) 그는 인턴 매뉴얼 인쇄비로 정상 가격을 지불할 것이다.
(C) 그가 행사 포스터를 직접 디자인했다.
(D) 그는 Daily Bureau를 구독한다.

188. 세부사항 – Mr. Asher의 요청사항 ★☆☆

해설 이메일의 마지막 단락을 보면, 'Please confirm that you have received my order.'라고 하면서 주문을 받았는지 확인해달라고 하고 있으므로, 정답은 (D)이다. 정답 (D)

표현 정리 review 검토하다 material 자료 participate 참여하다 verify 확인하다, 입증하다

해석 이메일에서 Mr. Asher가 Hypercolor에 요청하는 것은?
(A) 인턴들을 위한 자료를 검토하기
(B) 행사에 참여하기
(C) 광고를 디자인하기
(D) 그의 요청사항을 받았다는 것을 확인하기

189. 연계 문제 – 인턴 워크숍 날짜 ★☆☆

해설 이메일 두 번째 단락, 마지막 문장 'The completed manuals should be delivered three days ahead of the workshop, which will be held in the last week of April.'에서 워크숍이 열리기 3일 전에 배송해 달라고 했는데, 주문서의 'Delivery Date: April 20 and April 27'에 적힌 배송 일자를 보면 4월 27일에 매뉴얼이 배송될 것이고, 따라서 워크숍은 3일 후인 4월 30일에 개최된다는 것을 알 수 있으므로 정답은 (D)이다. 정답 (D)

해석 인턴 워크숍은 언제인가?
(A) 4월 20일
(B) 4월 24일
(C) 4월 27일
(D) 4월 30일

190. 연계 문제 – Mr. Asher의 주문에 대한 암시 내용 ★★☆

해설 첫 번째 지문에서 4월 프로모션가로 10장에 55달러인 포스터를 20장 주문했고, 가격은 알 수 없지만 매뉴얼도 100부 주문했기 때문에 총 주문액은 포스터

가격인 110달 이상이 될 것임이 확실하므로 정답은 (C)이다.　　　정답 (C)

🔍 **함정 분석** 이메일 두 번째 단락 'I would appreciate it if the posters are delivered a week before the manuals since we want to advertise the event beforehand.'에서 포스터와 매뉴얼의 배송일을 다르게 요청했으므로 (A)는 오답, 또한 같은 단락 'I saw your advertisement in the Daily Bureau paper and would like to hire your company to prepare our intern manuals.'에서 광고를 보고 Hypercolor Clarity에 인쇄 주문을 했다고 했기 때문에 이번이 처음임을 알 수 있으므로 (D) 역시 오답이다.

표현 정리 process 처리하다

해석 Mr. Asher의 주문에 대해 암시된 내용은?
(A) 그에게 모두 함께 보내질 것이다.
(B) 처리되지 않을 것이다.
(C) 110달러가 넘을 것이다.
(D) 이것이 그의 첫 번째 주문이 아니다.

문제 191-195번은 다음 전단지, 이메일, 그리고 공지를 참조하시오.

대중 연설 능력을 키우세요!

동기를 유발하고 고무시키는 연설을 하는 것이 당신의 일의 일부입니까? 대규모 집단의 사람들에게 간결한 메시지를 전달하는 것은 어떻습니까? 191당신의 직책이 무엇이든 말을 잘 한다는 것은 어떤 전문 직종에 있는 사람에게든 자산입니다. Better Business Bureau of Willmington이 제공하는 특별한 연설 시리즈와 함께 기술을 연마하십시오. 195모든 과정은 6주간 지속되며, 전문 커뮤니케이터인 James Mason이 가르칩니다.

연설 시리즈 과정

193Speaking 101: 대중 연설 소개 목요일, 오후 7시 30분 191장소: Garrick Hall	Speaking 102: 억양과 감정 화요일, 오후 6시 191장소: Lorie Hall
Speaking 103: 내용 만들기 금요일, 오후 5시 30분 191장소: James Hall	Speaking 104: 영감을 주고 동기를 유발하라 토요일, 오전 10시 30분 191장소: Kennedy Hall

가격표와 등록은 www.bbbwillmington.org를 방문해 확인하세요.

중요한 날짜:

1929월 1 - 30일	조기 등록 (5% 할인)
10월 1 - 31일	보통 등록
11월 1일	수업 시작

표현 정리 public speaking 대중 연설　motivational 동기를 부여하는　inspiring 고무시키는　speech 연설　concise 간결한　asset 자산　hone 연마하다

발신: Harriett Lyles ⟨hlyes@wunderlich.net⟩
수신: Registration ⟨registration@bbbwillmington.org⟩
날짜: 10월 3일
제목: 대중 연설 과정

안녕하세요. 192,193저는 2주 전에 대중 연설 능력을 향상시키고자 하는 희망을 갖고, 웹사이트를 방문해 Speaking 101 과정에 등록했습니다. 저는 회사 컨퍼런스에서 기조 연설을 자주 해야 하므로 이 과정은 저에게 매우 가치 있습니다.

195제가 이 과정을 위한 자료를 받을 수 있는지 여쭤보려고 이메일을 보냅니다. 미리 준비하고, 학습하기를 원합니다.

시간을 내주셔서 감사합니다.

Harriett Lyles

표현 정리 register for ~에 등록하다　in the hope of ~에 대한 희망으로　improve 개선시키다　give a keynote speech 기조 연설을 하다　valuable 가치 있는　beforehand 미리

194아래 열거된 과정들은 11월 13일로 강의 시작 날짜가 늦어지게 되었음을 참고하시기 바랍니다.

Speaking 101 – Garrick Hall

모든 과정에 필요한 책자들은 수업 첫날 구내 서점에서 구입하실 수 있습니다. 195만약 미리 책을 구입하시길 원하시면, 담당 강사에게 메일을 보내 긴급 주문할 수 있도록 하십시오. 여러분은 그들의 이메일 주소를 안내 책자에서 찾으실 수 있습니다.

표현 정리 note 참고하다, 주목하다　list 열거하다　pick up 얻다, 수령하다　campus bookstore 구내 서점　in advance 미리　instructor 강사　place an order 주문하다　expedited order 사전 주문　directory 안내 책자

---

191. 세부사항 – 대중연설 과정에 대한 내용　★☆☆

해설 전단지에서 수업이 진행되는 장소를 보면, 각각 Garrick Hall, Lorie Hall, James Hall, Kennedy Hall로 전부 다르다. 그래서 정답은 (C)이다.　정답 (C)

표현 정리 enroll 등록하다　certificate 수료증, 증서, 자격증

해설 대중연설 과정에 관해 언급된 것은?
(A) 11월에 끝날 것이다.
(B) 큰 규모의 그룹이 등록할 것이라고 예상된다.
(C) 각각 다른 장소에서 개최된다.
(D) 과정을 이수한 학생들은 수료증을 받을 것이다.

192. 연계 문제 – Ms. Lyles에 관한 암시 내용　★★★

해설 Ms. Lyles가 10월 3일에 보낸 이메일 'I registered for Speaking 101 at your Web site two weeks ago in the hope of improving my public speaking.'에서 2주 전에 해당 과정에 등록했음을 알 수 있는데, 이를 전단지 'September 1–30: Early registration(5% discount)'에서 확인해 보면 9월에 조기 등록할 경우 5% 할인이 되는 것을 알 수 있다. 따라서 Ms. Lyles는 수업료를 할인받았다고 볼 수 있으므로 정답은 (B)이다.　정답 (B)

🔍 **함정 분석** 이메일 첫 번째 단락 'I often have to give keynote speeches at company conferences'를 보면 이전에도 기조 연설을 했다는 것을 알 수 있으므로 (C)는 오답이다. Ms. Lyles이 연설을 했다는 사실을 알 수는 있지만 CEO인지는 알 수 없으므로 (A)는 오답이다.

표현 정리 tuition 수업료

해석 Ms. Lyles에 관해 암시된 내용은?
(A) 그녀는 회사 CEO이다.
(B) 그녀는 표준 수업료보다 더 적게 지불했다.
(C) 그녀는 대중 연설에 전혀 경험이 없다.
(D) 그녀는 일부 수업 일을 빠져야만 한다.

193. 연계 문제 – Ms. Lyles의 수업 시작 시간　★☆☆

해설 Ms. Lyles가 보낸 이메일 'I registered for Speaking 101 at your Web site two weeks ago in the hope of improving my public speaking.'에 따르면 Speaking 101 과정을 등록했다는 사실을 알 수 있는데, 첫 번째 지문인 전단지에서 Speaking 101은 목요일, 오후 7시 30분으로 예정되어 있으므로 정답은 (D)이다.　정답 (D)

해석 Ms. Lyles의 수업은 몇 시에 시작하는 것으로 일정이 잡혔는가?

(A) 오전 10시 30분
(B) 오후 5시 30분
(C) 오후 6시
(D) 오후 7시 30분

194. 주제 – 공지의 목적 ★☆☆

해설 세 번째 지문인 공지 첫 번째 문장 'Please note that the course listed below will have a later starting date of November 13. Speaking 101 – Garrick Hall'에서 11월 13일로 첫 강의 일자가 변경되었다고 했는데, 첫 번째 지문에서 보면 원래는 11월 1일에 시작하기로 일정이 잡혀 있었음을 알 수 있으므로 정답은 (A)이다. 정답 (A)

패러프레이징 |지문| have a later starting date 시작일을 늦추다 → |선택지 A| schedule adjustments 일정 조정

표현 정리 adjustment 조정 notify A of B A에게 B를 알리다 promote 홍보하다 cancellation 취소

해석 공지의 목적은?
(A) 일정 조정을 알리기 위해
(B) 독자들에게 새로운 과정을 알리기 위해
(C) 학생들을 위한 새로운 서비스를 홍보하기 위해
(D) 취소를 알리기 위해

195. 연계 문제 – Ms. Lyles가 11월 13일 이전에 할 일 ★★★

해설 이메일 두 번째 단락 'I am e-mailing you to ask if I will receive any materials for the course. I would like to prepare and study beforehand.'에서 자료를 미리 받아서 공부하고 싶다고 했고, 공지 사항 두번째 단락 'If you would like to purchase books in advance, please e-mail your course instructor to place an expedited order for you.'에서 책을 미리 구입하기를 원할 경우, 담당 강사에게 이메일을 보낼 것을 권유하고 있다. 그런데 Ms. Lyles가 수강하기를 원하는 연설 시리즈 코스는 첫 번째 지문 'All courses are taught by professional communicator James Mason.'에서 모두 James Mason이 담당하고 있음을 알 수 있으므로 정답은 (B)이다. 정답 (B)

표현 정리 switch 바꾸다

해석 Ms. Lyles가 11월 13일 이전에 할 일은?
(A) 온라인으로 자료를 주문한다.
(B) Mr. Mason에게 연락한다.
(C) 서점에 이메일을 보낸다.
(D) 과정을 바꾼다.

문제 196-200번은 다음 발표, 일정, 그리고 이메일을 참조하시오.

Ventures Hedge Fund: 사장 선거
날짜: 7월 1일

회사 직원들이 선출하는 신임 사장

Ventures Hedge Fund 직원들은 주목해 주십시오: 아시는 바와 같이, 현 사장은 개인적인 이유로 올 해 말 자리에서 물러날 것입니다. 196 **따라서 우리의 지도자를 선출할 때 새로운 민주적 접근법을 취하기로 결정했고, 처음으로 신임 사장을 위한 선거를 개최하려고 합니다.**

선거 행사에 전 직원이 참석해 줄 것을 부탁 드립니다. 197 **후보자들의 정견 발표를 들은 후에 세션 마지막에 투표를 할 것입니다.** 당선자의 이름이 그날 저녁 웹사이트에도 공지될 것입니다.

Greg Fry, 이사회 의장
Ventures Hedge Fund

표현 정리 presidential election 사장[대통령] 선거 attention 주목하세요 step down 물러나다 democratic 민주적인 in entirety 전체, 전부 nominee 후보 platform 정견 (발표) on the spot 현장에서 chairman 의장 board 이사회

Ventures Hedge Fund: 사장 선거 행사
197날짜: 7월 31일

오전 8시 15분	개회
오전 8시 25분	현 사장의 연설
오전 8시 45분	후보자 소개
198오전 8시 55분	**후보자 발표**
오후 12시 30분	점심
오후 1시 30분	회의장으로 복귀
오후 1시 45분	투표
오후 2시 30분	신임 사장 발표
198오후 3시	**신임 사장의 연설**

표현 정리 address 연설

발신: BrandonJiles@ventures.com
수신: MarshaPidjorn@ventures.com
제목: 축하
날짜: 8월 1일

Marsha,

Ventures Hedge Fund의 새로운 사장이 된 것을 개인적으로 축하하고 환영합니다. 당신은 우리 회사를 밝고 번영하는 미래로 인도하도록 열광적으로 선출되었습니다. 저는 우리 회사가 올바른 선택을 했다고 믿습니다.

199지난 12년 이상, 우리와 함께 한 경험과 우리의 가장 최근의 협력에 대한 당신의 소중한 기여를 생각하면, 저는 당신으로부터 오직 최고만을 기대합니다. 사장으로서의 첫 임무는 15층 중역실로 옮기는 것이 될 것입니다. Misty Allen이 당신의 재배치를 도울 수 있을 것입니다. 200저는 이번 주 화요일 다음 이사회에서 만날 수 있기를 기대합니다.

Brandon

표현 정리 enthusiastically 열광적으로 prosperous 번영하는 valuable 소중한, 귀중한 contribution 기여 collaboration 협력, 공동의 endeavor 노력, 시도 noting but 오직 executive office 중역실 relocation 재배치 board meeting 이사회

196. 세부사항 – Ventures Hedge Fund의 사장 선거에 대한 내용 ★★☆

해설 첫 번째 지문 첫 번째 단락 'As such, we have decided to take a new democratic approach to our leadership and will hold an election for our new president for the first time.'에서 처음으로 선거를 통해 사장을 선출하겠다고 했으므로 이전의 사장들은 선거로 선출된 적이 없다는 것을 짐작할 수 있어 정답은 (B)이다. 정답 (B)

🔍함정 분석 발표문 마지막 문장 'The winner will be announced on the spot.'에서 당선자는 현장에서 발표될 예정일 뿐, 추후에 발표되지 않으므로 (A)는 오답이다.

표현 정리 previous 이전의 biannual 연 2회의

해석 Ventures Hedge Fund의 사장 선거에 대해 언급된 것은?
(A) 신임 사장은 나중에 발표될 것이다.
(B) 이전 사장들이 선택된 방법이 아니었다.
(C) 선거에 관한 이사회가 열릴 것이다.
(D) 연 2회의 행사로 일정이 잡혀 있다.

(B) Ms. Allen이 자리 옮기는 것을 돕는다.
(C) 곧 있을 모임에 참석한다.
(D) 소지품을 옮길 사람을 찾는다.

197. 세부사항 – 신임 사장의 이름이 발표되는 시점 ★☆☆
해설 두 번째 지문, 사장 선거 행사의 일정을 보면 7월 31일에 선거가 있고, 당일 오후 2시 30분에 신임 사장 투표 결과를 발표하므로 정답은 (C)이다. **정답 (C)**

표현 정리 make public 공표하다

해석 신임 사장의 이름은 언제 발표되는가?
    (A) 7월 1일
    (B) 7월 30일
    (C) 7월 31일
    (D) 8월 1일

198. 연계 문제 – Ms. Pidjorn에 관한 암시 내용 ★★☆
해설 세 번째 지문은 Ms. Pidjorn이 신임 사장으로 선출된 것을 축하한다는 내용의 이메일인데, 두 번째 지문에서 7월 31일 사장 선거 일정을 보면 '8:55 A.M. Nominee Presentations'와 '3:00 P.M. New President's Address'라고 되어 있다. 그러므로 Ms. Pidjorn은 오전에 후보자로서 정견 발표를 하고, 오후에는 신임 사장으로서 두 번 연설을 했음을 알 수 있으므로 (B)가 정답이다. **정답 (B)**

🔍 **함정 분석** Mr. Jiles가 Ms. Pidjorn에게 보낸 축하 이메일 내용 중 'Your first order of presidential business will be to move to the executive office on the 15th floor.'에서 사무실 이전 작업을 하도록 지시하는 것이 첫 업무가 될 것이라고 했는데, 이것은 Mr. Jiles가 사장에게 내리는 임무가 아니기 때문에 (A)는 오답이다.

표현 정리 count the votes 표를 세다

해석 Ms. Pidjorn에 대해 암시된 내용은?
    (A) 그녀는 Mr. Jiles로부터 첫 임무를 받았다.
    (B) 그녀는 선거 행사 동안 두 번 연설했다.
    (C) 그녀는 직접적으로 Mr. Fry 아래서 일한 적이 있다.
    (D) 그녀는 선거 개표 과정을 도왔다.

199. 세부사항 – Mr. Jiles에 관한 내용 ★★☆
해설 이메일의 두 번째 단락에서, 'Given your experience with us over the past 12 years and your valuable contributions to our most recent collaborative endeavor,'라고 했기 때문에 최근에 같이 협력해서 일을 했다는 것을 알 수 있으므로, 정답은 (A)이다. **정답 (A)**

표현 정리 decade 10년

해석 Mr. Jiles에 관해 언급된 것은?
    (A) 전에 Ms. Pidjorn과 프로젝트를 같이 한 적이 있다.
    (B) 선거에서 투표를 할 수 없었다.
    (C) 약 10년 전쯤에 회사에서 일을 시작했다.
    (D) 그의 사무실은 Mr. Pidjorn의 사무실과 같은 층에 있을 것이다.

200. 세부사항 – Ms. Pidjorn이 할 것으로 예상되는 일 ★★☆
해설 이메일 마지막 문장 'We look forward to seeing you at the next board meeting this Tuesday.'에서 화요일에 있을 이사회에서 만날 것을 기대한다고 했으므로 (C)가 정답이다. **정답 (C)**

🔍 **함정 분석** 이메일 'Misty Allen will be available to help you with your relocation.'에서 Misty Allen은 Ms. Pidjorn이 사무실 옮기는 것을 도울 사람일 뿐, 도움을 받을 사람이 아니어서 (B)는 오답이다.

패러프레이징 |지문| the next board meeting 다음 이사회 → |선택지 C| an upcoming gathering 곧 있을 모임

표현 정리 relocate 이동하다   upcoming 곧 있을   gathering 모임
belongings 소지품

해석 Mr. Jiles는 Ms. Pidjorn이 무엇을 하기를 기대하는가?
    (A) 직원들에게 할 연설문을 작성한다.

TEST 04

문제 147-148번은 다음 이메일을 참조하시오.

발신: John Wilson 〈jwilson@vibrant.com〉
수신: Paul Vance 〈pvance@vibrant.com〉
날짜: 6월 9일, 월요일
제목: 주문

Paul,

148 저희 팀이 방금 두 번째 공장 조립라인 점검을 마쳤습니다. 점검하는 동안, 한 기계에서 금요일에 조립라인을 재가동하기 전에 교체돼야 할 부품들을 발견했습니다. 저희는 다양한 부품 재고를 보유하고 있습니다. 그러나 저희가 보유하고 있지 않은 몇 개의 부품이 있습니다. 저희 공급업체로부터 필요한 부품을 얻기 위해 다음 날 도착하는 속달로 주문해도 될까요? 147 이 문제로 비용이 상당히 증가할 것으로 보이지만, 마감기한까지 조립라인을 다시 가동시키기 위해서는 다른 방법이 없어 보입니다.

John

표현 정리 complete 완료하다, 끝마치다 inspection 점검 assembly line 조립라인 discover 발견하다 parts 부품 replace 교체하다 restart 재가동하다 have something in stock 재고로 보유하다 overnight order 다음 날 도착하는 속달 주문 place an order 주문하다 supplier 공급업체 substantially 상당히 run 작동하다 deadline 마감기한

147. 세부사항 – 이메일을 보낸 이유 ★☆☆
해설 이메일 후반 'Can I place an overnight order from our supplier to get the needed parts?'에서 조립라인을 재가동하기 위해 필요한 부품을 공급업체로부터 주문해도 되는지 허락을 구하고 있으므로 (B)가 정답이다. **정답 (B)**

표현 정리 repairperson 수리공, 정비사 permission 허락, 허가 order 주문 schedule 일정을 잡다 inspection 점검

해석 Mr. Wilson이 Mr. Vance에게 이메일을 보낸 이유는?
(A) 수리공을 찾기 위해
(B) 허락을 구하기 위해
(C) 주문을 점검하기 위해
(D) 점검 일정을 잡기 위해

148. 세부사항 – Mr. Wilson에 관해 언급된 내용 ★★☆
해설 첫 번째 문장 'My team has just completed its inspection of the factory's second assembly line.'에서 공장의 두 번째 조립라인 점검을 마쳤다고 했으므로 (C)가 정답이다. **정답 (C)**

🔍 **함정 분석** 'Can I place an overnight order from our supplier to get the needed parts?'에서 필요한 부품을 얻기 위해 공급업체로부터 다음 날 배달되는 속달 주문을 해도 되는지 허락을 구하고 있고, 이 허락을 받아야 교체 부품 주문이나 수리를 할 수 있으므로 (A), (B), (D)는 오답이다.

패러프레이징 |지문| have just completed its inspection 막 점검을 마쳤다 → |선택지 C| finished an examination 점검을 마쳤다

표현 정리 replacement parts 교체 부품 make a repair 수리를 하다 examination 점검 machine parts 기계 부품

해석 Mr. Wilson에 관해 나타난 내용은?
(A) 그는 교체 부품을 주문했다.
(B) 그는 필요한 수리를 했다.
(C) 그는 점검을 마쳤다.

(D) 그는 일부 기계 부품을 받았다.

문제 149-150번은 다음 광고를 참조하시오.

Frank 패밀리 레스토랑
149 10월 스페셜*

비프 커틀릿	4인분 치킨 디너
완벽하게 요리된 부드러운 비프 커틀릿. 모짜렐라 치즈와 홈메이드 소스를 얹음. 파스타, 샐러드, 빵이 옆에 있으며 탄산음료가 포함됨. 단 15달러!	포함: 구운 치킨 또는 프라이드 치킨 8조각 두 가지 사이드 메뉴 빵과 샐러드(드레싱은 선택) 음료 포함(탄산음료, 차, 커피) 모두 30달러!
슈프림 피자	애플 파이
얇은, 레귤러, 또는 두꺼운 크러스트를 선택하세요. 페퍼로니, 소시지, 페퍼, 올리브 및 양파가 있는 세 가지 치즈. 단 10달러!	전체(8조각) 8달러 하프(4조각) 4.5달러 조각 1.5달러 애플파이 한 조각에 아이스크림 한 스쿠프를 50센트에 추가하세요!

150 *10월 1 – 31일까지 유효함. 다른 할인과 함께 사용할 수 없음. 포장 또는 레스토랑에서 식사.

표현 정리 tender 부드러운 cutlet 커틀릿(고기, 생선, 야채 따위를 다져 납작하게 만든 뒤 튀김 옷을 입혀 익힌 것) cooked to perfection 완벽하게 요리된 topped with ~을 얹은 homemade 수제의 baked 구운 fried 튀긴 include 포함하다 crust 크러스트(빵 껍질) pepperoni 페퍼로니(소시지의 일종) pepper 페퍼, 피망 a scoop of ice cream 아이스크림 한 스쿠프 valid 유효한 combine with ~와 합치다 take out 포장해 가져가다 eat in 레스토랑에서 먹다

149. 주제 – 광고의 목적 ★☆☆
해설 Frank's 패밀리 레스토랑의 10월 스페셜에 대한 광고 내용이다. 4가지 메뉴에 대해 자세히 설명하는 동시에 저렴한 가격을 강조하고 있으므로 이 광고의 목적은 고객 유치를 위한 광고임을 알 수 있어 정답은 (C)이다. **정답 (C)**

표현 정리 promote 홍보하다 comment on ~에 대해 평하다 attract 유치하다, 끌어 모으다 announce 알리다 opening 개점

해석 광고의 목적은 무엇인가?
(A) 신 메뉴를 홍보하기 위해
(B) 서비스에 대해 평가하기 위해
(C) 고객을 유치하기 위해
(D) 개점을 알리기 위해

150. 세부사항 – specials에 대한 내용 ★★☆
해설 광고 하단 '*Valid from October 1 – October 31'에서 알 수 있듯이 10월 한 달 동안만 유효하다고 했으므로 (A)가 정답이다. **정답 (A)**

🔍 **함정 분석** '*Valid from October 1 – October 31. Cannot be combined with other offers. Take out or eat in.'에서 알 수 있듯이 10월 한 달 동안만 유효하며, 다른 할인 쿠폰과 사용할 수 없다. 그리고 포장 주문 및 레스토랑에서 식사할 경우에 모두 사용 가능하므로 (B)와 (C)는 오답이다.

패러프레이징 |지문| Valid from October 1 – October 31 10월 1일부터 31일까지 유효하다 → |선택지 A| available for one month 한 달 동안 이용 가능하다

표현 정리 available 이용 가능한 orders to go 포장 주문 be limited to ~에 한정되다

해석 스페셜에 대해 언급된 내용은?
(A) 한 달 동안 이용 가능하다.
(B) 포장 주문일 경우에만 해당된다.
(C) 다른 쿠폰과 함께 사용할 수 있다.
(D) 네 곳의 지점으로만 한정되어 있다.

문제 151-153번은 다음 정보를 확인하시오.

> ¹⁵¹National Center for Health and Wellness는 10대들의 주중 일과에 규칙적인 운동을 포함시킬 것을 권장한다. ¹⁵²작년에 진행된 설문조사에 따르면, 요즘 10대 중 45퍼센트가 과체중이다. 사회적으로 비난을 받는 것과 더불어, 과체중은 장단기적으로 건강 문제를 일으킬 수 있다. 그러므로 10대들은 건강식을 선택하고, 충분한 수면을 취하며, 규칙적으로 운동을 하는 것이 필수적이다.
>
> ¹⁵³규칙적으로 운동을 하는 10대들은 피부가 더 좋아지고, 근육과 뼈가 더 강해졌으며, 에너지가 더 많아졌다고 보고되었다. 10대들은 조직화된 스포츠 활동에 참여하거나 댄스나 피트니스 프로그램에 등록하거나, 아니면 단순히 일상에서 걷기를 많이 함으로써 규칙적인 운동 효과를 즐길 수 있다. 귀댁의 10대 자녀들이 건강해지도록 도울 수 있는 방법에 관한 자세한 정보는 www.nchw.org를 방문하면 알 수 있다.

표현 정리 recommend 권장하다 teenager 10대 incorporate A in(to) B A를 B에 포함시키다 regular exercise 규칙적인 운동 conduct a survey 설문조사를 하다 overweight 과체중의 in addition to ~에 더하여 frown upon ~에 눈살을 찌푸리다, 못마땅해 하다 lead to ~로 이어지다, 야기하다 essential 필수적인 adopt 채택하다 healthy diet 건강식 sufficient 충분한 muscles 근육 bones 뼈 organized 조직화된, 체계화된 daily routine 일상 생활 get fit 건강해지다(= stay fit)

151. 주제 – 정보의 목적 ★☆☆
해설 첫 번째 문장 'The National Center for Health and Wellness recommends that teenagers incorporate regular exercise into their weekly routines.'를 통해 이 정보는 10대들이 규칙적인 운동을 생활화함으로써 건강한 생활을 유지할 수 있다는 것을 알리는 내용이므로 정답은 (D)이다. 정답 (D)

🔍함정 분석 첫 번째 문장 'The National Center for Health and Wellness recommends that teenagers incorporate regular exercise into their weekly routines.'가 전하고자 하는 것은 10대들에게 규칙적인 운동을 권장하고자 함일 뿐, (A)나 (C)처럼 경고하거나 요구하고자 하는 것이 아니므로 오답이다.

패러프레이징 |지문| recommend that teenagers incorporate regular exercise into their weekly routines 십대들이 규칙적인 운동을 그들의 주중 일과에 포함시킬 것을 권장한다 → |선택지 D| promote healthy practices 건강한 운동을 홍보하다

표현 정리 incorrectly 부정확하게 inform A of B A에게 B를 알려주다 teen 십대(= teenager) demand 요구하다 weight loss 체중 감량 promote 홍보하다 healthy practices 건강 실천

해석 정보의 목적은 무엇인가?
(A) 잘못된 운동에 대해 경고하기 위해
(B) 10대들에게 새로운 프로그램에 대해 알려주기 위해
(C) 체중 감량 프로그램을 요구하기 위해
(D) 건강 실천을 홍보하기 위해

152. 세부사항 – 10대들에 대해 언급된 내용 ★★☆
해설 두 번째 문장 'According to a survey conducted last year, nearly 45% of teenagers today are overweight.'에서 오늘날 10대 중 45퍼센트가

과체중이라고 했으므로 정답은 (C)이다. 정답 (C)

패러프레이징 |지문| nearly 45% of teenagers today are overweight 오늘날 십대들 거의 45%가 과체중이다 → |선택지 C| almost half have weight problems 거의 절반이 체중 문제가 있다

표현 정리 dieting 다이어트 하는 것 refuse to ~을 거부하다 weight problem 체중 문제

해석 10대들에 대해 언급된 것은?
(A) 다이어트에 대해 배우지 않는다.
(B) 대부분은 운동을 거부한다.
(C) 거의 절반이 체중 문제를 갖고 있다.
(D) 피트니스 프로그램을 즐긴다.

153. 세부사항 – 10대들이 운동할 경우의 이점 ★★☆
해설 두 번째 단락, 첫 번째 문장 'Teenagers who regularly exercise report having better skin, stronger muscles and bones, and more energy.'에서 규칙적으로 운동하는 10대들은 피부가 더 좋아지고, 근육, 뼈가 더 강해지고, 에너지도 많아진다고 했으므로 정답은 (D)이다. 정답 (D)

패러프레이징 |지문| have better skin, stronger muscles and bones, and more energy 피부가 더 좋아지며 근육, 뼈가 더 강해지고 에너지도 더 많아진다 → |선택지 D| boost their energy levels 에너지 양을 증가시켜 준다

표현 정리 succeed 성공하다 improve 향상시키다 school performance 학업 성취 reduce 줄이다 caloric intake 칼로리 섭취 boost 북돋우다, 신장시키다

해석 10대들을 위한 운동 중 한 가지 장점은?
(A) 스포츠에서 성공하게 해 줄 수 있다.
(B) 학업 성취를 향상시켜 줄 수 있다.
(C) 칼로리 섭취를 줄여줄 수 있다.
(D) 에너지 레벨을 향상시켜 줄 수 있다.

문제 154-155번은 다음 회람을 참조하시오.

> **회람**
>
> 발신: Pauline Samuelson
> 수신: 모든 상점 매니저들
> 참조: Penny Bale
>
> Deborah's의 올 가을 제품 출시와 함께 새로운 마케팅 캠페인을 시작합니다. ^{155(D)}저희 광고 및 마케팅 팀은 소셜 미디어와 웹사이트에서 볼 수 있는 동영상 광고에 나오는 캐릭터가 등장하는 홍보 디스플레이를 디자인했습니다. ^{155(B)}이들 디스플레이는 다음 주에 모든 소매점으로 배송될 것입니다. ¹⁵⁴귀 상점 앞에 눈에 띄게 진열해 주십시오. ^{155(C)}저희는 고객들이 매장에 들어와 구경하는 동안 가을 패션 코너에서 의류를 구매하기를 바랍니다. 질문이 있으면, 제 비서인 Penny Bale (pbale@deborahs.com)에게 문의하시기 바랍니다.

표현 정리 in conjunction with ~와 함께 release 출시 a series of 일련의 promotional displays 홍보 디스플레이 featuring 등장하는 ship 배송하다 retail location 소매점 in the coming week 다가오는 주에 prominently 눈에 잘 띄게, 두드러지게 draw A into B A를 B에 끌어들이다 browse 둘러보다 purchase 구매하다 assistant 조수, 비서

154. 세부사항 – 매장 매니저들이 지시 받은 사항 ★★☆
해설 지문 중반 'Be sure to prominently display them at the front of your stores.'에서 본사에서 시작하는 홍보 디스플레이를 각 매장 앞에 눈에 띄도록 진열해 달라고 요청하고 있으므로 정답은 (B)이다. 정답 (B)

표현 정리 instruct 지시하다 submit 제출하다 place 놓다, 두다, 배치하다 marketing materials 마케팅 자료 inventory 재고 report on ~에 대해 보고하다

해석 매장 매니저들이 하도록 지시받은 것은?
(A) 소셜 미디어 마케팅을 위한 아이디어를 제출하라고
(B) 마케팅 자료를 눈에 띄는 곳에 배치하라고
(C) 상점 내 의류 재고를 교체하라고
(D) 광고의 성공에 대해 보고하라고

155. 세부사항 – 새로운 마케팅 캠페인에 대한 내용 ★★☆
해설 두 번째 줄 'Our advertising and marketing team has designed a series of promotional displays featuring characters from the video ads we are showing on social media and other Web sites.'에서 올 가을 새롭게 선보이는 마케팅 캠페인에는 소셜 미디어와 웹사이트와 같은 온라인에서 선보이는 동영상이 포함돼 있다는 것을 알 수 있으므로 정답은 (D)이다. 정답 (D)

🔍 **함정 분석** 새로운 마케팅 캠페인에는 실제 상점 직원들이 아닌 동영상의 캐릭터가 나오며, 지난주에 시작된 것이 아니라 현재 시작하고 있고, 쇼핑객 유치가 목표이긴 하지만 젊은 쇼핑객들로 한정되어 있는 지는 알 수 없다.

표현 정리 feature 특별히 포함하다, 특징으로 삼다 aim to ~하는 것을 목표로 하다 attract 유치하다 include 포함하다

해석 새로운 마케팅 캠페인에 대해 언급된 것은?
(A) 실제 상점 직원들이 나온다.
(B) 지난주에 시작되었다.
(C) 젊은 쇼핑객 유치를 목표로 한다.
(D) 온라인 요소를 포함한다.

문제 156-157번은 다음 문자 메시지를 참조하시오.

Necker, Jeff 156Forrest Avenue 지점이 다음 달에 폐점한다는 얘기 들었어요?	오후 3시 22분
Kirby, Irene 156농담해요?	오후 3시 23분
Necker, Jeff 장사가 잘 안 된대요. 지금 Mr. Ferguson과 창구 직원 한 명만 그곳에서 근무하고 있어요.	오후 3시 24분
Kirby, Irene 어머, 난 몰랐어요. Mr. Ferguson은 어떻게 되는 거예요?	오후 3시 27분
Necker, Jeff 157(A)Ferguson 씨는 Allen Avenue 지점으로 옮길 거예요. 또 다른 매니저가 필요하대요. 또한 다른 대출 담당직원도 찾고 있다고 들었어요. 관심 있어요?	오후 3시 31분
Kirby, Irene 157(C)물론이죠. 하지만 거기서 일하려면 두 개 언어를 구사할 줄 알아야 하는 것으로 알고 있어요.	오후 3시 32분
Necker, Jeff 특정 고객들과 의사소통할 때 도움이 되겠지만 꼭 그래야 되는 것은 아니에요.	오후 3시 33분
Kirby, Irene 지원한다고 손해 볼 건 없겠군요.	오후 3시 35분

표현 정리 be down to ~밖에 남지 않다, ~으로 줄어든다 teller (은행) 창구 직원 transfer to ~로 이전하다 loan officer 대출 담당직원 bilingual 두 개 언어를 할 줄 아는 communicate with ~와 의사 소통하다 apply 지원하다

156. 의도 파악하기 – Ms. Kirby의 반응과 관련된 내용 ★★☆
해설 Mr. Necker는 오후 3시 22분에 'Did you hear that the Forrest Avenue branch is closing next month?'라는 메시지를 Ms. Kirby에게 보냈고, 이에 대해 'You've got to be kidding.'이라고 반응했다. 이는 Mr. Necker가 한 말을 Ms. Kirby가 전혀 모르고 있었다는 것을 의미하므로 정답은 (B)이다. 정답 (B)

표현 정리 unexpected 예상치 못한 be worried about ~에 대해 걱정하다 be surprised to ~을 하게 되어 놀라다

해석 Ms. Kirby가 오후 3시 23분에 "농담해요?"라고 한 이유는?
(A) 그녀는 Mr. Necker가 재미있다고 생각한다.
(B) 그녀는 예상치 못한 소식을 들었다.
(C) 그녀는 일자리를 잃는 것에 대해 걱정하고 있다.
(D) Mr. Necker에게서 소식을 듣게 되어 놀랐다.

157. 유추 – Allen Avenue 지점에 대한 내용 ★★☆
해설 Ms. Kirby는 Allen Avenue 지점에서 대출 담당직원을 구한다는 얘기를 듣고 관심을 보이면서, 'Sure, but I thought you had to be bilingual to work there.'라며 두 개 언어를 할 줄 알아야 지원할 수 있는 것으로 알고 있다고 말한 것으로 보아 이 지점에는 비영어권 고객들이 있음을 알 수 있으므로 정답은 (C)이다. 정답 (C)

🔍 **함정 분석** Mr. Ferguson이 Allen Avenue 지점으로 발령받을 것이라고 한 것을 보면 그가 Allen Avenue 지점을 설립했다는 (A)는 오답이다. 이 지점이 최근 설치된 지점인지는 메시지 내용에 없으므로 (B) 역시 오답이다. 또 Mr. Necker가 현재 어느 지점에서 근무하는지에 대한 힌트가 없으므로 (D)도 오답이다.

표현 정리 found 설립하다 newest 최신의 non-English 비영어권의 currently 현재

해석 Allen Avenue 지점에 관해 암시된 것은?
(A) Mr. Ferguson이 설립했다.
(B) 이 은행의 최근 설치된 지점이다.
(C) 비영어권 고객들을 보유하고 있다.
(D) Mr. Necker가 현재 근무하는 곳이다.

문제 158-160번은 다음 공지 내용을 참조하시오.

TALENT SHOW

텔레비전 3번 채널은 4월 5일 토요일, 오후 6시 Albert Theater에서 탤런트 쇼를 개최합니다. 자신의 특별한 능력을 현장에 있는 관객과 함께 나누기를 원하는 사람은 누구나 참가 오디션에 초대됩니다. Bridgeport에서 처음 열리는 158이 특별 행사는 3번 채널 소속인 Mayra Corrigan이 진행할 것입니다. 티켓 판매 수익금은 경제적으로 빈곤한 아이들에게 무료 연기 및 댄스 수업을 제공하는 비영리단체 Sunflower Center에 기부될 것입니다.

모든 참가자들의 공연은 추후 방송을 위해 녹화되며, 기념 티셔츠를 받게 될 것입니다. 1603명의 우승자들은 전국 TV 프로그램인 'Talent Scout' 오디션을 위해 Las Vegas에 초대될 것입니다. 교통과 숙박은 쇼 제작사인 Miracle Entertainment가 지불할 것입니다.

159탤런트 쇼의 참가자가 50명으로 제한되기 때문에 오디션이 필요합니다. 신청을 위해서는 www.TV3.com에 있는 지원서를 작성해 주세요. 오디션은 5월 24-28일 한 주 동안 다른 장소에서 열릴 것입니다. 나이 제한은 없지만 18세 미만의 어린이들은 성인의 동반을 필요로 합니다. 참가자들은 지역 예술 커뮤니티 회원들과 3번 채널 관계자들이 포함된 판정단이 선정될 것입니다.

표현 정리 host a show 쇼를 진행하다 share A with B A를 B와 공유하다,

함께 하다 **live audience** 현장에 있는 관객 **participate** 참가하다 **proceeds** 수익금 **donate to** ~에게 기부하다 **non-profit** 비영리단체 **acting** 연기 **economically disadvantaged** 경제적으로 빈곤한 **participant** 참가자 **commemorative** 기념의 **be limited to** ~에 제한되다 **sign up** 신청하다 **application form** 지원서 **be held** 열리다, 개최되다 **venue** 현장, 장소 **age restrictions** 나이 제한 **accompany** 동반하다 **a panel of judges** 판정단 **personalities** 관계자들

158. 유추 – Albert Theater에 대한 내용 ★☆☆
해설 공지 첫 번째 단락 'This special event, the first of its kind in Bridgeport, will be hosted by Channel 3's own Mayra Corrigan.'에서 이 특별 행사가 Bridgeport에서는 최초로 열린다고 했으므로 Albert Theater는 Bridgeport에 위치한다고 볼 수 있어 정답은 (D)이다.　　　　정답 (D)

🔍 **함정 분석** 첫 번째 단락 'Channel 3 television is hosting a talent show at the Albert Theater on Saturday, April 5, at 6:00 P.M.'에서 Albert Theater는 행사가 열리는 장소일 뿐, 어린이들을 위한 행사를 후원하는 것은 아니므로 (A)는 틀리고, 'Because participation in the talent show is limited to fifty individuals, auditions are required.'에서 참가자가 50명으로 제한되는 것일 뿐, 좌석이 50개인 것은 아니므로 역시 오답, 'Auditions will be held during the week of March 24-28 at a different venue.'에서 오디션은 다른 장소에서 열린다고 했으므로 (C)도 오답이다.

표현 정리 **sponsor** 후원하다 **reserve** 예약하다, 보유하다 **be located in** ~에 위치하다

해석 Albert Theater에 대해 암시된 것은?
(A) 어린이들을 위한 행사를 후원하고 있다.
(B) 좌석이 50명을 위해 예약되어 있다.
(C) 오디션이 거기서 열릴 것이다.
(D) Bridgeport에 위치해 있다.

159. 세부사항 – 공지를 읽은 사람들에 관한 내용 ★★☆
해설 마지막 단락 'Because participation in the talent show is limited to fifty individuals, auditions are required. To sign up, complete an application form at www.TV3.com.'에서 탤런트 쇼의 참가자는 50명으로 한정되어 있으므로 지원서를 작성해 신청하라고 했으므로 참가할 수 있는 자격을 얻기 위해 경쟁을 해야 한다는 것을 알 수 있어 정답은 (B)이다.　정답 (B)

표현 정리 **apply for** ~에 지원하다, 신청하다 **compete for** ~을 위해 경쟁하다 **local celebrities** 지역 인사들

해석 공지를 읽은 사람들에게 요청되는 것은?
(A) 무료 수업을 신청한다.
(B) (일)자리를 위해 경쟁해야 한다.
(C) 지역 인사들과 만난다.
(D) TV 스튜디오를 방문한다.

160. 문장 위치 찾기 ★★☆
해설 두 번째 단락 'Three winners will be invited to go to Las Vegas to audition for the national TV program 'Talent Scout.''에서 우승자는 라스 베가스로 오디션을 보러 가게 될 것이라고 했으므로, 이 다음에 그들의 교통과 숙박 비용에 대한 내용이 나오는 것이 자연스러워 (C)가 정답이다.　정답 (C)

표현 정리 **transportation** 교통 **lodging** 숙박 **pay for** ~을 지불하다 **producer** 제작사

해석 [1], [2], [3], [4] 중 다음 문장이 들어가기에 가장 적합한 곳은?
　"교통과 숙박은 쇼 제작사인 Miracle Entertainment가 지불할 것입니다."
(A) [1]
(B) [2]
(C) [3]

(D) [4]

문제 161~163번은 다음 광고를 참조하시오.

> **곧 여름이 시작됩니다!**
> Polar로 시원하게 보내세요.
>
> 161 에어컨을 적절하게 유지 보수 줌으로써 현대적인 에어컨 시스템은 바깥 온도가 상승할 때 귀댁을 시원하게 유지해 줄 것입니다. 관리가 제대로 되지 않을 경우, 폭염 속에서 귀댁의 에어컨 시스템은 기능 발휘가 안 되거나 아예 작동이 멈출 수도 있습니다.
>
> Polar Heating & Cooling으로 전화번호 555-3033으로 전화주세요. 저희가 고객님 가족들이 편안한 여름을 보내실 수 있도록 도와 드릴 수 있습니다.
>
> 에어컨 예방 정비 기본 패키지 – 정가 99.99달러
> <u>현재가 75달러*</u>
>
> 포함:
> - 162(C) 에어컨 기기, 통풍구 및 전기 연결의 완벽한 점검
> - 에어컨 기기와 배수관 청소
> - 온도조절장치, 온도 범위, 기류 및 공기필터 체크
> - 모터 기름칠
> - 권장되는 추가적인 모든 작업에 대한 무료 견적 및 5% 할인
>
> 162(D) Polar Heating & Cooling은 30년 이상 Glendale 주민들과 주위 지역 사회에 우수한 서비스를 제공해 왔습니다. 162 저희는 가족이 운영하는 난방 및 냉방 설치, 유지 보수 및 수리 업체입니다. 저희는 Glendale 지역에서 최초로 정식으로 인가된 Carbon Furnace & Ice King 에어컨 설치 업체였습니다. 163 저희가 하는 모든 작업은 1년 보증이 지원됩니다.
>
> *5월 31일까지 할인 혜택 제공됨
>
> Polar Heating & Cooling
> 879 Harmony Avenue
> Glendale, AZ 09830
> (218) 555-3033
> 162(A) www.polarheatingcooling.com

표현 정리 **proper** 적절한 **maintenance** 유지 보수 **air conditioning** 에어컨 **underperform** 기능을 하지 못하다 **fail** 실패하다, 작동하지 않다 **in the middle of** ~도중에 **heat wave** 폭염 **ensure** 반드시 ~하게 하다, 보장하다 **air-conditioning unit** 에어컨 기기 **vent** 통풍구 **electrical connection** 전기 연결 **drain line** 배수관 **thermostat** 온도조절장치 **temperature range** 온도 범위 **air flow** 기류 **air filter** 공기 필터 **lubricate** 기름칠하다 **free quote** 무료 견적 **additional** 추가적인 **exceptional** 우수한 **residents** 주민들 **surrounding** 주위의 **family-owned** 가족 사업 **family-operated** 가족 운영의 **heating** 난방 **cooling** 냉방 **installation** 설치 **repair** 수리 **authorized** 정식으로 인가된 **installer** 설치 업체 **back** 지원하다 **warranty** 보증

161. 세부사항 – 광고의 대상 ★☆☆
해설 첫 번째 문장 'With proper maintenance, modern air-conditioning systems will keep your home cool when the temperature outside rises.'에서 에어컨을 제대로 유지해 줄 경우 바깥 온도가 상승할 때 집을 시원하게 해 줄 것이라고 했으므로 이 광고의 대상은 집주인들임을 알 수 있어 정답은 (A)이다.　정답 (A)

표현 정리 **homeowner** 집주인 **technician** 기술자 **business owner** 사업주 **job seeker** 구직자

해석 광고 대상은 누구인가?
(A) 집주인들
(B) 기술자들

(C) 사업주들
(D) 구직자들

162. 세부사항 – Polar Heating & Cooling에 관한 내용이 아닌 것 ★★☆

해설 광고 하단 'We are a family-owned, family-operated heating and cooling installation, maintenance, and repair company.'에서 이 회사는 설치, 정비 및 수리업체일 뿐, 구매 제품을 무료로 설치한다는 내용은 없으므로 (B)의 내용은 틀리다. **정답 (B)**

🔍 함정 분석 광고 제일 하단에 www.polarheatingcooling.com이라는 홈페이지 주소가 언급되었으므로 (A)는 사실이고, 기본 패키지 항목 'Complete inspection of air-conditioning unit, vents, and electrical connections'에서 에어컨 기기도 명시돼 있으므로 고장 난 에어컨 기기를 수리해 준다는 (C)도 맞다. 또한 광고 후반 'For over 30 years, Polar Heating and Cooling has been providing exceptional service to residents of Glendale and the surrounding communities.'에서 이 회사는 30년 넘게 운영해 왔음을 알 수 있으므로 (D)도 맞는 내용이다.

표현 정리 operate 운영하다 install 설치하다 purchase 구입한 제품 for free 무료로 broken 고장 난, 깨진 decades 수십 년

해석 Polar Heating & Cooling에 대해 언급되지 않은 것은?
(A) 웹사이트를 운영한다.
(B) 구입한 것은 무료로 설치해 준다.
(C) 고장 난 에어컨 기기를 수리해 줄 수 있다.
(D) 수십 년 전에 회사를 시작했다.

163. 세부사항 – Polar Heating & Cooling의 서비스에 대한 내용 ★☆☆

해설 광고 후반 'All of our work is backed by a one-year warranty.'에서 알 수 있듯이 1년 보증이 지원되므로 (C)가 정답이다. **정답 (C)**

패러프레이징 |지문| be backed by a one-year warranty 1년 보증이 지원된다 → be covered by a guarantee 보증서로 보장된다

표현 정리 be limited to ~로 제한되다 reduced price 할인 가격 guarantee 보증(서) replacement part 교체부품

해석 제공되는 서비스에 대해 언급된 내용은?
(A) 특정 에어컨 브랜드로 한정된다.
(B) 6월에는 가격이 할인될 것이다.
(C) 보증서로 보장된다.
(D) 교체 부품비도 포함한다.

문제 164~167번은 다음 온라인 채팅을 참조하시오.

Corinne Evans 시장님은 도시에 기업 유치를 위해 저희가 더 많은 것을 하기를 요구하고 있어요. 오전 11시 2분

Nate Greely 164음, 우리는 이미 City Vision Program 첫 해에 20여 개 회사들이 이곳으로 이전하도록 설득했죠. 그 정도면 성공이라고 생각해요. 오전 11시 6분

Colin Harrison 165그것은 좋은 첫걸음이죠. 하지만 우리는 지금까지 소기업들만 유치했잖아요. 오전 11시 8분

Deena Sojourner 맞아요, 그런 회사들은 소수의 인원만 채용하죠. 시장은 우리에게 크게 생각하라고 요청했어요. 오전 11시 17분

Corinne Evans 167그렇죠, City Vision의 목표들 중 하나가 시에 수백 개의 보수가 좋은 일자리를 창출하는 거죠. 대기업들을 유치할 필요가 있다는 의미죠. 다른 제안을 들어보고 싶네요. 오전 11시 21분

Nate Greely 저는 우리가 세금 혜택을 이용해야 한다고 생각해요. 세금을 감면하고, 심지어는 몇 년 동안은 기업들이 세금 면제를 받고 운영하도록 해 줄 수 있겠죠. 오전 11시 25분

Corinne Evans 그래요, Nate. 우리가 다음 회의에서 토론할 수 있게 세금 혜택 사항에 대해 고민해 주세요. 다른 제안 또 있나요? 오전 11시 26분

Colin Harrison 아이디어가 있어요. 166외부로 시선을 돌리기보다는 우리 시에서 사업을 시작하는 사람들에게 투자를 하는 것이 어떨까요? 대출과 멘토링을 제공해 그들이 성장할 수 있도록 돕는 거죠. 오전 11시 28분

Deanne Sojourner 166Colin의 생각에 동의해요. 그것이 정확히 우리가 필요로 하는 장기적인 성장 전략이죠. 오전 11시 32분

Corinne Evans 하지만 지금 우리는 시장님을 만족시킬 수 있는 즉각적인 결과들이 더 필요해요. 금요일에 있을 시장님과의 회의 전에 아이디어를 생각해 보도록 합시다. 오전 11시 40분

표현 정리 attract businesses 기업을 유치하다 convince 목+to do ···에게 ~하도록 설득하다 relocate 이전하다 consider 여기다, 생각하다 small business 소기업 bring in 영입하다, 데려오다 employ 채용하다 a handful of 소수의 think big 크게 생각하다 generate 창출하다 hundreds of 수 백의 good-paying jobs 보수가 좋은 일자리 be open to ~의 여지가 있다 suggestions 제안 tax incentive 세금 혜택 reduce taxes 세금을 감면하다 operate 운영하다 tax-free 세금 면제의 loans 대출 mentorship 멘토링 long term 장기적인 growth strategy 성장 전략 immediate 즉각적인 results 결과물 come up with an idea 아이디어를 생각해 내다

164. 유추 – 대화자들의 근무처 ★☆☆

해설 Corinne Evans의 첫 메시지 'The mayor is asking us to do more to attract businesses to the city.'에서 시장이 더 많은 기업들을 유치하라고 요구하고 있다고 하자, Nate Greely가 이어서 'Well, we have already convinced two dozen companies to relocate here in the first year of the City Vision Program.'이라며 우리가 이미 상당수 기업들을 이전하도록 설득했다고 말하는 것으로 보아 시청에 설치된 경제 개발부서임을 짐작할 수 있으므로 정답은 (C)이다. **정답 (C)**

표현 정리 development 개발 organization 조직, 회사 real estate 부동산

해석 대화자들이 근무하는 곳은?
(A) 온라인 광고회사
(B) 산업 엔지니어링 회사
(C) 경제 개발 추진부
(D) 상업 부동산 중개소

165. 의도 파악하기 ★★☆

해설 Colin Harrison이 보낸 메시지 'It's a good first step. But we have only brought in small companies so far.'에서 출발은 좋았지만, 소규모 기업들만을 유치했기 때문에 앞으로 더 많은 기업들을 유치해야 한다는 의미임을 유추할 수 있으므로 정답은 (A)이다. **정답 (A)**

표현 정리 point out 지적하다 suggest 제안하다 redefine 재정의하다 change A to B A를 B로 전환하다 propose 제안하다 extend 확장하다, 연장하다

해석 Mr. Harrison이 오전 11시 8분에 "그것은 좋은 첫 걸음이죠."라고 한 이유는?
(A) 더 많은 일이 행해져야 한다고 짚어주기 위해
(B) 목표를 재정의해야 한다고 제안하기 위해
(C) 소기업에 중점을 두기 위해
(D) 프로그램을 한 해 더 연장하자고 제안하기 위해

166. 유추 – Ms. Sojourner의 의도 파악하기 ★☆☆

해설 Mr. Harrison이 오전 11시 28분에 'Instead of looking outside, why not invest in people starting businesses here? Give them loans and provide mentorship to help them grow.'에서 외부에서 기업을 유치하려고 하기보다는 시에서 사업을 시작하려는 사람들을 지원하자고 하자, Ms. Sojourner가 그의 생각에 동의를 했으므로 정답은 (B)가 된다. 정답 (B)

패러프레이징 |지문| give them loans and provide mentorship to help them grow 대출과 멘토링을 제공해서 그들이 성장할 수 있도록 돕는다 → |선택지 B| support for ~를 지원하다

표현 정리 run a business 기업을 운영하다 entrepreneur 기업가, 사업가 relocate 이전하다 lend money 돈을 빌려주다

해석 Ms. Sojourner에 대해 암시된 것은?
(A) 소기업 운영을 한 경험이 있다.
(B) 지역 사업가들을 위한 더 많은 지원을 원한다.
(C) 최근에 이 도시로 이전했다.
(D) 돈을 대출해 주는 것에 대해 많이 안다.

---

167. 유추 – 시장의 의도 파악하기 ★☆☆

해설 Mr. Evans가 오전 11시 21분에 'Exactly. One of the goals of City Vision is to generate hundreds of good-paying jobs in the city.'에서 시장이 주도하는 City Vision 프로그램의 목표는 이 도시에 좋은 일자리를 많이 창출해내는 것이라고 했으므로 정답은 (B)이다. 정답 (B)

🔍 **함정 분석** Mr. Greely가 오전 11시 6분에 City Vision 프로그램의 첫 해 성과에 대해 언급했으므로 최근에 시장에 선출된 것은 아니라 (A)는 오답이고, 오전 11시 25분에 Mr. Greely가 주민들에게 세금 감면을 해 주자고 제안했는데, 이는 시장이 세금 감면 캠페인을 벌이지 않았음을 의미해 (C) 역시 오답이다.

패러프레이징 |지문| to generate hundreds of good-paying jobs in the city 이 도시에 좋은 일자리를 많이 창출해내는 것 → |선택지 B| to bring lots of jobs to the city 이 도시에 많은 일자리를 가져오는 것

표현 정리 elect 선출하다 bring jobs 일자리를 가져오다 reduce 줄이다 resident 주민 hire 고용하다 lead 이끌다

해석 시장에 대해 추론할 수 있는 것은?
(A) 최근에 시장으로 선출되었다.
(B) 이 도시에 많은 일자리를 가져오길 원한다.
(C) 주민들을 위해 세금 감면을 위한 캠페인을 벌였다.
(D) Mr. Greely를 고용하여 City Vision Project를 이끌게 했다.

문제 168-171번은 다음 기사를 참조하시오.

오늘날의 서비스업은 그 어느 때보다 기술에 의존하고 있다. 여행자들은 호텔에서 고속 무선 인터넷 접속을 기대하게 되었다. 그들은 스마트폰을 통해 항공편 및 숙박 예약을 할 수 있기를 원한다.

샌프란시스코에 위치한 Bayside Hotel은 기술을 새로운 단계로 끌어올렸다. 이 호화로운 호텔은 와이파이 기술을 이용해 객실 냉장고를 채우는 것에서부터 고객들이 깨끗한 타월을 사용 가능하게 하는 것에 이르기까지 모든 것을 조정한다. 169(B),(D)모든 직원에게 태블릿 또는 스마트폰이 배포되어 호텔의 Digital Management System(DMS)과 즉각적인 의사소통이 가능하다.

169(C)"저희는 호텔 관리부가 호텔 물품 공급 점검을 좀 더 수월하게 할 수 있도록 12개월 전에 DMS를 설치했습니다."라고 Sam Wayland 호텔 지배인은 말했다. "우리가 의사소통과 효율성을 향상시킬 수 있음이 곧 명백해졌기에 우리는 이 시스템을 확대했습니다." 그리고 그들은 정말로 효율성을 향상시켰다.

168Bayside 고객들은 자신의 태블릿이나 스마트폰을 통해 룸서비스를 주문하고 여분의 타월을 요청하며, 심지어 공항으로 가는 셔틀버스도 예약할

수 있다. 170새로운 프로그램은 분주한 비즈니스 여행객들이 호텔 레스토랑 식사를 미리 주문을 할 수 있게 해 준다. 그들이 메뉴를 클릭하고 식사 시간을 선택하고 나서 레스토랑의 예약된 좌석에 앉으면 바로 음식과 음료가 제공된다.

169세계적으로 소수의 호텔만이 Bayside의 DMS와 같은 시스템을 채택했지만, 171일부 업계 분석가들은 2020년이 되기 전에 이와 유사한 시스템이 주류를 차지하게 될 것이라고 예상한다.

표현 정리 hospitality industry 서비스업(호텔이나 식당 등) rely on ~에 의존하다 technology 기술 high-speed 고속 wireless 무선의 Internet access 인터넷 접속 book 예약하다 flight 항공편 room reservation 숙박 예약 take to a new level 새로운 단계로 끌어올리다 luxury 호화로운 coordinate 조정하다 stock 넣다, 두다 issue 배포하다 either A or B A나 B 둘 중 하나 communicate 의사소통하다 instantaneously 즉각적으로 install 설치하다 management 관리, 경영 supplies 물품 hotel manager 호텔 지배인 apparent 명백한, 분명한 improve 향상시키다 communication 의사소통 efficiency 효율성 expand 확장하다 order 주문하다 book a shuttle 셔틀버스를 예약하다 business traveler 비즈니스 여행객 select a dining time 식사시간을 선택하다 food and beverages 음식과 음료 serve 제공하다 reserved seat 예약된 좌석 a handful of 소수의 worldwide 세계적으로 adopt 채택하다 industry analysts 업계 분석가들 predict 예측하다 mainstream 주류의 decade 10년

---

168. 세부사항 – Bayside Hotel에 대한 내용 ★★☆

해설 네 번째 단락, 첫 번째 문장 'Bayside guests can order room service, request extra towels, and even book a shuttle to the airport via their tablet or smartphone.'에서 공항까지 셔틀버스를 제공하는 것을 알 수 있으므로 정답은 (D)이다. 정답 (D)

패러프레이징 |지문| shuttle to the airport 공항까지 셔틀 버스 → |선택지 D| transportation 교통수단

표현 정리 accept 받아들이다, 수용하다 reservation made online 온라인으로 한 예약 a decade ago 10년 전에 region 지역 transportation 교통 수단

해석 Bayside Hotel에 관한 사실 내용은?
(A) 온라인으로 한 예약만 접수한다.
(B) 10년 전에 문을 열었다.
(C) 그 지역에서 가장 빠른 와이파이를 보유하고 있다.
(D) 고객을 위해 교통 수단을 제공한다.

---

169. 세부사항 – Bayside Hotel의 DMS에 대한 내용 ★★☆

해설 다섯 번째 단락 'While only a handful of hotels worldwide have adopted systems like Bayside's DMS, some industry analysts predict similar systems will become more mainstream by th end of the decade.'를 통해 알 수 있듯이 Bayside 호텔에서 사용하는 DMS와 같은 시스템을 몇몇 호텔들이 이미 사용하고 있기 때문에 (A)는 틀린 내용이다. 정답 (A)

🔍 **함정 분석** 두 번째 단락 'Every staff member is issued either a tablet or smartphone so they can communicate instantaneously with the hotel's Digital Management System(DMS).'에서 이 호텔 직원들은 그들이 갖고 있는 태블릿이나 스마트폰 같은 기기를 이용해 DMS로 통신을 한다는 것을 알 수 있으므로 (B)와 (D)는 맞는 내용이고, 세 번째 단락 '"We installed the DMS twelve months ago to make it easier for management to monitor hotel supplies," said hotel manager Sam Wayland.'에서 DMS를 12개월 전에 설치했다고 했으므로 (C) 역시 맞다.

표현 정리 available 사용 가능한 communicate with appliances 기기와 통신하다

표현 정리 **contact** 연락을 취하다 **awardee** 수상자

해석 Greater Pittsburgh Arts Council은 언제 보조금 수상자들에게 연락을 취할 것인가?
(A) 5월 5일
(B) 5월 31일
(C) 7월 1일
(D) 7월 31일

175. 문장 위치 찾기 ★★☆

해설 두 번째 단락 'Grant applications will be evaluated based on several factors, not the least of which is the contribution your project will make to the local community.'에서 보조금 신청은 여러 요인에 근거해 평가될 것이라고 했으므로 이어지는 문장에서 그 평가 기준 목록과 관련된 문장이 언급되는 것이 자연스러우므로 (B)가 정답이다. 정답 (B)

표현 정리 **complete list** 완전한 목록, 모든 목록 **evaluative criteria** 평가 기준

해석 [1], [2], [3], [4] 중 다음 문장이 들어가기에 가장 적절한 곳은?

"평가 기준의 모든 목록은 www.gpac.org를 방문해 확인하세요."
(A) [1]
(B) [2]
(C) [3]
(D) [4]

문제 176-180번은 다음 회람과 이메일을 참조하시오.

회람

177수신: 마케팅부 팀장들
발신: Shawn Schaller
날짜: 5월 2일, 월요일
제목: 다가올 이사

176저희 건물 확장 공사를 감독하는 프로젝트 매니저인 Paul Stevens로부터 방금 소식을 들었습니다. 177그는 저희 사무실 공사가 거의 완성돼 다음 주에 이전을 할 수 있게 되었다고 했습니다. 그는 또한 저희를 도와줄 이삿짐 운송업자와 일정을 잡을 수 있었답니다. 그러나, 그들이 다른 부서들을 돕기로 이미 일정을 잡았기에 저희 모든 부서를 한 번에 도와줄 수는 없을 것입니다. 그러므로 사무실 이전을 위해 각 팀에 다른 시간 및 날짜를 정했습니다. 각 팀의 이사 날짜는 아래와 같습니다.

팀장	날짜/시간	새 위치
Andrew Cooper	5월 9일, 월요일, 오전 8시	1 - 4 구역
180Haley Quinn	5월 10일, 화요일, 오전 9시 30분	9 - 12 구역
179Sara Martinez	5월 11일, 수요일, 오후 1시 30분	5 - 8 구역
Chloe White	5월 12일, 목요일, 오전 11시 30분	13 - 15 구역

178예정된 이사 이전에 직원들에게 소지품을 박스에 넣고, 컴퓨터, 프린터, 전화 및 다른 전자 기기의 플러그를 뽑고 불필요한 물품은 버리게 해 주세요.

질문이나 관심 사항이 있으면, 가능한 빨리 저에게 알려주세요.

Shawn Schaller

표현 정리 **memorandum** 메모, 회람 **upcoming** 다가오는, 곧 있을 **move** 이사, 이전 **oversee** 감독하다 **expansion** 확장 **schedule** 일정을 잡다 **a crew of movers** 이삿짐 운송업자 팀 **assist** 도와주다 **department** 부서 **at once** 한 번에 **assign** 배정하다 **staff** 직원 **box up** 상자에 넣다 **belongings** 소지품 **unplug** 플러그를 뽑다 **electronic devices** 전자 기기 **discard** 버리다 **unnecessary item** 불필요한 물품 **concerns** 관심사

수신: Shawn Schaller 〈sschaller@optimumtech.com〉
발신: Haley Quinn 〈hquinn@optimumtech.com〉
날짜: 5월 3일 화요일
제목: 다가올 이사

안녕하세요, Shawn.

저는 이제 막 뉴욕에서 돌아와, 이사와 관련된 당신의 메모를 읽었습니다. 새로운 사무실이 마침내 준비돼 저는 정말 신이 납니다.

180당신이 저희에게 이사하라고 정해준 날에 저희 팀원들 중 Frank Lindower와 Misty Argyle가 교육 워크숍에 참석할 것입니다. 179Sara의 팀과 저희가 날짜를 변경할 방법이 있을까요? 오늘 아침에 Sara는 저에게 그녀의 팀이 저희 이사 날짜와 시간에 이사하는데 문제가 없다고 말했습니다.

Haley

표현 정리 **regarding** ~에 관하여 **finally** 마침내 **attend** 참석하다

176. 주제 - 메모의 목적 ★☆☆

해설 첫 번째 지문, 첫 번째 단락 'I have just received word from Paul Stevens, the project manager overseeing the expansion of our building. He said that our offices are almost complete and that we can begin moving in next week.'에서 프로젝트 매니저에게서 사무실 확장이 거의 완성돼 다음 주에 이사할 수 있게 됐다는 소식을 들었다고 전하면서 이사 계획에 대해 알려주고 있으므로 정답은 (A)이다. 정답 (A)

표현 정리 **communicate** 전달하다, 알리다 **announce** 발표하다 **request** 요청하다 **correct** 정정하다 **error** 오류

해석 메모의 목적은 무엇인가?
(A) 계획을 알려주기 위해
(B) 새로운 정책 발표를 위해
(C) 이삿짐 운송업체를 요청하기 위해
(D) 오류를 정정하기 위해

177. 유추 - Mr. Schaller에 관한 암시 내용 ★☆☆

해설 Mr. Schaller는 이 회람을 작성한 사람이며, 마케팅부 팀장들에게 이 회람을 보내고 있으므로 그가 마케팅부에서 근무한다는 것을 알 수 있다. 또한 회람 두 번째 문장 'He said that our offices are almost complete and that we can begin moving in next week.'에서 '저희 사무실'이라고 말한 것으로 보아 마케팅부에서 일한다는 것을 확신할 수 있으므로 정답은 (D)이다. 정답 (D)

🔍함정 분석 Mr. Schaller는 마케팅부에서 근무하는 사람이므로 이사용 박스를 보유하고 있지 않다. Mr. Steven은 건물 확장을 감독하는 프로젝트 매니저이므로 Mr. Schaller는 그의 팀 구성원이 될 수 없다. 또한 Mr. Schaller는 새 사무실 공간 디자인 일과는 무관하다.

표현 정리 **moving box** 이사용 박스

해석 Mr. Schaller에 대해 암시된 내용은?
(A) 이사용 박스를 보유하고 있다.
(B) Mr. Steven's 팀의 구성원이다.
(C) 새로운 사무실 공간을 디자인했다.
(D) 마케팅부에서 근무한다.

178. 세부사항 - Mr. Schaller가 요청한 내용 ★☆☆

해설 회람 'Please have your staff members box up their belongings, unplug computers, printers, phones, and other electronic devices and discard unnecessary items before your scheduled move.'에서 Mr. Schaller는 마케팅부 팀장들에게 이사하기 전에 해야 할 내용들을 요청하고 있으므로 정답은 (A)이다. 정답 (A)

패러프레이징 |지문| box up their belongings, ~ and discard unnecessary items before your scheduled move 예정된 이사 전에 소지품을 박스에 넣고 불필요한 물품은 버려라 → |선택지 A| complete preparations prior to moving 이사 전에 준비를 마쳐라

표현 정리 complete 마치다, 완성하다 preparation 준비 prior to ~전에 schedule 일정을 잡다 decide on ~을 결정하다

해석 Mr. Schaller가 팀장들에게 하라고 요청하는 것은?
(A) 이사 전에 준비를 마치라고
(B) Ms. Quinn과 이사 일정을 잡으라고
(C) 사무실 공간을 결정하라고
(D) 그에게 이삿짐 운송업체 팀을 보내 달라고

179. 연계 문제 – Ms. Martinez에 관한 사실 내용 ★★★

해설 이메일 하단 'She told me this morning her team has no problem moving on my scheduled date and time.'에서 She는 Sara를 의미하고, 메모를 참조하면 Sara의 성은 Martinez라는 것을 알 수 있다. 따라서 Ms. Martinez는 오늘 아침에 Ms. Quinn과 대화를 했음을 확인할 수 있으므로 정답은 (C)이다. **정답 (C)**

표현 정리 used to + 동사 ~이었다 lead 이끌다 recently 최근에 relocate 이전하다

해석 Ms. Martinez에 관한 사실 내용은?
(A) Mr. Quinn의 팀이었다.
(B) 워크숍을 이끌 것이다.
(C) 최근에 Ms. Quinn과 대화를 나눴다.
(D) 뉴욕에서 이사 왔다.

180. 연계 문제 – Mr. Lindower의 교육 날짜 ★★★

해설 Mr. Lindower는 두 번째 지문인 이메일을 보낸 Mr. Quinn의 팀원이다. 이메일 두 번째 단락 'Two of my team members, Frank Lindower and Misty Argyle, will be attending a training workshop on the day you have scheduled us to move.'에서 Mr. Lindower는 Mr. Quinn 팀이 받은 이사 날짜에 교육을 받을 예정이므로 (B)가 정답이다. **정답 (B)**

표현 정리 train 교육하다, 훈련하다

해석 Mr. Lindower는 언제 교육을 받을 것인가?
(A) 5월 9일
(B) 5월 10일
(C) 5월 11일
(D) 5월 12일

문제 181-185번은 다음 광고와 이메일을 참조하시오.

아쿠아 풀 청소 서비스

8940 Highway 12, Suite 8
San Esteban, NV 29940
555-3202
david@aquapoolcleaning.com
www.aquapoolcleaning.com

휴식을 취하시고 귀하의 수영장은 저희한테 맡겨 주세요.

San Esteban의 주택 소유자들이 이용 가능한 기본 및 고급 클리닝 패키지:

기본 패키지: 월 99달러*
• 20가지 점검 및 유지 보수
• 수화학 테스트 및 균형 잡기
• 물 필터 테스트 및 청소하기
• 펌프 시스템 테스트 및 조절하기

185**고급 패키지: 월 129달러***: 베이직 패키지를 포함하고 더불어
• 수영장 진공 청소하기
• 수영장 벽과 타일 닦기
• 그물망으로 모든 부스러기 제거하기

"David와 그의 팀은 저희 수영장 물을 수년 동안 깨끗하고 맑게 해주었습니다. 저는 다른 사람은 신뢰하지 않습니다." – Betty Herman

181**2018년 수영장 클리닝 서비스 최우수상 수상** – The San Esteban Register

184***견적 가격은 표준 사이즈 인그라운드 수영장(70 또는 그 이하 입방미터) 및 지상 수영장용입니다. 더 큰 인그라운드 수영장과 온수욕조 요금은 저희 웹사이트를 참조하세요.

표현 정리 relax 휴식을 취하다 take care of ~을 돌보다, 처리하다 available 이용 가능한 homeowner 주택 소유자 inspection 점검 maintenance 보수 water chemistry 수화학(水化學) adjust 조절하다 vacuum 진공 청소하다 remove 제거하다 debris 부스러기 net 그물망 for years 수년 동안 price quoted 견적 가격 standard size 표준 사이즈 in-ground 인그라운드의(땅을 파고 설치하는) swimming pool 수영장 cubic meters 입방미터 above ground 지상의 rates 요금 hot tubs 온수욕조

발신: "Penny Martin" pen88@globalmail.com
수신: "Aqua Pool Cleaning" david@aquapoolcleaning.com
제목: 서비스
날짜: 5월 21일, 월요일

David,

제 남편과 저는 이번 여름을 위해 막 수영장을 열었는데, 저희 근무 일정 변경 때문에 저희 수영장에 필요한 모든 정기 유지관리를 저희가 하기 어려울 것이라는 점을 알게 되었습니다. 185제 아들이 풀과 나뭇잎을 제거하고 수영장 벽 청소와 진공청소 작업을 도와줄 수 있습니다. 따라서 귀사가 그 서비스를 해주실 필요는 없습니다. 182저희는 다른 유지 보수 일을 하는데 귀사를 고용하고 싶습니다. 183,184웹사이트에 저희 것과 같은 큰 수영장용으로 게시된 요금은 상당히 합리적입니다. 향후 2주 내로 작업이 가능한지요?

덧붙여, 귀사의 웹사이트에는 귀사가 겨울 대비 수영장을 준비하는데 있어서 고객들을 도와줄 수 있는지에 대해서는 명확한 언급이 없군요.

Penny Martin

표현 정리 due to ~때문에 perform 수행하다 regular maintenance 정기적 유지관리 reasonable 합리적인 rates 요금 availability 작업 가능성 in addition 덧붙여

181. 세부사항 – Aqua Pool Cleaning에 대한 내용 ★☆☆

해설 광고 하단 'Winner of the 2018 Best Pool Cleaning Service Award : – The San Esteban Register'에서 업계 최우수상을 받았으므로 공개적으로 인정을 받았다고 볼 수 있어 정답은 (C)이다. **정답 (C)**

🔍 **함정 분석** 기본 패키지와 고급 패키지로 단일 요금제가 아니므로 (A)는 오답, 2018년에 설립된 것이 아니라 최우수상을 수상했으므로 (B) 역시 오답, 광고 "David and his team have made sure the water in my pool is clean and clear for years. I wouldn't trust anyone else."에서 David와 그의 팀이라고 했으므로 직원은 한 명 이상임을 알 수 있어 (D) 역시 오답이다.

표현 정리 single rate 단일 요금제 found 설립하다 public recognition 공개적 인정 employee 직원

해석 Aqua Pool Cleaning에 대해 언급된 내용은?
(A) 수영장 사이즈에 대해 단일 요금제이다.

64

(B) 2018년에 설립되었다.
(C) 공개적인 인정을 받았다.
(D) 한 명의 직원이 있다.

182. 주제 – Ms. Martin이 이메일을 보낸 목적 ★☆☆

해설 이메일 첫 번째 단락 'We would like to hire your company to do the other maintenance.'에서 Aqua Pool Cleaning 사의 서비스를 요청하고 있음을 확인할 수 있으므로 정답은 (D)이다. **정답 (D)**

표현 정리 reschedule 일정을 다시 잡다 contest a billing 청구서에 이의를 제기하다 request 요청하다

해석 Ms. Martin이 Aqua Pool Cleaning에게 이메일을 보낸 이유는?
(A) 클리닝 일정을 다시 잡기 위해
(B) 서비스를 변경하기 위해
(C) 청구서에 이의를 제기하기 위해
(D) 서비스를 요청하기 위해

183. 동의어 찾기 ★★☆

해설 이메일 'The rates posted for a big pool like ours on the Web site are quite reasonable.'에서 형용사 reasonable은 '합리적인, 적당한'이라는 뜻으로 쓰였으며, 보기에서 이와 의미가 가장 유사한 것은 '비싸지 않은, 저렴한'의 의미를 가진 (A)이다. **정답 (A)**

표현 정리 reasonable 합리적인 inexpensive 비싸지 않은 plausible 그럴듯한 logical 논리적인 irrational 비이성적인

해석 이메일 첫 번째 단락, 여섯 번째 줄의 "reasonable"과 의미가 가장 가까운 것은?
(A) 비싸지 않은
(B) 그럴듯한
(C) 논리적인
(D) 비이성적인

184. 연계 문제 – Martin 가족의 수영장에 관한 사실 내용 ★★★

해설 이메일 첫 번째 단락 후반 'The rates posted for a big pool like ours on the Web site are quite reasonable.'에서 수영장 크기가 꽤 크다는 것과 웹사이트를 확인했다는 것을 알 수 있는데, 첫 번째 지문인 광고 하단 '*Price quoted for standard size in-ground swimming pool (70 cubic meters or less) and above-ground pools. Rates for larger in-ground pools and hot tubs available on our Web site.'에서 70입방미터 또는 그 이하가 표준 사이즈이며, 그보다 큰 수영장 가격은 웹사이트를 참조하라고 했으므로, Martin 씨의 수영장은 70 입방미터보다 크다는 것을 알 수 있다. **정답 (B)**

표현 정리 attached 부착된 cubic meter 입방 미터 above-ground 지상의

해석 Martin 가족의 수영장에 관한 사실 내용은?
(A) 온수욕조가 부착되어 있다.
(B) 크기가 70 입방미터 이상이다.
(C) 벽에 타일이 있다.
(D) 지상 유형이다.

185. 연계 문제 – Ms. Martin에 관한 암시 내용 ★★★

해설 두 번째 지문인 이메일 첫 번째 단락 'My son can help with removing grass and leaves, cleaning the walls, and vacuuming. So we don't need those services from your company.'에서 Ms. Martin은 자신의 아들이 풀과 나뭇잎을 제거하고, 수영장 벽 청소와 진공청소 작업을 도와줄 수 있다고 하면서 그 서비스는 필요 없다고 했는데, 첫 지문 패키지 내용을 보면 아들이 하겠다는 서비스가 디럭스 패키지에 속하는 항목이므로 Ms. Martin이 선택한 패키지는 기본 패키지임을 알 수 있어 정답은 (B)이다. **정답 (B)**

표현 정리 work for ~에 근무하다 all year 일년 내내

해석 Ms. Martin에 관해 암시된 내용은?
(A) 남편이 Aqua Pool Cleaning에서 근무한다.
(B) 기본 패키지를 원한다.
(C) 매달 129달러 이상을 지불할 것이다.
(D) 일년 내내 수영장을 열어 놓는다.

문제 186-190번은 다음 웹페이지, 이메일, 그리고 정보를 참조하시오.

www.riveralandscaping.com			
Home	상업용	주택용	갤러리

리비에라 조경

- 188(D)1992년 이후 Haverford에서 수천 명의 고객들을 위해 자랑스럽게 일해 왔습니다.
- 25개 이상의 상 수상
- 186(A)National Association of Landscaping Professionals (NALP) 및 Haverford Commerce Council (HCC)의 회원

자신 있게 Rivera를 선택하세요. 저희는 인가를 받았고, 보험에 가입했습니다. 186(C)저희 사진 갤러리 페이지에서 저희가 작업한 샘플과 고객 추천 글을 확인하세요. 186(D)저희는 디자인, 설치, 유지 보수 및 기타의 풀 조경 서비스를 주택 및 상업 고객들에게 제공해 드립니다. 저희는 장기 서비스 계약뿐만 아니라 프로젝트 별로 작업을 하기도 합니다.

상담 예약을 하시려면 저희 고객 서비스부 clients@riveralandscaping.com으로 연락주세요.

표현 정리 proudly 자랑스럽게 winner 수상자 with confidence 자신 있게 licensed 인가를 받은 insured 보험을 든 testimonial 추천의 글 landscaping services 조경 서비스 residential 주택의 commercial 상업의 installation 설치 maintenance 유지 보수 project-by-project 프로젝트 별 long-term 장기의 set up an appointment 약속을 정하다 consultation 상담

발신: clients@riveralandscaping.com
수신: echarleston@gogetter.com
날짜: 10월 1일
제목: RE: quote
첨부: charleston_5

Mr. Charleston 님께,

188(C)월요일에 귀하를 만나 귀사에 필요한 내용들을 논의할 수 있어 기뻤습니다. 188(B)진입로를 따라 늘어서 있는 참나무와 느릅나무는 훌륭한 견본입니다. 188(A)처음에 누가 조경을 디자인했는지 모르겠지만 제대로 작업을 한 것 같습니다.

저희가 논의했던 서비스에 대한 견적은 첨부 파일을 참조하세요. 190 견적을 작성한 날짜로부터 일주일 동안 유효합니다. 견적 요금과 가격을 신중하게 준비한다고 하지만, 예기치 않은 상황 때문에 약간 변경될 수 있습니다. 187그러므로 제공된 견적가, 특히 벽에 대한 견적은 대략적인 것으로 생각해 주시기 바랍니다. 187예상치 못한 문제가 생기면 귀하께 알려드리고 노력할 것이며, 최종 비용에 영향을 미칠 수 있는 추가 작업을 마치기 전에 귀하의 허락을 구할 것입니다.

질문이 있으시면 주저하지 마시고 저에게 연락주세요.

Michael Ingles

표현 정리 oak tree 참나무 elm tree 느릅나무 driveway (도로에서 집, 차고까지의) 진입로 fine specimens 훌륭한 견본 landscape design 조경 디자인 quote 견적 quoted rates 견적 요금 carefully 신중하게

slightly 약간　due to ~때문에　unforeseen circumstances 예기치
못한 상황　estimates 견적가　consider 간주하다　rough 대충한, 대략적인
make every effort 최선의 노력을 하다　inform A of B A에게 B를 알리다
unexpected issues 예상치 못한 문제　obtain permission 허가를 얻다
additional work 추가작업　affect 영향을 미치다　final cost 최종 비용

Rivera Landscaping

견적서

고객명: Edward Charleston
190 작성일: 10월 1일, 화요일
작성자: Michael Ingles

논의한 서비스
▶주기적 유지 보수: 주당 150달러*
189(B) 매주 행해지는 잔디 깎기, 물주기 및 제초 포함
189(C) 최소 3개월 계약 필수

▶관개 설비: 2,800달러
나무, 화단 및 잔디에 물을 주는 자동 관개 시스템 디자인 및 설치

▶나무 가지치기: 나무 당 100달러
일반적으로 일 년에 한 번 행해짐

189(A) *12개월 계약 서명으로 5퍼센트 할인받으세요.

표현 정리　lawn mowing 잔디깎기　watering 물주기　weeding 제초　on
a weekly basis 주 단위로　automated irrigation system 자동 관개
시스템　normally 일반적으로　once every year 일 년에 한 번

186. 세부사항 – Rivera Landscaping에 관한 내용이 아닌 것　★★☆
해설 (A)는 첫 번째 지문 첫 번째 단락 'Member of the National Association
of Landscaping Professionals (NALP) and Haverford Commerce
Council (HCC).'에서 비즈니스 그룹 회원임을 확인할 수 있고, (C)는 두 번
째 단락 'Check out samples of our work and customer testimonials
on our photo gallery pages.'에서 확인되고, (D)는 'We offer full service
landscaping services to residential and commercial clients: design,
installation, maintenance, and more.'에서 주택 소유자들에게도 서비스를 제
공한다고 했으므로 맞는 내용이다. 사업체 이전에 대한 내용은 없으므로 (B)가 정
답이다.　　　　　　　　　　　　　　　　　　　　　　　　정답 (B)

표현 정리　belong to ~에 속하다　relocate 이전하다　showcase
소개하다, 전시하다　completed 완성된　homeowner 주택 소유주

해석 웹 페이지에서, Rivera Landscaping에 대해 언급된 내용이 아닌 것은?
(A) 비즈니스 그룹에 속해 있다.
(B) 1992년에 사업체를 이전했다.
(C) 완성된 프로젝트를 소개한다.
(D) 주택 소유자들에게 서비스를 제공한다.

187. 세부사항 – 추가작업에 수반되는 사항　★☆☆
해설 이메일의 두 번째 단락에서, 'We will make every effort to inform
you of any unexpected issues and will obtain your permission before
completing additional work that will affect the final cost.'를 통해 알 수 있
듯이 추가적인 일이 생길 경우, 허락을 받겠다는 말을 하고 있다. 따라서 본문에서
additional을 extra로 바꾼 (A)가 정답이다.　　　　　　　　정답 (A)

🔍 함정 분석 (D)에서 추가작업이 이루어지게 되면 Mr. Ingles가 Mr.
Charleston으로부터 허락을 얻는 것이며, 그 반대가 아니기 때문에 오답이다.

표현 정리　contract 계약(서)　at a reduced rate 할인된 가격으로
approval 승인, 허락

해석 이메일에 따르면, 만일 추가 작업이 이루어져야 한다면 Mr. Charleston은

무엇을 기대할 수 있는가?
(A) 일이 시작되기 전에 그에게 통지될 것이다.
(B) 새로운 계약서에 서명을 해야 할 것이다.
(C) 할인을 받을 것이다.
(D) Mr. Ingles에게서 승인을 받아야 할 것이다.

188. 연계 문제 – Mr. Charleston에 대한 사실 내용　★★★
해설 웹페이지 상단 'Proudly serving thousands of clients in Haverford
since 1992.'에서 Rivera Landscaping은 Haverford에 사는 고객들에게 서비
스를 제공해 왔다고 했으므로 이 회사에 근무하는 Mr. Ingles는 Haverford에서
일한다는 것을 알 수 있고, 이 회사의 고객인 Mr. Charleston도 Haverford에서
직장이 있다는 것을 알 수 있기 때문에, (D)가 정답이다.　　정답 (D)

🔍 함정 분석 두 번째 지문 이메일에서, 건축회사가 아니라 조경회사를 고용했
고, 'The oak and elm trees lining the drive way are fine specimens.
Whoever did the original landscape design knew what they were
doing.'에서 두 종류 나무가 언급됐지만 Mr. Charleston이 심은 것이 아
니라 전에 고용했던 조경회사가 심은 것이며, 'It was a pleasure to meet
you on Monday to discuss your company's needs.'에서 Mr. Ingles
가 driveway에 심어져 있는 나무들을 본 것이므로, 오히려 Mr. Ingles가 Mr.
Charleston를 방문했음을 짐작할 수 있어 (A), (B), (C)는 각각 오답이다.

표현 정리　hire 고용하다　architectural firm 건축회사　plant a tree
나무를 심다

해설 Mr. Charleston에 대한 사실 내용은?
(A) 건설회사를 고용했다.
(B) 두 종류의 나무를 심었다.
(C) Mr. Ingles의 사무실에 방문했다.
(D) Mr. Ingles와 같은 지역에서 근무한다.

189. 세부사항 – 주기적 유지보수 서비스에 대한 내용　★★☆
해설 세 번째 지문인 정보 두 번째 단락 내용인 '▶Routine maintenance: $150
per week'에 관한 문제이다. 두 번째 항목 'Minimum three-month contract
required'에서 알 수 있듯이 계약은 최소 3개월이므로 3개월 이상의 계약도 가
능하다는 것을 알 수 있어 정답은 (C)이다.　　　　　　　　　정답 (C)

🔍 함정 분석 하단 '*Get 5% off by signing a twelve-month contract'에
서 12개월 계약 서명을 하면 할인을 받을 수 있는 것일 뿐, 상업 고객만 할인
받는 것은 아니므로 (A)는 오답이다. 두 번째 단락 'Includes lawn mowing,
watering, and weeding performed on a weekly basis.'에서 매주 서비
스를 제공한다는 것이며, 조정 가능하다는 것은 아니므로 (B)도 오답이다. (D)
의 내용은 본문에 언급되지 않았다.

표현 정리　discounts 할인　available 이용 가능한　commercial client
상업 고객　adjust 조정하다　contract 계약　varying 다양한　length
(시간의) 길이　supervise 감독하다

해설 주기적 유지 보수 서비스에 대해 언급된 것은?
(A) 할인은 상업 고객들에게만 이용 가능하다.
(B) 서비스는 매주 조정될 수 있다.
(C) 다양한 기간의 계약이 제공된다.
(D) 작업은 Mr. Ingles에 의해 직접 감독된다.

190. 연계 문제 – 견적 가격의 만기일　★★★
해설 이메일 두 번째 단락 'It is good for one week from the date it was
prepared.'에서 견적서가 작성되고 일주일 동안 유효하다고 했는데, 세 번째 지
문인 정보 상단 'Prepared on: Tuesday, October 1'에서 견적 작성일이 10월 1
일임을 알 수 있다. 따라서 만기일은 10월 8일이고 정답은 (A)이다.　정답 (A)

표현 정리　quoted price 견적 가격　expire 만기되다

해석 견적 가격은 언제 만기될 것인가?
(A) 10월 8일
(B) 10월 10일
(C) 10월 31일
(D) 11월 1일

문제 191-195번은 다음 공지, 일정표, 그리고 이메일을 참조하시오.

직원 복리후생 공개 행사

192(B)Link Corporation 전 직원들에게 공개합니다.

- 193신입직원들은 건강보험, 치과 치료, 시력 관리, 생명보험, 상해보험, 은퇴 계획 등을 포함해 자신이 어떤 복리후생 옵션을 사용할 수 있는지 알 수 있습니다.
- 기존 직원들은 복리후생 옵션 보유하기, 변경하기 또는 취소하기에 대한 자세한 정보를 기초로 선택을 할 수 있습니다.
- 곧 이용 가능해질 새로운 건강 보험과 퇴직 계획 옵션에 대해 알아보세요.
- 보험료 인상에 대해 먼저 알아보세요.
- 퇴직 전문가들이 은퇴를 얼마 남겨 놓지 않은 직원들을 위해 참석할 것입니다.

직원들은 복리후생 옵션 변경 기회를 1년에 한 번 갖는다는 것을 알아 두세요. 195복리후생 변경 기간은 10월 1일부터 10월 31일까지입니다. 그 기간에 요청된 변경 사항은 1월 1일부터 효력이 발생합니다.

191이 행사는 9월 후반에 있을 예정이며, 시간, 날짜 및 장소는 공지될 것입니다. 업데이트는 Link Corporation 웹사이트를 참조하세요.

표현 정리 employee 직원 benefit 복리후생 new hires 신입 직원들 available 이용 가능한 including ~을 포함하여 health insurance 건강보험 dental plan 치과 치료 vision plan 시력 관리 life insurance 생명보험 disability insurance 상해보험 retirement plan 은퇴 계획 existing employees 기존 직원들 make a choice 선택하다 informed 정보에 근거한 retain 보유하다 find out 알아내다 soon to be available 곧 이용 가능한 heads-up 기회, 사전 정보 premium increases 보험료 인상 specialist 전문가 be on hand 참가하다, 함께 하다 in the latter stages 후기 단계에 take effect 효력이 발생하다

직원 복리후생 공개 행사

9월 21일, 수요일
192(A)Vincent Building
Link Corporation

시간	행사	장소
오전 9시 – 오후 12시	193복리후생 제공자 대표자들과 만나보세요.	로비
오후 12시 30분 – 오후 1시 30분	192(C)복리후생 등록 과정 이해하기 (Link Corporation 인사 부장 Chris Watson)	194강당
오후 2시 – 오후 3시 30분	은퇴 계획하기 (인력지원 전문가 Alan Wright)	12호실
오후 4시 – 오후 5시	복리후생 양식 작성법 도움받기 (Link Corporation 인사부 직원)	14호실

표현 정리 representatives 대표자 enrollment process 등록 과정 auditorium 강당 workforce support specialist 인력 지원 전문가 assistance 지원, 도움

발신: Christina Cartwright 〈ccartwright@linkcorp.com〉
수신: Benjamin Caseman 〈bcaseman@linkcorp.com〉
Re: 행사
날짜: 9월 22일

Ben,

저는 어제 행사가 매우 유익했다는 것을 말씀드리고 싶습니다. 저는 이제 생명보험과 상해보험의 차이와 왜 이 두 가지 옵션을 신청해야 하는 지도 알게 되었습니다. 복리후생 대표자들은 정말 친절했고, 제 모든 질문에 대해 답해 주었습니다. 게다가, 제가 참석했던 강연회는 제가 앞으로 근무할 날이 많이 남았음에도 은퇴를 대비해 저축을 시작할 필요가 있음을 알게 해주었습니다. 194Chris의 강연을 놓쳐서 유감스러울 뿐입니다.

제가 이러한 변경에 필요한 서류 양식 작성을 도와주셔서 특히 감사합니다. 195복리후생 변경 신청 기간이 시작되면 양식을 제출하겠습니다.

Christina Cartwright

표현 정리 extremely 굉장히, 매우 useful 유용한 difference between A and B A와 B의 차이 enroll in ~에 등록하다 friendly 친절한 saving 저축 miss 놓치다 especially 특히 fill out (서류, 양식)을 작성하다 return 제출하다

191. 세부사항 – 회사 웹사이트를 참고해야 하는 이유 ★★★

해설 공지 마지막 단락 'This event will be held in late September. The time, date, and location are to be announced. Check the Link Corporation Web site for updates.'에서 행사 시간, 날짜 및 장소가 회사 웹사이트에 공지되니 확인하라고 했으므로 정답은 (D)가 된다.　　**정답 (D)**

표현 정리 notice 공지 refer to (정보를 알아내기 위해) ~을 참고하다 register for ~에 등록하다 make an appointment 예약하다 request 요청하다

해설 공지에서, 직원들이 회사 웹사이트를 참고하라고 한 이유는?
(A) 행사에 등록하기 위해
(B) 예약하기 위해
(C) 복리후생 변경 양식을 요청하기 위해
(D) 행사 일정을 알기 위해

192. 세부사항 – 행사 일정에 관한 내용 ★☆☆

해설 일정표 상단에 Vincent Building이라고 건물명이 제시되어 있고, 표를 보면 로비, 강당, 12호실, 14호실로 장소가 공지되었으므로 한 건물에서 행사가 진행됨을 짐작할 수 있어 정답은 (A)이다.　　**정답 (A)**

> **함정 분석** 공지 첫 행 'Open to all Link Corporation employees'에서 알 수 있듯이 퇴직자가 아닌 직원들에게 공개되므로 (B)는 오답이고, 일정표 '오후 12시 30분 – 오후 1시 30분: Understanding the benefit enrollment process (Chris Watson, Director of Human Resources, Link Corporation)'에서 현 인사부 부장이 나오므로 (C)도 역시 오답이다.

표현 정리 single structure 단일 건축물 be open to ~에게 공개되다 retired employee 퇴직자 feature 출연하다, 나오다 executive 임원, 중역 lunch break 점심시간

해설 일정에 있는 행사에 관해 언급된 것은?
(A) 단일 건물에서 열린다.
(B) 퇴직자들에게 공개된다.
(C) 전임 Link 중역이 나온다.
(D) 점심 시간을 포함한다.

193. 연계 문제 – 시력 관리 제공자와 대화할 시간 ★★☆

해설 공지 첫 항목을 보면 Vision Plan이 복리후생 옵션에 포함되어 있음을 알

수 있는데, 일정표의 '오전 9시 – 12시: Meeting with representatives from benefit providers'에서 복리후생 제공자와의 대화 시간에 마련돼 있음을 알 수 있어 정답은 (A)이다.　　　　　　　　　　　　　　정답 (A)

표현 정리 talk with ~와 대화하다　provider 제공자

해석 Link 직원들이 몇 시에 시력 관리 제공자와 대화를 나눌 것 같은가?
(A) 오전 9시
(B) 오후 12시 30분
(C) 오후 2시
(D) 오후 4시

194. 연계 문제 – Ms. Cartwright가 방문하지 않은 장소　★★☆

해설 Ms. Cartwright은 세 번째 지문인 이메일을 보낸 사람이다. 이메일 첫 번째 단락 마지막 줄 'I'm just sorry I missed Chris's talk.'에서 Ms. Cartwright은 Chris의 강의를 듣지 못했음을 알 수 있는데, 일정표를 보면 Chris는 현재 인사 부장이며, 그의 강의는 강당에서 하기로 예정되어 있으므로 (A)가 정답이다.
　　　　　　　　　　　　　　정답 (A)

표현 정리 auditorium 강당　lobby 로비

해석 행사 동안 Ms. Cartwright이 참석하지 않은 장소는?
(A) 강당
(B) 로비
(C) 12호실
(D) 14호실

195. 연계 문제 – Ms. Cartwright의 서류 제출 시점　★★☆

해설 첫 번째 지문인 공지 후반 'The benefit change period is October 1 – October 31.'에 복리후생 변경 기간이 명시되어 있고, 이메일 후반 'I will return the forms as soon as the benefit change enrollment period begins.'에서 변경 기간이 시작하자마자 제출하겠다고 했으므로 정답은 (B)이다.　　정답 (B)

표현 정리 hand in ~을 제출하다　disability insurance 상해보험

해석 Ms. Cartwright은 상해보험을 들기 위해 언제 서류를 제출할 계획인가?
(A) 9월 23일
(B) 10월 1일
(C) 11월 1일
(D) 1월 1일

문제 196-200번은 다음 웹페이지, 송장, 그리고 이메일을 참조하시오.

www.metrooffice.com			
회사 소개	제품	지원	연락처

Metropolitan Office Equipment 〉 Business 〉 Copy Machines

196(B) 저희는 인가된 Highmark 딜러입니다!

Highmark 디지털 복사기
분당 45페이지
600 X 600 DPI 해상도
197 인쇄, 복사, 스캔, 팩스 기능
USB 포트

196(A) 저희는 비즈니스 고객들만을 대상으로 영업합니다. **196(C)** 모든 복사기는 대여와 구입 옵션이 딸린 대여가 가능합니다. 지금 구매하시는 복사기는 12개월 간 보증됩니다. 문제가 있으면, 저희 기술자들이 귀 영업 장소를 방문해 진단하고 가능하다면 현장에서 기기를 수리해 드립니다.

196(D) 무료 견적을 받아보시려면 여기 링크를 클릭하세요.

표현 정리 product 제품　support 지원　contact 연락처　copy machine 복사기　per minute 분 당　resolution 해상도　authorized 인가된　exclusively 전적으로, 독점적으로　business client 비즈니스 고객　copy machine 복사기　lease 대여　purchase 구매하다　come with ~이 딸려오다　warranty 보증(서)　place of business 영업 장소　diagnose 진단하다　repair 수리하다　on site 현장에서　get a quote 견적을 받다

송장

주문 번호 689434
주문자: Ned Katz
주문 날짜: 8월 29일
예상 배송일: 9월 5일

회사: Sanford Graphic Designs
연락 담당자: Eugene Petty
전화: (610) 555-3034
배송 주소: 7124 S. Waverly Street, Shillington, PA 19609
청구 받는 사람: 위와 동일

모델 번호	품목	비용
197 M7894	Highmark 디지털 복사기	3,750달러
M8945	먼지 덮개	75달러
M0001	배송, 설치 및 교정	50달러
M0008	**198** 연장 보증(+12개월)	200달러

소계: 4,075달러
세금: 305달러
합계: 4,380달러

Metropolitan Office Machines를 선택해 주셔서 감사합니다!

표현 정리 invoice 송장　order 주문　date ordered 주문 일자　expected delivery date 예상 배송일　dust cover 먼지 덮개　installation 설치　calibration 교정　extended warranty 연장 보증　subtotal 소계

발신: Kent Wirth 〈kwirth@metrooffice.com〉
수신: Eugene Petty 〈epetty@sandfordgraphic.com〉
날짜: 11월 16일
제목: Re: 트레이닝

Mr. Petty 님께,

200 고객님이 사용 중인 Highmark 복사기에 생긴 문제를 저희에게 알려 주셔서 감사합니다. 고객님이 제공해 주신 설명에 따르면, 그 문제는 사용설명서의 고장 수리 섹션을 참고해 직접 해결하실 수 있는 것이 아닌 듯합니다. 게다가 소프트웨어 문제가 아닌 것 같습니다. 기기를 살펴보기 위해서 기술자를 보내드릴 것입니다. **199** 급지장치를 새것으로 교체할 것이라고 생각합니다.

198 고객님이 기기를 구입한지 14개월 이상 되었지만, 고객님이 구입하신 추가 보호 서비스에 해당되어 비용은 없습니다. **200** 제가 직원을 고객님 사무실로 파견할 수 있는 가장 빠른 시간은 내일 오후입니다. 그 시간이 괜찮으신지 저희에게 알려주시기 바랍니다.

Kent Wirth

표현 정리 regarding ~에 관하여　based on ~에 근거하여　description 설명　resolve 해결하다　refer to ~을 참고하다　troubleshooting section 고장수리 섹션　manual 사용설명서　take a look at ~을 살펴보다　replace 교체하다　document feeder 급지 장치

196. 세부사항 – Metropolitan Office Machines에 관한 내용이 아닌 것
★☆☆

해설 웹페이지 중반 'We work exclusively with business clients. All of our copy machines are available for lease or lease with the option to purchase.'에서 비즈니스 고객들만을 상대로 거래를 하는 복사기 대여 업체라고 만했을 뿐, 여러 개의 소매점이 있다는 내용은 없다. 정답 (A)

🔍 **함정 분석** (B)는 웹페이지 상단 'We are an authorized Highmark dealer!'에서 인가된 Highmark 딜러라고 했으므로 맞고, (C)는 'All of our copy machines are available for lease or lease with the option to purchase.'에서 확인이 된다. (D) 역시 'Click on this link to get a free quote.'에서 무료 견적을 받을 수 있음이 확인되어 사실이다.

패러프레이징 |지문| an authorized Highmark dealer 인가된 Highmark 딜러 → |선택지 B| be approved to sell a certain brand 특정 브랜드 판매를 승인받았다
|지문| available for lease 대여가 가능하다 → |선택지 C| rent machines 기계를 대여해주다
|지문| a free quote 무료 견적 → |선택지 D| estimates at no cost 무료 견적

표현 정리 several 여러 개의   retail location 소매점   approve 승인하다, 허가하다   certain 특정한   rent A to B A에게 B를 대여하다   provide 제공하다   estimates 견적   at no cost 무료로

해석 Metropolitan Office Equipment에 대해 언급된 내용이 아닌 것은?
    (A) 여러 개의 소매점이 있다.
    (B) 특정 브랜드 판매를 승인받았다.
    (C) 회사에 기계를 대여한다.
    (D) 무료 견적을 제공할 수 있다.

197. 연계 문제 – M7894 제품에 대한 내용
★★☆
해설 송장에서 M7894 제품이 'Highmark 디지털 복사기'임을 알 수 있는데, 웹페이지 상단 'Print, copy, scan, fax functions'에서 보면 이 복사기의 기능 중 스캔 기능을 확인할 수 있으므로 정답은 (D)이다. 정답 (D)

표현 정리 lease 임대하다   ship 배송하다   at no extra charge 추가 비용 없이   at a discounted price 할인 가격에

해석 M7894 제품에 대해 암시된 것은?
    (A) 12개월 동안 대여된다.
    (B) 추가 비용 없이 배송되었다.
    (C) 할인 가격에 판매되었다.
    (D) 서류를 스캔하기 위해 사용될 수 있다.

198. 연계 문제 – Mr. Wirth가 Mr. Petty에게 제공하는 서비스 보증 비용
★★☆

해설 이메일 두 번째 단락 'Even though your machine was purchased more than fourteen months ago, this service will be covered by the additional protection you purchased.'에서 Mr. Petty가 복사기를 구입한지 14개월(보증 기간은 1년) 이상이 되었지만 서비스 비용이 무료가 될 것이라고 했는데, 이는 송장을 보면 Mr. Petty가 Extended warranty (+12 months), 즉 12개월 간 보증 기간을 연장할 수 있는 상품을 200달러에 구입했기 때문에 가능하다. 따라서 정답은 (C)이다. 정답 (C)

표현 정리 payment 지불(금)

해석 Mr. Wirth가 Mr. Petty에게 제공하는 서비스를 보증해 준 비용은?
    (A) 50달러
    (B) 75달러
    (C) 200달러
    (D) 305달러

199. 세부사항 – 기술자가 Mr. Petty를 위해서 할 일
★☆☆
해설 이메일에서 Mr. Worth는 기술자를 보낸다고 했고, 'I expect that he will have to remove the document feeder and install a new one.'에서 알 수 있듯이 기술자가 급지장치를 교체할 것이라고 생각한다고 했다. 그러므로 정답은 (D)이다. 정답 (D)

표현 정리 audio 오디오, 음성의   setting 세팅, 설정   replace 교체하다

해석 기술자가 Mr. Petty를 위해 무엇을 할 것이라고 Mr. Worth는 생각하는가?
    (A) 기기의 소프트웨어를 업데이트하기
    (B) 매뉴얼을 사용하는 방법을 Mr. Petty에게 알려주기
    (C) 기기의 오디오 세팅을 바꾸기
    (D) 복사기의 부품을 교체하기

200. 세부사항 – Mr. Wirth가 Mr. Petty에게 요청한 사항
★☆☆
해설 이메일 두 번째 단락 후반 'The soonest I can have someone come to your office is tomorrow afternoon. Please let us know if that time will work for you.'에서 Mr. Petty의 사무실로 내일 오후에 수리공을 파견하려고 하는데, 이 일정이 괜찮은지 확인해 달라는 내용이므로 정답은 (B)이다. 정답 (B)

패러프레이징 |선택지| let us know if that time will work for you 그 시간이 괜찮은지 알려주세요 → |선택지 B| confirm a suggested appointment 제안된 약속을 확인하다

표현 정리 detailed 상세한   documentation 참고 문서   confirm 확인하다   suggested 제안된   appointment 약속, 예약   refer to ~을 참고하다   official instructions 공식 지시사항   make a payment 지불하다   additional 추가적인

해석 Mr. Wirth가 Mr. Petty에게 요청하는 것은?
    (A) 상세한 문서를 제공해 달라고
    (B) 제시된 예약 일정을 확인해 달라고
    (C) 공식 지시사항을 참고하라고
    (D) 추가 비용을 지불하라고

문제 147-148번은 다음 양식을 참조하시오.

> www.printedplates.com
>
> ### 로고가 새겨진 그릇
>
> #### 모든 행사에 맞는 맞춤식 그릇
>
> 이름: *Josephine Warner*
>
> 이메일: *jwarner@medicare.org*
>
> 품목: *커피 머그컵*
>
> 색깔: *흰색*
>
> 수량: *100*
>
> 출력 서술: *남색의 회사 로고*
>
> 주문 세부 사항: 147*저희 회사 Medicare에서는 기념 선물로 직원들에게 나눠줄 남색 로고가 새겨진 100개의 흰 머그컵을 주문하려고 합니다. 우리 사무실에서는 고온의 식기 세척기를 사용하기 때문에, 식기 세척기에 사용해도 괜찮은지 확인이 필요합니다.* 148*긴급 배송에는 추가로 50달러가 더 든다는 것을 알고 있습니다. Medicare 기념 파티가 이번 주 토요일에 있을 예정이기 때문에 긴급 배송으로라도 이 머그컵들을 되도록 빨리 받길 원합니다.*

표현 정리 **plate** 접시 **personalized** 맞춤의, 개인이 원하는 대로 주문한 **occasion** 행사, 경우 **description** 설명, 서술 **order** 주문 **specifics** 세부 사항 **employee** 직원 **anniversary** 기념일 **make sure** 확실히 하다 **dishwasher** 식기 세척기 **utilize** 활용하다 **high-temperature** 고온 **expedited delivery** 긴급 배송 **extra** 추가의

147. 주제 – Ms. Warner가 양식을 작성한 목적 ★☆☆

해설 주문 세부 사항 첫 번째 문장 'My company, Medicare, would like 100 white coffee mugs printed with our company logo picture in navy blue to give to our employees as anniversary gifts.'에서 회사 로고가 인쇄된 머그컵을 직원들에게 기념 선물로 나눠줄 것이라고 했으므로 정답은 (D)이다.

정답 (D)

표현 정리 **complete the form** 양식을 작성하다 **place an order** 주문하다

해석 Ms. Warner가 양식을 작성한 이유는?

(A) 그녀의 주문을 확인하기 위해
(B) 정보를 요청하기 위해
(C) 주문을 변경하기 위해
(D) 주문하기 위해

148. 세부사항 – Ms. Warner가 동의한 것 ★☆☆

해설 세부사항 후반 'I understand that expedited delivery will cost an extra $50.00. I'm fine with that since Medicare's anniversary party is this Saturday, and we need these mugs as soon as possible.'에서 추가 비용을 지불하더라도 기념 파티가 열리는 시점에 맞게 주문 제품을 받고 싶어 하고 있음을 알 수 있으므로 정답은 (A)이다.

정답 (A)

패러프레이징 |지문| cost an extra $50.00 추가 50달러를 지불하다 → |선택지 A| pay an additional fee 추가 요금을 지불하다

표현 정리 **additional fee** 추가 요금 **add text to** ~에 글을 덧붙이다

해석 Ms. Warner가 동의한 것은?

(A) 추가 비용을 지불한다.
(B) 머그컵에 글을 덧붙인다.
(C) 머그컵 색깔을 바꾼다.
(D) 그녀의 주문을 취소한다.

문제 149-150번은 다음 정보를 참조하시오.

> ### 3층 화장실: 단수
>
> 다음 주 7월 2일, 월요일에 Rayburn 건물의 3층 화장실 수도가 단수될 예정입니다.
>
> 149배관 수리 작업으로 인해 3층의 모든 화장실에서 오후 1시에서 오후 6시까지 물이 공급되지 않습니다. 150남성과 여성 화장실은 1층과 5층을 이용해 주세요.
>
> 3층에 있는 전 직원들과 Rayburn 건물을 방문하신 분들은 위의 시간 동안 화장실을 사용할 수 없습니다.

표현 정리 **shutoff** 차단 **turn off** (전기, 가스, 수도 등을) 끄다

149. 세부사항 – 수리에 대한 내용 ★★☆

해설 두 번째 단락 'All restrooms on the 3rd floor will have no water from 1:00 P.M. to 6:00 P.M. as pipes will be repaired.'에서 파이프 수리가 오후에 진행될 예정임을 알 수 있으므로 정답은 (A)이다. 정답 (A)

🔍함정 분석 첫 번째 단락 'Be advised that next Monday, July 2, the water will be turned off for 3rd floor bathrooms in the Rayburn Office Building.'에서 7월 1일 하루 동안에만 공사가 있으므로 (C)는 오답이며, 3층에 있는 모든 화장실에서 공사가 진행될 예정이므로 (B)와 (D) 역시 오답이다.

표현 정리 **take place** 일어나다, 발생하다 **affect** 영향을 미치다 **last** 계속되다

해석 수리에 대해 언급된 것은?

(A) 수리는 오후에 할 것이다.
(B) 한 곳의 화장실만 영향을 받을 것이다.
(C) 수리는 며칠 동안 진행될 예정이다.
(D) 3개 층에서 이루어질 것이다.

150. 세부사항 – 조언 받은 내용 ★☆☆

해설 마지막 단락 'All 3rd floor employees and visitors to the Rayburn Building should not enter the restrooms during the hours listed above.'에서 3층 화장실 사용이 불가능하다고 했고, 두 번째 단락 'The men's and women's bathrooms can be found on the 1st and 5th floors.'에서 1층과 5층에 있는 화장실을 안내하고 있으므로 대체 가능한 화장실을 이용하도록 조언하고 있다고 볼 수 있어 정답은 (C)이다. 정답 (C)

표현 정리 **alternative** 대체 가능한 **bottled water** 병에 든 생수

해석 단수 기간 동안 직원들이 하도록 조언받은 것은?

(A) 3층 화장실을 사용하라고
(B) 재택 근무하라고
(C) 대체 가능한 화장실을 사용하라고
(D) 병에 든 생수만 마시라고

문제 151-153번은 다음 기사를 참조하시오.

> ### 송별회에서 은퇴하는 Winex CEO
>
> 152유명 창문 설계회사 Winex는 9월 30일, 토요일에 열리는 회사 연례 행사에서 CEO Leman Rhines에게 작별을 고할 것이다. 올해 행사는 Catamount 호텔에서 열리며, 8코스 요리와 라이브 재즈 밴드와 함께 하는 춤이 포함되어 있다.
>
> 152Rhines는 1998년에 Winex에 입사했다. 그 후로 그는 회사가 이익을 많이 낼 수 있게 만들었고, 오늘날에도 여전히 사용되는 디자인 기술을 혁명적으로 바꾸었다. Winex와 함께 전설적인 경력을 쌓았음에도 불구하고,

Rhines는 건강 문제 때문에 일찍 은퇴한다.

Winex에 새로 부임할 CEO는 아직 결정되지 않았지만, 직원들은 저녁식사 자리에서 발표가 있을 것으로 기대하고 있다. **151.전 직원들은 행사에 참석해 유쾌하게 행복을 빌면서 Rhines 씨를 배웅하도록 권유받았다. 153.직원 1인당 두 장의 티켓이 주어진다.** 인사부에 방문하면 티켓을 얻을 수 있다.

표현 정리 retire 은퇴하다 farewell dinner 송별연 renowned 유명한, 저명한 bid farewell 작별을 고하다 annual 연례의 gala 경축 행사 be held 열리다 be accompanied by ~을 동반하다, ~이 이어지다 profitable 수익성이 있는 revolutionize 혁명적으로 바꾸다, 대변혁을 일으키다 in use 쓰이고 있는 legendary 전설적인 due to ~때문에 issue 문제 announcement 발표 send off 배웅하다 jovial 유쾌한 stop by (~에) 잠시 들르다 Human Resources 인사부 pick up ~을 얻다, 수령하다

151. 유추 – 기사문을 접할 수 있는 매체 ★☆☆
해설 세 번째 단락 후반 'All employees are encouraged to attend to send Mr. Rhines off with jovial well wishes. There is a limit of two tickets per employee. Stop by Human Resources to pick up yours.'에서 전 직원에 행사에 참석해 Mr. Rhines의 퇴직을 즐거운 마음으로 축하해 달라고 조언하고 있으므로 정답은 (C)가 가장 적절하다.　　　　정답 (C)

해석 기사문이 실릴 곳은?
(A) 디자인 무역 저널
(B) 금융 잡지
(C) 회사 사보
(D) 창문 카탈로그

152. 유추 – Mr. Rhines에 대한 사실 내용 ★☆☆
해설 첫 번째 문장 'Renowned window design company Winex will bid farewell to its CEO, Leman Rhines, on Saturday, September 30, at the company's annual gala.'에서 이 행사가 연례 행사로 열리고 있음을 알 수 있고, 두 번째 단락에서 Mr. Rhines가 1992년에 입사했다고 했으므로 이전에도 이 연례 행사에 참석했을 것으로 짐작할 수 있어 정답은 (A)이다.　정답 (A)

표현 정리 previous 이전의 appoint 지명하다 successor 후임자

해석 Mr. Rhines에 대한 사실 내용은?
(A) 이전에 있었던 Winex 경축 행사에 참석한 적이 있다.
(B) 그는 아마추어 음악가이다.
(C) 회사의 창문을 만들었다.
(D) 그는 후임자를 지명했다.

153. 세부사항 – 티켓을 구할 수 있는 방법 ★☆☆
해설 본문 마지막 두 문장은 회사 연례 행사 참여를 위한 티켓에 대한 정보를 제공한다. 'There is a limit of two tickets per employee. Stop by Human Resources to pick up yours.'에서 티켓을 구하려면 인사부를 직접 방문하라고 했으므로 정답은 (D)이다.　　　　정답 (D)

패러프레이징 |지문| stop by Human Resources to pick up yours 당신 것을 얻기 위해서 인사부에 방문하라 → |선택지 D| get them in person 직접 그것들을 구하라

표현 정리 obtain 얻다 in person 직접

해석 티켓을 얻을 수 있는 곳은?
(A) 호텔에 전화함으로써
(B) 온라인으로 예약함으로써
(C) Mr. Rhines에게 요청함으로써
(D) 직접 수령함으로써

문제 154-155번은 다음 문자 메시지를 참조하시오.

Harry Fieldstine	Ms. Pinkie, 내일 열릴 이사회에 필요한 간식을 포함시키는 것을 잊었어요. 내 생각에는 회의가 길어질 것이기 때문에 이사들이 지루하지 않고 집중하도록 만들기 위해 약간의 다과가 제공돼야 할 것 같아요.　오전 11시 7분
Gina Pinkie	좋은 지적이에요. 사무실로 들어가기 전에 뭣 좀 구입해야겠어요. **155.생각해 두고 있는 거 있어요?**　오전 11시 8분
Harry Fieldstine	프레첼과 감자칩이면 좋을 거예요.　오전 11시 9분
Gina Pinkie	맛있겠네요. 하지만, 짠 간식이 목마르고, 불편하게 만들까 봐 걱정이에요.　오전 11시 12분
Harry Fieldstine	맞아요. 회의 동안 그들이 산만해지면 안 되죠. 그러면 간단하면서 달콤한 것을 구입합시다.　오전 11시 13분
Gina Pinkie	회의용으로 쿠키 모음을 사 갈게요.　오전 11시 15분
Harry Fieldstine	네, 그게 안전하겠어요. 내 대신 신경 써 줘서 고마워요. **154.회의에서 봐요.**　오전 11시 16분

표현 정리 forget to V ~하는 것을 잊다 board meeting 이사회 refreshments 다과 awake 깨어 있는 alert 생기 있는, 활발한 head into ~에 향하다 have in mind ~을 염두에 두다, 마음에 두다 distracted 산만해진 assortment 모음 a safe bet 확실한 것 take care of ~에 신경을 쓰다, ~을 처리해 주다

154. 유추 – Mr. Fieldstine에 대한 내용 ★☆☆
해설 메시지 후반 Gina에 대한 Harry Fieldstine의 마지막 대화 'See you at the meeting.'에서 회의에서 두 사람이 만날 것이라는 것을 짐작할 수 있으므로 정답은 (D)이다.　　　　정답 (D)

표현 정리 go out 외출하다

해석 Mr. Fieldstine에 대해 암시된 것은?
(A) 그는 외출해서 쿠키를 살 것이다.
(B) 배가 고프면 산만해진다.
(C) 달콤한 간식을 좋아하지 않는다.
(D) 이사회에 참석할 것이다.

155. 의도 파악하기 ★★☆
해설 Gina Pinkie가 오전 11시 8분에 'Good point. I can pick up something before heading into the office. What do you have in mind?'에서 사무실에 들어가기 전에 간식을 살 수 있는데, 혹시 무엇을 살 지 생각해 두고 있는 것이 있는지 묻는 내용이므로 (B)가 가장 적절한 정답이다.　정답 (B)

표현 정리 suggestion 제안 instruction 지시

해석 Ms. Pinkie가 오전 11시 8분에 보낸 메시지에서 "생각해 두고 있는 거 있어요?"라고 한 말의 의미는?
(A) 그녀는 간식을 위한 제안이 있다.
(B) 무엇을 살 것인지 알려 줄 것을 원한다.
(C) 간식 가게에 가는 길을 알아야 한다.
(D) 그녀는 무슨 간식이 사무실 안에 있는지 묻고 있다.

문제 156-158번은 다음 이메일을 참조하시오.

발신: customerservice@cleanair.com
수신: randymoones@nationaltrust.org
제목: 통풍관 공기통 청소
날짜: 10월 21일

Mr. Moones 님께,

156우리 기록에 의하면 이번 주 화요일인, 10월 25일 오후 5시에 National Trust 건물의 모든 통풍관 공기통을 대대적으로 청소하는 것으로 돼 있습니다. 정기 청소 외에도, 건물 유지 보수 계획에 상세히 나와 있는 것처럼 통풍관이 녹이 슬었거나 파손되지는 않았는지도 점검할 것입니다.

15725년이 넘은 건물을 위해 1년에 한 번 청소를 하는 것은 중요합니다. 지금까지 그렇게 해 왔기 때문에 통풍관 공기통에 문제가 있을 것이라고는 생각하지 않습니다. 이것은 예방 점검이기 때문에 걱정하지 않으셔도 됩니다.

청소와 점검을 간소화하기 위해, 이 시간에 모든 직원이 사무실을 비울 수 있도록 일정을 세워주실 것을 부탁 드립니다. **158**에어컨은 적어도 1시간 전에 미리 꺼 두셔야 합니다. 만약 이것이 불가능하다면, 일정 변경을 위해 555-2833으로 전화 주시기 바랍니다. 저희 기술자의 안전을 위해, 모든 공기 시스템들은 그들이 도착하기 전에 가동이 중단돼 식어 있어야 합니다.

유지 비용은 건물비에서 적용되지만, 추가 수리비 또는 작업이 필요하면 기술자가 그때 알려줄 것입니다.

Rhonda Lee
고객 서비스 대표

표현 정리 air duct 통풍관 공기통 indicate 나타내다 undergo 겪다, 받다 in addition to ~에 더해, ~외에 routine 정례적인, 일상적인 inspect 점검하다 rusting 녹이 스는 것 detailed 상세한 maintenance 유지 yearly 1년에 한 번씩 있는 preventative maintenance 예방 점검 streamline 간소화하다 appointment 약속 turn off 끄다 ahead 미리 technician 기술자 arrival 도착 expense 비용 representative 대표

156. 주제 - 이메일의 목적 ★☆☆

해설 첫 번째 단락 'Our records indicate that the National Trust Building will undergo a complete cleaning of all air ducts this coming Thursday, October 25, at 5:00 P.M.'에서 통풍관 공기통 청소가 예정돼 있음을 알리는 내용이므로 정답은 (C)이다. **정답 (C)**

표현 정리 give instructions 지시를 주다 notify A of B A에게 B를 알리다 recipient 받는 사람 bill 계산서

해석 이메일이 보내진 이유는?
(A) 기술자에게 지시를 하기 위해
(B) 새로운 청소 기술자를 환영하기 위해
(C) 수신자에게 일정을 알려주기 위해
(D) 청소 서비스 계산서를 제공하기 위해

157. 세부사항 - National Trust 건물에 관한 내용 ★☆☆

해설 두 번째 단락 'It is important to have the yearly cleaning done for buildings more than 25 years old.'에서 25년 이상된 건물을 1년에 한 번 청소하는 것이 중요하다고 했고, 이후 내용에서 이 건물은 그 동안 그렇게 해 왔다고 했으므로 정답은 (B)이다. **정답 (B)**

해석 National Trust Building에 관해 언급된 것은?
(A) 한 달에 한 번 청소를 한다.
(B) 적어도 25년 된 건물이다.
(C) 서비스를 취소할 것이다.
(D) 오후 5시 이후에 문을 닫는다.

158. 문장 위치 찾기 ★★☆

해설 세 번째 단락 'In order to streamline the cleaning and inspection processes, please plan to have your office empty of any employees at the appointment time. The air conditioning needs to be turned off at least an hour ahead.'에서 청소 및 점검을 위해 사전에 준비해야 하는 내용을 알려 주고 있는데, 문맥상 이것이 가능하지 않을 경우에는 청소가 불가능하고, 따라서 일정을 다시 정해야 하므로 연락을 달라는 내용이 이어지는 것이 적절해 정

답은 (C)이다. **정답 (C)**

표현 정리 reschedule 일정을 변경하다

해석 [1], [2], [3], [4] 중 다음 문장이 들어가기에 가장 알맞은 곳은?

"만약 이것이 불가능하다면, 일정 변경을 위해 555-2833으로 전화 주시기 바랍니다."
(A) [1]
(B) [2]
(C) [3]
(D) [4]

문제 159-161번은 다음 기사를 참조하시오.

소프트웨어에 주력하는 Sonar Technology
미래의 소프트웨어

시애틀(3월 8일) – **159**한때 하드웨어의 미래로 여겨졌던 신생 기업 Sonar Technology 사는 자사가 중점으로 삼는 분야에 변화를 주기로 했다고 발표했다.

"우리의 숙련된 기술자들이 자랑스럽지만, 기술 영역에서 막대한 이익을 창출할 방법은 획기적인 소프트웨어를 만드는 것이다."라고 설립자인 Jay Tolina가 올해 시애틀에서 열린 Pacific Tech 컨퍼런스에서 말했다. **160**Sonar는 1억 달러에 가까운 자금을 조성하고, California Sunnyvale에 있는 본사에 200명 이상의 직원들을 새로 고용했다.

원래 위치해 있던 Austin을 떠나 회사는 서부로 옮기기로 결정했고, 그것은 새로운 재능을 가진 인재들을 찾을 좋은 방법이 될 것이다. 1,000명 이상의 지원자들이 면접을 보았고, 직원 자리를 차지하기 위해 경쟁을 해야 했다. Sonar는 무료 현장 세탁, 직원 체육관, 보조금이 지급된 식사가 제공되는 24시간 카페테리아가 포함된 직원 복리후생으로 유명하다.

"저희는 소프트웨어 개발에 있어 여전히 초기 단계에 머물러 있지만, 우리가 비책을 보유하고 있다는데 자신감을 가지셔도 됩니다."라고 Tolina는 넌지시 말했다. 컨퍼런스에서의 그의 출현은 회사의 큰 변화에 대해 궁금해하던 많은 기술 팬들을 흥분시켰다. **161**Sonar가 받은 관심을 고려할 때, Sonar 주식은 가까운 미래에 급등할 것으로 예상된다.

표현 정리 focus on ~에 주력하다, ~초점을 맞추다 startup company 신생 기업 be hailed as ~로 묘사되다, 일컬어지다 announce 발표하다 pride on ~을 자랑하다 skilled 숙련된 founder 창립자 moneymaker 막대한 수익을 낳는 사업 innovative 획기적인 nearly 거의 headerquarters 본사 originally 원래 move out 이사를 나가다 applicant 신청자 be famous for ~로 유명하다 employee benefit 직원 복리후생 onsite 현장에서 subsidized 보조금을 받은 assured 자신감 있는 up one's sleeve 몰래 준비해 두고[둔], 비책의 hint 넌지시 알려주다 appearance 출현, 모습 excitement 흥분 buzz 소곤거리다, 윙윙거리다 publicity 매스컴의 관심 stock 주식 predict 예견하다 skyrocket 급등하다

159. 주제 - 기사의 주제 ★☆☆

해설 첫 번째 문장 'Startup company, Sonar Technology was once hailed as the future of hardware, but it has announced a change in its focus.'에서 Sonar Technology가 새로운 분야에 초점을 맞추기로 했다는 내용은 회사의 운영 방향에 변화가 있을 것임을 알 수 있으므로 정답은 (D)이다. **정답 (D)**

패러프레이징 |선택지| a change in its focus 목표의 변화 → |선택지 D| new directions for a company 회사를 위한 새로운 방향

표현 정리 unexpected 예기치 않은 innovative 혁신적인, 획기적인 motivate 동기를 부여하다 collaboration 공동 작업 industry 산업

해석 무엇에 관한 기사인가?
(A) 예기치 않은 리더십의 변화
(B) 직원들에 동기를 부여할 혁신적인 방법들
(C) 소프트웨어 산업에서의 공동 작업
(D) 회사를 위한 새로운 방향들

160. 세부사항 – Mr. Tolina의 회사 위치 ★★☆

해설 두 번째 단락의 마지막 문장 'Sonar has raised nearly 100 million dollars in funding and hired over 200 new employees at its new Sunnyvale, California headquarters.'에서 회사 본사가 캘리포니아 서니베일에 있다고 했으므로 정답은 (B)이다. 정답 (B)

🔍 함정 분석 세 번째 단락, 첫 번째 문장 'Originally based out of Austin, the company decided to move to the west and it would be a fresh start and a good way to find new talent.'에서 오스틴은 회사를 서부 Sunnyvale로 옮기기 전에 본사가 위치해 있던 장소이므로 (C)는 오답이다.

해석 기사에 따르면, Mr. Tolina의 회사는 어디에 위치해 있는가?
(A) 시애틀
(B) 서니베일
(C) 오스틴
(D) 뉴욕

161. 유추 – Sonar Technology에 관한 암시 내용 ★★☆

해설 본문 마지막 문장 'Given all the publicity it has received, Sonar stock is predicted to skyrocket in the near future.'에서 Sonar Technology의 대중들의 관심과 함께 주식이 급등할 것으로 예상된다고 말한 것으로 보아 이 회사가 언론으로부터 긍정적인 반응을 얻고 있음을 알 수 있으므로 정답은 (A)이다. 정답 (A)

🔍 함정 분석 'We are still in the early stages of software development, ~.'에서 곧 새로운 소프트웨어를 발매하기에는 아직 시기상조임을 알 수 있어 (B)는 오답이며, 'Originally based out of Austin, the company decided to move to the west and ~.'에서 본사를 이전했다는 정보만 알 수 있으므로 (C)도 오답이다. 'Sonar has raised nearly 100 million dollars in funding and hired over 200 new employees at its new Sunnyvale, California headquarters.'에서 직원들을 새로 고용했음을 알 수 있으므로 (D) 또한 오답이다.

패러프레이징 |지문| Given all the publicity it has received, ~ is predicted to skyrocket in the near future. 대중의 관심을 받는 것에 더불어, 가까운 미래에 주식이 급등할 것으로 예상되어 왔다 → |선택지 A| have received mostly positive publicity 주로 긍정적인 매스컴의 관심을 받아왔다

표현 정리 mostly 주로 positive 긍정적인 publicity 매스컴의 관심 release 발매하다 currently 현재 lay off 해고하다

해석 Sonar Technology에 관해 암시된 것은?
(A) 대부분 긍정적인 매스컴의 관심을 받았다.
(B) 곧 새로운 소프트웨어를 발매할 것이다.
(C) 현재 두 곳에 사무실을 갖고 있다.
(D) 최근 200명의 직원들을 해고했다.

문제 162-164번은 다음 편지를 참조하시오.

Maritime Harbor 호텔
New Hope, Maine

5월 19일

Julie Ramond
221 Wayward Lane

Bridgewater, NJ 23134

Ms. Ramond 님께,

164 6월 2일에 2박 일정의 New Hope로의 여행을 위해 Maritime Harbor 호텔을 선택해 주셔서 감사합니다. 온라인으로 예약하시면서 이곳에서 두 번째 숙박하신다고 말씀하셨더군요. 162 재방문에 감사하며, 추가 비용 없이 자동적으로 개인 스위트로 방이 업그레이드될 것입니다.

Express Diamond 신용카드로 룸 보증금 200달러가 부과되겠지만, 이 보증금은 예약을 위한 절차일 뿐이며, 룸이 파손되는 일이 없이 계산서가 완전히 지불되면 체크아웃 시에 환불될 것입니다.

163 호텔 내 편의 시설은 피트니스 센터, 건강 스파, 5성급 레스토랑을 포함합니다. 룸서비스와 다른 객실 내 서비스는 추가 비용으로 주문하실 수 있습니다. 숙박 또는 호텔 시설에 대해 궁금한 사항이 있으시면 (555) 232–8593로 언제든지 연락 주십시오.

Maritime Harbor 호텔을 선택해 주셔서 감사합니다.

Michelle Harwin
호텔 컨시어지

표현 정리 list 리스트에 언급하다 private suite 개인 스위트 charge 요금 amenities 편의 시설 regarding ~에 관하여 facilities 시설 hesitate 주저하다

162. 주제 – Ms. Harwin의 목적 ★☆☆

해설 첫 번째 단락 마지막 문장 'We appreciate your return business and will automatically upgrade your room to a private suite at no additional charge.'에서 추가 비용이 없는 개인 스위트로 방이 업그레이드 될 것이라고 안내하고 있으므로 정답은 (B)이다. 정답 (B)

패러프레이징 |지문| upgrade your room ~ at no additional charge 추가 비용 없이 업그레이드하다 → |선택지 B| offer her a free upgrade 무료 업그레이드를 제공하다

표현 정리 request 요청하다 additional payment 추가 지불 offer 제공하다 improvement 개선

해석 Ms. Harwin이 Ms. Ramond에게 편지를 보낸 이유는?
(A) 추가 비용을 요청하기 위해
(B) 무료 업그레이드를 제공하기 위해
(C) 새로운 호텔 서비스를 언급하기 위해
(D) 신용카드 상 문제를 설명하기 위해

163. 세부사항 – Maritime Harbor 호텔에 관한 내용 ★★☆

해설 세 번째 단락, 첫 번째 문장 'Amenities at our hotel include a fitness center, a health spa, and a 5-star restaurant.'에서 피트니스 센터 이용이 가능하다는 것을 알 수 있으므로 정답은 (A)이다. 정답 (A)

🔍 함정 분석 'Room service and other in-room services can be ordered for additional fees.'에서 룸서비스와 기타 서비스는 추가 비용이 필요하다는 것을 알 수 있으므로 (C)는 오답이다.

패러프레이징 |지문| include a fitness center 피트니스 센터가 포함되다 → |선택지 A| exercise facilities are available 운동시설을 이용 가능하다

표현 정리 exercise facilities 운동 시설 available 이용 가능한 deposit 보증금 nonrefundable 환불이 불가한 book 예약하다

해석 Maritime Harbor 호텔에 관해 언급된 내용은?
(A) 운동 시설은 이용 가능하다.
(B) 보증금은 환불이 불가능하다.
(C) 룸서비스는 방비에 포함되어 있다.
(D) 셔틀 서비스를 예약할 수 있다.

164. 세부사항 – Ms. Ramond의 체크아웃 날짜 ★☆☆

해설 첫 번째 문장 'We are pleased that you have chosen to stay with us for two nights at the Maritime Harbor Hotel for your trip to New Hope on June 2.'에서 6월 2일부터 2박 예정이므로 6월 4일에 체크아웃할 예정이어서 정답은 (C)이다. 정답 (C)

해석 편지에 따르면, Ms. Ramond는 언제 체크아웃을 하는가?
(A) 6월 2일
(B) 6월 3일
(C) 6월 4일
(D) 6월 5일

문제 165-167번은 다음 광고를 참조하시오.

증기 세탁하고, 일할 준비하세요

"성공을 위해 옷을 입어라!" 그것이 대중적인 진리인 것은 다 이유가 있습니다. 그것은 진실입니다. 165구겨진 유니폼을 입고 출근하겠다는 생각은 아예 하지 마십시오. 여러분은 스마트해 보임으로써 좋은 인상을 남기기 원합니다. 우리는 여러분이 일과 아이, 그리고 개인적인 삶을 살아가느라 바쁘다는 것을 알고 있습니다. 누가 자신의 옷을 직접 다림질할 시간을 갖고 있습니까? 165,167(D)Stanley's의 전문가가 여러분의 유니폼에서 주름을 없애는 일을 할 수 있게 해 주십시오.

그것을 어떻게 하는가?
여러분의 유니폼을 저희 10개의 편리한 지점 중 한 곳에 맡기시면 저희가 여러분을 위해 세탁하고 증기 다림질을 할 것입니다. 167(A)100개의 물품까지 맡기십시오! 저희는 그것들을 모두 세탁해 드립니다.

얼마나 오래 걸리는가?
아주 바쁘신가요? 문제 없습니다. 166저희는 근무 중인 직원들을 위한 신속 스티밍을 보유하고 있습니다. 167(C)10분이면, 완전 새 것처럼 보일 것입니다. 맡기면 5개 또는 그보다 적은 유니폼들을 바로 다음 날 받으실 수 있습니다!

모두 얼마인가?
가격은 유니폼의 상태에 따라 달라집니다.

표현 정리 **steam-cleaned** 증기 세탁된 **dress for** ~에 적합한 옷을 입다 **success** 성공 **popular** 인기있는, 대중적인 **mantra** 만트라(기도, 명상 때 외는 주문, 또리 진리, 진실한 말) **for a reason** 이유로 **truth** 진리 **go into work** 일하러 가다 **wrinkly** 구김살이 생긴 **make an impression** 인상을 주다 **look sharp** (옷을 잘 입어) 스마트해 보이다 **be busy -ing** ~하느라 바쁘다 **juggle** (두 가지 이상의 일을 동시에) 곡예하듯 하다 **iron** 다림질하다 **professional** 전문가 **drop off at** ~에 갖다 놓다 **convenient** 편리한 **steam-press** 증기 다림질 **up to** (특정한 수, 정도 등)까지 **in a rush** 아주 바쁘게 **express** 급행의, 신속한 **on the clock** 근무 중인 **brand new** 완전 새 것인 **pick up** ~을 가져가다 **the very next day** 바로 다음 날 **vary** 달라지다 **based on** ~에 근거하여 **state** 상태

165. 유추 – 광고의 대상 ★☆☆

해설 첫 번째 단락은 'Don't even think about going into work with a wrinkly uniform.'에서 구겨진 유니폼을 입고 출근하지 말라고 했고, 이어 'Let the professionals at Stanley's get the wrinkles out of your uniform.'에서는 Stanley's의 전문가들이 다림질로 주름을 펼 수 있게 해 달라고 요청하고 있으므로 광고 대상은 유니폼을 입는 직장인이라고 할 수 있어 정답은 (C)이다. 정답 (C)

표현 정리 **job seeker** 구직자 **deadline** 마감 일자 **self-employed** 자영업의, 독자적으로 일을 하는 **dress code** 복장 규정 **homemaker** 주부

해석 이 광고는 누구를 대상으로 하는가?
(A) 마감 일자가 있는 구직자
(B) 독자적으로 일을 하는 디자이너
(C) 복장 규정이 있는 직장인
(D) 바쁜 주부들

166. 세부사항 – Stanley's에 관한 내용 ★★☆

해설 세 번째 단락 'We have express steaming for employees on the clock. Just wait 10 minutes, and you'll look brand new.'에서 근무 중인 직장인들을 위해 10분이면 새 옷처럼 보이게 만들어 주는 신속 스티밍 서비스가 제공된다고 했으므로 정답은 (A)이다. 정답 (A)

패러프레이징 |선택지| express steaming ~. Just wait 10 minutes 10분이면 되는 신속 스티밍 서비스 → |선택지 A| same-day service 당일 서비스

표현 정리 **same-day service** 당일 서비스

해석 Stanley's에 관해 언급된 내용은?
(A) 당일 서비스를 제공한다.
(B) 지점 당 다섯 명의 직원들을 보유하고 있다.
(C) 해진 유니폼을 수선할 수 있다.
(D) 예약이 요구된다.

167. 세부사항 – Stanley's의 서비스에 대한 내용 ★★☆

해설 배달 여부는 언급되지 않았기 때문에 정답은 (B)이다. 정답 (B)

🔍 함정 분석 'Drop off up to 100 items!'에서 100개의 품목까지 맡길 수 있으므로 (A)는 사실이고, 'We have express steaming for employees on the clock. Just wait 10 minutes, and you'll look brand new.'에서 10분이면 끝나는 신속 스티밍 서비스가 제공되기 때문에 (C)도 사실이다. 그리고 'Let the professionals at Stanley's get the wrinkles out of your uniform.'에서 Stanley's의 전문가들이 다림질을 통해 유니폼의 구김을 없애는 것을 알 수 있으므로 (D)도 역시 사실이다.

패러프레이징 |지문| drop off up to 100 items 100개의 품목까지 맡김 → |선택지 A| bulk drop-off 대량으로 맡김
|지문| express steaming 신속 스티밍(다림질) → |선택지 C| steam-pressing completed in minutes 몇 분 안에 완료되는 증기 다림질
|지문| get the wrinkles out of your uniform 유니폼의 구김을 없앰 → |선택지 D| removing wrinkles from clothes 옷에서 구김을 제거함

표현 정리 **bulk** 큰 규모(양) **drop-off** 맡김 **delivery** 배달 **in minutes** 금방, 빨리 **remove** 없애다, 제거하다

해석 Stanley's가 제공하는 서비스로 언급되지 않은 것은?
(A) 대량으로 세탁물을 맡아 세탁
(B) 세탁된 유니폼의 배달
(C) 몇 분 안에 완료되는 증기 다림질
(D) 옷에서 구김을 제거

문제 168-171번은 다음 기사를 참조하시오.

3개의 지점을 새로 여는 Paperworks Prints
By Wendy Stein
7월 18일

Paperworks Print는 Arizona 주 Phoenix에 있는 가장 큰 셀프 복사 서비스 소매점이다. 168(B)주 도처에 이미 7개 지점이 영업을 하고 있고, 이미 계획된 3개 지점을 추가로 열 계획에 있으며, 앞으로 더욱 확장할 것이다.

Paperworks Print는 40년 전에 설립자인 Kale Logers가 대학생일 때 시작됐다. 그는 급한 마감일을 지켜야 했는데, 그의 서류를 출력할 곳이 없었다. 정신 없이 그의 과제를 출력하려고 그의 친구 대학 기숙사 방으로 달려

간 후, 그의 문제를 해결할 수 있는 사업 아이디어가 있음을 깨닫게 되었다.

168(A)다음 달, Logers와 그의 룸메이트들은 출력이나 서류들의 복사를 필요로 하는 다른 학생들에게 그들의 기숙사 방을 공개했다. 그들은 곧 여러 프로젝트를 완료하는데 필요한 스테이플러와 여러 도구들을 제공했다.

170(5)년 뒤, 첫 번째 Paperworks Print 점포가 그들의 대학 캠퍼스에서 2 킬로미터 떨어진 곳에 공식 문을 열었다. 이 매장의 엄청난 성공으로, 다른 여섯 개 지점이 연이어 생겨났다. 171회사는 Logers와 그의 룸메이트들이 기대했던 것보다 훨씬 이익이 좋았다.

168(D)그 후 Kale Logers는 은퇴했고, 그의 후임자인 Cal Smith가 회사를 이끌고 있다. Smith는 최근에 문을 연 지점들의 개업을 진두지휘해 왔다. 169새 위치는 아직 발표되지 않았지만, 많은 이들은 출력 점포들이 주의 경계를 넘어 Arizona 주 밖으로 진출할지 궁금해 하고 있다.

표현 정리 retailer 소매점 throughout 도처에 expand 확장하다
additional 추가적인 decade 10년 urgent 긴급한 deadline 마감 일자
dorm room 기숙사 방 frantically 정신 없이 서둘러서 assignment 과제
realize 깨닫다 dilemma 난제 following month 다음 달 make a
copy 사본을 만들다 paper 서류 assembly line 조립 라인 complete
마치다 clear the way for ~으로의 길을 열다 successor 후임자
oversee 감독하다 spearhead 진두지휘하다 have yet to 아직 ~하지
않다 state lines 주 경계

168. 세부사항 – Paperworks Print에 대한 내용이 아닌 것 ★★★
해설 세 번째 단락 'The following month, Logers and his roommates opened their dorm room to other students who needed to print or make copies of papers.'에서처럼 첫 공식 점포가 문을 열기 전에 그들의 사업이 대학교 기숙사 방에서 시작된 것은 맞지만, 새 지점이 대학 안에 있다고 보기는 어려우므로 (C)가 사실과 달라 정답이다. 정답 (C)

🔍 함정 분석 세 번째 단락 첫 번째 문장 'The following month, Logers and his roommates opened their dorm room to other students who needed to print or make copies of papers.'에서 (A)가 확인되고, 첫 번째 단락 마지막 문장 'With 7 locations already spread throughout the state, the print shop will soon expand even more with 3 additional locations planned.'에서 (B)가, 마지막 단락 첫 문장 'While Kale Logers has since retired, his successor, Cal Smith, oversees the company.'에서 (D)도 확인할 수 있다.

표현 정리 no longer 더 이상 ~아닌 manage 경영하다

해석 Paperworks Print에 관해 언급된 내용이 아닌 것은?
(A) 학생의 방에서 시작되었다.
(B) 곧 총 10개의 지점을 갖게 될 것이다.
(C) 새로운 지점은 대학 안에 있다.
(D) 더 이상 Mr. Logers에 의해 경영되지 않는다.

169. 유추 – Paperworks Print에 대한 내용 ★☆☆
해설 본문 마지막 문장 'The new locations have yet to be announced, but many wonder if the print shops will cross state lines and appear beyond the state of Arizona.'에서 Paperworks Print가 다른 주까지 영역을 확장할 것인지 사람들이 궁금해 하고 있다고 했으므로 정답은 (D)이다. 정답 (D)

패러프레이징 |지문| cross state lines and appear beyond the state 주의 경계를 넘어 주의 밖에 생겨나다 → |선택지 D| expand into new states 새로운 주로 확장하다

표현 정리 make a profit 이익을 내다 force A to B A가 B하게 하다
expand 확장하다

해석 Paperworks Print에 대하여 암시된 것은?
(A) 올해 수익을 내지 못할 것이다.

(B) 배달 서비스를 제공했었다.
(C) Kale Logers에게 은퇴하도록 강요할 것이다.
(D) 다른 주로 확장할 수도 있다.

170. 세부사항 – 공식 점포가 문을 열기까지 걸린 기간 ★☆☆
해설 네 번째 단락 'Five years later, the first official Paperworks Print shop opened just 2 kilometers from their college campus.'에서 공식 점포는 5년 뒤에 영업을 시작했음을 알 수 있으므로 정답은 (C)이다. 정답 (C)

해석 기사에 따르면, Printworks 지점이 공식적으로 문을 열기까지 얼마나 걸렸는가?
(A) 2년
(B) 3년
(C) 5년
(D) 7년

171. 문장 위치 찾기 ★★☆
해설 창업 당시 Logers와 그의 룸메이트들이 기대했던 것보다 이익이 훨씬 좋았다는 내용이므로 문맥상 본격적인 사업이 시작되면서 성공을 언급한 네 번째 단락 [3]에 주어진 문장이 들어가기가 가장 적절하다고 할 수 있으므로 정답은 (C)이다. 정답 (C)

표현 정리 profitable 수익성이 있는

해석 [1], [2], [3], [4] 중 다음 문장이 들어가기에 가장 알맞은 곳은?
"회사는 Logers와 그의 룸메이트들이 기대했던 것보다 훨씬 이익이 좋았다."
(A) [1]
(B) [2]
(C) [3]
(D) [4]

문제 172-175번은 다음 온라인 채팅을 참조하시오.

Joe Garcia	172오늘 아침 회사 셔틀버스에 플래너를 두고 왔어요. 그것이 보이는지 누군가 말해 줄래요?	오전 8시 25분
Jessica Burt	플래너가 어떻게 생겼죠? 방금 건물 B를 지나친 2번 버스를 타고 있어요.	오전 8시 26분
Danny Sails	지금 건물 G를 향해 가는 9번 버스를 타고 있어요. 어떤 버스를 탔나요?	오전 8시 29분
Joe Garcia	회색 가죽으로 된 플래너이고, 버스 앞쪽의 제 옆자리에 둔 것으로 생각해요. 174아쉽게도 급해서 버스 번호를 보지 못했어요.	오전 8시 49분
Danny Sails	지금 제 책상이에요. 미안해요, Joe. 하지만 9번 버스에서 플래너를 보지 못했어요.	오전 8시 55분
Jessica Burt	여기도 좋은 소식이 없어요. 173오늘 저녁 퇴근길에 셔틀버스를 탈 거니까, 그때 살펴볼게요.	오전 8시 58분
Joe Garcia	확인해 줘서 고마워요. 아무래도 사무실에 있는 분실물 보관소를 봐야겠어요.	오전 9시 5분
Danny Sails	좋은 생각이네요! 175누군가가 그것을 찾아서 갖다 놓았을지도 몰라요.	오전 9시 19분
Jessica Burt	왜 그걸 생각 못 했죠? 행운을 빕니다!	오전 9시 25분

표현 정리 head to ~로 향하다 place 놓다, 두다 toward ~쪽으로
front 앞 unfortunately 아쉽게도, 불행히도 in a hurry 서둘러, 급히
keep an eye out 살펴 보다 lost and found 분실물 취급소 turn in
~을 돌려주다

172. 주제 – 온라인 대화의 주제 ★★☆

해설 Joe Garcia가 먼저 'I left my planner on the company shuttle bus this morning. Will someone tell me if they see it?'이라고 하며 플래너를 버스에 두고 내렸다고 하자, Jessica Burt와 Danny Sails가 이에 응답하는 내용으로 대화가 진행되고 있으므로 (B)가 가장 적절한 답이다. **정답 (B)**

🔍 **함정 분석** Jessica Burt가 오전 8시 58분에 'I'll be taking the shuttle home tonight, too.'에서 퇴근길에 셔틀 버스를 탑승할 것이라고 했지만, 셔틀버스 탑승을 계획하는 것이 주제라고 보기는 어려우므로 (A)는 오답, Joe Garcia가 오전 9시 5분에 'I should probably try our office lost and found.'에서 사무실 분실물 취급소를 확인해 봐야 할 것 같다고 했지만 이것이 대화의 주제는 아니므로 (C)도 오답이다. Jessica Burt와 Danny Sails의 탑승 셔틀버스 번호가 언급되었지만 이는 플래너를 찾기 위한 대화의 일부분이므로 (D) 또한 오답이다.

표현 정리 misplaced 분실한, 잘못 둔 locate 위치를 찾아내다

해석 온라인 채팅은 주로 무엇에 대한 것인가?
(A) 셔틀버스 탑승을 계획하는 것
(B) 분실한 물건의 위치를 찾아내는 것
(C) 분실물 취급소에 연락하는 것
(D) 셔틀버스 번호를 비교하는 것

173. 의도 파악하기 ★☆☆

해설 Ms. Burt는 'I'll be taking the shuttle home tonight, too. I'll keep an eye out.'에서 퇴근길에 셔틀 버스를 이용할 건데, 그때 버스에 플래너가 있는지 살펴보겠다는 의미이므로 정답 (C)이다. **정답 (C)**

표현 정리 disagree 동의하지 않다 look for ~을 찾다 unsure 확신하지 못하는

해석 Ms. Burt가 오전 8시 58분에 "내가 눈여겨 볼게요."라고 한 말의 의미는?
(A) 그녀는 플래너를 분실했다는 것에 동의하지 않는다.
(B) 그녀는 다른 모든 셔틀 버스들을 확인할 것이다.
(C) 그녀는 계속 플래너를 찾을 것이다.
(D) 그녀는 플래너가 어떻게 생겼는지 확신하지 못한다.

174. 세부사항 – Mr. Garcia가 탔던 버스에 대한 내용 ★☆☆

해설 Joe Garcia가 오전 8시 49분에 보낸 내용에 따르면 'Unfortunately, as I was in a hurry, I didn't see the bus number.'에서 급한 나머지 버스 번호를 보지 못했다고 했으므로 정답은 (A)이다. **정답 (A)**

표현 정리 board 탑승하다 than usual 평소보다

해석 Mr. Garcia는 오늘 아침 그가 탑승했던 버스에 대해 뭐라고 말하는가?
(A) 몇 번 버스였는지 확신하지 못한다.
(B) 운전기사에게 분실 물품을 보고했다.
(C) 오늘 밤 집으로 돌아가면서 동일한 버스를 탈 것이다.
(D) 그는 평소보다 더 늦게 탑승했다.

175. 유추 – Mr. Sails가 암시한 내용 ★☆☆

해설 Danny Sails가 오전 9시 19분에 보낸 글 'Someone probably found it and turned it in.'에서 누군가 플래너를 발견해 분실물 보관소에 가져다 두었을 것이라고 말했으므로 정답은 (B)이다. **정답 (B)**

표현 정리 imply 암시하다

해석 Mr. Sails가 플래너에 관해 암시한 것은?
(A) 그것은 여전히 Mr. Garcia가 놓고 내린 버스에 있다.
(B) 어떤 직원이 그것을 분실물 취급소에 뒀다.
(C) 그것이 오늘 밤 집으로 돌아가면서 타는 버스에 있을 것이다.
(D) 그것은 9번 셔틀 버스에 있을 지도 모른다.

문제 176-180번은 다음 일정표와 이메일을 참조하시오.

Western 은행 훈련 세미나

훈련 일정 (2월 3 – 6일)

월요일	화요일	수요일	목요일
체크인 오전 8시	체크인 오전 8시	체크인 오전 8시	체크인 오전 9시
점심식사 오후 1시 15분	점심식사 오후 1시 15분	점심식사 오후 1시 15분	점심식사 오후 1시 15분
폐회사 Conference Room 1 오후 4시 30분	폐회사 Conference Room 2 오후 4시 30분	폐회사 Conference Room 1 오후 4시 30분	180폐회사 Conference Room 5 오후 3시

비즈니스 정장이 요구됩니다. 176늦은 체크인과 조기 퇴장은 용인되지 않을 것입니다. 모든 수업에 출석하지 않으면 훈련 마지막에 증명서를 받을 수 없습니다.

질문? 179주최자인 Vladimir Do에게 vdo@westernbank.com 또는 555-2827로 연락하십시오.

표현 정리 attire 복장 tolerate 용인하다 certification 증명 organizer 주최자

발신: Amber Collins
수신: Vladimir Do
날짜: 1월 29일
제목: 마지막 연설자

Mr. Do 님께,

저의 이름은 Amber Collins이고, 2월 6일 귀측의 세미나에서 연설해 줄 것을 요청 받았습니다. 179오래 전 함께 회계 수업을 들었던 당신의 상사인 Fred Samber로부터 부탁 받았습니다. 그는 우리 은행 지점의 성장과 성공적인 대출 프로그램에 대해 연설해 줄 것을 요청했습니다.

177세미나 폐회 연설을 하게 돼 즐겁지만, 어제 세미나 스케줄을 받고 고민에 빠졌습니다. 178컴퓨터를 끄고, 보안 시스템을 작동시키기 위해 은행 지점으로 오후 5시까지 돌아와야 하거든요. 이 일은 모든 은행 지점들을 연결해 주는 추가 보안 서버들과 연결되어 있기 때문에 매일 오후 5시에 정확히 이루어져야 합니다.

아쉽게도, 내 연설은 최소한 2시간 걸리는데, 내가 보여드릴 정보들은 반드시 상세하게 설명해야 하기 때문에 줄일 수 없습니다. 180내가 지점으로 돌아올 충분한 시간을 확보할 수 있도록 예정된 시간보다 30분 일찍 시작할 수 있을까요? 은행으로 5시까지 돌아올 수 없을 경우에는 유감스럽지만 폐회 연설을 취소할 수밖에 없습니다.

당신의 넓은 이해에 감사 드립니다.

Amber Collins
지점장
Granite 은행

표현 정리 recruit 채용하다, 고용하다 accounting 회계 loan 대출 deliver a speech 연설하다 shut off 정지시키다, 끄다 on the dot 정확히, 시간 맞춰 trim 잘라내다 present 보여주다 half an hour 30분 otherwise 그렇지 않으면

176. 세부사항 – Western 은행 세미나 스케줄에 대한 내용 ★★★

해설 첫 번째 지문인 일정표 하단 'Late check-in and leaving early will not be tolerated.'에서 세미나에 늦거나 일찍 자리를 뜨는 것은 용인되지 않을 것이라고 했으므로 정시에 도착해야 한다고 한 (A)가 정답이다. **정답 (A)**

🔍 **함정 분석** 식사 시간은 매일 오후 1시 15분으로 일정하므로 (B)는 오답이다. 폐회 장소도 Conference Room 1, 2, 5로 거의 매일 바뀌기 때문에 (C)도 오답이다. 'You will not receive certification at the end of the training if you do not attend all of the sessions.'에서 모든 수업에 출석한 사람에 한해 교육이 끝나는 시점에 증명서가 발급된다고 했으므로 매일 증명서가 발급된다고 한 (D) 역시 오답이다.

패러프레이징 |지문| Late check-in ~ will not be tolerated 세미나에 늦는 것은 용인되지 않는다 → |선택지 A| expected to arrive on time 정시에 도착할 것으로 예상된다

표현 정리 **participant** 참가자 **on time** 정각에 **vary** 달라지다 **from day to day** 그날그날 **hand out** 나눠주다, 배포하다

해석 Western 은행 세미나 스케줄에 관해 언급된 것은?
(A) 참가자들은 정각에 도착해야 한다.
(B) 식사 시간은 그날그날 달라질 것이다.
(C) 폐회사는 같은 장소에 있을 것이다.
(D) 증명서는 매일 발급될 것이다.

177. 주제 – 이메일의 목적 ★☆☆

해설 Ms. Collins는 이메일 두 번째 단락 'I received the seminar schedule yesterday from you and have a dilemma.'에서 세미나 스케줄을 받은 후, 고민에 빠졌다고 말한 후, 이어서 'I need to be back at my bank branch by 5:00 P.M.'에서는 오후 5시까지 은행으로 돌아와야 한다고 말하는 것으로 보아 (C)가 정답임을 알 수 있다. **정답 (C)**

표현 정리 **conflict** 충돌, 중복

해석 이메일의 목적은 무엇인가?
(A) 폐회사를 취소하기 위해
(B) 정책에 대해 불평하기 위해
(C) Mr. Do에게 일정이 겹친 것을 알리기 위해
(D) 일찍 온 것에 대해 사과하기 위해

178. 유추 – Granite 은행 보안 시스템에 대한 내용 ★★☆

해설 Ms. Collins는 이메일 'I need to be back at my bank branch by 5:00 P.M. in order to shut off our computers and turn on our security system,'에서 컴퓨터를 끄고 안전 시스템을 켜기 위해 오후 5시까지 지점으로 꼭 돌아와야 하는 상황을 설명했고, 이어 'I am afraid I must cancel my closing speech if I am unable to be back at my bank by 5:00.'에서는 그러지 못할 경우 폐회사를 할 수 없을 것이라고 한 내용으로 보아 Granite 은행의 보안시스템이 작동하려면 반드시 Ms. Collins가 있어야 한다는 것을 짐작할 수 있으므로 (C)가 정답이다. **정답 (C)**

🔍 **함정 분석** 'This task must be done at 5:00 P.M. on the dot every day.'에서 매일 같은 시간인 오후 5시에 시스템을 작동시켜야 한다고는 했지만 이것이 5시에 작동되도록 최근에 다시 설정된 것은 아니므로 (B)는 오답이다.

패러프레이징 |지문| turn on 켜다 → |선택지 C| activate 활성화하다

표현 정리 **remotely** 원격으로 **reset** 다시 맞추다 **activated** 활성화된

해석 이메일에서 Granite 은행 보안 시스템에 관해 암시된 것은?
(A) 때때로 원격으로 켜질 수 있다.
(B) 최근 오후 5시에 작동되도록 다시 맞춰졌다.
(C) 오직 지점장에 의해서만 활성화될 수 있다.
(D) Ms. Collin의 연설에서 논의될 것이다.

179. 연계 문제 – Mr. Samber의 근무처 ★☆☆

해설 Ms. Collins는 이메일 'I was recruited by your manager, Fred Samber, with whom I attended accounting school a number of years ago.'에서 Mr. Samber가 Mr. Do의 상급자인 것을 알 수 있었는데, 첫 번째 지

문 후반에서 Mr. Do는 Western 은행의 세미나를 담당하는 직원임을 알 수 있다. 따라서 Mr. Samber 역시 Western 은행에서 근무하는 것을 알 수 있으므로 정답은 (D)이다. **정답 (D)**

🔍 **함정 분석** Mr. Samber가 Mr. Do의 상급자이긴 하지만, 직접 Mr. Do를 고용했는지는 알 수 없다. 다른 부서에서 근무하다가 옮겨온 것일 수도 있기 때문에 (C)는 정답이 될 수 없다.

표현 정리 **send out** ~을 보내다 **itinerary** 일정표

해석 Mr. Samber에 대해 언급된 내용은?
(A) 그는 일정표를 보냈다.
(B) 그는 세미나를 이끌 것이다.
(C) 그는 Mr. Do를 고용했다.
(D) 그는 Western에서 근무한다.

180. 연계 문제 – Ms. Collins의 연설 시간 ★☆☆

해설 Ms. Collins는 이메일 서두 'My name is Amber Collins, and I was asked to speak at your seminar on February 6.'에서 2월 6일에 연설해 달라고 제안받았다고 했다. 그런데 Western 은행의 세미나 일정은 2월 3일 월요일부터 2월 6일 목요일까지 목요일에 있을 폐회 연설은 오후 3시로 예정되어 있다. 그런데 이메일 마지막 단락 'Perhaps I could start half an hour earlier than scheduled to allow me enough time to return to my branch?'에서 30분 일찍 연설을 할 수 있게 해 달라고 요청하고 있으므로 연설은 오후 2시 30분에 시작할 것임을 예상할 수 있어 정답은 (A)이다. **정답 (A)**

표현 정리 **propose** 제안하다

해석 Ms. Collins는 몇 시에 연설하는 것을 제안하고 있는가?
(A) 오후 2시 30분
(B) 오후 3시
(C) 오후 3시 30분
(D) 오후 4시

문제 181-185번은 다음 브로셔와 웹페이지를 참조하시오.

Better Business Trips Planner

회사 차원의 여행 계획을 갖고 있지만, 계획을 세울 시간이 없나요? 그렇다면 저희를 고용하세요! 저희는 50개 이상의 기업 휴가를 기획해 온 전문 여행 플래너입니다.

저희 임무는 귀사의 임직원들의 필요에 맞는 재미있고, 다채로운 여행 일정을 제공하는 것입니다. **181** 저희는 귀사의 필요에 따른 세부적 또는 여유 있는 여행 계획을 세울 수 있습니다.

여행 기간:
• **182(A)** 짧은 한두 시간의 여행
• 사무실 밖의 반나절 여행
• 대규모 인원을 위한 주말 여행
• 해외로 가는 장기 여행도 가능합니다!

상세한 옵션들:
• 교통
• 식사 계획
• 여행 간식
• 구급 상자

저희 기획자와 만나 상세한 논의를 하는데 관심이 있으시면, 저희 사무실에 들러주세요:

Better Business Trips Planner
184 Vera Tealie, 기획 매니저
293 Happyway Lane
San Jacinto, CA 13724

지난 여행들의 갤러리를 www.BetterBusinessTrips.net에서 찾아볼 수 있습니다.

표현 정리 in need of ~을 필요로 하는 company-wide 회사 전체의 put together 만들다, 세우다 corporate 기업의 getaway 휴가, 휴가지 flexible 융통성 있는 itinerary 일정표 loosely 엄격하지 않게, 느슨하게 duration 기간 excursion (보통 단체로 짧게 하는) 여행 abroad 해외로 stop by ~에 들르다

---

www.BetterBusinessTrips.net

회사 소개	추천의 글	갤러리 사진들	자주 묻는 질문들

"제 상관이 회사 5주년 기념을 위한 주말 직원 여행을 일주일 내로 세우라고 요구했습니다! 사전 예고도 없이, 저는 10명을 위한 교통, 숙소, 관광 및 음식을 기획할 방법을 고심해야만 했습니다. **183**블로그를 통해 Better Business Trips Planner를 찾기 전까지 그것은 불가능해 보였습니다. **184**저는 Vera에게 전화를 했고, 그녀는 그들의 주말 여행 플래너인 Jason과 연락시켜 줬고, 24시간 이내에 버스 회사 가격부터 **182(B)**그의 팀이 준비해 출발 당일 저희에게 전달될 간식에 이르기까지 모든 것이 적힌 옵션 목록을 이메일로 보내줬습니다. **182(D)**3일 후, 저희 여행은 회사의 예산 내에서 계획을 세울 수 있었습니다.

제 상사는 '저의' 빠르고 열심히 일한 모습에 매우 깊은 인상을 받았습니다. 저는 그들을 적극적으로 추천합니다. **185**친근하고, 조직적이고, 신속한 Better Business Trips Planner가 최고입니다."

Shelly Franks
Bitcoil 소프트웨어 기술자

표현 정리 stop by ~에 들르다 testimonials 추천의 글 frequently 자주 without notice 예고 없이 figure out 생각해 내다 lodging 숙소 sights 관광 impressed 깊은 인상을 받은 organized 조직적인 prompt 신속한 beat 이기다

---

181. 세부사항 – Better Business Trips Planner를 고용하는 것의 이점 ★☆☆

해설 브로셔 두 번째 단락 'We can plan in as much detail or as loosely as your company needs.'에서 회사의 필요에 맞게 상세하고, 여유 있게 여행 계획을 세울 수 있다는 점을 장점으로 내세우고 있으므로 정답은 (D)이다. **정답 (D)**

패러프레이징 |지문| plan in as much detail or as loosely as your needs 당신의 필요에 맞게 상세하게 또는 느슨하게 계획하다 → |선택지 D| customize trips for clients 고객에 맞춰 여행을 설계하다

표현 정리 customize 주문 제작하다

해설 브로셔에 따르면, Better Business Trips Planner를 고용하는 것의 이점은?
(A) 재미있는 시간을 보장한다.
(B) 그들의 경쟁자들보다 더 빨리 일한다.
(C) 스스로 준비하는 것보다 저렴하다.
(D) 고객을 위한 맞춤 여행을 세울 수 있다.

182. 세부사항 – Better Business Trips Planner에 대한 내용 ★★☆
해설 가격에 대한 언급은 없으므로 정답은 (C)이다. **정답 (C)**

🔍 **함정 분석** 첫 지문에서 짧은 여행부터 긴 해외 여행까지 준비가 가능하다는 것을 알 수 있으므로 (A)는 확인되고, Better Business Trips Planner가 제공하는 옵션에 음식도 포함되어 있는 동시에 두 번째 지문인 추천의 글에서 Ms. Franks는 'the snacks that can be assembled by his team and delivered to us on the day of departure'라며 스낵도 준비되었다고 했

으므로 (B)도 사실이다. 'Three days later, the entire trip was planned and within our company's budget.'에서 3일 후에 모든 여행 계획이 완료됐다고 했으므로 (D)도 확인이 된다.

표현 정리 multiple 다양한

해설 Better Business Trips Planner에 관해 언급된 내용이 아닌 것은?
(A) 그것은 짧은 여행을 준비한다.
(B) 그것은 음식 준비하는 것을 돕는다.
(C) 그것은 다양한 가격 수준을 제공한다.
(D) 그것은 며칠 내로 여행을 준비할 수 있다.

183. 세부사항 – Ms. Franks가 Better Business Trips Planner를 알게 된 계기 ★☆☆
해설 두 번째 지문 'It seemed impossible until I found Better Business Trips Planners through a blog.'에서 Ms. Franks가 Better Business Trips Planner를 알게 된 동기는 블로그를 통해서임을 알 수 있으므로 정답은 (B)이다. **정답 (B)**

패러프레이징 |지문| through a blog 블로그를 통해 → |선택지 B| online 온라인으로

해설 Ms. Franks는 Better Business Trips Planner를 어떻게 알게 되었나?
(A) 고객으로부터 소개받았다.
(B) 회사에 대해 온라인으로 읽었다.
(C) 회사 사무실에 갔다.
(D) 상사로부터 이야기를 들었다.

184. 연계 문제 – Ms. Franks에 대한 내용 ★☆☆
해설 두 번째 지문 'I called Vera, and she put me in touch with their weekend trip planner, Jason'에서 먼저 Vera Tealie에게 전화를 했다고 했는데, 첫 번째 지문인 브로셔 후반에서 Vera Tealie는 Planning Manager임을 알 수 있으므로 정답은 (A)이다. **정답 (A)**

표현 정리 advanced deposit 계약금

해설 Ms. Franks에 대해 암시된 것은?
(A) 기획 담당 매니저와 함께 이야기했다.
(B) 예약금을 지불해야 했다.
(C) San Jacinto로 여행을 계획했다.
(D) 비상사태를 위한 용품을 주문했다.

185. 동의어 ★★☆
해설 'Friendly, organized, and prompt, Better Business Trips Planner can't be beat.'에서 beat은 '능가하다, 물리치다'라는 뜻을 갖고 있는데, 보기에서 이와 가장 유사한 단어는 (C)이다. **정답 (C)**

표현 정리 abuse 남용하다 outsmart ~보다 한 수 앞서다 surpass 능가하다

해설 고객평 두 번째 단락, 두 번째 줄의 "beat"와 의미가 가장 가까운 것은?
(A) 남용된
(B) 한 수 앞선
(C) 능가하는
(D) 축소한

문제 186-190번은 다음 일정표, 공지, 그리고 의견서를 참조하시오.

점심 배달 일정
Bermington LLC (1 – 8번 건물)

일일 배달

Building 1	Building 2	Building 3	Building 4
오전 11시 25분	오전 11시 35분	오전 11시 45분	오전 11시 55분
오후 12시 50분	오후 1시	오후 1시 15분	오후 1시 25분
Building 5	189 Building 6	Building 7	Building 8
오후 12시 10분	오후 12시 25분	오후 12시 45분	오후 12시 55분
오후 1시 40분	오후 1시 55분	오후 2시 10분	오후 2시 25분

186(B) 이른, 그리고 늦은 점심 배달은 직원 회의 일정에 맞춰 매일 이용 가능합니다. 일별 메뉴는 직원 포털에 있는 Bermington 사 웹사이트에서 찾으실 수 있습니다.

만약 예정된 배달을 놓쳤다면, 중앙 식당에서 오후 12시 – 3시 사이에 찾아가실 수 있습니다.

표현 정리 accommodate 수용하다, 맞추다

알림

여름 동안 늦은 점심 배달을 중단합니다.
게시: 5월 29일

186(A),190 6월 1일 월요일부터 7월 30일까지, 늦은 점심 배달이 여름 동안 비용을 줄이기 위해 중단될 것입니다. 187 회사가 이 두 달 동안 가동을 절반으로 줄이기로 함에 따라, 경영진은 하루에 한 번 식사 배달을 제공하기로 했습니다. 186(C) 식당은 평소처럼 픽업 서비스를 계속 제공할 것입니다.

표현 정리 suspend 중단하다 take place 일어나다, 발생하다 cut costs 비용을 줄이다 operate 운영하다 capacity 용량 management 경영진 usual times 평소처럼

당신의 의견을 아래에 남겨주시기 바랍니다:

날짜: 7월 1일
이름: Connor Giles
189 부서: 판매부, 6번 건물
이메일: cgiles@bermington.net

논평/질문/제안:
정기 시즌 동안, 점심 배달은 항상 제 시간에 배달되었습니다. 이번 여름에는 식사가 산발적으로 배달되는 것을 알았습니다. 188 어제, 저는 평소 점심 배달 스케줄에 맞춰 회의를 일찍 끝내고 식사 후에 다음 회의에 참석하려고 했지만 배달이 20분 늦었고, 그로 인해 두 번째 회의를 놓쳤습니다. 배달 지연에 대해 알아봐 주시기 바랍니다.

표현 정리 show up 나타나다 sporadically 간헐적으로, 산발적으로 in line with ~와 함께 look into 조사하다, 살펴 보다

---

186. 세부사항 – Bermington 점심 배달 서비스에 대한 내용이 아닌 것 ★★★
해설 두 번째 지문 첫 번째 문장 'From Monday, June 1, through July 30, late lunch deliveries will not take place in order to cut costs during summer hours.'에서 6월 1일부터 7월 30일까지 배달 서비스가 하루 2회에서 1회로 중단될 예정이라고 했으므로 무기한 중단될 것이라고 한 (A)는 틀린 내용이다. **정답 (A)**

🔍 **함정 분석** 첫 번째 지문 'Early and late lunch deliveries are available every day to accommodate employee meeting schedules.'에서 (B)의 내용이 확인되고, 첫 번째 지문에서 언급되었던 배달 시간을 놓친 점심을 식당에 가서 찾아가는 서비스는 두 번째 지문 'The cafeteria will continue to offer its pickup service at the usual times.'에서 계속될 것이라고 했으므로 (C)도 확인된다. 첫 번째 지문인 일정표에서 오전 11시 25분에 건물 1을 시작으로 시작된 배달은 오후 12시 55분, 마지막 배달이 이루어지기까지 1시간 30분 걸린다고 볼 수 있어 (D)도 맞는 내용이다.

패러프레이징 |지문| Early and late lunch deliveries are available every day 매일 이른 점심 배달과 늦은 점심 배달 두 번 가능하다 → |선택지 B| There are two delivery times during most of the year 1년의 대부분 기간 동안 두 번씩 배달한다

표현 정리 indefinitely 무기한으로 most of ~의 대부분

해설 Bermington 점심 배달 서비스에 대해 언급된 것이 아닌 것은?
(A) 두 번째 배달을 무기한으로 취소했다.
(B) 1년의 대부분 기간 동안 두 번의 배달 시간이 있다.
(C) 놓친 배달은 여전히 7월에도 받을 수 있다.
(D) 8개 건물에 점심이 배달되는데 1시간 이상이 소요된다.

---

187. 유추 – Bermington LLC에 대한 내용 ★★☆
해설 두 번째 지문 'From Monday, June 1, through July 30, late lunch deliveries will not take place in order to cut costs during summer hours. As the company will be operating at half capacity during these months'에서 여름 두 달 동안 가동량을 반으로 줄일 것이라고 했으므로 6월에는 평상 시에 비해 적은 수의 직원들이 근무한다고 볼 수 있어 정답은 (C)이다. **정답 (C)**

표현 정리 value 소중하게 여기다 do away with ~을 그만두다 fewer 더 적은 capacity 용량

해설 Bermington LLC에 대해 암시된 것은?
(A) 직원 피드백을 소중하게 여기지 않는다.
(B) 점심식사 배달을 그만 둘 것이다.
(C) 6월에는 적은 수의 직원들을 보유하고 있다.
(D) 항상 최대한 가동하여 일한다.

---

188. 유추 – Mr. Glies에 대한 내용 ★★☆
해설 Mr. Giles는 평소 시즌에는 점심 서비스가 항상 제 시간에 제공되었다고 말한 후, 'Yesterday, I ended my meeting early in line with the usual lunch delivery schedule'에서 어제는 평소 배달 시간에 맞춰 회의를 일찍 끝냈지만 20분 늦게 점심이 배달돼 회의 일정에 차질이 생겼다고 말하고 있다. 여름 두 달 동안 늦은 점심 배달이 중단되고, 이른 점심 배달 서비스만 제공되기 때문에 그에 맞추기 위해 회의 일정을 변경했음을 유추할 수 있고, 평소에는 지연되는 일이 없었던 것을 알 수 있으므로 정답은 (D)이다. **정답 (D)**

표현 정리 be satisfied with ~에 만족하다 reinstated 다시 재개된, 부활된 right away 즉시 due to ~때문에

해설 Mr. Giles에 대한 사실 내용은?
(A) 새로운 배달 일정에 만족한다.
(B) 두 번째 배달이 즉시 재개되기를 원한다.
(C) 곧 Bermington LLC를 떠날 것이다.
(D) 5월에는 늦은 배달로 인해 회의를 놓치지는 않았다.

---

189. 연계 문제 – Mr. Giles가 점심을 받을 예정이었던 시간 ★☆☆
해설 Mr. Giles는 'Department: Sales, Building 6'에서 6번 건물의 판매부 소속인데, 이를 첫 번째 지문 일정표에서 보면 6번 건물의 이른 점심은 오후 12시 25분에 제공되기로 되어 있다는 것을 알 수 있으므로 정답은 (B)이다. **정답 (B)**

표현 정리 be supposed to ~하기로 되어 있다, ~할 예정이다

해설 Mr. Giles는 몇 시에 점심을 받기로 되어 있었나?
(A) 오후 12시 10분
(B) 오후 12시 25분
(C) 오후 12시 45분
(D) 오후 1시 55분

---

190. 연계문제 – Mr. Giles가 늦은 점심을 받을 수 있는 가장 빠른 시간 ★☆☆
해설 두 번째 지문의 첫 번째 문장, 'From Monday, June 1, through July 30, late lunch deliveries will not take place in order to cut costs during

summer hours.'에서 알 수 있듯이 늦은 점심 배달이 중단되는 기간이 6월 1일부터 7월 30일까지이므로, 7월 31일부터는 배달이 재개됨을 유추할 수 있다. 그러므로 늦은 점심을 받아 볼 수 있는 가장 빠른 날은 7월 31일이라는 것을 알 수 있다. 따라서 정답은 (C)이다. 정답 (C)

표현 정리 obtain 얻다, 획득하다

해석 Mr. Giles가 늦은 점심 배달을 받을 수 있는 가장 빠른 날은?
(A) 7월 1일
(B) 7월 30일
(C) 7월 31일
(D) 8월 1일

문제 191-195번은 다음 공지, 양식, 그리고 이메일을 참조하시오.

회사 배드민턴 팀 입단 테스트!

3단계 레벨: 오락, 중급, 경쟁

Sanders Storage Disks 직원들에게 가을 시즌 배드민턴 리그에 지원할 것을 초대합니다! 모든 사람들이 가입할 수 있는 3단계 레벨이 있습니다! 오락을 목적으로 하는 선수들은 입단 테스트를 받을 필요가 없지만, 연습 첫 날에 나오시면 됩니다.

수요일 연습 (중급, 경쟁)	오후 6시 30분 – 오후 8시 30분
목요일 연습 (오락)	오후 6시 30분 – 오후 8시
전 레벨 경기는 매주 토요일 아침에 열릴 것입니다.	오전 10시

191 가입에 관심이 있는 분들은 라켓과 운동화를 9월 13일, 금요일 오후 5시 30분에 회사 체육관으로 가져오세요.

Sanders 회사 체육관
배드민턴 입단 테스트
오후 5시 30분

표현 정리 tryout 입단 테스트 recreational 오락의 intermediate 중급의 competitive 경쟁을 하는 try out for ~에 지원하다 show up 나타나다 match 경기

Sanders 주식회사

시설 예약 서식

이름: *Michael Nealers*
이메일: *michael@sanders.com*
시설: *체육관*
192,193 예약 날짜: *9월 13일, 오후 5시 30분 – 7시 30분*
행사: *회사 배드민턴 팀 입단 테스트*

표현 정리 facility 시설 gym 체육관(= gymnasium)

수신: Michael Nealers [michael@sanders.com]
발신: Tara Walkins [facilitiesmanager@sanders.com]
제목: 체육관 예약 승인
날짜: 9월 9일

안녕하세요, Michael.

배드민턴 입단 테스트를 위해 회사 체육관을 예약하려는 당신의 서식을 받았습니다. 원하는 시간에 다른 예약이 없기 때문에, 당신의 요청은 승인되었습니다.

193 행사를 준비하기 위해 예약된 시간 한 시간 전에 체육관에 들어가셔도 좋습니다. **195** 그러나, 예약하신 전 날 오후 3시 이전에 저에게서 열쇠를 받아가야 합니다. 그 시간 이후, 월요일 아침까지 사무실 밖에 있을 것입니다.

저의 사무실은 서쪽 건물 4층에 있습니다.

194 체육관 사용을 마치면, 쓰레기를 치우고 모든 기구들을 원래 있던 장소에 돌려 놓는 것을 잊지 마세요. 작성해서 나중에 열쇠와 함께 제출해야 하는 장비 체크리스트가 있습니다. 모든 체육관 장비는 기록으로 확인돼야 합니다.

행사 후에, 제 사무실 밖에 있는 서류 투입함에 열쇠를 반납해 주십시오.

좋은 시간 보내세요.

Tara

표현 정리 approve 승인하다 fill out 작성하다 account for ~을 설명하다, 확인하다 drop box 서류 투입함

---

191. 세부사항 – Sanders 회사 배드민턴 프로그램에 대한 내용 ★☆☆

해설 첫 번째 지문 세 번째 단락 'If you are interested in joining, bring your racket and sneakers to the company gym on Friday, September 13, at 5:30 P.M.'에서 가입을 원하는 사람은 자신의 라켓과 운동화를 지참해서 회사 체육관으로 와야 한다고 했으므로 정답은 (C)이다. 정답 (C)

패러프레이징 |지문| bring your racket and sneakers 당신의 라켓과 운동화를 가져와라 → |선택지 C| participants must have their own equipment 참가자들은 그들 자신의 장비를 가지고 있어야 한다

표현 정리 participation 참가 general public 일반 대중 participant 참가자 competition 대회

해석 Sanders 사 배드민턴 프로그램에 대해 언급된 것은?
(A) 3개의 다른 팀들이 있을 것이다.
(B) 참가는 일반 대중에게 열려 있다.
(C) 참가자들은 그들 자신의 장비를 갖추고 있어야 한다.
(D) 대회는 한 달에 한 번 있다.

192. 유추 – 배드민턴 입단 테스트에 대한 내용 ★☆☆

해설 두 번째 지문의 회사 시설 예약 서식에 따르면 'Reservation Date: September 13, 5:30 P.M. – 7:30 P.M.'에서 9월 13일 오후 5시 30분부터 7시 30분까지 두 시간 동안 예약된 것을 알 수 있으므로 정답은 (D)이다. 정답 (D)

패러프레이징 |지문| 5:30 P.M. – 7:30 P.M. 오후 5시 30분부터 7시 30분까지 → |선택지 D| no more than two hours 2시간 정도

표현 정리 optional 선택적인 entail 수반하다 medical examination 건강 진단 last 계속되다 no more than ~일 뿐

해석 배드민턴 입단 테스트에 관한 사실 내용은?
(A) 1년에 세 차례 개최된다.
(B) 중급의 선수를 위해서는 선택적이다.
(C) 건강 진단을 수반한다.
(D) 2시간 정도만 진행될 것이다.

193. 연계 문제 – Mr. Nealers가 입단 테스트를 준비할 시간 ★☆☆

해설 세 번째 지문 두 번째 단락 'You may enter the gym to prepare for the event an hour before your scheduled time.'에서 예약 시간 한 시간 전부터 체육관에 들어갈 수 있다고 했는데, 두 번째 지문 양식에서 예약 시간은 오후 5시 30분이다. 따라서 이보다 한 시간 전은 오후 4시 30분이므로 정답은 (B)이다. 정답 (B)

해석 Mr. Nealers가 입단 테스트를 위해 가장 빨리 준비할 수 있는 시간은?
(A) 오후 3시
(B) 오후 4시 30분
(C) 오후 5시 15분
(D) 오후 5시 30분

194. 세부사항 – Ms. Walkins가 Mr. Nealers에게 요청한 사항 ★☆☆

해설 세 번째 지문의 세 번째 단락을 보면, 'Once you're done with the gym, please make sure to clean up any trash and place all equipment back where you found it.'이라고 되어 있는데, 쓰레기를 청소해야 하고, 사용한 기구들은 원래 장소에 돌려놓아야 한다고 했기 때문에, 정답은 (C)가 된다. 참고로 본문에서 clean up any trash라고 되어 있는 문장을 (C)에서 remove garbage로 바꿔놓은 것이다. **정답 (C)**

패러프레이징 |지문| clean up any trach 쓰레기를 치우다 → |선택지 C| remove garbage 쓰레기를 치우기

표현 정리 storage chest 수납상자 distribute 나누어주다, 분배하다 remove 제거하다 garbage 쓰레기

해석 Ms. Walkins가 Mr. Nealers에게 입단 테스트가 끝난 후에 하도록 요청한 것은?
(A) 수납상자를 잠그기
(B) 라켓을 나누어주기
(C) 쓰레기를 치우기
(D) 설문조사를 완료하기

195. 연계 문제 – Ms. Walkins가 직장에 있을 날 ★☆☆

해설 Ms. Walkins는 이메일 두 번째 단락 'However, you need to pick up the keys from me before 3 P.M. the day before your reservation. After that time, I will be out of the office until Monday morning.'에서 예약한 날 하루 전 오후 3시까지 열쇠를 받아가라고 했는데, 그 이유는 그 시간 이후부터 월요일 오전까지 사무실을 비울 것이라고 했다. 그런데 두 번째 지문에서 체육관을 사용하려고 예약한 날짜는 9월 13일이다. 따라서 Ms. Walkins는 예약한 날 하루 전인 9월 12일 오후 3시까지 직장에 있을 것임을 알 수 있으므로 정답은 (A)이다. **정답 (A)**

해석 Ms. Walkins가 직장에 있을 날은 언제인가?
(A) 9월 12일
(B) 9월 13일
(C) 9월 14일
(D) 9월 15일

문제 196-200번은 다음 광고, 영수증, 그리고 이메일을 참조하시오.

사무용품 가게

사무실에 필요한 모든 것을 한 매장에서!

주간 세일*
196(D)11월 1일 – 11월 7일

검은색 젤 잉크 펜 – 개당 1달러

깨끗하고 부드럽게 쓰입니다. 필요로 할 유일한 펜입니다.

11월 특별가:
• 프린터 잉크 리필 30퍼센트 할인: 검은색, 컬러
• 종이 한 상자를 사고, 두 번째 상자는 공짜로 받으세요!
• 새로운 컴퓨터 의자를 책상 구입과 함께 30달러를 할인받으세요.
• 200레이저젯 프린터가 지금 89.99달러! (원래 109.99달러!)

196*주간 세일 제한: 고객 1인 당 5개

쿠폰
10퍼센트 할인
총 구매가 150달러 이상일 때.
196(A)만료: 2018년 11월 30일
196(B)Stelton Street 매장에서만 유효함

표현 정리 office supply 사무용품 expire 만료되다 valid 유효한

사무용품 가게
3520 Stelton Street
555-1532

199**일자: 11월 6일**
시각: 5시 15분
구매: #25163
출납원: Bon Thornton

제품 번호	197품목	수량	가격
BG201	검은색 젤 잉크 펜	5	5달러
LJ0394	레이저젯 프린터	1	89.99달러
BP2391	종이	4	24달러
		소계:	118.99달러
		세금:	10.01달러
		총:	129달러
		수납:	130달러
		거스름돈:	1달러

Office Supply 매장을 이용해 주셔서 감사합니다!

표현 정리 cashier 출납원 subtotal 소계

발신: Barry Valentino
수신: customersupport@officesupply.com
제목: 프린터 환불

고객지원 담당자 분께,

199**저는 어제 신형 프린터(Item #LJ0394)를 Stelton Street 매장에서 구입했습니다.** 그러나, 그것을 제 컴퓨터에 연결하려고 했을 때, 작동시킬 수 없었습니다. 처음에는 그것이 결함 있는 제품인지 의심했습니다. 그러나 저희 직장에서 일하는 기술자가 그의 컴퓨터로 출력이 되는지 시험했고, 198**문제가 없었습니다.** 그는 쉽게 시험 종이를 인쇄할 수 있었습니다. 그의 결론은 단순히 제 컴퓨터에서 소프트웨어와 호환이 되지 않는다는 것이었습니다. 제 컴퓨터에 있는 모든 소프트웨어는 제가 일을 하는데 필수적이고, 귀사의 기술 지원 직원이 다른 해결책을 제공할 수 없기 때문에 저는 프린터를 사용할 수 없습니다.

200**구매한지 30일이 안 됐으므로 환불 받을 수 있습니다.** 199**내일 제 지역 매장으로 제품을 가지고 가겠습니다.**

Barry V.

표현 정리 customer support 고객 지원 hook up (전원, 인터넷 등에) 연결하다 suspect 의심하다 faulty 결함이 있는 compatible 호환이 되는 essential 필수적인 eligible ~을 할 수 있는

196. 세부사항 – 광고에 대한 내용이 아닌 것 ★★☆

해설 첫 번째 지문인 광고 후반 '*Weekly sales limit: 5 per customer'에 따르면 주간 할인 제품인 펜은 고객 1인 당 5개로 판매가 제한되기 때문에 (B)는 광고의 내용과 부합되지 않는다. **정답 (B)**

🔍**함정 분석** 광고 후반 쿠폰에서 10% 할인은 'Expires: November 30, 2018'에서 11월 30일 만료될 때까지 이루어지기 때문에 (A)는 맞는 내용이고, 쿠폰은 Stelton Street 지점에서만 사용 가능하므로 (C)도 역시 맞다. 펜 할인은 'Weekly Sales *November 1 - November 7, Black Gel Ink Pens – $1 each'에서 11월 1일에서 7일까지 일주일간 주간 할인으로 진행되므로, 11월 특별가로 진행되는 다른 할인 품목보다 행사가 일찍 끝이 나 (D)도 맞는 내용이다.

패러프레이징 |지문| Valid only at Stelton Street store Stelton Street 지점에서만 사용 가능하다 → |선택지 C| only be used at one location 쿠폰은 한

TEST 06

정답 및 해설 _ **81**

지점에서만 쓸 수 있다

해석 광고에서 언급된 내용이 아닌 것은?
(A) 고객은 한 달 내내 10% 할인을 받는다.
(B) 고객은 무제한으로 1달러짜리 젤 펜을 살 수 있다.
(C) 쿠폰은 한 지점에서만 쓰일 수 있다.
(D) 펜 가격은 나머지 할인 품목 전에 끝난다.

197. 연계 문제 – 구매번호 26163에 대한 내용 ★★☆

해설 두 번째 지문인 영수증에 언급된 '구매 번호 25163'에서 구입된 품목은 검은색 젤 잉크 펜과 레이저젯 프린터, 그리고 종이이며, 이 물품들은 광고에서 알 수 있듯이 모두 홍보 품목임을 알 수 있으므로 정답은 (D)이다.　　정답 (D)

표현 정리 promotional 홍보의

해석 구매번호 251163에 대해 암시된 것은?
(A) 고객은 쿠폰을 사용했다.
(B) 고객은 잔돈을 받지 않았다.
(C) 고객은 신용카드로 결제했다.
(D) 고객은 오직 홍보 품목만 구입했다.

198. 동의어 문제 ★★☆

해설 이메일 첫 번째 단락 'At first, I suspected that it was a faulty product. However, a technician at my workplace tested the printer on his computer, and there were no issues.'에서 issues는 문맥상 '문제'라는 의미로 사용되었다. 따라서 보기에서 이와 가장 유사한 의미로 쓰인 단어는 (C) problems이다.　　정답 (C)

표현 정리 distribution 분배　instruction 지시, 명령

해석 이메일 첫 번째 단락, 네 번째 줄의 "issues"와 의미가 가장 가까운 것은?
(A) 분배
(B) 지시
(C) 문제
(D) 결과

199. 연계 문제 – Mr. Valentino가 매장을 방문하는 날 ★☆☆

해설 이메일 첫 번째 단락 'I purchased a new printer (Item #LJ0394) from your Stelton Street store yesterday.'에서 Mr. Valentino가 프린터를 구입한 날은 영수증에 적힌 날짜에 따르면 11월 6일이고, 따라서 이메일을 쓰는 오늘은 11월 7일이다. 이메일 마지막 문장 'I plan to bring the product back to my local store tomorrow.'에서 내일 제품을 가지고 지역 매장을 방문할 것이라고 했으므로 정답은 (B)이다.　　정답 (B)

해석 Mr. Valentino는 언제 Office Supply 매장에 갈 것인가?
(A) 11월 7일
(B) 11월 8일
(C) 11월 10일
(D) 11월 11일

200. 연계 문제 – Mr. Valentino가 반품하려는 제품에 대한 사실 내용 ★☆☆

해설 세 번째 지문, 이메일 후반 'I made the purchase fewer than 30 days ago, so I am eligible for a refund.'에서 Mr. Valentino는 환불받겠다는 의사를 나타냈는데, 첫 번째 지문 광고문 'LaserJet printer now $89.99! (originally $109.99)'에서 레이저젯 프린터는 원래 109.99달러에 판매되던 제품이었으므로 (C)가 정답이다.　　정답 (C)

표현 정리 highly rated 일류의　on sale 할인 판매 중인

해석 Mr. Valentino가 반품하고 싶어하는 제품에 대한 사실 내용은?
(A) 일류 제품이다.
(B) 12월에 할인 판매될 것이다.
(C) 평상 시에는 100달러 이상에 판매된다.
(D) 사용자 매뉴얼이 포함되었다.

문제 147-148번은 다음 전단지를 참조하시오.

신장 개업!

King's 슈즈
새 Linford 지점!

148(A)Campbell 가 쇼핑센터
2890 Wilson Highway, Suite 23

147일주일 내내 개장!

148(B)우리는 주에서 가장 많은 종류의 신발을 보유하고 있습니다!
지금 Fast Walk와 Racer 브랜드 운동화를 판매합니다.

148(C)남성, 여성, 아이들
캐주얼, 정장, 운동용, 특제품, 그 이상

이 전단지를 계산원에게 보여주시고 10퍼센트 할인받으세요.*
*다른 할인권과 함께 사용하거나 148(D)온라인 주문에 활용할 수 없습니다.

표현 정리 selection 보유 제품　footwear 신발　entire 전체의　formal 격식을 차린　athletic 운동의　specialty 특제품　present 제시하다　flyer 전단　cashier 계산원　combine 결합하다　offer 할인(권)

147. 세부사항 – 가격 할인에 관한 내용 ★★☆

해설 Open 7 days a week!를 통해 매장이 일주일 내내 문을 연다는 사실을 알 수 있고, 할인 날짜에 제한 사항이 없으므로 주말에도 할인이 가능하다는 것을 유추할 수 있어 정답은 (A)이다.　　정답 (A)

함정 분석 할인 행사는 새로 개업한 New Linford Location 지점에서만 가능하므로 (B)는 오답이다. 할인 기간에 대한 언급은 없으므로 (D)도 오답이다.

표현 정리 reduction 할인　obtain 얻다　multiple 다수의　restrict 제한하다　valid 유효한

해석 가격 할인에 관해 언급된 내용은?
(A) 주말에 할인받을 수 있다.
(B) 다수의 장소에서 제공된다.
(C) 직원들로 한정된다.
(D) 한 달 동안 유효하다.

148. 세부사항 – King's 슈즈에 대한 내용이 아닌 것 ★★☆

해설 전단지 중반 'We have the largest selection of footwear in the entire state!'를 통해 다양한 신발을 취급하는 것일 뿐, 특이한 신발만 전문적으로 거래하는지는 확인할 수는 없으므로 정답은 (B)이다.　　정답 (B)

함정 분석 King's 슈즈의 새 지점은 Campbell 가 쇼핑 센터 내에 입점해 있으므로 (A)는 사실, Men's, Women's, Children's에서 아이들 신발도 취급하므로 (C)도 사실, 그리고 마지막 문장 'Cannot be combined with other offers or used for online orders'에서 온라인으로 주문할 때 중복해서 사용할 수 없다고 했으므로 온라인 판매도 하고 있음을 유추할 수 있어 (D)도 확인이 가능하다.

표현 정리 specialize in ~전문으로 하다　unusual 특이한　carry 취급하다　via ~을 통해, ~을 경유해

해석 King's 슈즈에 대해 언급된 내용이 아닌 것은?
(A) 몰 안에 매장이 있다.
(B) 특이한 신발들을 전문으로 취급한다.
(C) 아이들을 위한 제품을 취급한다.

(D) 인터넷을 통해 제품을 판매한다.

문제 149~150번은 다음 문자 메시지 내용을 참조하시오.

> **Farrell, Denise** 오늘 오후에 회의에 참석하라는 요청을 방금 받았어요. 나 대신 Mr. Qi를 공항에서 모셔 줄 수 있나요?　오전 10시 21분
>
> **Folkman, Owen** 물론이죠. 그의 비행 정보를 줄래요?　오전 10시 24분
>
> **Farrell, Denise** 149그는 National Airlines 894편으로 Philadelphia에서 오후 3시 25분에 도착합니다. 비행기가 정시에 도착하는지 다시 한 번 확인해야 할 거예요. 동북부에 눈보라가 일어 연착될지도 몰라요.
> 　오전 10시 25분
>
> **Folkman, Owen** 좋은 생각이에요. 다른 것은요?　오전 10시 27분
>
> **Farrell, Denise** 84번 가에 있는 Grand Continental 호텔에 그의 방을 예약했어요. 150체크인할 수 있도록 도와주세요. 내가 아침에 그를 사무실로 모실 수 있도록 택시를 준비할 거예요. 오전 8시 45분에 모시러 갈 겁니다. Mr. Qi에게 이 점을 이해시켜 주세요.
> 　오전 10시 29분
>
> **Folkman, Owen** 걱정 마세요.　오전 10시 34분

표현 정리 **flight** 비행(편)　**double-check** 다시 한 번 확인하다　**on time** 정각에　**delay** 지연, 연착　**arrange** 마련하다　**count on** ~을 믿다

149. 유추 – Mr. Qi에 대한 내용　★☆☆
해설 Denise Farrell이 오전 10시 25분에 보낸 메시지 'He's on National Airlines Flight 894 arriving from Philadelphia at 3:25 P.M.'에 따르면 Philadelphia에서 출발해 오후 3시 25분에 도착한다고 했으므로 정답은 (D)이다.
　정답 (D)

해석 Mr. Qi에 대한 사실 내용은?
(A) 그는 Ms. Farrell과 저녁을 먹을 것이다.
(B) 그가 호텔을 예약했다.
(C) 그는 운전면허가 없다.
(D) 그는 Philadelphia에서 온다.

150. 의도 파악하기　★★☆
해설 Denise Farrell이 오전 10시 29분에 보낸 메시지 'Help him check in. I'll arrange for a taxi to bring him to the office in the morning. Pickup's at 8:45. Make sure Mr. Qi understands that.'에 대한 답변으로 Mr. Folkman이 "You can count on me."라고 말했는데, 이는 문맥상 '걱정 말아라, 내가 당신의 요청을 그대로 실행하겠다.'는 내용이므로 정답은 (B)이다.　정답 (B)

🔍 **함정 분석** 오전 10시 29분에 보낸 Denise Farrell의 메시지 중 'I'll arrange for a taxi to bring him to the office in the morning.'을 통해 택시 회사에 연락하는 것은 Mr. Folkman이 아니라는 것을 알 수 있으므로 (D)는 오답이다.

표현 정리 **confirm** 확인하다　**relay** 전달하다

해석 Mr. Folkman이 오전 10시 34분에 보낸 "걱정 마세요."가 의미하는 것은?
(A) 그는 호텔 예약을 확인할 것이다.
(B) 그는 Mr. Qi에게 정보를 전달할 것이다.
(C) 그는 호텔로 가는 방법을 찾을 것이다.
(D) 그는 택시 회사에 연락을 할 것이다.

문제 151~153번은 다음 편지를 참조하시오.

> Eric Cardon
> 89 Blaine Road
> Seager, MD 99343

> 4월 16일
>
> Mr. Cardon 님께,
>
> 152이 편지는 어제 우리가 나눴던 전화 대화를 서면으로 확인하는 내용입니다. 당신은 Caldera Engineering에서 Cultural Resource Specialist II로서 시간제로 근무하는 것을 제안받았고, 이를 받아들였습니다. 그 직책 급여는 한 해에 총 1,400시간을 일하고 25,879달러 받습니다. 실제 업무 시간은 당신의 상관에 결정에 의해 매주 다를 수 있겠지만, 한 주에 32시간을 초과하지는 않을 것입니다. 153당신은 파트타임 자격에 따라 혜택을 받을 것입니다.
>
> 5월 3일, 월요일 오전 8시 30분에 업무를 시작하도록 일정을 정했습니다. 안내소에서 수속을 밟으시기 바랍니다. 151(A),(B)당신의 상관인 Roger Vance가 당신을 맞이해 보안부로 안내할 것이며, 그곳에서 지문을 찍고, 공식 신분증을 받을 것입니다. 151(C)그 후에 혼자서 건물에 출입할 수 있습니다.
>
> 모든 신입 직원은 오리엔테이션을 마쳐야 합니다. 151(D)이것은 온라인 교육과 저와 저의 직원들을 만나는 것으로 이루어집니다. 우리는 당신의 업무 첫날에 오리엔테이션을 진행하기로 했습니다. Mr. Vance와 만난 후에 2층에 있는 제 사무실로 와 주시기 바랍니다.
>
> 우리는 당신이 Caldera Engineering 팀에 함께 하게 돼 기쁩니다. 질문이나 도움이 필요하면 저에게 연락주세요.
>
> Cindy Fergus
> 부장, 인사과
> Caldera Engineering

표현 정리 **written confirmation** 서면 확인　**vary** 각기 다르다　**supervisor** 상관, 관리자　**exceed** 초과하다　**front office** 안내소　**sign in** 서명하고 들여보내다　**fingerprinted** 지문을 찍은　**Security** 보안부　**official ID** 공식 신분증　**access** 들어가다　**consist of** ~으로 이루어지다　**brief** 짧은　**assistance** 도움

151. 세부사항 – Mr. Cardon이 5월 3일에 할 일이 아닌 것　★★☆
해설 두 번째 단락, 마지막 문장 'After that, you will be able to access the building on your own.'에서 공식 신분증을 받은 후에 건물에 혼자서도 출입할 수 있으므로 정답은 (C)이다.　정답 (C)

🔍 **함정 분석** 두 번째 단락 'Your supervisor, Roger Vance, will need to sign you in and escort you to Security, where you will be fingerprinted and receive an official ID card.'에서 (A)와 (B)가 확인되고, 'This will consist of online training modules and a brief meeting with my staff and me.'와 하단 편지를 보낸 사람의 신분에서 편지를 보낸 사람은 인사 부장임을 알 수 있으므로 (D)도 확인된다.

패러프레이징 |지문| receive an official ID card 공식적인 신분증을 받는다 → |선택지 B| obtain an employee identification card 직원 신분증을 얻는다

표현 정리 **instruct** 지시하다　**section** 부분, 구역

해석 Mr. Cardon이 5월 3일에 하도록 지시받은 사항이 아닌 것은?
(A) 그의 새 관리자와 만나라고
(B) 직원 신분증을 수령하라고
(C) 혼자서 건물 구역에 들어가라고
(D) 인사과 직원들과 이야기하라고

152. 유추 – Mr. Cardon에 관한 암시 내용　★★☆
해설 편지 서두에서 Ms. Fergus가 'This letter provides written confirmation of our phone conversation yesterday.'라며 어제 전화로 나눈 대화에 대한 확인 내용을 서면으로 보낸다고 했는데, 편지를 보낸 날짜가 4월 16일이므로 전화 통화는 하루 전인 4월 15일에 있었음을 알 수 있으므로 정답은 (D)이다.　정답 (D)

표현 정리 full-time 전임의

해석 Mr. Cardon에 대하여 암시된 것은?
(A) 그는 전에 Mr. Vance와 함께 일한 적이 있다.
(B) 그는 전임직을 갖는 것을 선호한다.
(C) 그는 매주 5일을 일할 것이다.
(D) 그는 4월 15일에 Ms. Fergus와 대화를 했다.

153. 문장 위치 찾기 ★★☆

해설 시간제 근무자로서의 지위에 대해 언급하는 부분은 첫 번째 단락으로 한정할 수 있다. 'The salary for the position is $25,879 for a total of 1,400 hours worked per year.' 이하 부분을 보면, 연봉과 근로 조건 등에 관해 언급하고 있으므로, [2]의 자리에 주어진 문장이 들어가는 것이 가장 적합하다고 할 수 있어 정답은 (B)이다. **정답 (B)**

표현 정리 in accordance with ~에 따라서 status 지위, 상태

해석 [1], [2], [3], [4] 중 다음 문장이 들어가기에 가장 알맞은 곳은?

"당신은 파트타임 자격에 따라 혜택을 받을 것입니다."

(A) [1]
(B) [2]
(C) [3]
(D) [4]

문제 154-155번은 다음 기사를 참조하시오.

> Edgewood (4월 12일) – 154**Edgewood에서 샌드위치를 사랑하는 사람들은 다음 달에 대접을 받게 될 전망이다.** 155(B)**5월 첫 2주 동안, Sammy's 샌드위치는 선택 메뉴 가격을 절반으로 내릴 것이다.**
>
> 155(D) **회사 대변인인 Andrew Gilford는 가격 할인은 필라델피아에 위치한 체인이 영업 30주년을 기념하기 위한 것이라고 말했다.** "우리는 고객들이 오랫동안 우리를 지지해 준 것에 대해 고마움을 전하고자 한다.'고 Gilford는 말했다.
>
> 여러 인기 샌드위치, 사이드, 음료에 적용될 홍보 가격 외에도 Sammy's는 런던에 갈 수 있는 2인 여행에 당첨될 기회를 고객들에게 제공하고 있다. 고객들은 특정 장소에서 Sammy's 샌드위치를 먹는 장면을 찍은 사진을 올림으로써 추첨에 참여할 수 있다. 당첨자는 월말에 무작위로 선정될 것이다.
>
> 155(A)**첫 번째 음식점이 1985년 필라델피아, Phoenixville에서 문을 연 이래, Sammy's는 전국 28개 주에서 185개 지점을 운영하고 있으며,** 가장 인기 있는 샌드위치 체인들 중 하나가 되었다.

표현 정리 be in for ~을 맞게 될 상황이다 treat 대접 cut prices 가격을 내리다 in half 절반으로 promotional 홍보의 spokesperson 대변인 celebrate 기념하다 anniversary 기념일 in addition to ~에 더하여, ~외에 at random 무작위로 spread 퍼지다 across the country 전국에 걸쳐

154. 유추 – 기사가 게재된 매체 ★☆☆

해설 샌드위치 체인점인 Sammy's가 30주년을 기념하기 위해 실시하는 홍보행사와 관련된 내용이며, 첫 문장 'Sandwich lovers in Edgewood are in for a treat next month.'라는 내용으로 보아 Edgewood 지역과 관련된 지역 신문에 게재되었다고 볼 수 있으므로 정답은 (B)이다. **정답 (B)**

표현 정리 publish 게재하다, 출판하다 brochure 책자 financial 금융의

해석 기사가 게재된 매체는?
(A) 홍보 책자
(B) 지역 신문
(C) 음식점 안내 책자
(D) 금융 잡지

155. 세부사항 – Sammy's에 대한 내용 ★★☆

해설 두 번째 단락 'The promotional pricing, says company spokesperson Andrew Gilford, is a way for the Philadelphia-based restaurant chain to celebrate its 30th anniversary.'에서 30주년을 기념하기 위한 행사임을 알 수 있고, 마지막 단락 'Since opening its first restaurant in Phoenixville, PA, in 1985.'에서도 1985년에 첫 지점을 열었다고 했으므로 (D)가 정답이다. **정답 (D)**

표현 정리 nationwide 전국적인 found 설립하다 decades 수십 년

해석 Sammy's에 관해 언급된 것은?
(A) 전국적으로 28개 점포를 보유하고 있다.
(B) 한 달 동안 할인을 제공할 것이다.
(C) 여행사와 함께 제휴하고 있다.
(D) 수십 년 전에 설립되었다.

문제 156-157번은 다음 정보를 참조하시오.

> 마음이 울적하십니까? 156(D)**여기에 당신의 기분을 자연적으로 개선할 몇 가지 간단하지만 효과적인 방법들이 있습니다.**
>
> 긍정적인 것에 초점을 맞추세요. 어떤 상황에서 자동으로 부정적인 요소들에 대해 생각하는 사람들이 있습니다. 157**그러나, 긍정적인 것을 보는 것으로 초점을 바꿈으로써 당신은 당신 안에 긍정적인 느낌을 만들어 낼 수 있습니다.**
>
> 156(A)**충분한 수면을 취하세요.** 보통의 사람은 하루에 7.5에서 8.5시간의 수면을 필요로 합니다. 너무 많거나 너무 적은 수면은 몸에 해롭고 우울증으로 이어질 수 있습니다.
>
> 156(C)**균형 잡힌 식사를 하세요.** 많은 과일과 채소를 먹는 사람들은 더 건강하고 기분이 좋습니다.
>
> 규칙적으로 운동하세요. 운동은 우리의 기분을 좋게 하는 뇌의 화학물질인 엔도르핀을 방출합니다. 156(B)**하루 단 30분의 운동은 우리의 기분과 전반적인 건강을 개선하기에 충분합니다.**

표현 정리 feel down 마음이 울적하다 effective 효과적인 focus on ~에 초점을 맞추다 positive 긍정적인 negative 부정적인 element 요소 generate 만들어 내다 harmful 해로운 depression 우울증 balanced 균형 잡힌 regularly 규칙적으로 release 방출하다 overall 전반적인

156. 세부사항 – 더 나은 기분을 가지는 방법이 아닌 것 ★★☆

해설 두 번째 문장 'Here are some simple, but effective, ways to improve your mood naturally.'에서 자연적으로 기분을 좋게 해 줄 방법에 대해 말할 것이라고 했지만, 약물 복용에 대한 내용은 찾을 수 없으므로 정답은 (D)이다. **정답 (D)**

패러프레이징 |지문| between 7.5 and 8.5 hours of sleep a night 7.5에서 8.5 시간의 수면 시간 → |선택지 A| sleep around 8 hours 8시간 정도 자기
|지문| 30 minutes of exercise a day 매일 30분의 운동 → |선택지 B| move your body daily 매일 몸을 움직이기
|지문| eat a balanced diet 균형 잡힌 식사를 하다 → |선택지 C| consume nutritious meals 영양분이 풍부한 식사하기

표현 정리 consume 소비하다, 먹다 nutritious 영양분이 많은 medication 약물

해석 더 나은 기분을 가지는 방법으로 언급되지 않은 것은?
(A) 8시간 정도 수면 취하기
(B) 매일 몸을 움직이기
(C) 영양분이 많은 식사하기
(D) 약물 복용하기

157. 세부사항 – 긍정적인 생각의 이점 ★☆☆

해설 두 번째 단락 'However, by changing your focus to seeing the positive, you can generate positive feelings in yourself.'를 통해 긍정적인 생각으로 초점을 옮기면 긍정적인 감정을 만들어 낸다는 것을 알 수 있으므로 정답은 (D)이다. **정답 (D)**

패러프레이징 |지문| generate positive feelings 긍정적인 감정을 만들어 내다 → |선택지 D| creating good emotions 좋은 감정을 만들어 냄

표현 정리 replace 대체하다 generate 발생시키다 enhance 향상시키다

해석 정보에 따르면, 긍정적인 사고의 이점은 무엇인가?
(A) 놓친 수면을 대체함
(B) 새로운 아이디어를 발생시킴
(C) 활동들을 향상시킴
(D) 좋은 감정들을 만들어 냄

문제 158-160번은 다음 회람을 참조하시오.

수신: 직원들, Corrigan Building
발신: Sara Johnson
제목: 전자 카드
날짜: 6월 8일

¹⁵⁸신형 전자 도어 잠금 장치가 현재 설치 중에 있습니다. ¹⁵⁹⁽ᴬ⁾,⁽ᴮ⁾모든 현관문과 여러 내부 도어들의 전기 잠금 장치는 6월 15일까지 완료될 예정입니다. ¹⁵⁹⁽ᶜ⁾문이 닫히면 자동으로 잠기는 이 문을 통과하기 위해서는 자기 전자 카드가 필요합니다. ¹⁵⁹⁽ᴰ⁾다른 문들은 기존 열쇠 잠금 장치를 계속 사용할 것입니다.

전자 카드는 6월 10일부터 경비실에서 수령할 수 있습니다. ¹⁶⁰이를 위해, 첨부된 신청서를 작성해 경비실로 제출해 주시기 바랍니다. 신청서에 사용하게 될 문을 명시해 주십시오. 외부 문을 여는데 필요한 모든 카드들은 코드화될 것입니다. 그러나, 직원들은 그들이 접근할 수 있는 내부 문들을 여는 목적으로만 카드를 사용할 것입니다. 요청은 관리자의 서명 없이 처리될 수 없으며, 요청이 처리되기까지는 24에서 48시간이 필요합니다.

감사합니다.

Sara Johnson

사무 차장, 보안팀
Landis Corporation

표현 정리 swipe card (전자 장치로 인식하게 만든) 전자 카드 installation 설치 electronic 전자의 currently 현재 underway 진행 중인 exterior 외부의 interior 내부의 functioning 기능 magnetic 자석 같은, 자기의 existing 기존의 available 이용할 수 있는 security office 경비실, 보안실 attach 첨부하다 request form 신청서 specify 명시하다 code 코드화하다 permit 허가하다 access 접근하다 process 처리하다 signature 서명 allow 허락하다

158. 주제 – Ms. Johnson이 회람을 작성한 이유 ★☆☆

해설 'The installation of new electronic door locks is currently underway. All exterior doors and several interior doors are scheduled to have functioning electronic locking systems on them by June 15.'에서 잠금 장치가 설치되고 있고, 이 작업은 6월 15일까지 완료될 것이라고 했다. 그리고 'A magnetic swipe card will be needed to enter these doors, which will automatically lock when closed.'에서 출입을 위해서는 전자 카드가 필요할 것이라고 한 내용을 통해 정답은 (B)임을 알 수 있다. **정답 (B)**

표현 정리 announce 발표하다 completion 완료 malfunctioning 제대로 움직이지 않는

해석 Ms. Johnson이 회람을 작성한 이유는?
(A) 관리자들로부터 피드백을 요청하기 위해
(B) 곧 있을 변화들을 설명하기 위해
(C) 프로젝트 완료를 발표하기 위해
(D) 제대로 작동하지 않는 자물쇠를 보고하기 위해

159. 세부사항 – 전자 잠금 시스템에 대한 내용 ★★☆

해설 첫 번째 단락 'A magnetic swipe card will be needed to enter these doors, which will automatically lock when closed.'를 통해 전자 잠금 시스템이 사용되는 문을 통과하기 위해서는 코드화된 전자 카드가 필요하다는 것을 알 수 있으므로 정답은 (C)이다. **정답 (C)**

패러프레이징 |지문| A magnetic swipe card will be needed 코드화된 전자 카드가 필요하다 → |선택지 C| requires the use of coded cards 코드화된 카드의 사용이 필요하다

해석 전자 잠금 시스템에 관해 언급된 것은?
(A) 모든 내부 문에 설치될 것이다.
(B) 6월 15일에 테스트를 거칠 예정이다.
(C) 코드화된 카드의 사용을 필요로 한다.
(D) 기존의 모든 자물쇠를 대체할 것이다.

160. 세부사항 – 직원들에게 하도록 요청된 것 ★☆☆

해설 두 번째 단락 'To obtain one, return the attached request form to the security office.'에서 전자 카드를 발급 받기 위해 첨부된 서류를 제출할 것을 요청하고 있으므로 정답은 (A)이다. **정답 (A)**

패러프레이징 |지문| return the attached request form 첨부된 서류를 제출하기 → |선택지 A| submit paperwork 서류를 제출하기

표현 정리 submit 제출하다 paperwork 서류 turn in ~을 반납하다

해석 직원들이 하도록 요청받은 것은?

    (A) 서류를 제출하라고

    (B) 기존의 열쇠를 반납하라고

    (C) 그들의 문의 잠금 장치를 테스트하라고

    (D) 신분증을 받아가라고

문제 161-163번은 다음 광고를 참조하시오.

뮤지컬 핑거스

겨울, 봄, 여름, 그리고 가을 – Musical Fingers는 1년 내내 이용할 수 있습니다!

현재 5에서 18세 사이의 신입생들을 받고 있습니다!

Musical Fingers 공동체의 일원이 되도록 당신을 초대하고자 합니다. 161(D)전문적으로 개발된 저희 커리큘럼은 아이들의 기타 실력을 발전시켜 준다는 것이 입증되었습니다. 161(B)초급자에서 상급자에 이르는 학생들과 함께 하면서, Musical Fingers는 음악 수업 이상의 것들을 제공합니다. 161(C)저희는 음악에 대한 폭넓은 감상과 창조성, 그리고 자기 표현을 길러 줍니다. 162,163저희 Musical Fingers의 모든 강사들은 설립자이자 전 고등학교 음악 교사 출신인 Mike Parka가 개발한 교수법에 대한 종합적인 교육을 이수했습니다.

161(A)Camden, Ardmore, Wayne, and Germantown에 있는 지점들과 함께

www.musicalfingers.com

(412) 555-9894

전국 기타 교습 협회와 음악 교사회 회원

표현 정리 **available** 이용할 수 있는 **all year** 1년 내내 **currently** 현재 **accept** 받다, 접수하다 **professionally** 전문적으로 **developed** 개발된 **prove** 입증하다 **beginner** 초보자 **advanced** 상급의 **cultivate** 경작하다, 기르다 **broad** (폭이) 넓은 **appreciation** 감상 **creativity** 창조성 **self-expression** 자기 표현 **instructor** 강사 **comprehensive** 종합적인 **teaching methods** 교수법 **founder** 설립자 **former** 예전의 **aim to** ~를 목표로 하다 **creative** 창조적인 **instrument** 악기

161. 세부사항 – Musical fingers에 관한 내용이 아닌 것 ★★☆

해설 'Our professionally developed curriculum has been proven to help children develop their guitar skills.'를 통해 기타 수업을 전문으로 하고 있지만, 여러 가지 악기 수업을 제공한다는 것은 알 수 없으므로 정답은 (D)이다.

정답 (D)

🔍함정 분석 광고 후반 'With locations in Camden, Ardmore, Wayne, and Germantown'을 통해 다른 지점이 있음을 알 수 있으므로 (A)는 맞고, 'Working with beginner through advanced learners, Musical Fingers offers more than just music lessons.'를 통해 초급자부터 상급자에 이르는 다양한 수준의 학생들을 가르치고 있음을 알 수 있으므로 (B)도 맞다. 그리고 'We cultivate a broad appreciation for music, creativity, and self-expression.'에서 음악과 창의력, 자기 표현을 함양할 수 있도록 돕는다고 했으므로 (C)도 맞는 내용이다.

패러프레이징 |지문| with locations in Camden, Ardmore ~ Camden, Ardmore에 있는 지점들과 함께 → |선택지 A| at multiple sites 다수의 장소에서 |지문| beginner through advanced learners 초급자에서 상급자에 이르는 학생들 → |선택지 B| students of varying levels 다양한 수준의 학생들 |지문| cultivate a broad appreciation for music, creativity 음악에 대한 폭넓은 감상과 창의성을 기른다 → |선택지 C| aim to help students become creative 학생들이 창의적일 수 있도록 돕는 것을 목표로 한다

표현 정리 **multiple** 다수의 **varying** 가지각색의

해석 Musical Fingers에 관해 언급된 내용이 아닌 것은?

    (A) 다수의 장소에서 수업을 제공한다.

    (B) 다양한 수준의 학생들을 받는다.

    (C) 학생들이 창의성을 기르도록 돕는 것을 목표로 한다.

    (D) 여러 가지 악기 수업을 제공한다.

162. 유추 – 강사들에 대한 내용 ★★☆

해설 'All of our Musical Fingers instructors have completed comprehensive training in the teaching methods first developed by founder and former high school music teacher Mike Parka.'를 통해 모든 강사들이 교수법을 이수했음을 알 수 있고, 이들 강사들이 학생들을 가르치므로 정답은 (A)이다.

정답 (A)

🔍함정 분석 'All of our Musical Fingers instructors have completed comprehensive training in the teaching methods first developed by founder and former high school music teacher Mike Parka.'에서 모든 강사들이 교수법을 이수했다고 했을 뿐, 이들이 Musical Fingers의 졸업생인지는 알 수 없으므로 (B)는 오답이다.

표현 정리 **graduate** 졸업자

해석 강사들에 대해 암시된 것은?

    (A) 그들은 아이들과 함께 하도록 교육받는다.

    (B) 그들은 Musical Fingers의 졸업생들이다.

    (C) 그들은 전문적인 음악인들이다.

    (D) 그들은 현재 고등학교 학생들이다.

163. 세부사항 – Mike Parka에 대한 내용 ★★★

해설 'All of our Musical Fingers instructors have completed comprehensive training in the teaching methods first developed by founder and former high school music teacher Mike Parka.'에서 Mike Parka가 Musical Fingers에서 사용하는 교습 프로그램을 개발하고 발전시킨 사람이라는 것을 알 수 있어 정답은 (C)이다.

정답 (C)

🔍함정 분석 'former high school music teacher Mike Parka'를 보면 Mike가 전직 고등학교 음악 교사였음을 알 수 있지만, 현직 공립학교의 강사인지 여부는 알 수 없으므로 (B)는 오답이다.

표현 정리 **public school** 공립학교

해석 Mike Parka에 대하여 언급된 내용은?

    (A) 그는 오직 상급의 학생들만을 가르친다.

    (B) 그는 공립학교의 강사이다.

    (C) 그는 음악 교육 프로그램을 시작했다.

    (D) 그는 전문적인 집단의 리더이다.

문제 164-167번은 다음 온라인 채팅을 참조하시오.

Peck, Allison 164저는 2년 전에 컴퓨터 공학 학위를 받았으며, 대학을 다녔던 작은 도시에서 첫 직장을 구했습니다. 저는 제 경력을 쌓기 위한 변화를 맞이할 준비가 되었습니다. 저의 전 동급생들이 저에게 이사하라고 제안했지만, 지금 부모님과 함께 살고 있고, 그들을 그리워할 것이라고 생각합니다. 가장 가까운 대도시는 4시간 이상 떨어져 있습니다! 제가 무엇을 해야 할까요?   오전 8시 45분

Johnson, River 당신의 친구들이 타당한 충고를 해주고 있군요. 만약 경력을 쌓는 일을 진지하게 생각하고 있다면, 최고의 기술 회사들이 있는 곳으로 이사하는 것이 필요합니다.   오전 9시 1분

Evans, Nathan 그것은 전적으로 당신의 목표들에 달려 있습니다.
  오전 10시 10분

Johnson, River **165**하지만 가장 좋은 일자리들은 대도시에 있습니다.
오전 11시 1분

Evans, Nathan **166**River, 그것은 견해의 문제입니다. 컴퓨터 공학 분야에서 좋은 일자리들은 어디든지 많이 있습니다. 요즘에는, 거의 모든 회사들이 당신의 배경을 가진 직원들을 필요로 합니다.
오전 11시 10분

Uribe, Iris　　　Allison, 원한다면 집에서 가까이 머무르세요. **167**저는 5년 전에 같은 학위를 받고 졸업했습니다. 저의 첫 직장은 제가 자랐던 지역에 있는 회사였습니다. 저는 좋은 경험을 얻었고, 나중에 수도로 이사를 했습니다.
오전 11시 20분

Johnson, River　Allison, 어디로 가든, 열쇠는 좋은 직장을 얻어 일을 시작하는 것입니다. 당신 학교 동문 사무실을 네트워크로 이용하세요. 당신은 인근에 있는 다른 도시에서 훌륭한 직장을 찾을지도 모릅니다. 오후 12시 1분

Peck, Allison　　　많은 의견을 줘서 고맙습니다. 제가 결정한 것을 알려드리겠습니다.
오후 1시 45분

표현 정리 graduate 졸업하다　degree 학위　attend 다니다　advance 발전시키다, 향상시키다　career 경력　former 이전의　sound 타당한　depend on ~에 달려 있다　nowadays 요즘에는　nearly 거의　wherever 어디에나　get one's foot in the door 발을 들여놓다　employer 고용주　alumni 졸업생들　nearby 인근의; 인근에　consider 고려하다, 생각하다

164. 유추 – Ms. Peck에 대한 내용 ★★☆

해설 Ms. Peck은 첫 대화 'I graduated with a degree in computer science two years ago and took my first job in the same small city where I attended college.'에서 한 도시에서 대학을 졸업하고, 첫 직장을 구했다는 사실을 알 수 있다. 이어 'My former classmates suggest that I move, but I live with my parents now and think I would miss them.'에서는 현재 부모님과 함께 살고 있다는 사실을 알 수 있으므로, 대학을 다니기 위해 이사하지 않았을 것이라고 유추할 수 있어 정답은 (C)이다.　　**정답 (C)**

🔍**함정 분석** 'My former classmates suggest that I move, but I live with my parents now and think I would miss them.'에서 이전의 동급생들이 이사하라고 조언한 사실을 알 수는 있지만, 최근에 동급생을 방문했는지 여부는 알 수 없으므로 (D)는 오답이다.

표현 정리 mediocre 평범한, 썩 좋지는 않은

해석 Ms. Peck에 관한 사실 내용은?
(A) 그녀는 평범한 직원이다.
(B) 그녀는 대학에 고용되었다.
(C) 그녀는 학교에 가려고 이사하지 않았다.
(D) 그녀는 최근 이전의 동급생을 방문했다.

165. 유추 – 기술 회사들에 대한 내용 ★☆☆

해설 River Johnson이 언급한 대화 'You need to move to where the best technology companies are if you want to seriously advance in your career.'에서 진지하게 경력을 생각한다면 최고의 기술 회사들이 있는 곳으로의 이사를 생각해 보라고 했고, 이어 'But the best jobs are in the big cities.'에서도 최고의 직장들이 대도시에 있다고 했으므로 (A)가 정답으로 가장 적절하다.
정답 (A)

패러프레이징 |지문| in the big cities 큰 도시에 → |선택지 B| in major urban areas 주요 도시 지역에

표현 정리 leading 선두적인　urban 도시의　get hired 채용되다

해석 대화자들에 따르면, 기술을 선도하는 회사들에 관해 암시된 것은?
(A) 주요 도시 지역에 위치한다.
(B) 상위 학교들의 졸업생들은 그곳에 채용된다.
(C) 젊은 사람들을 고용하는 것은 선호한다.

(D) Mr. Evans는 그 회사들 중 한 곳을 위해 일한다.

166. 동의어 ★☆☆

해설 River Johnson이 오전 11시 1분에 'But the best jobs are in the big cities.'라며 최고의 일자리는 대도시들에 있다고 하자, Nathan Evans가 'that's a matter of opinion. Good jobs in computer science are available pretty much anywhere.'에서 Johnson의 의견에 이의를 제기하고 있음을 알 수 있으므로 정답은 (C)이다.　　**정답 (C)**

표현 정리 mildly 부드럽게　validity 타당성　statement 진술　criticize 비판하다

해석 Mr. Evans가 오전 11시 1분에 "그것은 견해의 문제입니다."라고 한 말의 의미는?
(A) 자신의 견해를 위한 지지를 제공하기 위해
(B) 부드럽게 동의를 표현하기 위해
(C) 진술의 타당성에 이의를 제기하기 위해
(D) 전문적인 판단을 비판하기 위해

167. 유추 – Ms. Uribe에 관한 내용 ★★☆

해설 채팅 내용 중 'I graduated with the same degree five years ago.'에서 5년 전에 컴퓨터 공학 학위를 받았다고 했으므로 정답은 (D)이다.　**정답 (D)**

🔍**함정 분석** 'My first job was in the area where I grew up. I gained good experience and later moved to the nation's capital.'에서 첫 직장을 고향에서 구했지만, 현재는 수도로 이사했다고 했기 때문에 (A)는 오답이다.

패러프레이징 |지문| graduated with the same degree(computer science) 컴퓨터 공학 학위를 받았다 → |선택지 D| studied computer science in college 대학에서 컴퓨터 공학을 공부했다

해석 Ms. Uribe에 관해 암시된 것은?
(A) 그녀는 현재 고향에서 일하고 있다.
(B) 그녀는 Ms. Peck과 같은 학교에 다녔다.
(C) 그녀는 동문회 직원이다.
(D) 그녀는 대학에서 컴퓨터 공학을 공부했다.

문제 168-171번은 다음 회람을 참조하시오.

회람

수신: 관리 팀
발신: Karl Urban
날짜: 3월 16일

168다음 달부터 제한된 예산을 사용해야 하기 때문에, 저희 부서는 지금까지 대학 교내에 적용해 왔던 관행을 변경해야 할 필요가 있습니다. 항상 최고의 상태를 유지하는 것이 필요하기는 하지만, 우리가 과거에 사용했던 자원과 인력을 줄이는 것이 필요해졌습니다. 다음의 경비 절감 방안은 즉시 시행될 것입니다:

· **170(C)**잔디는 매주가 아닌 격주에 한 번 깎습니다. **169**다만 대학 운동장은 기존 일정대로 진행될 것입니다.
· 모든 살수 장치를 점검할 것입니다. 새는 곳은 보수하고, 고장 난 부분은 발견 즉시 교체할 것입니다. **170(D)**불필요한 살수 장치들은 없애고, 그 부품들은 보관될 것입니다.
· **170(B)** 더 이상 도서관과 Chandler Hall, 기숙사 화단, 그리고 Graduate Avenue를 따라 꽃을 심지 않을 것입니다. **170(A)**대신 화단은 장식용 쇄석으로 덮을 것입니다.
· 관리 팀 직원들은 업무에만 이동용 차량을 사용하도록 제한됩니다. 모든 비공식적인 용무를 위해서는 개인 차량을 사용해야 합니다.

171 저희의 다른 업무에 영향을 미칠 추가 경비 절감 방안은 7월 회람에서 발표될 것입니다. 이 어려운 시기에 여러분들이 대학 시설과 교내 관리에 쏟은 헌신에 감사 드립니다. 만약 이러한 변화들에 대해 질문이 있으면, 바로 저에게 272-5120으로 연락 주십시오.

Karl Urban
시설 및 교내 부지 책임자
Paramount 대학교

표현 정리 memo 회람 maintenance 관리 due to ~때문에 budgetary 예산의 restriction 제한 take effect 효력이 발생하다, 실행되다 adjust 조정하다 practice 관행 essential 필수적인 at all times 항상 necessary 필요한 reduce 줄이다 resource 자원 manpower 인력 commit 쓰다 cost-saving measures 경비 절감책 lawn 잔디밭 mow (잔디를) 깎다 exception 예외 sprinkler 살수 장치 inspect 점검하다 leak 새는 곳 remove 없애다 storage 저장 bed 화단 dormitories 기숙사 decorative 장식용의 crushed stone 쇄석 assigned 할당된 nonofficial 비공식의 affect 영향을 미치다 commitment 헌신, 노력 challenging 어려운, 도전적인 directly 바로

168. 주제 – Mr. Urban이 메모를 작성한 이유 ★☆☆

해설 회람 서두 'Due to budgetary restrictions set to take effect next month, our department will be required to adjust our practices concerning the university grounds.'에서 다음 달부터 예산 제한으로 지금까지 진행해 오던 업무를 조정할 필요가 있음을 알리면서 다음 내용부터 경비 절감책에 대한 구체적인 설명을 하므로 정답은 (B)이다. 정답 (B)

표현 정리 propose 제안하다 budget cuts 예산 삭감

해석 Mr. Urban이 회람을 작성한 이유는?
(A) 일부 관례들을 비판하기 위해
(B) 변경 사항들을 발표하기 위해
(C) 예산 삭감을 제안하기 위해
(D) 추가적인 임무를 설명하기 위해

169. 동의어 ★★☆

해설 'The only exception is the university's sports fields, which will continue to be maintained on their current schedule.'에서 대학 운동장의 잔디는 기존 일정대로 매주 한 번씩 정리를 계속할 것이라는 의미이므로 단 하나의 예외라고 볼 수 있어 정답은 (A)이다. 정답 (A)

표현 정리 single 단 하나의, 단일의 mere 순전한

해석 두 번째 단락, 첫 줄의 "only"와 의미가 가장 가까운 것은?
(A) 단 하나의
(B) 공정한, 적절한(형용사)
(C) 순전한
(D) 간단한

170. 세부사항 – Mr. Urban이 직원들에게 요청하지 않은 것 ★★★

해설 즉시 시행되어야 하는 경비 절감 방안들 중 'Flowers will no longer be planted in the beds at the library, Chandler Hall, and the dormitories and along Graduate Avenue.'에서 화단에 더 이상 꽃을 심지 않을 것이라고 했지만, 이것이 나무와 관목을 적게 심으라는 내용은 아니므로 정답은 (B)이다. 정답 (B)

🔍 **함정 분석** 'Instead, the beds will be covered with decorative crushed stone.'에서 꽃을 심었던 화단은 장식용 쇄석으로 덮을 것이라고 했으므로 (A)는 요청한 내용이고, 'Lawns are to be mowed once every two weeks instead of weekly.'에서 (C)도 요청한 내용이다. 'Unnecessary sprinkler lines will be removed and their parts placed in storage.'에서 불필요한 스프링쿨러 관은 제거해 보관할 것이라고 했으므로 (D)도 요청한 내용이 맞다.

패러프레이징 |지문| the beds will be covered with decorative crushed stone 화단은 장식용 쇄석으로 덮일 것이다 → |선택지 A| replace flowerbeds with ornamental rocks 장식용 바위로 화단을 대체하다

|지문| lawns are to be mowed once every two weeks instead of weekly 잔디 깎기는 매주가 아닌 격주로 진행될 것이다 → |선택지 C| cut grass less frequently 덜 자주 풀을 베다

|지문| unnecessary sprinkler lines will be removed 불필요한 송수관은 제거될 것이다 → |선택지 D| remove unused water lines 사용하지 않는 송수관을 없애다

표현 정리 ornamental 장식용의 bush 관목 frequently 자주

해석 Mr. Urban이 그의 직원들에게 요청하지 않은 것은?
(A) 장식용 바위로 화단을 대체한다.
(B) 나무와 관목을 더 적게 심는다.
(C) 잔디를 덜 자주 깎는다.
(D) 사용하지 않는 송수관을 없앤다.

171. 유추 – Mr. Urban이 7월에 할 일 ★★☆

해설 마지막 단락 'Additional cost-saving measures affecting our other functions will be announced in a July memo.'에서 추가적인 경비 절감 방안을 7월 회람에서 발표할 것이라고 했으므로 (D)가 정답이다. 정답 (D)

패러프레이징 |지문| additional cost-saving measures ~ will be announced 추가적인 경비 절감책이 발표될 것이다 → |선택지 D| state other ways to save money 돈을 아낄 수 있는 다른 방법들을 말하다

표현 정리 participate in ~에 참가하다

해석 Mr. Urban이 7월에 할 일은?
(A) 내년도 예산을 더 얻는다.
(B) 기본적인 부지 유지에 참가한다.
(C) 그의 부서 차량을 개선한다.
(D) 비용을 절감할 수 있는 다른 방법들을 말한다.

문제 172-175번은 다음 전단지를 참조하시오.

San Andreas 커뮤니티 칼리지
일자리 연결 사무실 (JCO)

고용주 채용 행사

172(A) 매달 두 번째 주 목요일에 열림

11월 10일, 목요일
172(C) 오전 11시 – 오후 2시
172(D) 학생회관, Daniels 강당
중앙 캠퍼스

아래는 참가할 많은 고용주들의 일부만을 샘플로 제시한 내용임.

• San Andreas 시 경찰 당국에는 경찰관과 공무원, 강사와 행정직에 200 개 이상의 일자리가 열려 있습니다.
• Sally's 제과점은 45번가 생산 시설을 유지 보수할 직원을 찾고 있습니다.
• Guardian Angles는 가정 보건 보조원을 고용합니다.

다가오는 워크숍

신규 채용 행사 외에도 저희 JCO는 우리 지역사회의 모든 구성원들에게 개방된 무료 워크숍을 개최합니다. **172(B)** 사전 등록이 요구됩니다. 모든 워크숍은 중앙 캠퍼스 Penner 건물 2층에 위치한 JCO에서 열립니다. **173** 참가를 원하시면, 저희 웹사이트 www.sanandreas.edu/jco를 방문해 주십시오.

이력서 조정
11월 2일, 수요일

88

오후 1시 – 오후 5시

이 열린 워크숍 기간에 방문해 글쓰기 개인 지도 교사들 중 한 명과 이야기 나누세요. 이력서 복사본 또는 현재, 그리고 과거 고용 목록을 가지고 오시면, 저희가 그것을 훨씬 더 좋게 만들 수 있도록 돕겠습니다. **175참가하는 데 이전의 비즈니스 작문 경험은 필요하지 않습니다.**

헬스케어 일자리 소개
11월 4일, 금요일
오후 12시 – 오후 1시

174우리 지역에서 가장 빠르게 성장하고 있는 분야 중 하나에 관한 발표를 점심시간에 할 예정이니 우리와 함께 하세요. 매년 헬스케어와 관련된 일자리가 자리를 채우는 지원자들보다 더 많습니다. 병원, 건강 클리닉, 양로원 등에서 일할 기회에 대해 알아보세요. 역시 중요한 것으로, 성공적인 구직자가 되기 위한 교육과 기술들을 습득하기 위해 필요한 것들에는 무엇이 있는지 배우세요.

표현 정리 recruitment 신규 채용 auditorium 강당 below 아래에 sampling 샘플 be on hand 참가하다 service worker 공무원 maintenance 유지 aide 보조원 upcoming 다가오는 advance 사전의 resume 이력서 tune up 조정 stop by 들르다 tutor 개인 지도 교사 prior 이전의 career 직업 presentation 발표 sector 분야 job openings 구인 applicant 지원자 find out 알아내다 nursing home 양로원 job seeker 구직자

172. 세부사항 – 고용주 채용 행사에 관한 내용이 아닌 것 ★★☆

해설 'Advanced registration is required.'는 Upcoming Workshops에 관한 내용으로 고용주 채용 행사와 관련 있는 것이 아니기 때문에 (B)가 정답이다. **정답 (B)**

🔍 **함정 분석** 고용주 채용 행사의 내용을 살펴 보면 'Held the second Thursday of every month'에서 매달 두 번째 목요일에 개최된다는 것을 알 수 있으므로 (A)를 확인할 수 있고, '11:00 A.M. - 2:00 P.M.'에서 총 3시간 동안 진행되기 때문에 (C)도 확인된다. 그리고 'Student Resources Building, Daniels Auditorium, Central Campus'에서 중앙 캠퍼스의 학생회관에 위치한 강당에서 개최되기 때문에 교육 기관에서 개최된다고 할 수 있으므로 (D)도 맞는 내용이다.

패러프레이징 |지문| Held the second Thursday of every month 매 달 두 번째 목요일에 개최된다 → |선택지 A| organized on a regular basis 정기적으로 준비된다
|지문| 11:00 A.M. - 2:00 P.M. 오전 11시 ~ 오후 2시 → |선택지 C| lasts for a total of three hours 총 세 시간 동안 지속된다
|지문| Student Resources Building, Daniels Auditorium, Central Campus 중앙 캠퍼스의 학생 회관 건물에 위치한 강당 → |선택지 D| an educational institution 교육 기관

표현 정리 organize 준비하다 on a regular basis 정기적으로 institution 기관

해석 고용주 채용 행사에 관해 언급된 내용이 아닌 것은?
(A) 정기적으로 준비된다.
(B) 사전 등록을 요구한다.
(C) 총 3시간 동안 진행된다.
(D) 교육 기관에서 개최된다.

173. 세부사항 – 독자들이 웹사이트에 가야 하는 이유 ★☆☆

해설 'Advanced registration is required.'에서 사전 등록을 하라고 요청받았고, 'If you would like to participate, visit our Web site'에서 워크숍에 참석하기 원하는 사람은 웹사이트를 방문해 등록하라고 했으므로 정답은 (D)이다. **정답 (D)**

해석 전단지에 따르면, 독자들이 일자리 연결 사무실 웹사이트를 방문해야 하는 이유는?
(A) 취업 박람회에 참석하기 위해
(B) 일자리에 지원하기 위해
(C) 잠재적인 고용주와 연락하기 위해
(D) 워크숍에 등록하기 위해

174. 유추 – San Andreas 시에 관한 내용 ★☆☆

해설 헬스케어 관련 일자리를 위한 워크숍 안내 'Join us for a lunchtime presentation on one of the largest and fastest growing sectors of our local economy.'에서 지역 경제에서 가장 크고, 빠르게 성장하는 영역 중 하나로 헬스케어 분야를 소개하고 있으므로 시의 경제에서 중요한 부분을 차지한다고 볼 수 있어 정답은 (C)이다. **정답 (C)**

패러프레이징 |지문| one of the largest and fastest growing sectors of our local economy 지역의 경제에 있어 가장 크고, 빠르게 성장하는 영역 중 하나 → |선택지 C| an important part of its(local) economy 지역 경제의 중요한 부분

표현 정리 population 인구 decline 감소하다 graduate 졸업생

해석 San Andreas 시에 관해 암시된 내용은?
(A) 최근에 인구가 감소했다.
(B) 지역 고용주들은 대학 졸업생들만을 고용한다.
(C) 헬스케어 분야는 경제의 중요한 부분이다.
(D) 여러 큰 회사들이 위치해 있다.

175. 문장 위치 찾기 ★★☆

해설 "No prior business writing experience is necessary to participate."는 참가하는데 이전의 작문 경험은 필요하지 않다는 내용이므로 글쓰기와 관련된 워크숍에 포함된다고 볼 수 있다. 따라서 [3]에 들어가는 것이 적절해 정답은 (C)이다. **정답 (C)**

표현 정리 business writing 비즈니스 작문

해석 [1], [2], [3], [4] 중 다음 문장이 들어가기에 가장 알맞은 위치는?

"참가하는 데 이전의 비즈니스 작문 경험은 필요하지 않습니다."

(A) [1]
(B) [2]
(C) [3]
(D) [4]

문제 176-180번은 다음 기사와 정보를 참조하시오.

> **'모네의 정원': 사랑과 배신의 이야기**
> **180Sam Sheppard의 비평**
> 9월 8일, 월요일
>
> **180나는 가을 시즌 첫 작품에 초대를 받아 Kaliope 극장으로부터 무료 티켓을 받은 것을 책상에 두고 거의 잊고 있었다. 177Kaliope의 봄과 여름 시즌의 어느 작품도 주목할 만하지 않았다.** '모네의 정원'은 정반대이기 때문에 티켓을 찾은 것은 좋은 일이었다. 커튼이 열리는 순간부터 아름다운 무대에 감동받았다. 비록 '모네의 정원'이 다섯 명의 배우들만으로 구성돼 있지만, 각자가 놀라운 연기를 했다. 모네 역의 Todd Jordan과 헬레나 역의 Lindsay White의 호흡은 굉장했네! **176Rene Pilar의 팬들(나 역시 그들 중 하나이다.)은 이 작품에 실망하지 않을 것이다.** 만약 가을 시즌의 나머지도 이렇게 좋다면, 그때는 지역 극장에 가는 사람들은 대접받는 느낌을 받을 것이다.

표현 정리 betrayal 배신 noteworthy 주목할 만한 opposite 반대 impressed 감동을 받은 feature 포함하다, 출연하다 marvelous 놀라운

performance 공연   chemistry 조화, 잘 맞는 호흡   awesome 굉장한
goer ~에 다니는 사람   be in for ~을 받을 상황이다   treat 대접

Kaliope 극장
가을 시즌: 특별작
'모네의 정원'
179(B) Rene Pilar 작
Oliver Preston 연출

날짜: 9월 5 – 28일

178(D) **시간:** 금요일과 토요일, 오후 7시 30분; 일요일 오후 2시

179(A) **티켓:** 20달러

180 **특별 시사회 밤*:** 9월 4일, 목요일 – 오후 7시

178(A),179(D) Kaliope 극장은 가을 시즌을 여는 작품으로 새로운 장소에서 처음으로 '모네의 정원'을 공연하게 되어 매우 자랑스럽습니다!

'모네의 정원'은 어린 여학생인 헬레나와 사랑에 빠지는 프랑스 인상주의 화가 클로드 모네에 대한 이야기입니다. 모네는 결혼했기 때문에 그들의 만남을 그의 정원의 숨겨진 장소로 제한함으로써 헬레나와의 싹트기 시작하는 관계를 비밀로 해야만 했습니다.

178(C) 새 공연 장소! 890 Baker Way, Armadillo 대로에서 두 블록 남쪽

*179(C),180 초대장을 받은 Kaliope 클럽 멤버와 언론을 대상으로 하는 행사임

표현 정리 preview 시사회   impressionist 인상주의   budding 싹트기 시작하는   restrict 제한하다   press 언론

176. 세부사항 – Mr. Sheppard에 대한 내용 ★★☆

해설 Mr. Sheppard는 첫 번째 지문인 비평문을 쓴 사람으로 후반 'Fans of Rene Pilar (and I am one of them) are not going to be disappointed by this production.'에서 자신도 팬 중 한 명이라는 것을 밝히고 있으므로 Rene Pilar의 작품을 좋아한다고 볼 수 있어 정답은 (B)이다.   정답 (B)

🔍 **함정 분석** 기사 초반 'None of the productions in Kaliope's spring or summer seasons was noteworthy.'에서 지난 봄과 여름 시즌 작품에 대해 비판적인 평을 한 것으로 보아 극장에 가 본 적이 있다고 볼 수 있으므로 (A)는 오답이다.

표현 정리 sponsor 후원하다

해석 Mr. Sheppard에 관해 언급된 것은?
(A) 그는 Kaliope 극장에 가 본 적이 없다.
(B) 그는 Ms. Pilar의 작품들을 좋아한다.
(C) 그는 또 다른 티켓을 요청해야 했다.
(D) 그는 '모네의 정원' 제작을 후원했다.

177. 동의어 ★★☆

해설 기사 'None of the productions in Kaliope's spring or summer seasons was noteworthy. It was a good thing I found the ticket because Monet's Garden is quite the opposite.'에서 봄과 여름에 공연된 작품들과 가을에 공연된 '모네의 정원'이라는 작품이 정반대의 평을 받고 있음을 알 수 있다. noteworthy는 '주목할 만한'이라는 뜻을 갖고 있으므로 의미가 가장 가까운 것은 (C) remarkable이다.   정답 (C)

표현 정리 enterprising 기획력이 있는   artistic 예술의   remarkable 주목할 만한   unattractive 매력적이지 못한

해석 기사에서, 세 번째 줄의 "noteworthy"와 의미가 가장 가까운 것은?
(A) 기획력이 있는
(B) 예술의

(C) 주목할 만한
(D) 매력적이지 못한

178. 세부사항 – Kaliope 극장에 대한 내용 ★★☆

해설 두 번째 지문 'NEW LOCATION! 890 Baker Way, two blocks south of Armadillo Boulevard.'에서 새 장소인 Baker Way로 이사했음을 알 수 있으므로 정답은 (C)이다.   정답 (C)

🔍 **함정 분석** 'The Kaliope Theater is very proud to present Monet's Garden, the opening production of the fall season and the first at our new location!'에서 '모네의 정원'이 가을 시즌 첫 공연작임을 알 수 있지만, 유일한 공연인지는 알 수 없으므로 (A)는 오답이다. Times: Friday and Saturday 7:30 P.M.; Sunday 2:00 P.M.에서 금, 토, 일요일에 공연을 하는 것을 알 수 있으므로 주말에만 문을 연다고 할 수 없어 (D)도 오답이다.

패러프레이징 |지문| NEW LOCATION! 890 Baker Way 새로운 위치! 890 Baker Way에 → |선택지 C| It recently moved to Baker Way 최근 Baker Way로 이사했다

해석 Kaliope 극장에 관해서 언급된 것은?
(A) 이번 가을에 오직 하나의 공연을 한다.
(B) 새로운 감독을 고용했다.
(C) 최근 Baker Way로 이사했다.
(D) 주말에만 문을 연다.

179. 세부사항 – '모네의 정원'에 대한 내용이 아닌 것 ★★★

해설 클럽 멤버들에 대한 내용이 확인되는 곳은 지문 하단 'Invitation-only event for members of the Kaliope Club and the press'로 초대장을 받은 클럽 멤버와 기자들만이 참석하는 공연인 것은 알 수 있지만, 할인에 대한 언급은 없으므로 (C)가 정답이다.   정답 (C)

🔍 **함정 분석** 정보에서 Tickets: $20를 통해 입장료가 있음을 알 수 있으므로 (A)는 오답이다. 간단한 작품 소개에서 (B) Rene Pilar에 의해 쓰인 작품이라는 것을 알 수 있다. 'The Kaliope Theater is very proud to present Monet's Garden, the opening production of the fall season and the first at our new location!'에서 시즌 첫 작품이라는 것을 알 수 있으므로 (D)도 확인 가능하다.

패러프레이징 |지문| Tickets: $20 티켓: 20달러 → |선택지 A| an admission fee 입장료
|지문| the opening production of the fall season 가을 시즌의 시작(첫) 작품 → |선택지 D| the first show of the season 시즌의 첫 작품

표현 정리 admission fee 입장료

해석 정보에서, '모네의 정원'에 대해 언급되지 않은 것은?
(A) 입장료가 있다.
(B) Rene Pilar에 의해 쓰여졌다.
(C) 클럽 멤버들은 티켓을 할인받을 수 있다.
(D) 시즌 첫 작품이다.

180. 연계 문제 – Mr. Sheppard가 연극을 본 날 ★★☆

해설 첫 번째 지문 'Review by Sam Sheppard'를 통해 그는 비평가임을 알 수 있으며, 'When I received a free ticket from the Kaliope Theater inviting me to its first production of the fall season, I put it on my desk and nearly forgot about it.'에서 무료 티켓을 받았다고 했다. 두 번째 지문 '*Invitation-only event for members of the Kaliope Club and the press와 Special preview night*: Thursday, September 4 – 7:00 P.M.'에서 9월 4일 오후에 공연될 특별 시사회의 밤에 초대받았음을 유추할 수 있으므로 정답은 (A)이다.   정답 (A)

해석 Mr. Sheppard는 언제 연극을 봤는가?

90

(A) 9월 4일
(B) 9월 5일
(C) 9월 6일
(D) 9월 8일

문제 181–185번은 다음 이메일들을 참조하시오.

발신: Miranda Aubergine 〈aubergine@ncra.org〉
수신: Philippe Miro 〈mirror4@fastmail.com〉
제목: Royal 로스터 상
날짜: 8월 15일

Mr. Miro 님께,

축하합니다! 전국 커피 로스터 협회를 대신해 이 글을 보냅니다. **182(A)귀하가 저희 협회의 7회 연례 Royal 로스터 상 수상자로 선정되었습니다.** 매년 전국에 있는 독립 커피 로스터들은 상을 위해 지명을 받습니다. 저희 심사위원들은 로스팅된 커피 콩의 분석과 고객 만족도 조사, 커피숍과 소매점들로부터의 추천을 기초로 수상자를 선정합니다.

181저희는 상을 수상하기 위한 연례 모임에 귀하를 초대하고자 합니다. **182(C),185올해의 모임은 Washington 주 Seattle에서 10월 21일, 금요일과 10월 22일, 토요일에 열립니다.** **182(B)저희 귀빈으로 저희가 비행기와 호텔을 준비할 것이고, 모든 비용을 부담할 것입니다.** 또한 'The Bean'의 기자가 참석할 예정이며, 잡지에 실을 특별 기사를 위해 당신을 인터뷰하고 싶어 합니다.

참석 여부 및 저희가 귀하를 위해 할 수 있는 일이 있는지 알려주십시오.

Miranda Aubergine
전국 커피 로스터 협회 회장

표현 정리 award 상 on behalf of ~을 대신해 association 협회 nominate 지명하다 analyses 분석(단수형은 analysis) satisfaction 만족 survey 조사 recommendation 추천 retailer 소매업자 make arrangements for ~을 준비하다 expense 비용 in addition 게다가, 또한 feature 특집 기사

발신: Philippe Miro 〈mirror4@fastmail.com〉
수신: Miranda Aubergine 〈aubergine@ncra.org〉
제목: RE: Royal 로스터 상
날짜: 8월 16일

Ms. Aubergine 님께,

저는 오늘 아침 당신의 이메일을 보고 아주 기뻤습니다. 저는 당신의 훌륭한 단체로부터 상은 고사하고, 후보로 지명될 것이라고는 생각도 못했습니다. 이것은 정말 놀라운 일입니다!

185저는 틀림없이 참석할 것이며, 기자와의 만남을 즐길 것입니다. **183그러나, 작은 부탁을 하나 드리고자 합니다. 행사장에 Kingston 890 로스터를 구비해 주실 수 있습니까?** **184특별한 커피 콩을 로스팅해 다른 참석자들과 공유하기 위해 그것을 사용하고 싶습니다.** 또한 저의 로스팅에 대한 접근법에 대해 시연하고, 논의하고 싶습니다. 이것이 이 상을 위한 제 감사의 뜻을 표시할 최고의 방법이라 생각됩니다.

감사합니다!

Philippe Miro

표현 정리 be delighted to ~하게 돼 기쁘다 inbox 편지함 let alone ~커녕 fine 훌륭한 organization 단체 marvelous 놀라운 certainly 틀림없이 journalist 기자 batch 집단[무리] attendee 참석자 moreover 게다가 demonstrate 보여주다 appreciation 감사

---

181. 주제 – 첫 이메일의 목적 ★☆☆

해설 첫 번째 단락 'Congratulations! I am writing on behalf of the National Coffee Roasters Association. You have been selected to receive our seventh annual Royal Roaster Award.'를 통해 수상 사실을 알린 후 두 번째 단락 'We would like to invite you to join us at our annual meeting to present you with your award.'에서 초대하고 싶다는 의사를 나타내고 있으므로 정답은 (C)이다. 　정답 (C)

표현 정리 accept 받아들이다 application 지원서 recommendation 추천 extend an invitation 초대장을 보내다 reschedule 일정을 변경하다

해석 첫 번째 이메일의 목적은 무엇인가?
(A) 지원서를 받아들이기 위해
(B) 추천하기 위해
(C) 초대장을 보내기 위해
(D) 회의 일정을 변경하기 위해

182. 세부사항 – 전국 커피 로스터 협회에 대한 내용 ★★☆

해설 첫 번째 이메일 'Our panel of judges makes its selection based on independent analyses of roasted coffee beans, customer satisfaction surveys, and recommendations from coffee shops and retailers.'를 통해 패널들이 수상자를 결정할 때 커피숍과 소매점들의 추천도 고려한다는 사실을 알 수 있지만, 협회가 많은 소매점을 경영하는지는 알 수 없으므로 (D)가 정답이다. 　정답 (D)

🔍 **함정 분석** 'You have been selected to receive our seventh annual Royal Roaster Award.'를 통해 Mr. Miro가 7회 수상자로 결정된 사실을 알 수 있으므로 (A)는 맞는 내용이고, 'As our guest, we will make arrangements for your flight and hotel and will cover all of your expenses.'에서 (B)도 사실이다. 'This year's meeting will be held in Seattle, Washington, on Friday, October 21, and Saturday, October 22.'에서 행사는 10월 21일과 22일 양일에 걸쳐 개최됨을 알 수 있으므로 (C)도 언급된 사실이다.

패러프레이징 |지문| make arrangements for your hotel 숙박을 예약하다 → |선택지 B| pay for Mr. Miro's lodging Mr. Miro의 숙박 비용을 지불하다

표현 정리 lodging 숙소 operate 영업하다 retail 소매

해석 전국 커피 로스터 협회에 대해 언급된 내용이 아닌 것은?
(A) 여러 해 동안 상을 수여했다.
(B) Mr. Miro의 숙박 비용을 지불할 것이다.
(C) 이틀 동안의 행사를 개최할 것이다.
(D) 많은 소매 지점을 경영한다.

183. 세부사항 – Mr. Miro가 Ms. Aubergine에게 요청한 일 ★☆☆

해설 Mr. Miro가 보낸 두 번째 이메일 'However, I would like to make a small request. Would you be able to have a Kingston 890 roaster on site?'에서 로스터기를 행사장에 구비해 달라고 요청하고 있으므로 정답은 (A)이다. 　정답 (A)

표현 정리 obtain 구하다 equipment 장비 permit 허락하다

해석 Mr. Miro가 Ms. Aubergine에게 요청한 것은?
(A) 그를 위해 장비를 구해 달라고
(B) 바로 그의 비행기를 예약해 달라고
(C) 다른 손님들을 초대해 달라고
(D) 그녀의 단체에 그가 가입하는 것을 허락해 달라고

184. 세부사항 – Mr. Miro가 하기로 한 일 ★☆☆

해설 두 번째 이메일 'I would like to use it at the event to roast a special batch of coffee beans to share with the other attendees.'에서 커피 콩을

로스팅하는데 로스터를 사용하기를 원한다는 사실을 알 수 있으므로 정답은 (B)이다.

정답 (B)

패러프레이징 |지문| use it at the event ~ to share with the other attendees 다른 참가자들과 공유하기 위해 행사에서 사용하다 → |선택지 B| give a demonstration 시연을 하다

표현 정리 award winner 수상자   give a demonstration 시연하다

해석 Mr. Miro가 기꺼이 하기로 한 일은?
(A) 수상자를 선정한다.
(B) 시연을 한다.
(C) 무료 커피 콩을 제공한다.
(D) 기사를 작성한다.

185. 연계 문제 – Mr. Miro에 관한 내용 ★★☆

해설 Mr. Miro가 보낸 두 번째 이메일 'I most certainly will attend and would enjoy meeting with the journalist.'에서 행사에 참석할 의향이 있다고 했는데, Ms. Aubergine이 보낸 첫 번째 이메일 'This year's meeting will be held in Seattle, Washington, on Friday, October 21, and Saturday, October 22.'에서 행사는 10월에 Seattle에서 열릴 예정이므로 정답은 (B)이다.

정답 (B)

🔍 **함정 분석** 두 번째 이메일 'Would you be able to have a Kingston 890 roaster on site?'에서 로스팅 장비를 준비해줄 것을 부탁하고 있으므로 장비를 갖고 여행한다고 보기는 어려워 (A)는 오답이다. 첫 번째 이메일 'In addition, a reporter from The Bean will be present and would like to interview you for a special feature in that magazine.'에서 잡지사에서 나온 기자와 인터뷰를 하는 것뿐, Ms. Aubergine을 인터뷰하는 것이 아니므로 (D)도 오답이다.

표현 정리 conference 회의

해석 Mr. Miro에 관해 암시하는 것은?
(A) 그는 그의 로스팅 장비를 가지고 여행을 한다.
(B) 그는 10월에 Seattle에 가려는 계획을 갖고 있다.
(C) 그는 최근 새로운 제품을 만들었다.
(D) 그는 회의에서 Ms. Aubergine과 인터뷰를 할 것이다.

문제 186-190번은 다음 광고, 이메일, 그리고 양식을 참조하시오.

Top Tier Cakes

"당신의 특별한 경우를 위한 전문 케이크 회사"

저희가 만든 아름답고 맛있는 주문 제작 케이크는 당신의 행사를 더욱 더 특별하게 만들 것입니다. **188우리는 인공의 맛과 색을 사용하지 않고, 최고의 천연재료만을 사용합니다!** 모든 케이크는 건강에 좋은 것들로 구워지고, 스타일에 대한 안목으로 장식됩니다. 우리는 결혼식, 기념일, 졸업식, 그리고 다른 특별한 경우를 위해 층으로 이루어진 케이크를 전문으로 제작합니다. **186바닐라, 초콜릿 또는 아몬드 중에 선택하십시오.** 재능 있는 저희 직원들은 케이크를 당신의 주문대로 장식할 수 있습니다. 또는, 당신과 당신의 손님이 케이크를 예술 작품으로 변형시키는 장식 파티를 하도록 도와 드리겠습니다.

beth@toptiercakes.com으로 저희에게 연락 주십시오.

표현 정리 top tier 일류의   specialty 전문   occasion 행사, 경우   custom 주문 제작한   all the more 더욱 더   ingredient 재료   artificial 인공의   flavor 맛   wholesome 건강에 좋은   an eye for ~에 대한 안목   specialize in ~을 전문적으로 다루다   tiered 층으로 배열된   anniversary 기념일   graduation 졸업식   talented 재능 있는   crew 직원   specifications 명시   transform A into B A를 B로 변모시키다

수신: Linda Garcia 〈lgarcia@gomail.com〉
발신: Beth Xavier 〈beth@toptiercakes.com〉
날짜: 3월 28일
Re: RE: 질문
첨부: 상담 신청서

Ms. Garcia 님께,

Top Tier Cakes에 연락을 주셔서 감사합니다! 우리가 당신의 결혼식 케이크를 만들 수 있습니다. 우리는 모든 규모의 손님을 위한 여러 층의 케이크를 만들어 왔습니다. 제가 제안 드리는 것은 당신의 필요 사항을 논의하기 위한 무료 상담 일정을 잡으시라는 것입니다. **186상담 중, 우리가 과거에 만든 케이크를 보여드리고, 각각의 맛을 보실 수 있도록 샘플들을 준비할 수 있습니다. 187상담 일정을 준비하기 위해, 첨부된 서류를 작성하셔서 편하실 때 저에게 보내주십시오.**

질문이 있으시면, 저에게 이메일을 보내주십시오.

Beth Xavier
사장, Top Tier Cakes

표현 정리 consultation 상담   prepare 준비하다   taste 맛을 보다   attached form 첨부 양식   convenience 편의

Top Tier Cakes
주문서

고객 이름: *Linda Garcia*
고객 전화번호: *(412) 555-6736*
189(C)필요한 날짜: *5월 4일, 토요일*
188(C)주문 형태: [ ] 가져가기   [✓] 배달
189(A),190(A)배송지 주소: *Singleton 연회장, 88 Oak Way, Buford*

배송 지시사항:
오후 3시 전까지 준비돼야 함. Sharon Tate(555-2030)와 상세한 준비 지시사항을 상의할 것. Ms. Tate는 돕기 위해 현장에 있을 예정임.

189(B),190(C),(D)케이크 크기: *5층, 40cm, 손님 150명을 위한 추가 케이크*
케이크 형태: *아몬드*
아이싱 형태: *흰 버터 크림*

추가적인 지시사항:
188(A)*독특한 장식이 요청됨(뒤쪽의 그림을 볼 것), 신랑, 신부의 작은 얼굴상을 케이크 위쪽에 놓을 것*

표현 정리 banquet hall 연회장   instructions 지시   be on site 현장에 있다   drawing 그림   mini-statue 미니 조각상   bride 신부   groom 신랑   statue 조각상

186. 연계문제 – Ms. Garcia가 Ms. Xavier를 만날 때 하는 일 ★★☆

해설 첫 번째 지문 중반부에 있는 'Choose from vanilla, chocolate, or almond.'를 통해 알 수 있듯이 고객들은 케이크의 종류를 바닐라, 초콜릿, 아몬드 중에서 선택할 수 있다. 그리고 두 번째 지문 중반부에 있는 'During the consultation, I will show you some relevant past work and prepare samples of each of our flavors for you to taste.'에서 각 케이크의 샘플을 맛볼 수 있게 준비를 한다고 했으므로, Ms. Garcia는 아몬드 케이크를 먹는다는 (D)가 정답이다.

정답 (D)

표현 정리 decorate 장식하다   observe 보다, 목격하다

해석 Ms. Garcia가 Ms. Xavier를 만날 때 하는 일은?
(A) 그녀가 직접 케이크를 장식하기
(B) 케이크가 만들어지는 것을 관찰하기
(C) 졸업 케이크의 사진을 보기

(D) 아몬드 케이크를 먹기

187. 세부사항 – Ms. Xavier가 요청한 것 ★☆☆

해설 Ms. Xavier는 두 번째 지문인 이메일을 보낸 사람이며, 'To set up a consultation, please complete the attached form and return it to me at your convenience.'에서 상담을 하기 위해 첨부한 서류를 작성해 보내달라고 요청하고 있으므로 정답은 (D)이다. 정답 (D)

패러프레이징 |지문| complete the attached form and return it 첨부한 서류를 작성하여 보내다 → |선택지 D| submit a document 서류를 제출하기

표현 정리 describe 묘사하다 submit 제출하다 document 서류

해석 Ms. Xavier가 Ms. Garcia에게 요청한 것은?
(A) 행사 종류를 설명해 달라고
(B) 베이커리를 방문해 달라고
(C) 조수를 만나라고
(D) 서류를 제출해 달라고

188. 연계 문제 – Ms. Garcia에 대한 내용 ★★☆

해설 마지막 지문인 주문서 내용을 통해 Ms. Garcia가 Top Tier Cakes에서 케이크를 주문했음을 알 수 있는데, 광고문 'We only use the finest natural ingredients – no artificial flavors or colors!'에서 천연 재료만을 사용한다는 것을 알 수 있으므로 Ms. Garcia가 인공적인 재료가 들어가지 않은 케이크를 원했음을 유추할 수 있어 정답은 (B)이다. 정답 (B)

🔍함정 분석 주문서의 'Order type: [ ] pickup, [✓] delivery'를 보면 직접 찾아가는 게 아니라 배달을 원했음을 알 수 있으므로 (C)는 오답이다. 'Additional instructions: Unique decorations requested (see drawing on back), place mini-statue of bride and groom on top of cake.'에서 독특한 장식을 요구했다는 것은 확인할 수 있지만, 직접 디자인했는지 여부는 알 수는 없으므로 (A)도 오답이다.

패러프레이징 |지문| no artificial flavors or colors 인공적인 감미료나 색상이 없는 → |선택지 B| without artificial ingredients 인공적인 재료가 없는

표현 정리 do business 사업을 하다, 거래를 하다

해석 Ms. Garcia에 관한 사실 내용은?
(A) 그녀는 케이크 장식을 직접 디자인했다.
(B) 그녀는 인공적인 재료가 들어가지 않은 케이크를 원한다.
(C) 그녀는 주문한 것을 직접 찾아갈 것이다.
(D) 그녀는 Ms. Xavier와 전에 거래를 한 적이 있다.

189. 유추 – 결혼 축하 연회에 대한 내용 ★★☆

해설 마지막 지문 주문서에 나온 케이크를 필요로 하는 날짜는 'Date(s) needed: Saturday, May 4'에서 5월 4일, 토요일이므로 연회가 주말에 열린다고 할 수 있어 정답은 (C)이다. 정답 (C)

🔍함정 분석 배송지 주소는 'Delivery address: Singleton Banquet Hall, 88 Oak Way, Buford'로 되어 있으므로 호텔이라고 보기는 어려워 (A)는 오답이다. 주문서에 명시된 케이크 크기는 'Cake size: five tiers, 40cm base, additional cakes for 150 guests'에서 150명의 손님을 위한 케이크이므로 (B)도 오답이다.

표현 정리 reception 축하 연회 take place 개최되다, 열리다

해석 결혼 축하 연회에 대해 암시된 것은?
(A) 호텔에서 열릴 것이다.
(B) 200명 이상의 손님을 포함한다.
(C) 주말에 열릴 것이다.
(D) 라이브 음악이 연주될 것이다.

190. 세부사항 – 주문에 관한 내용이 아닌 것 ★★★

해설 마지막 지문 'Additional instructions: Unique decorations requested (see drawing on back), place mini-statue of bride and groom on top of cake.'에서 신부와 신랑의 작은 조각상을 케이크 상단에 올려달라고는 했지만, 이것이 먹을 수 있는 장식인지는 알 수 없으므로 (B)가 정답이다. 정답 (B)

🔍함정 분석 배송지 주소는 'Delivery address: Singleton Banquet Hall, 88 Oak Way, Buford'로 (A)는 주문 내용에 포함된다. 'Cake size: five tiers, 40cm base, additional cakes for 150 guests'에서 150명을 위한 추가 케이크가 있을 것임을 알 수 있고, 5층으로된 케이크이므로 (C)와 (D)의 내용을 확인할 수 있다.

패러프레이징 |지문| additional cakes for 150 guests 손님 150명을 위한 별도의 케이크들 → |선택지 C| more than one cake 하나 이상의 케이크 |지문| five tiers 다섯 줄 → |선택지 D| multiple layers 다수의 층

표현 정리 edible 먹을 수 있는 multiple 다수의

해석 주문에 관해 언급된 내용이 아닌 것은?
(A) Buford로 배달될 것이다.
(B) 먹을 수 있는 장식을 포함할 것이다.
(C) 한 개 이상의 케이크가 있을 것이다.
(D) 그것은 다수의 층을 가질 것이다.

문제 191-195번은 다음 공지, 양식, 그리고 이메일을 참조하시오.

공지

수신: 모든 세입자
RE: 현지 피트니스 센터 제안

Kensington 인근에 여러 피트니스 센터를 보유하고 있는 Defined Fitness가 Halcion 건물에 새 지점을 오픈하려고 고려 중입니다. 191, 192(B)Defined Fitness는 우리 건물 1층에 있는 500평방미터의 유휴 공간을 임대하려고 합니다. 계획을 추진하기 전에, Defined Fitness는 여러분들로부터 의견을 듣기를 원합니다. 193 2월 8일에서 14일까지 평일에 Halcion 건물에 근무하는 사람들에게 설문지를 보낼 것입니다. 192(D)설문지를 작성하셔서 늦어도 2월 28일까지는 로비에 있는 상자에 넣으시기 바랍니다.

Sam Rogan, 건물 관리자

표현 정리 tenant 세입자 onsite 현장의 proposal 제안 define 규정하다 lease 임대하다 square meters 평방미터 retail space 소매점 move forward 추진하다

설문지

이름(선택적): Colleen Leopardi
194(B)전화(선택적): 555-2903
고용주: Banek Designs

– 194(C)현재 체육관이나 피트니스 센터의 멤버입니까?
[ ] 네   [✓] 아니오

– 당신의 건물에 있는 피트니스 센터에 가입할 생각입니까?
[✓] 네   [ ] 아니오

– 195어떤 서비스를 피트니스 센터가 제공하기를 원합니까?
웨이트 기계, 운동 강좌, 수건과 개인 물품 보관함 임대

– 194(A)얼마나 자주 운동을 합니까? 대부분의 평일

– 194(D)언제 운동하는 것을 선호합니까?
[ ] 오전 8시 이전   [ ] 오전 8시 – 오전 10시

[ ] 오전 11시 – 오후 1시 [ ] 오후 1시 – 오후 6시 [✓] 오후 6시 이후

– 저희가 후속 질문과 함께 당신에게 연락을 해도 됩니까?

[✓] 네　　　　　[ ] 아니오

당신의 소중한 피드백에 감사합니다!

표현 정리 **currently** 현재　**consider** 고려하다　**locker** 개인 물품 보관함　**rental** 임대　**frequently** 자주　**prefer to** ~을 선호하다　**follow-up** 후속의　**valuable** 소중한

> 수신: Sam Rogan <srogan@halcionbuilding.com>
> 발신: Penny Ivans <penny.ivans@definedfitness.com>
> 제목: 조사 결과
> 날짜: 3월 8일
>
> Mr. Rogan 님께,
>
> 일정대로 설문지를 배부해 주신 당신의 도움에 감사 드립니다. 저희는 관심의 정도에 놀랐습니다. 192(A)우리가 배부한 1,480장의 조사 중 1,012장이 돌아왔습니다. 195저희가 받은 압도적으로 긍정적인 피드백을 기초로, 저희는 운동 기구, 교실, 개인 물품 보관실과 함께 당신의 건물에 새 지점을 여는 것을 추진하고 싶습니다. 다음 단계를 논의하는 것이 언제 가능한지 저에게 알려주시기 바랍니다.
>
> Penny Ivans

표현 정리 **assistance** 도움　**distribute** 배부하다　**on schedule** 예정대로　**overwhelmingly** 압도적으로

191.　세부사항 – Defined Fitness가 하려고 하는 것　★★☆

해설 첫 번째 지문인 공지 'It would lease 500 square meters of unused retail space on the first floor of our building.'에서 Defined Fitness가 건물 1층에 비어 있는 500평방미터의 공간을 임대할 계획을 세우고 있음을 알 수 있으므로 정답은 (D)이다.　정답 (D)

패러프레이징 |지문| lease 500 square meters of unused retail space on the first floor of our building 건물의 1층에 비어 있는 500평방미터의 구역을 임대하다 → |선택지 D| rent an interior area 내부 구역을 임대하다

표현 정리 **purchase** 구입　**relocate** 이전하다　**interior** 내부의

해석 공지에 따르면, Defined Fitness가 하려고 생각하는 것은?
(A) 건물 구매
(B) 조사 업체 고용
(C) 사업체 이전
(D) 내부 구역 임대

192.　연계 문제 – Halcion 건물에 대한 내용　★★☆

해설 공지 'During the week of February 8–14, it will send out a survey to each person working in the Halcion Building.'에서 건물에 근무하는 사람들에게 조사지가 배부될 것이라고 했고, 마지막 지문인 이메일 'Of the 1,480 surveys, we distributed, 1,012 were returned.'에서 건물 근무자가 1,500명 미만임을 알 수 있으므로 정답은 (A)이다.　정답 (A)

> 🔍 함정 분석 공지 'It would lease 500 square meters of unused retail space on the first floor of our building.'에서 사용하지 않는 500평방미터를 임대하려고 한다고 했지만 1층 전체가 비어있는지는 알 수 없으므로 (B)는 오답이다. 'Please complete the survey and place it in the secure box in the lobby no later than February 28.'에서 설문지를 로비에 있는 상자에 2월 28일까지 넣어달라고 했지만, 경비원들이 로비에 있는지는 알 수 없으므로 (D)도 오답이다.

표현 정리 **entire** 전체의　**vacant** 비어 있는　**management** 운영, 관리

94

---

renovate 보수하다

해석 Halcion Building에 관해 암시된 내용은?
(A) 1,500명 미만의 사람들이 그곳에 근무한다.
(B) 1층 전체가 비어 있다.
(C) 관리부는 3월에 그곳을 보수할 것이다.
(D) 경비원들이 로비에 있다.

193.　유추 – 설문에 관한 내용　★☆☆

해설 공지 내용 중 'During the week of February 8–14, it will send out a survey to each person working in the Halcion Building.'을 통해 설문지가 2월 8일에서 14일, 한 주 동안 배부될 예정이라고 했으므로 2월 15일 이전에 발송됐음을 알 수 있어 정답은 (C)이다.　정답 (C)

표현 정리 **send out** ~을 보내다　**conduct** (특정한 활동을) 하다

해석 설문에 관해 암시된 것은?
(A) Mr. Rogan이 준비했다.
(B) Ms. Ivans에게 직접 이메일로 보내졌다.
(C) 2월 15일 이전에 보내졌다.
(D) 온라인으로 실시되었다.

194.　세부사항 – Ms. Leopardi에 관한 내용이 아닌 것　★★☆

해설 두 번째 지문인 설문지 'How frequently do you exercise? *most weekdays*'에서 얼마나 자주 운동을 하는지 묻는 질문에 대부분 주중에 운동을 한다고 답했으므로 주말인 토요일에 운동한다는 (A)의 내용이 틀려 정답이다.　정답 (A)

> 🔍 함정 분석 'Phone (optional): 555-2903'에서 (B)가 확인되고, 'Are you currently a member of a gym or fitness center? [　] yes, [✓] no'에서 (C)도 확인된다. 'What hours do you prefer to exercise? [✓] after 6:00 P.M.'에서 주로 저녁에 운동하는 것을 좋아한다고 볼 수 있으므로 (D)도 사실이다.

표현 정리 **work out** 운동하다　**volunteer** 자원하다

해석 설문지에서 Ms. Leopardi에 관해 언급된 내용이 아닌 것은?
(A) 그녀는 토요일에 운동한다.
(B) 그녀는 자진해서 전화번호를 알려줬다.
(C) 그녀는 Defined Fitness 멤버가 아니다.
(D) 그녀는 저녁에 운동하는 것을 좋아한다.

195.　연계 문제 – Ms. Leopardi에 대한 내용　★★☆

해설 두 번째 지문인 설문지 'What services would you like a fitness center to provide?'라는 질문에 Ms. Leopardi가 'weight machines, exercise classes, towel and locker rentals'라고 답했고, 세 번째 지문인 이메일에서 Ms. Ivans가 'we would like to move forward with developing a new location in your building with exercise equipment, classrooms, and locker rooms'라고 말하며, 새 피트니스 시설에 운동 기구와 교실, 물품 보관실을 마련할 것이라고 했다. 이는 Ms. Leopardi가 설문지에서 요구한 의견을 그대로 수용하겠다는 의미이며, 다른 사람들도 역시 같은 의견을 개진했을 수 있을 것으로 추측할 수 있어 정답은 (B)이다.　정답 (B)

표현 정리 **used to** (과거) ~했다　**intend to** ~할 작정이다　**coworker** 동료

해석 Ms. Leopardi에 관해 암시된 것은?
(A) 그녀는 Ms. Ivans를 위해 일했었다.
(B) 그녀가 요청한 서비스들은 대중적이다.(다른 사람들도 원한다)
(C) 그녀는 Mr. Rogan을 만날 예정이다.
(D) 그녀의 동료들은 모두 새로운 체육관을 원한다.

문제 196-200번은 다음 기사, 이메일, 그리고 공지를 참조하시오.

Barkwood(4월 15일) – 어제 아침, 수백 명의 쇼핑객들이 Colorado의 Boulder에 소재한 자연 식품 소매 체인인 Mother Earth Market의 개점을 줄 서 기다렸다. **196Maiden Creek 쇼핑센터에 위치한 이 마켓은 Barkwood에서 문을 여는 첫 매장이다.**

자연 식품은 농약이 건강에 미치는 영향에 관심을 갖는 소비자들이 늘면서 지난 10년 넘게 성장해 왔다. Mother Earth Foods는 농약이 없는, 유기농 인증을 받은 농산물을 판매한다. 게다가 가게에서 판매되는 고기와 유제품의 최소 25%가 인근 농장에서 온 것이다.

Barkwood에 있는 Mother Earth Market은 매일 오전 8시부터 오후 9시까지 문을 연다.

표현 정리 line up 줄을 서다 grand opening 개장 retail 소매 popularity 인기 decade 10년 consumer 소비자 concerned 염려하는 effect 영향 pesticide-free 농약이 들어있지 않은 certified organic 인증받은 유기농의 in addition 게다가 a minimum of 최소한의 dairy products 유제품 nearby 인근의

수신: Kelly Giles' 〈kgiles@marvelousshoes.com〉
발신: Kyle Lowe 〈klowe@bluemoon.com〉
제목: RE: 주차 문제
날짜: 5월 12일

Ms. Giles 님께,

Maiden Creek에 있는 주차장의 혼잡 문제로 저희에게 연락을 주셔서 감사합니다. **197새로 문을 연 자연 식품 가게의 인기는 모두를 깜짝 놀라게 했습니다.** 피크타임에는 거의 매일 주차장이 수용 능력을 넘어 포화 상태인 것을 알고 있습니다. **200저희는 Marvelous Shoes를 포함한 각 입점 업체**가 고객을 위한 충분한 주차 공간을 확보하도록 하기 위해 Barkwood 주차 당국뿐 아니라 새 매장의 경영진과 의논하고 있습니다. 이에 대한 자세한 내용이 곧 나올 것입니다.

198Kyle Lowe

Blue Moon 관리회사

표현 정리 regarding ~에 관하여 congestion 혼잡 parking lot 주차장 catch off guard 깜짝 놀라게 하다, 허점을 찌르다 capacity 수용력 Parking Authority 주차 당국 ensure 보장하다 tenant 세입자 adequate 충분한

공지

날짜: 5월 29
발신: Blue Moon 부동산
수신: Maiden Creek 쇼핑센터의 모든 입점 업체

199주차 문제를 해결하고, 여러분의 사업에 끼치는 영향을 최소화하기 위하여, 저희는 해결책을 다음과 같이 제시합니다. 200첫째, 각 세입자는 그들의 고객들만이 사용할 수 있는 주차 공간을 지정받을 것입니다. 이 공간들은 바로 각 매장 앞에 위치할 것이며, 표지판으로 분명하게 표시될 것입니다. 위반자들은 Barkwood 주차 당국(위반자 보고를 위한 전화 555-9303)에 의해 위반 티켓을 발부받을 것입니다. 둘째, 시청 측은 늘어나는 주차 문제를 해결하기 위해 쇼핑센터 뒤쪽 공터를 우리가 사용하도록 허용했습니다. 쇼핑객들이 알 수 있도록 안내 표지판을 설치할 것입니다.

표현 정리 address 다루다, 해결하다 minimize 최소화하다 impact on ~에 대한 영향 propose 제안하다 exclusively 독점적으로 clearly 분명히 violator 위반자 ticket 딱지를 발부하다 permit 허용하다

vacant lot 공터 post 배치하다

196. 유추 – Barkwood에 대한 내용 ★☆☆
해설 기사 첫 번째 단락 'Located in the Maiden Creek Shopping Center, this is the first store of its kind in Barkwood.'에서 Barkwood 지역의 유일한 자연 식품점이라는 것을 알 수 있으므로 정답은 (B)이다. **정답 (B)**

패러프레이징 |지문| the first store of its kind 유일한 자연 식품점 → |선택지 B| one health food store 오직 하나의 건강 식품 가게

표현 정리 rural 시골의 numerous 많은

해석 Barkwood에 관해 나타난 내용은?
(A) 시골 지역에 위치한다.
(B) 오직 하나의 건강 식품 매장을 갖고 있다.
(C) 많은 작은 사업체들을 가지고 있다.
(D) Colorado의 Boulder에 가깝게 있다.

197. 세부사항 – 주차 문제의 이유 ★☆☆
해설 이메일 'The popularity of the new natural food store has caught everyone off guard.'에서 새로 문을 연 자연 식품점의 인기가 예상치 못했던 주차 문제를 일으켰다는 사실을 알 수 있으므로 정답은 (D)이다. **정답 (D)**

패러프레이징 |지문| The popularity of the new natural food store has caught everyone off guard 새로운 자연 식품점의 인기가 깜짝 놀랄 정도다 → |선택지 D| A new store is drawing more customers than expected 새로운 가게가 예상했던 것보다 더 많은 고객을 끌고 있다

표현 정리 construction 공사

해석 Maiden Creek에 주차 문제가 발생한 이유는?
(A) 주차 공간이 최근 없어졌다.
(B) 새 입점 업체가 주차 공간을 추가로 요구했다.
(C) 쇼핑센터는 공사 중에 있다.
(D) 신규 매장이 예상보다 더 많은 고객을 끌고 있다.

198. 연계 문제 – Mr. Lowe의 직업 ★☆☆
해설 이메일에서 Kyle Lowe는 Kelly Giles에게 이메일을 보낸 사람이며, 이메일 하단 'Kyle Lowe, Blue Moon Properties'에서 건물 관계자임을 알 수 있으므로 정답은 (C)이다. **정답 (C)**

표현 정리 supervisor 관리자

해석 Mr. Lowe는 누구인가?
(A) 소매점 관리자
(B) 지방 공무원
(C) 건물 관리인
(D) 경찰관

199. 동의어 ★★☆
해설 공지 첫 번째 문장 'In order to address the parking issue and to minimize its impact on your business, we propose the following solutions.'에서 주차 문제에 대한 해결책을 제시하고 있음을 알 수 있다. 여기서 동사 address는 '다루다, 해결하다'라는 뜻으로 쓰였으므로 (A) resolve가 가장 유사한 단어라고 볼 수 있어 정답이다. **정답 (A)**

표현 정리 resolve 해결하다 elevate 올리다

해석 공지에서, 첫 번째 줄의 "address"와 의미가 가장 가까운 것은?
(A) 해결하다
(B) 올리다
(C) 위치하다
(D) 논의하다

TEST 07

정답 및 해설 _ 95

200. 연계 문제 – Marvelous Shoes에 대한 내용　★★★

해설 두 번째 지문인 이메일 후반 'each of our tenants, Marvelous Shoes included, has adequate parking for customers'에서 알 수 있듯이 Marvelous Shoes는 the Maiden Creek Shopping Center에 입주해 있는 업체임을 알 수 있고, 세 번째 지문인 공지 'First, each tenant will receive a set number of parking spaces reserved exclusively for their customers.'에서 각 매장은 자신들의 고객만이 이용할 수 있는 주차 공간을 할당받을 것이라고 했으므로 (D)가 정답이다.　정답 (D)

🔍 함정 분석 주차 문제를 항의하기 위해 Ms. Giles는 이미 Mr. Lower에게 이메일을 보낸 적이 있고, 이에 답하기 위해 Mr. Lower가 보낸 이메일 내용에 'each of our tenants, Marvelous Shoes included, has adequate parking for customers'라는 내용이 언급된 것으로 보아 Ms. Giles가 현재 Marvelous Shoes를 운영하는 주인이라는 것을 짐작할 수 있으므로 (A)는 오답이다.

패러프레이징 |지문| receive a set number of parking spaces 할당된 주차 공간을 받는다 → |선택지 D| get assigned parking spaces 할당된 주차 공간을 얻는다

표현 정리 assigned 할당된

해석 Marvelous Shoes에 관해 제시된 내용은?
(A) Ms. Giles는 그 매장의 이전 주인이다.
(B) 그것은 Mother Earth Market 옆에 위치해 있다.
(C) 고객들은 매장의 새 위치를 찾을 수 없다.
(D) 그것은 할당된 주차 공간을 얻을 것이다.

문제 147-148번은 다음 광고를 참조하시오.

Professional Edits
말하고자 하는 내용을 적절한 단어로 전달하세요.

서비스에 포함된 내용:
– 147(B) 기존 내용의 오탈자, 철자 오류, 문법 오류 수정
– 마케팅이나 프로모션 용으로 새로운 글 작성
– 147(D) 웹사이트로 더 많은 고객들을 유도하기 위한 매력적인 블로그 포스트 글 작성

Professional Edits는 모든 사람들이 글쓰기를 전공하거나 교정에 필요한 매의 눈을 갖고 있지는 않다는 것을 잘 알고 있으며, 147(A)따라서 저희는 똑똑하고, 신속하며, 부지런한 작가들로 하여금 귀하의 사업을 돕고 있습니다. 작은 수정이든, 새로운 콘텐츠를 작성하는 것이든, Professional Edits는 귀하의 모든 교정 관련 문제를 도와드립니다.

148저희의 교정 포트폴리오를 확인하시려면, 3252 Merryway Lane에 위치한 저희 사무실을 방문해 주세요.

표현 정리 professional 전문적인　existing 기존의　typo 오탈자　draft 초안을 작성하다　engaging 매력적인　draw 끌어오다, 유도하다, 유인하다　major in ~을 전공하다　eagle eye 매의 눈(관찰력이 예리한 눈)　diligent 부지런한　help (someone) out 누군가를 돕다　correction 수정　be here for ~를 위해 존재하다　needs 필요성　portfolio 포트폴리오　stop by ~에 들르다

147. 세부사항 – Professional Edits에 관해 언급되지 않은 내용　★☆☆

해설 'that is why we have a smart, quick, and diligent staff of writers to help your business out'에서 사업을 위해 서비스를 제공한다는 점, 'editing existing content for typos, spelling errors, and grammar problems'에서 실수를 고쳐준다는 점, 'writing engaging blog posts to draw more customers to your Web site'에서 온라인 블로그와 관련된 작문 또한 제공한다는 점 등을 알 수 있다. 작성한 글의 단어 별로 단가를 책정한다는 부분은 나와있지 않으므로 (B)가 정답이다.　정답 (B)

패러프레이징 |지문| edit existing content for typos, spelling errors, and grammar problems 기존 내용의 오탈자, 철자 오류, 문법 오류를 수정하다 → |선택지 C| correct writing mistakes 작문 실수를 고쳐 주다
|지문| write engaging blog posts 매력적인 블로그 포스트를 작문하다 → |선택지 D| write for online audiences 온라인 고객을 위해 작문한다

표현 정리 indicate 지시하다, 나타내다　commercial 상업적인　charge 청구하다, 받다　correct 수정하다　audience 청중, 대상

해석 Professional Edits에 관해 언급된 내용이 아닌 것은?
(A) 상업적인 고객들을 위해 서비스를 제공한다.
(B) 작성된 모든 단어 당 대가를 받는다.
(C) 작문 실수를 고쳐 준다.
(D) 온라인 고객을 위해 글을 작성해 준다.

148. 세부사항 – 독자들이 주소를 참조해야 하는 이유　★★☆

해설 'To see our editorial portfolio, please stop by our office at 3252 Merryway Lane.'은 서비스와 관련된 포트폴리오를 견학하기 위해서 사무실을 방문해 달라는 요청이다. 따라서, 작문 예시를 보기 위해서라고 볼 수 있으므로 정답은 (D)이다.　정답 (D)

패러프레이징 |지문| to see our editorial portfolio 우리의 편집 관련 포트폴리오를 견학하기 위해서 → |선택지 B| to view writing samples 작문 예시를 보

기 위해서

표현 정리 refer to ~을 참조하다, 참조하게 하다 make an appointment 약속을 잡다 view 보다 sample 예시

해석 독자들이 주소를 참조해야 하는 이유는?
(A) 무료 브로셔를 받기 위해
(B) 블로그 포스트를 작성하기 위해
(C) 약속을 정하기 위해
(D) 작문 예시를 보기 위해

문제 149-150번은 다음 카드를 참조하시오.

Paperworks 주식회사
귀하에게 필요한 모든 종이 수요를 위해!

종이			
기본 종이	두꺼운 종이	인쇄 용지	판지
흰색	흰색/황백색	흰색/검은색	흰색/갈색
500장	300장	200장	100장
50달러	75달러	100달러	150달러

Ms. Simone, 다음은 귀사의 행사를 위한 초대장과 관련된 최종적인 종이 선택지입니다. 149어떤 종이에 초대장을 인쇄하실 것인지와 색상을 함께 명시해 주십시오. 초대장을 인쇄하는 데는 하루, 혹은 이틀 정도가 소요되기 때문에, 150적어도 10월 2일까지는 연락을 주시는 편이 좋습니다. 이후 저희 은행 계좌 2342-13282-5232로 총 금액을 송금해 주십시오. 문의 사항이 있으시면 저에게 알려주세요.

테리 고메즈(tgomez@paperwork.net)

표현 정리 cardstock 인쇄 용지 cardboard 판지 piece 장 invitation 초대장 specify 명시하다 at the latest 늦어도 wire 송금하다 total amount 총 금액 bank account 은행 계좌

149. 주제 – 카드의 목적 ★☆☆
해설 'Please let me know which paper you would like the invitations printed on and specify the color.'에서 이 카드를 보내는 목적이 고객의 선택과 관련된 지시 사항을 전달받기 위해서임을 알 수 있으므로 정답은 (C)이다.
정답 (C)

표현 정리 purpose 목적 deny 거부; 거절하다 request 요청 correct 수정하다 mistake 실수 instruction 지시 사항 delay 지연, 지체

해석 이 카드의 목적은 무엇인가?
(A) 요청을 거절하기 위해
(B) 실수를 바로잡기 위해
(C) 지시 사항을 요청하기 위해
(D) 지연을 알리기 위해

150. 유추 – 행사에 대한 내용 ★☆☆
해설 'so it is best to contact me by October 2 at the latest.'에서 늦어도 10월 2일까지 연락을 달라고 했으므로 초대장이 필요한 행사는 적어도 10월 2일 이후에 진행된다는 것을 알 수 있어 정답은 (B)이다.
정답 (B)

🔍함정 분석 흰색 종이를 사용해야 한다는 것은 언급되지 않았으므로 (A)는 오답이며, Paperworks 사가 아닌 Ms. Simone의 행사이므로 (C)도 오답이다. 또한, 누구를 위한 행사인지는 명시되어 있지 않으므로 (D)도 정답이 될 수 없다.

표현 정리 occur 나타나다, 발생하다 organize 기획하다, 준비하다

해석 행사와 관련해 암시된 것은?

(A) 흰색 종이를 필요로 한다.
(B) 10월 2일 이후에 개최된다.
(C) Paperworks에 의해 기획되었다.
(D) 회사의 직원과 가족을 위한 행사이다.

문제 151-153번은 다음 기사를 참조하시오.

어린 아이들과 여행하는 것이 꼭 악몽일 필요는 없다. 실제로, 많은 가족들이 어린 아이들과 함께 성공적으로 여행을 한다. 151성공의 비밀은 바로 계획에 있다.

성공적으로 여행하는 가족들은 시간을 충분히 가진다. 이런 가족들은 공항, 기차역, 버스 터미널에 일찍 도착하여 예측하지 못한 응급 상황에 필요한 충분한 시간을 확보한다. 일찍 도착하는 것은 가족 구성원 모두가 느끼는 스트레스를 줄여준다.

어린 아이들은 집중력이 제한되어 있다. 따라서 차량이나 비행기로 이동하는 긴 시간 동안에는 게임, 퍼즐, 색칠 공부 책을 비롯한 여러 활동 도구를 챙겨 아이들을 집중시키는 것이 좋다. 153어떤 부모들은 태블릿 컴퓨터나 스마트폰에 있는 이동식 오락에 의존하기도 한다. 어느 쪽을 선호하든지 아이들이 재미있게 할 수 있는 것들을 생각해 보면 이동 중 머리 아플 일이 줄어들 것이다.

마지막으로, 하지만 무시해서는 안 될 것은 아이들의 일과를 최대한 따라야 한다. 어린 아이가 아침 10시에 간식을 먹는다면, 어느 곳에 있던 간에 간식을 먹도록 해 주는 게 좋다. 낮잠, 목욕, 동화 읽어주기 등도 마찬가지다. 152익숙한 일과가 유지될수록, 어린 아이들은 새로운 환경에 더 쉽게 적응할 것이다.

물론, 모든 아이들이 똑같지는 않으며, 새로운 경험에 좀 더 잘 적응하는 아이들도 있다. 그렇지만, 계획하는 것은 아이들과 여행하는 것을 수월하게 할 수 있다.

표현 정리 nightmare 악몽 in fact 실제로 successfully 성공적으로 secret 비법, 비밀 planning 계획하는 것 take one's time 시간을 충분히 가지다 airport 공항 train stations 기차역 bus terminals 버스 터미널 sufficient 충분한 available 사용 가능한 unforeseen 예측하지 못한 emergency 응급 상황 reduce 줄이다 limited 제한된 attention span 집중력 coloring books 색칠공부 책 occupied ~에 집중한 during ~동안 portable 가지고 다니는 prefer 선호하다 think ahead 미리 내다보다 last but not least 마지막으로, 그렇지만 중요한 stick to ~를 따르다 routine 일과 as much as possible 최대한 familiar 익숙한 remain intact 온전한 상태로 유지되다 adjust to ~에 적응하다 with ease 수월하게 deal with ~에 대처하다

151. 주제 – 글의 목적 ★☆☆
해설 기사 내용은 아이들과 함께하는 여행을 수월하게 만드는 방법을 소개하는 것으로, (B)와 같이 아이들과 여행하는 것에 대한 조언을 하기 위해서 쓰여진 글이며, 따라서 정답은 (B)이다. (A)는 아이들의 양육 방식 설명, (C)는 비행기 여행을 권장, (D)는 여행을 위해 계획을 하지 않는 사람에 대한 비판이므로 오답이다.
정답 (B)

표현 정리 raise 키우다, 양육하다 give advice 조언을 주다 encourage 권장하다 air 비행 criticize 비판하다

해석 이 글의 목적은 무엇인가?
(A) 아이들의 양육 방식을 설명하기 위해
(B) 아이들과 함께 하는 여행에 대한 조언을 하기 위해
(C) 비행기 여행을 권장하기 위해
(D) 여행을 계획하지 않는 사람들을 비판하기 위해

152. 세부사항 – 일과의 중요성에 대해 명시된 내용 ★★☆

해설 네 번째 단락 'The more familiar routines remain intact, the more likely your little one will adjust to the new environment with ease.'에서 익숙한 일과가 유지될수록, 어린 아이들은 새로운 환경에 더 쉽게 적응할 수 있다고 했으므로 정답은 (A)이다. 　　　　　정답 (A)

🔍 함정 분석 (B)에서 부모들이 천천히 움직일 수 있게 한다는 점은 명시되어 있지 않다. 또한, (C)의 휴식과 관련된 내용도 찾아볼 수 없으며, (D)와 같이 아이들의 흥미를 유지시키는 것은 일과가 아니라 재미있는 장난감들이기 때문에 (D)는 오답이다.

패러프레이징 |지문| adjust to the new environment with ease 새로운 환경에 더 쉽게 적응할 것이다 → |선택지 A| adapt to changes 변화에 적응하다

표현 정리 according to ~에 따르면 help A B A를 B하게 돕다 adapt to ~에 적응하다 changes 변화 allow A to B A가 B하도록 허락하다 ensure 확실히 하다 enough 충분한 rest 휴식 keep A B A를 B하게 유지하다

해석 본문에 따르면, 아이들과 여행할 때 일과가 중요한 이유는?
(A) 아이들이 변화에 적응하는 것을 도와준다.
(B) 부모들이 더 천천히 움직이도록 해 준다.
(C) 아이들이 충분한 휴식을 가질 수 있도록 해 준다.
(D) 아이들을 재미있게 해 준다.

153. 세부사항 – 스마트폰에 대한 내용 ★★☆

해설 스마트폰과 관련된 문장 'Some parents rely on the portable entertainment available on their tablet computers and smartphones.'에서 아이들의 집중력이 제한적이라는 부분을 설명하기 위해 사용되었다. 따라서, 아이들이 쉽게 싫증을 내는 것과 관련하여 주의를 딴 데로 돌려 부모들이 이동 중에 편하도록 하는 도구로 명시되었으므로 정답은 (B)이다. 　　　정답 (B)

🔍 함정 분석 스마트폰은 원래 소통을 위해 필요한 도구이므로 (A)를 답으로 착각하기 쉽다. 그러나 본문에서는 스마트폰의 소통 기능보다는 아이들에게 놀이감을 제공하기 위한 도구로 등장했으므로 (A)는 오답이다. 또한, (C)는 essential이라는 단어가 틀렸다. 단지 권고 사항일 뿐이다. (D)는 일과와 관련된 세 번째 단락과 스마트폰이 나온 두 번째 단락을 혼합해 오답을 유도한 것이므로 오답이다.

표현 정리 useful for ~에 유용한 communicate 소통하다 used to ~에 사용되다 distract 주의를 분산시키다(딴 데로 돌리다) essential 필수적인 track (여정 등을) 기록하다, 체크하다

해석 스마트폰에 관해 언급된 것은?
(A) 아이들과 소통하는데 유용하다.
(B) 아이들의 주의를 딴 데로 돌리는데 사용된다.
(C) 여행하는 가족에게 필수적이다.
(D) 여행 일과를 체크할 수 있게 해 준다.

문제 154-155번은 다음 문자 메시지를 참조하시오.

Helms, Joe 안녕하세요. 154Rick. 요청하신 비슷한 로고들을 한 파일로 합치는 작업을 마무리했습니다. 공유 드라이브에서 확인할 수 있습니다. 　　　오전 9시 11분

Tocher, Rick 몇 개의 로고가 포함되어 있습니까? 고객을 위해 만들어야 하는 새로운 로고를 위해 많은 영감이 필요합니다. 　　　오전 9시 20분

Helms, Joe 10개입니다. 충분한가요? 여러 가지 텍스트 폰트도 포함시켰습니다. 155아이디어가 떠오르게 해 줄 거예요. 　　　오전 9시 21분

Tocher, Rick 좋은 생각이네요! 좋은 시작처럼 보입니다. 오전 9시 35분

Helms, Joe 다른 것이 필요한 경우 알려주세요. 당신이 알려준 특징을 가진 회사 로고를 찾는 일은 즐겁거든요. 　　　오전 9시 36분

Tocher, Rick 더 필요하면 말할게요. 　　　오전 9시 47분

Helms, Joe 언제든지 연락주세요. 　　　오전 9시 48분

Tocher, Rick 고마워요. 　　　오전 9시 50분

표현 정리 put together 모으다, 합치다 similar 비슷한, 유사한 logo 로고 access 접근하다 shared drive 공유 드라이브 include 포함하다 inspiration 영감 create 새롭게 만들다 client 고객 font 폰트, 서체 spark 영감을 주다, 떠오르게 하다 specifics 세부사항 lay out 제시하다

154. 유추 – Helms 씨의 사업 분야 ★★☆

해설 Helms가 오전 9시 11분에 Rick에게 보낸 메시지 'I finished putting together the file of similar logos you requested. You can access it on the shared drive.'에서 유사한 로고들 파일을 합치는 작업을 마쳤다고 했다. 이는 Rick이 새로운 로고를 만드는 것에 영감을 주기 위해 사용하는 것으로, Helms는 그래픽 디자인과 관련된 업종에 종사하고 있을 가능성이 가장 높아 정답은 (B)이다. 　　　정답 (B)

표현 정리 type of business 사업 분야 graphic design 그래픽 디자인 firm 회사 government 정부 clothing 의류

해석 Mr. Helms가 일하는 업종으로 가장 적절한 것은?
(A) 패밀리 레스토랑
(B) 그래픽 디자인 회사
(C) 정부 기관
(D) 옷가게

155. 의도 파악하기 ★★☆

해설 "That should spark some ideas."는 Rick이 새로운 영감을 받도록 해당 자료를 전달했다는 점을 보여주는 문장으로, 바로 앞에서 'I also included various text fonts.'라며 여러 서체도 함께 포함시켰다고 했는데, 이 서체들이 Rick으로 하여금 영감을 받게 해 줄 것이라는 의미이다. spark는 불꽃이 튀는 모습을 나타내며, 영감에 불을 붙인다는 식으로 해석될 수 있으므로 가장 가까운 (C)가 정답이다. 　　　정답 (C)

🔍 함정 분석 (A)는 내용상 오답으로, 첫 번째 줄의 'I finished putting together the file of similar logos you requested.'에서 자료를 모으는 작업이 끝났음을 보여준다. Mr. Helms는 (B)에 나와 있는 것처럼 Tocher에게 의견을 제시하고 있는 것이 아니며, (D) 또한 언급되지 않은 내용으로, 새로운 서체를 디자인한 것이 아니라 여러 가지 서체 자료를 포함하여 전달했기 때문에 오답이다.

표현 정리 collect 모으다 at the moment 현재 take A seriously A를 진지하게 여기다 inspire 영감을 주다 project 프로젝트

해석 Mr. Helms가 오전 9시 21분에 "아이디어가 떠오르게 해 줄 거예요."라고 한 이유는?
(A) Mr. Helms는 지금도 로고를 모으고 있다.
(B) Mr. Helms는 자신의 아이디어가 진지하게 받아들여지길 원한다.
(C) Mr. Helms는 자신이 준 여러 서체가 Tocher 씨에게 영감을 줄 것이라고 생각한다.
(D) Mr. Helms는 Tocher 씨의 프로젝트를 위한 새로운 서체를 디자인했다.

문제 156-158번은 다음 공지를 참조하시오.

Better-Tech PowerView 컨퍼런스

행사 이름: Better-Tech PowerView 컨퍼런스
시작일: 1월 12일　　　시간: 오전 9시

종료일: 1월 13일　　　　시간: 오후 5시

담당자: Sally Gales

연락처: 555-8921

이메일: sgales@bettertech.com

157.(C) 참가 비용: 100달러

첨부 자료: 참가 신청서, 지불 관련 지시 사항

행사에 관하여: PowerView 프레젠테이션은 전반적으로 대기업, 중소기업에 의해 충분히 활용되지 않고 있는 도구입니다. PowerView 프레젠테이션을 작성하는 기본을 알고 있는 사용자들에게 이 컨퍼런스는 해당 소프트웨어의 좀 더 숙련된 활용법을 알려드릴 것입니다. 또한, **156.여러분의 프레젠테이션을 만드는 것뿐만 아니라, 프레젠테이션을 전달하는 방법에 대해서도 팁과 조언을 받게 됩니다.** Better-Tech 사의 획기적인 PowerView 컨퍼런스와 함께 무대에서 자신감을 가지고 연설을 하고, 당신의 마케팅 전략을 극대화하세요. **158.컨퍼런스의 참가 신청 마감일은 1월 3일입니다.** 장소가 제한되어 50명을 수용할 수 있습니다. **157.(B),(D)서명된 참가 신청서를 Sally Gales의 이메일 주소 sgales@bettertech.com으로 보내셔야 합니다.** 만약 관심이 저희의 예상을 넘어서는 경우, 추가적으로 좌석이 확보될 수 있습니다. 해당 공지나 다른 변경 사항은 1월 4일 저희 웹사이트인 www.bettertech.com에 공지될 것입니다.

표현 정리 registration 참가 신청, 등록　fee 비용　attached 첨부된　application form 참가 신청서　payment 비용 지불　instructions 주의 사항, 지시 사항　underutilized 충분히 활용되지 못한　tool 도구　advanced 고급의, 숙련된　application 활용법　pointers 조언　beyond ~를 넘어서는　delivery 전달　maximize 극대화하다　strategy 전략　revolutionary 획기적인　deadline 기한　signed 서명된　via ~를 통해　exceed 넘어서다　expectation 기대, 기대치　notification 공지, 알림　changes 변경 사항

156. 세부사항 – PowerView 컨퍼런스에 관한 내용 ★★☆

해설 PowerView 컨퍼런스는 'you will receive tips and pointers on both the creation of your presentation and also on the presentation delivery.'처럼 연설과 관련된 tips and pointers를 제공한다는 내용이 본문에 명시되어 있으므로 정답은 (D)이다.　**정답 (D)**

🔍 **함정 분석** Better-Tech의 행사 대상은 따로 명시되어 있지 않기 때문에, 이를 회사의 직원에 한정한 (A)는 오답이다. 또한, 프레젠테이션과 관련된 기술을 가르쳐준다는 부분인 'this conference will teach you more advanced applications of the software.'를 확인해 보면, (B)에 나온 기본적인 컴퓨터 스킬과는 관련이 없다는 것을 알 수 있다. 그리고 (C)에서 언급된 소프트웨어 개발자들은 본문에 언급된 적이 없으므로 오답이다.

패러프레이징 |지문| both the creation of your presentation and also on the presentation delivery 프레젠테이션을 만드는 것뿐만 아니라, 프레젠테이션을 전달하는 방법 → |선택지 D| information on public speaking 연설에 관한 정보

표현 정리 open to ~에게 열려 있는　directed at ~를 대상으로 한　software developer 소프트웨어 개발자　offer 제공하다　training 트레이닝, 교육　public speaking 연설

해설 PowerView 컨퍼런스에 관해 언급된 내용은?
(A) Better-Tech의 직원들만을 대상으로 한다.
(B) 기본적인 컴퓨터 스킬을 가르쳐준다.
(C) 소프트웨어 개발자들을 대상으로 한다.
(D) 연설에 관한 정보를 제공한다.

157. 세부사항 – 컨퍼런스 참가와 관련이 없는 것 ★☆☆

해설 컨퍼런스에 참가하기 위해서는 참가 신청서에 서명을 해야 하며(signed applications need to be sent), 이를 담당자인 Sally Gales에게 이메일로 보

내고(sent via e-mail to Sally Gales at sgales@bettertech.com), 참가 비용 100달러를 지불해야 한다(Registration fee: $100). 이 세 단계는 모두 (B), (C), (D)에 명시되어 있는 반면, (A)에 등장한 온라인 양식은 본문에 나와있지 않으므로 (A)가 정답이다.　**정답 (A)**

패러프레이징 |지문| signed applications 서명한 신청서 → |선택지 B| signing a document 서류에 서명하기
|지문| sent via e-mail to Sally Gales 이메일을 Sally Gales에게 보내라 → |선택지 D| e-mailing a contact person 담당자에게 이메일 보내기

표현 정리 attend 참석하다　complete 완성하다, 작성을 완료하다　form 양식　sign 서명하다

해설 컨퍼런스에 참가하기 위해 요구되는 것이 아닌 것은?
(A) 온라인 양식 작성
(B) 서류 서명
(C) 비용 지불
(D) 담당자에게 이메일 송부

158. 세부사항 – 참가 신청서 제출 기한 ★☆☆

해설 본문 내용 중 'The registration deadline for the conference is January 3.'에서 해당 신청서는 1월 3일까지 제출돼야 한다고 언급되어 있으므로 정답은 (A)이다.　**정답 (A)**

표현 정리 latest 가장 늦은　submit 제출하다

해설 참가 신청서가 이메일로 제출되는 마지막 기한은 언제인가?
(A) 1월 3일
(B) 1월 4일
(C) 1월 12일
(D) 1월 13일

문제 159-161번은 다음 편지를 참조하시오.

Direct Delivery

Keifer Jones

KJ 로펌

2214 34th Avenue

Oklahoma City, OK

11월 9일

Mr. Jones 님께,

귀하의 비서실장인 Jessica Klein은 제 친한 지인입니다. 그녀는 귀 로펌에서 회사의 기밀 서류를 배달해 줄 개인 배송 서비스를 찾고 있다는 것을 언급한 적이 있습니다. 저희는 귀사의 사업적 특성을 잘 이해하고 있으며, 법적인 문제에 있어서 시간이 생명이라는 사실 또한 잘 알고 있습니다.

저희 배송 회사인 Direct Delivery는 소규모 사업의 배송 서비스에 특화되어 있습니다. 특히 저희는 소규모 회사들만을 대상으로 사업을 진행하여 세부사항에 신경을 쓸 수 있고, 과도한 업무량을 맡지 않고 있습니다. **160.귀하는 배송을 위해 긴 줄에 서 있는 또 다른 회원으로 취급되지 않을 것입니다.**

159.저희는 각 고객사의 특별한 업무 특성에 서비스를 맞출 수 있습니다. 근거리 배송을 위해서는 교통 체증을 피하고 작은 물품을 신속하게 배달할 수 있는 자전거 배송 서비스를 제공합니다. 좀 더 규모가 큰 배송이나 장거리 배송을 위해서는 밴을 보유하고 있으며, 귀사의 사무실에 언제라도 물품을 가지러 갈 수 있습니다. 저희 회사는 일주일 내내, 하루 24시간 운영됩니다.

저희 서비스가 KJ 로펌에 잘 맞는다고 생각되시면, 언제라도 저희에게 전화 주셔서 계약 조건을 상의하실 수 있습니다. 귀하의 사무실에 들러 저희가 제공할 수 있는 서비스와 관련하여 직접 찾아 뵙고 말씀드릴 수도 있습니다. 부디 Ms. Klein에게 제 안부를 전해주십시오.

Harry Pines
Direct Delivery

표현 정리 delivery 배송, 배달 law firm 로펌, 법률회사 head ~의 장
administrative assistant 행정 비서 close 가까운 acquaintance 지인
private 개인적인 practice 사업 confidential 기밀의 paperwork
서류, 문서 nature 특징, 본성, 성향 essence 가장 중요한 가치 legal
법적인 specialize in ~을 전문으로 하다 specifically 특히 do
business with ~와 거래하다 pay attention to ~에 관심을 기울이다
detail 세부사항 inundated 과부하가 되는 adjust ~에 맞게 조정하다
unique 특별한 needs 필요 courier service 배달 서비스 avoid 피하다
traffic jam 교통 체증 farther 더 멀리 pick up 가지러 가다, 수거하다
directly 직접적으로 run 운영하다 good fit 잘 맞음

159. 세부사항 – Direct Delivery에 대한 내용 ★★☆

해설 본문 세 번째 단락 'We can adjust our services to each client's
unique needs.'에서 회사가 고객의 필요에 따라 서비스를 맞출 수 있다는 것을
알 수 있으므로 정답은 (C)가 된다. **정답 (C)**

🔍 **함정 분석** Direct Delivery는 지인인 Jessica Klein의 얘기를 듣고 처음으로
Mr. Jones에게 연락을 했기 때문에 (A)는 오답이다. 또한, 1인용 자전거 서비
스는 'For close deliveries, we offer a bike courier service'에서 확인할
수 있는 것처럼 근거리 배송을 위한 서비스일 뿐, Direct Delivery의 서비스 전
체가 1인용 자전거 서비스는 아니기 때문에 (B)도 오답이다. 마지막으로, 회사
의 규모나 확장 계획에 관해서는 언급된 바가 없기 때문에 (D) 역시 오답이다.

패러프레이징 |지문| adjust our services to each client's unique needs 각
고객의 필요에 따라 서비스를 맞추다 → |선택지 C| offer customized services
to clients 고객들에게 맞춤 서비스를 제공하다

표현 정리 one-man 1인용 customized 맞춤의 expand 확장하다 in
the near future 조만간

해석 Direct Delivery에 관해 암시된 내용은?
(A) 전에 Mr. Jones와 일한 경험이 있다.
(B) 1인용 자전거 배송 서비스이다.
(C) 고객들에게 맞춤 서비스를 제공한다.
(D) 조만간 사업 규모를 확장할 것이다.

160. 문장 위치 찾기 ★☆☆

해설 해당 문장 바로 앞의 내용 'We specifically only do business with
small companies so that we can pay attention to detail and not be
inundated with work.'에서 고객의 수를 적게 유지해 세세한 부분까지 신경 쓸
수 있는 Direct Delivery의 장점을 표현하는 내용이므로, 이 문장의 뒤에 주어진
문장이 들어가는 것이 가장 적절해 (B)가 정답이다. **정답 (B)**

표현 정리 position 위치 marked 표시된

해석 [1], [2], [3], [4] 중 다음 문장이 들어가기에 가장 적절한 곳은?

"귀하는 배송을 위해 긴 줄에 서 있는 또 다른 회원으로 취급되지 않을 것입
니다."

(A) [1]
(B) [2]
(C) [3]
(D) [4]

161. 세부사항 – KJ 로펌에 대한 내용이 아닌 것 ★☆☆

해설 본문 도입부 'your law firm is looking for a private delivery service
for your practice's confidential paperwork'에서 KJ 로펌은 비밀 서류를 배
송해 줄 사업상 소규모의 개인적인 배송 서비스를 필요로 한다는 것을 알 수 있
다. 따라서, 대규모 배송 서비스를 이용한다는 (D)는 관련이 없어 정답이다.
정답 (D)

🔍 **함정 분석** 첫 번째 문장 'Your head administrative assistant, Jessica
Klein, is a close acquaintance of mine'에서 Klein은 이 회사 직원이므로
(A)는 확인되고, 'your law firm is looking for a private delivery service for
your practice's confidential paperwork'에서 (B)도 확인된다. 또한 (C)는 본
문 세 번째 단락의 내용이 이에 해당한다고 볼 수 있어 역시 맞는 내용이다.

패러프레이징 |지문| confidential paperwork 기밀 서류 → |선택지 B|
sensitive documents 민감한 서류

|지문| that time is of the essence for legal matters 법적인 문제에 관해서는
시간이 중요하다 → |선택지 C| require timely deliveries 시기적절한 배송을 필
요로 한다

표현 정리 employer 고용주 sensitive 민감한 timely 시기 적절한, 때맞춘

해석 KJ로펌에 관해 언급된 내용이 아닌 것은?
(A) Klein의 고용주이다.
(B) 민감한 서류를 다룬다.
(C) 시기적절한 배송을 필요로 한다.
(D) 대규모 배송 서비스를 이용한다.

문제 162–164번은 다음 광고를 참조하시오.

Wilson's 사무실 창문 청소와
함께
당신의 하루를 빛내 보세요.

문지르고 가 버리는 그저 그런 청소 서비스를 참고 계시지 마세요. 대신
Wilson's를 부르세요! **164**저희 팀의 전문가들은 고층빌딩을 20년 간 청소
해 왔습니다. 최신식 기술 장비와 함께 하는 Wilson's가 닿지 못하는 창문은
없습니다. 작은 회사를 운영하고 계신가요? **164**Wilson's는 모든 크기의 창
문을 청소합니다. 사무실 전망을 먼지 층으로 덮고 있을 필요가 없습니다. 깨
끗한 창문이 오고 있어요.

만족 보장: **163**서비스를 받은 창문에 비친 자신의 모습을 볼 수 없으면, 다
시 청소하고 무료 청소 약속을 정하겠습니다.

먼지 하나 없는 창문이 바로 Wilson's의 서비스입니다. 3개월 동안 주간 청
소 서비스를 예약하시고 10% 할인을 받으세요. **162**해당 할인은 11월 30일까
지 유효합니다.

전화번호: (713) 555-2152

표현 정리 brighten 밝게 하다 put up with ~를 참다, 견디다 mediocre
그저 그런 swipe 쓱 문지르다 instead 대신 professional 전문가
skyscrapers 고층빌딩 latest 최신의 array 집단 high-tech 신기술
equipment 장비 reach 닿다 accept 받아들이다 shrouded 뒤덮인
layer 층 dust 먼지 satisfaction 만족 guarantee 보장하다
reflection 반사 spotless 흠 없는 schedule 예약하다, 스케줄을 잡다
discount 할인 valid 유효한 until ~까지

162. 세부사항 – 할인에 대한 내용 ★★☆

해설 광고 후반에서 할인은 'Offer valid until November 30.' 즉, 11월 30일까
지만 유효하다. 따라서 12월에는 이용할 수 없으므로 (B)가 정답이다. **정답 (B)**

🔍 **함정 분석** 'Schedule 3 months of weekly cleanings and get a 10%
discount.'에 따르면 3개월 동안 주간 청소를 신청하는 경우 할인이 적용되는
것을 알 수 있기 때문에, 세 번의 청소로 한정된다고 한 (A)와 연간 계약에만
해당한다는 (C)는 오답이다. 또한, 대상 사무실의 크기는 정해져 있지 않으므
로 (D) 또한 오답이다.

패러프레이징 |지문| valid until November 30 11월 30일까지만 유효하다 →
|선택지 B| It cannot be used in December 12월에는 이용할 수 없다

해석 할인에 관한 사실 내용은?
    (A) 세 번의 청소로 한정된다.
    (B) 12월에는 이용할 수 없다.
    (C) 연간 계약을 필요로 한다.
    (D) 작은 사무실에만 적용된다.

163. 동의어 ★★☆

해설 두 번째 단락 'If you can't see your reflection in any of your serviced windows, we'll clean it again and give you a free cleaning appointment.'에서 청소를 마친 창문에 얼굴이 비칠 정도로 깨끗하지 않을 경우 무료로 청소를 해 주겠다는 의미이다. 따라서 반사된 형상을 뜻하는 reflection과 가장 가까운 단어는 (A) image이다.   정답 (A)

표현 정리 reflection 반사 image 형상 sign 표시, 서명 surface 표면 thoughts 생각

해설 광고 두 번째 단락, 첫 번째 줄의 "반사"와 의미가 가장 가까운 것은?
    (A) 형상
    (B) 표시
    (C) 표면
    (D) 생각

164. 유추 – Wilson's 사무실 창문 청소에 대한 내용 ★★☆

해설 "Our team of professionals has been cleaning skyscrapers for over 20 years."라는 문장과 "Wilson's cleans windows of all sizes."라는 문장에서 알 수 있듯이, 회사는 폭넓은 경험을 가지고 서비스를 제공한다고 했으므로 정답은 (C)이다.   정답 (C)

🔍 함정 분석 (A)에 명시된 온라인 예약은 본문에서 언급된 적이 없다. 또한, (B)에 명시된 서비스 가능 시간도 언급된 바가 없으며, (D)에 나온 여러 표면 관련 서비스도 언급되지 않았다. 단지 다양한 사이즈의 표면을 닦는다고 했다. 그리고 이 회사는 창문 청소회사이므로 표면은 유리라는 것을 유추할 수 있다.

표현 정리 extensive 포괄적인, 폭넓은 be capable of ~이 가능하다 a variety of 여러 개의 surface 표면

해설 Wilson's 사무실 창문 청소에 관해 암시된 내용은?
    (A) 회사는 온라인으로 예약을 받는다.
    (B) 회사의 직원들은 하루 중 언제든지 서비스 제공이 가능하다.
    (C) 회사는 폭넓은 경험을 갖추고 있다.
    (D) 여러 표면을 닦을 수 있다.

문제 165–167번은 다음 회람을 참조하시오.

수신: Freugers 회계부
발신: Nancy Digly, IT 관리자
날짜: 2월 10일
제목: 회계부의 새로운 전화

165우리 Freugers 사에서 여러분들이 현재 사용하는 휴대 전화기가 다음 주 모두 교체될 예정임을 알려드립니다. 166(A),(C)회사는 Clearcom Telecoms 사와 전화 사용에 관해 5년 간 새로운 계약을 체결하였습니다. 이는 현재 저희가 사용하는 서비스 회사인 Green Line Communications 와의 종료를 뜻합니다.

여러분께서는 회사 휴대 전화기 안에 있는 사진, 연락처, 업무 파일과 같이 보관하고자 하는 파일을 따로 저장해 두셔야 합니다. 166(D)IT부는 해당 파일들을 회사 클라우드의 추가 저장 공간에 옮기기를 권장합니다. 새로운 회사 휴대 전화기를 수령하면, 클라우드 저장공간에서 휴대 전화로 저장된 파일들을 다운로드하실 수 있습니다. 휴대 전화기 내의 데이터를 임시적으로 클라우드에 저장하는 것은 여러분에게 할당된 총 저장 공간에 영향을 끼치

지 않을 것입니다.

167데이터 이동이나 새로운 휴대 전화기 수령과 관련하여 도움이 필요하신 경우, IT부의 내선 번호 5번을 눌러서 제게 연락 주십시오.

Nancy Digly
IT 관리자

표현 정리 accounting 회계 replace 교체하다 contract 계약 bring an end ~를 종료하다 back up 백업하다, 따로 저장하다 transfer 옮기다 extra storage space 추가 저장 공간 store 저장하다 temporarily 임시적으로, 일시적으로 affect 영향을 끼치다 allot 할당하다 assistance 지원, 도움 dial 번호를 누르다 extension 내선번호 reach ~에 닿다

165. 주제 – 회람의 목적 ★☆☆

해설 첫 번째 문장 'Be advised that your current Freugers company cell phone will be replaced next week.'에서 다음 주에 회사에서 사용하던 휴대 전화기를 교체할 것이라고 통보하고 있다. 따라서 이는 변동 사항을 직원들에게 알리려는 목적이 있으므로 정답은 (C)이다.   정답 (C)

표현 정리 data 데이터 announce 발표하다

해설 회람을 보낸 이유는 무엇인가?
    (A) 새로운 데이터 저장 시스템에 대해 설명하기 위해
    (B) 새로운 직원을 소개하기 위해
    (C) 직원들에게 변동 사항에 대해 알리기 위해
    (D) 행사 진행을 발표하기 위해

166. 세부사항 – Freugers에 대한 내용이 아닌 것 ★☆☆

해설 Freugers에 관한 문장 중 신형 전화기를 개발해 공개했다는 내용은 언급되지 않았으므로 정답은 (B)이다.   정답 (B)

🔍 함정 분석 Freugers 사는 'The company has signed a new 5-year contract with Clearcom Telecoms for all of our phone service.'에서 새로운 회사와 거래를 체결했다고 했으므로 (A)는 명시된 내용이다. 또한, 같은 문장에서 5년간의 계약에 대한 내용이 있으므로 (C) 또한 타당한 내용이다. 마지막으로, 'The IT Department suggests that you transfer the files to the extra storage space on the company cloud.'에서 클라우드 공간에 백업을 받으라는 권장 사항이 명시되어 있으므로 (D) 또한 맞는 내용이다.

표현 정리 release 발표하다, 선보이다 partner with ~와 협업하다

해설 Freugers에 관해 언급된 내용이 아닌 것은?
    (A) 곧 새로운 서비스 제공자를 갖게 될 것이다.
    (B) 최근 새 전화기를 공개했다.
    (C) Clearcom 사와 5년 동안 거래를 유지할 것이다.
    (D) 클라우드 저장 공간을 제공한다.

167. 유추 – Digly에 관한 암시 내용 ★★☆

해설 IT 관리자인 Ms. Digly는 해당 메모를 보낸 발신자로, 마지막 단락 'If you need assistance with the data transfer or need to arrange to pick up your new phone, dial extension 5 on the IT Department phone line to reach me.'에서 새로운 휴대 전화기를 수령할 때 찾게 될 사람이므로 정답은 (A)이다.   정답 (A)

🔍 함정 분석 Ms. Digly가 기존의 핸드폰을 수거한다는 부분은 명시된 바가 없어 (B)는 오답이며, dial extension 5 on the IT Department phone line to reach me에서 전화 연락을 바란다고 했기 때문에 (C) 역시 오답이다. 또한, Ms. Digly는 도움을 필요로 하는 사람을 지원하는 역할을 하기 때문에 도움이 필요하다고 한 (D) 역시 오답이다.

표현 정리 in charge of ~를 담당하다 distribution 분배 collect 수거하다 outdated 유행이 지난, 구식의 prefer ~를 선호하다

해석 Ms. Digly에 관해 암시된 내용은?
(A) 새로운 휴대 전화 배급을 담당한다.
(B) 모든 기존의 휴대 전화기를 수거할 것이다.
(C) 이메일로 연락을 받는 것을 선호한다.
(D) 데이터 이동과 관련해 도움이 필요하다.

문제 168-171번은 다음 웹페이지를 참조하시오.

http://www.officedecorators.com

| 회사 소개 | 서비스 | 갤러리 & 정보 | 가격 | 문의하기 |

**사무실의 장식을 업그레이드하고,
고객들에게 가장 멋진 (건물) 모습을 보여주세요!**

첫인상은 매우 중요하고, 특히 사업과 관련해서 고객들이 여러분의 사무실에 들어온 순간 느끼는 감정은 다시 방문할 것인지를 결정하는데 중요한 역할을 합니다. 이것이 바로 사무실을 멋지고 트렌디한 최신 스타일로 유지해야 하는 이유입니다. 저희를 믿으세요. 171 Office Decorators 디자인의 전문성이 여러분의 눈앞에서 여러분의 작업 공간을 변신시켜 드립니다.

168 Office Decorators에서는 저희가 도색, 밋밋한 벽의 장식 작업부터 여러분의 사업에 알맞은 최적의 가구를 선택하는 것까지 모두를 담당합니다. 저희는 전문 산업을 위한 고객 맞춤의 쇼핑, 스타일링을 제공하며, 여러분의 사무실이 멋지게 보일 때까지 장식을 멈추지 않습니다! 여러분의 특별한 스타일 또한 반영됩니다. 여러분의 새로운 사무실은 여러분과 여러분이 하는 일을 대표하게 될 것입니다.

169(A) 저희의 쇼룸을 방문하셔서 대여를 위해 전시된 나무 책상, 169(B) 손수 제작한 의자와 같은 대표적인 작품과 함께 169(D) 저희가 작업했던 기존의 회사들의 사진 갤러리를 확인해 보시기 바랍니다. 갤러리 운영 시간은 월요일부터 목요일, 오후 1시부터 4시까지입니다.

170 Office Decorators는 인테리어 디자이너 Pierre Niels가 설립했습니다. Pierre와 특별 상담을 예약하시려면 555-2164로 전화 주십시오. Pierre와의 예약은 5%의 보증금을 필요로 한다는 점을 알려드립니다. 다른 모든 상담은 무료로 진행됩니다.

표현 정리 office decor 사무실 장식 first impression 첫인상 when it comes to ~에 관해서라면 on-trend 트렌디한, 유행을 따르는 adorn 장식하다 bare walls 빈 벽, 밋밋한 벽 represent 대표하다 showroom 쇼룸 signature piece 대표적인 작품 wooden 나무로 만들어진 handcrafted 수제의 on display 전시된 rent 대여 exclusive 특별한 consultation 상담 deposit 보증금

168. 주제 – 웹페이지의 목적 ★★☆
해설 해당 웹페이지는 광고를 위해 작성되었으며, 두 번째 단락 'At Office Decorators, we do it all, from painting and adorning bare walls to selecting the best furniture appropriate for the kind of work you do.'에서 회사가 제공하는 서비스를 상세하게 설명하고 있으므로 (B)가 정답이다.
정답 (B)

🔍 함정 분석 (A)에서 언급된 새로운 위치 소개나 (C)에서 언급된 고객의 후기 등은 명시된 바가 없으며, 새로운 인테리어 담당자에 대해 언급한 (D) 또한 명시된 적이 없으므로 세 선택지 모두 오답이다.

표현 정리 recruit 모집하다

해석 웹페이지의 목적은 무엇인가?
(A) 새로운 위치를 소개하기 위해
(B) 회사의 서비스를 상세히 설명하기 위해
(C) 고객의 후기를 설명하기 위해
(D) 새로운 인테리어 담당자를 모집하기 위해

169. 세부사항 – Office Decorators에 대한 내용이 아닌 것 ★★☆
해설 회사의 서비스와 관련하여 건축가가 포함되어 있다는 말은 언급되지 않았으므로 (C)가 정답이다.
정답 (C)

🔍 함정 분석 'Stop by our showroom to see signature pieces'에서 사무실에 들러 전시된 가구를 볼 수 있다는 점을 알 수 있고, 'including wooden desks and handcrafted chairs'에서 Office Decorators는 수제품 가구를 가지고 있고, 'extensive photo gallery of companies we have worked with in the past'에서 지난 작업에 관한 사진을 통해 샘플을 확인할 수 있으므로 (A), (B), (D)는 모두 사실 내용들이다.

패러프레이징 |지문| our showroom to see signature pieces 대표적인 제품들을 보기 위한 전시장 → |선택지 A| have special furniture on view 특별한 가구를 전시해 놓았다
|지문| handcrafted chairs 수공예 의자 → |선택지 B| handmade furniture 손으로 만든 가구
|지문| photo gallery ~ we have worked with in the past 과거에 작업했던 것에 관한 사진 → |선택지 D| examples of past work 지난 작업의 샘플

표현 정리 on view 전시된 architect 건축가

해석 Office Decorators에 관해 언급되지 않은 것은?
(A) 특별한 가구를 볼 수 있게 해 놓았다.
(B) 수제품인 가구를 가지고 있다.
(C) 직원 중 건축가가 있다.
(D) 지난 작업의 샘플이 있다.

170. 세부사항 – Mr. Niels에 관한 내용 ★★☆
해설 마지막 단락 'Office Decorators was started by interior designer Pierre Niels.'에서 Niels 씨가 회사를 설립했음을 알 수 있으므로 정답은 (D)이다.
정답 (D)

🔍 함정 분석 Neils 씨가 디자이너라는 사실은 마지막 단락 'Office Decorators was started by interior designer Pierre Niels.'에서 확인이 되지만, 의자를 직접 디자인했다는 언급은 찾아볼 수 없다. 또한, (B)에서 언급된 상담 가능 시간은 명시된 적이 없으며, 'Please be advised that appointments with Pierre require a 5% deposit.'에 따르면 다른 상담과는 별개로 Niels 씨와의 상담은 초기 상담 비용이 발생한다는 것을 알 수 있으므로 (A), (B), (C)는 모두 오답이다.

패러프레이징 |지문| Office Decorators was started by interior designer Pierre Niels Office Decorators는 인테리어 디자이너 Pierre Niels 씨에 의해 시작되었다 → |선택지 D| He is the founder of the company 그는 회사의 설립자이다

표현 정리 design 디자인하다, 설계하다 on display 전시된 initial 초기의 founder 설립자, 창립자

해석 Mr. Niels에 관해 언급된 것은?
(A) 전시된 의자를 디자인했다.
(B) 주로 오후에 상담이 가능하다.
(C) 초기 상담은 무료로 제공한다.
(D) 회사 설립자이다.

171. 문장 위치 찾기 ★★☆
해설 제공된 문장 'Office Decorator's design expertise will transform your workspace right before your eyes.'는 포괄적인 내용으로, 회사의 전문성을 부각시키는 내용이므로 도입부에 들어가는 것이 적절하다.
정답 (A)

🔍 **함정 분석** 두 번째 단락은 첫 번째 단락과는 달리 세부적인 서비스 내용을 다루고 있기 때문에 포괄적인 내용의 문장이 들어가기에 적합하지 않다. 세 번째 단락은 회사 자체의 사무실 방문을 주제로 하고 있기 때문에 문장을 사용할 수 없으며, 마지막 단락은 설립자에 대한 설명과 설립자가 진행하는 상담을 주제로 하므로 마찬가지로 문장이 추가되기에 적절하지 않다.

표현 정리 expertise 전문성 transform 변신시키다, 변화시키다 workspace 업무 공간 right before 바로 앞에서

해석 [1], [2], [3], [4] 중 다음 문장이 들어가기에 가장 적절한 곳은?

"Office Decorators 디자인의 전문성이 여러분의 눈앞에서 여러분의 작업 공간을 변신시켜 드립니다."
(A) [1]
(B) [2]
(C) [3]
(D) [4]

문제 172-175번은 다음 온라인 채팅을 참조하시오.

Linda Ambers	저는 2시간 후에 파리 사무실과 전화 통화가 있어서 일찍 토론토에 와 있어요. 172 미식가들을 대상으로 한 음식을 마케팅하려고 하는 중요한 회사와 계약을 체결하려고 합니다. 그런데 방금 컨퍼런스 룸 프로젝터를 테스트한 적이 없다는 걸 깨달았어요. 저와 테스트 전화를 할 사람이 있나요?　오전 6시 29분
Barbara Summers	175저는 베를린 사무실에서 초과근무 중입니다. 저희 컨퍼런스 룸에 갈 테니 저에게 영상으로 전화를 해 볼 수 있을 거예요. 제가 그쪽 프로젝터의 영상을 볼 수 있는지 확인할게요.　오전 6시 30분
Linda Ambers	정말 좋아요. 제가 파리로 거는 전화가 3자 통화가 될 가능성이 있습니다. 173혹시 다른 분 또 있나요?　오전 6시 32분
Paula Rubio	안녕하세요, Linda. 저는 멕시코 사무실의 Paula입니다. 제가 도와드릴 수 있어요.　오전 6시 34분
Linda Ambers	안녕하세요, Paula. 3자 통화를 위해 준비를 할 수 있게 잠깐만 시간을 주세요.　오전 6시 36분
Paula Rubio	물론이죠. 174준비되면 사무실로 전화 주세요.　오전 6시 37분
Linda Ambers	Barbara, Paula. 그쪽에서 제 프레젠테이션이 보이나요?　오전 6시 39분
Barbara Summers	베를린에서는 깨끗하게 보입니다. 프로젝터가 괜찮은 것 같아요.　오전 6시 41분
Paula Rubio	아주 깔끔해요. 파리 회의는 잘 될 것 같아요. 행운을 빌어요!　오전 6시 43분

표현 정리 in two hours 2시간 후에 land a contract 계약을 체결하다 gourmet 미식가, 식도락가 projector 프로젝터 overtime 근무시간 외 three-way call 3자 통화 jump in 뛰어들다 give someone a hand 도움을 주다 crisp 깔끔한

172. 유추 – Ms. Ambers가 일하는 분야 ★☆☆
해설 첫 번째 단락에서 Ambers 씨는 'We are trying to land a contract with a major player to market its gourmet food products.'와 같이 고객 회사와 계약을 체결하고, 그 회사 제품의 마케팅을 해 주는 사람임을 짐작할 수 있다. 또한, 토론토, 베를린, 멕시코 등 여러 국가에서 일하는 것으로 보아 국제 시장의 마케팅을 담당하고 있을 가능성이 높으므로 정답은 (B)이다. **정답 (B)**

표현 정리 field 분야 film 영화 production 제작 luxury 호화로운

해석 Ms. Ambers가 근무하는 분야는?

(A) 영화 제작
(B) 국제 마케팅
(C) 호화 여행
(D) 기술 디자인

173. 의도 파악하기 ★★☆
해설 베를린에 있는 Barbara가 테스트를 도와준다고 한 상황에서, Ms. Ambers는 'My call to Paris might end up being a three-way call.'이라고 말하면서 3자 통화가 될 수도 있다고 했다. 따라서 3자 통화는 각각 다른 나라에서 이루어질 가능성이 높다는 것을 알려준다. 이에 다른 나라 사무실의 도움을 받아야 한다는 의미로 한 얘기이므로 다수의 국가에서 작동하는지를 확인하는 절차라고 볼 수 있다. **정답 (D)**

🔍 **함정 분석** 현재의 프로젝터 테스트에 참여할 사무실을 찾고 있다고 했으므로 이후에 있을 회의에 참석할 사무실을 찾는 (A)는 오답이다. 또한, 테스트를 꼭 하고 싶어하는 마음을 피력하고 있으므로 (B) 또한 답이 될 수 없다. 그리고 파리와는 2시간 후에 전화 회의가 있으므로 (C)는 오답이다.

표현 정리 jump in 뛰어들다, 참여하다 multiple 다수의

해석 Ms. Ambers가 오전 6시 32분에 보낸 "혹시 다른 분 또 있나요?"의 의미로 가장 적절한 것은?
(A) 이후에 있을 회의에 다른 사무실을 초대하고 있다.
(B) 테스트를 하지 않고도 프로젝터가 잘 작동하기를 바라고 있다.
(C) 파리에 일찍 전화해 프로젝터를 점검하고 싶어한다.
(D) 프로젝터가 여러 나라에서 작동하는지를 확인하고자 한다.

174. 세부사항 – Ms. Rubio가 Ms. Ambers를 위해 하는 것 ★☆☆
해설 Ms. Rubio가 'Call my office when you're ready.'라고 한 부분은 Ms. Ambers가 'Give me a minute to set everything up for a three-way call.'이라고 한 말에 대한 대답으로, 준비가 되면 전화해 달라는 의미로 답변한 것이다. 따라서, 궁극적으로는 장비가 잘 작동하는지를 확인하기 위한 것이므로 (A)가 정답이다. **정답 (A)**

패러프레이징 |지문| set everything up for a three-way call 삼자 통화를 위해 모든 준비를 하다 → |선택지 A| confirms that some equipment is working 장비가 작동하는지 확인하다

표현 정리 confirm 확인하다, 확정하다 equipment 도구, 장비 assist 지원하다 personal 개인적인

해석 Ms. Rubio가 Ms. Ambers를 위해 하는 것은?
(A) 장비가 작동하는지 확인한다.
(B) 회의하는데 도움을 주겠다고 제안한다.
(C) 영상을 보내달라고 요청한다.
(D) 개인적인 전화로 연락한다.

175. 유추 – Ms. Summers에 대한 내용 ★☆☆
해설 Ms. Summers가 'I'm still here in the Berlin office working overtime.'에서 초과 근무를 하고 있다고 말했는데, 이는 결국 사무실이 문을 닫은 뒤에도 남아 일을 하고 있다는 것을 의미하므로 정답은 (C)이다. **정답 (C)**

패러프레이징 |지문| here in the Berlin office working overtime 야근을 하느라 Berlin 사무실에 있다 → |선택지 C| stayed at the office after closing 업무가 끝난 이후에도 사무실에 남아있다

표현 정리 fix 고정하다, 고치다 closing 닫힘 travel for business 출장을 가다

해석 Ms. Summers에 관해 암시된 내용은?
(A) 프로젝터를 전에 고쳐본 경험이 있다.
(B) 파리 통화에 나중에 참여할 것이다.
(C) 사무실이 닫힌 후 남아있었다.

(D) 출장 중이다.

사무실 카펫을 오늘 교체하세요!

Fantastic Flooring은 비교할 수 없는 9월 특가를 진행하고 있습니다. 기존의 카펫을 수거하고 원래 가격의 반값에 해당하는 가격에 새로운 카펫으로 교체해 드립니다. **176모두 하루 안에 가능합니다!** 그리고 설치 비용도 따로 들어가지 않습니다. 대단하죠!

나무나 타일 바닥 또한 같은 특가로 제거 가능하지만 **178작업 비용 500달러가** 청구되며, 추가로 하루 더 작업 일이 필요합니다.

기본 카펫 제거 *특가*	0.00달러
베이지 카펫	350달러/방
갈색 카펫	450달러/방
178네이비 카펫	**500달러/방**

위에 명시된 색상들만 9월 할인 이벤트에 해당됩니다! 무료 카펫 제거 서비스 가격은 명시된 대로입니다. 해당 특가에 참여하고 싶으나 다른 색상의 카펫을 설치하고 싶으시다면, **177새 카펫 가격에서 30퍼센트 할인된 가격과 무료 제거 서비스를 제공해** 드릴 수 있습니다.

설치 기사와 예약을 하고 싶으시다면 사이트 www.FantasticFlooring.com을 방문해 주세요. 특가는 9월 30일날 종료되지만, 모든 주문은 배송과 설치 기간 때문에 9월 20일까지 완료되어야 합니다.

표현 정리 replace 교체하다 unbeatable 비교할 수 없는 pull up 뜯어내다 existing 기존의 half the usual price 기존 가격의 반값 installation fee 설치 비용

수신: Bernard Derk 〈customerservice@fantasticflooring.com〉
발신: Janice Weggin 〈jweggin@polytech.com〉
제목: 바닥재 약속 다시 잡기
일자: 9월 2일

안녕하세요, Bernard.

2주 전 제 원룸 사무실의 바닥을 새로 하고자 약속을 잡기 위해 통화한 적이 있습니다. 그런데, 방금 9월 가격에 관한 전단지를 보았고, 다른 직원에게서 저도 제가 한 주문에 특가를 적용 받을 수 있다는 얘기를 들었습니다.

177원래 타일 바닥 제거는 내일로 예정하고 있었고, 검은 카펫이 9월 4일 특가로 설치되는 걸로 되어 있었습니다. 178샘플을 본 뒤 저는 카펫의 색상을 네이비로 바꾸고 싶어졌습니다. 179그리고 타일 제거도 9월 6일로 재예약을 진행하고, 그 다음날 카펫 설치를 하면 좋겠습니다. **180이게 가능한지 알려** 주시고, 특가를 바탕으로 새로운 송장을 이메일로 보내주세요.

감사합니다.

Janice Weggin

표현 정리 flooring 바닥재 redone 다시 한 representative 직원 reschedule (예약) 날짜를 변경하다 invoice 송장

176. 세부사항 – 카펫 설치에 대한 내용 ★☆☆
해설 첫 번째 단락의 'all on the same day!'에서 하루 안에 모든 작업이 가능하다는 점을 알 수 있으므로 (C)가 정답이다. **정답 (C)**

🔍**함정 분석** 광고 마지막 단락 'The promotion ends on September 30, but orders must be made by September 20 due to delivery and installation time.'에서 할인 행사가 9월 30일에 끝나기 때문에 할인을 원하다면 9월 20일까지 주문해야 한다는 것일 뿐, 모든 주문이 10일 전에 이루어져야

하는 것은 아니므로 (A)는 오답이다. 그리고 'Please note wooden or tile flooring can be removed with the same promotion'에서 나무나 타일 바닥도 같은 가격으로 제거가 가능하다고 했으므로 (B)도 오답이다.

패러프레이징 |지문| all on the same day 하루 안에 모두 하다 → |선택지 C| be completed in a single day 하루 안에 완료되다

표현 정리 in advance 미리 single day 하루에 labor 작업량, 노동력

해설 광고에 의하면, 카펫 설치와 관련하여 맞는 내용은?
(A) 10일 전 미리 주문해야 한다.
(B) 나무 바닥에는 작업할 수 없다.
(C) 하루 안에 작업이 완료될 수 있다.
(D) 두 명의 설치 기사의 노동력을 요구한다.

177. 연계 문제 – Ms. Weggin에 대한 내용 ★☆☆
해설 두 번째 지문인 이메일 'Originally, I was scheduled to have my tile floor removed tomorrow and black carpet installed on September 4 at the promotional price.'에서 9월 특가를 제공받았음을 알 수 있다. 광고에서 'we can offer you free removal plus a 30% discount on the new carpet price.'에서 광고에 언급된 색이 아닌 카펫의 경우 30%의 할인을 해 준다고 했으므로 정답은 (A)가 된다. **정답 (A)**

🔍**함정 분석** 선택지 (A)를 보면 시제가 과거완료형이므로, 카펫의 색을 navy로 바꾸기 전의 상황을 말하고 있는 것을 알 수 있다.

표현 정리 out of town 마을에 없는

해설 Ms. Weggin에 관해 알 수 있는 것은?
(A) 원래 30%의 할인을 제공받았다.
(B) 7월에 카펫 설치를 예약했다.
(C) 며칠 간 지역을 떠나 있을 것이다.
(D) Mr. Derk에게 비용을 지불했다.

178. 연계 문제 – Ms. Weggin이 지불할 가격 ★☆☆
해설 Ms. Weggin은 이메일에서 타일 바닥을 제거하고, 'I have decided I would like to change the carpet's color to navy.'에서 원래 주문한 블랙 카펫을 네이비 카펫으로 바꿔 주문하고 싶다고 했다. 따라서 타일 바닥 제거하는데 필요한 노동 비용 500달러와 네이비 색상의 카펫을 구매하는데 청구되는 500달러를 합해 총 1,000 달러를 지불해야 함을 알 수 있으므로 정답은 (D)이다. **정답 (D)**

해설 Ms. Weggin이 지불할 가격으로 가장 알맞은 것은?
(A) 450달러
(B) 500달러
(C) 950달러
(D) 1,000달러

179. 세부사항 – Ms. Weggin이 원하는 카펫 설치 날짜 ★★☆
해설 이메일 마지막 단락 'I would also like to reschedule the tile removal for September 6 and the carpet installation for the following day.'에서 타일 제거 작업은 9월 6일, 그리고 카펫 설치는 그 다음 날로 일정을 조정하고 싶다고 했으므로 카펫 설치하는 날은 9월 7일이 돼서 정답은 (D)이다. **정답 (D)**

🔍**함정 분석** 이메일 마지막 단락 'Originally, I was scheduled to have my tile floor removed tomorrow and black carpet installed on September 4 at the promotional price.'에서 9월 4일은 이미 주문했던 블랙 카펫을 설치하기로 예정된 날이었으므로 (B)를 답으로 고르지 않도록 해야 한다.

해설 Ms. Weggin이 카펫 설치를 원하는 날짜는 언제인가?
(A) 9월 3일

(B) 9월 4일

(C) 9월 6일

(D) 9월 7일

180. 세부사항 – Ms. Weggin이 Mr. Derk에게 요청한 것 ★☆☆

해설 이메일 마지막 단락 'Please let me know if this will work and e-mail me an updated invoice with the promotional pricing.'에서 변경된 날짜에 작업이 가능한지를 알려달라고 하는 것을 알 수 있으며, 또한 특가 가격을 반영한 새로운 송장을 요청하는 것을 알 수 있다. 따라서 새로운 청구서를 요청한다는 (B)가 정답이다. **정답** (B)

패러프레이징 | 지문 e-mail me an updated invoice 새로운 송장을 보내주세요 → **선택지 B|** send her a new bill 새로운 청구서를 보내다

표현 정리 supervise 감독하다 bill 청구서 refund 환불하다

해설 Ms. Weggin이 Mr. Derk에게 요청한 것은 무엇인가?

(A) 설치 감독

(B) 새로운 청구서 송부

(C) 지불 내역 환불

(D) 카펫 샘플 제공

문제 181~185번은 다음 발표와 이메일을 참조하시오.

우수 직원상

182Vexus 사는 매년 진행되는 우수 직원상을 위한 후보를 찾고 있습니다. 우수 직원상은 Vexus 사의 성공에 훌륭한 기여를 한 직원을 인정하는 상입니다.

후보들은:

– 185Vexus 사에서 최소 2년간 정직원으로 근무했어야 합니다.

– 본인의 일상 업무와 책임 사항 이상의 성과를 보였어야 합니다.

– 183이전에 우수 직원상을 받지 않았어야 합니다.

후보들은 다음 사항들에 의해 평가됩니다.:

– 회사의 목표에 대한 이해와 실천

– 직장에서의 혁신

– 리더로서의 자질

– 동료들과의 관계

181직원을 추천하기 위해서는, 직원의 이름, 사원번호와 함께 해당 직원이 우수 직원상을 받아야 하는 이유를 설명하는 한 장짜리 설명서를 보내주십시오. 후보 추천은 HR 사무실로 제출하거나 Benita Kito에게 팩스나 이메일로 제출하시면 됩니다(555-8930 / bkito@vexus.com).

후보 추천은 4월 15일까지 전달되어야 합니다. 수상자는 6월에 발표될 예정이며, 7월 연례 회사 야유회에서 시상식이 열립니다.

표현 정리 excellence 우수 award 상 seek 찾다 nomination 후보 추천 annual 연례 acknowledge 인정하다 exceptional 뛰어난, 훌륭한 contributions 기여 nominee 후보 full-time employee 정직원 performance 성과 responsibility 책임감 demonstrate 보이다 evaluate 평가하다 implementation 실행 innovation 혁신 coworker 동료 nominate 추천하다 employee ID 직원 신분증 narrative 묘사 statement 성명서, 진술서 deserve ~를 받아 마땅하다, ~할 자격이 있다

수신: Benita Kito 〈benita.kito@vexus.com〉

발신: Robert Wilson 〈robert.wilson@vexus.com〉

제목: 추천

첨부파일: nomination_wells

Benita 님께,

저는 우수 직원상에 Jason Wells(사원번호 485003)를 추천하고자 이메일을 씁니다. 185Jason은 저희 부서에서 3년간 기술자로 근무해 왔습니다. 저나 다른 상사가 요청하지 않더라도 Jason은 솔선하여 효율성과 안전을 극대화하기 위해 시험 연구소를 재조직하였습니다. 사실, 184그의 제안을 이행한 이후 사고는 35퍼센트 감소하였으며, 고장은 85퍼센트 감소하였습니다. Jason은 그의 동료들과 상사들에게 매우 좋은 평을 받고 있습니다. 그가 이대로 일을 계속 한다면, 몇 년 안에 매니저 자리로 승진한다고 해도 이상할 것이 없을 것입니다. 그의 추천을 위한 진술서를 첨부합니다. 질문이 있으시면 이 이메일이나 제 내선번호인 3456으로 연락 주십시오.

Robert Wilson

팀장

제품 시험부

표현 정리 technician 기술자 department 부서 take the initiative to ~에 솔선수범하다 reorganize 재조직[재편성]하다 lab 연구소 maximize 극대화하다 efficiency 효율성 safety 안전 implement 도입하다 reduce 감소하다 breakage 고장 path 길 promote 승진하다 managerial 관리직

181. 세부사항 – 동료를 수상자로 추천하는 방법 ★☆☆

해설 첫 번째 지문 'To nominate an individual, please send that person's name, employee ID number, and a one-page narrative statement describing why the nominee deserves an Employee Excellence Award.'에서 추천을 위해서는 직원의 이름, 사원 번호 , 추천 이유에 대한 진술서가 필요하다고 했으므로 정답은 (D)가 된다. **정답** (D)

🔍**함정 분석** 'Nominations can be submitted to the HR office or faxed / e-mailed to Benita Kito (555-8930 / bkito@vexus.com).'에서 후보 추천서는 인사부로 제출하거나 Benita Kito에게 팩스나 이메일로 보내라고 했다. 이는 이미 작성된 추천서를 보내는 방법일 뿐, 온라인 상으로 추천서를 작성하는 것이 아니므로 (A)와 (B)는 오답임을 알 수 있다.

패러프레이징 | 지문 please send that person's name, employee ID number, and a one-page narrative statement 직원의 이름, 사번, 추천 이유에 대한 한 장짜리 진술서를 보내라 → **선택지 D|** submit a written statement 글로 쓴 진술서를 제출하라

표현 정리 colleague 동료 complete 완료하다 supervisor 상사 submit 제출하다

해설 동료를 수상자로 추천하기 위해서는 어떻게 해야 하는가?

(A) HR의 누군가와 회의를 함으로써

(B) 온라인 신청서를 제출함으로써

(C) 해당 직원의 상사와 얘기함으로써

(D) 글로 쓴 진술서를 제출함으로써

182. 세부사항 – 우수 직원상에 대한 내용 ★★☆

해설 첫 번째 지문 첫 번째 단락 'The Vexus Corporation is currently seeking nominations for our annual Employee Excellence Awards.'에서 매년 진행되는 우수 직원상을 위한 후보를 찾고 있다고 한 부분에서 연례 행사임을 알 수 있으므로 정답은 (A)이다. **정답** (A)

패러프레이징 |지문| our annual event ~ 연례 행사 → |선택지 A| the event once a year 일년에 한번 행사

표현 정리 once a year 한 해에 한 번 autumn 가을

해석 우수 직원상에 대해 언급된 내용은?
(A) 1년에 한 번 수여된다.
(B) 인사과의 직원에게 수여된다.
(C) 시상식 만찬에서 수여된다.
(D) 가을에 수여된다.

183. 세부사항 – 후보들에게 요구되지 않은 것 ★★☆
해설 첫 번째 단락 Nominees 항목 세 번째 'cannot have received a previous Employee Excellence Award'에서 이 상의 수상 경력이 없어야 한다. 이로써, 수상 실적이 없어야 대상자로 선정될 수 있으므로 (D)가 정답이 된다.
정답 (D)

패러프레이징 |지문| full-time employees of the Vexus Corporation with at least 2 years Vexus 사에서 적어도 2년간 일한 정직원 → |선택지 C| more than 2 years of working at Vexus 최소 2년간 Vexus 사에서 일한 경력
|지문| excellent performance above their normal duties and responsibilities 본인의 일상 업무와 책임사항 이상의 성과 → |선택지 B| exceptional job performance 뛰어난 업무 성과

해석 후보들에게 요구되지 않은 것은 무엇인가?
(A) 동료의 추천
(B) 뛰어난 업무 성과
(C) 최소 2년간의 Vexus 사에서 일한 경력
(D) 수상 경력

184. 동의어 ★☆☆
해설 두 번째 지문인 Jason의 추천 이메일 'In fact, after implementing his suggested changes, accidents have been reduced by 35% and breakage by 85%.'에서 그가 제안한 방법을 실행한 후에 사고와 고장이 모두 감소했다고 한 내용인데, 여기서 implementing과 의미가 가장 가까운 것은 (A) performing이라고 할 수 있다.
정답 (A)

표현 정리 perform 실시하다 evaluate 평가하다 notice 알아차리다 confuse 혼동하다

해석 이메일에서 네 번째 줄의 "실행한"과 의미가 가장 가까운 것은?
(A) 실시한
(B) 평가한
(C) 알아차린
(D) 혼동시키는

185. 연계 문제 – Mr. Wells에 대해 알 수 있는 것 ★★☆
해설 두 번째 지문 'Jason has worked as a technician in my department for three years.'에서 확인할 수 있듯이, Mr. Wilson이 추천하는 직원 Jason

은 해당 부서에서 3년간 근무했음을 알 수 있는데, 후보자 선정의 조건 중 'must be full-time employees of the Vexus Corporation with at least 2 years at the company' 즉, 정직원으로 근무하고 있어야 한다는 조건을 충족시키고 있으므로 Jason은 정직원임을 알 수 있어 정답은 (C)이다.
정답 (C)

표현 정리 multitasking 멀티태스킹, 한 번에 여러 가지 일을 하는 것

해석 Mr. Wells에 관해 알 수 있는 내용은?
(A) 관리직을 위해 연수를 받고 있다.
(B) 멀티태스킹을 잘 한다.
(C) Vexus에서 정직원으로 근무한다.
(D) Mr. Wilson에 의해 고용되었다.

문제 186–190번은 다음 회람, 일정표, 그리고 이메일을 참조하시오.

회람

수신: A팀, B팀
발신: Hayley Narco, 매니저
일자: 3월 2일

186(D),189직원들의 주말 여행이 3월 23일에서 30일로 변경되었음을 알립니다. 이는 계절에 맞지 않게 추워진 날씨 때문입니다.

여행 일정은 그대로이며, 모두 오전 9시까지 버스에 탑승해야 합니다. 버스가 기다리고 있을 것이며, 오전 9시 5분에 이름을 호명할 것입니다. 시간 관리가 중요하므로, 모두 늦지 않도록 주의해 주십시오. **188늦어질 것 같으면, 저에게 메시지를 보내 주세요.**

Hayley

표현 정리 unseasonably 계절에 맞지 않게, 때 아니게 itinerary 일정 managing time 시간 관리

회의 안건: 출발일
일자: 3월 30일, 금요일 *변경 사항 주의 요망*
출발 시각: 오전 9시
참가자: **186(A)**Directco A팀과 B팀

체크인	오전 8시 30분 – 9시	**189집합 장소: 선적 부두 #8** **187Hayley와 체크인해 주십시오**
버스 출석 점검	오전 9시 5분	**186(C)**모두 지정된 버스에 앉아 주십시오.
화장실 휴식	오전 11시 15분	15분간 휴식
점심식사	오후 1시	팀 내 점심식사
도착	오후 3시 45분	Yosemite 공원에 도착합니다. 숙소 안내에 주의해 주세요.
저녁식사	오후 6시 15분	팀 내 저녁식사 저녁 시간 동안 다음 날 일정을 확인합니다.

모든 문의 사항은 Hayley Narco에게 전달해 주십시오: hnarco@directco.com

표현 정리 dock 부두 roll call 출석 확인 assigned 지정된 assignment 배정

표현 정리 reschedule 날짜가 변경되다 originally 원래 reserve 예약하다 soccer match 축구 게임 attend 참가하다 drop someone off 차로 태워 어딘가에 내려주다 cutoff 마감 heads-up 미리 알림 in case ~의 경우에 대비해

---

186. 세부사항 – 주말 여행에 대한 내용이 아닌 것 ★★☆

해설 회사 행사와 관련된 내용으로, 해당 행사의 음식과 숙소 비용을 누가 지불할 것인지에 대한 내용은 찾아볼 수 없으므로 (B)가 정답이다. **정답 (B)**

🔍**함정 분석** 두 번째 지문 'Directco Teams A and B'라는 표현에서 이 행사는 두 팀을 위한 행사임을 알 수 있으므로 (A)는 맞고, 이어서 'Please be seated on your assigned bus.'에서 교통 수단을 마련했으므로 (C)도 맞는 내용이다. 첫 번째 지문인 회람 "Please note the weekend trip for employees of Directco Deliveries has been moved from March 23 to March 30.'에서 날짜가 변경되었으므로 (D)도 역시 맞는 내용이다.

패러프레이징 |지문| your assigned bus 당신의 지정된 버스 → |선택지 C| arranged transportation 준비된 교통수단
|지문| have been moved from March 23 to March 30 3월 23일에서 30일로 변경되다 → |선택지 D| The departure date has been modified 출발일이 변경되었다

표현 정리 organize 조직하다, 준비하다 lodging 숙소

해석 회람에서, 주말 여행에 관해 언급된 내용이 아닌 것은?
(A) 두 팀을 위해 조직되었다.
(B) Directco가 음식과 숙소 비용을 지불한다.
(C) Directco가 직원들을 위한 교통을 준비하였다.
(D) 출발일이 변경되었다.

---

187. 유추 – Ms. Narco에 대한 내용 ★★☆

해설 Ms. Narco는 해당 행사를 준비한 인물로, 두 번째 지문인 일정표에서 체크인 시간은 8시 30분으로 공지되어 있다. 또한, '"Please check in with Hayley,"'에서 Hayley Narco에게 체크인하라는 언급이 있는 것으로 보아 Ms. Narco는 8시 반부터 모임 장소에 있을 것이라는 것을 알 수 있다. **정답 (D)**

🔍**함정 분석** 마케팅부에서 근무하는 사람은 Susie Vines로, 이메일의 서명에서 확인할 수 있으므로 (A)는 오답이다. Yosemite에 가 본 경험에 대한 설명이 없으므로 (B)는 알 수 없으며, 해당 여행을 준비하고 체크인 시점부터 자리에 있는 Narco 씨가 여행에 가지 않는다는 것을 본문 내용으로는 알 수 없으므로 (C)도 오답이다.

표현 정리 arrive by ~시까지 도착하다

해석 Ms. Narco에 관해 암시된 내용은?
(A) 그녀는 마케팅부에서 근무한다.
(B) 그녀는 Yosemite에 가 본 적이 있다.
(C) 그녀는 여행을 가지 않을 것이다.
(D) 그녀는 8시 30분까지 도착할 것이다.

---

188. 연계 문제 – 이메일의 목적 ★★★

해설 Ms. Vines는 세 번째 지문인 이메일을 보낸 사람이다. 이메일 하단 'but I want to give you a heads-up just in case I arrive a few minutes late'에서 Vines 씨가 Narco 씨에게 약속 시간에 늦을 수도 있다는 점을 미리 알리기 위해 이메일을 작성했다는 것을 알 수 있는데, 첫 번째 지문인 회람 'if you know you will be late, please send me a message.'에 대한 답변으로 이메일을 보냈음을 알 수 있으므로 정답은 (A)가 된다. **정답 (A)**

표현 정리 respond 답변하다 cancel 취소하다

해석 Ms. Vines의 이메일의 목적은 무엇인가?
(A) 요청에 답변하기 위해
(B) 다른 여행에 참가하는 것을 요청하기
(C) 공지 사항을 알리기 위해
(D) 그녀의 여행 계획을 취소하기 위해

---

189. 연계 문제 – Ms. Vines가 3월 30일에 할 일 ★☆☆

해설 먼저 첫 번째 지문 회람에서 주말 여행이 3월 23일에서 30일로 변경되었음을 알 수 있다. 그리고 이메일 후반 'I believe there is time for me to drive from the stadium to our departure spot before the 9:00 A.M.'에서 출발 지점에 시간에 맞춰 갈 것이라고 했는데, 두 번째 지문인 일정표에 보면, 출발 지점은 'Meeting Point: Delivery Dock #8'이므로 그녀는 선적 부두 #8로 갈 것임을 알 수 있어 정답은 (C)가 된다. **정답 (C)**

표현 정리 attend 참가하다 board 탈것에 타다

해석 Vines 씨는 3월 30일에 무슨 일을 할 예정이라고 하는가?
(A) 축구 경기에 참가한다.
(B) 경기장에서 버스를 탄다.
(C) 선적 부두 #8로 간다.
(D) 여행 중 A팀을 이끈다.

---

190. 동의어 ★★☆

해설 이메일 'I believe there is time for me to drive from the stadium to our departure spot before the 9:00 A.M. cutoff'에서 cutoff는 '마감, 기한' 등의 뜻으로, 출발을 위한 모임 시간에 정확히 맞춰 도착할 것이라는 뜻임을 유추해 볼 수 있어 이와 가장 유사한 단어는 (B) deadline이다. **정답 (B)**

해석 이메일에서 두 번째 단락, 두 번째 줄의 "마감"과 의미가 가장 가까운 것은?
(A) 축소, 감소
(B) 마감 기한
(C) 제약
(D) 출발

문제 191-195번은 다음 편지, 회람, 그리고 가이드라인을 참조하시오.

저희는 적어도 10년간 IT 분야에서 근무한 소프트웨어 엔지니어를 필요로 합니다. 후보들은 모든 주요 컴퓨터 언어에 능통해야 하며, IT 문제를 진단하는 능력도 있어야 합니다.

학업과 관련하여, 저희는 후보자가 어느 학교를 나왔는가에 대해서는 크게 개의치 않습니다. 위의 조건에 부합하는 후보들의 이력서를 송부해 주십시오. 최대한 빨리 면접을 하고자 합니다.

Teddy Gershwin

표현 정리 **look for** ~를 찾다 **talent** 인재 **list** 목록을 만들다 **job opening** 일자리 **temporary** 일시적인 **agency** 대리인 **candidates** 후보 **on hand** 이미 가지고 있는 **counterpart** 상대자, 담당자 **recommend** 추천하다 **at least** 최소한 **proficient** 능숙한 **competent** 유능한 **school experience** 학력 **diagnose** 진단하다 **fit** ~에 들어맞다

회람

발신: Julie Moore, **193채용 담당자**
수신: Solid Staffing 인재 전체
일자: 10월 14일
RE: 소프트웨어 엔지니어 구인

Halifax 주식회사는 경험이 많은 소프트웨어 엔지니어를 고용하고자 하고 있습니다. 본인이 10년 이상의 경력을 가졌다면, 첨부한 해당 지원 절차를 위한 안내를 읽어보시고 면접에 관심이 있으시면 제게 알려주십시오.

194지원 준비를 마쳤다면, Ben Turner에게 연락을 하십시오. 그가 여러분과 고객과의 연결 담당자가 될 것입니다. 행운을 빌어요!

표현 정리 **seasoned** 노련한 **attached** 첨부된 **application process** 지원 과정 **point of connection** 연결 담당자

Solid Staffing

취업 지원 안내:
업데이트됨: 10월 14일

– 지난 경력을 모두 나열하는 이력서를 준비하세요. 귀하의 기술, 학력, 성과 등을 포함해야 합니다. **194이 서류를 저희에게 직접 제출해 주시면 고용주에게 전달하도록 하겠습니다.**

– **195(B)면접 시 물어볼 수 있는 모든 질문에 대한 대답을 연습하십시오.** 저희 웹사이트에서 자주 하는 질문 목록을 여러분이 사용할 수 있도록 찾으실 수 있습니다.

– **195(C)면접을 위해 전문적이고 보수적인 복장을 선택하세요.** 깔끔한 헤어스타일과 메이크업을 추천합니다. 편하고 깨끗한 신발을 신으시고, 액세서리는 최소한으로 착용하세요.

– **195(D)고용주가 면접을 제안하면, 일찍 도착하도록 하십시오.** 좋은 인상을 남기는 편이 좋습니다. 면접 일정, 시간과 날짜를 다시 한 번 확인하십시오.

193우리 인턴 중 한 명과 대면 모의면담을 예약하려면 555-3120으로 채용 담당자에게 연락하십시오. 이 서비스는 무료입니다.

표현 정리 **resume** 이력서 **past work experience** 업무 경력 **achievement** 성과 **forward** 전달하다 **conservative** 보수적인 **outfit** 복장 **minimal** 최소한의 **impression** 인상 **doublecheck** 다시 한 번 확인하다

191. 유추 – Mr. Gershwin의 직업 ★☆☆

해설 첫 번째 이메일 하단 서명란에 Teddy Gershwin이라는 사람의 이름이 있는 것으로 보아 이 사람은 편지 첫 문장 'Our company, Halifax, Inc., is

---

looking for new talent.'에서 회사에서 고용을 담당하는 관리자임을 알 수 있으므로 정답은 (B)이다. **정답 (B)**

해설 Mr. Gershwin은 누구인가?
　(A) 소프트웨어 엔지니어
　(B) 고용 담당자
　(C) 전문 통역사
　(D) 고용 대행사 오너

192. 유추 – Signal Design에 대한 내용 ★☆☆

해설 첫 번째 지문, 이메일 첫 번째 단락 'My counterpart at Signal Design recommended your company after having a great experience working with you.'에서 Signal Design은 전에 Solid Staffing의 도움을 받아 직원을 채용한 경험이 있고, 이에 만족해 Halifax, Inc. 직원인 Teddy Gershwin에게 추천을 했음을 알 수 있으므로 정답은 (C)가 된다. **정답 (C)**

표현 정리 **satisfy** 만족하다

해설 Signal Design에 관해 암시된 내용은?
　(A) Ms. Moore를 위해 직원을 물색했다.
　(B) 인터넷에 구인 광고를 올렸다.
　(C) Solid Staffing에 만족했다.
　(D) Mr. Turner의 이전 고용주였다.

193. 연계문제 – 인터뷰 연습을 하고 싶은 구직자가 할 일 ★★☆

해설 마지막 지문의 마지막 문장을 보면, 'To schedule a face-to-face mock interview with one of our interns, contact the Staffing Director at 555-3120.'이라고 하며, 모의 인터뷰를 하길 원하는 사람은 채용담당자에게 연락하라고 되어 있다. 그런데 두 번째 지문의 발신을 보면, 채용담당자는 Julie Moore이기 때문에 (D)가 정답이 된다. **정답 (D)**

표현 정리 **stop by** ~에 잠시 들르다

해설 구직자는 직접 인터뷰를 연습하고 싶으면 무엇을 해야 하는가?
　(A) 인턴직에 지원하기
　(B) Solid Staffing에 방문하기
　(C) 수수료를 지불하기
　(D) Ms. Moore에게 전화하기

194. 연계 문제 – 인물의 다음 행동 유추하기 ★★☆

해설 두 번째 지문, 회람 'Once you've prepared your application, contact Ben Turner. He will be your point of connection with the client.'에서 Ben Turner라는 인물이 중간에서 Halifax와의 연결을 담당한다는 것을 알 수 있는데, 세 번째 지문, 가이드라인 'Submit that directly to us, and we will forward it to the employer.'에서 연결자는 이력서를 받아 고용주 즉, Halifax Inc.에게 전달할 것임을 알 수 있으므로 정답은 (C)이다. **정답 (C)**

해설 Mr. Turner가 할 일로 가장 적절한 것은?
　(A) 모의 면접을 진행한다.
　(B) Moore 씨에게 고객을 소개한다.
　(C) Halifax에 이력서를 보낸다.
　(D) 구인 광고를 준비한다.

195. 세부사항 – 지원자들에게 추천하지 않는 것 ★★★

해설 세 번째 지문 가이드라인에서 "인터뷰에 이력서를 지참하고 가야 한다는 내용은 언급된 바가 없다. 이력서는 Mr. Turner가 전달하게 되며, 이력서를 면접에 가져가야 하는지에 대한 내용은 나와있지 않으므로 정답은 (A)이다. **정답 (A)**

🔍 **함정 분석** 가이드라인 내의 'Practice your answers for any questions'에서 예상 질문에 대한 답변을 연습하는 편이 좋다는 부분이 언급되어 있어 (B)가, 'Pick a professional, conservative outfit to wear for your interview.'에서 (C)가, 그리고 'When you are offered to interview with the employer, be sure to arrive early.'에서 시간 약속을 지키는 것이 중

요하다는 점이 언급되어 있으므로 (D)가 확인된다.

식 전날 제 집에 주차되어 있을 것입니다.

신용카드 번호(예약 시 필요): XXX-XXXX-XXXX-7840

196(A)참고: 요청 서비스가 완료될 때까지 카드에 청구되지 않습니다.

양식을 제출해 주셔서 감사합니다. 직원이 24시간 안에 귀하에게 연락을 드릴 것입니다.

패러프레이징 |지문| practice your answers for any question 답변을 연습하다 → |선택지 B| rehearse their answers 답변을 먼저 연습하다(리허설하다)
|지문| pick a professional, conservative outfit to wear 전문적이고 보수적인 복장을 선택하다 → |선택지 C| dress appropriately 적절한 옷을 입다
|지문| be sure to arrive early 일찍 도착하다 → |선택지 D| be punctual 시간을 엄수하다

표현 정리 rehearse 리허설하다, 미리 연습하다 punctual 시간 약속을 잘 지키는

표현 정리 spotless 흠이 없는 license plate 번호판 bill 청구하다
completion 완성 representative 대표, 직원 be in touch with ~에게 연락하다

해석 지원자들에게 추천하지 않는 것은 무엇인가?
(A) 면접에 이력서를 가지고 가야 한다.
(B) 답변을 먼저 연습해 보아야 한다.
(C) 적절한 옷을 입어야 한다.
(D) 면접 시간에 맞춰 가야 한다.

발신: dgrail@aquaauto.com
수신: mhoven@jetmail.com
제목: 귀하의 최근 서비스
일자: 5월 11일

Mr. Hoven 님께,

Aqua Auto 주식회사에 연락해 주셔서 감사합니다. 요청하신 날짜에 귀하의 차량을 저희 세차 스케줄에 추가하였습니다. **199서비스 기술자 중 한 명**이 오전 9시 30분에서 10시 30분 사이에 알려주신 주소에 도착할 것입니다.

196(C)서비스를 위해 준비하려면, 다음 지시사항을 따라 주십시오.
– 차량을 외부의 평평한 포장된 바닥에 주차해 주십시오. (예. 사유 차도, 주차장, 길)
– 차량 주변에 적어도 1 미터의 방해가 없는 공간이 있도록 해 주십시오.
– **200차량의 내부에서 짐을 제거해 주십시오.**

문의 사항이 있으시면 555-9834로 언제든지 연락 주십시오.

Dane Grail
서비스 관리자

문제 196-200번은 다음 광고, 양식, 그리고 이메일을 참조하시오.

Aqua Auto 주식회사

이동식 자동차 세차 서비스

199저희는 여러분의 집이나 일터로 찾아가
그 자리에서 차량을 청소해 드립니다.

196(B)지난 25년 동안 Carbondale의 시민들에게 서비스 제공

196(D)저희 인기 서비스의 일부는 다음과 같습니다.
• 기본 세차 – 차량의 내부와 외부를 청소합니다.
• Armor Guard™ 왁스 – 비바람으로부터 추가로 보호합니다.
• 앞 유리 수리 – 유리에 난 작은 흠집을 메웁니다.
• **197슈퍼 세차 – 기본 세차와 같지만 훨씬 좋습니다.**

가격과 같은 세부 사항이나 다른 서비스에 관해서는 www.aquaauto.com을 방문하세요. 서비스를 예약할 수도 있습니다.

1985월에 10% 할인을 받으세요. 이 광고를 서비스 시 보여주셔야 합니다. 차량 한 대에 한합니다.

표현 정리 vehicle 차량 serve ~를 모시다, 봉사하다 interior 내부
exterior 외부 protection 보호 elements 비바람 chips 흠집
pricing 가격 schedule 스케줄을 정하다 present 제출하다, 보여주다
limit 제한하다

표현 정리 flat 평평한 paved 포장된 surface 표면 unobstructed 방해가 없는 belongings 짐

196. 세부사항 – Aqua Auto 주식회사에 대한 내용이 아닌 것 ★★☆
해설 두 번째 지문인 양식 후반 'Note: Your credit card will not be billed until completion of the requested service(s).'에서 세차 서비스가 완료되기 전에는 비용 청구를 하지 않는다고 했으므로 (A)의 미리 전액을 지불해야 한다는 내용은 사실이 아니므로 정답이다. **정답 (A)**

🔍 **함정 분석** 첫 번째 지문 "Proudly serving residents of Carbondale for the past 25 years."에서 수십 년 동안 운영해 왔다는 것을 알 수 있으므로 (B)는 언급된 내용. 또한, 마지막 지문의 'To prepare your vehicle for service, please follow these guidelines'와 같은 세부 설명을 통해 차량 청소 전에 필요한 부분을 안내하고 있으므로 (C)도 언급된 내용이며, 첫 번째 지문 'Some of our most popular services'라는 표현에서 해당 회사의 모든 서비스를 광고한 것이 아님을 알려주고 있으므로 (D) 역시 사실 내용이다.

패러프레이징 |지문| serving ~ for the past 25 years 25년 동안 서비스해 오다 → |선택지 B| in business for decades 수십 년 동안 경영해 온
|지문| To prepare your vehicle for service, please follow these guidelines 차량 서비스를 준비하기 위해서는 이 가이드를 따르세요 → |선택지 C| gives tips for preservice preparations 서비스 전의 준비 사항에 대해 팁을 주다

www.aquaauto.com

서비스 요청 양식

이름: *Michael Hoven*
전화번호: *(512) 555-6743*
이메일: *mhoven@jetmail.com*
198,199 서비스 필요 일자: *5월 18일, 금요일*
서비스 지역: *787 Harper Lane, Carbondale*

차량 타입: *세단*
회사/모델: *Hanata Edge*
색상: *검정*
번호판 #: *HJT 619*

어떤 서비스(들)가 필요하세요?
제 사촌이 다음 주 결혼합니다. 사촌과 사촌의 미래 부인을 리셉션 장소까지 데려다 줄 예정입니다. 197내부와 외부 모두 완벽하게 흠이 없어야 하기 때문에, 귀사의 최고 세차 서비스를 필요로 합니다. 제 차량은 결혼

해석 Aqua Auto 주식회사에 관해 언급된 내용이 아닌 것은?
(A) 미리 전액을 지불해야 한다.
(B) 수십 년간 사업을 진행해 왔다.
(C) 서비스 전 준비 사항에 대해 주의 사항을 준다.
(D) 전체 서비스를 다 광고한 것이 아니다.

197. 연계 문제 – Mr. Hoven이 요청한 서비스 ★☆☆

해설 두 번째 지문 'We need the vehicle to look absolutely spotless inside and out, so we want your best cleaning service.'에서 Mr. Hoven은 신랑과 신부를 태워다 주기 위해 차량의 내부와 외부가 모두 먼지 한 톨 없이 깨끗해야 하기 때문에 청소 서비스를 원한다고 했는데, 첫 번째 지문에서 이 요구에 맞는 서비스 항목으로는 'Super car wash – like the basic car wash but only better'에서 Super Car Wash를 필요로 한다. 따라서 정답은 (D)이다. 정답 (D)

해석 Hoven 씨가 요청한 서비스는 무엇인가?
(A) 기본 세차
(B) Armor Guard™ 왁스
(C) 앞 유리 수리
(D) 슈퍼 세차

198. 연계 문제 – Mr. Hoven에 대한 내용 ★★☆

해설 두 번째 지문에서 Mr. Hoven은 자신의 차량을 서비스 받기 위해 양식을 작성한 사람으로, 5월 18일에 서비스를 받기를 원하고 있는데, 첫 번째 광고 후반 'Get 10% off in May.'라는 부분을 참고하면 5월에 서비스를 신청하면 할인을 받는다는 것을 알 수 있으므로 정답은 (D)가 된다. 정답 (D)

🔍 함정 분석 Mr. Hoven이 해당 서비스를 사용해 본 적이 있는지에 관한 내용은 언급된 바가 없어서 (A)는 오답. 또한, Carbondale로 이사를 왔다는 부분도 명시되지 않았으며, "parked at my house"라는 표현이 있으나 차고에 주차를 한다는 말이 없으므로 (B)와 (C) 모두 오답이다.

해석 Mr. Hoven에 대해 암시된 내용은?
(A) 이동식 세차 서비스를 이용해 본 적이 있다.
(B) Carbondale로 최근 이사했다.
(C) 차고에 차량을 주차할 것이다.
(D) Aqua Auto 주식회사에서 할인을 받을 것이다.

199. 연계 문제 – 5월 18일에 일어날 일 ★☆☆

해설 두 번째 지문 'Date(s) services needed: Friday, May 18'에서 Mr. Hoven이 서비스를 원하는 날이 5월 18일이라는 것을 알 수 있는데, 첫 번째 지문인 광고 '"We go to your home or place of work and wash your vehicle on site."'에서 회사 직원이 직접 방문할 것이라고 했고, 또 세 번째 지문인 이메일 'One of our service technicians will arrive at the address provided between 9:30 A.M. and 10:30 A.M.'에서도 양식에 적힌 Mr. Hoven의 주소로 직원이 찾아갈 것이라고 했으므로 정답은 (B)가 된다. 정답 (B)

해석 5월 18일에는 무슨 일이 있을 것인가?
(A) Mr. Hoven이 결혼을 한다.
(B) Mr. Hoven의 집에 기술자가 간다.
(C) Mr. Hoven이 Aqua Auto 주식회사로 차를 가져간다.
(D) Mr. Hoven에게 청구서가 보내진다.

200. 세부사항 – Mr. Grail이 Mr. Hoven에게 요청한 것 ★☆☆

해설 마지막 지문의 지시사항 중, 'remove your belongings from the vehicle's interior'를 통해 차량의 내부에서 짐을 제거해야 한다는 사실을 알 수 있다. 따라서 remove를 empty로 바꾼 (C)가 정답이다. 정답 (C)

표현 정리 confirm 확인하다 measurement 치수[크기/길이/양] vehicle 차량 empty 비우다 parking permit 주차권

해석 Mr. Grail이 Mr. Hoven에게 요청한 것은?
(A) 약속을 전화로 확인하기
(B) 그의 차량의 치수를 제공하기
(C) 서비스가 제공되기 전에 차를 비우기
(D) 주차권을 요청하기

문제 147–148번은 다음 초대를 참조하시오.

> ### Weston Park에서 열리는 지역사회 축하행사!
> 5월 6일, 토요일 오후 1시 – 8시
>
> ¹⁴⁷보수를 위해 폐쇄되었던 Weston Park가 6개월이 지나 일반인에게 다시 개방될 예정입니다! Tom Stafford 시장님과 지역 사회 구성원들과 함께 축하하는 자리에 참석해 주시기 바랍니다. 새로운 산책로와 자전거 길, 새로 단장된 운동장, 그리고 시의 최신 수영장을 둘러 보시기 바랍니다.
>
> #### ¹⁴⁸Shirley Winston, Alex's Band of Fools, 그리고 The Jokers Wild의 라이브 음악 공연
> 페이스 페인팅, 곡예사, 그리고 아이들을 위한 게임
>
> 지역 요식업체들이 피크닉을 위해 마련한 임시 구조물 옆에서 음식을 판매할 예정입니다.
>
> 자세한 문의 사항은 Ted Flinders에게 555-3020으로 전화 주시기 바랍니다.

표현 정리 celebrate 축하하다, 기념하다 community 지역 사회 closure 폐쇄 renovation 재단장, 보수 public 일반 대중 mayor 시장 local 지역의 check out ~을 확인하다 trail 오솔길 improve 개선되다 athletic field 경기장, 운동장 perform 공연하다 juggler 곡예사 caterer (행사의) 음식 공급자 pavilion (공공 행사, 전시회의) 가설 건물, 임시 구조물 detail 세부 사항

147. 주제 – 행사의 목적 ★☆☆

해설 첫 번째 문장 'After 6 months of closure for renovations, Weston Park will once again be open to the public!'에서 알 수 있듯이 Weston Park는 6개월의 보수 기간을 마치고 다시 시민들에게 개방하려고 하므로 정답은 (A)이다. 정답 (A)

패러프레이징 |지문| Weston Park will once again be open to the public Weston 공원을 다시 일반인에게 개방한다 → |선택지 A| reopen a recreational area 휴식 공간을 다시 열다

표현 정리 event 행사 reopen 다시 열다 recreational 오락의, 휴식의 welcome 환영하다 hold (회의, 시합 등을) 열다, 개최하다 athletic 육상, 경기의 competition 운동 대회, 시합

해석 이 행사의 목적은 무엇인가?
(A) 휴식 공간을 다시 열기 위해
(B) 새로운 지역 지도자를 환영하기 위해
(C) 공원의 변경 사항을 계획하기 위해
(D) 운동경기를 개최하기 위해

148. 유추 – The Jokers Wild의 정체 ★☆☆

해설 본문 'Live music performed by Shirley Winston, Alex's Band of Fools, and The Jokers Wild'에서 The Jokers Wild는 라이브 음악을 공연하는 그룹임을 알 수 있으므로 정답은 (C)이다. 정답 (C)

표현 정리 vendor 행상인 troupe 공연단

해석 The Jokers Wild는 무엇인가?
(A) 음식 판매인
(B) 코미디 공연단
(C) 음악 공연 단체
(D) 스포츠 팀

---

¹⁴⁹Carter and Case가 이메일 마케팅 자료와 더불어 가끔 신문, 잡지 광고를 제작할 그래픽 디자이너를 찾고 있습니다. 또한 Dartmore 지점에 생긴 이 자리는 이메일 마케팅 작업 준비를 돕는 것도 포함합니다. 그래픽 디자이너는 주로 Plato 소프트웨어를 사용해 그래픽이 많이 포함된 자동 이메일을 제작하게 됩니다. 이 일은 유동적인 근무 시간을 가진 파트타임 자리이고, 일부 업무의 경우 재택 근무를 하는 경우도 있습니다.

^{151(B)}지원자들은 그래픽 디자인이나 관련 분야의 학사 학위를 갖고 있어야 합니다. ^{151(A)}여러 가지 일을 할 수 있는 뛰어난 능력과 준비 능력이 요구됩니다. ^{151(D)}꼼꼼해야 합니다. Plato, Insight 및 그 외의 일반 그래픽 디자인 소프트웨어를 사용해 본 경험은 필수입니다.

¹⁵⁰1909년 설립된 Carter and Case는 26개국에 있는 회사에 광고 및 마케팅 전략을 제공하고 있습니다.

이력서와 자기소개서는 Shawn Livermore의 이메일 slivermore@carterandcase.com으로 보내주시기 바랍니다.

표현 정리 material 자료 along with ~와 함께 occasional 가끔 ad 광고 position 지위 involve 수반하다, 관여하다 launch 시작하다, 개시하다 automate 자동화하다 flexible 탄력적인 potential 가능성 complete 완료하다 applicant 지원자 bachelor's degree 학사 학위 related field 관련 분야 multitasking 동시에 여러 가지 일을 하는 organizational 조직적인, 준비가 잘 된 require 필요하다, 요구하다 detail oriented 꼼꼼한, 세심한 standard 일반적인, 표준의 found 설립하다 advertise 광고하다 solution 해결책, 전략 resume 이력서 cover letter 자기소개

149. 세부사항 - 그래픽 디자이너가 할 일 ★☆☆

해설 첫 번째 줄 'Carter and Case is seeking a graphic designer to create e-mail marketing materials along with occasional newspaper and magazine ads.'에서 이메일 마케팅 자료와 신문 및 잡지 광고를 제작할 그래픽 디자이너를 구하고 있음을 알 수 있으므로 정답은 (C)이다. 정답 (C)

표현 정리 advertisement 광고 communicate 연락을 주고받다 multiple 다수의, 다양한 obtain 얻다, 달성하다

해석 광고에 의하면 그래픽 디자이너는 무슨 일을 하게 되는가?
(A) 다수의 사무실과 연락을 주고 받는다.
(B) 온라인 영상을 준비한다.
(C) 광고를 만든다.
(D) 새로운 소프트웨어 프로그램에 대한 교육을 받는다.

150. 유추 - Cater and Case에 대한 내용 ★★☆

해설 세 번째 단락 'Founded in 1909, Carter and Case provides advertising and marketing solutions to companies in 26 countries.'에서 Carter and Case는 26개국에 걸쳐 고객을 두고 있음을 알 수 있으므로 정답은 (D)이다. 정답 (D)

🔍 함정 분석 (A)의 경우 'This position in our Dartmore office also involves helping to launch e-mail marketing campaigns.'에서 Dartmore가 언급되기 했으나 이곳이 본사인지는 알 수 없으므로 (A)는 오답이다.

표현 정리 headquarters 본사 leader 선두 full-time 상근의, 전임의 international 국제적인, 해외의 client 고객

해석 Carter and Case에 관해 암시된 것은?
(A) 본사는 Dartmore에 위치해 있다.
(B) 온라인 마케팅 분야의 선두주자이다.
(C) 정규직을 가지고 있지 않다.
(D) 해외 고객을 보유하고 있다.

151. 세부사항 - 지원자에게 요구되는 사항이 아닌 것 ★☆☆

해설 두 번째 단락에서 지원자가 갖추어야 할 조건들이 나열되어 있다. (A)는 'Strong multitasking and organizational skills required.'에, (B)는 'Applicants must have a bachelor's degree in graphic design or a related field.'로 확인된다. 그리고 (D) 역시 'Must be detail oriented.'에서 확인되지만 (C)는 본문에서 언급되지 않아 정답이다. 정답 (C)

패러프레이징 |지문| have a bachelor's degree 학사 학위를 가지고 있어야 한다 → |선택지 B| having earned a college degree 대학학위를 취득할 것 |지문| must be detail oriented 반드시 꼼꼼해야 한다 → |선택지 D| being attentive to details 세부적인 것에 신경을 쓸 것

표현 정리 earn 획득하다, 얻다 degree 학위 professional 전문적인 attentive 주의 깊은, 세심한, 신경을 쓰는

해석 이 자리의 지원자에게 요구되는 사항이 아닌 것은?
(A) 다양한 일을 할 수 있는 능력
(B) 대학 학위 취득
(C) 전문적인 글쓰기 코스 완료
(D) 세부적인 일에 대한 관심

Nixon, Clarissa	Asa, Scitech 사에 점심 도시락 배달을 완료했어요. 문제는 그들이 충분한 양을 주문하지 않았다는 거예요. 누군가 수량을 너무 적게 잡은 것 같아요.	오전 9시 31분
Cramer, Asa	추가분이 몇 개인가요?	오전 9시 32분
Nixon, Clarissa	일반 도시락 7개와 채식주의자 도시락 2개입니다.	오전 9시 33분
Cramer, Asa	잠시만요. ¹⁵²오늘 주문량을 준비하면서 남은 음식이 있는지 직원에게 확인해 볼게요.	오전 9시 34분
Cramer, Asa	잘 됐네요. 당신이 가져갈 수 있도록 30분 안에 도시락을 포장할 수 있어요. 그러면 괜찮을까요?	오전 9시 39분
Nixon, Clarissa	¹⁵³그럴 거예요. 주문서에는 점심이 12시에 제공될 거라고 돼 있어요. 그때까지 Scitech 사에 돌아갈 수 있어요. 고마워요.	오전 9시 41분

표현 정리 boxed lunch 도시락 corporation 기업, 법인 turn out ~인 것으로 드러나다, 밝혀지다 underestimate 너무 적게 잡다 quantity 양, 수량 extra 여분의, 추가의 regular 일반적인, 평범한 vegetarian 채식주의자; 채식주의의 leftover 남은 package 포장하다 half an hour 반 시간, 30분 pick up ~을 찾다, 찾아오다 work 효과가 있다 serve 제공하다 get back 돌아가다, 돌아오다

152. 세부사항 - Mr. Cramer의 근무처 ★☆☆

해설 Cramer, Asa (9:34 A.M.)의 문자 메시지 'I'm going to check with the staff to see if they had any leftover food when preparing today's orders.'에서 Mr. Cramer가 직원에게 오늘의 주문을 준비하면서 남은 음식이 있는지 확인하겠다고 했으므로 그가 근무하는 곳은 음식 주문을 받고 공급하는 음식 공급업체임을 알 수 있어 정답은 (D)가 된다. 정답 (D)

표현 정리 packaging 포장재, 포장 manufacturer 생산회사 grocery store 식료품점, 슈퍼마켓 catering 음식 공급, 공급업체

해석 Mr. Cramer가 근무하는 곳은 어디인가?
(A) 포장재 제조회사
(B) 식료품점
(C) 기술 회사
(D) 음식 공급업체

TEST 09

(D) Fitch Avenue

153. 의도 파악하기 ★☆☆

해설 Mr. Cramer가 오전 9시 39분에 'They can have the meals packaged within half an hour for you to pick up. Will that work for you?'라고 하자, Ms. Nixon이 'I'm pretty sure.'라고 답했고, 이후에 이어지는 내용은 12시에 점심이 제공될 예정인데 그때까지 도시락을 갖고 Scitech 사에 돌아갈 수 있는 시간이 충분하다는 것을 의미하므로 정답은 (B)이다. 정답 (B)

표현 정리 item 항목, 물품 fairly 꽤, 아주 certain 확신하는

해석 Ms. Nixon이 오전 9시 41분에 "그럴 거예요."라고 한 말은 무슨 의미인가?
(A) 그녀는 Scitech 사가 점심을 나중에 먹을 수 있을 거라고 생각한다.
(B) 그녀는 배달을 하기에 충분한 시간이 있다고 생각한다.
(C) 물건을 일찍 배달하는 것이 중요하다고 느낀다.
(D) 직원이 포장을 할 수 있다고 전적으로 확신하고 있다.

문제 154-155번은 다음 공지를 참조하시오.

안내문: 지하철역 폐쇄

North 노선 중 일부 역이 다음 달부터 시작되는 보수공사로 인해 폐쇄될 예정입니다. 이 역들을 이용하는 승객들께서는 도시 버스를 이용해 줄 것을 권합니다. 지하철 탑승권 소지자들은 폐쇄된 역에서 무료 버스 탑승권을 받을 수 있으며, 이는 폐쇄 기간 동안 유효합니다. 이를 위해서는 지하철 탑승권을 발매기에 넣고, 코드 5668을 입력하면 됩니다.

지하철역	폐쇄 기간	가까운 버스 노선	가까운 버스 정류장
89th Street	3월 2일 – 3월 10일	84B	89th, Ellis
155 Belmont	3월 11일 – 3월 15일	82C	Pullman, 12th
154 Greely	3월 16일 – 3월 29일	78	Oak, Main
Fitch Avenue	3월 30일 – 4월 8일	116	Freemont, Fitch
Woolworth Road	4월 9일 – 4월 16일	14A	Woolworth, Franklin

표현 정리 notice 공고문, 안내문 closure 폐쇄 line 노선 renovation 수리, 보수 normally 보통 advise 조언하다, 권유하다 holder 소지자 obtain 얻다, 구하다 pass 탑승권 good for (~기간) 유효한 duration 기간 insert 넣다 ticketing 매표 stop 정류장

154. 세부사항 – 3월 20에 일어날 일 ★☆☆

해설 공지에 제시된 표에서 3월 20일이 포함되는 폐쇄 기간은 March 16 – March 29로, 이 기간에 폐쇄되는 지하철역은 Greely 역임을 알 수 있어 (C)가 정답이다. 정답 (C)

표현 정리 reopen 다시 문을 열다, 재개하다 construction 건설, 공사 rider 타는 사람

해석 안내문에 따르면 3월 20일에 무슨 일이 있을 것인가?
(A) 새로운 버스 노선이 생길 것이다.
(B) Fitch Avenue 역이 다시 운행될 것이다.
(C) Greely 역에 공사가 있을 것이다.
(D) 버스 승객들은 지하철을 타야 할 것이다.

155. 세부사항 – Fullman과 12th 정류장에서 가장 가까운 지하철 역 ★☆☆

해설 공지의 표에서 가장 가까운 버스정류장을 나타내는 Nearest Bus Stop 목록 중 Pullman, 12th과 가장 가까운 역에 해당하는 지하철역은 Belmont임을 알 수 있으므로 정답은 (B)이다. 정답 (B)

해석 Pullman 정류장과 12th 정류장에 가장 가까운 지하철 역은?
(A) 89th Street
(B) Belmont
(C) Greely

문제 156-157번은 다음 이메일을 참조하시오.

수신: Karen Grisham ⟨kgrisham@getmail.net⟩
발신: Customer Service ⟨custserve@zephyrcomputers.com⟩
날짜: 10월 12일
제목: 귀하의 주문

157(B),(C) 국내 최대 온라인 컴퓨터 하드웨어 공급업체인 Zephyr Computers를 선택해 주셔서 감사합니다. 156 현재 재고가 있는 경우 48시간 안에 배송됩니다. 귀하의 주문 내역은 www.instantshipment.com/zephyr에서 배송 조회 번호를 입력하시면 추적이 가능합니다.

배송조회 번호: 78–90454–0430
주문 번호: HJ9300430
날짜: 10월 12일
고객명: Karen Grisham
청구서 발송지: 1920 Whitney Avenue, New Haven, CT 06501
배송 주소: 위의 주소와 동일
구매 내역: Kayman USB drive, 16MB
상태: 재고 있음
총액: 8.99달러 (무료 배송*)
157(D) 끝 번호 3940인 신용카드로 청구

환불을 원하실 경우 개봉되지 않은 제품은 구매일로부터 30일 이내에 반품이 가능합니다. 반품 정책 전체를 확인하시려면 www.zephyrcomputers.com으로 이동하시기 바랍니다.

157(A) *특가 할인

표현 정리 supplier 공급회사 item 물품, 품목 currently 현재 stock 재고품 ship 보내다, 수송하다 track 추적하다 billing 청구서[계산서] 발부 purchase 구입, 구매 status 상태 amount 총액 bill 청구서[계산서]를 보내다 unopened 개봉하지 않은 return 반납하다, 돌려보내다 refund 환불 special offer 특가 판매, 특가 할인

156. 세부사항 – Ms. Grisham의 주문에 대한 내용 ★★☆

해설 이메일 첫 번째 단락 'Items currently in stock ship within 48 hours.'에서 재고가 있는 제품의 경우에는 48시간 내에 배송이 가능하다고 했고, Ms. Grisham이 주문을 한 날짜가 10월 12일이므로 늦어도 10월 14일까지는 배송이 될 것이다. 따라서 정답은 (D)이다. 정답 (D)

🔍 함정 분석 'Thank you for choosing Zephyr Computers, the nation's largest online supplier of computer hardware.'에서 Zephyr Computers는 온라인 컴퓨터 하드웨어를 판매하는 곳으로 이곳에서 배송을 보내게 되므로 (B)는 오답이다.

표현 정리 include 포함하다 no later than 늦어도 ~까지는

해석 Ms. Grisham의 주문에 관한 사실 내용은?
(A) 10월 10일에 주문되었다.
(B) Zephyr Computers로 배송될 것이다.
(C) 무료 선물이 포함되어 있다.
(D) 늦어도 10월 14일까지는 배송될 것이다.

157. 유추 – Zephyr Computers에 관한 사실 내용 ★★☆

해설 주문 정보 'Billed to credit card number ending in 3940'에서 Ms. Grisham의 결제 금액은 끝자리 번호가 3940인 신용카드로 청구가 됐을 알 수 있다. 따라서 Zephyr Computers는 신용카드 지불방식을 택하고 있음을 알 수 있으므로 정답은 (D)이다. 정답 (D)

🔍 **함정 분석** (A) Amount: $8.99 (w/free shipping*)과 하단 *Special offer 에서 해당 상품이 특가 할인을 제공하는 품목이기 때문에 무료 배송을 해 준 다는 것을 알 수 있다. 따라서 평소에도 배송비를 부과하지 않는지는 알 수 없다. (B), (C)는 'Thank you for choosing Zephyr Computers, the nation' s largest online supplier of computer hardware.'에서 매장에서 판매하 는 업체가 아니라 온라인 판매를 주로 하는 곳임을 알 수 있고, 컴퓨터 프로그 램을 설계하는 곳이 아니라 컴퓨터 하드업체를 공급하는 곳임을 알 수 있다.

표현 정리 charge 청구하다, 부담시키다 retail 소매 accept 받다 payment 지불

해석 Zephyr Computers에 관해 암시된 것은?
(A) 배송비를 부과하지 않는다.
(B) 많은 소매점에서 상품을 판매한다.
(C) 컴퓨터 프로그램을 설계한다.
(D) 신용카드 결제를 받는다.

문제 158-160번은 다음 이메일을 참조하시오.

발신: Robert Navarro <rnavarro@diynetwork.com>
수신: Lena Rivers <lrivers@getmail.net>
날짜: 11월 2일
제목: 회신: 주문에 관해

Ms. Rivers 님께,

158귀하의 주문 내역(#13849)에서 하나의 품목(PM48994)이 현재 재고가 없는 상태임을 알려 드립니다. 159그 외 다른 물품은 귀하께 보내 드렸습니 다. 저희는 5~7일 이내로 빠진 품목이 입고될 것으로 예상합니다. 159빠진 물품이 저희 창고로 입고되자마자 추가 비용 없이 익일 배송으로 바로 보내 드리겠습니다. 일단 물품이 배송되면 이 이메일 주소로 통지 받으실 것이며, 배 송 추적 번호도 받게 됩니다.

160DIY Network는 고객 만족을 소중히 여깁니다. 만약 귀하께서 제품에 대해 만족하지 않으신다면 30일 이내로 반품해 주십시오. 그러면 귀하의 금 액을 환불해 드릴 것입니다. 아무 것도 묻지 않겠습니다. 저희의 환불 및 교 환 정책에 대해 더 알고 싶으시다면 www.diynetwork.com을 방문해 주세 요.

DIY Network를 선택해 주셔서 감사 드리고, 다음 주문 시에 10퍼센트 할인 혜택을 제공해 드리겠습니다. 계산하실 때 쿠폰 코드 GET10을 사용하시면 됩니다. 이 코드는 한 번만 사용이 가능합니다.

다른 질문이 있으면 알려주십시오.

Robert Navarro

표현 정리 out of stock 재고가 떨어진, 품절된 anticipate 예상하다 missing 빠진, 누락된 in stock 비축되어, 재고로 as soon as ～하자마자 warehouse 창고 directly 곧장, 즉시 via ～을 통해 overnight shipping 익일 배송 extra 추가의 charge 요금 notification 알림, 통지 track 추적하다 pleased 만족해 하는 purchase 구매 return 반품 exchange 교환 offer 제공하다 discount 할인 check out (호텔 등에서 비용을 지불하고) 나가다

158. 주제 – Mr. Navarro가 이메일을 보낸 목적 ★☆☆
해설 첫 번째 문장 'I am writing to let you know that one of the items (PM48994) from your order (#13849) is currently out of stock.'에서 특정 품목의 재고가 없다는 점과, 'As soon as it arrives at our warehouse, it will be sent directly to you via overnight shipping at no extra charge to you.'에서 재고가 입고되는 대로 즉시 배송해 주겠다는 내용이므로 정답은 (A)이다. **정답 (A)**

표현 정리 delay 지연, 연기 additional 추가의 payment 지불 replacement 교체, 대체 confirm 확인하다, 확정하다 receipt 영수증 backorder (재고가 없어) 뒤로 미룬 주문, 이월 주문

해석 Mr. Navarro가 이메일을 보낸 이유는?
(A) 배달이 지연된 점을 설명하기 위해
(B) 추가적인 지불을 요청하기 위해
(C) 대체 품목을 제공하기 위해
(D) 이월 주문에 대한 영수증을 확인하기 위해

159. 유추 – Ms. Rivers에 관한 사실 내용 ★★★
해설 두 번째 줄 'The other items have just been sent to you.'에서 재고가 없는 물품을 제외한 나머지 품목은 이미 보냈다고 했고, 'As soon as it arrives at our warehouse, it will be sent directly to you via overnight shipping at no extra charge to you.'에서 재고가 들어오는 대로 익일 배송으로 보내겠다고 했으므로 주문품을 따로따로 받을 것이라는 것을 알 수 있어 정답은 (D)이다. **정답 (D)**

🔍 **함정 분석** 'As soon as it arrives at our warehouse, it will be sent directly to you via overnight shipping at no extra charge to you.'에서 별도의 비용을 지불하지 않아도 됨을 알 수 있으므로 (A)가, (B) 'To thank you for choosing DIY Network, we would like to offer you a 10% discount on your next order.'에서 PM48994 상품이 아니라 다음 주문 시에 할인을 해 주겠다고 했으므로 (B)가, 환불이 아니라 재고가 들어오는 대로 배송해 주겠다고 했으므로 (C)가 각각 오답이다.

표현 정리 shipping cost 발송비 refund 환불 separate 분리된, 서로 다른 shipment 수송

해석 Ms. Rivers에 대한 사실 내용은?
(A) 추가적인 배송비를 지불해야 할 것이다.
(B) PM48994 상품에 대해 가격 할인을 받을 것이다.
(C) 빠진 물품에 대해 환불을 받을 것이다.
(D) 두 번의 배송으로 물건을 각각 받을 것이다.

160. 문장 위치 찾기 ★★☆
해설 "DIY Network values customer satisfaction."의 의미가 고객 만족을 소 중히 여긴다는 뜻이므로 뒤에 이어지는 내용 역시 'If you are not fully pleased with any purchase, return it within 30 days, and we will give you your money back.'과 같이 앞의 내용을 부연 설명하는 문장이 이어지는 것이 자연스 러워 (C)가 정답이다. **정답 (C)**

표현 정리 value 소중하게 생각하다 satisfaction 만족

해석 [1], [2], [3], [4] 중 다음 문장이 들어가기에 가장 적합한 곳은?

"DIY Network는 고객 만족을 소중히 여깁니다."
(A) [1]
(B) [2]
(C) [3]
(D) [4]

문제 161-163번은 다음 편지를 참조하시오.

5월 14일

Colin Hayes
793 Coulter Pace
Minneapolis, MN 55423

Mr. Hayes 님께,

161Gruber 사는 귀하를 전기 기술직원으로 채용하기로 결정했음을 알려

TEST 09

드리게 되어 기쁩니다. 163(D)공식 근무 시작일은 5월 28일, 월요일입니다. 그날 오전 8시 30분에 상관인 상품 시험부 David McGrath에게 출근을 알리기 바랍니다. Mr. McGrath를 만난 후, 저를 만나 계약서에 서명해야 합니다. 유효한 신분증명서와 사회 보장 카드를 지참하고 오시기 바랍니다. 의무적으로 참석해야 하는 신입사원 오리엔테이션이 6월 5일, 화요일 오전 8시 30분에서 오후 4시 30분으로 예정되어 있습니다.

163(C)이 자리는 성과에 따라 계약이 매년 연장되는 12개월 계약직입니다. 163(B)급여는 48,750달러이며, 2주마다 지급됩니다. 162(A)상근직으로 건강보험, 치과보험, 안과 진료 제도, 생명보험, 연금제도, 유급 휴가, 유급 병가, 교육비 변제 등 회사의 일반 복리후생 혜택을 받으실 자격이 됩니다. 162(B)오리엔테이션 기간 동안 복리후생 제도에 대한 세부사항을 추가로 듣게 될 것입니다. 162(D)복리후생 옵션의 일부 또는 전체를 등록할 기간은 근무 시작일로부터 60일입니다.

직책에 대해 질문 사항이 있으면, 224-8940으로 언제든지 연락 주십시오.

Mayra Greene
차장
인사부

표현 정리 inform 알리다 hire 고용하다, 채용하다 official 공식적인 report (직장, 회의 등에 도착을) 알리다, 보고하다 supervisor 감독관, 관리자 valid 유효한 proof 증명(서) identification 신원 확인, 신분 증명 social security card 사회 보장 카드 mandatory 의무적인, 필수의 employee 피고용인 renewable 갱신[연장] 가능한 annually 매년 performance 실적, 성과 bi-weekly 2주에 한 번의, 격주의 eligible 자격이 있는 benefit 복리후생 급부 insurance 보험 dental 치과의 vision 시력, 눈 plan (특정 연금, 보험금 등 필요한 자금을 위한) 제도 life insurance 생명보험 retirement plan 연금제도[계획] paid 유급의, 보수가 주어지는 sick leave 병가 reimbursement 변제, 상환 regarding ~에 관하여 benefits package 복리후생 제도 enroll 등록하다 assistant 보조원, 비서 director 임원, 책임자 personnel 인사부

161. 주제 – 편지의 목적 ★☆☆
해설 첫 번째 문장 'I am pleased to inform you that the Gruber Corporation has agreed to hire you as a junior electrical engineer.'에서 서신을 보낸 의도를 확인할 수 있다. 즉, Gruber 사에서 Mr. Hayes를 전기 기술 직원으로 채용하기로 했음을 알리는 편지이므로 정답은 (C)이다. 정답 (C)

표현 정리 announce 발표하다, 알리다 promotion 승진 modify 수정하다, 변경하다 employment 고용 offer 제의, 제안 recommend 추천하다

해석 이 편지를 쓴 목적은 무엇인가?
(A) 승진을 알리기 위해
(B) 고용 계약서를 수정하기 위해
(C) 일자리를 제의하기 위해
(D) 직원을 추천하기 위해

162. 세부사항 – 복리후생에 대한 내용이 아닌 것 ★★★
해설 두 번째 단락 'health insurance, dental insurance, vision plan, life insurance, retirement plan, paid vacation, paid sick leave, educational reimbursement, etc.'에 나열된 복리후생 종류에 (C)의 차량보험에 관한 내용은 포함되어 있지 않으므로 정답은 (C)이다. 정답 (C)

🔍 함정 분석 (A)는 두 번째 단락 'As a full-time position, it is eligible for standard company benefits: ~.'에서 복리후생 혜택은 상근직 직원에게 해당됨을 알 수 있고, (B)는 'You will receive additional details regarding the benefits package during the orientation.'에서 복리후생에 대한 자세한 내용은 오리엔테이션 당일에 설명해 줄 것이라고 했는데, 오리엔테이션 날은 6월 5일임을 알 수 있다. (D)는 'You will have 60 days from your starting

date to enroll in some or all of the options.'에서 복리후생 혜택을 등록하는데 60일이라는 기간이 주어짐을 알 수 있다.

표현 정리 mention 언급하다 available 이용할 수 있는 vehicle 차량 sign up 가입하다

해석 복리후생 제도에 대해 언급되지 않은 것은?
(A) 상근직으로 근무하는 직원들이 이용 가능하다.
(B) 6월 5일에 설명을 받게 될 것이다.
(C) 차량에 대한 보험을 포함한다.
(D) 등록하는데 기한이 있다.

163. 유추 – Mr. Hayes에 관한 내용 ★★☆
해설 첫 번째 단락 'Your official starting date is Monday, May 28. ~. After meeting with Mr. McGrath, you need to see me to sign your contract.'에서 첫 출근 일은 월요일임을 알 수 있고, 계약서에 사인을 하기 위해 자신을 만나라고 했는데, 편지 하단 'Mayra Greene, Assistant Director, Personnel Office'에서 이 서신을 작성한 사람은 인사부에서 근무하고 있음을 알 수 있으므로 정답은 (D)이다. 정답 (D)

🔍 함정 분석 이 서신은 채용이 결정되었음을 알리기 위한 것이며, 온라인 지원서 작성을 했는지는 알 수 없으므로 (A)가, 'The salary is $48,750 and will be paid bi-weekly.'에서 급여는 2주마다 지급된다고 했으므로 (B)가, 'This is a twelve-month contract position renewable annually based on performance.'에서 매년 연장이 되는 계약직이라고 했으므로 (C)가 각각 오답이다.

표현 정리 complete 완료하다, 끝마치다 application 지원

해석 Mr. Hayes에 관해 암시된 것은?
(A) 온라인 지원서 작성을 마쳤다.
(B) 한 달에 한 번 급여를 받을 것이다.
(C) 1년 근무 후 그만둬야 한다.
(D) 월요일에 인사부에 갈 것이다.

문제 164-167번은 다음 온라인 채팅을 참조하시오.

Don Shemilt	저희 사무실 건물 청소 용역업체와의 계약 만료가 5주 남았습니다. 164(B)Paul Owens는 이 용역업체에 만족하고 있다며, 계약을 연장할 계획이라고 했어요. 165하지만 여러분의 의견을 듣고 싶어하십니다. 오전 8시 52분
Noah Morgan	Commercial Custodial이 청소를 시작한지 이제 6개월 정도 된 것으로 알고 있습니다. 하지만 그들은 냄새가 꽤 강한 세제를 한 번 사용했었습니다. 오전 8시 54분
Betty Freidman	그것은 표준 청소용 제품이었습니다. 164(A)직원들이 냄새가 거슬린다고 말한 후에는 덜 자극적인 제품으로 교체했습니다. 저는 사실 그들이 꽤 협조적이라고 생각합니다. 오전 8시 56분
Noah Morgan	말이 나와서 말인데, 우리 직원이 먼지 털기를 추가로 요청하자 그들은 즉시 해줬습니다. 오전 8시 57분
Betty Freidman	164(D)3층에는 신입 직원들이 많이 있습니다. 그들은 재활용이 가능한 물품들을 해당 쓰레기통에 넣는 것을 잊어버릴 때가 있습니다. 164(C)Commercial Custodial은 그러한 실수를 바로 잡느라 힘들 텐데도 한 번도 불평을 한 적이 없습니다. 오전 9시 2분
Don Shemilt	165아주 도움이 됐습니다. 감사합니다. 166 4층은 어때요? 오전 9시 7분
Jocelyn Rich	이곳은 아무런 불만이 없습니다. 사무실 공간이 정기적으로 청소되고 있습니다. 늦게까지 사무실에 남아있을 때 청소하시는 여성분과 이야기를 나눌 때가 있습니다. 그분은 아주 친근하고 그녀의 일을 진지하게 받아들이는 것 같았습니다. 오전 9시 8분

표현 정리 contract 계약   expire 만료되다, 끝나다   satisfy 만족시키다
renew 갱신하다, 연장하다   cleaner 세제   commercial 상업의, 시판용의
irritate 거슬리다, 자극하다   switch 바꾸다   pungent (허를) 강하게
자극하는   accommodating 협조적인   responsive 반응하는, 대응하는
extra 추가의   dusting 먼지 털기   correct 바로잡다, 정정하다
recyclable 재활용할 수 있는   disposal (무엇을 없애기 위한) 처리, 처분
bin 쓰레기통   complain 불평하다   involve 관여하다, 개입하다   chat
이야기를 나누다, 수다를 떨다   seriously 진지하게   relay 전달하다

164. 세부사항 – Commercial Custodial에 관한 내용이 아닌 것 ★★☆

해설 Commercial Custodial은 대화자들이 속한 회사와 계약을 체결하고 청소
해 주는 용역업체이다. (D)의 내용은 대화를 나누고 있는 직원들이 근무하는 회
사와 관련된 내용으로, Betty Freidman (9:02 A.M.)의 대화 'We have a lot of
new employees on the third floor.'에서 현재 3층에 신입사원이 많이 있음을
알 수 있으므로 (D)가 정답이다.   **정답 (D)**

🔍**함정 분석** (A)는 Betty Freidman(8:56 A.M.)의 대화 'After we told them
that it was irritating some employees, they switched to a less
pungent product.'에서 맞는 내용이고, (B)는 Don Shemilt (8:52 A.M.)의
대화 'Paul Owens says he is satisfied with the company and plans
to renew the contract, but he wants to hear your opinions.'에서 Paul
Owens가 계약을 연장할 계획이라는 것을 언급하고 있어 가능성이 있고, (C)
의 경우 Betty Freidman(9:02 A.M.)의 대화 'Commercial Custodial has
never complained about the extra work involved in correcting those
mistakes.'에서 신입직원들이 재활용 쓰레기를 잘못 넣었을 때 분류를 다시
했음을 알 수 있다.

패러프레이징 |지문| switched to a less pungent product 덜 자극적인 제품
으로 바꾸다 → |선택지 A| changed its cleaning chemicals 청소용 화학제품
을 변경했다
|지문| plans to renew the contract 계약을 갱신할 계획이다 → |선택지 B| Its
contract might be extended 계약이 연장될 수도 있다
|지문| put recyclable materials in the correct waste disposal bin 재활용
품을 올바른 쓰레기 수거함에 넣다 → |선택지 C| sort trash properly 쓰레기를
올바로 분리하다
|지문| a lot of new employees 많은 새로운 직원 → |선택지 D| a lot of new
staff members 많은 신입 직원

표현 정리 chemical 화학 제품   extend 연장하다   sort 분류하다, 구분하다
trash 쓰레기   properly 제대로, 올바로

해석 Commercial Custodial에 관해 언급된 내용이 아닌 것은?
    (A) 청소용 화학제품을 변경했다.
    (B) 계약이 연장될 수도 있다.
    (C) 쓰레기를 올바로 분리했다.
    (D) 많은 신입직원들이 있다.

165. 의도 파악하기 ★☆☆

해설 Don Shemilt (8:52 A.M.)의 대화 'but he wants to hear your opinions'
에서 Paul Owens가 직원들의 의견을 듣고 싶어함에 따라, Mr. Shemilt가 일부
직원들과 대화를 나눈 후에 'This is all very helpful.'이라고 말했다. 따라서 이
는 의견을 말해 줘서 고맙다는 의미이므로 (B)가 정답이다.   **정답 (B)**

표현 정리 appreciate 고마워하다

해석 Mr. Shemilt가 오전 9시 7분에 "아주 도움이 되었습니다."라고 한 내용의
의미는?
    (A) 청소 직원이 한 일을 정말 마음에 들어 한다.
    (B) 대화자들이 의견을 얘기해 줘서 고마워한다.

    (C) Mr. Friedman의 직원을 교육시키기를 원한다.
    (D) Commercial Custodial에 대한 그의 의견이 바뀌고 있다.

166. 세부사항 – Ms. Rich에 대한 내용 ★★☆

해설 Don Shemilt가 오전 9시 7분에 'How are things going on the fourth
floor?'라고 질문하자, Ms. Rich가 'No complaints for any one up here.'라고
답한 것으로 보아 Ms. Rich는 4층에서 근무하는 직원임을 알 수 있으므로 정답은
(D)이다.   **정답 (D)**

🔍**함정 분석** (A)는 Jocelyn Rich (9:08 A.M.)의 대화 'When I stay late, I
chat with one of the cleaning ladies.'에서 매일 야근을 한다고는 볼 수 없
고, (B)는 Don Shemilt가 'How are things going on the fourth floor?'라
고 물은 것으로 보아 두 사람은 같은 층에서 일하지 않는다는 것을 추측할 수
있다.

표현 정리 frequently 자주   overtime 초과근무, 야근   generally 대체로
serious 진지한

해석 Ms. Rich에 관해 언급된 내용은?
    (A) 그녀는 매일 야근을 한다.
    (B) 그녀는 Mr. Shemilt의 사무실에서 일한다.
    (C) 그녀는 대체로 진지한 사람이다.
    (D) 그녀는 4층에서 근무한다.

167. 세부사항 – Mr. Shemilt가 할 일 ★☆☆

해설 Don Shemilt가 오전 9시 11분에 한 대화 'I'll relay that to Paul.'에서 Don
Shemilt는 직원들로부터 들은 의견을 Mr. Owens에게 전달할 것임을 알 수 있으므
로 정답은 (A)이다.   **정답 (A)**

패러프레이징 |지문| relay that to ∼에게 전달하다 → |선택지 A| share the
responses with ∼와 반응을 공유하다

표현 정리 response 반응, 응답   recommend 권고하다, 권하다   hire
쓰다, 고용하다

해석 Mr. Shemilt는 무엇을 할 계획인가?
    (A) 직원들의 반응을 Mr. Owens와 공유한다.
    (B) 새 회사를 고용할 것을 권한다.
    (C) 매니저에게 문제를 보고한다.
    (D) Commercial Custodial의 대표와 이야기를 나눈다.

문제 168-171번은 다음 정보를 참조하시오.

> ### Masterson 화이트보드
>
> **168Masterson은 건식 지움과 습식 지움 화이트보드 시장의 글로벌 리더
> 입니다.** 저희 모든 화이트보드 제품은 내구성과 사용 편의성을 목표로 만들
> 어졌습니다. 저희 제품은 전 세계 기업, 대학교, 병원에서 매일 사용되고 있
> 습니다.
>
> Masterson 화이트보드는 내구성을 지닌 섬유 유리와 함께 긁힘 방지 표면
> 으로 구성되어 있고, 가볍지만 견고한 알루미늄 틀에 **171설치되어 있습니다.**
> **화이트보드는 자석층을 포함하거나 또는 포함하지 않고 주문할 수 있습니다.**
> Masterson에서는 표준 규격 이외에도 고객 사양에 부합하기 위해서 고객
> 의 요구에 맞춘 화이트보드도 생산이 가능합니다. 저희 모든 화이트보드 제
> 품은 조절 가능한 설치 시스템을 사용함으로써 대부분의 벽 표면에 가로 또
> 는 세로로 손쉽게 설치가 가능합니다. 또한 다수의 표준 규격 화이트보드
> 이 저희 접이식 스탠드에 설치가 가능합니다.
>
> Masterson에서는 최상의 결과를 위해서 저희 화이트보드와 함께
> Masterson 공식 제품만을 사용할 것을 권해 드립니다. **169저희는 12가지
> 색상과 5가지 사이즈의 건식 지움과 습식 지움 마커펜의 완전한 제품을 생
> 산하고 있습니다. 또한 저희는 화이트보드 지우개, 세정액, 그리고 표면 복구**

TEST 09

도구 세트도 생산하고 있습니다.

170 **저희 웹사이트(www.masterson.com)에서는 화이트보드 상품 전체 목록과 관련 제품들을 이들의 기술 사양 및 사진과 함께 확인하실 수 있습니다.** 주문을 하시려면 저희 판매 담당자 1-888-456-0940으로 전화 주시기 바랍니다.

표현 정리 dry-erase 지우개나 천으로 지우는 방식 wet-erase 젖은 천을 이용해서 지우는 방식 durability 내구성 ease 쉬움, 용이함, 편의성 daily 매일, 날마다 construct 조립하다, 구성하다 scratch 긁힌 자국, 긁기 resistant 저항력 있는, ~에 잘 견디는[강한] surface 표면 durable 내구성이 있는, 오래가는 fiberglass 섬유 유리 backing 뒤 판, 안감 house 집에 넣다, 넣다 lightweight 가벼운 sturdy 튼튼한, 견고한 frame 틀 magnetic 자석의 layer 막, 층 customize 주문 제작하다 specification 사양 mount 설치하다 horizontally 가로로 vertically 수직으로, 세로로 adjustable 조절[조정] 가능한 folding 접을 수 있는 manufacture 제조하다, 생산하다 complete 완전한 line (상품의) 종류 marker 마커펜 solution 용액 restoration 복원, 복구 kit (특정한 목적용 도구, 장비) 세트 representative (판매) 대리인, 대표자

168. 주제 – 글의 주제 ★☆☆
해설 본문 제목과 첫 번째 단락에서 알 수 있듯이 이 내용은 Masterson 회사에서 생산하는 화이트보드에 대한 내용임을 알 수 있으므로 정답은 (C)이다.
정답 (C)

표현 정리 mainly 주로, 대부분 presentation 발표, 설명; 프레젠테이션 overview 개관, 개요 process 절차

해석 이 정보는 주로 무엇에 관한 것인가?
(A) 새로운 프레젠테이션 기술
(B) 국제적 기업의 중요성
(C) 기업의 상품에 대한 개요
(D) 주문을 하는 절차

169. 세부사항 – Masterson에 관한 내용 ★★☆
해설 세 번째 단락 'We manufacture a complete line of wet-erase and dry-erase markers in twelve colors and five sizes.'에서 이 회사에서는 마커펜도 생산하고 있음을 알 수 있으며, 이어 'In addition, we produce erasers, cleaning solutions, and surface restorations kits.'에서 화이트보드 지우개, 세척액, 표면복구 도구세트도 생산하고 있다고 했으므로 정답은 (A)이다. 정답 (A)

🔍 **함정 분석** (B)는 두 번째 단락 'All of our whiteboard products can be easily mounted horizontally or vertically on most wall surfaces by using our adjustable mounting system.'에서 손쉽게 설치가 가능하다고 한 것으로 보아 고객이 직접 설치하는 것이 가능할 것이라고 생각되며, 회사에서 화이트보드를 설치해 준다는 언급은 없다.

표현 정리 mount 설치하다 offer 제공하다 lifetime 일생, 평생 warranty (품질 등의) 보증, 보증서

해석 Masterson에 관해 언급된 내용은?
(A) 화이트보드만 판매하는데 그치지 않는다.
(B) 고객을 위해 화이트보드를 설치할 수 있다.
(C) 회사 제품에 대해 평생 품질보증을 제공한다.
(D) 다른 여러 나라에 사무실을 가지고 있다.

170. 세부사항 – Masterson의 웹사이트에 대한 내용 ★☆☆
해설 네 번째 단락 'A complete list of our whiteboards and related products, along with their technical specifications and photographs, can be found on our Web site (www.masterson.com).'에서 Masterson 웹사이트에서 알 수 있는 내용은 전체 상품 목록과 관련 제품, 그리고 이것들의 기술 사양과 사진에 관한 내용임을 알 수 있으므로 정답은 (B)이다. 정답 (B)

패러프레이징 |지문| photographs, can be found on our Web site 웹사이트에서 사진을 찾아볼 수 있다 → |선택지 B| provide pictures of its products 상품의 사진을 제공한다

표현 정리 installation 설치 procedure 절차

해석 Masterson의 웹사이트에 관해 언급된 것은?
(A) 설치 절차를 설명하고 있다.
(B) 상품의 사진을 제공한다.
(C) 회사로 가는 길을 제공한다.
(D) 고객들로부터 피드백을 받는다.

171. 동의어 ★★☆
해설 본문에 쓰인 housed는 '집에 넣다, 집에 구비하다'라는 의미로 '설치하다, 배치하다'라는 의미를 가진 (D) placed와 비슷한 의미로 쓰였으므로 정답은 (D)이다. 정답 (D)

표현 정리 manufacture 제조하다, 생산하다 complete 모든 것이 갖춰진, 완전한 place 설치하다, 배치하다

해석 두 번째 단락, 두 번째 줄의 "housed"와 의미가 가장 가까운 것은?
(A) 생산된
(B) 배달된
(C) 완료된
(D) 설치된

문제 172~175번은 다음 기사를 참조하시오.

TARNTON(3월 3일) – Oak Park 인근 주민들은 거의 50년간 자신들의 주택을 보수 유지하는데 Harrison Hardware에 의지해 왔다. 172**사람들은 이곳이 문을 닫을 것이라고 말해 왔는데, 마침내 주인인 Tom Carrol은 상점을 올 여름 새로운 장소로 이전할 것이라고 공식적으로 밝혔다.**

"저는 Oak Park를 사랑합니다. 저의 최대 고객은 저의 이웃입니다."라고 Mr. Carrol은 말했다. 173**주민들은 지난 5년간 수십여 개의 소규모 사업체들이 문을 닫는 것을 보아왔다.** 상점들의 폐업으로 지역 사회의 중심 거리는 텅 비게 되었다. "저희가 Ivy 가에 남아 있는 마지막 상점입니다. 다른 지역 쇼핑객들은 더 이상 오지 않아요. 그로 인해 사업에 타격을 입고 있죠. 저희를 버틸 수 있게 해 주는 것은 지역의 단골 고객들입니다."라고 Mr. Carrol은 설명했다.

175**Mr. Carrol의 결정에 영향을 미친 것은 단지 경제적 상황만은 아니다.** 그는 몇 년 후에 은퇴할 준비를 하고 있다고 말했다. "저는 이 사업을 저의 아버지로부터 배웠습니다. 그리고 지금은 제 사위 Alex Romansky에게 넘겨주려고 준비하고 있습니다."

새로운 위치는 아직 알려지지 않았지만, Mr. Carrol은 그가 Oak Park에 살기 때문에 근처에 있는 건물을 고려하고 있다고 말했다. "Alex가 이전 절차를 도와주고 있습니다."라고 Mr. Carrol은 덧붙였다. "이것은 그에게 있어서 커다란 움직임입니다. 174**그리고 제가 최종적으로 매도할 준비가 되었을 때, Alex가 인수받을 준비가 되어 있기를 바랍니다.**"

또한 Harrison Hardware는 지난해 시작한 온라인 사업에 투자를 늘릴 계획을 갖고 있다. 새로운 상점에서는 지역 고객들에게 최고의 서비스를 제공하면서 온라인 판매 비중을 늘릴 것으로 예상된다.

표현 정리 resident 거주민, 주민 neighborhood 근처, 인근, 주민 turn to (도움, 조언 등을 위해) ~에 의지하다 maintenance 유지 보수 need 필요(성) shut (상점, 식당 등이) 문을 닫다 state (정식으로) 말하다, 진술하다 publically 공개적으로 dozens of 수십 개의, 다수 stretch (특히 길게) 뻗은 지역[구간] afloat (사업 등이) 빚을 안 질 정도의, 도산을 안 당하는 retire 은퇴하다 pass on (~에게) 넘겨 주다 son-in-law 사위 look at ~을 고려하다, 찾아보다 nearby 인근의, 가까운 곳의 transition 이동, 변화 step 움직임 take over (기업 등을) 인수하다 launch

시작하다 **expectation** 기대, 예상 **handle** (상품을) 취급하다, 거래하다 **exceptional** 우수한, 특별한

172. 주제 – 기사의 주제 ★☆☆
해설 첫 단락 'People have been saying that it was going to shut its doors, but owner Tom Carrol has finally stated publically that the business will be moving to a new part of the city this summer.'에서 이 상점이 올 여름 새로운 장소로 이전하기로 결정했다고 했으므로 정답은 (B)이다.
정답 (B)

표현 정리 **rise** 증가, 상승 **commerce** 상업(= business), 통상 **relocate** 이전하다, 이동하다 **decline** 감소, 하락

해석 기사는 주로 무엇에 관한 것인가?
(A) 인터넷 상거래의 증가
(B) 이전을 준비하는 사업체
(C) 성장을 위한 도시의 계획
(D) 주민의 감소

173. 세부사항 – Oak Park에 대한 내용 ★★☆
해설 두 번째 단락 'The neighborhood has seen dozens of small businesses close in the past five years.'에서 지난 5년간 소규모 사업체들이 문을 닫았다고 한 내용으로 보아 정답은 (B)이다.
정답 (B)

🔍 **함정 분석** (A) Oak Park는 Mr. Carrol이 옮겨갈 장소가 아니라 현재 가게가 위치하고 있는 곳이다. (C), (D)의 내용은 본문의 내용을 통해 추측할 수가 없다.

패러프레이징 |지문| dozens of small businesses close in the past five years 지난 5년간 소규모 사업체들이 문을 닫았다 → |선택지 B| have fewer stores than in the past 과거보다 상점의 수가 더 적다

표현 정리 **no longer** 더 이상 ~아닌 **demand** 수요 **hardware** 철물, 철물류 **attraction** 관광 명소

해석 Oak Park에 대해 언급된 것은?
(A) Mr. Carrol이 옮겨갈 장소이다.
(B) 과거보다 상점의 수가 더 적다.
(C) 철물점에 대한 수요가 더 이상 없다.
(D) 인기 있는 관광지가 아니다.

174. 유추 – Mr. Romansky에 대한 내용 ★★☆
해설 네 번째 단락 'and I hope it prepares him to take over when I am finally ready to sell'에서 Mr. Carrol은 사위인 Mr. Romansky에게 자신의 상점을 매도하려고 하고 있음을 알 수 있으므로 정답은 (C)이다.
정답 (C)

🔍 **함정 분석** (B)는 세 번째 단락 'now I am ready to pass it on to my son-in-law, Alex Romansky'에서 Mr. Romansky는 Harrison Hardware의 수석 매니저가 아니라 Mr. Carrol의 사위임을 알 수 있다.

표현 정리 **head** (단체, 조직의) 책임자

해석 Mr. Romansky에 관해 암시된 것은?
(A) Tarnton에서 평생을 보냈다.
(B) Harrison Hardware의 수석 매니저이다.
(C) Harrison Hardware를 매입하는 것을 고려하고 있다.
(D) 최근 Mr. Carrol과 일하기 시작했다.

175. 문장 위치 찾기 ★★☆
해설 세 번째 단락 'It's not just economics that has driven Mr. Carrol's decision.'에서 Mr. Carrol이 이러한 결정을 하게 된 것이 경제적 상황만이 아니라고 했다. 그렇다면 이 문장 앞쪽에는 경제적인 상황에 대한 설명이 언급되었을 것이고, 뒤에는 경제적인 상황이 아닌 그 외의 이유가 나오게 될 것이다. [2]의 뒤

에 나온 문장 'He says he is getting ready to retire in the next few years.'에서 그가 몇 년 후 은퇴할 것이라는 내용이 언급된 것으로 보아 이 역시 그가 이러한 결정을 한 또 다른 이유에 해당한다는 것을 알 수 있으므로 정답은 (B)이다.
정답 (B)

표현 정리 **economics** (어떤 산업 분야, 사회의) 자본 환경[조건], 경제 상태 **drive** (사람을 특정한 방식의 행동을 하도록) 만들다 **decision** 결정

해석 [1], [2], [3], [4] 중 다음 문장이 들어가기에 가장 적합한 곳은?

"Mr. Carrol의 결정에 영향을 미친 것은 단지 경제적 상황만은 아니다."
(A) [1]
(B) [2]
(C) [3]
(D) [4]

문제 176-180번은 다음 안내문과 이메일을 참조하시오

초안

미래를 위해 나무를 심자!

Green City Initiative에서는 ¹⁸⁰4월 18일, 토요일 오전 11시 – 오후 4시에 Glendale's Gateway Park에서 열리는 제12회 식목일 연례 기념행사에 귀하를 초대하고자 합니다. 재미있고, 교육적인 이번 행사에는 연설, 워크숍, 게임, 그리고 라이브 공연이 포함되어 있습니다. 많은 지역 노점상이 음식, 예술 작품, 의류 등을 판매하기 위해 참가할 것입니다. ¹⁷⁶참여하는 모든 분들은 공원 특별 구역 또는 가정에 심을 수 있는 소나무와 오크나무 묘목을 무료로 받게 됩니다. ¹⁷⁷일부 지역 사업체와 지역사회 단체가 후원하는 가족 친화적인 이 행사는 무료이며, 일반인들에게 열려있습니다. 더 많은 정보를 원하시면 이 사이트를 방문해 주십시오. www.greencity.org.

표현 정리 **draft** 초안, 초안을 작성하다 **initiative** 계획, 주도 **annual** 매년의, 연례의 **Arbor Day** 식목일 **feature** 특별히 포함하다, 특징으로 삼다 **dozen** 다수, 여러 개 **vendor** (거리의) 행상인, 노점상 **be on hand** 참여하다 **pine** 소나무 **oak** 오크나무 **sapling** 묘목 **family-friendly** 가정 친화적인

발신: Andrew Gates 〈agates@greencity.org〉
수신: Mayra Olivas 〈molivas@jetmail.net〉
날짜: 3월 27일
제목: 공연자들에 관하여

Mayra,

¹⁷⁹방금 올해의 식목일 행사에 관해 당신이 작성한 안내문을 검토했습니다. 모든 것이 괜찮아 보입니다. 내일 이것을 인쇄소로 보낼 예정입니다.

¹⁷⁸4월 2일 기획 회의가 있기 전에 공연자들에게 전화로 일정을 확인해 주시겠습니까? 저희는 웹사이트 상의 정보가 정확하기를 원합니다.

공연자	시간	장소
곡예사	종일	돌아다니면서 공연
페이스 페인팅	종일	피크닉 구역
이야기꾼	오후 12시 45분	Dawson Creek 무대
아일랜드 댄서	오후 1시	야외 무대
소다 크래커	오후 2시 15분	Dawson Creek 무대
Dan의 빅밴드	오후 3시	야외 무대

올해 행사 준비를 도와주는 Mayra와 자원 봉사자 분들의 노고에 정말 감사드립니다. ¹⁸⁰행사 당일에 여러분의 가족들과 만나길 기대합니다.

감사합니다.

Andrew

표현 정리 review 검토하다 send off ~을 발송하다 printer 인쇄업자
verify 확인하다 juggler 곡예사 storyteller 이야기꾼, 만담가 Irish
아일랜드의 soda cracker 소다 크래커(담백한 맛이 나는 살짝 구운 비스킷)
wandering 돌아다니는, 걸어 다니는 bandstand (지붕이 있는) 야외 무대
appreciate 고마워하다 volunteer 자원 봉사자 organize (어떤 일을)
준비하다, 조직하다 look forward to ~을 기대하다

176. 세부사항 – 식목일 기념 행사에서 나누어 줄 것   ★☆☆
해설 안내문 'Everyone attending will receive a free pine or oak sapling,
which can be planted in a special area of the park or at home.'에서 참
석자 전원은 소나무나 오크나무 묘목을 무료로 받게 됨을 알 수 있으므로 정답은
(C)이다.   정답 (C)

표현 정리 give away ~을 선물로 주다, 기부하다

해설 식목일 기념 행사에서 나누어 주는 것은 무엇인가?
(A) 티켓
(B) 음식
(C) 나무
(D) 돈

177. 세부사항 – 기념행사에 대한 내용   ★★☆
해설 첫 번째 지문인 안내문 'Sponsored by several area businesses and
community groups, this family-friendly event is free and open to the
public.'에서 이번 가족 친화적인 행사는 무료이며, 대중에게 열려있다고 했는데
(C)의 온라인으로만 구매 가능하다는 제약은 나와있지 않다.   정답 (C)

함정 분석 (A)는 'The Green City Initiative would like to invite you
to attend our twelfth annual Arbor Day celebration in Glendale's
Gateway Park on Saturday, April 18, from 11 A.M. to 4 P.M.'에서 매년
열리는 연례 행사이므로 확인이 되고, (B)는 'Sponsored by several area
businesses and community groups'에서 지역 사업체와 지역 단체 후원
을 받고 있으므로 역시 맞는 내용이며, (D)는 'Dozens of local vendors will
be on hand selling food, art, clothing, and more.'에서 지역 노점상들이
참여해 음식, 예술 작품, 의류 등을 판매할 것이라고 해서 사실이다.

표현 정리 hold 개최하다, 열다 purchase 구입하다

해설 기념 행사에 관해 언급된 것이 아닌 것은?
(A) 과거에도 열렸다.
(B) 지역 후원자가 있다.
(C) 티켓은 온라인으로 구매가 가능하다.
(D) 음식을 구입할 수 있다.

178. 주제 – 이메일의 목적   ★☆☆
해설 이메일 두 번째 단락 'Before our April 2 planning meeting, can you
call the performers and verify their schedules?'에서 공연자들에게 전화해
일정을 확인해 달라고 요청하고 있으므로 정답은 (A)이다.   정답 (A)

표현 정리 delegate 위임하다, 부여하다 place an order ~을 주문하다
communicate 전달하다, 전하다 inquire 묻다, 알아보다 availability
유효성, 가능성

해설 이메일의 목적은 무엇인가?
(A) 자원 봉사자에게 임무를 부여하기 위해
(B) 인쇄를 주문하기 위해
(C) 일정 변경을 알리기 위해
(D) 가능 여부를 물어보기 위해

179. 동의어   ★★☆
해설 이메일 'I just reviewed the announcement you drafted for this
year's Arbor Day event.'에서 drafted는 '초안을 작성하다, 기안하다'라는 의
미를 가진 동사의 과거로, 선택지에서 이와 가장 가까운 단어는 '쓰다, 작성하다'

라는 뜻의 (B) wrote이다.   정답 (B)

표현 정리 advertise 광고하다 perform 수행하다, 공연하다

해설 이메일에서 첫 번째 단락, 첫 번째 줄의 "drafted"와 의미가 가장 가까운 것
은?
(A) 광고한
(B) 작성한
(C) 보고한
(D) 수행한

180. 연계 문제 – Mr. Gates가 Ms. Olivas의 가족을 만나는 날   ★★☆
해설 이메일 마지막 단락 'I'm looking forward to meeting all of your
families at the event.'에서 Mr. Gates는 행사 당일에 Mayra의 가족들과 만나
길 기대한다고 했는데, 첫 번째 지문인 안내문 'The Green City Initiative would
like to invite you to attend our twelfth annual Arbor Day celebration in
Glendale's Gateway Park on Saturday, April 18, from 11 A.M. to 4 P.M.'에
서 4월 18일에 행사가 있을 예정임을 알 수 있으므로 정답은 (D)이다.   정답 (D)

함정 분석 (A)는 Andrew Gates가 Mayra Olivas에게 이메일을 보낸 날
이고, (C)는 'Before our April 2 planning meeting, can you call the
performers and verify their schedules?'에서 기획 회의를 하기로 한 날이
다.

해설 Mr. Gates는 Ms. Olivas의 가족을 언제 만날 것인가?
(A) 3월 27일
(B) 3월 28일
(C) 4월 2일
(D) 4월 18일

문제 181-185번은 이메일과 일정표를 참조하시오.

발신: Kalib Schwan (kalib.schwan@luckman.com)
수신: Sales Team (salesteam@luckman.com)
제목: 곧 있을 수련회에 관하여
날짜: 3월 19일
첨부파일: 일정표

안녕하십니까!

Whispering Pines에서 열릴 예정인 수련회가 저뿐 아니라 여러분들에게
도 신날 거라고 생각합니다. 이 장소에서 행사를 하는 것은 이번이 처음일
것입니다. 182(B)하지만 Sam Richards가 지난해 그곳 행사에 참석했었
고, 시설과 직원들에 대해 칭찬을 많이 했습니다.

181(D),182(C)운송부의 Gary Bane이 우리에게 회사용 밴과 차량을 제공
해 주기로 했습니다. 여러분께서는 가능한 한 빨리 운전자 또는 탑승자로 신
청해 주시기 바랍니다. 신청서는 책상 위에 있습니다. 운전자들은 열쇠를 받
기 전에 운전면허증 복사본을 Gary에게 제출해 주십시오.

181(B)이맘때쯤 산의 날씨는 쌀쌀할 수 있습니다. 그러니 모두들 따뜻한 옷
을 가져오시고, 특히 로프 코스를 위해 모자와 장갑을 지참하실 것을 권해
드립니다. 181(C)복장은 이틀 모두 편리한 복장입니다. 편안한 운동화가 좋
을 거라고 전해 들었습니다. 184Whispering Pines에는 자유 시간에 즐길
수 있는 산책로와 정원이 있습니다.

첨부된 일정을 확인해 보시고 복사본을 인쇄하시기 바랍니다. 182(D)만약
궁금한 점이 있으면 회사 행사 담당자인 Paul Orpheus에게 555-6998로
연락 주시기 바랍니다.

182(A)수련회에서 모두 뵙게 되기를 기대합니다.

Kalib

표현 정리 attachment 첨부파일 greetings 안녕하십니까 upcoming

다가오는, 곧 있을 **retreat** 수련회, (평상시의 생활에서 벗어나서 갈 수 있는) 조용한 곳, 휴양지 **speak highly of** ~을 극구 칭찬하다 **facility** 시설 **urge** 강력히 권고[촉구]하다 **sign up** 참가하다, 가입하다 **passenger** 탑승객 **signup** 서명에 의한 등록 **sheet** (종이) 한 장, (서류의) 1매 **driver's license** 운전 면허증 **receive** 받다 **advise** 조언하다, 권고하다 **rope** 밧줄, 로프 **dress** 복장 **comfortable** 편한 **trail** 오솔길, 산길 **attach** 첨부하다 **coordinator** 책임자, 진행자 **look forward to** ~을 기대하다

185(C) 영업 팀 연례 수련회

185(A) 3월 26 – 27일

Whispering Pines 컨벤션 센터와 호텔
Conestoga, PA19040

3월 26일, 금요일

오전 11시	숙소 배정을 위해 180호 방에 집합*
오전 11시 30분	Luckman 본사 출발
오후 1시	Whispering Pines 도착
오후 1시 30분	점심식사 및 환영
오후 2시 30분	팀 오리엔테이션
184 오후 4시 30분	자유 시간
오후 6시 30분	저녁 식사

3월 27일, 토요일

오전 8시	아침 식사
오전 8시 45분	건물 주변 둘러보기
오전 9시	교육 세미나
오전 10시	팀 활동
오전 11시 30분	로프 코스
오후 12시 30분	점심 식사
오후 1시 30분	A팀 발표
오후 2시 15분	B팀 발표
오후 3시	휴식
오후 3시 15분	C팀 발표
오후 4시	맺음말
오후 4시 30분	Whispering Pines 출발
오후 6시	Luckman 본사 도착

183(C) *개인실 이용 불가, 2인실만 가능

표현 정리 **annual** 매년의, 연례의 **assemble** 모이다, 집합시키다 **lodge** 묵다, 숙박하다 **assignment** 배정, 배치 **depart** 출발하다 **headquarters** 본사 **unscheduled** 미리 계획되지 않은 **ground** (건물 주위의) 구내 **exercise** 활동 **presentation** 발표 **remark** (말이나 글로 의견, 생각 등을 표하는) 발언

181. 세부사항 – 영업 팀 구성원들에게 전달된 것 ★★★

해설 이메일 두 번째 단락 'Gary Bane in Transportation has agreed to provide us with company vans and cars.'에서 회사용 밴과 차량을 이용해 이동할 예정임을 알 수 있으므로 정답은 (D)이다. 정답 (D)

🔍 **함정 분석** (B)는 'The weather can be cool in the mountains this time of year.'에서 비가 오는 날씨가 아니라 쌀쌀한 날씨에 대비하라는 내용이고, (C)는 'Dress is casual for both days.'에서 편리한 복장을 입으면 된다는 내용이다.

패러프레이징 |지문| company vans and cars 회사용 밴과 차량 → |선택지 D| company vehicles 회사 차량

표현 정리 **electronic** 전자의 **device** 장치, 기구 **wet** 비가 오는 **attire** 의복, 복장 **vehicle** 차량

해석 영업 팀 구성원들에게 전달된 사항은?
(A) 전자기구를 가져온다.
(B) 비 오는 날씨에 대비한다.
(C) 비즈니스 정장을 입는다.
(D) 회사 차량으로 이동한다.

182. 유추 – 3월에 Conestoga에 갈 사람 ★★☆

해설 두 번째 지문인 일정표에서 Conestoga는 수련회가 열리는 장소이며, 이 문제는 수련회에 참석하는 사람을 고르는 문제이기도 하다. 첫 번째 지문인 이메일 'I look forward to seeing you all at the retreat!'에서 수련회에서 뵙기를 기대한다고 말한 것으로 보아 이메일을 작성한 Kalib가 Conestoga에 갈 것임을 알 수 있으므로 정답은 (A)이다. 정답 (A)

🔍 **함정 분석** Sam Richard는 이메일 'Sam Richards attended an event there last year and spoke very highly of the facilities and staff'에서 지난해에 Conestoga에 갔던 사람이므로 (B)가, Gary Bane는 'Gary Bane in Transportation has agreed to provide us with company vans and cars.'에서 운송부에 근무하는 직원이므로 (C)가, Paul Orpheus는 'If you have any questions, contact our company's event coordinator, Paul Orpheus, at 555-6998.'에서 행사 준비를 담당하는 직원이므로 (D)가 오답이다.

해석 3월에 Conestoga에 가게 될 사람은 누구인가?
(A) Kalib Schwan
(B) Sam Richards
(C) Gary Bane
(D) Paul Orpheus

183. 유추 – 일정에 대한 내용 ★★☆

해설 두 번째 지문인 일정표 마지막 줄 '*Private rooms not available. Doubles only.'에서 직원들은 개인실 이용이 불가능하며, 2인실 사용이 가능하므로 정답은 (C)이다. 정답 (C)

🔍 **함정 분석** (D)는 일정표 'Saturday, March 27, 11:30 A.M. Rope Course'에서 로프코스에서 야외 활동이 계획되어 있음을 알 수 있다.

패러프레이징 |지문| Private rooms not available. Doubles only 개인실 이용이 불가능하며 2인실만 사용 가능하다 → |선택지 C| have to share hotel rooms 호텔 방을 함께 써야만 한다

표현 정리 **prepare** 준비하다 **share** 함께 쓰다 **remain** 머무르다 **indoors** 실내에서

해석 일정에 대해 암시된 것은?
(A) 직원들은 팀을 선택할 수 있다.
(B) 직원들은 음식을 준비하는 것을 도울 것이다.
(C) 직원들은 호텔 방을 함께 써야 한다.
(D) 직원들은 행사 전체 기간 동안 실내에 머무를 것이다.

184. 연계 문제 – 직원들이 정원을 돌아볼 수 있는 시간 ★☆☆

해설 일정표 상에서 금요일, 오후 4시 30분은 Unscheduled Time 즉, 자유 시간인데, 첫 번째 지문인 이메일 세 번째 단락 마지막 문장 'Whispering Pines has walking trails and gardens you can enjoy in your free time.'에서 자유 시간에 공원에 산책하며 즐길 수 있다고 했으므로 정답은 (B)이다. 정답 (B)

🔍 **함정 분석** (A)는 Pines Whispering Pines에 도착하는 시간이며, (C)는 교육 세미나가 잡혀 있는 시간이다. 또한 (D)는 로프 코스 활동이 예정돼 있는 시간이다.

표현 정리 **explore** 답사하다, 탐사하다

해석 직원들은 언제 정원을 돌아볼 수 있나?

(A) 금요일, 오후 1시
(B) 금요일, 오후 4시 30분
(C) 토요일, 오후 9시
(D) 토요일, 오후 11시 30분

185. 세부사항 – 수련회와 관련된 내용이 아닌 것 ★★☆

해설 일정표에서 3월 26일 금요일의 일정은 오후 6시 30분에 끝이 나고, 3월 27일 토요일의 경우도 오후 6시 이후에는 아무런 일정이 없다. 야간 관광에 관한 일정은 찾아 볼 수 없으므로 (B)가 정답이다. 정답 (B)

🔍 함정 분석 (A)의 경우 일정표에서 'March 26 – 27'로 수련회가 이틀간 진행됨을 알 수 있고, (C)는 일정표 제목 'Sales Team Annual Retreat'에서 매년 열리는 연례 행사임을 알 수 있다. 그리고 (D)는 금요일에는 점심과 저녁 식사시간이, 토요일에는 점심 식사 시간이 잡혀 있음을 알 수 있다.

표현 정리 take place 개최되다, 일어나다 feature 특별히 포함하다 scheduled 예정된, 표에 기입된

해석 수련회에 대해 언급된 내용이 아닌 것은?
(A) 이틀간 열릴 것이다.
(B) 저녁 관광이 포함되어 있다.
(C) 매년 열린다.
(D) 식사가 예정되어 있다.

문제 186-190번은 다음 웹페이지, 온라인 양식, 그리고 이메일을 참조하시오.

---

http://www.alpahemployment.com/home/aboutus

홈	구직자	고용주	재원

Alpha Employment Agency

186(D)1995년에 설립된 이후, 수십 년간 Marston 지역에서 고객들께 서비스를 제공하는 가장 큰 채용 대행업체가 되었습니다. 186(B)저희는 보건, 제조, 운송, 소매, 사무실, 그리고 이 외의 분야에서 연간 평균 2,000명이 일자리를 찾는 것을 돕고 있습니다.

일자리를 찾으시나요?
저희가 도와드리기 위해 여기 있습니다. 186(C)저희 온라인 지원서를 작성해 보안 웹사이트로 증빙 서류를 업로드해 주세요. 자격에 맞는 일자리가 생기면 최대한 빨리 여러분께 알려드릴 것입니다. 190(B)이 서비스에 대한 비용은 없습니다.

직원을 찾고 계십니까?
필요하신 내용을 저희에게 제공해 주십시오. 188그러면 최소 자격을 충족하는 지원자만 보내드릴 것입니다. 지원서를 보내드리고 면접을 주선해 드립니다. 저희가 보내드린 지원자를 채용하는데 동의하실 경우에만 비용이 청구됩니다.

표현 정리 job seeker 구직자 employer 고용인 resource 자원, 재원 employment 채용 agency 대리인, 대행자 found 설립하다 serve (상품, 서비스를) 제공하다 client 고객 fill (어떤 일자리에 사람을) 채우다 average 평균의 position (일)자리, 직위 health care 의료 서비스, 보건 manufacturing 제조업 transportation 운송 retail 소매 setting 환경, 장소 complete 기입하다, 작성하다 application 지원서 upload 업로드하다 supporting (사실임을) 뒷받침하는 documentation 서류 secure 안전한, 보안이 철저한 notify (공식적으로) 알리다, 통지하다 qualify 자격이 있다 available 이용할 수 있는 charge 비용 applicant 지원자 qualification 자격 material 자료 set up (어떤 일이 있도록) 마련하다 bill 청구서[계산서]를 보내다 candidate 후보자, 지원자 refer (남을 ~에게) 보내다

직원 채용 요청 서식

일자리
직책: 공항 셔틀버스 운전기사
일자리 유형: [✓] 임시직 [ ] 파트타임 [ ] 정규직
190(A)시간: 화요일 – 금요일, 오전 6시 – 오후 1시
교육/자격증: 고등학교 졸업 이상, 1종 운전 면허 선호
188경력: 동일 직종이거나 관련 직종에서 3개월 근무
190(C)업무: 정확한 장소에서 승객을 태우고 목적지에 내려주기, 승객의 짐을 싣고 내려주기(최대 100킬로그램까지), 187(A)공항 주차장 직원과의 의사소통, 정확한 일일 작업 일지를 작성하고 매주 제출하기
190(D)위치: Franklin
그 외 정보: 3개월 근무 평가 후 정규직으로 전환 가능함. 그 시점부터 복리후생 이용 가능
저희에 대해서 어떻게 알게 되셨나요? Franklin Register에서 광고를 보았음

고용주
회사: Jetside Airport Parking
연락처: Molly Ringer
전화번호: (410) 555-2903
이메일: molly.ringer@jetsideparking.com

표현 정리 temporary 일시적인, 임시의 credentials 자격증 diploma 졸업장 commercial driver's license 1종 운전 면허(증) prefer 선호하다 related 관련된 duty 업무 pick up ~를 (차에) 태우다 drop off ~을 내려주다 passenger 승객 destination 목적지 load (자동차, 선박 등에서) (짐을) 싣다 unload (자동차, 선박 등에서) (짐을) 내리다 luggage (여행용) 짐 up to ~까지 communicate 의사소통을 하다, 연락을 주고받다 parking lot 주차장 keep 일기, 장부, 기록 등을 쓰다[적다] accurate 정확한 daily 일일, 매일 activity 활동, 작업 log 일지 submit 제출하다 weekly 매주 permanent 영구적인, 종신의 review 검토하다 benefit (회사에서 직원에게 제공하는) 복리 후생 advertisement 광고

발신: jobs@alphaemployment.com
수신: cnewbery@safemail.net
날짜: 9월 8일

Mr. Newbery 님께,

189귀하가 계시는 지역의 채용 기회가 최근 저희 웹사이트에 게시되었습니다(공항 셔틀버스 운전기사 #290334). 세부사항을 보시고, 지원하시려면 저희 보안 웹사이트에 로그인하거나 555-2834로 전화 주십시오. 만약 고용주가 면접을 원할 경우 저희가 시간, 날짜, 장소를 알려드릴 것입니다.

Alpha 채용 대행사

표현 정리 advertisement 광고 opportunity 기회 locale (사건 등의) 현장, 장소 recently 최근에 post 게시하다

186. 세부사항 – Alpha Employment Agency에 대한 내용이 아닌 것 ★★☆

해설 Alpha Employment Agency는 구직자와 직원 채용을 필요로 하는 회사 사이를 연결해 주는 직업 소개소인데, (A)의 채용 담당자는 직원을 구하고자 하는 회사의 인사 담당자를 말하는데, 웹페이지에서 이러한 내용은 찾아 볼 수 없으므로 정답이다. 정답 (A)

함정 분석 (B)는 웹페이지 첫 번째 단락 'We fill an average of 2,000 positions a year in health care, manufacturing, transportation, retail, office, and other settings.'에서 확인되고, (C)는 웹페이지 두 번째 단락 'Complete our online application and upload supporting documentation onto our secure Web site.'에서 확인되며, (D)는 웹페이지 첫 문장 'We were founded in 1995 and have become the largest employment agency serving clients in the greater Marston area for decades.'에서 확인할 수 있다.

패러프레이징 |지문| fill an average of 2,000 positions a year in health care, manufacturing 보건, 제조업 등 다양한 산업 분야에 2,000여 개의 일자리를 알선해 주다 → |선택지 B| place workers in a variety of industries 다양한 산업 분야에 근로자들을 알선해 주다

|지문| serving clients ~ for decades 수년간 고객들에게 서비스하다 → |선택지 D| have been operating for many years 수년간 운영되어 왔다

표현 정리 directly 곧장, 바로 hiring 고용 place (사람에게 집, 직장 등을) 찾아주다, 구해주다 variety 다양성, 여러 가지 industry 산업 collect 모으다, 수집하다 operate 운영하다, 경영하다

해석 Alpha Employment Agency에 관해 언급된 내용이 아닌 것은?
(A) 채용 담당자와 직접 일하는 것을 선호한다.
(B) 다양한 산업 분야에서 근로자들을 알선해 준다.
(C) 구직자들로부터 정보를 수집한다.
(D) 수년간 운영되어 왔다.

---

187. 세부사항 – 셔틀버스 운전기사 일자리에 대한 내용 ★★☆
해설 두 번째 지문의 Position 내용 중 'Duties: Pick up and drop off passengers at correct destinations; ~ communicate with parking lot crew at airport; keep accurate daily activity log and submit weekly'에서 공항 셔틀버스 운전 기사가 수행해야 할 업무들이 나열되어 있다. 이 중 'communicate with parking lot crew at airport'가 (A)에 해당한다고 볼 수 있으므로 정답이다. 정답 (A)

함정 분석 (B)는 Position 내용 중 'Hours: 6:00 A.M. – 1:00 P.M., Tuesday through Friday'를 통해 볼 때 근무 요일은 화요일에서 금요일까지임을 알 수 있고, (C)는 'Other Information: Position may be made permanent after a three-month review; benefits available at that time'에서 3개월 근무 평가 후 정규직으로 전환된 다음부터 가능하고, (D)는 'Education/Credentials: High school diploma or higher; commercial driver's license preferred'에서 1종 면허를 선호한다고만 나와 있으므로 오답이다. commercial driver's를 특수 면허로 혼동하지 않도록 한다.

패러프레이징 |지문| communicate with parking lot crew at airport 공항에서 주차장 직원과 소통하다 → |선택지 A| coordinate with airport employees 공항 직원과 협력해 일하다

표현 정리 entail 수반하다 coordinate 협력하다, 조정하다 insurance 보험 right away 곧바로, 즉시 obtain 얻다, 획득하다

해석 셔틀기사 운전기사 일자리에 관해 언급된 내용은?
(A) 공항 직원들과 협력해 업무를 진행해야 한다.
(B) 주말 근무를 포함한다.
(C) 건강보험을 즉시 제공한다.
(D) 특수 면허 취득이 요구된다.

---

188. 연계 문제 – Ms. Ringer에 대한 내용 ★★☆
해설 Ms. Ringer는 두 번째 지문 하단에서 직원을 채용하려고 하는 회사의 채용 담당자임을 알 수 있다. 두 번째 지문 POSITION 내용 중 'Experience: Three months in the same or related position'에서 동일 또는 관련 직종에서 3개월 근무를 한 사람을 원한다고 했는데, 웹페이지 세 번째 단락 'We will only send applicants meeting your minimum qualifications.'에서 채용할 회사의 최소

조건을 충족시키는 지원자를 보낼 것이라고 했으므로 (B)가 정답이다. 정답 (B)

함정 분석 (A)는 이메일 'To view the details and apply, please log on to our secure Web site or call 555-2834.'에서 아직 지원을 한 상태가 아니기 때문에 Ms. Ringer가 Mr. Newbery를 고용할지는 아직 알 수 없다. (C), (D)의 경우 이메일 'If the employer wants to interview you, we will provide you with the time, date, and location.'에서 고용주가 면접을 원할 경우 채용 대행사에서 시간, 날짜, 장소를 지원자에게 알려줄 것이라고 했으므로 전화 면접이 아니라 대면 면접임을 알 수 있다.

표현 정리 certainly 확실히, 틀림없이 hire 고용하다 adequately 적절히, 충분히 skilled 숙련된, 노련한 applicant 지원자 personally 직접, 개인적으로 conduct (특정한 활동을) 하다, 수행하다

해석 Ms. Ringer에 대해 암시된 내용은?
(A) Mr. Newbery를 확실히 고용할 것이다.
(B) 적절히 숙련된 지원자를 받게 될 것이다.
(C) 개인적으로 지원자에게 연락할 것이다.
(D) 전화 면접을 진행할 것이다.

---

189. 세부사항 – Alpha에서 Mr. Newbery에게 연락한 이유 ★☆☆
해설 세 번째 지문인 이메일 첫 번째 줄 'An opportunity in your locale has recently been posted (Airport Shuttle Bus Driver # 290334) to our Web site.'에서 공항 셔틀버스 운전기사 일자리가 웹사이트에 올라왔으니 살펴보라는 뜻으로 Mr. Newbery에게 알려주고 있으므로 정답은 (B)이다. 정답 (B)

패러프레이징 |지문| an opportunity 채용 기회 → |선택지 B| a job opening 채용 공고

표현 정리 confirm 확인하다 opening 빈자리, 공석, 결원 remind 상기시키다 submit 제출하다

해석 Alpha에서 Mr. Newbery에게 연락한 이유는?
(A) 지원서 수령을 확인하기 위해
(B) 채용 공고를 알려주기 위해
(C) 면접 일정을 잡기 위해
(D) 서류를 제출하는 것을 상기시켜주기 위해

---

190. 연계 문제 – Mr. Newbery에 대한 내용이 아닌 것 ★★★
해설 첫 번째 지문인 웹페이지 'There is no charge for this service.'에서 구직자에게는 직업 소개 비용을 받지 않는다고 했는데, 이메일에서 Mr. Newberry는 구직자임을 알 수 있으므로 (B)는 사실이 아니어서 정답이다. 정답 (B)

함정 분석 이 문제는 구직자인 Mr. Newbery가 고용주가 요구하는 최소한의 요구 조건을 충족시킨다는 전제 하에 문제를 풀어야 하는 까다로운 문제이다. (A)는 두 번째 지문 POSITION 내용 중 'Hours: 6:00 A.M. – 1:00 P.M., Tuesday through Friday'에서 오전 6시에서 오후 10시까지 근무할 수 있는 사람을 원하고 있음을 알 수 있고, (C)는 POSITION 내용 중 'Duties: ~ load and unload passengers' luggage (up to 100 kilograms)'에서 최고 100킬로그램까지 나가는 승객의 짐을 싣고 내려주는 업무도 포함되어 있음을 알 수 있다. (D)는 POSITION 내용 중 'Location: Franklin'에서 근무지가 Franklin임을 나타내고 있어, Mr. Newberry 역시 Franklin에 거주한다는 것을 추론할 수 있다.

패러프레이징 |지문| load and unload passengers' luggage (up to 100 kilograms) 최고 100kg까지 나가는 승객의 짐을 싣고 내려준다 → |선택지 C| lift heavy bags 무거운 짐을 든다

표현 정리 lift 들어올리다

해석 Mr. Newberry에 관한 사실 내용이 아닌 것은?
(A) 아침에 근무할 수 있다.
(B) Alpha Employment에 비용을 지불했다.

(C) 무거운 가방을 들어 올릴 수 있다.
(D) Franklin에 거주한다.

문제 191-195번은 다음 회람, 일정표, 그리고 이메일을 참조하시오.

회람

수신: 모든 영업부 직원

발신: Gordon Mosher, 영업부 부사장

날짜: 4월 10일

다음 달에 우리 회사의 새 재고정리 소프트웨어를 만드는 TrackPro가 Williamsport에 옵니다. **192그들의 숙련된 교육 담당자가 일일 워크숍을 진행하기 위해 멀리 Jefferson City에 있는 본사에서 옵니다.** **191저는 Sigma 직원들을 위해 TrackPro가 4개의 워크숍 자리를 확보할 수 있게 했습니다.** 다른 지역 회사들 역시 선발된 직원들을 보낼 예정입니다.

Sigma에서는 교육에 대한 모든 비용을 부담하고 출장비도 지급할 것입니다. 참석하는데 선발된 직원은 다음 부서 회의에서 Numera에 대한 발표를 해야 합니다.

194만약 워크숍에 참가하고 싶다면 여러분의 자격 요건을 적은 편지를 보내주시기 바랍니다. 또한 부서가 여러분에게 투자하는 것이 어떤 이점이 있는지를 편지에 설명해야 합니다. 편지를 4월 20일까지 저에게 보내 주십시오. 참석자들의 명단은 5월 1일에 발표될 예정입니다.

표현 정리 **vice president** 부사장 **inventory** 물품 목록, 재고품, 재고조사 **experienced** 노련한, 숙련된 **come all the way** 먼 길을 오다 **headquarters** 본사 **space** 공간, (빈) 자리 **as well** 또한, 역시 **cover** (무엇을 하기에) 충분한 돈을 대다 **fee** 요금, 수업료 **reimburse** 상환하다, 되물어내다 **expense** 비용 **qualification** 자격 요건, 자질, 능력 **benefit** 이익, 이득 **attendee** 참석자

Numera 교육

날짜: 5월 23일, 금요일

시간: 오전 8시 – 오후 4시 30분

장소: Williamsport 컨벤션 센터, 205호

오전 8시	환영 (진행자: Doug Popovich)
192오전 8시 15분	Numera의 기초 정복 (발표자: Tim Song)
195오전 10시	Numera의 고급 기능 사용 (발표자: Jill Yen)
오전 11시 45분	점심 시간 (점심 식사 포함)
오후 12시 15분	하드웨어/소프트웨어 충돌 문제 다루기 (발표자: Norma Lee)
오후 2시 30분	사용자의 요구에 맞춘 기록 생성 (발표자: Doug Popovich)
오후 4시	질의응답 (모든 발표자)

참석자들은 TrackPro로부터 공식적인 수료증을 받게 됩니다.

표현 정리 **presenter** 진행자, 발표자 **master** 정복하다, 습득하다 **advanced** 고급의, 상급의 **address** (어려운 문제 등을) 다루다, 처리하다 **conflict** 갈등, 충돌 **customize** 주인이 원하는 대로 만들다 **Q&A** 질의응답(= Question and Answer)

수신: Betina Richards ⟨brichards@wagogo.com⟩

발신: Kim Jordan ⟨kjordan@sigmatechnologies.com⟩

날짜: 5월 27일, 화요일

Betina 님께,

194지난주 Numera 워크숍에서 만나서 반가웠습니다. Wagogo에 근무하

는 당신과 당신 동료들도 Sigma에서 저희가 겪는 문제와 같은 소프트웨어 문제를 갖고 있어서 놀랐습니다.

195Ms. Yen의 발표는 아주 유용했습니다. 상품의 가용성 확인을 할 때 시각을 조정하는 방법에 대해 가르쳐주시는 부분이 마음에 들었습니다. 하지만 Ms. Yen이 알려주신 방법대로 해 보았으나 변경 사항을 어떻게 저장하는지 생각이 나지 않습니다. **193그 부분에 대한 상세 내용을 메모하셨는지 궁금합니다.** 만약 그러시다면 어떻게 하는지 방법을 알려주실 수 있으시겠습니까?

Kim

표현 정리 **participant** 참석자 **official** 공식적인 **certificate** 수료증서 **completion** 수료 **colleague** 동료 **extremely** 아주, 대단히 **adjust** 조정하다 **availability** 가용성 **direction** 사용법, 지침서 **take notes** 기록하다, 필기를 하다

---

191. 동의어 ★★☆

해설 첫 번째 지문인 회람 'I was able to get TrackPro to hold four spaces in the workshop for Sigma employees.'에서 hold는 '보유하다, 마련하고 있다'의 의미를 가지고 있으므로 이와 가장 유사한 단어는 (D) reserve이다.
정답 (D)

표현 정리 **grasp** 꽉 잡다, 완전히 이해하다 **host** 주최하다 **reserve** (자리 등을) 따로 잡아두다, ~을 마련해 두다

해석 회람에서 첫 번째 단락, 세 번째 줄의 "hold"와 의미가 가장 가까운 것은?
(A) 꽉 잡다
(B) 주최하다
(C) 소유하다
(D) 따로 잡아 두다

192. 연계 문제 – Mr. Song에 대한 내용 ★★☆

해설 두 번째 지문인 일정표에서 Mr. Song은 교육을 진행하는 TrackPro의 직원으로 오전 8시 15분에 예정된 발표자인데, 회람 첫 번째 단락 'Its experienced trainers are coming all the way from the company's headquarters in Jefferson City to lead a one-day workshop.'에서 TrackPro 교육 담당자들이 워크숍을 진행하기 위해 Williamsport에 왔음을 알 수 있으므로 정답은 (B)이다.
정답 (B)

🔍 **함정 분석** (D)는 일정표 하단 'Participants will receive an official certificate of completion from TrackPro.'에서 노트가 아니라 수료증을 받게 되며, 나누어 주는 사람이 Mr. Song인지는 알 수 없으므로 오답이다.

표현 정리 **hire** 고용하다 **organize** 준비하다 **distribute** 나누어 주다, 배부하다 **participant** 참석자

해석 Mr. Song에 관해 암시된 것은?
(A) 최근 TrackPro에 고용되었다.
(B) 5월 23일 교육을 위해 이동을 했다.
(C) TrackPro를 위한 워크숍을 준비한다.
(D) 참석자들에게 노트를 나눠 주었다.

193. 주제 – Ms. Jordan의 목적 ★☆☆

해설 이메일 내용을 통해 Ms. Jordan은 워크숍에 참가했던 Sigma 직원(이메일 주소를 보면 힌트를 얻을 수 있다.)임을 알 수 있다. 이메일 두 번째 단락 'I wonder if you took notes on that detail. If so, could you tell me how to do it?'에서 Ms. Jordan은 강의 내용에 대한 메모를 했는지 궁금해 하면서 만약 했다면, 그것에 대해 알려줄 수 있는지 묻고 있으므로 정답은 (C)이다. 정답 (C)

표현 정리 **schedule** 일정을 잡다 **provide** 주다, 공급하다 **assistance** 도움

해석 Ms. Jordan이 이메일을 보낸 이유는?
(A) 회의 일정을 잡으려고

(B) 피드백을 주려고
(C) 도움을 요청하려고
(D) 교육을 추천하려고

194. 연계 문제 – Mr. Jordan에 대한 내용　★★★

해설　먼저 Ms. Jordan은 워크숍에 참석했던 Sigma의 직원이며, Gordon Mosher는 직원들에게 회람을 보낸 Sigma의 영업 담당 부사장이다. 회람 세 번째 단락 'If you would like to be considered for the workshop, send me a letter listing your qualifications.'에서 Mr. Mosher는 직원들에게 교육에 참석하고 싶으면 자신이 왜 참가 자격이 있는지를 편지에 적으라고 했는데, Ms. Jordan이 보낸 이메일 'It was nice to meet you at the Numera workshop last week.'에서 워크숍에 참석했음을 알 수 있는데, 이는 결국 Gordon Mosher에게 편지를 보내 워크숍에 참가할 수 있게 선택을 받았음을 의미하므로 정답은 (A)이다.　정답 (A)

표현 정리　lead 이끌다, 지휘하다　used to (과거) ～했다

해석　Ms. Jordan에 관해 암시된 것은?
(A) Mr. Mosher에게 글을 썼다.
(B) 워크숍을 이끌었다.
(C) 영업부장이다.
(D) Wagogo에서 일한 적이 있다.

195. 연계 문제 – Ms. Richards가 Numera의 시각 조정을 배운 시간 ★★☆

해설　Ms. Richards는 이메일 수신인이며, Kim Jordan과 같이 교육에 참석했음을 알 수 있다. 이메일 두 번째 단락 'The presentation by Ms. Yen was extremely useful. I like that she taught us how to adjust the view when checking product availability.'에서 이 둘은 Ms. Yen의 발표를 같이 들었고 상품의 가용성을 확인할 때 시각을 조정하는 방법에 대해 배웠음을 알 수 있는데, 일정표에서 Ms. Yen이 강의하는 시간은 오전 10시임을 알 수 있으므로 정답은 (B)이다.　정답 (B)

표현 정리　adjustment 조정, 조절, 수정

해석　Ms. Richards는 몇 시에 Numera의 시각 조정 메뉴에 대해 배웠나?
(A) 오전 8시 15분
(B) 오전 10시
(C) 오전 12시 15분
(D) 오전 2시 30분

문제 196-200번은 다음 웹페이지, 리뷰, 그리고 이메일을 참조하시오.

http://www.dominorecords.com/				
Domino Records				
회사소개	아티스트	뉴스	쇼핑	구독

도미노 레코드

196Domino Records는 Chuck Mille가 1943년 뉴욕 Queens에 있는 그의 작은 스튜디오에서 지역 음악가들을 대상으로 녹음 작업을 하는 것으로 시작했습니다. 이후 저희 회사는 세계적인 대형 재즈 음반사 중 하나로 성장했습니다. 뉴욕, 런던, 도쿄에 있는 본사와 함께 저희는 전통 재즈와 그 외의 멋진 음악을 26개 국가의 고객들에게 제공하고 있습니다. Domino를 선택한 아티스트로는 Sam Harris, The Golden Trio, Skip Tracer가 있습니다. 197저희는 6월에 전 세계적인 가수인 Betty Raygun과 계약을 체결했습니다. 새롭게 발매되는 음반 외에도 저희는 창립일까지 거슬러 올라가는 초기 녹음 목록을 보관하고 있으며, 이들 중 다수는 여전히 구매가 가능합니다.

표현 정리　subscribe 구독　label 음반사　forefront 선두　sign (운동선수, 음악가 등과[이]) 계약하다　world-famous 세계적으로 유명한　release (레코드, 책 따위)를 발매하다　maintain 유지하다, 보존하다　founding

days 설립 초기 시절

Easton Times	12월 1일, 수요일

Betty Raygun의 'Bright Lights'

Betty Raygun의 목소리는 실크처럼 부드러우며, 진정한 재즈팬이라면, 누구나 알고 있듯이 그녀는 항상 열정을 갖고 노래한다. 197그녀가 새로 계약한 회사와 작업한 음반인 'Bright Lights'를 통해서도 이를 확실히 알 수 있다. 198앨범 타이틀에도 불구하고 이 앨범에 실린 8곡의 노래는 상실, 갈망, 후회라는 주제를 다룬다. 아마 그녀는 음악을 공부하는 어린 시절을 파리에서 보낸 시간을 회상했을 것이다. 이 앨범은 그녀의 열성 팬들과 아직 그녀의 이전 작품에 친숙하지 않은 많은 이들에게 공감을 불러일으킬 것이다. 199이런 양쪽에 걸친 그녀의 매력은 힙합 아티스트인 To Go Bros와 함께 순회공연을 하기로 한 것을 이해하는데 도움이 된다. 그들은 1월부터 전국 22곳을 돌며 순회공연을 할 것이다.　- Shawn Price

표현 정리　describe 묘사하다, ～을 평하다　serious 진지한, 진정한　evident 분명한, 눈에 띄는　despite ～에도 불구하고　touch on ～을 간단히 언급하다, 다루다　loss 상실　longing 갈망, 열망　regret 후회　recall 기억해내다, 생각나게 하다　appeal 불러일으키다, 관심을 끌다　diehard 끝까지 버티는, 오래가는　crossover 양쪽에 걸친 것, 크로스오버(활동이나 스타일이 두 가지 이상의 분야에 걸친 것)　tour 순회공연　hit the road 길을 나서다, 여행을 떠나다

발신: Ed O'Neal
수신: Kate Magus
날짜: 12월 2일
제목: 새로운 음악에 관하여

Kate,

저는 어제 Betty Raygun이라는 재즈 가수에 대한 평론을 읽었습니다. 199그녀는 제가 가장 좋아하는 밴드와 함께 곧 순회공연을 할 예정입니다. 이 사실이 나를 흥미롭게 만들었고, 그녀의 곡 중에서 하나인 "Downtown"을 무료로 www.soundvoyage.com에서 다운로드하였습니다. 그 노래는 정말 놀라웠습니다! 200한번 들어볼 것을 추천합니다. 새로운 앨범에 있는 모든 다른 노래도 마찬가지로 좋았습니다. 만약 그것이 마음에 든다면, 그녀의 새 CD를 구입해 우리 고객들을 위해 커피숍에서 틀어도 될 것 같습니다.

Ed

표현 정리　review 비평, 평론　curious 호기심이 강한, 알고 싶어하는　download 다운로드하다　track (음반, 테이프에 녹음된 음악) 한 곡　amazing 놀라운　suggest 추천하다, 제안하다　check out (흥미로운 것을) 살펴보다

196. 세부사항 – Domino Records에 대한 내용　★★★

해설　첫 번째 지문인 웹페이지 'Domino Records began when Chuck Miller started recording local musicians in 1943 in his small studio in Queens, New York.'에서 Domino Records는 1943년 Chuck Miller가 뉴욕 Queens에서 시작했음을 알 수 있으므로 정답은 (C)이다.　정답 (C)

함정 분석　(A)는 'We have since grown into one of the largest and best-known jazz labels in the world.'에서 전 세계적인 재즈 음반사가 됐다고는 했지만 재즈 음악만을 녹음하는지는 알 수 없으므로 혼동해서는 안 된다. (B)는 'With main offices in New York, London, and Tokyo, ～.'에서 뉴욕, 런던, 도쿄에 본사를 두고 있다고 했지만, 본사를 이전했다는 내용은 없다. (D)는 ' ～, many of which are still available for purchase.'에서 초기 녹음 목록 중 다수가 여전히 구매가 가능하다고 했는데, 이것이 온라인으로만 판매되는지는 알 수 없다.

패러프레이징 |지문| Chuck Miller started ~ Chuck Miller가 시작하다 → |선택지 C| founded by Mr. Miller Miller 씨에 의해 설립되었다

표현 정리 **musician** 음악가 **headquarters** 본사 **found** 창립하다, 설립하다

해설 Domino Records에 대해 언급된 것은?
    (A) 재즈 음악만 녹음한다.
    (B) 본사를 이전했다.
    (C) Mr. Miller가 설립했다.
    (D) 온라인에서만 음악을 판매한다.

197. 연계 문제 – 'Bright Lights'에 대한 내용   ★★☆

해설 두 번째 지문인 리뷰에서 'Bright Lights'는 Betty Raygun의 신규 앨범 타이틀임을 알 수 있다. 'This is evident, once again, on her newest recording 'Bright Lights' with her new company.'에서 그녀는 새로 계약한 회사와 녹음 작업을 했음을 알 수 있는데, 첫 번째 지문 'We signed world-famous vocalist Betty Raygun in June.'에서 6월에 Betty Raygun과 계약했다고 했으므로 Bright Lights는 Dominoo에서 발매된 것을 알 수 있다. 정답은 (B)이다.   정답 (B)

🔍 함정 분석 (C)는 'This album will appeal both to her diehard fans and many who are not yet familiar with her earlier work.'에서 이번 앨범이 첫 번째 앨범이 아님을 알 수 있다. (D) 역시 'That crossover appeal may help explain her decision to go on tour with hip-hop artists To Go Bros.'에서 그녀가 힙합 아티스트와 함께 순회공연을 한다는 것일 뿐, 그녀의 음악이 힙합인 것은 아니다.

표현 정리 **produce** (영화, 연극 등을) 제작하다 **release** (레코드, 책 따위)를 발매하다 **debut** 데뷔, 첫 출연 **consider** ~으로 생각하다, 여기다

해설 'Bright Lights'에 관한 사실 내용은?
    (A) Tokyo에서 제작되었다.
    (B) Domino에서 발매되었다.
    (C) Ms. Raygun의 데뷔 앨범이다.
    (D) 힙합 앨범으로 여겨진다.

198. 세부사항 – Ms. Raygun에 관한 내용이 아닌 것   ★★☆

해설 두 번째 지문 'Despite the title, the eight songs on this album touch on themes of loss, longing, and regret.'에서 Ms. Raygun은 이번 앨범에 8곡을 수록했을 뿐, 8개의 앨범을 녹음한 것이 아니므로 정답은 (D)이다.   정답 (D)

🔍 함정 분석 (A)는 두 번째 지문 'Perhaps she was recalling her years spent in Paris as a young music student.'에서 그녀가 어린 시절에 파리에서 공부했음을 알 수 있다. (B)는 첫 번째 지문 'We signed world-famous vocalist Betty Raygun in June.'에서 세계적인 가수임을 알 수 있다. (C)는 두 번째 지문 'They will hit the road in January for twenty-two stops across the country.'에서 1월부터 전국 22곳을 순회공연할 것이라고 했으므로 맞는 내용이다.

패러프레이징 |지문| her years spent in Paris as a young music student 어린 음악 학도로 파리에서 보냈던 시간 → |선택지 A| She studied in Paris 그녀는 파리에서 공부했다
|지문| world-famous vocalist 세계적으로 유명한 보컬리스트 → |선택지 B| an acclaimed artist 호평을 받고 있는 아티스트
|지문| will hit the road in January 1월부터 전국을 순회공연하다 → |선택지 C| will be traveling next year 내년부터 순회를 하다

표현 정리 **acclaimed** 칭찬(갈채, 환호, 호평)을 받고 있는

해설 Ms. Raygun에 관해 언급된 내용이 아닌 것은?
    (A) 파리에서 공부했다.
    (B) 호평을 받고 있는 아티스트이다.

    (C) 내년에 여러 곳을 순회할 것이다.
    (D) 8개의 앨범을 녹음했다.

199. 연계 문제 – Mr. O'Neal에 관한 내용   ★★☆

해설 세 번째 지문인 이메일 'She is touring soon with one of my favorite bands.'에서 자신이 가장 좋아하는 밴드가 Betty Raygun과 순회공연을 할 것이라고 했는데, 두 번째 지문 'That crossover appeal may help explain her decision to go on tour with hip-hop artists To Go Bros.'에서 Betty Raygun이 함께 순회공연을 할 아티스트가 To Go Bros임을 알 수 있으므로 정답은 (A)이다.   정답 (A)

🔍 함정 분석 (B)는 이메일 'That made me curious, so I downloaded one of her tracks.'에서 Ms. Raygun의 음악을 다운로드해 들었음을 알 수 있다. (C)는 'Yesterday, I read a review about a jazz singer named Betty Raygun.'에서 Mr. O'Neal이 Betty Raygun이라는 재즈 가수에 대한 평론을 읽었다는 것은 알 수 있지만, 그가 Easton Times를 구독한 시점은 알 수 없다. (D)는 '~, maybe we could purchase her new CD and play it for our customers in the coffee shop.'에서 Mr. O'Neal은 이미 커피숍을 운영하고 있다고 할 수 있다.

해석 Mr. O'Neal에 관해 암시된 것은?
    (A) To Go Bros의 팬이다.
    (B) Ms. Raygun을 라이브 공연으로 보았다.
    (C) Easton Times를 12월에 구독했다.
    (D) 커피숍을 열 계획을 하고 있다.

200. 세부사항 – Mr. O'Neal이 Ms. Magus에게 이메일을 보낸 이유   ★★☆

해설 마지막 지문에서, Downtown이라는 노래를 무료로 다운로드하여 들어보고, 'I suggest you check it out.'이라고 했기 때문에, 노래를 추천하기 위해서 이메일을 보낸 것을 알 수 있다.   정답 (D)

표현 정리 **music recording** 음반 **promote** 홍보하다 **upcoming** 다가오는, 곧 있을

해석 Mr. O'Neal이 Ms. Magus에게 이메일을 보낸 이유는?
    (A) 음반을 주문하기 위해
    (B) 새로운 웹 사이트에 관해 말하기 위해
    (C) 다가오는 투어를 홍보하기 위해
    (D) 노래를 추천하기 위해

문제 147-148번은 다음 발표를 참조하시오.

Shipley's가 Branford에 옵니다!

"신선한 농산물, 훌륭한 음식"

147**7월 1일, 월요일에 478 State Street in Branford, CT에 저희 최신 지점을 오픈할 예정이니 함께 해 주세요.**
148**첫 고객 50분께는 재사용할 수 있는 쇼핑 가방을 무료로 드립니다!**

개장 특별가 (7월 1일 – 7월 7일)

달콤한 하얀 복숭아 99센트/파운드

큰 씨 없는 대형 수박 개당 단 3.99달러

과즙이 많은 귤 79세트/파운드

그래놀라(엄선된 품종들) 1.99달러/파운드

말린 과일과 견과류 혼합 2.99달러부터

주차는 State Street를 따라, 그리고 가게 뒤 부지에 가능.

표현 정리 **reusable** 재사용할 수 있는 **lb** (무게를 나타내는) 파운드 **jumbo** 아주 큰 **seedless** 씨 없는 **juicy** 즙이 많은 **tangerine** 귤 **select** 엄선된 **variety** 품종 **along** ～을 따라 **lot** (특정 용도용) 부지

147. 세부사항 – 7월 1일에 일어날 일 ★☆☆

해설 첫 문장 'Join us on Monday, July 1, for the grand opening of our newest location at 478 State Street in Branford, CT.'를 통해 7월 1일에 새 지점을 오픈할 예정임을 알 수 있으므로 정답은 (C)이다. **정답 (C)**

해석 7월 1일에 일어날 일은?
(A) 채소가 할인되어 팔릴 것이다.
(B) 할인 품목은 더 이상 이용이 가능하지 않을 것이다.
(C) 새로운 지역에 매장이 문을 열 것이다.
(D) 새 주차장이 개방될 것이다.

148. 세부사항 – Shipley's에 대한 내용 ★★☆

해설 'The first 50 customers will receive a free reusable shopping bag!'을 통해 50명의 고객에게 재사용이 가능한 쇼핑 가방을 제공할 것이라고 했으므로 정답은 (B)이다. **정답 (B)**

🔍**함정 분석** 특별가로 제공되는 물품들을 고급 식료품이라고 보기는 어려우므로 (A)는 오답이다. 'Join us on Monday, July 1, for the grand opening of our newest location at 478 State Street in Branford, CT.'를 통해 Branford에 처음으로 매장을 오픈하는 것을 알 수 있으므로 (C)는 오답이다.

표현 정리 **specialize in** ～을 전문적으로 다루다 **gourmet food** 고급 식료품 **currently** 현재

해석 Shipley's에 관해 언급된 것은?
(A) 고급 식료품을 전문적으로 다룬다.
(B) 일부 고객을 위한 선물들을 갖추고 있다.
(C) Branford에 다른 매장들을 갖고 있다.
(D) 현재 직원들을 고용하고 있는 중이다.

문제 149-150번은 다음 일자리 기사를 참조하시오.

요즘 높은 실업률에도 불구하고 일부 직종은 일자리 수요가 많다. 간호직이 한 예이다. 1999년 이후, 인구가 평균적으로 고령화되면서 간호사의 수요가 급증했다. 149한편 이 분야로 진출하는 간호사 수가 적다 보니, 병원과 의료

시설에 간호사 인력이 부족하게 되었다. 사실, 사용자들은 직원을 새로 끌어 오기 위해 2,000달러 이상의 현금을 보너스로 제공하기도 한다. 150그 분야로 진출하기 위한 교육은 간호조무사 자격을 위해 적게는 3개월에서 6개월 정도면 마칠 수 있다.

표현 정리 **unemployment** 실업률 **profession** 직업 **demand** 수요 **nursing** 간호 업무, 간호직 **prime** 주요한 **spike** (가치가) 급등하다 **population** 인구 **on average** 평균적으로 **in the meantime** 한편, 또한 **result in** ～을 야기하다 **shortage** 부족 **facility** 시설 **frequently** 자주 **attract** 끌어 모으다, 유치하다 **nursing assistant** 간호조무사

149. 세부사항 – 간호사 부족의 원인 ★☆☆

해설 'In the meantime, fewer people entering the field has resulted in shortages of nurses at some hospitals and medical facilities.'에서 해당 분야로 진출하려고 하는 사람의 수가 적기 때문이라고 했으므로 정답은 (B)이다.
정답 (B)

패러프레이징 |지문| fewer people entering the field has resulted in shortages of nurses 그 분야에 진출하는 사람의 수가 적은 것이 간호사 부족을 야기시킨다 → |선택지 B| Not enough people are becoming nurses 충분 치 않은 사람들이 간호사가 되고 있다

해석 기사에 따르면, 간호사 부족의 원인은?
(A) 간호사에 대한 수요가 줄고 있다.
(B) 간호사가 되려고 하는 사람들이 충분하지 않다.
(C) 적은 보수를 받고 싶은 사람은 거의 없을 것이다.
(D) 많은 경험이 있는 간호사들이 은퇴하고 있다.

150. 세부사항 – 간호조무사가 되기 위해 필요한 것 ★☆☆

해설 마지막 문장 'Training to enter the field can be completed in as little as 3 to 6 months for nursing assistant positions.'에서 간호조무사가 되기 위해서는 3개월에서 6개월 정도 교육을 받아야 한다고 했으므로 있으므로 정답은 (A)이다. **정답 (A)**

패러프레이징 |지문| Training ～ can be completed in as little as 3 to 6 교 육은 3개월에서 6개월 정도로 마칠 수 있다 → |선택지 A| Finishing several months of study 수 개월 동안의 공부를 마치는 것

표현 정리 **sponsorship** 후원 **degree** 학위 **specialized** 전문화된

해석 간호조무사가 되기 위해 필요한 것은?
(A) 몇 개월의 교육 수료
(B) 의료시설로부터의 후원
(C) 대학 학위 취득
(D) 전문화된 면허를 취득

문제 151-152번은 다음 문자 메시지 내용을 참조하시오.

| Randy Zerber | Holloman 고객 건은 어떻게 되고 있죠? | 오후 1시 45분 |

| Niki Holinka | 그렇게 좋진 않아요. 저는 약간 좌절감을 느끼고 있어요. | |
| | | 오후 1시 48분 |

| Randy Zerber | 무엇이 문제인가요? | 오후 1시 49분 |

| Niki Holinka | Mr. Johnson이 저에게 Newport 호텔을 보수하는데 드 는 비용 견적서를 준비해 달라고 요청했어요. 하지만 제가 견적서를 작성해 제시하자, 그는 제가 비용을 지나치게 부풀렸다고 하며 다시 해 달라고 했어 요. | |
| | | 오후 1시 50분 |

| Randy Zerber | 우리 회사의 표준 청구율을 참고했나요? | 오후 1시 52분 |

| Niki Holinka | 151네. 제가 항상 준비하는 모든 견적서들과 같은 기준을 참고해 작성했어요. 왜 Mr. Johnson이 그렇게 반응을 했는지 이해가 가지 | |

	오후 1시 54분

Randy Zerber **152그분답지 않네요. 제가 전화를 걸어 무슨 일이 있는지 알아 볼게요. 걱정 말아요. 모든 것은 잘 될 겁니다.** 오후 1시 57분

Niki Holinka 고마워요. 오후 1시 58분

표현 정리 account 단골, 고객 (계정) frustrated 좌절감을 느끼는 estimate 견적(서), 추정 renovate 개조하다, 보수하다 present 제시하다 overinflate 지나치게 올리다 expense 비용 redo 다시 하다 standard 일반적인, 표준의

151. 유추 – Ms. Holinka에 대한 내용 ★★☆
해설 Ms. Holinka는 견적서를 작성할 때, 표준 청구 기준율을 사용했다고 했고, 'I did exactly what I do for every other estimate I prepare'를 통해 다른 견적서를 작성할 때 하는 방식 그대로 했다고 했으므로 정답은 (C)이다. **정답 (C)**

패러프레이징 |지문| standard billing rates 일반적인 청구율 → |선택지 C| a quote in the regular way 통상적인 견적서

표현 정리 calculation 계산 quote 견적 turn in ~을 제출하다

해석 Ms. Holinka에 관해 암시된 것은?
(A) 그녀의 계산에 실수가 있었다.
(B) Holloman과 전에 일한 적이 있다.
(C) 일반적인 방법으로 견적서를 준비했다.
(D) 그녀의 추정치를 늦게 제출했다.

152. 의도 파악하기 ★★☆
해설 오후 1시 54분에 보낸 메시지 'I don't understand why Mr. Johnson reacted that way.'에서 Ms. Holinka는 Mr. Johnson이 왜 그렇게 반응을 했는지 이해하지 못하겠다고 했고, 이에 대해 Mr. Zerber가 'That's not like him. I'll give him a call and see what's going on.'이라고 말하며, 자신이 연락해 확인해 보겠다고 했으므로 Mr. Johnson이 평소와는 다르게 행동했다고 생각하고 있음을 알 수 있어 (A)가 정답이다. **정답 (A)**

표현 정리 strangely 이상하게 suspect 의심하다 disapprove 못마땅해하다 reasonable 합리적인

해석 Mr. Zerber가 오후 1시 57분에 "그분답지 않네요."라고 한 말의 의미는?
(A) Mr. Johnson이 이상하게 행동했다고 생각한다.
(B) Mr. Johnson이 프로젝트를 좋아하지 않는다고 의심한다.
(C) Mr. Johnson이 그의 일을 못마땅해 한다고 생각한다.
(D) Mr. Johnson이 합리적이었다고 믿는다.

문제 153-155번은 다음 회사 뉴스레터를 참조하시오.

다가오는 행사들

새해 복 많이 받으세요! 많은 분들이 건강을 위한 많은 결심을 했습니다. 그것이 10파운드를 줄이는 것이든, 한 주에 세 번 운동을 하겠다는 것이든, 저희는 여러분이 목표를 달성하도록 돕기를 원합니다. 2월 8일, 오전 11시에서 오후 3시까지 2층 아트리움에서 무료 건강 보건 박람회가 있을 예정이니 함께 해 주세요. **153모든 Dili 사 직원들도 이용할 수 있는 건강과 보건에 관해 배우세요.** Blue Star 보험, St. Margaret's 병원, Total Fitness, Mega Nutrition, Sarah's Natural Foods 등에서 온 직원들과 대화를 나누세요. **155(A)건강 검진(혈압, 맥박, 키, 몸무게, 체질량 지수)을 받으세요.** 간단하고, 맛있고, 건강한 식사를 요리하는 방법을 배우세요. **155(C)Gates 조리학교 학생들이 매 30분마다 수업을 할 것입니다. 155(B)Bamboo 스파 방문권, 2인을 위한 Manny's 저녁 식사, 그 이상을 얻으려면 등록하세요.** **154추가 정보는 Sherry Wilson에게 555-3112로 전화 주십시오.**

그곳에서 여러분을 보길 바랍니다!

표현 정리 upcoming 다가오는 make a resolution 결심을 하다 wellness 건강 fair 박람회 atrium 아트리움(현대식 건물 중앙 높은 곳에 보통 유리로 지붕을 한 넓은 공간) resource 자원 Inc. 주식회사 representative 직원, (판매) 대리인, 외판원 insurance 보험 checkup 검진, 검사 blood pressure 혈압 pulse 맥박 BMI 체질량 지수 Culinary Arts 조리 give lessons 수업을 하다

153. 주제 – 행사의 대상 ★☆☆
해설 'Learn about the health and wellness resources available to all Dili, Inc. employees.'를 보면 건강 보건 박람회 참가자들은 Dili 주식회사 직원들이라는 것을 알 수 있으므로 정답은 (C)이다. **정답 (C)**

해석 이 행사는 누구를 대상으로 하는가?
(A) 보건 분야 직원
(B) 잠재적인 학생들
(C) Dili의 직원들
(D) 보험 설계사들

154. 유추 – Ms. Wilson의 직업 ★★☆
해설 본문의 마지막 문장 'For more information, call Sherry Wilson at 555-3112.'에서 행사에 대한 자세한 사항을 Sherry Wilson에게 연락하라고 했으므로 Ms. Wilson은 행사를 담당하는 사람이라는 것을 알 수 있어 정답은 (B)이다. **정답 (B)**

해석 Ms. Wilson은 누구인가?
(A) 뉴스레터 편집자
(B) 행사 준비자
(C) St. Margaret's의 간호사
(D) Bamboo 스파의 직원

155. 세부사항 – 행사의 일부가 아닌 것 ★★☆
해설 본문에서 제품 샘플을 제공한다는 내용은 찾을 수 없으므로 정답은 (D)이다. **정답 (D)**

🔍 **함정 분석** (A)는 'Get a health checkup (blood pressure, pulse, height, weight, BMI).'에서, (B)는 'Register to win a visit to the Bamboo Spa, dinner for two at Manny's, and more.'에서, (C)는 'Students from the Gates School of Culinary Arts will be giving lessons every half hour.'에서 확인이 가능하다.

표현 정리 a prize draw 상품 추첨

해석 행사의 일부로 언급되지 않은 것은?
(A) 혈압 검사
(B) 상품 추첨
(C) 요리 수업
(D) 제품 샘플

문제 156-157번은 다음 영수증을 참조하시오.

Gordon's
78 Mithos Road
Edgewood, NM 89943
(505) 555-5673

날짜: 7월 28일
등록 #: 4
157(B)출납원: Jason Smith

제품 번호	156품목	수량	가격
05642	줄넘기	1	5달러
29045	운동용 반바지	2	26달러
03434	육상용 탱크톱	3	30달러
54455	스니커즈 운동화 (정리 세일)	1	85달러
		소계:	146달러
		세금:	10.22달러
		총:	156.22달러
		지불:	160달러
		157(D) 거스름돈:	(3.78달러)

Gordon's를 이용해 주셔서 감사합니다!

영수증을 지참하시면, 물품은 30일 이내에 반품이 가능하며, 포인트로 적립해 드립니다.

157(C) *할인 제품은 반품이 되지 않습니다.

표현 정리 cashier 출납원 description 품목 이름 quantity 수량 jump rope 줄넘기 shorts 반바지 subtotal 소계 change 거스름돈 receipt 영수증 store credit 상점 포인트(반품할 때 현금으로 돌려받는 것이 아니고 상점 포인트로 적립하는 것) clearance 정리 세일

156. 세부사항 – Gordon's의 업종 ★☆☆
해설 Description에 포함된 물품을 보면 운동용품점이라는 것을 알 수 있으므로 정답은 (C)이다. **정답 (C)**

표현 정리 convenience 편의 goods 상품

해석 Gordon's는 무엇인가?
(A) 편의점
(B) 신발 가게
(C) 스포츠 상품 가게
(D) 피트니스 센터

157. 세부사항 – 영수증에 나타나지 않은 것 ★★☆
해설 영수증에 쿠폰을 사용해 해당 서비스를 제공받은 내용이 없으므로 정답은 (A)이다. **정답 (A)**

🔍**함정 분석** 'Cashier: Jason Smith'에서 계산을 담당한 직원이 Mr. Smith 이므로 (B)가 확인되고, 구입 물품 목록에서 스니커즈 운동화는 'sneakers (clearance)'로, 하단 '*No returns on clearance items.'에서 반품이 될 수 없는 할인 상품으로 분류된 것을 알 수 있으므로 (C)가 확인된다. 'Change: ($3.78)'를 통해 거스름돈을 받았음을 알 수 있으므로 (D)도 확인된다.

해석 영수증에 나타나지 않은 것은?
(A) 고객은 쿠폰을 사용했다.
(B) 고객은 Mr. Smith의 도움을 받았다.
(C) 스니커즈 운동화는 반품될 수 없다.
(D) 고객은 약간의 돈을 받았다.

문제 158-160번은 다음 이메일을 참조하시오.

발신: Lionel Opher〈lionel@excelcatering.com〉
수신: Kim Reininger〈kim.reininger@hopesprings.com〉
제목: 설치 계약
날짜: 3월 2일

Ms. Reininger 님께,

어제 당신과 대화를 나눌 수 있어 즐거웠습니다. 곧 있을 시상식 연회와 관련해 당신이 갖고 있는 계획들은 꽤 인상적이었습니다. 159(A) 저는 당신 동료들이 그것을 즐길 것이라고 확신합니다. 저는 제 파트너와 이야기를 했고,

당신의 행사를 위해 주문 제작한 디저트를 저희가 준비할 수 있게 돼 매우 기쁘다는 점을 알려 드립니다.

158당신의 요청 사항을 확인해 보도록 하겠습니다. 159(C)당신은 95명의 손님들에게 제공될 대형 케이크를 저희가 만들기를 원하고 있습니다. 버터크림 아이싱과 함께 아몬드 맛이 나는 케이크가 될 것입니다. 160당신은 또한 당신이 제공한 꽃무늬로 그것을 장식하고 앞쪽에 회사 이름을 새기기를 원합니다. 또한, 당신의 회사 로고가 맨 위에 놓여질 것입니다.

159(B),(D)케이크는 12월 3일, 토요일, 늦어도 오후 3시까지는 Mihalski 호텔로 배달될 것입니다. 그곳에서 연락할 사람은 Dereck Turner (555-3403)입니다.

위의 정보가 맞는지, 또는 변경할 필요가 있는지 저에게 알려주시기 바랍니다.

Lionel Opher

표현 정리 installation 설치 contract 계약 pleasure 즐거움 upcoming 다가오는 awards banquet 시상식 연회 impressive 인상적인 colleague 동료 custom-made 주문 제작한 review 재검토하다 floral pattern 꽃무늬 deliver 배달하다

158. 주제 – 이메일의 목적 ★☆☆
해설 이메일 두 번째 단락 'Let me take a moment to review your request.'에서 요청 사항이 있음을 알 수 있으므로 정답은 (C)이다. **정답 (C)**

표현 정리 reschedule 일정을 변경하다 confirm 확인해 주다 place an order 주문하다

해석 이메일이 보내진 이유는?
(A) 초대에 응하기 위해
(B) 배달 일정을 변경하기 위해
(C) 요청을 확인하기 위해
(D) 주문하기 위해

159. 세부사항 – Ms. Reininger의 행사에 대한 내용이 아닌 것 ★★☆
해설 세 번째 단락 'The order will be delivered to the Mihalski Hotel'에서 Mihalski 호텔은 언급돼 있지만 행사가 레스토랑에서 열린다는 내용은 찾아 볼 수 없으므로 (B)가 정답이다. **정답 (B)**

🔍**함정 분석** 첫 번째 단락 'I'm sure your colleagues will enjoy it.'에서 행사를 동료들도 즐길 것이라고 했으므로 (A)는 확인되고, 두 번째 단락 'You would like us to make a large cake to serve all ninety-five guests.'에서 95명에게 제공될 케이크를 주문했음을 알 수 있으므로 (C)도 확인되며, 'The order will be delivered to the Mihalski Hotel on Saturday, December 3, no later than 3:00 P.M.'에서 토요일에 행사가 개최된다는 사실을 알 수 있으므로 (D)도 확인된다.

패러프레이징 |지문| colleagues 동료 → |선택지 A| coworkers 동료
|지문| all ninety-five guests 총 95명의 참석자 → |선택지 C| fewer than 100 attendees 100명 미만의 참석자

표현 정리 coworker 동료 attendee 참석자 take place 개최되다

해석 Ms. Reininger의 행사에 관해 언급된 것이 아닌 것은?
(A) 그녀의 동료를 포함할 것이다.
(B) 레스토랑에서 열릴 것이다.
(C) 100명 미만의 참석자를 가질 것이다.
(D) 주말에 개최될 것이다.

160. 문장 위치 찾기 ★★☆
해설 주어진 문장은 케이크 장식과 관련된 내용으로 볼 수 있다. Ms. Reininger 가 요청한 내용을 확인하는 두 번째 단락 'You would also like us to decorate

it with the floral pattern you provided and to write your company's name across the front.'에서 꽃무늬 장식과 회사 이름을 앞에 새길 것이라고 한 다음에 본 문장이 오는 것이 가장 적절해 정답은 (B)이다.　　　정답 (B)

표현 정리 in addition 게다가

해석 [1], [2], [3], [4] 중 다음 문장이 들어가기에 가장 알맞은 곳은?

　　　"또한, 당신의 회사 로고가 맨 위에 놓여질 것입니다."

　　　(A) [1]
　　　(B) [2]
　　　(C) [3]
　　　(D) [4]

문제 161-163번은 다음 편지를 참조하시오.

King Heating Oil
894 Green Street
Baltimore, MD 21231

3월 7일

Susan Miller
2894 Reisterstown Road
Owings Mills, MD 21283

Ms. Miller 님께,

고객님께서 3월 3일 보내신 요금을 수령했음을 알려 드립니다. 그러나 보내 주신 총 금액은 2월 19일 댁으로 배달된 난방용 연료 가격에 비해 적은 금액입니다. 162저희는 고객님이 납부하셔야 할 금액 195.65달러에서 159.65달러를 받은 것으로 처리했습니다. 25달러의 연체료를 피하려면, 161잔액 36달러를 3월 15일까지 납부해 주시기 바랍니다. 납부는 저희 사무실이나 메일로 보내 주시거나, 아니면 안전한 웹사이트 www.kingheatingoil.com을 통해 보낼 수 있습니다. 저희는 신용카드, 개인 수표, 우편환, 유효한 은행 계좌를 통해 전자 이체(EFT)를 받습니다. 163올해 1월 1일부터 더 이상 현금 결제는 받지 않습니다.

이 문제에 관해 질문이 있으면, 저에게 연락 주시기 바랍니다.

Fred Parker
계정 기술자
(410) 555-0367
fparker@kingheatingoil.com

표현 정리 inform 알리다 payment 지불, 납부 amount 총액 balance due 납부해야 할 금액 credit 입금하다 late fee 연체료 remaining 남은, 잔액 administrative office 행정실 post 발송하다 secure 안전한 check 수표 money orders 우편환 electronic funds transfers 전자 이체 valid 유효한 account 계좌 as of ~일자로 concerns 관심사

161. 주제 – 편지의 목적　　★☆☆

해설 첫 번째 문장 'I am writing to inform you that the payment you sent on March 3 was received.'에서 입금을 확인했다고 했고, 'However, the amount sent was less than the balance due'에서 적은 금액이 납부되었다고 했으며, 'please pay the remaining balance of $36.00 by March 15'에서는 남은 잔액을 납부해 달라고 요청하고 있으므로 정답은 (D)이다.　　정답 (D)

표현 정리 refund 환불하다 inquiry 문의, 조사 negotiate 협상하다

해석 편지의 목적은?
　　　(A) 돈을 환불하기 위해
　　　(B) 문의하기 위해
　　　(C) 가격을 협상하기 위해
　　　(D) 납부를 요청하기 위해

162. 세부사항 – 난방용 기름의 총 비용　　★☆☆

해설 'We have credited your payment of $159.65 toward the balance of $195.65.'에서 Ms. Miller가 지불해야 했던 총 금액은 $195.65임을 알 수 있으므로 정답은 (D)이다.　　정답 (D)

해석 난방용 연료의 총 비용은 얼마인가?
　　　(A) 25달러
　　　(B) 35달러
　　　(C) 159.65달러
　　　(D) 195.65달러

163. 유추 – King Heating Oil에 대한 내용　　★★☆

해설 King Heating Oil은 지금까지 여러 방식으로 기름 값을 받아왔지만, 'As of January 1 this year, we no longer accept cash payments.'에서 올해 1월 1일부로 현금을 받지 않을 것이라고 했으므로 이전에는 현금을 받았다는 의미가 돼 정답은 (B)가 된다.　　정답 (B)

패러프레이징 |지문| No longer accept cash payments 더 이상 현금을 받지 않는다 → |선택지 B| used to let customers pay with cash 고객이 현금으로 지불하게 했다

표현 정리 quantity 양 incorrect 맞지 않는

해석 King Heating Oil에 관해 암시된 것은?
　　　(A) 잘못된 양의 기름을 배달했다.
　　　(B) 고객이 현금으로 지불하도록 했다.(이제는 아니다)
　　　(C) Baltimore에 여러 지점을 갖고 있다.
　　　(D) Ms. Miller에게 맞지 않는 청구서를 보냈다.

문제 164-167번은 다음 온라인 채팅을 참조하시오.

Tom Jones　　방금 지역 본부로부터 분기별 매출액을 받았습니다. 164신 메뉴와 홍보로 인해 매출이 급증했습니다. 여러분 모두 매우 바빴을 줄로 압니다. 각 지점에 대해 저에게 간단히 보고해 주시겠습니까?
　　　　　　　오전 9시 48분

Lynn Westerberg　정말 바빴습니다. 저희는 지난 달에 매출이 125퍼센트 증가했습니다. 165몇 주 전에 한 명의 새 요리사와 두 명의 서빙하는 사람을 고용한 것이 정말 다행이었습니다.　　　오전 9시 49분

Tom Jones　　Bleecher Avenue를 위해 다행이군요! 98th Street은 어떤가요?　　　오전 9시 52분

Josh Phan　　Lynn처럼 저희도 매우 바빴습니다. 저희의 주된 문제는 재료가 계속 부족하다는 것입니다. 밀가루, 기름, 그리고 기타 다른 것들을 구입하느라 제 사비를 사용해야 했습니다.　　오전 9시 53분

Vijay Rao　　돈을 되돌려 받기를 바랍니다.　　오전 9시 55분

Josh Phan　　166요청했지만 지점 관리자가 승인해 주기를 아직 기다리고 있습니다. 그는 2주 안에 저에게 연락할 것이라고 했습니다.
　　　　　　　오전 9시 58분

Vijay Rao　　저희가 여분의 물품을 보낼 수 있을 겁니다. Oliver Road는 당신의 지점만큼 바쁘지는 않습니다.　　오전 10시 1분

Josh Phan　　그렇게 해야겠네요.　　오전 10시 4분

Lynn Westerberg　그것은 단지 일시적인 해결책일 뿐입니다. 167당신은 정말로 더 큰 예산이 필요합니다.　　오전 10시 6분

Josh Phan　　제가 요청하면 지역 본부가 승인할지 확신이 없습니다.
　　　　　　　오전 10시 7분

Tom Jones　　제가 할 수 있는 일을 찾아 보겠습니다. 오전 10시 8분

표현 정리 quarterly 분기별의 figure 수치 district 지역

128

headquarters 본부, 본사   drive 만들다, 몰다   give a report 보고를 하다
understatement 과소 평가   server 서빙하는 사람   run low on
~이 적어지다   supplies 물품, 공급품   reimburse 배상하다, 변제하다
approval 승인   up for 기꺼이 ~하려고 하는   temporary 임시의
budget 예산   authorize 승인하다, 인가하다

164. 유추 – 대화자들의 근무처   ★★☆
해설 Tom Jones가 첫 대화 'Our new menu and promotions have driven sales through the roof!'에서 메뉴와 홍보로 인해 판매가 급증했다고 한 후, 'Can you give me a short report on each location?'에서 각 지점별 상황 보고를 요청하고 있으므로 음식점 체인임을 짐작할 수 있어 정답은 (C)이다.
정답 (C)

표현 정리 distributor 유통 회사   warehouse 창고   cafeteria 구내식당

해설 대화자들이 근무하는 곳은?
(A) 식품 유통회사
(B) 창고
(C) 음식점 체인
(D) 공장 구내식당

165. 세부사항 – Bleecher Avenue 지점에 대한 내용   ★★☆
해설 Lynn Westerberg가 오전 9시 49분에 보낸 메시지 마지막 문장 'Thank goodness I hired a new cook and two servers a few weeks back.'에서 몇 주 전에 고용한 직원들의 도움으로 바쁜 상황에 대처할 수 있었음을 유추할 수 있으므로 정답은 (B)이다.
정답 (B)

🔍 **함정 분석** 98th Street 지점의 상황을 묻는 Mr. Jones의 질문에 Josh Phan이 'Our main issue is that we keep running low on supplies.'라며 재료 부족이 큰 문제라고 했는데, 이 지점은 98th Street이므로 (D)는 오답이다.

패러프레이징 |지문| hired a new cook and two servers a few weeks back 몇 주 전에 요리사와 2명의 서빙 직원을 고용했다 → |선택지 B| recently hired additional employees 최근에 직원 몇 명을 고용했다

표현 정리 loyal 충실한   additional 추가의   dissatisfied 불만스러워 하는

해설 Bleecher Avenue 지점에 관해 언급된 것은?
(A) 그곳의 고객은 매우 충성스럽다.
(B) 최근 직원들을 추가로 고용했다.
(C) 그곳의 직원들은 불만스러워 한다.
(D) 그곳은 여전히 물품을 추가적으로 필요로 한다.

166. 주제 – Mr. Phan이 연락한 이유   ★☆☆
해설 Mr. Phan이 오전 9시 58분에 보낸 메시지 'I put in a request, but I am still waiting for approval from our district manager.'에서 본인이 사비로 지불한 금액을 상환 요청했고, 지역 관리자의 승인을 기다리고 있는 중이라고 말했다. 따라서 그가 지역 관리자에게 연락한 이유는 물건을 구입하는데 사용한 자신의 돈을 돌려 받기 위함임을 알 수 있으므로 정답은 (C)이다.
정답 (C)

표현 정리 propose 제안하다   reassignment 재발령, 재배치   repayment 상환   complaint 불만

해설 Mr. Phan이 지역 관리자에게 연락한 이유는?
(A) 재발령을 제안하기 위해
(B) 음식을 주문하기 위해
(C) 상환을 요구하기 위해
(D) 불만을 말하기 위해

167. 의도 파악하기   ★★☆
해설 재료 부족을 해결하기 위해 더 많은 예산이 필요할 것이라는 Ms. Weterberg의 말에 Mr. Phan이 'I'm not sure district headquarters would authorize that even if I asked them.'이라고 말하며 지역 본부에서 승인해 줄

지 모르겠다고 했다. 이에 대한 응답으로 Mr. Jones가 말한 내용이므로 '예산을 더 확보할 수 있도록 도울 수 있는 방법을 찾아보겠다'는 의미로 볼 수 있어 정답은 (D)이다.
정답 (D)

표현 정리 pick up 얻다

해설 Mr. Jones가 오전 10시 8분에 '제가 할 수 있는 일을 찾아 보겠습니다.'라고 말한 이유는?
(A) 98th Street 지점에서 일하겠다고 제안하기 위해
(B) Mr. Phan이 관리자와 이야기하도록 격려하기 위해
(C) 그가 재료들을 얻을 수 있도록 제안하기 위해
(D) 더 많은 돈을 확보하도록 도움을 주기 위해

문제 168-171번은 다음 회람을 참조하시오.

회람

수신: 모든 건물 운영 직원들
발신: Leonard Piot
날짜: 1월 15일
제목: 연간 실적 평가

다음 주부터 연간 실적 평가 일정을 잡기 시작할 예정입니다. 이전과 같이, 평가는 저와 1대 1 대면 평가가 될 것이며, **170(B)각 직원이 맡고 있는 책임 분야에 따라 30분에서 1시간 정도가 걸릴 것입니다. 170(D)평가는 다음 달에 시작해 4월까지 계속됩니다.** 각 부서에 지장을 미치는 것을 최소화하는 방법으로 평가 일정을 정하겠지만, 관리자들은 담당 직원의 일시적인 부재를 감안해야 할 것입니다.

168,170(A)올해의 실적 평가 절차에는 몇 가지 변동 사항이 있습니다. 169직원들은 이제 평가 기간 동안 마친 모든 교육과 취득한 증명서 또는 자격증 서류를 제출해야 합니다. 또한 여러 가지 새로운 기준이 실적 평가 양식에 추가되었습니다. 이에 대한 상세 내용은 온라인 교육 모듈에 설명되어 있습니다.

직원들이 리뷰를 준비하는 것을 돕기 위해 인사부가 개발한 온라인 교육 모듈을 참고할 것을 적극 권유합니다. "온라인 교육" 링크를 클릭하면, "연간 실적 평가 준비 교육" 모듈을 찾을 수 있습니다.

171Viro Corporation의 전 직원들은 매년 실적 평가에 참가하도록 요구 받습니다. 만약 회사 정책에 관해 질문이 있다면, 구내전화 478번 인사부의 Michael Parker에게 연락해 주세요.

표현 정리 annual 연례의   performance evaluation 실적 평가   one on one 1대 1로   responsibility 책임   depend on ~에 달려 있다   make every effort 모든 노력을 하다   minimize 최소화하다   disruption 지장   supervisor 관리자   temporary 일시적인   absence 부재   submit 제출하다   documentation 서류   certification 증명   criteria 기준   Human Resources 인사부   assist in ~을 돕다   participate in ~에 참가하다   extension 내선, 구내전화

168. 주제 – 메모의 목적   ★☆☆
해설 본문 첫 번째 문장 'Starting next week, I will begin scheduling annual performance evaluations.'에서 다음 주부터 연간 실적 평가 일정을 잡을 것이라고 한 다음, 두 번째 단락부터 회람을 보낸 목적을 설명하기 시작했는데, 'Please be aware that some changes have been made to this year's performance evaluation process.'에서 올해부터 평가 과정에 변화가 있다고 말한 다음, 이에 대한 부연 설명이 이어지고 있으므로 정답은 (B)이다.
정답 (B)

해설 회람의 목적은?
(A) 평가를 확인하기 위해
(B) 과정을 설명하기 위해

(C) 새로운 웹사이트를 소개하기 위해
(D) 회의 일정을 잡기 위해

169. 동의어 ★★☆

해설 두 번째 단락 'Employees are now required to submit documentation for all training completed during the period under evaluation and for any new certifications or licenses obtained.'에서 documentation은 '서류'라는 의미로 쓰였으므로 이와 가장 유사한 단어는 (A) records라고 할 수 있다. **정답 (A)**

표현 정리 permission 허가

해석 두 번째 단락, 두 번째 줄의 "documentation"과 의미가 가장 가까운 것은?
(A) 기록
(B) 비디오
(C) 공지
(D) 허가

170. 세부사항 – 실적 평가에 대한 내용이 아닌 것 ★★☆

해설 본문에서 온라인과 관련된 내용은 세 번째 단락인데, 첫 문장 내용 'Employees are strongly advised to view the online training module developed by the Human Resources (HR) Department to assist in preparing for their review.'는 온라인 교육 모듈을 참고하라고 적극 요청하는 내용일 뿐, 온라인 시험을 포함한다는 내용이 아니므로 혼동하지 않도록 한다. 따라서 정답은 (C)이다. **정답 (C)**

🔍 **함정 분석** (A)는 두 번째 단락 'Please be aware that some changes have been made to this year's performance evaluation process.'에서 확인되고, (B)는 첫 번째 단락 'will take between thirty minutes and an hour to complete'에서 확인되며, (D)는 첫 번째 단락 'Evaluations will begin next month and continue through April.'에서 다음 달에 시작될 것이라고 했는데, 회람이 보내진 시점이 'Date: January 15'이므로 사실 내용임을 알 수 있다.

패러프레이징 |지문| some changes have been made to this year's 올해 몇몇 변화가 생겼다 → |선택지 A| differ from last year 작년과는 다르다
|지문| will take between thirty minutes and an hour 30분에서 한 시간 정도의 시간이 걸린다 → |선택지 B| take an hour or less 한 시간 미만이 걸린다

표현 정리 differ from ~와 다르다 commence 시작되다

해석 실적 평가에 관해 언급된 내용이 아닌 것은?
(A) 작년과는 다르다.
(B) 한 시간 가량 걸린다.
(C) 온라인 시험을 포함한다.
(D) 2월에 시작될 것이다.

171. 유추 – Mr. Piot에 대한 내용 ★★★

해설 마지막 단락 'All employees at the Viro Corporation are required to participate in a performance evaluation annually.'에서 모든 직원들이 매년 실적 평가를 받아야 한다는 것을 알 수 있고, 본문 첫번째 단락에서 "evaluations will be done one on one with me"를 통해 1대 1로 만나 평가를 진행한다고 했으므로 정답은 (B)이다. **정답 (B)**

표현 정리 procedure 절차

해석 Mr. Piot에 관해 암시된 것은?
(A) 그는 새로운 실적 평가 절차를 개발했다.
(B) 그는 그의 부서 내 전 직원들을 만날 것이다.
(C) 그는 이미 그의 실적 평가를 했다.
(D) 그는 인사부에 근무한다.

문제 172-175번은 다음 웹페이지를 참조하시오.

---

http://www.vacationguide.com

당신의 검색 기준과 프로필에 기초해, 저희는 다음을 추천합니다:

172당신이 Bright Mountain 국립공원을 방문할 계획이라면, Grizzly Gulch에 오두막집을 빌리는 것을 고려하세요. 그곳에서 당신은 숲 속 깊은 곳에 있는 소박한 오두막집에 머물면서 최고의 자연을 경험할 수 있습니다. 28개의 모든 오두막집들은 감각있게 장식되었고 **173(B)완비된** 주방, 조절 가능한 냉난방 시설, 위성 TV와 Wi-Fi와 같은 현대적인 편의 시설들을 제공합니다. 당신이 바깥에 앉아 경치를 보고 야생동물을 보는 것을 선호한다면, 대부분의 오두막집들은 지붕 덮인 현관을 갖추고 있습니다. **173(D)혼자 오시는 손님에서 여러 명 또는 더 많은 분들을 위한 숙소 옵션도 이용 가능합니다.**

173(C)오두막집들은 Grizzly Gulch 시가 소유하고 있고, 운영하고 있습니다. 공원 측이 운영하는 오두막집과는 달리, 최대 3달 전에 예약할 수 있습니다. 그러나 꽤 많은 보증금이 요구된다는 것을 알아두기 바랍니다. 게다가, 취소할 경우 환불되지 않습니다.

Grizzly Gulch 오두막집들은 공원 지역을 탐사하는 것에 흥미를 가진 방문객들에게 매우 편리하도록 **173(A),174공원 남쪽 입구에서 12마일 떨어진 곳에 있습니다.** 그것은 또한 공원의 북쪽 절반을 방문하기에 적합한 출발점이기도 합니다. 그러나 가장 인기 있는 명소들에 도달하려면 상당 시간 운전할 준비가 돼 있어야 합니다.

175Grizzly Gulch 오두막집에 머무는 것을 선택하신다면, 음식을 요리 하거나 나가서 사 먹어야 합니다. 식사는 포함되지 않습니다. 이것은 본 인이 손수 해결해야 하는 일이지만, 그렇더라도 매우 즐거운 일입니다.

148명의 독자들이 이 리뷰가 유용하다고 했습니다.

표현 정리 based on ~에 기초해 criteria 기준 profile 프로필, 개요 national park 국립공원 cabin 오두막집 rustic 소박한 at its best 가장 좋은 상태에 tastefully 감각있게 amenity 편의시설 fully equipped 완비된 adjustable 조절 가능한 satellite 위성 porch 현관, 베란다 wildlife 야생 동물 lodging 숙소 privately 개인적으로 in advance 미리 sizable 꽤 많은 deposit 보증금 moreover 게다가 refundable 환불 가능한 in the event of 만약 ~하면 cancellation 취소 convenient 편리한 explore 탐사하다, 답사하다 suitable 적합한 jumping-off point 출발점 considerable 상당한 sight 명소 strictly 엄격히 do-it-yourself 스스로 하는, 본인이 직접 하는 pleasant 즐거운 nonetheless 그렇더라도

172. 주제 – 웹페이지의 목적 ★★☆

해설 첫 번째 단락 'If you are planning a visit to Bright Mountain National Park, consider renting a cabin in Grizzly Gulch.'에서 Grizzly Gulch에 있는 오두막집을 숙소로 고려해 볼 것을 권유하면서 숙박과 관련한 구체적인 사항들에 대해 설명하고 있으므로 숙박 옵션을 평가하고 있다고 한 (B)가 정답이다. **정답 (B)**

표현 정리 promote 홍보하다 evaluate 평가하다 criticize 비판하다

해석 웹페이지의 목적은?
(A) 지역 명소를 홍보하기 위해
(B) 숙박 옵션을 평가하기 위해
(C) 고객 피드백을 요청하기 위해
(D) 호텔 회사를 비판하기 위해

173. 세부사항 – Grizzly Gulch 오두막집에 대한 내용이 아닌 것 ★★★

해설 세 번째 단락 'The Grizzly Gulch cabins are twelve miles outside the park's southern entrance'를 통해 오두막집은 공원 남쪽 입구에서 외곽으로 12마일 정도 떨어진 곳에 위치한 것을 알 수 있으므로 국립공원 안에 위치하고

있다는 (A)는 틀린 내용이다. 　　　　　정답 (A)

🔍 **함정 분석** (B)는 'All twenty-eight cabins are tastefully decorated and offer modern amenities like fully equipped kitchens, adjustable heating and cooling units, satellite TV, and Wi-Fi.'에서 요리 시설이 갖춰져 있음이 확인 가능하고, (C)는 'The cabins are privately owned and managed by the town of Grizzly Gulch.'에서 시가 운영한다는 사실을 알 수 있어 맞는 내용이고, (D) 역시 'Lodging options for single guests to parties of a dozen or more are available.'에서 단체 숙박이 가능하다는 사실을 알 수 있다.

패러프레이징 |지문| fully equipped kitchens 완비된 주방 → |선택지 B| cooking facilities 요리할 수 있는 시설
|지문| managed by the town of Grizzly Gulch Grizzly Gulch 시에 의해 운영된다 → |선택지 C| be run by a municipality 지방 당국에 의해 운영된다
|지문| Lodging options for single guests to parties of a dozen or more are available 혼자 오는 손님에서 여러 명 또는 더 많은 분들을 위한 숙소 옵션 → |선택지 D| can accommodate groups 단체를 수용할 수 있다

표현 정리 municipality 지방 당국 accommodate 수용하다

해석 Grizzly Gulch 오두막집에 관해 언급되지 않은 것은?
　(A) 국립공원 안에 위치해 있다.
　(B) 요리 시설을 갖추고 있다.
　(C) 지방 당국에 의해 운영된다.
　(D) 단체를 수용할 수 있다.

174. 유추 – Bright Mountain 국립 공원에 대한 내용　★☆☆

해설 세 번째 단락 'The Grizzly Gulch cabins are twelve miles outside the park's southern entrance'에서 공원 남쪽 입구가 언급된 것으로 보아 국립공원으로 진입하는 출입구가 여러 개임을 짐작할 수 있으므로 정답은 (C)이다. 　　　　　정답 (C)

🔍 **함정 분석** 두 번째 단락 마지막 문장 'it is not refundable in the event of a cancelation'에서 오두막 예약을 취소하는 경우에 환불이 되지 않으므로 (D)는 틀린 내용이다.

표현 정리 takes reservations 예약을 받다 multiple 다수의

해석 Bright Mountain 국립 공원에 관해 암시된 것은?
　(A) 캠핑을 위해 예약을 받는다.
　(B) 두 개의 유명한 명소를 가지고 있다.
　(C) 여러 곳의 출입구를 가지고 있다.
　(D) 환불이 되는 보증금을 요구한다.

175. 문장 위치 찾기　★★☆

해설 네 번째 단락 'If you choose to stay at the Grizzly Gulch cabins, be prepared to either make your own food or to eat out.'에서 직접 요리를 하거나 외식을 해야 한다고 말하고 있으므로, 이후의 내용에서는 이에 대한 부연 설명이 이어지는 것이 자연스럽다. 즉, 숙박 비용에 식사는 포함되어 있지 않다는 것을 부연 설명하고 있으므로 정답은 (D)이다. 　　　　　정답 (D)

해석 [1], [2], [3], [4] 중 다음 문장이 들어가기에 가장 알맞은 곳은?
　"식사는 포함되지 않습니다."
　(A) [1]
　(B) [2]
　(C) [3]
　(D) [4]

문제 176-180번은 다음 이메일과 정보를 참조하시오.

발신: Sandra Magsaysay 〈smagsaysay@pacificair.com〉
수신: Alan Hao 〈alan.hao@coastaindustries.com〉
날짜: 10월 18일
제목: 귀하의 회원 자격

Mr. Hao 님께,

Pacific Airlines 상용 고객 클럽에 가입해 주셔서 감사합니다. 귀하는 올해 귀하의 이름으로 예약된 전 항공편에 대한 마일을 적립받았습니다.

회원 번호: 8300-534-9920
선호 비행 클래스: 비즈니스
179,180 비행 마일: 27,000

귀하의 Coastal Industries 직원 신용카드(XXX-XXXX-3893)로 등록비로 19.99달러가 청구되었습니다. 만약 회원 자격 등급을 언제라도 승급시키기를 원하신다면, 저희 웹사이트에서 추가 마일을 구입하실 수 있습니다.

176 3, 4주 내로 우편을 통해 귀하의 회원카드를 받으실 겁니다. **177** 그 동안 이메일 복사본을 출력해 주십시오. 체크인을 하고, 공항 보안 검색대를 통과할 때, 회원 자격 증거로 그것을 사용하십시오.

질문 사항은 저희 고객 서비스 1-888-555-3000으로 연락하시거나 www.pacificair.com/frequentflyers를 방문해 주십시오.

Sandra Magsaysay
회원 서비스

표현 정리 membership 회원 자격 enroll 등록하다 frequent flyer (비행기의) 단골 고객, 상용 고객 account 계정 be credited for ~로 인정받다 charge 청구하다 at any time 언제라도 purchase 구입하다 in the meantime 또한, 그 동안 proof 증거 check in 탑승 수속을 밟다 pass through 거치다, 통과하다

Pacific Airlines 상용 고객 클럽

고객님의 이용에 감사 드립니다. 저희 단골 고객들에 대한 감사의 표시로 상용 고객 혜택을 4단계로 제공합니다.

자격	다이아몬드	플래티넘	골드	프리미어
178 최소 비행 마일*	40,000	30,000	20,000	10,000
혜택				
우선 탑승	✓	✓	✓	✓
여행 관련 상품 구입 시 보너스 마일 취득	✓	✓	✓	✓
무료 Wi-Fi	✓	✓	✓	
VIP 라운지 입장	✓	✓	✓	
179 가방 3개까지 체크인 가능	✓	✓		
무료 업그레이드**	✓			

*올해의 달력을 기준으로 계산됨 (1월 1일 - 12월 31일)
**탑승 시간에 이용할 가능성을 기초로 함

Pacific Airlines는 상용 고객 클럽 회원이 추가 마일을 구입함으로써 그들의 등급을 승급시킬 수 있도록 허용합니다.

필요한 마일	구매 가격
1 - 1,000	179달러
1,001 - 2,000	329달러
180 2,001 - 3,000	**479달러**
3,001 - 4,000	629달러
3,001 - 5,000	779달러

표현 정리 **loyalty** 충성 **benefit** 혜택 **eligibility** 자격 **priority** 우선 **boarding** 탑승 **complimentary** 무료의 **access** 입장, 접근 **availability** 이용 가능성

176. 유추 – Mr. Hao에 대한 내용 ★★☆
해설 이메일 네 번째 단락 'You should receive your membership card in the mail within 3 – 4 weeks.'에서 3, 4주 후에 회원 카드를 받을 것이라고 했는데, 이메일을 보낸 날짜가 'Date: October 18'이므로 11월에 받을 것이라고 한 (D)가 정답이다. 정답 (D)

🔍 함정 분석 이메일 'Thank you for enrolling in the Pacific Airlines frequent flyer club. Your account has been credited for all flights booked under your name in the current calendar year.'에서 상용 고객으로 이제 등록을 한 상태이지만, 올해만 해도 이미 여러 번 항공편을 이용했음을 알 수 있으므로 (C)는 오답이다.

표현 정리 **renew** 갱신하다

해석 Mr. Hao에 관해 암시된 것은?
(A) 그는 아시아로 빈번히 여행을 한다.
(B) 그는 그의 회원 자격을 갱신했다.
(C) 그는 Pacific Airlines를 처음 이용하는 승객이다.
(D) 그는 11월에 그의 카드를 받을 것이다.

177. 세부사항 – Mr. Hao가 지시 받은 일 ★☆☆
해설 회원 카드 발급까지 3, 4주가 걸릴 예정이기 때문이라고 한 뒤, 'In the meantime, please print a copy of this e-mail. Use it as proof of membership when checking in and passing through airport security screenings.'에서 이메일 복사본을 출력해 탑승 수속과 공항 보안 검색대를 통과할 때 증거로 사용하라고 했으므로 정답은 (A)이다. 정답 (A)

표현 정리 **instruct** 지시하다

해석 Mr. Hao가 하도록 지시받은 것은?
(A) 이메일 복사본을 탑승 수속할 때 사용하라고
(B) 공항 보안에 등록하라고
(C) 그의 등급을 즉시 업그레이드하라고
(D) 신용카드 결제를 하라고

178. 세부사항 – 상용 고객 회원 등급에 대한 내용 ★★☆
해설 두 번째 지문인 정보 'Minimum miles flown*'에서 올해의 달력을 기준으로 한 최소 비행 마일에 따라 회원 등급을 나눈다는 것을 알 수 있으므로 정답은 (C)이다. 정답 (C)

🔍 함정 분석 'we offer frequent flyer benefits at four levels'를 통해 네 가지 등급에 따라 회원 혜택이 달라진다는 사실을 알 수 있으므로, 비즈니스와 퍼스트 클래스 탑승자들로 한정되었다고 보기는 어려워 (A)는 오답이다.

표현 정리 **restrict** 한정하다, 제한하다

해석 상용 고객 회원 등급에 관해 나타난 것은?
(A) 비즈니스와 퍼스트 클래스 탑승자들에 한정되어 있다.
(B) 그들의 혜택은 일부 공항에만 적용된다.
(C) 올해 비행한 마일의 숫자에 기반한다.
(D) 그것들은 한 해의 시작 전에 구매되어야 한다.

179. 연계 문제 – Mr. Hao가 이용할 수 있는 혜택이 아닌 것 ★★☆
해설 첫 번째 지문에서 Mr. Hao의 비행 마일은 'Miles Flown: 27,000'에서 27,000마일임을 알 수 있는데, 이를 두 번째 지문 표에서 살펴 보면 골드 등급으로 분류된 사실을 알 수 있다. 체크인 시 3개 이상의 가방 탑승 수속이 가능한 등급은 'Can check in up to 3 bags'를 보면 다이아몬드와 플래티넘이므로 (D)는 Mr. Hao가 이용할 수 있는 혜택이 아니다. 정답 (D)

해석 Mr. Hao가 현재 이용할 수 있는 혜택이 아닌 것은?
(A) 우선 탑승
(B) 무료 Wi-Fi
(C) VIP 라운지 입장
(D) 3개 가방 탑승 수속

180. 연계 문제 – 다음 등급으로 승급하기 위해 지불해야 할 금액 ★☆☆
해설 골드 등급인 Mr. Hao가 다음 등급인 플래티넘으로 승급되기 위해서는 Minimum miles flown에서 30,000마일이 필요한데, 현재 27,000마일을 보유하고 있으므로 추가로 3,000마일이 필요하다. 추가 마일 구입 표를 확인해 보면 2,001에서 3,000마일을 구입하려면 479달러가 필요하므로 정답은 (C)이다. 정답 (C)

해석 다음 회원 등급으로 승급하기 위해 Mr. Hao는 얼마를 지불해야 하는가?
(A) 179달러
(B) 329달러
(C) 479달러
(D) 629달러

문제 181-185번은 다음 광고와 이메일을 참조하시오.

Pro를 이용해 컴퓨터를 점검받으세요
컴퓨터 Pros, LLC.

완벽한 컴퓨터 조정, 지금 49.99달러 (181(A)**보통 74.99달러**)

저희 완벽한 조정은 다음을 포함합니다:
• 바이러스, 스파이웨어, 악성코드 검사 및 제거
• 레지스트리 청소와 불필요한 파일 및 프로그램 제거
• 하드 드라이브 검사 및 점검 (그리고 만약 필요하다면 조각을 모음)
• 컴퓨터를 켜고 끄는 것을 간소화
• 182업데이트, 바이러스 퇴치 소프트웨어, 그리고 보안 프로그램 업데이트 (그리고 해당되면 무료 버전 설치)

이 요금을 받는 서비스 일정을 잡을 때 이 광고를 언급해야 합니다.
181(C)**다른 광고, 쿠폰, 또는 특가 제공과 결합해 사용할 수 없습니다.**
할인은 가정용 서비스만을 위해 해당됩니다.
11월 30일에 제공은 만기됩니다.

이번 달 하드웨어와 소프트웨어 가격 조건에 관해 저희에게 문의하세요! 저희는 할인 중인 휴대용 컴퓨터, USB 드라이브, 그 이상을 가지고 있습니다!

181(B)**help@computerpros.com**
1-888-555-4040

표현 정리 **tune-up** 조정 **malware** 악성코드 **unnecessary** 불필요한 **defragment** 조각 처리된 것을 연계하여 배열하다 **streamline** 간소화하다 **startup** 시작 **shutdown** 끄기 **firewall** 방화벽 **applicable** 해당되는 **rate** 요금 **be combined with** ~와 결합되다 **residential service** 가정용 서비스 **expire** 만기가 되다

수신: Computer Pros ⟨help@computerpros.com⟩
발신: Allison Parker ⟨aparker@topmail.com⟩
제목: 서비스 예약
날짜: 11월 14일 월요일

안녕하세요,

185저희 집에 있는 컴퓨터를 귀사의 특별 광고 가격으로 튠업하고 싶습니다. 184컴퓨터는 2년이 되었고, 최근까지 문제가 없었습니다. 저는 9월쯤에 제 컴퓨터가 평소보다 느리다는 것을 인식하기 시작했습니다. 프로그램을 열고 닫는데 오랜 시간이 걸렸습니다. 한 친구가 SunClean이라고 불리는 무료 바이러스 제거 프로그램을 실행할 것을 제안했습니다. 그것은 잠시 도움

이 되는 것처럼 보였지만, 잠시 후 컴퓨터는 다시 작동이 늦어졌습니다. **183예를 들면, 컴퓨터를 시동시키거나 끄는데 2분이 안 걸렸습니다.** 그러나 지금은 5분 이상이 걸립니다! 저는 이번 주 아침 10시 전에 컴퓨터를 검사받을 수 있습니다.

또한 이번 달에 외장 하드드라이브를 할인 판매하는지 알고 싶습니다. 저는 제 컴퓨터 파일을 백업할 수 있는 500GB 모델을 찾고 있습니다.

감사합니다.

Allison Parker

표현 정리 **tune-up** 튠업, 조정 **up until** ~까지 **hassle** 성가신, 번거로운 **notice** 의식하다 **boot up** 컴퓨터를 시동하다 **external** 외부의

181. 세부사항 – 광고에 포함되지 않은 내용 ★★☆
해설 서비스가 제공되는 컴퓨터 유형에 대한 내용은 언급되지 않아 정답은 (D)이다. 정답 (D)

🔍 함정 분석 (A)는 광고에 보면 'Now $49.99 (Reg. $74.99)'로 정상 가격을 명시하고 있다. (B)는 이메일 주소와 전화번호가 'help@computerpros.com, 1-888-555-4040'과 같이 제시되어 있다. (C)는 광고 'Cannot be combined with other ads, coupons, or special offers. ~.'의 내용을 보면 다른 광고, 쿠폰, 특가 제공과 함께 사용될 수 없으며, 가정용에만 할인이 적용되고, 11월 30일이라는 날짜 제한을 두고 있으므로 (C)도 답이 될 수 없다.

패러프레이징 |지문| Cannot be combined with other ads, coupons, or special offers 다른 광고, 쿠폰, 특가 제공과 함께 사용될 수 없다 → |선택지 C| Restrictions placed on an offer 특가 제공에 제한이 있다

해석 광고에 포함되지 않은 정보는?
(A) 서비스의 정상 가격
(B) 회사를 위한 연락 정보
(C) 제공에 대한 제한 사항
(D) 점검을 받는 컴퓨터들의 유형

182. 세부사항 – 완벽한 컴퓨터 조정에 대한 내용 ★★★
해설 첫 번째 지문인 광고 'Update firewalls, antivirus software, and security programs (and install free versions when applicable)'에서 조정 서비스에는 방화벽, 바이러스 퇴치 소프트웨어, 보안 프로그램의 업데이트를 포함하며, 해당되는 경우 무료 버전을 설치하는 것이 포함되었다는 사실을 알 수 있으므로, 선택적인 소프트웨어 설치를 포함한다고 볼 수 있어 정답은 (C)이다. 정답 (C)

🔍 함정 분석 광고 하단 'Offer expires November 30'를 보면 특가로 제공되는 서비스가 11월 30일로 만기된다는 것일 뿐, 컴퓨터 튠업 자체는 12월에도 계속 이용할 수 있다고 볼 수 있어 (D)는 오답이다. 단 12월부터는 정상 가격인 74.99달러를 지불해야 한다.

표현 정리 **inspection** 점검 **mobile** 이동식의 **device** 장치 **optional** 선택적인

해석 완벽한 컴퓨터 조정에 관해 알 수 있는 것은?
(A) 다른 하드웨어의 점검을 포함한다.
(B) 이동식 장치를 위해 사용될 수 있다.
(C) 선택적인 소프트웨어 설치를 포함한다.
(D) 12월에는 더 이상 이용 가능하지 않을 것이다.

183. 세부사항 – Ms. Parker의 컴퓨터에 대한 내용 ★★☆
해설 두 번째 지문인 이메일 'To give you an example, it used to take less than 2 minutes for the computer to boot up or shut down. It now takes 5 minutes or longer!'에서 예전에는 컴퓨터를 켜거나 끄는데 2분이 안 걸렸는데, 지금은 5분 이상 걸린다고 말했으므로 정답은 (D)이다. 정답 (D)

🔍 함정 분석 이메일 'A friend suggested that I run a free virus-removal program called SunClean.'에서 성능이 저하된 컴퓨터에 무료 바이러스 제거 프로그램을 설치하도록 친구가 제안했다는 것을 알 수 있지만 친구가 수리했다고 보기는 어려워 (A)는 오답이다.

패러프레이징 |지문| it used to take less than 2 minutes for the computer to boot up or shut down. It now takes 5 minutes or longer 예전에는 컴퓨터를 켜거나 끄는데 2분이 안 걸렸다면 지금은 5분 이상이 걸린다 → |선택지 C| have reduced performance 성능이 저하되다

표현 정리 **reduce** 줄이다 **performance** 성능

해석 Ms. Parker의 컴퓨터에 대한 사실은?
(A) 친구가 수리했다.
(B) 더 이상 작동하지 않고 있다.
(C) 전원을 끌 수 없다.
(D) 성능이 감소했다.

184. 동의어 ★☆☆
해설 **hassle**은 '귀찮은, 번거로운 상황'이라는 뜻을 갖는다. 'It is a two-year-old PC that, up until recently, had been hassle free'에서 2년이 지난 컴퓨터로 최근까지는 귀찮은 상황이 없었다고 했으므로, 'hassle free'는 '편리한'이라는 뜻을 가진 convenient와 의미가 가장 유사하다고 볼 수 있어 정답은 (A)이다. 정답 (A)

표현 정리 **up to date** 현대식의 **problematic** 문제가 있는 **complex** 복잡한

해석 이메일 첫 번째 단락, 두 번째 줄의 "hassle free"와 의미가 가장 가까운 것은?
(A) 편리한
(B) 현대식의
(C) 문제가 있는
(D) 복잡한

185. 연계 문제 – Ms. Parker에 관한 내용 ★☆☆
해설 Ms. Parker는 이메일 첫 번째 문장 'I would like to schedule a tune-up for my home computer at your special advertised rate.'에서 광고에 언급된 특별 가격으로 자신의 컴퓨터를 튠업하고 싶다고 했는데, 이메일을 보낸 날짜는 11월 14일이다. 첫 번째 지문인 광고 하단에 특별 가격은 11월 한 달 동안에만 해당된다고 했기 때문에 Ms. Parker는 특별 가격인 49.99달러를 청구받을 것이라고 한 (B)가 정답이다. 정답 (B)

표현 정리 **lack** ~이 없다, ~이 부족하다 **damage** 손상을 주다

해석 Ms. Parker에 관해 암시된 것은?
(A) 그녀는 오후에 일한다.
(B) 그녀는 49.99달러를 청구 받을 것이다.
(C) 그녀의 컴퓨터는 하드 드라이브가 없다.
(D) SunClean은 그녀의 컴퓨터를 손상시켰다.

문제 186-190번은 다음 웹페이지, 일정표, 그리고 이메일을 참조하시오.

www.janus.org			
홈	전시품	달력	연락처

Waterbury에 위치한, Janus 미술관은 전 지역에서 가장 훌륭한 북아메리카 미술품들을 소장하고 있습니다. 미술관은 1898년 Herbert Janus에 의해 대중들이 그의 가족 소유의 소장품들을 감상할 수 있도록 하려는 목적으로 설립되었습니다

원형 홀: 안내 데스크, 매표소, 초상화

서관: 유럽 미술, 아시아 미술, 아프리카 미술

별관: 조각 작품, 임시 전시

186시간: 월요일 – 금요일, 오전 11시 – 오후 4시,

토요일, 오후 12시 – 오후 5시

입장료: 5달러, 5세 이하 어린이 무료

표현 정리 collection 수집품   rotunda 원형 홀   portrait 초상화   modernism 모더니즘, 현대주의   annex 별관   sculpture 조각품   temporary 임시의   admission 입장료

Janus 미술관

캘린더

8월 7일

미술 대화: "수채화: 과거와 현재" Amanda Gaines 박사

Pierce 강당: 오후 3시

8월 11일

전시회 개막: "현대의 도시 화가들"

별관: 오후 1시

1898월 15일

미술 대화: "다양한 예술적 전통에서의 풍경" Devon Roland

Pierce 강당: 오후 3시

8월 22일

미술가를 만나요: "현대의 도시 화가들"에 포함된 Jan Jansen

Pierce 강당: 오후 2시 30분

엄선된 갤러리들의 안내 투어는 주 단위로 제공되며, 입장료 가격에 포함됩니다. 투어는 안내 데스크에서 만나며, 50분 정도 걸립니다.

화요일, 오전 10시 – 유럽 미술관

수요일, 오후 2시 – 아시아 및 아프리카 미술관

금요일, 오후 1시 – 조각품 전시장

187 토요일, 정오 – 아메리카 미술관

질문/논평:

188지원 및 행사 코디네이터, Paula Garcia(pgarcia@janus.org)에게 연락해 주세요.

표현 정리 watercolors 수채화   auditorium 강당   contemporary 현대의   urban 도시의   landscape 풍경   artistic 예술적인, 예술의   last 지속되다   approximately 대략   outreach 지원

발신: Frank Eggers ⟨eggy@livemail.com⟩

수신: Paula Garcia ⟨pgarcia@janus.org⟩

날짜: 8월 21일

Ms. Garcia 님께,

저는 지난주에 출장으로 인해 당신이 거주하는 도시에 있었습니다. **189운이 좋게도 회의가 일찍 끝났고, Mr. Roland가 이끈 대화에 참석할 수 있었습니다.** 그의 미술사에 대한 지식은 인상적이었습니다. **190그의 이야기가 끝난 후, 완전히 새로운 시각으로 여러 작품들을 감상했습니다.** 다음에 이 지역에 오게 되면 다시 방문할 수 있기를 기대합니다.

감사합니다.

Frank Eggers

표현 정리 business trip 출장   let out 끝나다   look forward to ∼을 기대하다

---

186. 세부사항 – 미술관에 대한 내용 ★★☆

해설 첫 번째 지문 하단 'Hours: Monday – Friday, 11:00 A.M. – 4:00 P.M. and Saturday, noon to 5:00 P.M.'에서 월요일에서 토요일까지 일주일에 6일을 개관한다는 사실을 알 수 있으므로 정답은 (B)이다.   **정답 (B)**

🔍**함정 분석** 웹페이지 첫 번째 단락 'The museum was founded in 1898 by Herbert Janus to make his family's collection of art available for the public to enjoy.'에서 Herbert Janus가 1898년에 미술관을 설립했지만, 그가 예술가였는지는 알 수 없으므로 (D)는 오답이다.

표현 정리 senior 어르신   found 설립하다

해석 미술관에 관해 언급된 것은?

(A) 어르신들에게 할인을 제공한다.

(B) 일주일에 6일을 연다.

(C) 영화관을 가지고 있다.

(D) 유명한 예술가에 의해 설립되었다.

187. 연계 문제 – 토요일 가이드 투어에 대한 내용 ★★☆

해설 두 번째 지문 후반, 미술 관람 일정에 따르면 토요일에는 'Saturdays, noon – American Art Galleries'에서 정오에 '아메리카 미술 투어'가 예정돼 있음을 알 수 있는데, 첫 번째 지문에서 아메리카 미술은 'East Wing: Early American Art, American Modernism'에서 동관에 위치해 있음을 알 수 있으므로 정답은 (A)이다.   **정답 (A)**

해석 토요일 가이드 투어에 관한 사실 내용은?

(A) 미술관의 동관을 방문한다.

(B) 미술관 큐레이터가 안내한다.

(C) 한 시간 이상 걸린다.

(D) 사전 등록을 요구한다.

188. 유추 – Ms. Garcia에 대한 내용 ★☆☆

해설 Ms. Garcia는 두 번째 지문 하단에 언급되어 있는데, 'Questions/Comments: Contact our outreach and events coordinator, Paula Garcia (pgarcia@janus.org)'에서 지원 및 행사 코디네이터로 미술관 직원임을 알 수 있으므로 정답은 (D)이다.   **정답 (D)**

패러프레이징 |지문| events coordinator 행사 코디네이터 → |선택지 D| a member of the museum's staff 미술관 직원 중 한 명

표현 정리 sculptor 조각가

해석 Ms. Garcia에 관해 암시된 것은?

(A) 그녀는 금요일에 투어를 안내할 것이다.

(B) 그녀는 조각가로서 그녀의 일을 시작했다.

(C) 그녀의 작품은 별관에 걸려 있다.

(D) 그녀는 미술관 직원의 일원이다.

189. 연계 문제 – Mr. Eggers가 미술관을 방문한 날짜 ★☆☆

해설 Mr. Eggers가 보낸 이메일에서 'Luckily, my meetings let out early, and I was able to attend the talk by Mr. Roland.'에서 Mr. Roland가 연사로 참여한 대화에 참석했음을 알 수 있는데, 두 번째 지문에서 Mr. Roland와 함께 하는 행사는 'August 15, Art Talk: "Landscapes in Different Artistic Traditions" by Devon Roland'에서 8월 15일임을 알 수 있으므로 정답은 (C)이다.   **정답 (C)**

해석 Mr. Eggers가 미술관을 방문한 날짜는?

(A) 8월 7일

(B) 8월 11일

(C) 8월 15일

(D) 8월 22일

190. 동의어 ★☆☆

해설 이메일 'After his talk, I looked at several pieces in your collection in a whole new light.'에서 light은 '방식, 시각' 등의 뜻을 내포하고 있어 이와 가장 가까운 단어는 (C) manner이다. 즉, 미술품을 완전히 새로운 시각[방식]에서 감상할 수 있었다는 내용이다. **정답 (C)**

표현 정리 brightness 밝음 gleam 흐릿한 빛 manner 방식

해석 이메일 세 번째 줄의 "light"와 의미가 가장 가까운 것은?
(A) 밝음
(B) 흐릿한 빛
(C) 방식
(D) 시야

문제 191-195번은 다음 광고, 이메일, 그리고 온라인 쇼핑 카트를 참조하시오.

> ### 디 엣지
> www.theedge.com
> **최고의 온라인 쇼핑 클럽!**
>
> 3월 거래
>
> | | |
> |---|---|
> | 191(D)당신이 선택하는 모든 상품을 10퍼센트 할인받으세요.* | 191(B)이미 낮은 가격으로 판매되는 음악을 35퍼센트까지 할인된 가격에 다운로드하세요. |
> | Ace 또는 Mile의 운동화 한 켤레를 구입하고, 두 번째는 반값으로 얻으세요. | 195100달러 이상 구입하시고, The Edge의 열쇠고리를 무료로 받으세요.** |
>
> The Edge는 회원제로 운영되는 온라인 쇼핑 클럽입니다. 191(A)새로운 혜택이 매달 제공됩니다. 지금 참여하셔서 이 훌륭한 거래를 이용하세요. 게다가, 신규 회원들은 첫 번째 주문에 대해 무료 배송을 받습니다(돌아온 회원들에게는 적용되지 않음). 193회비는 한 달에 2달러입니다.***
>
> TheEdge.com으로 가셔서 지금 쇼핑을 시작하세요!
>
> *3월에 거래 한 번만 적용. 다른 제공들 또는 쿠폰들과 중복 사용 불가.
> **한 명의 고객 당 하나로 제한됨.
> ***3개월의 시험 회원제를 위해 등록을 할 때.

표현 정리 premier 최고의 members-only 회원제 take advantage of ~을 이용하다 free shipping 무료 배송 applicable 적용되는 be combined with ~와 결합되다 sign up for ~에 등록하다

> 발신: 고객 서비스 ‹custserv@theedge.com›
> 수신: Norman Greer ‹norm.greer@ezmail.com›
> 날짜: 3월 12일
>
> Mr. Greer 님께,
>
> The Edge에 오신 것을 환영합니다! 고객님은 현재 최고의 온라인 쇼핑을 할 수 있는 엘리트 쇼핑 그룹의 일원입니다.
>
> 192,1933개월 체험 회원으로 등록해 주셔서 감사합니다. 고객님의 회원번호는 2890338입니다. 당장 쇼핑을 시작할 수 있습니다. 이달의 특가를 이용하시려면 www.theedge.com을 방문해 주세요. 194첫 구매를 하기 전에 먼저 계정을 만드는 것이 필요합니다. 단순히 회원번호를 입력하세요. 그 다음에, 사용자 이름과 비밀번호를 결정해 입력하세요.
>
> 만약 체험 회원 기간이 끝날 무렵, The Edge가 마음에 든다면, 아무것도 하지 마세요. 그러면 저희가 매달 고객님의 신용카드로 청구서를 보낼 것입니다. 체험 기간 후에, 저희에게 연락함으로써 고객님은 언제든 회원가입을 취소할 수 있습니다. 아무 것도 묻지 않습니다.

> 저희는 회원의 피드백을 환영합니다. custserv@theedge.com으로 저희에게 연락 주십시오.
>
> The Edge

표현 정리 have access to ~에 접근할 수 있다, ~이 가능하다 sign up for ~에 등록하다 trial 시험 account 계정 bill 청구서를 보내다 drop a line 몇 줄 써 보내다

> www.theedge.com
>
> 주문번호: YU8495
> 날짜: 3월 15일, 금요일
> 회원 번호: 2890338
>
> 배송처: Norman Greer
> 222 Lily Lane
> Canton, OH 39034
> 전화번호: (808) 555-9303
>
> **쇼핑 카트**
>
> | 수량 | 코드 | 상품 | 가격 | 합계 |
> |---|---|---|---|---|
> | 1 | 63343 | Ace "Tiger" 운동화 | 58달러 | 58달러 |
> | 1 | 59856 | Ace "Puma" 운동화 | 50달러 | 25달러 |
> | 1 | 35935 | Rigo 운동용 반바지 | 14.25달러 | 14.25달러 |
> | 1 | 90698 | Rigo 운동용 상의 | 17.99달러 | 17.99달러 |
>
> 195총: 115.24달러가 7934로 끝나는 신용카드로 청구됨
>
> 고객님의 주문이 처리되었습니다. 다음 24시간 내에 배송될 것입니다. 주문은 www.theedge.com/tracking에서 추적될 수 있습니다.
>
> 구매해 주셔서 감사합니다!

표현 정리 bill 청구하다 process 처리하다 track 추적하다

---

191. 세부사항 – 광고에서 언급되지 않은 것 ★★☆

해설 쿠폰 코드와 관련된 내용은 광고 내용에서 찾을 수 없으므로 정답은 (C)이다. **정답 (C)**

함정 분석 (A)는 광고 'New offers every month.'에서 특가는 매달 제공되는데, 광고 상단에 March Deals라고 적혀 있어 이번 달은 3월 특가 행사임을 알 수 있다. (B)는 3월 특가 내용 중 'Download select music for up to 35% off our already low prices.'에서 신규 회원 역시 할인가로 음악을 다운로드 할 수 있다. (D) 'Get 10% of any item off your choice.*'와 'Applicable to a single transaction in March.'에서 어떤 상품이든 3월에는 1회 할인을 받을 수 있다는 것을 알 수 있다.

패러프레이징 |지문| download select music for up to 35% off 35% 할인된 가격으로 음악을 다운로드하다 → |선택지 B| get discounted music 할인된 음악을 구입하다

해석 광고에서 언급된 내용이 아닌 것은?
(A) 특가는 한 달 동안 유효하다.
(B) 신규 회원은 할인된 음악을 얻을 수 있다.
(C) 쿠폰 코드는 주문할 때 사용돼야 한다.
(D) 어떤 상품이든 1회 할인이 제공되고 있다.

192. 세부사항 – Mr. Greer가 6월에 할 수 있는 일 ★☆☆

해설 두 번째 지문인 이메일 두 번째 단락 'Thank you for signing up for a three-month trial membership.'에서 Mr. Greer가 3개월 체험 회원으로 등록했다는 것을 알 수 있는데, 이메일을 받은 시점이 3월 12일이므로 3개월 뒤인 6월에는 회원 가입을 취소할 수 있어 정답은 (D)이다. **정답 (D)**

표현 정리 terminate 종료하다

해석 Mr. Greer가 6월에 할 수 있는 일은?
    (A) 무료 배송을 받는다.
    (B) 특별한 쿠폰을 받는다.
    (C) 요금의 환불을 요청한다.
    (D) 그의 멤버십을 종료한다.

193. 연계 문제 – Mr. Greer에 대한 내용 ★☆☆

해설 이메일 'Thank you for signing up for a three-month trial membership.'에서 Mr. Greer는 3개월 체험 회원으로 가입했음을 알 수 있는데, 첫 번째 지문 광고 'Membership costs just $2 a month! When you sign up for a three-month trial membership.'에서 체험 회원으로 등록하면 매달 2달러를 회비로 내야 하므로 정답은 (A)이다.　　　　　　　　　정답 (A)

표현 정리 formerly 전에

해석 Mr. Greer에 관해 암시된 것은?
    (A) 그는 회원 가입비로 6달러를 청구 받았다.
    (B) 이메일을 통해 제안 사항을 제공했다.
    (C) 모든 쇼핑을 온라인으로 한다.
    (D) 전에 The Edge 회원이었다.

194. 세부사항 – Mr. Greer가 3월 15일 구매 전 한 일 ★☆☆

해설 두 번째 지문인 이메일 'There, you need to create an account before you can make your first purchase.'에서 첫 구매를 하기 전에 홈페이지 상에서 계정을 만드는 것이 필요하다고 했으므로 Mr. Greer는 3월 15일 첫 구매 전에 온라인 계정을 만들었을 것으로 유추할 수 있어 정답은 (C)이다.　　　정답 (C)

패러프레이징 |지문| visit www.theedge.com. There, you need to create an account www.theedge.com을 방문해 계정을 만들어라 → |선택지 C| set up an online account 온라인 계정을 설정하라

해석 Mr. Greer가 3월 15일에 구매를 하기 전에 한 일은?
    (A) 새로운 번호를 선택했다.
    (B) 고객 서비스에 연락했다.
    (C) 온라인 계정을 설정했다.
    (D) 제품을 추적했다.

195. 연계 문제 – 주문 YU8495에 대한 내용 ★★☆

해설 첫 번째 지문인 광고 'Get a free The Edge key chain with any single purchase of $100 or more.**'에서 한 번 구매 금액이 100달러 이상일 경우 The Edge 열쇠를 무료로 제공한다고 했으므로 정답은 (B)이다.　정답 (B)

🔍 함정 분석 (A)는 세 번째 지문에서 총 물품 구입 금액 115.24달러 외에 배송 비용에 관한 내용은 언급되지 않아 오답이고, (C)는 첫 번째 지문에서 음악을 다 운로드하면 35퍼센트 할인해 준다고 했는데, 구입 품목에 보면 음악을 구입하지 않았음을 알 수 있어 오답이다. (D)는 24시간 내로 배송을 할 것이라고 했을 뿐, 하루 안에 물건이 도착할 것이라고 한 것은 아니므로 오답이다.

표현 정리 be eligible for ~에 대한 자격이 있다

해석 주문 YU8495에 관해 사실인 내용은?
    (A) 배송비가 청구되었다.
    (B) 무료 선물을 받을 자격이 있다.
    (C) 35퍼센트 할인을 받았다.
    (D) 하루 만에 도착할 것이다.

문제 196-200번은 다음 발표, 일정표, 그리고 이메일을 참조하시오.

이제 온라인 교육이 가능합니다!
Desanti 주식회사

Desanti 주식회사는 직원 모두가 최신 지식과 기술을 갖추기를 원합니다. 200그것이 저희가 일련의 온라인 교육 모듈을 개발하는 NetLearn과 계약한 이유입니다. 첫 번째 시리즈는 이번 가을에 이용 가능하게 될 것입니다.

각 교육 모듈은 오늘의 빠르게 변화하는 직장에서 유용한 특정 논제에 초점을 맞춥니다. 교실과 강사의 제약에서 자유로운, 이 과정들은 직원 자신의 속도에 맞춰 완료할 수 있습니다.

196재능 발달 팀의 웹사이트에서 신청하세요: https://www.desanti.com/talentdevelopment

---

표현 정리 ensure 보장하다 up-to-date 최신의 contract 계약하다 a series of 일련의 available 이용할 수 있는 specific 구체적인 topic 논제 utility 유용성 constraint 제약 instructor 강사 pace 속도 sign up 등록하다

온라인 교육 모듈
Desanti 주식회사

그룹 1

OT 101: 신입 직원 오리엔테이션
이 온라인 코스는 대면 오리엔테이션에 이어 반드시 이수해야 하는 과정으로 회사의 웹 사이트와 웹에 기반한 프로그램을 소개합니다. 197오직 신입 직원들에게만 열려있습니다.

OT 203: 디지털 기술의 이용
직접 해 보는 이 과정은 스마트폰 또는 다른 디지털 기기를 최대한 활용하는 방법을 가르쳐 줍니다. 시간을 더 잘 관리하고, 전문적으로 의사소통을 하는 방법 등을 배우십시오.

199OT 301: 디지털 보안 *
디지털화된 모든 사항과 관련된 회사 정책을 배웁니다: 파일 저장, 전자 통신, 데이터 전송 등등

OT 403: 감기의 시즌에 건강을 유지하는 법
이 모듈은 당신과 다른 사람들을 질병으로부터 보호하는 실질적인 방법들을 가르쳐 줄 것입니다.

*199전 직원은 온라인 버전 또는 교실 버전 중 하나를 12월 31일까지 마쳐야 합니다.

그룹 1 교육 모듈은 9월 10일에서 12월 31일까지 이용 가능합니다. 직원들이 성공적으로 교육을 완료하면 증명서가 수여될 것입니다.

표현 정리 required 필수의 follow-up 후속편 leverage 이용하다, 활용하다 hands-on 직접 해 보는 make the most of ~을 최대한 활용하다 professionally 전문적으로 storage 저장 and so forth 등등 stay healthy 건강을 유지하다 practical 실질적인 certificate 증명서 completion 완료

발신: nlewis@desanti.com
수신: phartman@desanti.com
제목: 교육 모듈
날짜: 10월 1일

Mr. Hartman님께,

199저는 의무적인 온라인 교육 모듈을 어제 마쳤습니다. 그것은 저희가 몇 년 전에 받아야 했던 유사한 실내 교육보다 확실히 편리했습니다. 한 가지 문

제가 있는데, 저의 이수 수료증을 출력하는데 문제가 있어서입니다. **200과**정을 준비한 회사에 이메일을 보냈는데, 회사 사람은 작은 결함이 있어서 출력하는데 문제가 있다고 합니다. **198**문제가 해결될 때까지, 당신만이 수료증을 출력할 권한이 있다고 말하더군요. 저에게 사내 메일로 제 수료증을 보내주실 수 있습니까?

Ned Lewis

표현 정리 mandatory 의무적인 definitely 확실히 convenient 편리한 put together 합하다 due to ~때문에 glitch 작은 문제 work out 해결하다 be authorized to ~에 대한 권한이 있다 interoffice 사내

196. 세부사항 – 독자들이 웹사이트를 주목해야 하는 이유   ★☆☆
해설 첫 번째 지문 후반 'Sign up on the Talent Development Team's Web site'에서 재능 개발 팀의 웹사이트에 등록하라고 했으므로 정답은 (D)이다.
정답 (D)

표현 정리 be referred to ~을 참조하게 하다, 알아보게 하다 participate in ~에 참가하다

해석 발표에서, 독자들이 웹사이트를 참조해야 하는 이유는?
(A) 교육을 위한 제안들을 제공하기 위해
(B) 행사를 위한 좌석을 예약하기 위해
(C) 온라인 조사에 참가하기 위해
(D) 일련의 교육 과정들에 등록하기 위해

197. 세부사항 – 교육 모듈에 대해 언급된 것   ★☆☆
해설 두 번째 지문에서 OT 101과정을 보면, 'Only open to new hires.'라고 제시되어 있다. 이 과정은 신입 사원에게만 적용되기 때문에 정답은 (C)이다. 참고로 이 교육 모듈이 온라인과정이긴 하지만, OT 301인 경우, 'Either the online version or the classroom version of this training must be completed by all employees by December 31'에서 보듯이, 교실 버전도 있기 때문에 (D)는 오답이다.
정답 (C)

표현 정리 be restricted to ~에게만 국한되다

해석 교육 모듈에 대해 언급된 것은?
(A) 끝내는데 수개월이 걸린다.
(B) 교육 모듈 중 2개는 데이터 입력에 관해 가르친다.
(C) 하나의 교육 모듈은 특정 스태프에게만 국한된다.
(D) 온라인에서만 사용 가능하다.

198. 주제 – Mr. Lewis의 목적   ★★☆
해설 Mr. Lewis가 이메일을 보낸 이유는 교육을 마친 후, 수료증을 출력하는 과정에서 문제가 있었다고 했고, 이메일 마지막 문장 'Would you be able to send mine to me via interoffice mail?'에서 수료증을 출력해 사내 메일을 통해 자신에게 보내 달라고 요청하고 있으므로 정답은 (B)이다.
정답 (B)

표현 정리 inaccessible 접근하기 어려운

해석 Mr. Lewis가 Mr. Hartman에게 이메일을 보낸 이유는?
(A) 또 다른 교육 과정에 등록하기 위해
(B) 서류의 복사본을 요청하기 위해
(C) 회사에 관해 불평하기 위해
(D) 접근할 수 없는 과정을 보고하기 위해

199. 연계 문제 – Mr. Lewis가 끝마친 훈련 모듈   ★★☆
해설 이메일 첫 번째 문장 'I completed the mandatory online training module yesterday.'에서 의무적인 온라인 과정을 마쳤다고 했는데, 두 번째 지문인 일정표에서 의무적으로 반드시 마쳐야 하는 과정은 (*) 표시가 있는 OT 301이다. 왜냐하면, 일정표 마지막 부분 '*Either the online version or the classroom version of this training must be completed by all employees by December 31.'에서 알 수 있듯이 (*) 표시가 되어 있는 과정은 반드시 이수해

야 한다고 했기 때문이다. 따라서 정답은 (C)이다.
정답 (C)

해석 Mr. Lewis가 끝마친 교육 모듈은?
(A) OT 101
(B) OT 203
(C) OT 301
(D) OT 403

200. 연계 문제 – Mr. Lewis에 대한 내용   ★★★
해설 Mr. Lewis는 이메일에서 수료증을 출력하려고 교육 모듈을 개발한 회사에 이메일을 보냈지만 사소한 문제가 있어 출력이 어렵다는 말을 들었다고 했다. 그런데 첫 번째 지문인 발표 'That's why we have contracted with NetLearn to develop a series of online training modules.'에서 온라인 교육 모듈을 개발한 회사 이름이 NetLearn임을 알 수 있다. 따라서 Mr. Lewis가 이메일을 보내 수료증을 부탁했던 회사 이름이 곧 NetLearn임을 알 수 있으므로 (A)가 정답이다.
정답 (A)

함정 분석 이메일 'It was definitely more convenient than the similar in-class training program we had to do a few years back.'에서 몇 년 전에 받았던 교육에 관해 언급하고 있으므로 신입 직원이라고 보기는 어려워 (C)는 오답이다.

해석 Mr. Lewis에 관해 암시된 것은?
(A) NetLearn과 접촉했다.
(B) Mr. Hartman의 부서에서 일한다.
(C) 신입 직원이다.
(D) 소프트웨어 기술자이다.

문제 147-148번은 다음 이메일을 참조하시오.

발신: Alexis Polan
수신: Dale Fisher
제목: 불만사항 #892201
날짜: 10월 5일

Mr. Fisher 귀하

저희는 귀사에 제기된 고객불만사항(#892201)을 해결하려는 시도에 있어서 이를 성실하게 수행했다고 판단했습니다. 147 그 결과, 귀 업체가 저희 최고 등급인 골드 등급을 유지하는 것으로 결정했습니다. 그러나 귀사의 온라인 프로필에는 메모가 추가될 것입니다. 이는 불만사항의 성격을 설명할 것입니다. 148 귀사가 그 사항을 해결하기 위해 성실하게 임한다는 것 역시 언급될 것입니다. 불만사항의 세부내용은 대중에게 공개되지 않습니다.

Alexis Polan 드림
ConsumerReviews.com

표현 정리 determine 결정하다 in good faith 성실하게 resolve 풀다, 해결하다 complaint 항의, 불만 file (소송 등을) 제기하다 retain 유지하다, 보유하다 rating 등급 nature 성격 mention 말하다, 언급하다 details 세부사항 visible 보이는, 가시적인

147. 주제 – Ms. Polan이 이메일을 보낸 이유 ★☆☆
해설 결과를 나타내는 'As a result, we have decided that your business shall retain our Gold rating, our highest level.'에서 업체가 최고 등급을 유지하도록 결정했다는 말이 나온다. 뒤이어 이에 대한 추가 내용이 언급되므로 결정에 대한 결과를 알린다는 (D)가 정답이다. 정답 (D)

🔍 함정 분석 'retain our Gold rating, our highest level'에서 retain은 '(계속) 유지[보유]하다(to keep someone or something)'라는 뜻이다. 최고 등급을 유지하고 있을 뿐, 자격이 상승한 것이 아니므로 'a status upgrade'로 표현한 (B)는 오답이다.

표현 정리 alert 경고하다, 알리다 status 지위, 자격 additional 추가의 decision 결정

해석 Ms. Polan은 왜 Mr. Fisher에게 연락을 취하고 있는가?
(A) 그에게 불만사항을 알리기 위해
(B) 자격 상승을 보고하기 위해
(C) 추가 정보를 요청하기 위해
(D) 결정된 결과를 설명하기 위해

148. 유추 – Mr. Fisher의 회사에 대한 내용 ★★☆
해설 첫 번째 문장 'We have determined that your company acted in good faith in attempting to resolve the customer complaint filed against you (#892201).'와 후반부 'It will also mention that you attempted to resolve it in good faith.'에서 회사가 고객불만을 성실히 해결해왔다는 내용이 나오므로 'attempting to resolve the customer complaint', 'attempted to resolve it'을 'tried to respond to an unhappy customer'로 바꿔 표현한 (B)가 정답이다. 정답 (B)

패러프레이징 |지문| attempted to resolve it 그 문제를 해결하려고 시도했다 → |선택지 B| tried to respond to an unhappy customer 불만족스러운 고객에게 대응하기 위해 노력했다

표현 정리 review 리뷰, 후기 respond to ~에 대응하다 conduct (특정한 활동을) 하다

해석 Mr. Fisher의 회사에 대해 암시된 것은?
(A) Ms. Polan을 위해 제품 후기를 준비한다.
(B) 불만족스러운 고객에게 대응하기 위해 노력했다.
(C) 고객들에게서 많은 불만사항을 받아왔다.
(D) 온라인으로만 사업한다.

문제 149-150번은 다음 광고를 참조하시오.

Grover Towers
149(B) 현재 70~90평방미터의 침실 하나짜리 아파트와 침실 두 개짜리 아파트를 임대하고 있습니다!

월임대 또는 연간임대 옵션 중에서 선택하십시오.

149(D) 한 달에 800달러부터!
합리적인 임대보증금.

고속도로에서 몇 분 거리에 있는 Grover Towers는 조용한 주거 지역에 위치해 있습니다.
149(C) 세입자는 공원과, 쇼핑센터, 은행, 도서관까지 걸어갈 수 있습니다.

주차는 문이 있는 주차장에 추가 비용 없이 모든 세입자가 이용할 수 있습니다.
149(A) 동전 투입식 세탁기와 건조기는 1층에 있습니다.

건물 관리자는 24시간 상주하여 도움을 제공합니다.

사진과 평면도는 www.grovertowers.com에서 확인하실 수 있습니다.

150 무료 방문을 예약하시려면 555-0303으로 건물 관리자에게 전화하십시오.

표현 정리 currently 현재 for rent 임대함, 세놓음 annual 연간의, 한해의 lease 임대차계약 option 선택 reasonable 합리적인 security deposit 임대보증금 located ~에 위치한 residential 주거의 tenant 세입자 available 이용 가능한 at no additional charge 추가 비용 없이 gated 문이 있는(운전자가 여닫게 되어 있음) lot 지역, 부지 ground floor 1층 on site 현장의, 현지의 assistance 도움, 지원 floor plan (건물의) 평면도 set up (어떤 일이 있도록) 마련하다 free 무료의

149. 세부사항 – Grover Towers에 대해 언급되지 않은 것 ★★☆
해설 'Coin-operated washer and dryers are located on the ground floor.'에서 (A)를, 'We currently have one-and two-bedroom apartments for rent ranging from 70 to 90 square meters in area!'에서 (B)를, 'Tenants can walk to a park, a shopping center, a bank, and a library.'에서 (C)를 모두 확인할 수 있다. '$800 a month and up!'은 월 임대료가 800달러 이상이라는 말이고, 'Reasonable security deposits.'에서 보증금은 구체적으로 명시되지는 않았다. 따라서 보증금을 800달러로 표현한 (D)가 잘못된 내용이다. 정답 (D)

패러프레이징 |지문| We currently have one-and two-bedroom apartments for rent ranging from 70 to 90 square meters in area 현재 70~90평방미터의 침실 하나짜리 아파트와 침실 두 개짜리 아파트를 임대하고 있습니다 → |선택지 B| It rents out different-sized units 다양한 크기의 아파트를 임대한다

표현 정리 appliances 가전제품 unit (아파트 같은 공동주택 내의) 한 가구 charge 부과하다

해석 Grover Towers에 대해 언급되지 않은 것은?
(A) 아파트에 가전제품을 제공한다.
(B) 다양한 크기의 아파트를 임대한다.
(C) 쇼핑 장소 가까이에 위치해 있다.

(D) 모든 세입자들에게 800달러의 임대보증금을 부과한다.

150. 세부사항 – 아파트를 볼 수 있는 방법 ★☆☆

해설 광고 하단 'Call the building manager at 555–0303 to set up a free tour.'에서 아파트를 둘러보려면 전화로 예약하라고 하므로 정답은 (A)이다.

정답 (A)

표현 정리 prospective 장래의, 유망한 make a phone call 전화하다 fill out 작성하다 form 양식 stop by ~에 들르다

해석 광고에 따르면, 장래 세입자는 어떻게 아파트를 볼 수 있는가?
(A) 전화하여
(B) 온라인 양식을 작성하여
(C) 이메일을 발송하여
(D) 사무실에 방문하여

문제 151–152번은 다음 문자 메시지 내용을 참조하시오.

> Karen Griggs Seth, 저는 사람들을 몇 명 더 인터뷰하기 위해 마을에 하루 더 머물기로 했어요. 어젯밤에 저와 이야기를 나눈 현지 관리가 흥미로운 단서들을 알려주었어요. 그게 제 기사에 깊이를 더해줄 것 같아요. 151그리고 그 기사를 다음 호에 늦지 않게 맞추어 완료할 계획이에요.
>
> 오전 9시 50분
>
> Seth Malone 금요일까지는 초안이 필요하다는 점 유념하세요.
>
> 오전 9시 51분
>
> Karen Griggs 알고 있어요. 152기차로 3시간이면 시내로 돌아갈 수 있어요. 기사를 작성할 시간이 충분히 있습니다. 돌아가기 전에 끝낼 수도 있어요.
>
> 오전 9시 52분
>
> Seth Malone 알겠어요. 좋은 내용 기대하고 있겠어요. 오전 9시 53분
>
> Karen Griggs 그렇게 될 거예요. 오전 9시 54분

표현 정리 extra 추가의 local 현지의, 지역의 lead 실마리, 단서 depth 깊이 article 글, 기사 in time for 시간에 맞게 issue (잡지 등의) 호 draft 초고, 초안 plenty of 많은 expect 기대하다

151. 유추 – 대화의 대상 찾기 ★☆☆

해설 Karen Griggs (9:50 A.M.)의 대화 중 'And I plan to have the article finished in time for the next issue.'에서 다음 호에 기사가 실리게 할 것이라는 내용이 나온다. 또한 지문에 등장하는 report, draft 등의 단어도 화자가 기사를 작성하는 일을 하고 있음을 알 수 있다. 따라서 정답은 잡지사인 (C)가 가장 적절하다.

정답 (C)

표현 정리 most likely 아마도 travel agency 여행사 railway 철도

해석 Ms. Griggs는 아마도 어떤 유형의 사업에 종사하겠는가?
(A) 광고회사
(B) 여행사
(C) 잡지사
(D) 철도회사

152. 의도 파악하기 ★★☆

해설 Seth Malone (9:51 A.M.)의 대화인 'Remember that we need a draft by Friday.'에서 금요일까지 초안이 필요하다고 하자, 이에 대한 화답으로 Karen Griggs가 'It's a three–hour train ride back to the city. I'll have plenty of time to write.'라고 말하면서 'I might even finish before I get back.'이라고 하므로, 기차를 타는 3시간 동안 작업할 수 있다는 말이라는 것을 알 수 있다.

정답 (A)

표현 정리 overtime 초과근무, 잔업 deadline 기한, 마감일자

해설 오전 9시 52분에 Ms. Griggs가 "기사를 작성할 시간이 충분히 있어요."라고 쓴 의미는 무엇인가?
(A) 이동 중에 쓸 계획이다.
(B) 필요하다면 초과근무를 할 것이다.
(C) 마감기한을 연장할 수 있다고 생각한다.
(D) 기사 작성을 거의 끝마쳤다.

문제 153–154번은 다음 공지를 참조하시오.

> **컨퍼런스 공지**
>
> 153(A) 프로 스포츠 사진작가 협회(APSP)는 5월 7–9일 Florida주 Naples에 소재한 Manatee 호텔에서 제62차 연례 컨퍼런스를 개최할 계획입니다. 153(C)전문 사진작가라면 모두 APSP 회원이 되실 수 있습니다.
>
> 컨퍼런스 기간 동안 사진 클리닉, 프레젠테이션 및 워크숍이 열립니다. 153(C)5월 8일 금요일 오후 6시에 회원 저녁 식사 동안 Mitch Bullard에게 올해의 평생 회원상이 수여됩니다. 153(D)저녁 식사 후에는 Mr. Bullard가 자신의 경력에 대해 강연할 것입니다.
>
> APSP 회원 등록은 1월 31일에 시작됩니다. 3월 1일 이전에 등록하시는 회원에게는 10% 할인이 제공됩니다. 154등록하려면 www.apsp.org를 방문하십시오. 워크숍 및 기타 행사 목록과 Naples 지도, Naples의 추천 호텔 및 식당 후기를 보실 수 있습니다.
>
> 한정된 수의 Manatee 호텔 객실이 APSP 단체 특별요금으로 이용 가능합니다. 예약은 전화 1–888–555–1277번으로 하실 수 있습니다.

표현 정리 conference 학회, 회의 announcement 공지 association 협회 hold 개최하다 annual 연례의 lifetime 일생, 평생 give a talk 강연하다 career 직업, 경력 registration 등록 receive 받다 discount 할인 happening 행사 recommend 추천하다 available 이용 가능한 make a reservation 예약하다

153. 세부사항 – Mr. Bullard에 대해 언급되지 않은 것 ★☆☆

해설 첫 번째 문장인 'The Association of Professional Sports Photographers (APSP) plans to hold its sixty–second annual conference on May 7–9 at the Manatee Hotel in Naples, Florida.'에서 (A)를 먼저 확인할 수 있다. 다음으로, 'APSP membership is open to all professional photographers.'와 'An annual lifetime membership award will be given to Mitch Bullard'에서 (C)도 확인할 수 있다. 두 번째 단락 중 'After dinner, Mr. Bullard will give a talk about his career.'에서 (D)를 확인할 수 있다. 컨퍼런스 일정 중에 워크숍이 포함되어 있지만 Mr. Bullard가 이 행사를 직접 진행하는 것은 아니므로 (B)가 잘못된 사실이다.

정답 (B)

패러프레이징 |지문| After dinner, Mr. Bullard will give a talk about his career 저녁식사 후에는 Mr. Bullard가 자신의 경력에 대해 강연할 것입니다 → |선택지 D| He will speak in the evening 그가 저녁에 연설을 할 것이다

표현 정리 lead 이끌다 work as ~로서 일하다

해석 Mr. Bullard에 대해 언급되지 않은 것은?
(A) 5월에 Florida주에 있을 것이다.
(B) 워크숍을 진행할 것이다.
(C) 사진작가로 일해왔다.
(D) 저녁에 연설을 할 것이다.

154. 세부사항 – 독자가 웹사이트에서 할 수 있는 일 ★★☆

해설 'Visit www.asps.org to register. There, you can also find a list of workshops and other happenings, a map of Naples, and reviews of recommended hotels and restaurants in Naples.'에서 웹사이트를 통해 협회의 여러 행사 목록을 확인할 수 있다고 하므로 (C)가 정답이다.

정답 (C)

표현 정리 book 예약하다 activity 활동

해석 공지에 따르면, 이 글을 읽는 사람은 협회의 웹사이트에서 무엇을 할 수 있는가?
(A) 회원 명단을 찾는다.
(B) 호텔 객실을 예약한다.
(C) 컨퍼런스 활동에 대해 읽는다.
(D) 협회에 가입한다.

문제 155-157번은 다음 소식지 기사를 참조하시오.

> 직원 스포트라이트: Anna Ferguson   156**5월호**
>
> 156**Miranda Chen 씀**
>
> 156지난달에 Anna Ferguson과 자리를 같이 하여 그녀의 일에 대해 몇 가지 질문을 했습니다. 만약 기업 커뮤니케이션 부서 내 팀인 문서 서비스에 연락한 적이 있다면, Anna와 함께 작업했을 것입니다. 155그녀는 Maria Tate가 감독하는 세 명의 문서 제작 전문가팀의 수석 팀원입니다. 다른 팀원인 Cara Bailey와 Trish Landis가 그래픽 디자인 등의 업무를 처리하는 동안 Anna는 문서 서식 및 레이아웃에 주력합니다. 교정이나 기본 편집과 관련하여 도움이 필요하다면 Anna가 믿을 수 있는 사람입니다.
>
> 157(A)Anna는 8년 전 Lighthouse Enterprises에 영업부 인턴으로 입사해 6개월 후 커뮤니케이션 부서에 고용되었습니다. 157(B)2년 후에는 회사의 재정 지원으로 학교로 돌아가 석사 학위를 받았습니다. 품질에 대한 헌신은 그녀를 돋보이게 했습니다. 157(D)작년에 Anna는 우수 직원상을 수상했습니다.

표현 정리 employee 직원, 고용인 contact 연락하다 document 문서, 서류 specialist 전문가 supervise 감독하다, 지휘하다 formatting 서식 설정 handle 다루다, 처리하다 task 업무 proofreading 교정 editing 편집 turn to ~에 의지하다 intern 인턴 hire 고용하다 master's degree 석사 학위 financial 재정의 commitment to N ~에 대한 전념, 헌신 stand out 두드러지다

155. 유추 – Cara Baily에 대한 내용 ★★☆
해설 질문의 키워드인 Cara Baily가 언급되는 첫 번째 단락 중 'She is the senior-most member of the team of three document production specialists supervised by Maria Tate. Anna focuses on document formatting and layout while the other members of the team, Cara Bailey and Trish Landis, handle graphic design and other tasks.'에서 Maria Tate가 지휘하는 팀원들에 Cara Bailey가 속해 있다. 따라서 'supervised by Maria Tate'를 'under Maria Tate's direction'으로 표현한 (C)가 정답이다.
정답 (C)

🔍 **함정 분석** 'If you need help with proofreading or basic editing, Anna is the person to turn to.'와 'Anna joined Lighthouse Enterprises eight years ago as an intern in the Sales Department'에서 소개되는 사람은 직원 스포트라이트의 주인공인 Anna Ferguson이다. 질문은 Anna Ferguson이 아닌 팀 동료 Cara Bailey에 대해 묻기 때문에 주의해야 한다.

패러프레이징 |지문| supervised by Maria Tate Maria Tate가 감독하는 → |선택지 C| under Maria Tate's direction Maria Tate의 감독 하에

표현 정리 mostly 대개 spelling 철자법 under somebody's direction ~의 감독[지휘] 하에 used to (예전에는) ~이었다

해석 Cara Baily에 대해 언급된 것은?
(A) Anna Ferguson보다 먼저 고용되었다.
(B) 주로 철자법 오류를 확인한다.
(C) Maria Tate의 감독 하에 일한다.
(D) 영업부에서 일한 적이 있다.

156. 세부사항 – Miranda Chen에 대한 내용 ★☆☆
해설 헤드에 나온 'by Miranda Chen'에서 기사 작성자임을 알 수 있다. 도입부 'Last month, I sat down with Anna Ferguson and asked her a few questions about her job.'에서 Anna Ferguson을 지난달에 인터뷰했다고 나온다. 'May Issue'에서 기사가 5월호에 실리고 있으므로 4월에 인터뷰했다는 (D)가 정답이다.
정답 (D)

표현 정리 editor 편집자 press release 보도자료

해석 Miranda Chen에 대해 언급된 것은?
(A) 신문사의 편집자이다.
(B) 세 명의 직원들이 있는 그룹에서 일한다.
(C) 보도자료를 쓰기 위한 도움이 필요했다.
(D) Anna Ferguson을 4월에 인터뷰했다.

157. 세부사항 – Lighthouse Enterprises에 대해 언급되지 않은 것 ★★☆
해설 마지막 단락 중 'Anna joined Lighthouse Enterprises eight years ago as an intern ~.'에서 (A)를, 'After two years, she returned to school to earn a master's degree thanks to financial support from the company.'에서 (B)를, 'Last year, Anna was given an employee excellence award.'에서 (D)를 각각 확인할 수 있다. Lighthouse Enterprises가 고급 제품 판매로 명성이 있다는 내용은 찾을 수 없으므로 (C)가 정답이다.
정답 (C)

표현 정리 apprenticeship 견습기간, 견습직 have a reputation for ~로 유명하다, ~라는 평판을 얻다 recognize 인정하다

해석 Lighthouse Enterprises에 대해 언급되지 않은 것은?
(A) 과거에 견습직을 제공했다.
(B) 직원의 교육비를 지불했다.
(C) 고급 제품을 판매하는 것으로 유명하다.
(D) Ms. Ferguson의 업무를 인정했다.

문제 158-160번은 다음 편지를 참조하시오.

> 8월 8일
>
> Gerhard Essen
> Camello Corporation
> 1209 Merrimack Road
> Manchester, NH03101
>
> Mr. Essen 귀하,
>
> 저는 뉴욕시에서 자전거 메신저 서비스 일을 하고 있습니다. 매주 저는 자전거로 수백 킬로미터를 달립니다. 예상하시겠지만, 제 자전거 타이어는 꽤 손상을 입습니다.
>
> 5년 전에 이 일을 시작했을 때 저는 Camello 500 타이어를 처음 구입했습니다. 이제 저희 회사의 거의 모든 직원들이 이 타이어를 사용합니다. 158**부드러운 고무는 도시의 거리가 젖거나 건조하거나, 뜨겁거나 차갑거나에 관계없이 접지력이 우수합니다.** 또한 그렇게 탁월한 성능의 타이어인 데 비해 가격이 합리적입니다.
>
> 159**약 1년 전쯤에, 동료들과 저는 Camello의 타이어가 평소보다 더 빨리 마모된다는 것을 알게 되었습니다.** 160**그뿐 아니라 타이어에 펑크와 찢어짐이 더 많이 발생하고 있습니다.** 고무가 예전만큼 내구성이 없습니다. 또한 더 뻣뻣한 느낌이 납니다.
>
> 충실한 고객으로서, 저는 귀사의 타이어 품질에 무슨 일이 있었는지 알고 싶습니다. 기존의 Camello 500 타이어로 가능한 한 빨리 되돌려주시길 바랍니다.
>
> 답변 기다리겠습니다.

Gabe Aspen 드림

표현 정리 take a beating 손상을 입다, 타격을 받다   nearly 거의   rubber 고무   grip (기계·장치 따위의) 그립, 붙드는 힘   reasonably priced 적당한 가격의   coworker 동료   wear out (낡아서) 떨어지다   durable 내구성이 있는   stiff 뻣뻣한   look forward to ~을 고대하다

158. 유추 – Mr. Aspen에 대한 내용   ★☆☆

해설 본문 두 번째 단락 중 'The soft rubber provides an excellent grip on city streets whether they are wet, dry, hot, or cold.'에서 다양한 도로 상태에서도 접지력이 우수하다고 말하고 있다.   정답 (D)

표현 정리 found 설립하다   compete 경쟁하다   a variety of 다양한   condition 상태, 조건

해석 Mr. Aspen에 대해 암시된 것은?
(A) 5년 전에 회사를 설립했다.
(B) 뉴욕시에 산 적이 있다.
(C) 자전거 경주에 참가한다.
(D) 다양한 조건에서 자전거를 탄다.

159. 세부사항 – 타이어에 대한 불만사항   ★☆☆

해설 본문 세 번째 단락인 'About a year or so ago, my coworkers and I noticed that our Camello tires were wearing out faster than normal. The rubber is not a durable as it used to be. It also feels stiffer.'에서 타이어의 품질이 계속 저하되고 있음을 여러 예시로 전달하고 있다. 따라서 이를 less robust로 표현한 (B)가 정답이다.   정답 (B)

패러프레이징 |지문| our Camello tires were wearing out faster than normal Camello의 타이어가 평소보다 더 빨리 마모된다 → |선택지 B| They have become less robust 그것들은 덜 튼튼해졌다

표현 정리 complaint 항의, 불평   robust 튼튼한, 강력한   dwindle (점점) 줄어들다   no longer 더 이상 ~않는

해석 Mr. Aspen은 Camello 타이어에 대해 어떤 불만을 가지고 있는가?
(A) 현재 너무 비싸다.
(B) 덜 튼튼해졌다.
(C) 인기가 줄어들고 있다.
(D) 더 이상 구할 수 없다.

160. 문장 위치 찾기   ★★☆

해설 'Not only that'에서 대명사 that이 가리키는 내용을 찾아야 하는데 'more punctures and tears'에서 타이어에 펑크가 많이 발생한다고 하므로 타이어의 품질 저하를 설명하는 단락에 들어가야 함을 알 수 있다. 특히 tears와 동의어인 wearing out이 명시된 세 번째 단락의 [3]에 들어가면 앞에 나온 마모를 that으로 받고 이와 연관되어 펑크가 많이 생긴다는 주어진 문장이 이어지는 것이 흐름상 자연스럽다.   정답 (C)

표현 정리 puncture (타이어의) 펑크   tear 찢어진 데, 구멍

해석 [1], [2], [3], [4]로 표시된 곳 중에서 다음 문장이 들어가기에 가장 적합한 곳은 어디인가?

"그뿐 아니라, 타이어에 펑크와 찢어짐이 더 많이 발생하고 있습니다."
(A) [1]
(B) [2]
(C) [3]
(D) [4]

문제 161-164번은 다음 온라인 채팅을 참조하시오.

Jason Newman   Colin Traynor 관련해서 어떻게 되어가고 있나요? 이번주 금요일 저녁에는 우리 프로그램에 그 부분을 포함시키고자 하므로 목요일 아침까지는 미리 보고 싶은데요.   오전 10시 2분

Todd Pulaski   그 부분의 제작은 거의 끝났습니다. 인터뷰는 편집했는데 그래픽을 좀 추가하고 싶어요. 162그가 소유한 농장과 과수원이 위치한 곳을 보여주는 지도를 보게 되면 161시청자들에게 도움이 될 것 같아요.   오전 10시 5분

Jason Newman   163그렇게 해주세요. 도움이 필요하면 알려주세요. Sandra, 맡고 계신 부분은 어떻게 진행되고 있나요?   오전 10시 6분

Sandra Ling   여러 유소년 축구팀의 코치와 학부모, 선수들을 인터뷰했습니다. 161Daniel이 지난 토요일에 녹화한 경기의 비디오 클립을 저에게 가져다줘야 해요. 그걸 받는 대로 편집을 마칠 겁니다.   오전 10시 8분

Todd Pulaski   Daniel은 저와의 업무 때문에 나와 있어요. 점심 식사 이후에 돌아갈 거예요.   오전 10시 11분

Sandra Ling   164잘됐네요. 저도 그 시간 즈음에 사무실로 돌아갈 거예요. 그때 그의 자리에 들르겠다고 전해주세요. 고마워요!   오전 10시 12분

표현 정리 segment 부분, (프로그램) 구분, 세그먼트   preview 미리 보다   edit 편집하다   benefit from ~로부터 이득을 보다   orchard 과수원   own 소유하다   go for it 단호히 목적을 추구하다, 자, 해봐   match 경기   assignment 임무, 과제   stop by 들르다

161. 유추 – 화자들의 직업 찾기   ★☆☆

해설 'I think the viewers would benefit from seeing a map showing where the farms and orchards he owns are located.'에서 시청자(viewers)라는 말을 했고, 'Daniel still has to get me the video clips from the matches he recorded this past Saturday. As soon as I have them, I will finish the editing.'에서 영상을 녹화하고 편집하는 것을 유추할 수 있으므로 화자들이 일하는 곳은 TV 방송국이 적절하다.   정답 (A)

표현 정리 station 방송국   magazine 잡지

해석 화자들은 아마도 어디에서 일하겠는가?
(A) 텔레비전 방송국에서
(B) 신문사에서
(C) 라디오 방송국에서
(D) 스포츠 잡지사에서

162. 세부사항 – Mr. Traynor에 대한 내용   ★☆☆

해설 키워드인 Mr. Traynor는 대화 초반에 등장하는데, 특히 Todd Pulaski(10:05 A.M.)의 대화 중 'I think the viewers would benefit from seeing a map showing where the farms and orchards he owns are located.'에서 he가 Mr. Traynor이다. 이 사람이 농장과 과수원을 소유하고 있다고 하므로 이를 agricultural land로 표현한 (A)가 정답이다.   정답 (A)

패러프레이징 |지문| the farms and orchards 농장과 과수원 → |선택지 A| agricultural land 농지

표현 정리 agricultural land 농지   journalist 기자

해석 Mr. Traynor에 대해 언급된 것은?
(A) 농지를 가지고 있다.
(B) 목요일에 Mr. Newman을 만날 것이다.
(C) Ms. Ling과 인터뷰를 했다.
(D) 기자이다.

163. 의도 파악하기   ★★☆

해설 go for it은 '단호히 목적을 추구하다, 자, 해봐' 등의 의미로 쓰인다. 보통 열

심히 하도록 용기를 북돋을 때 쓰인다. Todd Pulaski가 그래픽을 추가해서 시청자들에게 도움을 주고 싶다고 하자, 이에 대해 해보라고 말하므로 아이디어를 허가한다는 (B)가 정답이다.　　　　　　　　정답 (B)

표현 정리 permit 허가하다　take time off 휴가를 내다　voice 표현하다　approval 인정, 찬성　request 요청하다　additional 추가적인

해석 오전 10시 6분에 Mr. Newman이 "그렇게 해주세요"라고 말한 이유는 무엇인가?
(A) Mr. Pulaski가 휴가를 내는 것을 허가하기 위해
(B) 아이디어에 허가를 표하기 위해
(C) 추가 인터뷰를 요청하기 위해
(D) Mr. Pulaski가 한 곳 이상의 장소를 방문하도록 권유하기 위해

164. 세부사항 – Ms. Ling이 나중에 할 일　★☆☆
해설 Sandra Ling의 마지막 대화 'I should be back at the office at around that time too. Please tell him I'll stop by his desk then.'에서 오후에 사무실에 돌아가면 Daniel을 만나겠다고 하므로 정답은 (D)이다.　　정답 (D)

표현 정리 conduct (특정한 활동을) 하다　colleague 동료

해석 Ms. Ling은 오늘 늦게 무엇을 할 것이라고 말하는가?
(A) 친구와 점심을 먹는다.
(B) 인터뷰를 한다.
(C) 업무차 외근한다.
(D) 동료와 만난다.

문제 165-167번은 다음 웹페이지를 참조하시오.

Fredericksburg 모형 열차 클럽			
소개	가입	행사	문의

165 46년 전 현지 모형 열차 애호가들에 의해 설립된 Fredericksburg 모형 열차 클럽(FMRC)은 교육과 후원, 사회적 교류를 통해 모형 열차 취미를 발전시키는 데 전념하고 있습니다.

저희는 월간 소식지 Riding the Rails를 발행합니다. 이번호와 과월호는 저희 웹사이트의 회원 전용 섹션에 게시됩니다.

저희는 주로 회원들의 회비로 운영됩니다. 또한 167 누구나 모형 열차, 서적, 포스터 등을 구입할 수 있는 상점인 Train Depot도 운영합니다.

저희는 월례 모형 열차 교환과 매년 12월에 열리는 인기있는 휴일 기차쇼를 포함한 여러 가지 행사를 개최합니다. 이 행사들은 일반에게 공개됩니다. 비회원에게는 입장료가 부과됩니다.

개인 회원권

Apprentice $5/년
• 청소년 전용 할인 회원권(18세 이하)
• 모든 행사에 무료 입장
• 166(A) Riding the Rails 수령

Supporter $20/년
• 166(B) Apprentice의 모든 혜택과 Train Depot에서 판매되는 모든 모형 열차, 용품 등에 10% 할인

Conductor $50/년
• 166(C) Supporter의 모든 혜택. 또한 당사 웹사이트에 회원명 게시

Engineer $100/년
• Conductor의 모든 혜택 및 Baltimore의 열차 박물관 입장권 두 장

기업 후원

후원업체가 되고 싶으신가요? 후원업체는 저희 소식지와 행사에 기업체가 소개됩니다. 자세한 내용은 Pat Gaston(555-8101)에게 문의해 주십시오.

표현 정리 establish 설립하다　enthusiast 애호가, 팬　be committed to ~에 전념하다, ~에 헌신하다　advance 진전시키다　advocacy 후원, 지지, 옹호　interaction 상호작용　publish 발행하다　monthly 월간의　members-only 회원제의　primarily 주로　fund 자금[기금]을 대다　dues 회비, 요금　operate 운영하다　swap 교환　admission 입장료　charge 청구하다　apprentice 초보자, 견습생　attend 참석하다　for free 무료로　sponsor 후원자　feature 특별히 포함하다, 특징으로 삼다　contact 연락하다

165. 세부사항 – Fredericksburg Model Railroad Club에 대한 내용　★☆☆

해설 도입부인 'Established 46 years ago by a group of local model train enthusiasts, the Fredericksburg Model Railroad Club (FMRC) is committed to advancing the hobby of model railroading through education, advocacy, and social interaction.'에서 46년 전에 설립되었다고 하므로 수십 년간 운영되고 있다는 (B)가 정답이다.　정답 (B)

패러프레이징 |지문| 46 years ago 46년 전 → |선택지 B| for decades 수십 년 동안

표현 정리 decade 10년　branch 지사, 분점　locality 인근　raise (돈을) 모으다

해석 Fredericksburg 모형 열차 클럽에 대해 사실인 것은?
(A) 자체 박물관을 운영한다.
(B) 수십 년 동안 운영되어 왔다.
(C) 여러 지역에 지부가 있다.
(D) 기차 탑승권을 판매해 돈을 모금한다.

166. 세부사항 – Conductor 회원권에 대해 언급되지 않은 것　★☆☆
해설 Apprentice 회원권은 월간 소식지를 수령(Receive *Riding the Rails*)한다고 하므로 (A)를 먼저 확인할 수 있다. Supporter회원권은 Train Depot에서 할인 혜택을 받는다고 하므로 (B)도 사실이다. Conductor 회원권은 'Get all the benefits of Supporter. Plus, we will post your name on our Web site.'에서 Supporter 회원권 혜택에 온라인으로 이름까지 게시된다고 나온다. 따라서 (C)를 확인할 수 있다. Conductor 회원권의 연령 제한은 찾을 수 없으므로 (D)가 정답이다. 연령 제한이 있는 회원권은 Apprentice이다.　정답 (D)

표현 정리 publication 출판물　acknowledge 인정하다

해석 Conductor 회원권을 가진 사람에 대해 언급되지 않은 것은?
(A) 매달 출간물을 받게 될 것이다.
(B) 클럽 상점에서 가격 할인을 받을 수 있다.
(C) 온라인으로 인정받을 것이다.
(D) 특정 연령대보다 어려야 한다.

167. 세부사항 – 비회원이 할 수 있는 일　★★☆
해설 중반부 'In addition, we operate a store, the Train Depot, where anyone can buy model trains, books, posters, and more.'에서 누구라도 Train Depot을 이용할 수 있다고 했으므로 (A)가 정답이다. 'Both current and past issues are posted on the members-only section of our Web site.'에서 소식지를 읽을 수 있는 것은 회원 전용 섹션에서 가능하다고 했으므로 (C)는 오답이다. 'Admission is charged to nonmembers.'에서 알 수 있듯이 비회원은 입장료를 내야 하므로 (D)도 오답이다.　정답 (A)

표현 정리 purchase 구입하다　article 기사

해석 웹페이지에 따르면, 비회원이 할 수 있는 것은?
(A) 모형 열차 구입하기
(B) 할인받기
(C) 온라인으로 과월호 읽기
(D) 행사에 무료로 참석하기

문제 168-171번은 다음 이메일을 참조하시오.

> 발신: Owen Medan 〈owen.medan@labova.com〉
> 수신: Henry Chinaski 〈hchinaski@dreamland.com〉
> 제목: 2차 전형
> 날짜: 1월 27일
>
> Mr. Chinaski 귀하,
>
> 축하드립니다! Labova Corporation의 1차 면접에 통과하셨습니다. **168그 결과, 귀하는 2차 채용 전형을 치르시게 됩니다.**
>
> **169 2차 전형의 후보자는 본사 사무실에 다시 와서 실기시험을 치르셔야 합니다.** 시험은 컴퓨터를 통해 시행되며 약 2시간이 소요됩니다. 최소 점수 이상을 받게 되면, 귀하의 시험 결과와 지원서를 부서 관리자에게 전달할 것입니다. 부서 관리자가 귀하에게 관심이 있다면, 최종 면접을 요청할 것입니다. 이번에 면접을 요청받지 못한다면, 귀하의 지원서는 이후 6개월 동안 유효한 상태로 보관됩니다.
>
> **170실기시험에 합격한 지원자들 중 75% 가까이가 최종적으로 채용되어 10년 이상 저희 회사에서 일합니다.** 사실 저희는 업계에서 이직률이 가장 낮습니다. 이는 저희 회사의 신중한 심사와 높은 급여 및 복지혜택 때문입니다.
>
> **171 555-1122번으로 전화해 실기시험을 치를 시간을 정하십시오.**
>
> Owen Medan 드림

표현 정리 initial 처음의, 초기의 screening interview 면접심사, 면접전형 advance 앞으로 나아가다, 전진하다 hiring 채용, 고용 candidate 후보자, 응시자 skills test 실기시험 administer 실행하다, 실시하다 approximately 거의, 약 forward 전달하다 application 지원(서) active 유효한 applicant 지원자 turnover rate 이직률 generous 후한, 넉넉한

168. 주제 – 이메일의 목적 ★★☆

해설 도입부의 'As a result, you will advance to the second round of our hiring process.'에서 1차 면접에 통과해 2차 시험을 치르게 된다고 말한다. 뒤이어 2차 시험의 진행과정이 소개되므로 글의 목적은 다음 절차를 설명한다 (D)이다.
정답 (D)

🔍 **함정 분석** 'If you get above the minimum score for the test, we will forward your test results and application materials to a department manager. If the manager is interested in you, he or she will invite you back for a final interview.'에서 실기시험에서 일정 점수 이상을 받은 후 부서 관리자가 관심을 보일 때 면접을 진행하게 되므로 (B)는 오답이다.

표현 정리 arrange 정하다, 주선하다 employment interview 취직 면접 documentation 서류 procedure 절차, 수순

해석 이메일의 목적은 무엇인가?
(A) 지원자에게 일자리를 제공하려고
(B) 취업 면접을 정하려고
(C) 추가 서류를 요청하려고
(D) 과정의 다음 단계를 설명하려고

169. 유추 – Mr. Chinaski에 대해 유추할 수 있는 것 ★☆☆

해설 Mr. Chinaski는 회사 지원자인데 두 번째 단락 중 'Candidates who advance to the second round are invited to return to our offices to take a skills test.'에서 회사에 다시 와야 한다는 내용이 나온다. return to는 '~로 돌아오다'라는 의미로 이미 1차 시험을 위해 회사에 방문한 적이 있음을 유추할 수 있다.
정답 (A)

표현 정리 currently 현재, 지금 employ 고용하다

해석 Mr. Chinaski에 대해 암시된 것은?

(A) 전에 Labova Corporation을 방문했다.
(B) 부서 관리자와 이야기했다.
(C) 6개월 전에 처음 면접을 봤다.
(D) 현재 Mr. Medan의 회사에 고용되어 있다.

170. 세부사항 – Labova Corporation에 대한 내용 ★★☆

해설 'Nearly 75% of all applicants who pass our skills test are eventually hired and stay with the company for over ten years.'에서 실기시험을 통과한 합격자들의 75%가 회사에서 오랫동안 일하고 있다고 나온다. 이를 통해 많은 신입사원들이 회사를 떠나지 않고 계속 근무를 한다(retain)는 것을 알 수 있다.
정답 (C)

🔍 **함정 분석** 'This is due to our careful screening as well as our generous salaries and benefits.'에서 회사의 이직률이 낮은 이유로 높은 급여와 복지혜택이 언급되지만 업계 최고의 급여인지, 또 이전보다 더 나아진 혜택인지는 알 수 없으므로 (A)와 (D)는 오답이다.

패러프레이징 |지문| Nearly 75% of all applicants who pass our skills test are eventually hired and stay with the company for over ten years. 실기시험에 합격한 지원자들 중 75% 가까이가 최종적으로 채용되어 10년 이상 저희 회사에서 일합니다. → |선택지 C| It retains many of its new hires 많은 신입 직원들을 유지한다

표현 정리 opportunity 기회 retain 유지하다, 보유하다

해석 Labova Corporation에 대해 언급된 것은?
(A) 업계에서 임금이 가장 높은 일자리를 가지고 있다.
(B) 온라인 교육 기회를 제공한다.
(C) 많은 신입 직원들을 유지한다.
(D) 지금은 훨씬 더 많은 혜택을 제공한다.

171. 요청 – Mr. Chinaski가 해야 하는 일 ★☆☆

해설 마지막 문장인 'Please call me at 555-1122 to set up a time to take the skills test.'에서 전화해서 실기시험 일정을 잡으라고 하므로 (D)가 정답이다.
정답 (D)

표현 정리 complete 작성하다 form 양식 attend 참석하다 schedule 일정을 정하다

해석 Mr. Medan은 Mr. Chinaski에게 무엇을 하도록 요청하는가?
(A) 관리자에게 전화하기
(B) 온라인 양식 작성하기
(C) 1차 면접에 참석하기
(D) 시험 일정 잡기

문제 172-175번은 다음 메모를 참조하시오.

> **메모**
>
> 발신: David Gresh, 시설 관리자
> 수신: 모든 직원
> 날짜: **174 5월 3일**
> 제목: 피트니스 센터
>
> 우리 회사는 4년 전 건물 5층에 피트니스 센터를 열었습니다. 이 시설은 모든 직원이 무료로 사용할 수 있습니다. 처음에는 피트니스 센터를 월요일부터 금요일까지 오전 7시부터 9시와 오후 5시부터 7시에 개방했습니다. **172하지만 직원들의 요청으로 3개월간의 시험기간 동안 오전 7시부터 오후 7시까지 시간대를 변경했습니다.** 새로운 시간대에 대한 반응이 무척 좋았기 때문에 이를 새로운 정규시간으로 만들기로 결정했습니다. **174신임 부사장님의 지원 덕분에 곧 토요일과 일요일 오전에도 피트니스 센터를 열 수 있게 될 것입니다.** 정확한 시간대는 다음달 이 변경사항이 적용되기 전에 공지

될 것입니다. 또한 피트니스 센터가 확장될 예정임을 알려드리고자 합니다. 다음 주부터 옆방의 창고에 있는 물품을 모두 치울 것입니다. **175두 방 사이의 벽은 허물 것입니다.** 이로 인해 공간이 거의 두 배가 될 것입니다. **173더 넓은 공간이 생기면 새로운 운동기구와 웨이트 장비를 구입할 수 있습니다.** 작업은 이달 말까지 완료될 것으로 예상됩니다. 그때까지 기존의 운동시설 중 일부의 사용이 제한될 것입니다.

표현 정리 fitness center 피트니스 센터, 헬스클럽   floor 층   facility 시설   initially 처음에   request 요청, 요구   trial period 시험기간   regular hours 정상 영업[근무] 시간   vice president 부사장   announce 발표하다, 알리다   take effect 효력을 발휘하다   inform 알리다   enlarge 확대하다, 확장하다   storage room 저장고, 창고   expect 예상하다   complete 완료하다   portion 부분, 일부   existing 기존의   restrict 제한하다

172. 세부사항 – 피트니스 센터에 생긴 변화 ★☆☆

해설 첫 번째 단락 중 'However, due to requests from employees, we changed the hours to 7:00 A.M. to 7:00 P.M. for a three-month trial period.'에서 직원들의 요청으로 운영시간을 변경했다고 나온다. 기존에 2시간씩 총 2회 운영하던 것이 하루 12시간으로 연장되었으므로 정답은 (A)이다. **정답 (A)**

🔍**함정 분석** 두 번째 단락의 'I would also like to inform you that the fitness center is going to be enlarged.'에서 옆방 창고 벽을 허물면서 센터의 공간이 확장되는 것일 뿐, 위치를 변경하는 것은 아니므로 (C)는 오답이다.

표현 정리 in response to ~에 응하여, 답하여   extend 연장하다   fee 요금   location 위치

해석 직원 의견에 응하여 피트니스 센터에 어떤 변화가 생겼는가?
(A) 시간이 연장되었다.
(B) 요금이 인하되었다.
(C) 위치가 옮겨졌다.
(D) 웨이트 장비가 개선되었다.

173. 세부사항 – 신규 장비를 설치하는 이유 ★☆☆

해설 두 번째 단락 중 'With more room, we can purchase some new exercise machines and weights.'에서 추가 공간 덕분에 새 운동장비를 구매할 수 있다고 하므로 정답은 (C)이다. **정답 (C)**

표현 정리 equipment 기기, 장비   outdated 구식인, 낡은   available 이용 가능한   on sale 할인[세일] 중인

해석 메모에 따르면, 회사는 왜 새로운 장비를 설치할 계획인가?
(A) 직원들이 요청했다.
(B) 기존 장비가 구식이었다.
(C) 추가 공간이 생길 것이다.
(D) 장비가 할인 판매되었다.

174. 유추 – 6월에 피트니스 센터에 생기는 일 ★☆☆

해설 'DATE: May 3'에서 메모를 쓴 날짜는 5월 3일이다. 첫 번째 단락 후반부 중 'Thanks to support from our new vice president, we will soon be able to keep the fitness center open on Saturday and Sunday mornings as well. The exact hours will be announced before this change takes effect next month.'에서 다음달(6월)에 주말 운영이 실시됨을 알 수 있다. **정답 (B)**

패러프레이징 |지문| we will soon be able to keep the fitness center open on Saturday and Sunday mornings as well 토요일과 일요일 오전에도 피트니스 센터를 열 수 있게 될 것입니다 → |선택지 B| It will be open on weekends 주말에 문을 열 것이다

표현 정리 construction 공사   feature 특별히 포함하다, 특징으로 삼다

daytime 낮, 주간

해석 6월에 피트니스 센터에 대해 무엇이 사실이겠는가?
(A) 공사를 위해 폐쇄될 것이다.
(B) 주말에 문을 열 것이다.
(C) 새로 게시된 정보가 있을 것이다.
(D) 새로운 낮시간대 운영을 시도할 것이다.

175. 문장 위치 찾기 ★★☆

해설 제시된 문장에서 the two rooms가 가리키는 부분을 찾아야 하는데 두 번째 단락 초반부 중 'Starting next week, we will remove all the items in the storage room next door.'에서 옆 방 창고가 언급된다. 그리고 그 다음에 'That will give us almost twice the amount of space.'에서 공간이 두 배가 될 것이라는 결론 문장이 나오므로 두 방 사이의 벽을 허물어 공간이 확대될 것이라는 흐름으로 연결되는 것이 자연스럽다. **정답 (C)**

표현 정리 tear down 허물다, 해체하다

해설 [1], [2], [3], [4]로 표시된 곳 중에서 다음 문장이 들어가기에 가장 적합한 곳은 어디인가?
"두 방 사이의 벽은 허물 것입니다."
(A) [1]
(B) [2]
(C) [3]
(D) [4]

문제 176-180번은 다음 정보와 이메일을 참조하시오.

High Plains Engineering
www.highplainsengineering.com

180공인 대학 또는 종합대학에서 학사 학위 과정의 최종 학년에 있는 학생들에게 무급 인턴직을 제공합니다. 환경공학, 토목공학, 측량, 프로젝트 관리 **179분야의 팀 중에서 일하기를 희망하는 지원자를 받습니다.** 인턴직은 가을 또는 봄에 열리며 참가자의 일정에 따라 6주에서 12주간 진행됩니다. 인턴직은 기존 프로젝트에 협력할 예정입니다. **176또한 인턴직은 하루에 6시간에서 8시간 동안 저희 사무실에서 주 2일 근무해야 합니다. 1779월에 시작하는 인턴직 지원은 5월 31일까지, 1월에 시작하는 인턴직 지원은 10월 31일까지 마감합니다.**

지원하시려면, 당사 웹사이트에서 지원서를 다운로드하시기 바랍니다. 지원서 양식을 작성한 후에, 지원자는 자기소개서, 성적증명서 사본, 현재 또는 전 교수나 지도교수가 쓴 추천서 3장과 함께 양식을 우편으로 제출해야 합니다.

표현 정리 unpaid 무보수의, 무급의   internship 인턴십   bachelor's degree 학사 학위   accredited 승인 받은, 공인된   applicant 지원자   civil engineering 토목공학   surveying 측량   be held 열리다   last 지속되다   depending on ~에 따라   contribute to ~에 기여하다   commit to ~에 할당하다, ~에 전념하다   due ~하기로 되어있는[예정된]   submit 제출하다   letter of interest 자기소개서(cover letter와 비슷하지만, cover letter는 특정 일자리에 지원할 때 이력서와 함께 보내는 것이고, letter of interest는 회사가 직원을 뽑는지에 관계없이, 회사에 본인을 소개하고 일자리를 알아볼 때 보내는 것)   transcript 성적증명서   reference letter 추천서   former 이전의   supervisor 지도교수

수신: 토목공학 팀 〈allcivil@highplainsengineering.com〉
발신: Eldon Charlie 〈echarlie@highplainsengineering.com〉
날짜: 12월 8일
제목: 인턴직
첨부: 서신

안녕하세요,

180 Kyle Richardson이 1월에 우리 회사에서 인턴직을 시작하고자 합니다. 그는 고속도로 건설 프로젝트 작업에 관심을 보였습니다. 그는 교과과정에서 우수함을 보였습니다. 또한 두 해 여름을 측량 보조원으로 일했으므로 관련 경험을 가지고 있습니다. 그를 선발할 것을 강력히 추천하는 바입니다.

그의 자기소개서를 첨부합니다. **178**살펴보시고 그가 우리 팀에 잘 맞는다고 생각하시면 알려주십시오. 그럴 경우, 그를 어떤 프로젝트에 배정하는 것이 좋을지 추천해 주시겠어요? 12월 15일 다음 팀 회의에서 그의 지원서를 논의할 것입니다.

감사합니다.

Eldon

표현 정리 express 표현하다 highway 고속도로 construction 건설, 공사 excel 뛰어나다, 탁월하다 surveyor 측량사 assistant 조수, 보조원 relevant 관련 있는, 적절한 attach 첨부하다 assign (일·책임 등을) 맡기다[배정하다/부과하다] discuss 논의하다

176. 세부사항 – 인턴이 해야 하는 일 ★☆☆

해설 첫 번째 지문 중반부의 'Moreover, they must commit to working two days a week at our offices for between six and eight hours per day.'에서 지원자는 주 2회 사무실에 출근해야 한다고 하므로 (B)가 정답이다. **정답 (B)**

🔍 **함정 분석** 'Internships are held in either the fall or the spring and can last from six to twelve weeks, depending on the schedule of the participant.'에서 근무기간이 참가자의 일정에 따라 최소 6주, 최대 12주이므로 (D)는 오답이다.

패러프레이징 |지문| commit to working two days a week at our offices 저희 사무실에서 주 2일 근무 → |선택지 B| Come to the workplace twice a week 일주일에 두 번 직장에 출근하기

표현 정리 participate in ~에 참가[참여]하다 workplace 직장 propose 제안하다 at least 최소한

해석 정보에 따르면, 인턴은 무엇을 할 수 있어야 하는가?
(A) 주간 회의에 참석하기
(B) 일주일에 두 번 직장에 출근하기
(C) 프로젝트 아이디어 제시하기
(D) 최소 12주간 근무하기

177. 세부사항 – 인턴직 지원서에 대한 내용 ★★☆

해설 정보의 첫 번째 단락 마지막 문장 'Applications are due by May 31 for internships starting in September and by October 31 for internships starting in January.'에서 지원서 마감이 5월과 10월에 두 번 있다고 하므로 이 중 참여하고 싶은 기간에 맞춰 제출해야 함을 알 수 있다. **정답 (A)**

🔍 **함정 분석** 첫 번째 지문의 두 번째 단락 'To apply, download an application packet from our Web site. After filling out the application form, applicants must submit it by mail along with a letter of interest, copies of their transcripts, and three reference letters from current or former professors or supervisors.'에서 다운로드해서 양식을 작성한 후에 다른 서류들과 함께 우편으로 보내라고 했으므로 (C)는 오답이다.

표현 정리 deadline 마감, 기한 proof 증명, 증거 graduation 졸업

해석 인턴직 신청서에 대해 언급된 것은?
(A) 두 마감일 중 한 마감일까지 제출해야 한다.
(B) 졸업증명서가 필요하다.
(C) 온라인으로 작성할 수 있다.
(D) 수수료 지불이 필요하다.

178. 주제 – 이메일의 목적 ★☆☆

해설 이메일의 첫 번째 단락은 Kyle Richardson이 인턴직을 희망한다는 내용이고, 두 번째 단락 중 'Please take a look at it and let me know if you think he would be a good fit for our team. If so, which project would you recommend assigning him to?'에서 이 사람의 자기소개서를 본 다음 팀에 어울리는 인재인지 파악 후 관련 업무까지 추천해 달라고 한다. 이를 피드백을 요청한다고 표현한 (A)가 이메일의 목적으로 적절하다. **정답 (A)**

표현 정리 feedback 피드백

해석 이메일의 목적은?
(A) 지원자에 대한 피드백을 요청하려고
(B) 팀 회의 일정을 정하려고
(C) Mr. Richardson을 위한 프로젝트를 제안하려고
(D) 인턴직 시작일을 요청하려고

179. 동의어 찾기 ★★☆

해설 'We accept applicants interested in working on one of our teams in the following fields: environmental engineering, civil engineering, surveying, and project management.'에서 fileds의 예로 관련 분야가 제시된다. 관련 분야의 성격상 과목이 제일 적합하므로 (C)가 정답이다. **정답 (C)**

표현 정리 agricultural 농업의 worksites 일터, 직장

해석 정보에서 첫 번째 단락 3행의 "fields"와 의미상 가장 가까운 단어는?
(A) 농업 지역
(B) 실외 공간
(C) 과목
(D) 직장

180. 연계 문제 – Mr. Richardson에 대해 사실인 내용 ★★☆

해설 이메일 도입부의 'Kyle Richardson would like to start an internship with us in January.'에서 Kyle Richardson은 인턴직 지원자임을 알 수 있다. 정보의 도입부 문장 'We offer unpaid internships for students in their final year of their bachelor's degree program at an accredited college or university.'에서 인턴직 제공은 학사 학위 최종 학년의 학생들에게 무급으로 제공된다고 나온다. Mr. Richardson 역시 인턴직 지원자로서 아직 졸업한 것은 아님을 유추할 수 있으므로 (B)가 정답이다. **정답 (B)**

🔍 **함정 분석** 'We offer unpaid internships for students ~.'에서 무급 인턴직이므로 (C)는 오답이다. Kyle Richardson이 측량 보조원으로 일한 것일 뿐, 측량 수강자인지 환경공학 전공자인지는 명시되지 않으므로 (A)와 (C)도 오답이다.

표현 정리 course 강의, 강좌 earn 벌다, 얻다 salary 급여, 월급

해석 Mr. Richardson에 대해 아마도 사실인 것은?
(A) 측량 강의를 수강했다.
(B) 아직 학사 학위를 받지 못했다.
(C) 인턴으로서 급여를 받을 것이다.
(D) 환경공학을 전공하고 있다.

문제 181-185번은 다음 정보와 양식을 참조하시오.

이벤트룸 대여

The Cherry Hills Community Center Great Room은 비영리 단체 및 지역사회 주민에게 대여 가능합니다. **181**Great Room은 최대 100명까지 수용할 수 있으며, 강연, 연수, 공연, 수업, 파티 등을 위해 대여하실 수 있습니다.

요금:
184**20달러/최대 1시간**
60달러/최대 4시간
100달러/최대 8시간
150달러/8시간 이상

제한된 수의 테이블과 의자를 Great Room에서 사용하실 수 있습니다. 이벤트 주최자는 185**Peterson Rentals(555-9332)에서 추가 가구를 빌리실 수 있습니다.** Peterson Rentals는 수년간 저희와 함께 일했으며 합리적인 가격을 제공합니다. 이 업체에서 배달, 설치, 분해를 해줍니다.

The Cherry Hills Community Center는 월요일부터 금요일까지 오전 9시부터 오후 8시까지, 그리고 토요일과 일요일은 오전 10시부터 오후 5시까지 운영합니다. 182**일반 운영시간 이외에 개최되는 행사에는 community center를 열고 닫기 위해 직원이 있어야 합니다.** 이 서비스에 대해서는 추가 요금이 부과됩니다.

표현 정리 rental 임대, 임차, 대여 nonprofit 비영리적인 performance 공연 rate 요금 a limited number of 제한된 수의 organizer 조직자, 주최자 additional 추가의 furniture 가구 reasonable 합리적인 take care of ~을 처리하다 delivery 배달 teardown 해체, 분해 charge 청구하다

Community Center 행사 예약 양식

오늘 날짜: 6월 7일

행사명: 183**태극권 초보 수업**
주최자 이름: Juliette Masetta
단체: Soto Martial Arts
전화번호: 555-0033
이메일: julie@sotomartialarts.com

신청 이벤트룸: Great Room
날짜: 월요일(8주간: 7월 9일 - 8월 17일)
시간: 184**오후 6시 - 오후 6시 50분**
참석자 수: 미정

추가 요구사항/지침: 지역사회 주민들에게 태극권 운동의 건강상 이점을 배우고 경험할 수 있는 기회를 제공하는 것에 대해 Beverly Varney와 이야기했습니다. 그녀는 참가자들에게 수업당 5달러를 부과하도록 허가했습니다. 185**바닥 면적을 넉넉하게 사용할 수 있도록 모든 가구를 이벤트룸에서 빼거나 남쪽 벽을 따라 배치할 필요가 있습니다.**

저희 직원 중 한 명이 귀하의 요청을 접수한 시간으로부터 48시간 이내에 연락드릴 것입니다.

표현 정리 reservation 예약 tai chi 태극권 martial arts 무술 attendee 참석자 requirement 필요조건 instructions 지침 opportunity 기회 benefit 이점 participant 참가자 remove 치우다, 제거하다 contact 연락하다

181. 세부사항 – Great Room에 대한 내용 ★☆☆
해설 정보의 첫 번째 단락 마지막 문장 'The Great Room can hold up to 100 people and can be rented for talks, trainings, performances, classes, parties, and more.'에서 Great Room에서 파티를 열 수 있다고 하므로 생일 축하행사에 사용할 수 있다는 (D)가 정답이다. **정답 (D)**

표현 정리 weekday 평일 individual 개인 celebration 축하행사

해석 Great Room에 대해 언급된 것은?
(A) 평일에만 이용 가능하다.
(B) 개인은 대여할 수 없다.
(C) 모든 가구를 대여해야 한다.

(D) 생일 축하행사를 위해 사용할 수 있다.

182. 세부사항 – 운영시간 외에 Great Room을 빌리기 위해 해야 할 일 ★★☆
해설 정보 마지막 단락 중 'Events held outside our normal business hours will require a staff member to be present to unlock and lock the community center. An additional fee will be charged for this service.'에서 일반 운영시간 외에는 직원이 있어야 해서 추가 요금이 필요하다고 나온다. 따라서 이를 정리한 (D)가 정답이다. **정답 (D)**

🔍 **함정 분석** 직원(a staff member)이 있어야 한다고 했는데, 이것은 보안요원을 고용하는 것이 아니고 센터의 직원 한 명이 있으면 되기 때문에 (C)는 오답이다.

패러프레이징 |지문| An additional fee will be charged 추가 요금이 부과됩니다 → |선택지 D| Make an extra payment 추가 요금 지불하기

표현 정리 in advance 미리 hire 고용하다 security guard 경비원, 보안요원 make a payment 지불하다 extra 추가의

해석 Great Room을 오후 8시 이후에 사용하려면 주최자는 무엇을 해야 하는가?
(A) 미리 임대료 지불하기
(B) 출입문 열쇠 요청하기
(C) 보안요원 고용하기
(D) 추가 요금 지불하기

183. 세부사항 – Ms. Masetta가 준비하는 행사 종류 ★☆☆
해설 키워드 Ms. Masetta는 'Organizer's Name: Juliette Masetta'에서 행사 주최자인데 행사명인 'Event Name: Beginning Tai Chi Class'에서 태극권 수업이라고 나온다. 추가 요구사항/지침의 'the health benefits of tai chi exercises'에서도 한번 더 단서를 확인할 수 있다. **정답 (B)**

표현 정리 organize 준비하다, 조직하다 fair 박람회 demonstration 시연 lecture 강연

해석 Ms. Masetta는 어떤 종류의 행사를 준비하고 있는가?
(A) 건강 박람회
(B) 운동 교실
(C) 시연
(D) 강좌 시리즈

184. 연계 문제 – 대여 비용 ★☆☆
해설 예약 양식에서 'Hours: 6:00 P.M. - 6:50 P.M.'에서 이용시간은 총 50분이다. 정보의 요금표에서 '$20 for up to 1 hour'에서 1시간 미만은 20달러이다. **정답 (A)**

해석 Ms. Masetta는 행사 비용으로 매주 얼마가 청구되겠는가?
(A) 20달러
(B) 60달러
(C) 100달러
(D) 150달러

185. 연계 문제 – Ms. Masetta에 대한 내용 ★★☆
해설 예약 양식의 추가 요구사항/지침에서 'We need all of the furniture either removed from the room or placed along the south wall so that we can have enough floor space.'에서 이벤트룸에 비치된 가구를 모두 치워서 공간을 늘릴 것이라고 한다. 첫 번째 지문의 'Event organizers can rent additional furniture from Peterson Rentals (555-9332).'에서는 추가 가구를 대여하고 싶을 때 Peterson Rentals에 연락하라고 나와 있다. Ms. Masetta는 가구를 추가 대여할 필요가 없으므로 이 업체에 연락하지 않을 것이라는 (A)가 정답이다. **정답 (A)**

표현 정리 raise (돈을) 모으다   charitable 자선의

해석 Ms. Masetta에 대해 암시된 것은?
(A) Peterson Rentals에 연락하지 않을 것이다.
(B) 자선단체를 위해 돈을 모금하려고 한다.
(C) community center의 직원이다.
(D) 7월 9일에 Ms. Varney의 연락을 받을 것이다.

문제 186-190번은 다음 공지, 온라인 양식, 그리고 이메일을 참조하시오.

문헌정보학 전문가협회(ALISP)는 186(A)4월 18일부터 4월 22일까지 Colorado주 Denver의 Great Western Convention Center에서 186(D)제35회 연례 컨퍼런스를 개최합니다. 모든 현 ALISP 회원이 초대됩니다. *189올해 Heritage Tours는 단체로 지역 유적지로 모십니다.

www.alisp.org/conference에서 컨퍼런스에 등록하시기 바랍니다. 현직에서 활동하고 있는 전문가들은 188발표와, 워크숍 진행, 공개 토론회 참가를 통해 "발표자" 할인을 받으실 수 있습니다.

186(C)등록비:
학생 150달러
187전문가 400달러
발표자 300달러
은퇴자 250달러

*186(B)이 행사는 ALISP 회원만 참석할 수 있습니다. ALISP에 가입하려면 저희 웹사이트 www.alisp.org를 방문하십시오. 저희 회원에는 학생 뿐만 아니라 대학과 기업에서 근무하는 현직 문헌정보학 전문가들도 포함되어 있습니다.

표현 정리 association 협회   Library and Information Science 문헌정보학   professional 전문가   hold 개최하다   annual 연례의, 연간의   attend 참석하다   register 등록하다   practicing 현직에서 활동하고 있는, 개업하고 있는   discount 할인   participate in ~에 참가하다   retiree 은퇴자   institution 기관, 시설

ALISP 연례 컨퍼런스
등록 양식

이름: Kelsey Walton
직함: 부사서
조직: McManus Medical Center
187등록 유형: 전문가
전화번호: (412) 555-7718
이메일: k.walton@mcmanus.org
지불 방법: 신용카드(끝자리 5653)
발표하실 겁니까? [ ] 예 [x] 아니오
발표하실 경우, 발표/강연/토론회 주제를 기술해 주시오: _____

아래 "제출" 버튼을 클릭하기 전에 등록 양식을 확인해 주시기 바랍니다. 등록이 처리되면, 확인 메일이 위의 이메일 주소로 발송됩니다. 문제가 있을 경우 1-888-555-7830번으로 기술지원 부서에 문의하십시오.

제출

표현 정리 associate 준(準)[부/조]   librarian 사서   review 검토하다   process 처리하다   confirmation 확인

발신: Kelsey Walton 〈k.walton@mcmanus.org〉
수신: Brenda Pierce 〈b.pierce@hoffman.edu〉
날짜: 4월 27일
제목: 컨퍼런스

Brenda,

Denver에서 다시 만나게 되어 반가웠습니다. 우리가 Sinclair Corporation에서 함께 일한 지 10년이 지났다니 믿기 어렵군요. 189전 동료들 몇몇과 Heritage Tours 여행을 함께 갈 수 있어서 정말 기뻤습니다.

당신의 대학에서 사용하고 있는 클라우드 기반 저장 시스템에 대한 이야기는 정말 잘 들었습니다. 저희 직장에도 유사한 시스템을 설치하려고 합니다. 기회가 생기면 188,190당신의 발표 개요를 제게 이메일로 보내주실 수 있을까요?

Kelsey 드림

표현 정리 catch up with 따라잡다, 쫓다   excursion 여행   former 예전의, 과거의   colleague 동료   storage 저장, 보관   install 설치하다   workplace 직장   outline 개요

---

186. 세부사항 – ALISP 컨퍼런스에 대한 내용   ★☆☆
해설 공지 도입부 'The Association of Library and Information Science Professionals (ALISP) will hold its thirty-fifth annual conference at the Great Western Convention Center in Denver, Colorado, from April 18 to April 22.'에서 18~22일의 총 5일간 열리므로 (A)는 사실이고, 올해 제35회라고 하므로 (D)를 확인할 수 있다. 'The event is only for ALISP members.' 라고 했으므로 (B)도 사실이다. 등록비인 'Registration Fees' 부분을 보면 지역주민에게 무료인지는 알 수 없으므로 (C)가 사실과 달라 정답이다.   정답 (C)

패러프레이징 |지문| The event is only for ALISP members 이 행사는 ALISP 회원만 참석할 수 있습니다 → |선택지 B| It is only open to people who have joined the group 단체에 가입한 사람들만 참석할 수 있다

표현 정리 run 진행되다   local 주민   decade 10년

해석 ALISP 컨퍼런스에 대해 언급되지 않은 것은?
(A) 5일 동안 열릴 것이다.
(B) 단체에 가입한 사람들만 참석할 수 있다.
(C) 지역주민들에게 무료 등록을 제공한다.
(D) 30년 이전에 처음 개최되었다.

187. 연계 문제 – 컨퍼런스 등록비   ★★☆
해설 등록 양식의 'Registration type: Professional'에서 전문가로 등록했으며, 첫 번째 지문의 요금표에서 전문가는 'Professional $400'임을 확인할 수 있다.   정답 (D)

표현 정리 pay 지불하다

해석 Ms. Walton은 컨퍼런스에 등록하기 위해 얼마를 지불했는가?
(A) 150달러
(B) 200달러
(C) 300달러
(D) 400달러

188. 연계 문제 – Ms. Pierce에 대한 내용   ★★☆
해설 Ms. Pierce는 이메일 수신인(TO: Brenda Pierce)인데, 본문 마지막 문장 'When you have a chance, could you kindly e-mail me the outline of your presentation?'에서 발표 자료를 보내달라는 요청을 받고 있다. 첫 번째 지문의 'Practicing processionals can receive a "Presenter" discount by giving a presentation, by leading a workshop, or by participating in a panel discussion.'에서 발표할 경우 할인을 받는다고 하므로 두 가지 내용을 통해 정답은 (C)임을 알 수 있다.   정답 (C)

표현 정리 design 설계하다, 디자인하다   supervise 감독하다, 지도하다

해석 Ms. Pierce에 대해 암시된 것은?
(A) 컴퓨터 네트워크를 설계했다.
(B) 소프트웨어 회사에서 일한다.
(C) 등록비 할인을 받았다.
(D) Ms. Walton을 감독했다.

189. 연계 문제 – Ms. Walton이 Denver에서 한 일   ★★☆
해설 이메일 첫 번째 단락 중 'I'm so glad we were able to go on a Heritage Tours excursion together with some of our former colleagues.'에서 동료들과 Heritage Tours를 했다고 나오는데 첫 번째 지문의 'This year, Heritage Tours will be taking groups to visit local historical sites.'에서 이 여행을 통해 지역 유적지를 방문한다고 나온다. 이들 내용을 종합할 때 (A)가 정답이다.   정답 (A)

표현 정리 attraction 명소   lecture 강의

해석 Ms. Walton은 Denver에서 아마도 무엇을 했겠는가?
(A) 문화명소를 방문했다.
(B) 연수를 진행했다.
(C) 역사 강의를 했다.
(D) 새 일자리를 얻었다.

190. 요청 – Ms. Walton이 Ms. Pierce에게 요청한 사항   ★☆☆
해설 이메일의 'When you have a chance, could you kindly e-mail me the outline of your presentation?'에서 발표한 자료를 이메일로 보내달라고 부탁하고 있기 때문에 정답은 (D)가 된다.   정답 (D)

표현 정리 talk 연설   technology 기계, 장비, 기술

해석 Ms. Walton이 Ms. Pierce에게 요청한 것은 무엇인가?
(A) 그녀의 회사에서 강연하기
(B) 새로운 기술을 설치하는 것을 도와주기
(C) 시스템 추천하기
(D) 정보 보내기

문제 191-195번은 다음 정보, 주문서, 그리고 이메일을 참조하시오.

H&R Building Supplies
78 Allen Street
Salish, WA78331
(608) 555-1249
www.hrbuildingsupplies.com

당사는 Wasatch Valley에서 목재와, 벽돌, 콘크리트 및 기타 건축자재의 최대 공급업체입니다.

저희 비즈니스 계정에 가입하십시오. 간단합니다! 전화해서 회계부서에 이 야기하시면 됩니다. 당사 보안 웹사이트에 접속하는 데 사용하실 수 있는 사용자명과 암호가 제공될 것입니다. **191**여기서 현재 재고를 검색하고, 구매하고, 주문을 추적하고, 픽업 및 배달을 예약하실 수 있습니다. 또한 계정을 이용하면, 결제가 아주 쉬워집니다!

당사는 직접 주문품을 배달해드릴 수 있습니다. 요금은 트럭당으로 청구되며 저희 창고에서 귀사 근무처까지의 거리를 기준으로 합니다.

거리	요금
0-20km	150달러
19221-40km	200달러
41-80km	350달러
81-200km	500달러

표현 정리 supplier 공급자, 공급회사   lumber 재목   brick 벽돌   concrete 콘크리트   construction 건축   sign up for ~에 가입하다   account 계정   accounting 회계   access 접근하다, 접속하다   secure 안전한   inventory 재고(품)   make a purchase 구매하다   track 추적하다   order 주문   billing 계산서 발부   cinch 아주 쉬운 일   truckload 트럭 한 대 분량   distance 거리   warehouse 창고

주문서 — H&R Building Supplies

고객 정보
계정 번호: 89532
이름: Kenny Barlow
회사: Drummond Construction
전화번호: (608) 555-1832
이메일: kbarlow@drummond.com

주문 정보

품목 번호	내역	수량
4893	골조용 목재	100개
3322	콘크리트 블록	500개
7873	모르타르	20개
2921	합판	40개

배송 정보
194날짜: 7월 12일 금요일
주소: 170 Coburn Road, Andersville, WA
크기: 트럭 한 대
192요금: 200달러

표현 정리 customer 고객   framing lumber 골조용 목재   cinder block 콘크리트 블록   plywood 합판

발신: Kenny Barlow ⟨kbarlow@drummond.com⟩
수신: Steve Thompson ⟨sthompson@hrbuildingsupplies.com⟩
194날짜: 7월 11일
제목: 주문 #128977

Steve,

194어제 주문을 넣어서 내일 배달되도록 요청했습니다. **193**이는 내일 심한 뇌우가 예상되는 것을 알기 전이었습니다. 저희 직원들이 들어올리기에 훨씬 더 무거워질 것이므로 목재를 젖게 할 수 없습니다. 그러니 제 주문품을 대신 다음 주 월요일에 배달해주실 수 있겠습니까? 작업 일정을 맞출 수 있도록 아침 일찍 배달되면 좋겠습니다. **195**하지만 귀하의 일정에 맞지 않을지도 모르겠네요. 이 요청사항을 맞춰줄 수 있는지 알려주시기 바랍니다.

감사합니다.

Kenny 드림

표현 정리 place an order 주문하다   expect 예상하다, 추측하다   thunderstorm 뇌우   afford ~할 여유가 되다   lift 들어올리다   ideal 이상적인   stick to ~을 계속하다, ~을 고수하다   accommodate 수용하다, 부응하다   request 요청, 요구사항

191. 세부사항 – 고객이 이용 가능한 상품을 확인하는 방법   ★☆☆
해설 첫 번째 지문의 두 번째 단락 중 'There, you can search our current inventory, make purchases, track your orders, and schedule pickups

and deliveries.'에서 There는 앞에 나온 our secure Web site로 이 사이트를 통해 현재 재고를 알 수 있다고 하므로 (A)가 정답이다. **정답 (A)**

표현 정리 available 구할 수 있는, 이용할 수 있는   sales associate 영업사원

해석 정보에 따르면, 고객은 H&R Building Supplies에서 현재 이용 가능한 상품을 어떻게 알 수 있는가?
(A) 웹사이트에 로그인해서
(B) 영업사원에게 전화해서
(C) 창고에 방문해서
(D) 이메일을 보내서

---

192. 연계 문제 – 보관 시설에서 고객 회사까지의 거리 ★★☆

해설 주문서의 배송 정보 중 'Charges: $200'에서 요금은 200달러를 지불했음을 알 수 있다. 첫 번째 지문의 'Rates are per truckload and are based on the distance from our warehouse to your job site.'에서 배송료는 창고부터 주문처까지의 거리를 기준으로 한다고 나오는데 200달러는 21–40km에 해당하는 요금이다. **정답 (B)**

표현 정리 storage facility 저장 시설

해석 H&R의 보관 시설에서 Andersville까지의 거리는 얼마이겠는가?
(A) 0–20km
(B) 21–40km
(C) 41–80km
(D) 81–200km

---

193. 세부사항 – Mr. Barlow가 일정을 변경하려는 이유 ★☆☆

해설 이메일 초반부의 'That was before I learned that we are expecting severe thunderstorms tomorrow. I really can't afford to have the wood get wet because then it will be a lot heavier for my employees to lift.'에서 뇌우로 목재가 젖으면 운반하기 어렵다고 말한다. 따라서 날씨로 인해 일정 변경을 요청하므로 (C)가 정답이다. **정답 (C)**

표현 정리 reschedule 일정을 변경하다   deadline 기한, 마감기한   move up 앞당기다   recalculate 다시 계산하다, 재검토하다   be concerned about ~을 걱정하다   additional 추가적인

해석 Mr. Barlow는 왜 배송 일정을 변경하고 싶어 하는가?
(A) 작업 마감기한이 앞당겨졌다.
(B) 필요한 자재의 양을 다시 계산했다.
(C) 날씨에 대해 우려하고 있다.
(D) 추가 작업자를 찾아야 한다.

---

194. 연계 문제 – 이메일 작성 요일 ★★☆

해설 이메일 작성일은 'Date: July 11'에서 7월 11일임을 알 수 있고, 본문의 'I placed an order yesterday and asked to have it delivered tomorrow.'에서 어제 7월 10일에 주문하고 배송은 내일 7월 12일로 요청했다고 나온다. 주문서를 보면 'Date: Friday, July 12'에서 배송일 7월 12일은 금요일임을 알 수 있으므로 이메일을 쓴 요일은 목요일이다. **정답 (B)**

해석 Mr. Barlow는 무슨 요일에 이메일을 작성했는가?
(A) 월요일
(B) 목요일
(C) 금요일
(D) 토요일

---

195. 세부사항 – Mr. Barlow가 알고 있는 사항 ★★☆

해설 이메일 마지막 부분의 'However, I realize that may not fit your schedule. Please let me know if you can accommodate this request.'에서 일정 변경을 요청하기는 했지만 상대 일정에 맞지 않을 수도 있을 것이라는 내용이 나온다. **정답 (C)**

표현 정리 be aware of ~을 알다   appeal 호소

해석 Mr. Barlow는 무엇을 알고 있다고 말하는가?
(A) 추가 요금을 지불해야 한다.
(B) 요청하기에는 너무 오래 기다렸다.
(C) 그의 요청이 받아들여지지 않을 수도 있다.
(D) 이메일을 Mr. Thompson이 읽지 않을 수도 있다.

문제 196–200번은 다음 이메일과 일정을 참조하시오.

발신: Carla Jensen <cjens@bixtechnologies.com>
수신: Alex Rondeaux <arond@bixtechnologies.com>
날짜: 3월 7일
제목: 여행 준비
첨부: 일정

Mr. Rondeaux 귀하,

Sunshine Airlines에 다음 비행편을 예약했습니다(예약번호 #7883):

6월 6일 월요일	1622편	**196오전 9시 3분 Albuquerque 출발**
		오후 12시 45분 Minneapolis 도착
6월 9일 목요일	788편	오후 5시 23분 Minneapolis 출발
		오후 8시 9분 Albuquerque 도착

항공사 웹사이트에서 전자 항공권을 보실 수 있습니다. 체크인할 때 예약번호를 제시하고 사진이 있는 신분증을 보여주시면 됩니다.

또한 Winchester Hotel에 싱글룸을 예약해 드렸습니다(예약번호 #HJ763). 호텔 셔틀버스는 공항까지 다닙니다. 유감스럽게도 Logan Hotel에는 귀하의 요구사항을 충족시키는 객실이 없었습니다. 귀하의 호텔은 Logan Hotel과 같은 시내에 위치해 있습니다. **197따라서 도보 거리에 극장과, 식당, 커피숍이 많이 있습니다.**

마지막으로, **199Minneapolis의 잠재 고객들과 회의를 잡았습니다**(첨부 일정 참조).

제가 도와드릴 다른 일이 있으면 알려주시기 바랍니다.

Carla Jensen 드림
여행부
Bix Technologies

표현 정리 travel arrangement 여행 준비   make a reservation 예약하다   depart 출발하다   electronic 전자의   book 예약하다   meet a requirement 요구사항을 만족시키다   available 이용 가능한   plenty of 많은   within walking distance 걸어서 갈 수 있는 거리에   potential 잠재적인   attached 첨부된

회의 일정

1986월 6일
오후 2시 30분   Sam Harrison (Gleeson Corporation)

6월 7일
오전 9시 30분   **199**Tracy Ericson (STX Inc.)
오후 1시 30분   Devon White (Lighthouse Medical Supply)

6월 8일
오전 9시 45분   Paul Corby (Haberstam Ltd.)
오후 2시   Elaine Shew (St. Vincent Hospital)

6월 9일
오전 10시 30분   Patricia Linklater (CRX Transportation)

표현 정리 technical specification 기술명세서, 기술규격서 attachment 첨부(물) rearrange 재조정하다 originally 원래, 본래 appreciate 고마워하다 fit somebody in 시간을 내어 ~을 만나다 appointment 약속 document 문서 supervisor 감독관 direct ~에게 보내다 response 응답 advise (정식으로) 알리다

196. 세부사항 – Mr. Rondeaux의 여행 일정 ★☆☆

해설 첫 번째 지문에서 항공 일정을 보면 첫 번째 비행기가 'Departing Albuquerque at 9:03 A.M.' 즉 아침 9시 3분에 Albuquerque를 출발함을 알 수 있기 때문에 정답은 (B)가 된다. **정답 (B)**

표현 정리 layover (비행기를 갈아타기 위한) 도중 하차 initial 처음의, 초기의

해석 Mr. Rondeaux의 여행 준비에 관해 언급된 것은?
(A) 돌아오는 항공편에서 중간에 내린다.
(B) 처음 항공편은 아침에 출발한다.
(C) 항공권을 프린트해야 한다.
(D) 호텔까지 택시를 타야 한다.

197. 세부사항 – Winchester Hotel에 대한 내용 ★☆☆

해설 첫 번째 이메일의 'I also booked you a single room at the Winchester Hotel(reservation #HJ763).'에서 Winchester Hotel을 예약했다고 하고 'So there are plenty of theaters, restaurants, and coffee shops within walking distance.'에서 도보 거리에 즐길거리가 많다고 하므로 (C)가 정답이다. **정답 (C)**

패러프레이징 |지문| there are plenty of theaters, restaurants, and coffee shops within walking distance 도보 거리에 극장과, 식당, 커피숍이 많이 있습니다 → |선택지 C| It is near entertainment venues 여흥을 즐길 수 있는 장소가 근처에 있다

표현 정리 entertainment venue 여흥을 즐길 수 있는 장소 meeting room 회의실

해석 Winchester Hotel에 대해 언급된 것은?
(A) 온라인으로만 예약을 받는다.
(B) 고객들에게 식사를 제공한다.
(C) 여흥을 즐길 수 있는 장소가 근처에 있다.
(D) 고객들을 위한 회의실이 있다.

198. 연계 문제 – Mr. Corby가 Mr. Rondeaux를 만난 날짜 ★★☆

해설 세 번째 지문의 이메일 첫 번째 단락 중 'I appreciate your fitting me in after your appointment at the Gleeson Corporation.'에서 Gleeson Corporation 일정 후에 만나주었다고 하는데, 두 번째 지문의 회의 일정 중

'June 6 2:30 P.M. Sam Harrison (Gleeson Corporation)'에서 이 회사와 만난 날은 June 6이다. **정답 (A)**

해석 Mr. Corby는 Mr. Rondeaux를 언제 만났는가?
(A) 6월 6일에
(B) 6월 7일에
(C) 6월 8일에
(D) 6월 9일에

199. 연계 문제 – Ms. Ericson에 대한 내용 ★★☆

해설 첫 번째 지문의 'Finally, I set up meetings with some potential buyers in Minneapolis (see attached schedule).'에서 Minneapolis에 있는 잠재 고객들과 회의가 잡혀 있다고 했다. 두 번째 지문의 일정을 보면 Ms. Ericson과의 약속이 6월 7일에 잡혀 있기 때문에 Ms. Ericson은 Minneapolis에서 일한다는 것을 유추할 수 있다. **정답 (D)**

표현 정리 existing 기존의

해석 Ms. Ericson에 대해 암시된 것은?
(A) 약속을 바꿔야 했다.
(B) 현재 Bix Technologies의 고객이다.
(C) Mr. Rondeaux가 묵는 호텔에서 그를 만났다.
(D) Minneapolis에서 일한다.

200. 세부사항 – Mr. Rondeaux가 해야 할 일 ★★★

해설 세 번째 지문인 이메일 후반부의 'Could you direct your response to Erik Markman (emarkman@haberstam.com)?'에서 답변을 다른 직원에게 직접 보내라고 하므로 (C)가 정답이다. **정답 (C)**

🔍 **함정 분석** 'The lead supervisor had a few questions about your products, which I have attached.'에서 첨부 파일은 제품에 관한 몇 가지 질문이라고 했고, 이 질문에 대한 답변을 요청하고 있다. 질문에 대한 답변이 '제안사항'은 아니므로 suggestion으로 표현한 (A)는 오답이다.

표현 정리 suggestion 제안, 제의 colleague 동료

해석 Mr. Corby는 Mr. Rondeaux가 무엇을 하기를 바라는가?
(A) 그에게 제안하기
(B) 기술 문서 보내기
(C) 답변하기
(D) 동료와 만나기

문제 147-148번은 다음 기사를 참조하시오.

전문가 뉴스

147(A)공인 검안사 협회(SCO)는 Louisiana주 New Orleans에 소재한 Mac Douglas 컨벤션 센터에서 제9회 연례 컨퍼런스를 개최했습니다. 147(D)5월 3일부터 5월 5일까지 개최된 올해 행사에는 전국에서 450명 이상의 참가자들이 모였습니다.

Sampson 시력검안 대학 총장 Dr. Frieda Olsen은 "시력 검안의 미래구상"이라는 제목으로 기조 연설을 했습니다. 이 행사에는 24개의 연설과, 18회의 전문성 신장 워크숍, 5회의 공개 토론회도 포함되었습니다. 147(B)선도기업들에서 나온 80명 이상의 직원들이 현장에서 신제품을 선보였습니다.

148현 SCO 회원은 www.sco.org에서 연설문과, 프레젠테이션, 워크숍 노트 사본을 이용하실 수 있습니다.

표현 정리 professional 전문가(의) certified 공인된 optometrist 검안사, 시력측정 의사 hold 주최하다 annual 연례의 take place 일어나다, 발생하다 attendee 참석자 keynote address 기조 연설 entitled ~라는 제목의 envision 마음 속에 그리다[상상하다] panel discussion 공개 토론회 vendor 판매업자, 판매상인, (특정한 제품) 판매회사 leading 선두의 on site 현장의, 현지의 showcase 소개하다 access 접근하다

147. 세부사항 – 컨퍼런스에 대한 내용 ★☆☆

해설 첫 번째 문장 'The Society of Certified Optometrists (SCO) held its ninth annual conference at the Mac Douglas Convention Center in New Orleans, Louisiana.'에서 제9차 컨퍼런스라고 하므로 (A)를 확인할 수 있으며, 'This year's event, which took place from May 3 to May 5'에서 3일간 진행되므로 (D)를 확인할 수 있다. 두 번째 단락의 'Over eighty vendors from leading companies were on site to showcase new products.'에서 현장에서 신제품을 선보인 공급상을 product representatives로 표현한 (B)도 사실이다. 기조 연설가가 검안대학 총장이긴 하지만, 대학생을 대상으로 한 워크숍이 있다는 내용은 찾을 수 없으므로 (C)가 사실과 다른 내용으로 정답이다.

정답 (C)

패러프레이징 |지문| The Society of Certified Optometrists (SCO) held its ninth annual conference 공인 검안사 협회(SCO)는 제9회 연례 컨퍼런스를 개최했습니다 → |선택지 A| It has been held for almost ten years 거의 10년간 개최되어 왔다

|지문| Over eighty vendors form leading companies were on site to showcase new products 선도 기업들에서 나온 80명 이상의 직원들이 현장에서 신제품을 선보였습니다 → |선택지 B| It included product representatives 제품 판매원들이 참여했다

|지문| took place from May 3 to May 5 5월 3일부터 5월 5일까지 개최된 → |선택지 D| took place over three days 3일 이상 개최된

표현 정리 almost 거의 representative (판매) 대리인

해설 컨퍼런스에 관해 언급되지 않은 것은?
(A) 거의 10년간 개최되어 왔다.
(B) 제품 판매원들이 참여했다.
(C) 대학생들을 위한 워크숍을 마련했다.
(D) 3일 이상 개최되었다.

148. 세부사항 – 회원들이 연설문을 얻을 수 있는 곳 ★☆☆

해설 마지막 문장 'Current SCO members can access copies of speeches, presentations, and workshop notes at www.sco.org.'에서 웹

사이트에서 연설문 사본을 볼 수 있다고 하므로 (D)가 정답이다. 정답 (D)

패러프레이징 |지문| at www.sco.org www.sco.org에서 → |선택지 D| By going to a Web site 웹사이트를 방문하여

표현 정리 sign up for ~을 신청[가입]하다 order 주문하다

해설 기사에 따르면, SCO 회원들은 Dr. Olsen의 연설문을 어떻게 읽을 수 있는가?
(A) 소식지를 신청하여
(B) Sampson 시력검안 대학에 편지를 써서
(C) SCO로부터 사본을 주문하여
(D) 웹사이트를 방문하여

문제 149-150번은 다음 문자 메시지 내용을 참조하시오.

George Benson Irma, 점심 식사하러 나가신 동안 죄송한데, 프린터에 문제가 생겨서요. 149제 보고서에 실린 일부 차트 내용이 잘려나가고 있어요. 오후 12시 44분

Irma Kramer 컴퓨터에서 인쇄 레이아웃을 확인하셨어요? 프린터의 용지와 동일한 크기로 설정해야 해요. 오후 12시 46분

George Benson 네. 설정은 일치합니다. 오후 12시 47분

Irma Kramer 음. 그러면 제가 프린터를 살펴봐야 할 것 같아요. 150잠시만 기다려 주시겠어요? 점심 식사를 거의 마쳤어요. 오후 12시 48분

George Benson 그러죠. 149오후 2시 30분까지는 보고서가 필요없어요. 그때 고객과 만나기로 했거든요. 오후 12시 49분

표현 정리 have a problem with ~에 문제가 있다 cut off ~을 자르다, ~을 차단하다 setting (기계의 속도·고도·온도 등을 조절하는) 설정[세팅] match 일치하다, 서로 맞다 take a look at ~을 보다

149. 세부사항 – 남자가 시도하고 있는 사항 ★☆☆

해설 George Benson의 첫 문자 중 'but I am having a problem with the printer'에서 프린터에 문제가 있음을 말하는데, 다음 문장이 'Some of the charts in my report are getting cut off.'에서 보고서 일부 내용이 잘린다고 덧붙인다. 마지막 문자 중 'I don't need to have a copy of the report until 2:30.'에서 보고서 사본이 필요하다고 말하므로 이를 'a paper version'으로 표현한 (A)가 정답이다. 정답 (A)

함정 분석 지문의 내용을 보면, 프린터가 고장난 것이 아니다. 어떤 이유인지는 모르지만, 보고서의 차트가 출력을 할 때 잘려나간다는 문제가 있다는 것일 뿐, 프린터 자체는 정상이므로 (D)를 고르지 않도록 한다.

표현 정리 obtain 얻다 version 버전 repair 수리하다 broken 고장난

해설 Mr. Benson은 무엇을 하려고 시도하는가?
(A) 보고서를 종이로 뽑는다.
(B) 컴퓨터를 프린터에 연결한다.
(C) 차트의 내용을 수정한다.
(D) 고장 난 프린터를 수리한다.

150. 의도 파악하기 ★☆☆

해설 남자가 프린터에 문제가 있다고 하자 점심 식사를 하던 여자가 'Can you wait a few minutes? I'm almost done with lunch.'와 같이 식사를 거의 끝마치므로 조금만 기다리면 사무실로 돌아가 프린터를 확인해 주겠다는 의도로 말하는 것임을 알 수 있다. 정답 (B)

표현 정리 right now 지금 당장 impatient 성마른, 성급한, 참을성이 없는

해설 오후 12시 48분에 Ms. Kramer가 "잠시만 기다려 주시겠어요?"라고 말한 의미는 무엇인가?

(A) 지금 당장 무엇을 해야 할지 모른다.
(B) 곧 사무실로 돌아올 것이다.
(C) 인쇄 레이아웃을 바꾸기 위해 시간이 필요하다.
(D) Mr. Benson이 인내심이 없다고 생각한다.

문제 151-152번은 다음 공지를 참조하시오.

> 고객 여러분,
>
> Shore Bird는 12월 22일부터 1월 31일까지 개조공사를 위해 문을 닫습니다. 매년 여름 관광 시즌마다 Casey Beach를 방문하는 고객들이 늘어서 확장을 결정했습니다.
>
> **151 개인 파티용으로 예약할 수 있는 별도의 다이닝룸이 레스토랑 뒤편에 추가됩니다.** 또한 야외 식사 구역을 두 배로 확장해 더 많은 손님이 파도소리를 즐기고 바닷바람을 느끼실 수 있도록 계획하고 있습니다. 주방을 개조하고, 스토브, 레인지, 냉장고를 에너지 효율이 좀 더 큰 모델로 교체할 것입니다.
>
> 하지만 염려하지 마십시오. 수상 경력이 있는 메뉴는 그대로 지킬 것입니다.
>
> **152 2월 1일 재개장을 달력에 표시해 두십시오. 대표적인 모든 메인 요리가 10% 할인됩니다.**
>
> Andrea D'Abrosso

표현 정리 renovation 수선, 수리, 개조, 보수 additional 추가적인 expand 확장하다 reserve 예약하다 double 두 배로 하다 outdoor 야외의 diner (특히 식당에서) 식사하는 사람[손님] breeze 산들바람, 미풍 replace 교체하다 energy-efficient 에너지 효율적인 have every intention of ~할 충분한 의향이 있다 mark 표시하다 entrée 앙트레(식당이나 만찬에서 주요리, 또는 주요리 앞에 나오는 요리)

151. 세부사항 – Shore Bird에 대한 내용 ★★☆
해설 두 번째 단락 첫 번째 문장인 'Another dining room, which can be reserved for private parties, will be added to the back of the restaurant.'에서 개인 파티용으로 예약할 수 있는 식사 공간이 추가된다고 하므로 (D)가 정답이다. 　정답 (D)

🔍 **함정 분석** 'The Shore Bird will be closed from December 22 to January 31 for renovations.'에서 12월 22일부터 공사가 시작되므로 12월 내내 문을 닫는 것은 아니다. 따라서 (B)는 오답이다.

패러프레이징 |지문| Another dining room, which can be reserved for private parties, will be added to the back of the restaurant 개인 파티용으로 예약할 수 있는 별도의 다이닝룸이 레스토랑 뒤편에 추가됩니다 → |선택지 D| It will be adding a space for private dining 개인 식사를 위한 공간을 추가할 것이다

표현 정리 location 위치, 장소 no longer 더 이상 ~아닌 purchase 구매하다, 매입하다

해석 Shore Bird에 대해 암시된 것은?
(A) 새로운 위치로 이전할 것이다.
(B) 12월에 더 이상 문을 열지 않을 것이다.
(C) Ms. D'Abrosso가 2년 전에 매입했다.
(D) 개인 식사를 위한 공간을 추가할 것이다.

152. 세부사항 – 2월 1일에 발생할 일 ★☆☆
해설 마지막 두 문장 'Mark your calendars for our grand reopening on February 1. All of our classic entrées will be 10% off.'에서 2월 1일은 식당 재개장 날짜이고 이날 앙트레 메뉴가 할인된다고 하므로 (D)가 정답이다. 　정답 (D)

패러프레이징 |지문| All of our classic entrées will be 10% off 대표적인 모든 메인 요리가 10% 할인됩니다 → |선택지 D| A discount will be offered 할인이 제공될 것이다

표현 정리 award 상 debut 데뷔하다, 첫무대에 서다

해석 2월 1일에는 어떤 일이 발생할 것인가?
(A) 상이 수여될 것이다.
(B) 새로운 메뉴가 선보일 것이다.
(C) 개인 파티가 열릴 것이다.
(D) 할인이 제공될 것이다.

문제 153-154번은 다음 안내문을 참조하시오.

> 발신: Greg Miller 〈gmiller@furniturewarehouse.com〉
> 수신: 모든 영업사원 〈sales@furniturewarehouse.com〉
> 제목: 안내 – 판매 경연대회!
> 날짜: 4월 18일
>
> 다시 한번 우리 Furniture Warehouse에서는 판매 시즌을 준비하고 있습니다. 올해에는 일찍 시작하기 위해, 판매 경연대회를 알려드리고자 합니다.
>
> **153 Dallas-Fort Worth 지역 내 9개 매장에서 일하는 영업사원들을 모두 초대합니다.**
>
> 참가자는 파트너가 배정되어 팀을 구성하게 됩니다. 팀은 판매 합산에 대해 점수를 받게 됩니다. 대회가 끝날 때 가장 많은 점수를 얻은 팀이 우승자로 선정됩니다. **154(A) 1등상은 파트너당 250달러가 지급됩니다.** 2등상은 Stetson Steakhouse 식사권 두 장입니다. 3등상은 영화표 2장입니다.
>
> **154(C) 대회는 공식적으로 5월 1일 오전 9시에 시작되어, 5월 30일 오후 5시에 종료됩니다.** 마감기한까지 제출된 실제 판매 영수증 및 서명된 판매 계약서만 합산됩니다.
>
> **154(B) 신청하시려면 dbacon@furniturewarehouse.com으로 David Bacon에게 연락하십시오.**

표현 정리 gear up for ~을 위한 준비를 하다 announce 발표하다 sales associate 영업사원 participate 참가하다 assign 배정하다 form 형성하다 combined 결합된, 합동의 declare 선언[선포/공표]하다 certificate 상품권, 증서, 증명서 officially 공식적으로[정식으로] receipt 영수증 sign 서명하다 contract 계약서 submit 제출하다 deadline 마감일

153. 세부사항 – Furniture Warehouse에 관한 내용 ★☆☆
해설 첫 번째 단락 마지막 문장 'Sales associates working at any one of our nine stores in the Dallas-Fort Worth area are invited to participate.'에서 9개 지점 중 어느 지점에서나 일하는 직원은 모두 대회에 참가할 수 있다고 나온다. 따라서 1개 이상의 지점을 가지고 있다는 (B)가 정답이다. 　정답 (B)

🔍 **함정 분석** 'Once again, we are gearing up for our sales season here at Furniture Warehouse.'에서 대회가 다시 열리는 것은 확인할 수 있지만 연례 행사인지는 언급되지 않으므로 (C)는 오답이다.

표현 정리 location 위치, 장소 hire 고용하다 additional 추가의

해석 Furniture Warehouse에 관해 언급된 것은?
(A) 다음 달에 큰 할인판매가 있을 것이다.
(B) 하나 이상의 지점이 있다.
(C) 매년 판매 경연대회를 연다.
(D) 추가 직원을 고용할 계획이다.

154. 세부사항 – 대회에 대한 내용 ★★☆

해설 두 번째 단락의 'First prize is $250 for each partner.'에서 (A)는 사실임을 알 수 있다. 세 번째 단락의 'The contest officially begins at 9:00 A.M. on May 1 and ends at 5:00 P.M. on May 30.'에서 대회기간이 5월 1일부터 30일까지 한 달이므로 (C)도 사실이다. 마지막 문장 'To sign up, contact David Bacon at dbacon@furniturewarehouse.com.'에서 이메일 접수가 필요하므로 (B)도 사실이다. 9개 지점 중 어느 지점에서나 일하는 직원은 대회에 참가할 수 있지만 전 직원의 의무사항이라는 내용은 찾을 수 없으므로 (D)가 사실과 달라 정답이다. **정답 (D)**

패러프레이징 |지문| First prize is $250 for each partner 1등상은 파트너 당 250달러가 지급됩니다 → |선택지 A| The top sales team will be awarded cash 최고 판매팀은 현금을 수상한다

|지문| The contest officially begins at 9:00 A.M. on May 1 and ends at 5:00 P.M. on May 30 대회는 공식적으로 5월 1일 오전 9시에 시작되어, 5월 30일 오후 5시에 종료됩니다 → |선택지 C| It takes place over one month 한 달 동안 열린다

표현 정리 **award** 주다, 수여하다 **cash** 현금 **register** 등록하다 **compete** 경쟁하다

해석 대회에 대해 사실이 아닌 것은?
(A) 최고 판매팀은 현금을 수상한다.
(B) 직원들은 등록을 위해 이메일을 보내야 한다.
(C) 한 달 동안 열린다.
(D) 모든 판매직원이 참가해야 한다.

문제 155-157번은 다음 정보를 참조하시오.

> **Delta Materials**
>
> Delta Materials는 Canada의 Montreal에 본사를 둔 스테인리스 스틸 제조업체입니다. 당사는 특수한 용도로 사용하는 다양한 스테인리스 스틸 합금을 제작합니다. ¹⁵⁵저희 합금은 항공 우주, 자동차, 의료기기 산업의 제조업체에서 사용됩니다. ¹⁵⁶Delta 제품은 17개국의 고객들에게 판매되며, 북미 시장은 당사 전체 매출의 60% 가까이 차지합니다.
>
> Delta Materials는 전 세계적으로 600명 이상의 직원을 고용하고 있으며, Canada에서만 400명을 고용하고 있습니다. Montreal에 소재한 본사와 생산시설 외에도, British Columbia주 Vancouver와 Michigan주 Detroit에 유통 센터가 있습니다. 당사는 Europe과 Asia, 남미의 여러 주요 도시에 영업 직원들을 두고 있습니다.
>
> Delta Materials는 2013년부터 최고경영자인 George McClelland가 이끌어왔습니다. Mr. McClelland의 지휘하에 Delta는 고객을 위해 주문을 맞춤화하는 데 주력해왔습니다. ¹⁵⁷또한, Mr. McClelland는 Enhance라는 프로그램을 통해 직원 교육을 강화해왔습니다. 2년 전에 이 프로그램이 시작된 이래로 생산성은 50% 증가했습니다.

표현 정리 **manufacturer** 제조업체 **headquartered in** ~에 본사를 둔 **a range of** 다양한 **alloy** 합금 **specialized** 전문적인, 전문화된 **application** 적용, 응용 **aerospace** 항공우주 산업 **automotive** 자동차의 **device** (특정 작업을 위해 고안된) 장치[기구] **account for** ~을 차지하다 **nearly** 거의 **employ** 고용하다 **production facility** 생산시설 **distribution** 유통 **sales representative** 영업사원 **based in** ~에 기반을 둔, 근거지로 한 **under one's leadership** ~의 지휘하에 **customize** 주문 제작하다 **launch** 시작[개시/착수]하다 **productivity** 생산성

155. 유추 – 회사의 고객 대상 찾기 ★☆☆

해설 첫 번째 단락의 'Our alloys are used by manufacturers in the aerospace, automotive, and medical device industries.'에서 자사에서 만

든 합금이 자동차 산업에서도 활용된다고 하므로 (B)가 정답이다. **정답 (B)**

표현 정리 **travel agency** 여행사 **furniture** 가구

해석 어떤 유형의 회사가 Delta Materials의 고객이 되겠는가?
(A) 여행사
(B) 자동차 제조업체
(C) 치과 병원
(D) 가구 제조업체

---

156. 세부사항 – Delta Materials에 대한 내용 ★☆☆

해설 첫 번째 단락 마지막 문장 'Delta products are sold to customers in 17 countries, with the North American market accounting for nearly 60% of all of our sales.'에서 북미 지역이 판매의 60% 가까이 차지한다고 하므로 (C)가 정답이다. **정답 (C)**

🔍**함정 분석** 마지막 단락의 'Delta Materials has been led by CEO George McClelland since 2013.'에서 2013년은 회사 설립 연도가 아닌 George McClelland가 CEO를 맡은 해이므로 (A)는 오답이다. 첫 번째 단락의 'Delta products are sold to customers in 17 countries'에서 17은 제품을 판매하는 국가 수를 나타내므로 (B)도 오답이다. 두 번째 단락의 'we have distribution centers in Vancouver, British Columbia, and Detroit, Michigan'에서 유통센터는 2곳이므로 (D)도 오답이다.

표현 정리 **found** 설립하다

해석 Delta Materials에 대해 언급된 것은?
(A) 2013년에 설립되었다.
(B) 17개국에 지사가 있다.
(C) 북미에서 많은 사업을 하고 있다.
(D) 3개의 유통센터가 있다.

---

157. 세부사항 – Delta Materials가 2년 전에 한 일 ★★☆

해설 마지막 두 문장 'Mr. McClelland has also increased employee training through a program called Enhance. Since the program was launched two years ago, productivity has increased by 50%.'에서 직원 교육 프로그램을 2년 전에 시작했다고 하므로 employee training through a program을 a worker training initiative로 표현한 (D)가 정답이다. **정답 (D)**

패러프레이징 |지문| employee training through a program 프로그램을 통한 직원 교육 → |선택지 D| a worker training initiative 직원 교육 계획

표현 정리 **select** 선발하다, 선택하다 **additional** 추가의 **initiative** (특정한 문제 해결 · 목적 달성을 위한 새로운) 계획

해석 정보에 따르면, Delta Materials는 2년 전에 무엇을 했는가?
(A) 새 지도자를 선임했다.
(B) 직원 급여를 인상했다.
(C) 추가 직원을 고용했다.
(D) 직원 교육 계획을 수립했다.

문제 158-160번은 다음 메모를 참조하시오.

> 발신: Carlton Farmer
> 수신: 전 직원
> 날짜: 5월 3일
> 제목: 매장 이전
>
> 3개월 전에 임대주가 우리 건물을 팔 계획이라고 알렸습니다. 그가 구매자를 찾았는데 그는 건물을 레스토랑으로 개조할 계획입니다. 그 결과, 우리는 어쩔 수 없이 이전하게 됐습니다. 저는 Empire Realty의 중개인과 협력해왔습니다. 그들은 대학에서 가까운 2층짜리 건물을 찾아 주었습니다. ¹⁵⁸임대

료는 여기보다 약간 비싸지만 그 지역의 보행자 통행량이 상당히 많습니다.

새 임대주와 협상해서 여기까지 6월 30일까지 머무르기로 했습니다. 159**새 건물의 임대는 6월 15일에 시작됩니다.** 옮겨야 할 재고량을 줄이기 위해 6월 1일부터 2주간 세일을 진행할 예정입니다. 159**새 임대일 첫날에 7117 Davis Avenue의 새 건물로 나머지 재고와, 진열대, 간판을 옮기기 시작했으면 합니다.**

모든 직원은 곧 있을 세일을 준비해야 합니다. 그러나 2주간의 이전 기간 동안의 근무는 자발적입니다. 160**그 기간에 일하는 것을 선택하면 정규 급여를 받게 될 것입니다.** 선택사항을 알려주시기 바랍니다.

표현 정리 relocation 이전　landlord (방·집·사무실 등을 빌려주는) 주인, 임대주, 임대회사　convert 전환시키다[개조하다]　be forced to 어쩔 수 없이 ~하다　property 건물　slightly 다소, 약간　pedestrian 보행자　negotiate 협상하다　lease 임대차계약　inventory 물품 목록, 재고품　remaining 남아있는, 남은　display rack 진열용 선반　signage 신호들[신호체계]　prepare for ~을 준비하다　voluntary 자발적인, 임의적인, 자진한　preference 선호

158. 세부사항 – 새 건물에 대한 내용　★☆☆

해설 첫 번째 단락의 마지막 문장 'The rent is slightly higher than here, but there is heavy pedestrian traffic in the area.'에서 보행자 통행량이 많다고 하므로 'heavy pedestrian traffic'을 'busy area'로 표현한 (B)가 정답이다.　정답 (B)

패러프레이징　|지문 there is heavy pedestrian traffic in the area 그 지역의 보행자 통행량이 상당히 많습니다 → |선택지 B| It is located in a busy area 붐비는 지역에 있다

표현 정리 used to 과거 한때는[예전에는] ~이었다[했다]　eatery 음식점, 식당　entrance 입구

해석 7117 Davis Avenue의 건물에 대해 언급된 것은?
(A) 전에는 음식점이었다.
(B) 붐비는 지역에 있다.
(C) 학교 건너편에 있다.
(D) 두 개의 입구가 있다.

159. 세부사항 – Mr. Farmer가 6월 15일에 계획한 일　★★☆

해설 두 번째 단락의 'Our lease at the new location starts on June 15.'에서 6월 15일에 새 건물의 임대차계약이 시작된다고 하며 'I would like to start moving the remaining inventory, display racks, and signage to our new building at 7117 Davis Avenue starting on the first day of our new lease.'에서 임대차계약 첫날부터 물건을 옮기고 싶다고 하므로 (A)가 정답이다.　정답 (A)

패러프레이징　|지문 start moving the remaining inventory, display racks, and signage to our new building 새 건물로 나머지 재고와, 진열대, 간판을 옮기기 시작하다 → |선택지 A| Begin transporting things to the new location 물건을 새 매장으로 옮기기 시작한다

표현 정리 transport 이동시키다[실어나르다]　professional 전문의　deal 거래　real estate 부동산

해석 Mr. Farmer는 6월 15일에 무엇을 할 계획인가?
(A) 물건을 새 매장으로 옮기기 시작한다.
(B) 전문 이삿짐회사를 고용한다.
(C) 부동산 회사와 거래를 협상한다.
(D) 새 임대주와 임대계약서에 서명한다.

160. 문장 위치 찾기　★★☆

해설 주어진 문장의 that time이 가리키는 부분을 찾아야 한다. that time은 2주 간의 이전 기간(the two-week move)을 가리키므로 이때 직원이 일하면 정규

급여를 받는다고 해야 의미가 연결된다.　정답 (D)

표현 정리 regular 정기적인　rate 요금

해석 [1], [2], [3], [4]로 표시된 곳 중에서 다음 문장이 들어가기에 가장 적합한 곳은 어디인가?

"그 기간에 일하는 것을 선택하면 정규 급여를 받게 될 것입니다."

(A) [1]
(B) [2]
(C) [3]
(D) [4]

문제 161-163번은 다음 광고를 참조하시오.

Fallstaff Theater

161(A)*East St. Louis의 가장 오래된 극장*

161(D)올해는 창립 100주년입니다. 161(B)이를 기념하고자 일년 내내 무료 음악공연, 연극, 강연, 영화 상영을 제공합니다.

162Paolo Grimaldi의 가장 유명한 영화 4편으로 축하행사를 시작합니다. Mr. Grimaldi는 Fallstaff에서 멀지 않은 곳에서 이탈리아 이민자 부모에게서 태어났습니다. 그는 Central High School을 졸업한 후, California주 Hollywood로 이주해 촬영 기사와, 음향 엔지니어, 배우로 일하다가 자신의 영화를 만들었습니다. 그의 영화는 실존주의적인 주제를 탐구하고 종종 자신의 삶에서 얻은 경험을 활용합니다.

Husbands and Wives (1956) 163**1월 8일 토요일** 오후 2시	The Long Walk Home (1958) 1월 15일 토요일 오후 7시
Finding Faith (1955) 1월 22일 토요일 오후 2시	Open and Closed (1960) 1월 28일 금요일 오후 6시

163각 상영 시 무료 팝콘과 음료가 제공됩니다. 최고의 좌석을 얻으려면 일찍 도착하십시오. 티켓을 구하려면 매표소나 www.falstafftheater.org를 방문하십시오.

표현 정리 mark (중요 사건을) 기념[축하]하다　anniversary 기념일　celebrate 축하하다　performance 공연　lecture 강연　all year long 일년 내내　kick off (~을) 시작하다　immigrant 이민자　camera operator 촬영 기사, 촬영 감독　sound engineer 음향 기사　explore 탐구하다　existential 존재에 관한[관련된]　draw on 의지하다

161. 세부사항 – Fallstaff Theater에 대한 내용　★☆☆

해설 'The oldest theater in East St. Louis'에서 (A)를, 첫 문장 'This year marks our 100th anniversary.'에서 (D)를, 'To celebrate, we will be offering free music performances, plays, lectures, and film showings all year long.'에서 (B)를 확인할 수 있다. Mr. Grimaldi는 100주년 기념으로 상영되는 영화의 감독일 뿐 극장의 설립자가 아니다. 따라서 (C)가 사실과 다르므로 정답이 된다.　정답 (C)

패러프레이징　|지문 To celebrate, we will be offering free music performances, plays, lectures, and film showings all year long 이를 기념하고자 일년 내내 무료 음악공연, 연극, 강연, 영화 상영을 제공합니다 → |선택지 B| It will offer events over the next twelve months 앞으로 12개월 동안 이벤트를 제공할 것이다

|지문 This year marks our 100th anniversary 올해는 창립 100주년입니다 → |선택지 D| It opened a century ago 1세기 전에 문을 열었다

표현 정리 located in ~에 위치한　found 설립하다

해석 Fallstaff Theater에 관해 언급되지 않은 것은?
(A) East St. Louis에 있다.
(B) 앞으로 12개월 동안 이벤트를 제공할 것이다.
(C) Mr. Grimaldi가 설립했다.
(D) 1세기 전에 문을 열었다.

162. 세부사항 – Mr. Grimaldi에 대한 내용 ★☆☆

해설 두 번째 단락의 'Kicking off the celebration are four of the best-known films by Paolo Grimaldi.'에서 유명한 작품들 중 4편을 상영하겠다는 것이므로, 여러 편을 만들었다는 (B)가 정답이다. 정답 (B)

🔍 함정 분석 이탈리아 이민자 부모에게서 태어난 것은 맞지만 이탈리아에서 시간을 보냈다는 것은 알 수 없으므로 (D)는 오답이다.

해석 Mr. Grimaldi에 대해 암시된 것은?
(A) Hollywood에서 태어났다.
(B) 여러 편의 영화를 만들었다.
(C) 배우가 되기 위해 공부했다.
(D) Italy에서 시간을 보냈다.

163. 유추 – 1월 8일에 극장에서 일어날 일 ★★☆

해설 'January 8'은 지문에 나와 있는 상영표의 영화 상영일 중 하루인데, 상영표 아래에 'Free popcorn and drinks will be provided at each showing.'에서 상영일에 무료 팝콘과 음료를 제공한다고 하므로 (A)가 정답이다. 정답 (A)

패러프레이징 |지문| Free popcorn and drinks will be provided at each showing. 각 상영 시 무료 팝콘과 음료가 제공됩니다 → |선택지 A| Refreshments will be served 다과가 제공될 것이다

표현 정리 refreshments 다과, 음식물 give a talk 강연하다

해석 1월 8일에 Fallstaff Theater에서는 무슨 일이 일어날 것인가?
(A) 다과가 제공될 것이다.
(B) 감독이 그의 인생에 대해 강연할 것이다.
(C) 극장이 재개관할 것이다.
(D) 티켓을 온라인에서 구매할 수 없을 것이다.

문제 164~167번은 다음 온라인 채팅을 참조하시오.

Shelia Cotter	167방금 Luxa 직원 Rachel Simmons와 점심 식사를 했어요. 164우리가 그 회사 제품 판매에 관심이 있는지 궁금해 하더군요. 어떻게 생각하세요? 오후 1시 23분
Elaine Nguyen	Luxa요? 그 회사 샴푸와 컨디셔너는 미용실에서만 판매되는 줄 알았어요. 오후 1시 24분
Shelia Cotter	현재는 허가 받은 미용실에서만 그 회사 제품을 구입할 수 있어요. 164그런데 Luxa에서 백화점에서 판매할 새로운 제품 라인을 만들었어요. 오후 1시 25분
Nancy Saba	제 스타일리스트가 그 회사 제품을 사용해요. 저는 결과물이 정말 마음에 들어요. 그 제품을 사용하면 제 머리카락이 건강하고 윤기가 나는 걸 느껴요. 그 제품을 판매해야 한다고 봐요. 오후 1시 27분
Elaine Nguyen	잠시만요. Luxa에서 무엇 때문에 소매 샴푸 시장에 진입할 수 있다고 생각할까요? 오후 1시 28분
Shelia Cotter	그 회사는 많은 제품 테스트를 시행했어요. 165소비자 그룹에게 새로운 샴푸와 컨디셔너 샘플을 사용해 보도록 제공했는데, 그들이 매우 호의적인 반응을 보였어요. 또한 이 회사는 자사 브랜드를 이용해서 판매를 촉진하고 있습니다. 오후 1시 29분
Elaine Nguyen	가격 책정은 어떤가요? 오후 1시 31분

Shelia Cotter	Luxa 제품은 주요 경쟁사 제품보다 조금 더 비쌀 것으로 예상됩니다. 450ml 병의 경우, 주요 브랜드의 샴푸는 약 9.50달러에 판매됩니다. Luxa의 샴푸 소매가는 10.25달러가 될 거예요. 오후 1시 32분
Nancy Saba	166그 정도면 별거 아니에요. 소비자들이 알아차리지도 못할 거예요. 소비자들은 브랜드 이름에 주목할 테니까요. 오후 1시 33분
Shelia Cotter	Nancy, 그게 제 결론이기도 해요. 167Rachel에게 전화해서 그녀에게 알리도록 하겠습니다. 오후 1시 34분

표현 정리 representative 대표, 직원 be interested in ~에 흥미를 느끼다 beauty salon 미용실, 미장원 currently 현재 licensed 허가를 받은 go for it 단호히 목적을 추구하다. 사생 결단으로 덤비다 break into 잠입하다 retail 소매의 focus group 포커스 그룹(시장조사나 여론조사를 위해 각 계층을 대표하도록 뽑은 소수의 사람들로 이루어진 그룹) respond 대답[응답]하다 favorably 우호적으로 count on ~에 의존하다 pricing 가격 책정 competitor 경쟁사 leading 선두의 notice 알아차리다 conclusion 결론

164. 유추 – 화자들의 근무지 찾기 ★☆☆

해설 Shelia Cotter의 첫 대화 중 'She wants to know if we are interested in selling its products.'에서 화자들은 물건을 판매하는 곳에서 일하고 있음을 알 수 있다. 다음으로, [1:25 P.M.]의 대화 중 'But Luxa has created on a new line of products for sale in department stores.'에서 백화점이 구체적으로 언급되므로 정답은 (A)이다. 정답 (A)

표현 정리 cosmetics 화장품 manufacturer 제조업체 grocery store 식료품점

해석 화자들은 아마도 어디에서 일하겠는가?
(A) 백화점
(B) 화장품 제조업체
(C) 미용실
(D) 식료품점

165. 세부사항 – 새로운 제품 라인에 대한 내용 ★★☆

해설 Shelia Cotter [1:29 P.M.]의 대화 중 'Consumer focus groups were given samples of its new shampoos and conditioners to try, and they responded very favorably.'에서 포커스 그룹에 제공된 신제품 라인 샘플의 반응이 호의적이었다고 하므로 'responded very favorably'를 'well received'로 표현한 (C)가 정답이다. 정답 (C)

표현 정리 be well received 호평을 받다

해석 Luxa의 새로운 제품 라인에 대해 언급된 것은?
(A) 스타일리스트들이 사용한다.
(B) 현재 일부 상점에서만 판매되고 있다.
(C) 일부 소비자들에게 호평을 받았다.
(D) 할인 판매될 것이다.

166. 의도 파악하기 ★☆☆

해설 Shelia Cotter [1:32 P.M.]의 대화 중 'For a 450ml bottle, the leading brand's shampoo sells for about $9.50. Luxa's retail shampoo will be $10.25.'에서 Luxa 제품가가 경쟁사 가격보다 조금 더 비싸다고 하자, 이에 대해 그 정도 차이는 아무것도 아니라고 말하고 있으므로 (D)가 정답이다. 정답 (D)

표현 정리 impressed with ~에 감명을 받은 charge 부과하다 profit 이득 insignificant 대수롭지 않은, 사소한, 하찮은

해석 오후 1시 33분에 Ms. Saba가 "그 정도면 별거 아니에요"라고 말한 의미는 무엇인가?
(A) 그녀는 Luxa의 브랜드 이름에 감명을 받지 못했다.
(B) 그녀는 Luxa가 훨씬 더 비싸게 받아야 한다고 생각한다.
(C) 그녀는 Luxa 제품을 판매함으로써 얻어지는 이익이 거의 없다고 생각

(D) 그녀는 가격 차이는 대수롭지 않다고 생각한다.

167. 유추 – Ms. Cotter가 다음에 할 일 ★★☆

해설 Shelia Cotter의 마지막 대화 중 'Let me give Rachel a call and let her know.'에서 Rachel에게 연락한다고 나오는데, 첫 대화 중 'I just had lunch with Rachel Simmons, a representative from Luxa.'에서 이 직원은 Luxa 영업사원임을 알 수 있다. 따라서 영업사원에게 연락한다는 (C)가 정답이다. 정답 (C)

표현 정리 cancel an order 주문을 취소하다 distribute 배포하다
salesperson 영업사원

해석 Ms. Cotter는 아마도 다음에 무엇을 할 것인가?
(A) 주문을 취소한다.
(B) 제품 샘플을 배포한다.
(C) 영업사원에게 연락한다.
(D) 소비자와 대화한다.

문제 168-171번은 다음 기사를 참조하시오.

Brinn의 신간 소설 출간 예정
Jennifer Andres
168, 170 2월 7일

Karl Brinn이 새로운 소설을 작업 중이라는 소문이 사실로 확인되었습니다. **168, 170** Brinn의 출판사인 Brickhouse Books는 다음 달 쯤에 그의 신간 소설 〈Light and Darkness〉를 출간할 예정이라고 어제 확인해 주었습니다. 이 소설은 Brinn의 고향인 Connecticut주 Bainbridge를 무대로 하며, 한 청년의 성장기를 담고 있습니다.

22년 전 첫 번째 소설을 출간한 이래로 Brinn은 전 세계적으로 수백만 명의 팬을 확보했습니다. **169** 그의 베스트셀러 소설 〈Kim's Game〉은 12개 언어로 번역되었습니다.

170 Brickhouse Books의 보도자료는 Brinn이 오랜 친구인 Dale Carradine이 진행하는 New York의 지역 라디오 프로그램에 출연한 지 하루만에 나온 것입니다. 생방송 인터뷰에서 Brinn은 자신의 신간에 대해 언뜻 내비쳤습니다. 인터뷰와 보도자료의 시기는 소셜미디어에서 많은 추측을 불러 일으켰습니다.

Brinn은 신중하게 의도적으로 대중 앞에 모습을 드러내지 않으며 개인적인 생활과 관련한 정보를 거의 밝히지 않습니다. **171** 그러나 Carradine과 라디오에서 이야기를 나누는 동안 그는 자신의 해군 시절 경험담을 공유했습니다. San Francisco에서 휴가를 보내는 동안 그는 한 클래식 음악 콘서트에 참석했습니다. 그날 밤, Brinn은 작가가 되기로 결심했다고 말했습니다.

표현 정리 on the way 진행되어, 도중에 verify 확인하다 release 발표[공개]하다 come of age 성년이 되다 gain 얻다 translate 번역하다 press release 보도자료 hint at ~을 암시하다 speculation 추측, (어림)짐작 studiously 신중하게 의도적으로 public appearance 공개 출연 rarely 드물게, 좀처럼 ~하지 않는 converse with ~와 이야기하다 on leave 휴가로 attend 참석하다

168. 세부사항 – Light and Darkness에 대한 내용 ★★☆

해설 첫 번째 단락의 'Brinn's publisher, Brickhouse Books, confirmed yesterday that it plans to release his newest novel, *Light and Darkness*, sometime next month.'에서 책이 다음 달에 출간된다고 하는데 기사를 쓴 날짜가 February 7이므로 정답은 (D)이다. 정답 (D)

🔍 **함정 분석** 'The novel is set in Brinn's hometown of Bainbridge, Connecticut, and tells the story of a young man's coming of age.'에서 청년의 성장기를 담았다고 하므로 어린 시절에 관한 이야기라는 (B)는 오답이다. 또한 작가의 고향인 Connecticut이 책의 무대가 되지만, 이곳에서 소설을 쓴 것은 아니므로 (C)도 오답이다.

표현 정리 youth (성인이 되기 전의) 어린 시절 on sale (특히 상점에서) 판매되는[구입할 수 있는]

해석 〈Light and Darkness〉에 대해 언급된 것은?
(A) Mr. Brinn의 23번째 소설이다.
(B) Mr. Brinn의 어린 시절에 관한 것이다.
(C) Connecticut에서 쓰였다.
(D) 3월에 판매될 예정이다.

169. 유추 – 작가의 이전 소설에 대한 내용 ★☆☆

해설 두 번째 단락을 보면 'Brinn has gained millions of fans worldwide'에서 전 세계적으로 수백만 명의 팬을 확보했고, 'His best-selling novel, *Kim's Game*, has been translated into 12 different languages.'에서 작가의 책이 12개 언어로 번역되었다고 하므로 (B)가 정답이다. 정답 (B)

표현 정리 multiple 다수의 be based on ~을 토대로 하다

해석 Mr. Brinn의 이전 소설에 대해 암시된 것은?
(A) Brickhouse Books에서 출간했다.
(B) 다수의 국가에서 판매되었다.
(C) 전 세계의 도시를 배경으로 한다.
(D) Mr. Brinn의 삶의 경험을 토대로 한다.

170. 세부사항 – Mr. Brinn이 Mr. Carradine과 인터뷰한 날짜 ★★☆

해설 먼저 기사의 첫 번째 단락 중 'Brinn's publisher, Brickhouse Books, confirmed yesterday that it plans to release his newest novel, *Light and Darkness*, sometime next month.'에서 기사 작성일(2월 7일)보다 하루 전인 어제(2월 6일) 신간 출시를 확인했다는 내용이 나온다. 다음으로 세 번째 단락의 'The press release from Brickhouse Books came out just one day after Brinn appeared on a local radio program in New York hosted by his longtime friend, Dale Carradine.'에서 보도자료는 두 사람이 라디오 인터뷰를 한지 하루 뒤에 나온 것이라고한다. 즉, 보도자료가 2월 6일에 나왔으므로 하루 전인 2월 5일에 인터뷰가 있었다는 것을 알 수 있다. 정답 (B)

해석 Mr. Brinn은 언제 Mr. Carradine과 인터뷰했는가?
(A) 2월 4일에
(B) 2월 5일에
(C) 2월 6일에
(D) 2월 7일에

171. 세부사항 – 라디오 인터뷰 내용 ★☆☆

해설 마지막 단락의 'However, while conversing with Carradine on the radio, he shared a story about his time in the Navy. While on leave in San Francisco, he attended a classical music concert. That night, Brinn explained, he decided to become a writer.'에서 자신의 인생에 대해 이야기하던 중 작가가 되기로 결심한 계기가 언급되므로 (C)가 정답이다.
정답 (C)

표현 정리 private 사적인, 비공개의 join the military 군대에 가다

해석 라디오 인터뷰에서 논의된 내용은 무엇인가?
(A) 클래식 음악에 대한 Mr. Brinn의 평생의 애정
(B) Mr. Brinn이 그렇게 개인적인 사람이 된 이유
(C) Mr. Brinn의 삶을 변화시킨 경험
(D) Mr. Brinn이 군에 입대한 이유

시내 사무실 건물 개관

HAYWOOD (10월 3일) – CKY Properties 소유의 새로운 사무실 건물이 월요일 선을 보였다. 20층짜리의 Santos Building은 도심 스카이라인에서 가장 높은 건물 중 하나이다.

유명 지역 건축회사인 Seagrams가 설계한 Santos Building은 아르데 코 사조를 연상하게 한다. 곡선을 이루는 라인과 조각으로 이루어진 외관은 1920년대에 New York과 Chicago에 세워진 고층건물들을 떠올리게 한다. 172동시에, 자연 통풍과 같은 최첨단 기능을 포함하여, 냉난방에 에너지를 적게 소비한다. 사실, Seagrams는 이 건물의 공과금이 시내의 비슷한 크기의 건물들보다 45% 저렴할 것이라고 예상한다. "고객의 요청에 따라, 지붕에 태양광 패널을 설치했습니다. 173저와 저희 팀은 그것을 최종 건축 설계에 포함시켰고, 그래서 전기를 생산할 뿐만 아니라 건물의 외관도 향상시켰습니다."라고 Seagrams의 Marc Cassidy는 설명했다.

개관하기 전에 CKY Properties는 이미 19곳의 입주업체와 계약을 맺었다. 175입주업체 두 곳은 현재 검토 과정에 있다. 174이 두 곳을 제외하면 현재 점유율은 약 65%이다. 그에 반해, 보통 새 건물 소유주가 이용 가능한 사무실의 대부분을 임대하려면 최대 12개월이 걸린다.

표현 정리 own 소유하다 claim 주장하다 urban 도시의 renowned 유명한 evoke (감정·기억·이미지를) 떠올려주다[환기시키다] sweeping 곡선 모양의, 만곡을 이루는, 전면적인, 광범위한[포괄적인] sculpted 조각된 reminiscent of ~을 회상하게 하는 skyscraper 마천루 incorporate 포함하다 state-of-the-art 최신의, 최근의 passive air circulation 자연환기[통풍] predict 예측하다 utility (수도·전기·가스 같은) 공익사업 install 설치하다 photovoltaic panel 광전지 패널 generate 만들어내다 electricity 전기 sign 서명하다 contract 계약서 tenant 세입자 excluding ~을 제외하고 occupancy rate 객실 용률 around 대략 rent out ~을 임대하다 available 이용 가능한

172. 세부사항 – Santos Building에 대한 내용 ★☆☆
해설 두 번째 단락의 'At the same time, it incorporates state-of-the-art features, such as passive air circulation, so that it will require less energy to heat and cool. In fact, Seagrams predicts its utility bills will be 45% lower than similar-sized buildings in the city.'에서 냉난방에 에너지가 적게 들고 공과금도 동급 건물에 비해 저렴하다고 하므로 (D)가 정답이다. 정답 (D)

🔍 **함정 분석** 첫 번째 단락의 'The 20-story Santos Building claims its place among the tallest buildings in the urban skyline.'에서 이 건물은 가장 높은 건물 중 하나일 뿐, 가장 높은 건물은 아니므로 (B)는 오답이다. 두 번째 단락 마지막 문장 "they not only generate electricity for the building but also improve the building's appearance."에서 전기를 생산하는 것은 맞지만 모든 전기를 생산한다는 말은 없으므로 (C)도 오답이다.

패러프레이징 |지문| it will require less energy to heat and cool 냉난방에 에너지를 적게 소비한다 → |선택지 D| It is designed to be energy-efficient 에너지 효율적으로 설계되었다

표현 정리 energy-efficient 에너지 효율적인

해석 Santos Building에 대해 사실인 것은?
(A) 1920년대에 지어졌다.
(B) 시내에서 가장 높은 건물이다.
(C) 필요한 모든 전기를 만들어낼 것이다.
(D) 에너지 효율적으로 설계되었다.

173. 유추 – Marc Cassidy에 대한 정보 ★☆☆
해설 Santos Building은 건축회사인 Seagrams에서 설계했는데(Designed by renowned local architectural firm Seagrams, the Santos Building ~), 두 번째 단락의 'My team and I incorporated them in our final architectural designs'에서 Mr. Cassidy와 그의 팀이 설계 관련 업무를 했다는 것을 알 수 있으므로, 건물을 설계하는 사람임을 알 수 있다. 정답 (C)

표현 정리 property 건물 real estate agent 부동산 중개인

해석 Mr. Cassidy는 아마도 누구이겠는가?
(A) 사무실 관리자
(B) 부동산 소유주
(C) 건물 설계자
(D) 부동산 중개인

174. 유추 – CKY Properties에 대해 암시되는 내용 ★★☆
해설 마지막 단락의 'Prior to opening, CKY Properties had already signed contracts with nineteen tenants.'에서 이 건물은 지금 문을 열기도 전에 이미 19곳이 계약되어 있다고 하고, 'the current occupancy rate is around 65%'에서 점유율이 65%라고 한다. 마지막 문장 'In contrast, it normally takes up to twelve months for the owners of new buildings to rent out the majority of their available office space.'에서 일반적으로 다른 경우에 새 건물이 임대의 대부분을 완료하려면 최대 12개월은 걸린다고 나온다. 즉, 다른 곳보다 계약율이 좋으므로 이를 filling up faster than usual로 표현한 (C)가 정답이다. 정답 (C)

표현 정리 completely 완전히, 전적으로 fill up ~을 가득 채우다 house 수용하다

해석 CKY Properties에 대해 암시된 것은?
(A) 임차인은 1년 계약서에 서명해야 한다.
(B) 곧 모든 임대가 완료될 것이다.
(C) 평소보다 빨리 채워지고 있다.
(D) 60개 이상의 사업체를 수용한다.

175. 문장 위치 찾기 ★★☆
해설 마지막 단락의 'Excluding the latter'는 the latter(후자)가 가리키는 것이 앞에 나와야 한다. 또한 주어진 문장에 나온 Two more가 가리키는 것을 찾아야 한다. 'Prior to opening, CKY Properties had already signed contracts with nineteen tenants.'에서 건물이 문을 열기 전에 이미 19곳의 입주업체와 계약을 맺었다고 하므로 이 뒤에 문장이 들어가서, 추가적으로 2곳의 입주업체가 현재 검토 중이라고 하는 것이 흐름상 자연스럽다. 그렇게 되면 the latter(후자)가 검토 중인 2곳의 입주업체를 가리키게 되어 문맥에 어울린다. 정답 (C)

표현 정리 currently 현재 review 검토, 심사

해석 [1], [2], [3], [4]로 표시된 곳 중에서 다음 문장이 들어가기에 가장 적합한 곳은 어디인가?
"입주업체 두 곳은 현재 검토 과정에 있다."
(A) [1]
(B) [2]
(C) [3]
(D) [4]

TEST 12

문제 176-180번은 다음 이메일과 정보를 참조하시오.

발신: Wendy Brooks 〈wendy.brooks@aml.org〉
176수신: Patricia Hui 〈p.hui@achievingexcellence.com〉
날짜: 6월 3일
제목: ANA 컨퍼런스

Patricia,

오늘 아침에 만나서 즐거웠습니다. 11월에 Atlanta에서 열리는 연례 컨퍼런스에서 연설을 하기로 수락해 주셔서 다시 한번 감사드립니다. **176우리 회원들은 Africa와 남미의 대학을 위한 최첨단 컴퓨터 네트워크를 설계하는 일에 관해 듣는 것을 매우 흥미로워할 것입니다.**

이 이메일은 우리가 전화로 논의한 내용을 확인하는 것입니다. **178귀하는 컨퍼런스 두 번째날 오후 또는 저녁에 50분간 연설을 하실 것입니다.** 정확한 시간은 확정되면 알려드리겠습니다. ANA는 귀하의 항공료와 숙박비를 부담할 것입니다. 또한, 2,000달러의 연설료를 지불해 드릴 것입니다.

177제 비서인 Tamara Keller가 앞으로 몇 주 동안 연락을 드릴 것입니다. 그녀가 모든 초청 연사들의 여행 준비를 담당합니다. 귀하가 도착하시면 그녀가 마중을 나가고 컨퍼런스 장소까지 모셔다 드릴 것입니다.

궁금한 점이 있으시면 언제든지 저에게 연락해 주십시오.

Wendy

표현 정리 **agree** 동의하다 **annual** 연례의 **state-of-the-art** 최신식의, 최첨단의 **confirm** 확인하다 **determine** 결정하다 **cover** (돈을) 대다 **airfare** 항공료 **lodging** 숙박 **speaking fee** 연설료 **assistant** 비서 **responsible for** ~에 책임이 있는 **travel arrangement** 여행 준비 **guest speaker** 초청 연사 **hesitate** 주저하다

네트워크 분석가 협회(ANA)
제17회 연례 컨퍼런스
Bascomb Convention Center
Atlanta, Georgia
17811월 6일 – 11월 9일

ANA 연례 컨퍼런스는 컴퓨터 네트워크 분석가들의 국내 최대 규모의 모임입니다. 저희 회원들은 정부기관, 비영리 단체뿐만 아니라 다양한 업계에서 일합니다. 컨퍼런스에는 수백 가지의 프레젠테이션과, 워크숍, 전시 및 초청 연사가 마련되어 있습니다.

등록은 7월 1일에 시작되어 10월 31일에 종료됩니다. **1798월 15일 이전에 등록하면 10% 할인을 받으실 수 있습니다.** 활동중인 ANA 회원만이 컨퍼런스에 참석할 수 있으므로 등록하기 전에 반드시 회원자격을 갱신해 주십시오.

180(A)시외에서 오시는 회원은 Kenworth Hotel에서 특별 할인을 받으실 수 있습니다. 혜택에 대한 자세한 내용은 저희 웹사이트 www.ana.org를 방문하시기 바랍니다. **180(B/D)또한 웹사이트에서 컨퍼런스 장소까지 오시는 길과, 인근 추천 레스토랑 및 Atlanta에서 할 만한 것의 목록을 확인하실 수 있습니다.** 또한 온라인 컨퍼런스 프로그램이 준비되는 대로 게시될 것입니다.

표현 정리 **analyst** 분석가 **gathering** 모임 **nonprofit** 비영리적인 **organization** 단체, 기구 **feature** 특징으로 하다 **registration** 등록 **active** 활동[진행] 중인 **attend** 참석하다 **renew** 갱신하다 **membership** 회원자격 **rate** 요금 **recommended** 추천된 **nearby** 근처의

176. 유추 – Ms. Hui에 대한 정보　　　　★☆☆

해설 Ms. Hui는 'To: Patricia Hui'에서 이메일 수신인인데, 'Our members would be very interested in hearing about your work designing state-of-the-art computer networks for universities in Africa and South America.'에서 최첨단 컴퓨터 네트워크를 설계하는 일에 종사하는 사람이라는 것을 알 수 있으므로 (B)가 정답이다.　　　**정답 (B)**

표현 정리 **administrator** 관리자, 행정인 **instructor** 강사

해석 Ms. Hui는 누구이겠는가?
(A) 정부 관리
(B) 기술 전문가
(C) 대학 강사

(D) 여행작가

177. 유추 – Ms. Keller에 대한 내용　　　　★☆☆

해설 이메일의 'My assistant, Tamara Keller, will contact you in the coming weeks. She is responsible for making travel arrangements for all of our guest speakers. She will pick you up when you arrive and bring you to the conference.'에서 비서인 Tamara Keller가 공항 마중을 나가서 연설자인 you(=Ms. Hui)를 픽업한다고 하므로 (B)가 정답이다.　　**정답 (B)**

표현 정리 **organizer** 주최자 **give a talk** 강연하다

해석 Ms. Keller에 대해 암시된 것은?
(A) 전에 Ms. Hui와 함께 일한 적이 있다.
(B) 공항에서 Ms. Hui를 만날 것이다.
(C) 주요 컨퍼런스 주최자이다.
(D) 컨퍼런스에서 연설할 것이다.

178. 연계 문제 – Ms. Hui의 연설 날짜　　　　★★☆

해설 이메일의 'You will give a fifty-minute talk in the afternoon or evening of the second day of the conference.'에서 컨퍼런스 두 번째 날 강연한다고 하는데, 두 번째 지문인 정보의 상단 'November 6 – November 9'에서 컨퍼런스 두 번째 날은 11월 7일이므로 (B)가 정답이다.　**정답 (B)**

해석 Ms. Hui는 언제 연설할 것인가?
(A) 11월 6일에
(B) 11월 7일에
(C) 11월 8일에
(D) 11월 9일에

179. 세부사항 – 할인을 받을 수 있는 방법　　　　★★★

해설 정보의 두 번째 단락 'Save 10% if you register before August 15.'에서 8월 15일 전에 등록할 경우 10% 할인을 받게 되므로 (D)가 정답이다.　　**정답 (D)**

🔍 **함정 분석** 'Only active ANA members can attend the conference, so be sure to renew your membership before registering.'에서 컨퍼런스 참가를 위해 회원자격을 갱신하는 것이고 할인을 받기 위한 방법은 아니므로 (C)는 오답이다.

표현 정리 **attendee** 참석자 **get a discount** 할인을 받다 **fill out** 작성하다 **form** 양식 **deadline** 기한, 마감일자

해석 정보에 따르면, 컨퍼런스 참석자는 어떻게 할인을 받을 수 있는가?
(A) 온라인 양식을 작성하여
(B) 연설을 수락하여
(C) 회원자격을 갱신하여
(D) 마감기한 전에 등록하여

180. 세부사항 – ANA 웹사이트에서 찾을 수 없는 내용　　　　★★☆

해설 정보의 마지막 단락 'Members traveling from out of town can receive special rates at the Kenworth Hotel. To find out more about this offer, visit our Web site at www.aml.org.'에서 호텔 할인을 웹사이트에서 확인하라고 하므로 (A)는 사실이다. 'There, you can also find which roads to take to get to the conference, recommended restaurants nearby, and a list of things to do in Atlanta.'에서 (B)와 (D)의 두 가지 사항도 알 수 있다. 제공되는 워크숍 목록에 관한 내용은 없기 때문에 정답은 (C)가 된다.　**정답 (C)**

표현 정리 **instructions** 지침 **directions** 길 안내 **suggested** 제안된

해석 정보에 따르면, 현재 ANA 웹사이트에 게시되어 있지 않은 것은?
(A) 숙박 할인 안내
(B) 컨벤션 센터까지 운전해서 가는 길 안내
(C) 제공되는 워크숍 목록
(D) 추천 먹거리 장소

문제 181-185번은 다음 송장과 이메일을 참조하시오.

발신: Electronics Outlet 〈orders@electronicsoutlet.com〉
수신: Sam Rayburn 〈samr12@adventurouslife.com〉
날짜: 8월 13일
제목: Electronics Outlet 주문 확인서(#12843)

주문해 주셔서 감사합니다!

주문 ID #: 12843

청구서 발송지	배송지
Sam Rayburn	Sam Rayburn
118 Howe Street	184 118 Howe Street
Lincoln, NE68501	Lincoln, NE68501

주문 내역

장바구니 품목	SKU #	수량	제품 가격	제품 총액
Tobashi 8700 노트북 컴퓨터	TB2934	1	550.00달러	$550.00
Tobashi 8700 추가 배터리	TB7494	1	50.00달러	$50.00
Singha USB 드라이브, 32GB	SH1323	2	15.00달러	$30.00
182 Singha 무선 헤드폰	SH8995	1	24.00달러	$24.00

소계 654.00달러
세금 32.70달러
배송비 12.75달러
총액 699.45달러

결제 신용카드 xxxx-xxxx-xxxx-3472

주문품은 일반적으로 주문 후 48시간 이내에 배송됩니다. 제품이 재고가 없는 경우 배송이 지연될 수 있습니다. 181 www.electronicsoutlet.com에서 예상 도착일을 포함하여 주문 상태를 확인하십시오. 주문에 대한 질문은 orders@electronicsoutlet.com으로 문의해 주십시오.

표현 정리 billing address 청구서 발송지　contain 포함하다　extra 추가의　wireless 무선의　subtotal 소계　grand total 총계　typically 보통, 일반적으로　out of stock 재고가 없는　shipment 선적　delay 지연시키다　status (진행과정 상의) 상황　estimated 견적의, 추측의

발신: Electronics Outlet 〈orders@electronicsoutlet.com〉
수신: Sam Rayburn 〈samr12@adventurouslife.com〉
날짜: 8월 14일
제목: 귀하의 요청사항

Mr. Rayburn 귀하,

주문과 관련하여 문의해 주셔서 감사합니다. 고객님의 요청사항이 저에게 전달되었습니다. 다음과 같이 변경사항을 적용했습니다. 182 품목 SH8995는 품목 SH8999로 대체되었습니다. 배송은 일반배송에서 빠른배송으로 변경되었습니다. 183 주문품은 이제 영업일 기준 5~7일이 아닌 영업일 기준 2~3일 이내에 도착하게 됩니다. 배송 예정일은 이제 8월 16일입니다. 184 주문품은 이제 고객님의 집 대신 직장으로 배송될 것입니다. 또한 배달 시 고객님의 서명이 필요하다는 지침을 포함했습니다.

위의 변경사항으로 인해, 고객님의 주문 금액은 이제 705.65달러로 185 됩니다. 곧 업데이트된 송장이 이메일로 발송됩니다. 질문이나 궁금한 점이 있으시면 알려주시기 바랍니다.

Veronica Tiller
고객서비스 직원
Electronics Outlet

표현 정리 forward 전달하다　following 다음의　replace 교체하다　standard 일반적인, 보통의　express 급행의, 속달의　business day

---

영업일, 평일　estimated 견적의, 추측의　delivery 배달　instructions 지침, 지시사항　signature 서명　shortly 곧, 즉시　additional 추가의

---

181. 세부사항 – 고객이 회사 웹사이트에서 할 수 있는 사항 ★★☆

해설 송장 하단의 'Check the status of your order, including its estimated date of arrival, at www.electronicsoutlet.com.'에서 웹사이트를 통해 예상 도착일을 알 수 있다고 하므로 (A)가 정답이다.　　　　**정답 (A)**

패러프레이징 |지문| Check the status of your order, including its estimated date of arrival 예상 도착일을 포함하여 주문 상태를 확인하십시오 → |선택지 A| Find out when an order will be delivered 주문품이 언제 배송되는지 파악한다

표현 정리 existing 기존의　communicate with ~와 연락하다, 대화를 나누다

해석 송장에 따르면, 고객은 회사 웹사이트에서 무엇을 할 수 있는가?
(A) 주문품이 언제 배송되는지 파악한다.
(B) 기존 주문을 변경한다.
(C) 고객서비스 부서와 소통한다.
(D) 품절된 품목을 주문한다.

182. 연계 문제 – Mr. Rayburn이 구매하지 않기로 결정한 품목 ★★☆

해설 이메일 본문 첫 번째 단락의 'Item SH8995 has been replaced with item SH8999.'에서 Item SH8995 대신 SH8999로 교체하는데, 송장의 주문 품목 표에서 Item SH8995는 Singha wireless headphones이므로 정답은 (B)이다.　　　　**정답 (B)**

해석 Mr. Rayburn이 구매하지 않기로 결정한 품목은?
(A) 배터리
(B) 헤드폰
(C) 노트북 컴퓨터
(D) USB 드라이브

183. 세부사항 – Mr. Rayburn이 요청한 사항 ★★☆

해설 먼저 이메일 도입부의 'Thank you for contacting us regarding your order.'에서 고객이 주문과 관련해 문의했고, 이에 대한 답변임을 알 수 있다. 다음으로, 'Shipping has been changed from standard to express. Your order should now arrive in 2–3 business days rather than in 5–7 business days.'에서 일반배송에서 빠른배송으로 변경되면서 도착일이 빨라진다고 나오므로 고객이 주문품 배송을 더 서둘렀음을 유추할 수 있다. 따라서 (C)가 정답이다.　　　　**정답 (C)**

표현 정리 free 무료의　pay 결제하다

해석 Mr. Rayburn은 이메일에서 무엇을 요청했는가?
(A) 무료 배송을 받고 싶다.
(B) 주문품을 다른 사람에게 보내고 싶다.
(C) 주문품이 일찍 도착하기를 원한다.
(D) 다른 신용카드로 지불하고 싶다.

184. 연계 문제 – Mr. Rayburn에 대한 내용 ★☆☆

해설 이메일의 'The order will now be shipped to your place of work instead of your home.'에서 주문품이 이제 집 대신 직장으로 배송된다고 나온다. 송장에 있는 표를 보면 고객의 변경 요청 전 주문 정보인 청구서 발송지와 배송지가 모두 동일하다. 즉, 처음에는 고객이 주문품을 집으로 배송해 주기를 원해 두 주소지가 동일한데, 요청 후 집이 아닌 직장으로 변경했음을 알 수 있다. 즉, 집 주소가 '118 Howe Street'임을 알 수 있으므로 (B)가 정답이다.　　　　**정답 (B)**

표현 정리 gift card 기프트 카드(상품권의 기능과 신용카드의 편리함을 합친 선불 카드)　move 이사하다

해석 Mr. Rayburn에 대해 암시된 것은?
(A) 주문에 상품권을 사용했다.

(B) Howe Street에 살고 있다.
(C) Electronics Outlet에서 일한다.
(D) 곧 이사할 것이다.

185. 동의어 찾기 ★☆☆

해설 come to something은 '(총계가) ~이 되다'라는 의미이므로 (D) totals가 의미상 가장 유사하다. **정답 (D)**

해석 이메일에서 두 번째 단락 1행에 나온 "comes to"와 의미상 가장 가까운 어구는?
(A) ~에 도착하다
(B) 결합하다
(C) ~로 증가하다
(D) 총액이 ~가 되다

문제 186-190번은 다음 광고, 온라인 장바구니, 그리고 이메일을 참조하시오.

Petstore.com

Petstore.com에서 여러분의 애완동물을 소중히 보살피세요.

186(A)당사는 개, 고양이, 새, 물고기, 이국적 애완동물을 위한 1,000종 이상 브랜드의 식료품, 장난감, 간식, 액세서리를 취급합니다.

186(B)50달러 이상 주문하시면 고객님의 가정이나 사업장으로 무료로 주문품을 직접 배송해 드립니다.*

특별 혜택

187다음 번 100달러 이상 주문시 25달러 할인

다음 쿠폰 코드를 입력하세요:

187J7434BH1

유효기간: 3월 1일부터 3월 31일까지

---

* 일반배송에 한함(영업일 기준 3–5일). 빠른배송(영업일 기준 1–2일)으로 업그레이드하려면 요금이 부과됩니다. 186(D)미국 이외의 주소는 해외 배송료가 부과됩니다.

표현 정리 pamper 소중히 보살피다. 애지중지하다 treat 특별한 즐거움을 주는 것 exotic 이국적인 order 주문하다 directly 바로 at no charge 무료로 enter 입력하다 following 다음의 valid 유효한 standard 표준의 shipping 배송, 선적 business day 영업일 charge 부과하다 rate 요금

---

www.petstore.com

187주문번호: M78331   날짜: 3월 18일

고객 정보
이름: Jessica D'Francesca
188주소: 37 Penn Avenue, Apartment 8, New York City, NY, USA
전화번호: (412) 555–8933
이메일: jessica20@megafac.net

주문 요약

제품 번호	제품 내역	수량	가격
F6733	Homer 강아지 사료, 13.5kg들이	2	64.00달러
A3034	물어뜯는 장난감, 3개	1	5.50달러
A5237	강아지 침대, 미디엄	1	22.25달러
190F1223	강아지 간식, 24개들이	2	19.00달러

187소계: 110.75달러

187쿠폰 코드: J7434BH1

160

〈뒤로〉 장바구니 변경 지금 결제〈다음〉

표현 정리 summary 요약, 개요 description 내역 quantity 수량

수신: Pet Store 〈custserv@petstore.com〉
발신: Jessica D'Francesca 〈jessica20@megafac.net〉
제목: 주문
날짜: 4월 2일

저는 Goldie라는 이름의 골든 리트리버 강아지의 새로운 주인으로, 아직도 Goldie에게 필요한 것을 구해줄 최선의 방법을 찾고 있습니다. 189우편으로 귀사의 광고를 접했을 때, 귀사 제품을 한번 시도해 봐야겠다고 생각했습니다. 그렇게 한 것이 다행이었습니다. 귀사의 웹사이트 쇼핑은 매우 쉬웠습니다. 제 주문품은 약속된 시간 내에 도착했습니다. Goldie는 사료와, 간식, 물어뜯는 장난감을 좋아합니다. 처음에는 새 침대에 무관심했지만, 천천히 익숙해지고 있습니다. 처음 귀사에 대해 제게 이야기해준 제 여동생이 곧 주문을 할 예정입니다. 190그녀가 일전에 방문했을 때, 여동생의 강아지들에게 간식 몇 개를 줬는데 너무나 좋아했습니다!

Jessica D'Francesca

표현 정리 give something a try ~을 한번 해보다 timeframe (어떤 일에 쓰이는) 시간[기간] initially 처음에 uninterested in ~에 무관심한 get used to ~에 익숙해지다

186. 세부사항 – Petstore.com에 대한 내용 ★★☆

해설 광고의 'We carry over 1,000 brands of food, toys, treats, and accessories for dogs, cats, birds, fish, and exotic pets.'에서 다양한 동물을 위한 먹을거리를 판매하므로 (A)를 확인할 수 있고, 'If you order $50 or more, we will deliver your order directly to your home or business at no charge.'에서 50달러 이상 구매시 배송이 무료이므로 (B)를 확인할 수 있다. 하단의 'Addresses outside the United States will be charged our international shipping rates.'에서 해외로도 배송하므로 (D)를 알 수 있다. 'We carry over 1,000 brands' 에서 1,000여 종의 브랜드를 취급한다고만 나와 있으므로 인기 브랜드만 취급한다는 (C)가 사실과 달라 정답이다. **정답 (C)**

패러프레이징 |지문| We carry over 1,000 brands of food, toys, treats, and accessories for dogs, cats, birds, fish, and exotic pets 당사는 개, 고양이, 새, 물고기, 이국적 애완동물을 위한 1,000종 이상 브랜드의 식료품, 장난감, 간식, 액세서리를 취급합니다 → |선택지 A| It sells edible items for a variety of animals 다양한 동물을 위한 먹을거리를 판매한다

|지문| If you order $50 or more, we will deliver your order directly to your home or business at no charge 50달러 이상 주문하시면 고객님의 가정이나 사업장으로 무료로 주문품을 직접 배송해 드립니다 → |선택지 B| It offers free shipping on certain orders 특정 주문에 대해 무료 배송을 제공한다

표현 정리 edible 먹을 수 있는 a variety of 다양한 multiple 다수의

해석 광고에서 Petstore.com에 관해 언급되지 않은 것은?
(A) 다양한 동물을 위한 먹을거리를 판매한다.
(B) 특정 주문에 대해 무료 배송을 제공한다.
(C) 가장 인기있는 브랜드만 취급한다.
(D) 여러 나라의 고객에게 배송한다.

187. 연계 문제 – M78331 주문에 대한 내용 ★★☆

해설 온라인 장바구니의 'ORDER NUMBER: M78331'의 주문 금액은 'SUBTOTAL: $110.75'이며 그 아래 'Coupon Code: J7434BH1'과 같이 쿠폰 코드가 입력되어 있다. 광고의 박스 내용 중 'Get $25 off your next order of $100 or more'에서 다음 주문시 100달러 이상인 경우 할인 혜택을 받는다고 나오고, 그 아래 같은 쿠폰 코드가 명시되어 있다. 이들 내용을 종합할 때 이 주문은 할인 대상이 되므로 (C)가 정답이다. **정답 (C)**

표현 정리 **sales tax** 판매세, 물품세 **be eligible for** ~할 자격이 있다

해설 M78331 주문에 대해 암시된 것은?
  (A) 3일 이내에 배송될 것이다.
  (B) 판매세가 부과될 것이다.
  (C) 할인 대상이다.
  (D) 배송료를 지불해야 했다.

188. 유추 – Ms. D'Francesca에 관한 내용 ★☆☆
해설 두 번째 지문의 주소 부분을 보면 'New York City, NY, USA'에서 알 수 있듯이 New York City에서 살고 있기 때문에 city를 urban area로 바꿔 놓은 (D)가 정답이 된다. 정답 (D)

표현 정리 **rarely** 좀처럼, 드물게 ~하지 않는 **urban** 도시의, 도회지의

해설 Ms. D'Francesca에 대해 암시된 것은?
  (A) 한 마리 이상의 애완동물을 가지고 있다.
  (B) 전에 Petstore.com에서 주문했다.
  (C) 인터넷으로는 거의 쇼핑하지 않는다.
  (D) 도시에 살고 있다.

189. 주제 – Ms. D'Francesca가 이메일을 쓴 목적 ★☆☆
해설 이메일 중반부의 'When I received your advertisement in the mail, I thought I would give your company a try. I am glad I did.'에서 제품을 한번 사봤는데 좋았다고 하므로 정답은 (B)이다. 정답 (B)

표현 정리 **express** 표현하다 **satisfaction** 만족 **complain about** ~에 대해 불평하다 **inquire about** ~에 대해 문의하다

해설 Ms. D'Francesca가 이메일을 쓴 이유는?
  (A) 새로운 고객을 환영하기 위해
  (B) 주문에 대한 만족을 표현하기 위해
  (C) 제품에 대해 불만을 표하기 위해
  (D) 배달 지연에 대해 문의하기 위해

190. 연계 문제 – 여동생이 주문할 제품 ★★☆
해설 이메일 마지막의 'She was over the other day, and I let her dogs try some of the treats, which they loved!'에서 여동생의 강아지들이 간식을 좋아했다고 나온다. 온라인 장바구니 품목 중 간식에 해당하는 제품번호는 F1223, Dog Treats이다. 정답 (C)

해석 Ms. D'Francesca의 여동생이 주문할 제품은 아마도 무엇이겠는가?
  (A) A3034
  (B) A5237
  (C) F1223
  (D) F6733

문제 191-195번은 다음 웹사이트와 이메일을 참조하시오.

HUNTINGTON DINING CLUB			
홈페이지	소개	로그인	회원 가입

193Huntington에서 최고의 햄버거
Sally Twinning
게시일: 8월 7일 화요일

191매주 저는 시내의 다른 장소나, 음식 스타일, 주제에 초점을 맞춥니다. 이번 주는 햄버거입니다. 저는 시내에 갈 때마다 Sammy's Café에서 식사를 합니다. 단돈 7달러에 감자튀김과 음료수와 함께 햄버거를 먹을 수 있습니다. 같은 지역에서 좀더 고급스러운 것을 찾는다면 Harris Grill에 가보십시오. 베이컨 아보카도 햄버거가 아주 맛있습니다. 192제가 가장 좋아하는 점심 식사 장소 중 하나는 Allison's인데, 제 사무실과 가깝

기 때문만은 아닙니다. 그 곳에서는 단돈 8달러에 고구마 튀김과 함께 수상 실적이 있는 햄버거를 먹을 수 있습니다. 손님이 많으니까 일찍 도착하세요! 그러나 194시내 최고의 햄버거는 Main Street Diner에서 발견할 수 있습니다.

191회원은 로그인하여 이 글을 비롯한 다른 모든 평가를 읽을 수 있습니다.

표현 정리 **focus on** ~에 주력하다, 초점을 맞추다 **fancy** (비교급 fancier) 값비싼, 고급의, 품질 높은, 일류의 **delicious** 아주 맛있는 **award-winning** 수상 실적이 있는 **review** 비평, 평가

HUNTINGTON DINING CLUB			
홈페이지	소개	로그인	회원 가입

회원 양식

Huntington Dining Club의 회원이 되어 돈을 절약하세요. 192저희 웹사이트에서 평가한 모든 레스토랑에서 5% 할인을 받으실 수 있는 회원카드를 보내 드립니다. 또한 매주 목요일 받은편지함에 특별 할인정보를 받으시게 됩니다.

날짜: 8월 8일
이름: Jennifer Landis
전화: (412) 555-7393
이메일: jennytenny@aimhigh.net
연회비: 50달러
결제 방법: 6283으로 끝나는 신용카드
결제하기

표현 정리 **save** 절약하다, 아끼다 **entitle** 자격[권리]을 주다 **special offer** 특별 할인 **inbox** 받은편지함

발신: Jennifer Landis 〈jennytenny@aimhigh.net〉
수신: Huntington Dining Club 〈feedback@hdc.com〉
제목: 신규 회원
일시: 8월 15일 수요일

193저는 약 6개월 전에 이 지역으로 이사 왔고 종종 외식을 합니다. 귀사의 클럽에 더 일찍 가입했다면 좋았을 것이라고 생각합니다. 귀사의 평가 덕분에 좋은 장소 목록을 갖게 되었습니다.

지난주 Sally Twinning의 게시글로 저는 시작하게 되었습니다. 지난 주말에 194그녀의 최고 등급의 햄버거 가게에 가보았습니다. 195햄버거와 감자튀김은 맛있었지만, 종업원들은 너무 느렸습니다. 또한 너무 붐벼서 주차하는 데 어려움을 겪었습니다. 평가가 이러한 면에 초점을 맞췄다면, 테이크아웃을 주문했을 겁니다.

Jennifer Landis

표현 정리 **eat out** 외식하다 **top-ranked** 최상위의, 최고 등급의 **joint** 음식점[술집] **waitstaff** 종업원 **pack** (사람, 물건으로) 가득 채우다 **aspect** 측면, 양상 **takeout** 테이크아웃, (사서 식당에서 먹지 않고) 가지고 가는 음식

191. 유추 – Sally Twinning의 직업 ★☆☆
해설 첫 번째 웹사이트를 보면 'Each week, I focus on a different part of town, style of food, or theme.'에서 보듯이 Sally Twinning은 본인이 쓰고 싶은 주제에 대해서 자기 의견을 올리고 있고, 'Members can log in to read this and all of our other reviews.'에서 회원이 되면 이런 평가를 볼 수 있다는 내용

으로 보아 Sally Twinning은 웹사이트에 글을 올리는 블로거라는 것을 알 수 있다. **정답 (A)**

표현 정리 **blogger** 블로거(인터넷의 blog를 만드는 사람) **coordinator** 조정자, 코디네이터

Sally Twinning은 누구이겠는가?
(A) 블로거
(B) 요리사
(C) 회원 관리자
(D) 사무실 관리자

192. 연계 문제 – Allison's에 관한 내용 ★★☆

첫 번째 지문의 'One of my favorite places for lunch, and not just because it is close to my office, is Allison's.'에서 알 수 있듯이 Allison's는 Sally Twinning이 평가한 음식점이다. 두 번째 지문의 'We'll send you a membership card, which entitles you to 5% off at any restaurant reviewed on our Web site.'에서 회원들은 웹사이트에서 평가된 모든 음식점에서 5% 할인을 받을 수 있다고 했기 때문에, Allison's에서 회원들이 할인을 받을 수 있다는 것을 알 수 있다. **정답 (D)**

패러프레이징 |지문| We'll send you a membership card, which entitles you to 5% off at any restaurant reviewed on our Web site 저희 웹사이트에서 평가한 모든 레스토랑에서 5% 할인을 받으실 수 있는 회원카드를 보내 드립니다 → |선택지 D| Huntington Dining Club members can get a discount there Huntington Dining Club 회원들은 그곳에서 할인을 받을 수 있다

표현 정리 **district** 지역[지구] **side dish** 곁들여 나오는 음식[요리]

Allison's에 관해 암시된 것은?
(A) 상업 지역 중심에 위치해 있다.
(B) 그곳에서 판매되는 모든 햄버거에는 사이드로 나오는 음식이 있다.
(C) Ms. Twinning은 매주 그곳에서 식사를 한다.
(D) Huntington Dining Club 회원들은 그곳에서 할인을 받을 수 있다.

193. 세부사항 – Ms. Landis에 관한 내용 ★☆☆

이메일의 'I moved to the area about six months ago'를 보면, 그 지역에 이사한 지 6개월이 되었다고 하고 있다. 그 이하 내용을 보면 Sally Twinning이 쓴 글에 있는 음식점을 가본 경험을 말하고 있다. 첫 번째 지문의 'Best Burgers in Huntington'에서 알 수 있듯이, Sally Twinning이 평가하고 있는 것은 Huntington에 있는 음식점이므로 정답은 (B)이다. **정답 (B)**

🔍 **함정 분석** 이메일의 마지막 부분을 보면 'It was also packed, so I had trouble parking.'이라고 되어 있는데, 답을 (A)로 하면 안된다. 본문의 내용은 너무 붐벼서 주차공간을 못 찾았다는 것이고, (A)의 내용은 Ms. Landis가 주차를 하는 데 불편함을 느낀다는 것이다(운전이 미숙해서 그럴 수도 있다). 또한 시제를 보면, 본문의 내용은 과거의 시점에서 주차하기가 어려웠다는 것이기 때문에 (A)는 오답이다.

패러프레이징 |지문| moved to the area six months ago 6개월 전에 이사 왔다 → |선택지 B| has lived in Huntington for less than a year Huntington에 산 지 1년이 되지 않았다

표현 정리 **renew** 갱신하다 **regularly** 정기적으로

Ms. Landis에 대해서 언급된 것은?
(A) 주차하는 것이 쉽지 않다.
(B) Huntington에 산 지 1년이 되지 않았다.
(C) 최근에 회원권을 갱신했다.
(D) 자주 저녁 식사를 테이크아웃으로 주문한다.

194. 연계 문제 – Ms. Landis가 최근에 식사한 장소 ★★★

첫 번째 웹사이트에서 Sally Twinning의 글에 따르면, 최고의 햄버거를 맛볼 수 있는 곳은 Main Street Diner이고, 이메일을 보면 'This past weekend, I tried her top-ranked burger joint.'에서 Ms. Landis가 가본 음식점은 Sally Twinning이 최고 등급을 매긴 음식점이므로 Main Street Diner에 갔다는 것을 알 수 있다. **정답 (C)**

Ms. Landis가 최근에 식사한 장소는?
(A) Allison's
(B) Harris Grill
(C) Main Street Diner
(D) Sammy's Café

195. 세부사항 – Ms. Landis가 좋아한 점 ★☆☆

이메일에서 음식점에 대해서 좋은 평가를 내리는 부분은 'The burger and fries were delicious'에서 알 수 있듯이 음식 맛이다. **정답 (D)**

표현 정리 **mood** 분위기 **taste** 맛, 미각

Ms. Landis가 최근의 식사에서 무엇을 좋아했는가?
(A) 서비스 속도
(B) 식사 가격
(C) 음식점 분위기
(D) 음식 맛

문제 196-200번은 다음 기사, 이메일, 그리고 편지를 참조하시오.

CAPE GIRARDEAU – (9월 11일) **197** 유일하게 지역민이 소유하고 운영하는 데이터 저장 솔루션 제공업체인 Data Solutions Corporation이 지난주에 3주년을 기념했다. 이 회사는 데이터 저장 솔루션과, 클라우드 컴퓨팅, 데이터 복구 서비스를 제공한다. 또한 Data Solutions Corporation 시설에 공간을 빌리기보다는 자체 개별 데이터 센터를 구축하고자 하는 회사들에게 컨설팅을 제공한다. Benjamin Ochs 사장은 "우리 사업의 대부분은 여전히 다른 사람들의 데이터를 저장하는 것으로부터 비롯됩니다."라고 말했다. **196** "그러나 작년부터는 더 많은 기업들이 자체 저장 시설을 구축하기 위해 저희 회사를 고용해왔습니다."

표현 정리 **locally** 지역적으로 **own** 소유하다 **operate** 운영하다 **storage** 보관, 저장 **provider** 제공업체 **celebrate** 기념하다 **recovery** 회복, 복구 **consult with** ~와 협의하다 **establish** 구축하다, 설립하다 **lease** 임대 **facility** 시설 **store** 저장하다 **set up** 설치하다

199 발신: Greg Towner 〈greg@bullionfinancial.com〉
수신: Owen Wissler 〈owen@bullionfinancial.com〉
제목: 데이터 저장
날짜: 10월 8일

Owen,

Accenture의 IT 부이사인 Richard Deacon과 방금 점심 식사를 했습니다. 대화가 진행되는 동안, 데이터 보안에 관한 이야기가 나왔습니다. **197** Richard는 Data Solutions Corporation을 추천했는데, 이 회사는 서비스를 처음 제공하기 시작한 이래로 계약해온 업체입니다. 그 전에 Accenture는 현재 우리 회사 공급업체인 Mega Storage를 이용했습니다.

Richard는 전국 규모의 큰 회사들은 종종 더 저렴한 비용으로 서비스를 제공하지만, 그의 회사가 Data Solutions Corporation에서 받는 맞춤 서비스를 제공하지 못한다고 하더군요.

199 Richard는 Data Solutions의 계정 관리자와 연락하게 해주었습니다. 그녀가 전화로 준 견적이 우리 예산 범위 내에 있으며 현재 우리가 받고 있

는 것보다 더 많은 서비스를 제공합니다. **198직접 만나서 이 부분을 논의하고 싶습니다. 언제 시간이 괜찮으시겠어요?**

Greg

표현 정리 **data security** 데이터 보안 **come up** 나오다 **recommend** 추천하다 **contract with** ~와 계약하다 **current** 현재의 **national company** 전국의 고객을 대상으로 사업을 하는 회사 **rate** 요금 **unable to** ~할 수 없는 **personalized** 개인이 원하는 대로 할 수 있는 **attention** 주의 **in touch with** ~와 접촉하여 **quote** 견적액 **budget** 예산 **in person** 직접

10월 28일

Owen Wissler
Bullion Financial Advisors
1212 State Street
Cape Girardeau, MO 63703

Mr. Wissler 귀하

Bullion Financial Advisors에 장기 데이터 저장 서비스를 제공하도록 Data Solutions Corporation을 선택해 주셔서 감사합니다.

계약 조항의 일부로서, 귀사는 저희 서버에 지정된 공간을 받으시게 됩니다. 또한 기술 지원 담당자가 기존 공급업체에서 저희 서버로 데이터를 이전하는 작업을 감독합니다. 이 계약의 **200전체** 내용은 첨부된 서비스 계약서에서 확인하실 수 있습니다. 꼼꼼히 살펴보시고 서명한 사본을 보내주십시오.

질문이 있으시면 언제든지 555-7070이나 paula@datasolutions.com으로 저에게 연락해 주십시오.

Paula Ochs
199계정 관리자
Data Solutions Corporation

표현 정리 **long-term** 장기적인 **agreement** 합의, 계약서 **designated** 지정된 **technical support** 기술 지원 **oversee** 감독하다 **migration** (컴퓨터 시스템·프로그램의) 이송 **existing** 기존의 **details** 세부사항 **attached** 첨부된 **review** 검토하다 **signed** 서명된

196. 세부사항 – Data Solutions Corporation에 대한 내용 ★☆☆
해설 기사의 마지막 부분인 회사 소유주의 인용문 중 "Starting last year, however, more companies have hired us to help them set up their own storage facilities."에서 작년부터 컨설팅하는 업체가 늘게 되었다고 하므로 (C)가 정답이다. **정답 (C)**

표현 정리 **buy out** 인수하다 **competitor** 경쟁자 **multiple** 다수의

해설 기사에 따르면, Data Solutions Corporation에 관해 사실인 것은?
(A) 모든 지역 경쟁사들을 인수했다.
(B) 지역 회사들에 컴퓨터 하드웨어를 판매한다.
(C) 작년에 컨설팅 사업이 성장했다.
(D) 여러 개인 데이터 센터를 소유하고 있다.

197. 연계 문제 – Accenture에 대한 내용 ★★☆
해설 이메일 첫 번째 단락의 'Richard recommended the Data Solutions Corporation, which his company has contracted with since it first started offering its services.'에서 Data Solutions Corporation이 데이터 저장 서비스를 처음 제공하기 시작했을 때부터 이 회사와 계약하고 있다고 나와 있다. 그리고 기사 첫 번째 문장 'The Data Solutions Corporation, the only locally owned and operated data storage solutions provider, celebrated its third anniversary last week.'에서 Data Solutions Corporation이 3주년을 기념했다고 나온다. 이들 내용을 종합할 때 Accenture

가 Data Solutions Corporation을 3년 전부터 이용했음을 알 수 있으므로 (D)가 정답이다. **정답 (D)**

해설 Accenture에 대해 아마도 사실인 내용은?
(A) Mr. Deacon이 소유하고 있다.
(B) 전국을 대상으로 사업하는 회사이다.
(C) 자체 개별 데이터 저장 시설을 가지고 있다.
(D) 3년 전에 Data Solutions Corporation을 고용했다.

198. 주제 – Mr. Towner가 이메일을 쓴 목적 ★☆☆
해설 이메일 마지막 부분 'I would like to discuss it with you in person. What would be a good time for you?'에서 직접 만나 논의하고 싶다고 하면서 시간을 묻고 있으므로 (D)가 정답이다. **정답 (D)**

표현 정리 **respond to** ~에 반응하다, 응답하다 **criticize** 비난하다 **face-to-face** 대면의

해설 Mr. Towner가 Mr. Wissler에게 이메일을 쓴 이유는?
(A) 연락처를 소개하기 위해
(B) 요청에 응답하기 위해
(C) 현재의 서비스 제공업체를 비판하기 위해
(D) 대면 회의를 요청하기 위해

199. 연계 문제 – Mr. Towner에 대한 내용 ★★★
해설 먼저 질문의 키워드인 Greg Towner는 이메일 발신인이다. 이메일 마지막 단락의 'Richard put me in touch with the account manager at Data Solutions.'와 그 이하 문장에서 Data Solutions의 계정 담당자와 연락하게 되어 전화 통화를 했다는 내용이 나온다. 그 다음, 편지 하단에 보면 Paula Ochs는 Data Solutions Corporation의 계정 담당자이다. 따라서 이들 내용을 종합할 때 Mr. Towner가 계정 담당자인 Ms. Ochs와 이야기했다는 (A)가 정답이다. **정답 (A)**

표현 정리 **supervisor** 상사 **be in charge of** ~을 담당하다 **used to** 예전에는 ~이었다

해설 Mr. Towner에 대해 언급된 것은?
(A) Ms. Ochs와 이야기했다.
(B) Mr. Wissler의 상사이다.
(C) 예산을 책임지고 있다.
(D) 과거에 Accenture에서 일했다.

200. 동의어 찾기 ★☆☆
해설 'The full details of this agreement'에서 full은 '전체의'라는 뜻이므로 (B) complete가 의미상 가장 유사하다. **정답 (B)**

해설 편지에서 두 번째 단락 3행의 "full"과 의미상 가장 가까운 단어는?
(A) 추가적인
(B) 완전한
(C) 큰
(D) 수많은

시험에 나오는 것만 공부한다!

시나공 토익

파트 **7**
실전문제집 시즌 **2**

2007년 ~ 2018년
〈파트별 실전문제집〉 분야 부동의 누적 판매 1위!

 정답, 오답의 이유까지 자세하게 설명한 해설집!

 독해 실력을 한층 높여주는 독학용 복습 노트!

 기본 독해 실력을 키워주는 의미 단위 해석 훈련!

 추가 고난도 100문제 PDF!

 파트 7 문제풀이의 핵심인 패러프레이징 암기장!

* 〈추가 고난도 100문제 PDF〉, 〈독학용 복습 노트〉 다운로드 안내

　길벗 홈페이지(www.gilbut.co.kr)에 접속하신 후, 해당 교재의 자료실에서 무료로 다운로드하실 수 있습니다.

| 이 책을
권장하는 점수대 | 400 ┼┼┼┼ 500 ┼┼┼┼ 600 ┼┼┼┼ 700 ┼┼┼┼ 800 ┼┼┼┼ 900 |

| 이 책의 난이도 | 쉬움 ┼┼┼┼┼┼┼┼ 비슷함 ┼┼┼┼┼┼┼┼ 어려움 |

03740

9 791159 242229

ISBN 979-11-5924-222-9

시나공 토익

파트 7 실전문제집 시즌 2

Do it yourself!

Part 7 Actual Tests (Season 2)

가격 16,000원 (해설집 포